Supply Chain Logistics Management

The McGraw-Hill/Irwin Series Operations and Decision Sciences

OPERATIONS MANAGEMENT

Beckman and Rosenfield, **Operations, Strategy: Competing in the 21st Century,** *First Edition*

Benton, **Purchasing and Supply Management,** *First Edition*

Bowersox, Closs, and Cooper, **Supply Chain Logistics Management,** *Third Edition*

Burt, Petcavage, and Pinkerton, **Supply Management,** *Eighth Edition*

Cachon and Terwiesch, **Matching Supply with Demand: An Introduction to Operations Management,** *Second Edition*

Finch, **Interactive Models for Operations and Supply Chain Management,** *First Edition*

Finch, **Operations Now: Supply Chain Profitability and Performance,** *Third Edition*

Fitzsimmons and Fitzsimmons, **Service Management: Operations, Strategy, Information Technology,** *Sixth Editon*

Gehrlein, **Operations Management Cases,** *First Edition*

Gray and Larson, **Project Management: The Managerial Process,** *Fourth Edition*

Harrison and Samson, **Technology Management,** *First Edition*

Hayen, **SAP R/3 Enterprise Software: An Introduction,** *First Edition*

Hill, **Manufacturing Strategy: Text & Cases,** *Third Edition*

Hopp, **Supply Chain Science,** *First Edition*

Hopp and Spearman, **Factory Physics,** *Third Edition*

Jacobs and Chase, **Operations and Supply Management: The Core,** *First Edition*

Jacobs, Chase, and Aquilano, **Operations and Supply Management,** *Twelfth Edition*

Jacobs and Whybark, **Why ERP?** *First Edition*

Leenders, Johnson, Flynn, and Fearon, **Purchasing and Supply Management,** *Thirteenth Edition*

Melnyk and Swink, **Value-Driven Operations Management: An Integrated Modular Approach,** *First Edition*

Olson, **Introduction to Information Systems Project Management,** *Second Edition*

Pinto and Parente, **SimProject: A Project Management Simulation for Classroom Instruction,** *First Edition*

Schroeder, **Operations Management: Contemporary Concepts and Cases,** *Fourth Edition*

Seppanen, Kumar, and Chandra, **Process Analysis and Improvement,** *First Edition*

Simchi-Levi, Kaminsky, and Simchi-Levi, **Designing and Managing the Supply Chain: Concepts, Strategies, Case Studies,** *Third Edition*

Sterman, **Business Dynamics: Systems Thinking and Modeling for Complex World,** *First Edition*

Thomke, **Managing Product and Service Development: Text and Cases,** *First Edition*

Ulrich and Eppinger, **Product Design and Development,** *Fourth Edition*

Vollmann, Berry, Whybark, and Jacobs, **Manufacturing Planning & Control for Supply Chain Management,** *Fifth Edition*

Webster, **Principles and Tools for Supply Chain Management,** *First Edition*

Zipkin, **Foundations of Inventory Management,** *First Edition*

QUANTITATIVE METHODS AND MANAGEMENT SCIENCE

Hillier and Hillier, **Introduction to Management Science: A Modeling and Case Studies Approach with Spreadsheets,** *Third Edition*

Kros, **Spreadsheet Modeling for Business Decisions,** *First Edition*

Stevenson and Ozgur, **Introduction to Management Science with Spreadsheets,** *First Edition*

Supply Chain Logistics Management

Third Edition

Donald J. Bowersox
David J. Closs
M. Bixby Cooper
Michigan State University

Boston   Burr Ridge, IL   Dubuque, IA   Madison, WI   New York   San Francisco   St. Louis
Bangkok   Bogotá   Caracas   Kuala Lumpur   Lisbon   London   Madrid   Mexico City
Milan   Montreal   New Delhi   Santiago   Seoul   Singapore   Sydney   Taipei   Toronto

SUPPLY CHAIN LOGISTICS MANAGEMENT
International Edition 2010

10   09   08   07   06   05   04   03   02   01
20   09
CTP   BJE

When ordering this title, use ISBN 978-007-127617-7 or MHID 007-127617-3

Printed in Singapore

www.mhhe.com

This book is dedicated to our wives Terry, Noel, and Ann, and families for their time, encouragement, and patience for it is the authors' families who ultimately pay the dearest price, and to Dr. Donald A. Taylor, deceased, who was a guiding force in all our careers.

About the Authors

Donald J. Bowersox is University Professor and Dean Emeritus at Michigan State University. He received his Ph.D. at Michigan State and has worked in industry throughout his career. He is the author of numerous articles in publications such as the *Harvard Business Review, Journal of Marketing, Journal of Business Logistics,* and *Supply Chain Management Review.* He is coauthor of *Start Pulling Your Chain: Leading Responsive Supply Chain Transformation,* published in 2008. Dr. Bowersox has led a number of industry-supported research studies investigating the best practices of logisticians in North America and around the world. He is a frequent speaker at industry and academic meetings.

David J. Closs is the John H. McConnell Chaired Professor of Business Administration and Chairperson in the Department of Supply Chain Management at Michigan State University. He received his Ph.D. in marketing and logistics from Michigan State. Dr. Closs is the author and coauthor of many publications in journals, proceedings, and industry reports. He was also a principal researcher for *World Class Logistics: The Challenge of Managing Continuous Change* and *21st Century Logistics: Making Supply Chain Integration a Reality.* Dr. Closs is a frequent speaker at industry and academic conferences and presenter at executive education programs. Dr. Closs formerly served as the editor of the *Journal of Business Logistics* and is currently the executive editor of *Logistics Quarterly.*

M. Bixby Cooper is an Associate Professor in the Department of Supply Chain Management at Michigan State University. He is coauthor of three texts on distribution and logistics, including *World Class Logistics: The Challenge of Managing Continuous Change* and *Strategic Marketing Channel Management.* He also served for four years on the Executive Board of the International Customer Service Association as Head of the Research and Education Committee.

Preface

Over the last seven decades, the discipline of business logistics has advanced from the warehouse floor and transportation dock to the boardroom of leading global enterprises. We have had the opportunity to be actively involved in this evolution through research, education, and advising. *Supply Chain Logistics Management* encompasses the development and fundamentals of the logistics discipline within a supply chain structure. It also presents our vision of the future of business logistics and supply chain management and their role in enterprise competitiveness.

Although individually and collectively the three authors have written extensively on various aspects of logistics, the decision to initially write and subsequently revise *Supply Chain Logistics Management* represents the synthesis of many years of research, augmenting and, in many ways, supplanting earlier works of the authors published by McGraw-Hill. The union of ideas presented in this text provides an integrated supply chain framework for the study of logistics, serves to expand the treatment of supply chain management by placing it firmly in the context of integrated business strategy, and highlights the increasing importance of logistics in the supply chains supporting a global economy.

Logistics includes all the activities required to move product and information to, from, and between members of a supply chain. The supply chain provides the framework for businesses and their suppliers to jointly deliver goods, services, and information efficiently, effectively, relevantly, and in a sustainable manner to customers. *Supply Chain Logistics Management* presents the mission, business processes, and strategies needed to achieve integrated logistical management. We hope the text achieves three fundamental objectives: (1) presents a comprehensive description of existing logistical practices in a global economy, (2) describes ways and means to apply logistics principles to achieve competitive advantage, and (3) provides a conceptual approach for integrating logistics as a core competency within enterprise supply chain strategy.

For their specific suggestions regarding the manuscript, our appreciation goes to Hugh Turner, University of Maryland; Soonhung Min, University of Oklahoma; Ted Stank, University of Tennessee; Robert Novack, Penn State University; David Borst, Concordia University; Charles Peterson, Northern Illinois University; John Mawhinney, Duquesne University; Elliot Rabinovich, Arizona State University; Chris I. Enyinda, Alabama A&M University; and Hugh S. Turner, University of Maryland, all of whom provided detailed reviews and offered numerous suggestions for improving the presentation.

We also wanted to acknowledge the staff at McGraw-Hill/Irwin for their guidance and efforts on behalf of the book: Richard Hercher, Executive Editor, Operations and Decision Sciences; Rebecca Mann and Christina Lane, Editorial Coordinators; Dana Pauley, Project Manager; and Jaime Halteman, Marketing Manager. Further assistance was provided by Michelle Gardner, Project Manager, Laserwords Maine.

As active members of the Council of Supply Chain Management Professionals, we have been the fortunate recipients of contributions by many council members to the development of this manuscript. In particular, we wish to acknowledge the assistance of Rick Blasgen, president and CEO of the Council of Supply Chain Management Professionals, and the CSCMP staff who maintain an open door to the academic community.

Over the past 45 years, the business executives who have attended the annual Michigan State University Logistics Management Executive Development Seminar have been exposed to the basic concepts presented in the text and have given freely of their time and experience. We also acknowledge the long-standing support to Michigan State logistics, through the funding of the endowed chairs, provided by the late John H. McConnell, founder of Worthington Industries.

The number of individuals involved in teaching logistics around the world expands daily. To this group in general, and in particular to our colleagues at Michigan State University, whose advice and assistance made it possible to complete and enhance this text, we express our sincere appreciation.

Teachers receive continuous inspiration from students over the years, and in many ways the day of judgment in an academic career comes in the seminar or classroom. We have been fortunate to have the counsel of many outstanding young scholars who currently are making substantial impact on the academic and business worlds. In particular, we appreciate the input of students who have used this text in manuscript form and made suggestions for improvement. We also acknowledge the contributions of current and former doctoral students, particularly Drs. Judith Whipple and Thomas Goldsby, who participated extensively in case development and editorial support. Student Research Assistant John Bowersox provided valuable support throughout manuscript preparation and managed the complex process of obtaining publication permissions. Appreciation is extended to Major G. Scott Webb and Brian Pease, who assististed in updating materials for this edition.

We wish to acknowledge the contributions of Felicia Kramer and Pamela Kingsbury, for manuscript preparation on several earlier versions of this text, and Cheryl Lundeen, who prepared many drafts of the manuscripts. Without Felicia, Pam, and Cheryl, this long published text in its many variations would not be a reality.

With so much able assistance, it is difficult to offer excuses for any shortcomings that might appear. Any faults are solely our responsibility.

Donald J. Bowersox
David J. Closs
M. Bixby Cooper

Brief Contents

Contents

PART ONE

Supply Chain Logistics Management

Part 1 establishes the strategic importance of logistics to achieving business success by creating value throughout domestic and global supply chains. The initial chapter scopes the current business attention to supply chain management. The supply chain provides the framework within which logistical strategies are developed and executed. Logistics, the primary topic of this book, is introduced in Chapter 2. The concept of integrated logistics is developed by discussing the ways specific work tasks combine to support customer accommodation, manufacturing, and procurement. Chapter 3 describes the importance of customer accommodation to successful logistics. The value created by logistics can serve as a powerful driver of customer success. Chapter 4 introduces procurement and manufacturing. The combination of customer accommodation, procurement, and manufacturing represents the supply chain operational areas that are linked and supported by logistics. Chapter 5 presents an overview of information technology that is specifically applicable to supply chain logistics. A framework is developed to serve as a format for presenting specific technology applications in supply chain logistics operation and design. Part 1 concludes in Chapter 6 with a discussion of integrated operations planning. One of the key challenges in integrated supply chain management is cross-functional and cross-enterprise planning and operational implementation.

21st-Century Supply Chains

As recently as the 1990s, the average time required for a company to process and deliver merchandise to a customer from warehouse inventory ranged from 15 to 30 days, sometimes even longer. The typical order-to-delivery process involved order creation and transfer, which was usually via telephone, fax, electronic data interchange (EDI), or public mail; followed by order processing, which involved the use of manual or computer systems, credit authorization, and order assignment to a warehouse for processing; followed by shipment to a customer. When everything went as planned, the average time for a customer to receive items ordered was lengthy. When something went wrong, as it often did, such as inventory out-of-stock, a lost or misplaced work order, or a misdirected shipment, total time to service customers escalated rapidly.

To support this lengthy and unpredictable time to market, it became common practice to accumulate inventory. For example, inventories of identical products were typically stocked by retailers, wholesalers, and manufacturers. Despite such extensive inventory, out-of-stocks and delayed deliveries were common due in part to the large number of product variations.

These accepted business practices of the 20th century, as well as the distribution channel structure used to complete delivery, evolved from years of experience dating from the industrial revolution. Such long-standing business practices remained in place and unchallenged because no clearly superior alternative existed. The traditional distribution process was designed to overcome challenges and achieve benefits that long ago ceased to be important. The industrialized world is no longer characterized by scarcity. Consumer affluence and desire for wide choice of products and services continue to grow. In fact, today's consumers want a wide range of product and source options they can configure to their unique specifications. The desires of customers have shifted from passive acceptance to active involvement in the design and delivery of specific products and services. Transportation capacity and operational performance have increasingly become more economical and reliable. Today's transportation is supported by sophisticated information systems that facilitate predictable and precise delivery.

Massive change has occurred as a result of available information technology. During the decade of the 1990s, the world of commerce was irrevocably impacted by computerization, the Internet, and a range of inexpensive information transmission capabilities. Information characterized by speed, accessibility, accuracy, and most of all relevancy became the norm. The Internet has become a common and economical way to complete business-to-business (B2B) transactions. An increasing number of consumers are directly connected to firms via the Internet. Driven by these fundamental forces, a global economy rapidly emerged.

What began during the last decade of the 20th century and will continue to unfold well into the 21st century is what historians are increasingly characterizing as the dawning of the **information** or **digital age.** In the information age the reality of business connectivity continues to drive a new order of relationships called **supply chain management.** Managers are increasingly improving traditional marketing, manufacturing, purchasing and logistics practices. In this new order of affairs, products can be manufactured to exact specifications and rapidly delivered to customers at locations throughout the globe. Logistical systems exist that have the capability to deliver products at precise times. Customer order and delivery of product assortments can be performed in hours. The frequent occurrence of service failures that characterized the past is increasingly being replaced by a growing managerial commitment to zero defect or what is commonly called **six-sigma** performance.[1] **Perfect orders**—delivering the desired assortment and quantity of products to the right location on time, damage-free, and correctly invoiced—once the exception, are now becoming the expectation. Perhaps most important is the fact that such high-level performance is being achieved at lower total cost and with the commitment of fewer financial resources than was characteristic of the past. All of this fundamental change in business enterprise structure and strategy is primarily being driven by information technology.

In this initial chapter, the supply chain management business model and value proposition is introduced as a growing strategic posture of contemporary firms. The chapter reviews the development of the supply chain revolution in business practice. Next, the supply chain concept is presented in a strategic framework. The chapter then examines integrative management, responsiveness, financial sophistication, and globalization as forces driving the emergence of supply chain logic. The overall objective of Chapter 1 is to position the logistical challenges of supporting a 21st century supply chain strategy. The supply chain is positioned as the strategic framework within which logistical requirements are identified and related operations managed.

---

[1] Six-sigma performance reflects a level of achievement having an error rate of 3.4 defects per million, or 99.99966 percent perfect.

The Supply Chain Revolution

What managers are experiencing today we choose to describe as the **supply chain revolution** and a related **logistical renaissance.** These two massive shifts in expectation and practice concerning best-practice performance of business operations are highly interrelated. However, they are significantly different aspects of contemporary strategic thinking.

Supply chain management consists of firms collaborating to leverage strategic positioning and to improve operating efficiency. For each firm involved, the supply chain relationship reflects a strategic choice. A supply chain strategy is a channel and business organizational arrangement based on acknowledged dependency and collaboration. Supply chain operations require managerial processes that span functional areas within individual firms and link suppliers, trading partners, and customers across organizational boundaries.

Within a firm's supply chain management, **logistics** is the work required to move and geographically position inventory. As such, logistics is a subset of and occurs within the broader framework of a supply chain. Logistics is the process that creates value by timing and positioning inventory. Logistics is the combination of a firm's order management, inventory, transportation, warehousing, materials handling, and packaging as integrated throughout a facility network. Integrated logistics serves to link and synchronize the overall supply chain as a continuous process and is essential for effective supply chain connectivity. While the purpose of logistical work has remained essentially the same over the decades, the way the work is performed continues to radically change.

The fundamental focus of this book is integrated logistics management. However, to study logistics, a reader must have a basic understanding of supply chain management. Supply chain strategy establishes the operating framework within which logistics is performed. As will be reviewed shortly, dramatic change continues to evolve in supply chain practice. Accordingly, logistics best practice, as described in this book, is presented as a work in progress, subject to continuous change based on the evolving nature of supply chain structure and strategy. Chapter 2, Logistics, examines the renaissance taking place in logistics best practice and sets the stage for all chapters that follow.

At first blush, supply chain management may appear to be a vague concept. A great deal has been written on the subject without much concern for basic definition, structure, or common vocabulary. Confusion exists concerning the appropriate scope of what constitutes a supply chain, to what extent it involves integration with other companies as contrasted to integrating internal operations, and how to best implement it in terms of competitive practices and legal constraints. For most managers, the supply chain concept has intrinsic appeal because it envisions new business arrangements offering the potential to improve competitiveness. The concept also implies a highly effective network of business relationships that serve to improve efficiency by eliminating duplicate and nonproductive work. Understanding more specifically what constitutes the supply chain revolution starts with a review of traditional distribution channel practice.

To overcome challenges of commercial trading, firms developed business relationships with other product and service companies to jointly perform essential activities. Such acknowledged dependency was necessary to achieve benefits of specialization. Managers, following the early years of the industrial revolution, began to strategically plan core competency, specialization, and economy of scale. The result was realization that working closely with other businesses was essential for continued success. This understanding that no firm could be totally self-sufficient contrasted to some earlier notions of vertical ownership integration.[2] Acknowledged dependence between business firms created the study of what became known as **distribution** or **marketing channels.**

---

[2] Henry Ford, *Today and Tomorrow* (New York: Doubleday, Page, and Company, 1926). Reprinted by Productivity Press (Portland, OR, 1988).

Because of the high visibility of different types of businesses, the early study of channel arrangements was characterized by classification based on specific roles performed during the distributive process. For example, a firm may have been created to perform the value-added services called wholesaling. Firms doing business with a wholesaler had expectations concerning what services they would receive and the compensation they would be expected to pay. In-depth study of specific activities quickly identified the necessity for leadership, a degree of commitment to cooperation among all channel members, and means to resolve conflict. Scholars who conduct research in channel structure and strategy developed typologies to classify observable practice ranging from a single transaction to highly formalized continuous business relationships.

The bonding feature of channel integration was a rather vague concept that all involved would enjoy benefits as a result of cooperating. However, primarily due to a lack of high-quality information, the overall channel structure was postured on an adversarial foundation. When push came to shove, each firm in the channel would first and foremost focus on its individual goals. Thus, in final analysis, channel dynamics were more often than not characterized by a dog-eat-dog competitive environment.

During the last decade of the 20th century, channel strategy and structure began to shift radically. Traditional distribution channel arrangements moved toward more integration and collaboration. Prior to reviewing the generalized supply chain model, it is important to understand why integration creates value.

Why Integration Creates Value

To explain the basic benefits and challenges of integrated management, it is useful to point out that customers have at least three perspectives of value.

The traditional perspective of value is **economic value.** Economic value builds on economy of scale in operations as the source of efficiency. Economy of scale seeks to fully utilize fixed assets to achieve the lowest, total landed cost. The focus of economic value is efficiency of product/service creation. Economic value is all about doing things as well as possible. The customer take-away of economic value is high quality at a low price.

A second value perspective is **market value.** Market value is about presenting an attractive assortment of products at the right time and place to realize effectiveness. Market value focuses on achieving economy of scope in product/service presentation. The creation of multimerchant shopping malls, large-scale mass-merchandising retail stores, and multivendor Internet fulfillment operations are all initiatives to achieve **market value.** The customer's take-away in terms of market value is **convenient product/service assortment and choice.**

Realization of both economic and market value is important to customers. However, increasingly firms are recognizing that business success also depends upon a third perspective of value, referred to as **relevancy.** Relevancy involves customization of value-adding services, over and above product and positioning, that make a real difference to customers. Relevancy value means the right products and services, as reflected by market value, at the right price, as reflected by economic value, modified, sequenced, synchronized, and otherwise positioned in a manner that creates valuable segmental diversity. In a consumer context, for example, relevancy means transforming ingredients into ready-to-eat meals. In general merchandise retailing, relevancy means transforming products into fashionable apparel. In manufacturing and assembly, relevancy is achieved by integrating specific components into products to increase functionality desired by a specific customer. The customer's take-away in terms of relevancy is a unique product/service bundle.

The simultaneous achievement of economic value, market value, and relevancy value requires total integration of the overall business process and is known as the integrative management value proposition, as illustrated in Table 1.1

TABLE 1.1
Integrative
Management Value
Proposition

Economic Value	Market Value	Relevancy Value
• Lowest total cost	• Attractive assortment	• Customization
• Economy-of-scale efficiency	• Economy-of-scope effectiveness	• Segmental diversity
• Product/service creation	• Product/service presentation	• Product/service positioning
Procurement/Manufacturing Strategy	**Market/Distribution Strategy**	**Supply Chain Strategy**

Generalized Supply Chain Model

The general concept of an integrated supply chain is often illustrated by a line diagram that links participating firms into a coordinated competitive unit. Figure 1.1 illustrates a generalized model adapted from the supply chain management program at Michigan State University.

The context of an integrated supply chain is multifirm collaboration within a framework of key resource flows and constraints. Within this context, supply chain structure and strategy results from efforts to operationally align an enterprise with customers as well as the supporting distributive and supplier networks to gain competitive advantage. Business operations are therefore integrated from initial material purchase to delivery of products and services to customers.[3]

[3] Customers are defined as destination points in a supply chain. Customers either consume a product or use it as an integral part or component of an additional process or product. The essential point is that the original product loses its unique configuration when consumed. Business entities that purchase products from manufacturers for resale, for example, wholesalers and retailers, are referred to as intermediate customers.

FIGURE 1.1 The Integrated Supply Chain Framework

Value results from the synergy among firms constituting a supply chain as a result of five critical flows: information, product, service, financial, and knowledge (see the bidirectional arrow at the top of the Figure 1.1). Logistics is the primary conduit of product and service flow within a supply chain arrangement. Each firm engaged in a supply chain is involved in performing some aspects of overall logistics. Achievement of logistical integration and efficiency is the focus of this text. The generalized supply chain arrangement illustrated in Figure 1.1 logically and logistically links a firm and its distributive and supplier network to customers. The message conveyed by the figure is that the integrated value-creation process must be aligned and managed from material procurement to end-customer product/service delivery.

The integrated supply chain perspective shifts traditional channel arrangements from loosely linked groups of independent businesses that buy and sell inventory to each other toward a managerially coordinated initiative to increase market impact, overall efficiency, continuous improvement, and competitiveness. In practice, many complexities serve to cloud the simplicity of illustrating supply chains as directional line diagrams. For example, many individual firms simultaneously participate in multiple and competitive supply chains. To the degree that a supply chain becomes the basic unit of competition, firms participating in multiple arrangements may confront loyalty issues related to confidentiality and potential conflict of interest.

Another factor that serves to add complexity to understanding supply chain structure is the high degree of mobility and change observable in typical arrangements. It's interesting to observe the fluidity of supply chains as firms enter and exit without any apparent loss of essential connectivity. For example, a firm and/or service supplier may be actively engaged in a supply chain structure during selected times, such as a peak selling season, and not during the balance of a year.

The overarching enabler of supply chain management is information technology. In addition to information technology, the rapid emergence of supply chain arrangements is being driven by four related forces: (1) integrative management and supply chain process (2) responsiveness, (3) financial sophistication, and (4) globalization. These forces will continue, for the foreseeable future, to drive supply chain structure and strategy initiatives across most industries. A brief discussion of each supply chain driver provides a foundation to understand the challenges supply chain management places on exacting logistical performance.

Integrative Management and Supply Chain Processes

Across all aspects of business operations, attention is focused on achieving improved integrative management. The challenge to achieving integrated management results from the long-standing tradition of performing and measuring work on a functional basis. Since the industrial revolution, achieving best practice has focused managerial attention on functional specialization.[4] The prevailing belief was the better the performance of a specific function, the greater the efficiency of the overall process. For well over a century, this fundamental commitment to functional efficiency has driven best practice in organization structure, performance measurement, and accountability.

In terms of management, firms have traditionally been structured into departments to facilitate work focus, routinization, standardization, and control. Accounting practices were developed to measure departmental performance. Most performance measurement focused on individual functions. Two examples of common functional measurement are the cost per unit to manufacture and the cost per hundredweight to transport. Cross-functional

[4] Frederick W. Taylor, *Scientific Management* (New York: W. W. Norton, 1967).

TABLE 1.2
Eight Supply Chain Integrative Processes

Process	Description
Demand planning responsiveness	The assessment of demand and strategic design to achieve maximum responsiveness to customer requirements.
Customer relationship collaboration	The development and administration of relationships with customers to facilitate strategic information sharing, joint planning, and integrated operations.
Order fulfillment/service delivery	The ability to execute superior and sustainable order-to-delivery performance and related essential services.
Product/service development launch	The participation in product service development and lean launch.
Manufacturing customization	The support of manufacturing strategy and facilitation of postponement throughout the supply chain.
Supplier relationship collaboration	The development and administration of relationships with suppliers to facilitate strategic information sharing, joint planning, and integrated operations.
Life cycle support	The repair and support of products during their life cycle, including warranty, maintenance, and repair.
Reverse logistics	The return and disposition of inventories in a cost-effective and secure manner.

measurements and allocations were typically limited to costs common to all functional areas of work, such as overhead, labor, utilities, insurance, interest, and so on.

Excellence in supply chain performance requires the simultaneous achievement of eight key processes. Table 1.2 identifies the eight key processes and provides a brief description of each. Although these integrative processes are not the exclusive domain of supply chain logistics, some critical elements of such performance are integral to a firm achieving high-level operational success. Therefore, supply chain structure, strategy, and continuous operational execution must be focused on achieving and continuously improving these essential eight processes. Simultaneous operational achievement of these eight processes forms the essence of achieving operational integration and performance excellence.

The fundamental challenge of integrated management is to redirect traditional emphasis on functionality in an effort to focus on process achievement. Over the past few decades, it has become increasingly apparent that functions, individually performed best in class, do not necessarily combine or aggregate to achieve lowest total cost or highly effective processes. Integrative process management seeks to identify and achieve lowest total cost by capturing trade-offs that exist between functions. To illustrate using a logistical example, a firm might be able to reduce total cost to serve a customer as a result of spending more for faster, dependable transportation because the overall cost of inventory associated with the process may be reduced by an amount greater than that being spent for premium transportation. The focus of integrated management is **lowest total process cost,** which is not necessarily the achievement of the lowest cost for each function included in the process.

The concept of trade-off and the goal of lowest total cost have logical appeal. While deceptively simple, managers continue to find the identification, measurement, and implementation of a process to minimize total cost a difficult task in day-to-day operations. The unavailability of process performance data and cost measures capable of quantifying cross-functional trade-offs served to stimulate development of such integrative tools as Total Cost Analysis, Process Engineering, and Activity-Based Costing (ABC).

Three important facets of supply chain logic resulted from increased attention to integrated management: (1) collaboration, (2) enterprise extension, and (3) integrated service providers.

Collaboration

As discussed earlier, the history of business has been dominated by a desire to cooperate but always couched within a competitive framework. Whereas competition remains the dominant model guiding free market economies, the increasing importance of collaboration has positioned the supply chain as a primary unit of competition. In today's global economy, supply chain arrangements compete with each other for customer loyalty. Supply chains dominated by Sears Holding, Target, and WalMart* are direct competitors in many markets. Similar supply chain alignments can be observed in industries ranging from entertainment to food to automobiles to chemicals. The global strategic reach of Limited Logistics Services is an example of the complexity of modern supply chain management. Garments are manufactured throughout the world and are sold in all fashion seasons to worldwide consumers.

The general impetus to institutionalized collaborative working arrangements was the 1984 enactment of the National Cooperative Research and Development Act, which was expanded in scope by the Production Amendments of 1993 and 2004.[5] This national legislation and its subsequent modification signaled fundamental change in traditional Justice Department antitrust philosophy. The basic legislation, as supplemented by administrative rulings, encouraged firms to develop collaborative initiatives in an effort to increase the global competitiveness of U.S.-based firms. Widespread realization that cooperation is both permissible and encouraged served to stimulate formation of supply chain arrangements.

While all forms of price collusion remain illegal, the collaborative legislation served to facilitate cross-organizational sharing of operating information, technology, and risk as ways to increase competitiveness. The response was a wide variety of new and innovative operating arrangements. One such development was the growing vision of the extended enterprise.

Enterprise Extension

The central thrust of enterprise extension expanded managerial influence and control beyond the ownership boundaries of a single enterprise to facilitate joint planning and operations with customers and suppliers. The fundamental belief is that collaborative behavior between firms that integrate processes will maximize customer impact, reduce overall risk, and greatly improve efficiency. Enterprise extension builds on two basic paradigms: information sharing and process specialization.

The **information sharing paradigm** is the widespread belief that achieving a high degree of cooperative behavior requires that supply chain participants voluntarily share operating information and jointly plan strategies. The scope of cross-enterprise collaboration should span beyond sales data to include plans detailing promotion, new product introduction, and day-to-day operations. It's important to emphasize that information sharing to

---

[5] On October 11, 1984, President Reagan signed into law the National Cooperative Research Act of 1984 (Public Law 98-462) in an effort "to promote research and development, encourage innovation, stimulate trade, and make necessary and appropriate modifications in the operation of the antitrust laws." This law enables research and development activities to be jointly performed up to the point where prototypes are developed. The law further determined that antitrust litigation would be based on the rule of reason, taking into account all factors affecting competition. An extension to this act was signed into law by President Clinton on June 10, 1993. The extension, National Cooperative Production Amendments of 1993 (Public Law 103-42), allows joint ventures to go beyond just research to include the production and testing of a product, process, or service. This created a new act called the National Cooperative Research and Production Act of 1993 to replace the 1984 act. Furthermore, this new act established a procedure for businesses to notify the Department of Justice and the Federal Trade Commission of their cooperative arrangement in order to qualify for "single-damages limitation on civil antitrust liability." In 2004 President Bush signed into law the Standards Development Organization Advancement Act (SDOAA, H. R. 1086) which amended the 1993 act to include immunity for standards development organizations and thereby further validated the collaborative doctrine.

support collaboration must not be limited to historical or even accurate current sales data. Of greater importance is a willingness to share information about future strategic initiatives to facilitate joint operations. The guiding principle is that information sharing is essential among supply chain participants to collectively do the things customers demand faster and more efficiently.

The **process specialization paradigm** is commitment to focusing collaborative arrangements on planning joint operations with a goal of eliminating nonproductive or non-value-adding redundancy by firms in a supply chain. The basic idea is to design the overall supply chain processes in a manner that identifies a specific firm's competencies along with the responsibility and accountability to perform each element of essential work in a manner that maximizes overall results.

Firms participating in a supply chain have specific roles and share strategic goals. Sharing information and joint planning can reduce risk related to inventory positioning. Collaboration can eliminate duplicative or redundant work, such as repetitive quality inspection, by designating and empowering a specified member of the supply chain to be fully responsible and accountable. Such extended enterprise integration introduces new challenges regarding measurement, benefit and risk sharing, trust, leadership, and conflict resolution. It is clear that the challenges of collaboration and enterprise extension constitute new managerial horizons. A third contributing force to supply chain development is the rapidly changing managerial attitude toward integrated service providers.

Integrated Service Providers

As noted earlier, the origins of contemporary business were grounded in functional specialization. It is not surprising that firms developed the practice of **outsourcing** work to businesses that are specialists in the performance of specific functions. The two traditional logistics service providers are transportation and warehousing specialists.

The for-hire transportation industry consists of thousands of carriers who specialize in product movement between geographic locations. Over the years, a comprehensive carrier network has emerged, providing shippers a broad assortment of services, utilizing all available forms or modes of transportation and related technology. The value proposition of for-hire transportation is based on specialization, efficiency, and scale economies. Value is generated by a carrier's capability to provide shared transportation services for multiple shippers. The transport alternatives for shippers are either to invest capital in transportation equipment and operations or to engage the services of for-hire carriers. Naturally, a large number of firms develop transportation solutions that combine benefits of these alternatives.

In addition to transportation, a large number of service companies have traditionally provided warehouse services. Traditionally called **public warehouses,** these firms provide product storage supplemented with other specialized services. Two significant benefits are gained when shippers use public warehouses. First is elimination of capital investment in warehouse buildings. The second is the ability to consolidate small shipments for combined delivery with products of other firms that use the same public warehouse. Such multishipper consolidation achieves transportation efficiency not typically available when firms ship from their own warehouses. Many firms combine private and public warehouses into go-to-market and product supply networks.

In 1980 the landscape of for-hire services in the United States changed dramatically. Within a few short months, the economic and political regulatory infrastructure of transportation in the United States shifted from economic to social regulation as a result of the passage of the Motor Carrier Regulatory Reform and Modernization Act (MCA-80) and the Staggers Rail Act.[6] These regulatory changes served to initiate a trend toward an open

---

[6] Public Laws 96-296 and 96-488, respectively. These laws, as well as others briefly noted here, are discussed in greater detail in Chapter 8.

transportation market that ultimately resulted in less government economic regulation for all forms of transportation. Over time, this trend extended worldwide to deregulate transportation in most free-market industrialized nations.

In contrast to transportation, firms engaged in public warehousing were not operationally regulated by federal or state governments. Most warehouse firms did not offer transportation services so as to avoid regulation. However, with the deregulation of transportation, that practice soon changed. Overnight, warehousing firms began to offer transportation services. Likewise, many transport carriers began to offer customers warehouse services.

What occurred in the logistics service industry was a radical shift from single function to multifunctional outsourcing. **Integrated service providers (ISPs)** began to market a range of logistics services that included all work necessary to accommodate customers, ranging from order entry to product delivery. In many situations the foundation of transportation and warehouse services was augmented by the performance of a wide range of special services. These customized services are typically described as **value-added services (VAS).** For example, United Parcel Service (UPS) stocks Nike shoes and warm-ups at its Louisville warehouse and processes orders hourly. All related communication and financial administration are handled by a UPS call center. Thus, Nike has effectively outsourced basic logistics and related value-added service to UPS.

The common name used throughout industry to describe ISPs is **third-party and fourth-party service providers.** In a general sense, ISPs are commonly classified as being either **asset-** or **nonasset-based,** the distinction being that asset-based (third-party) firms own and operate transportation equipment and warehousing buildings. In contrast, nonasset service (fourth-party) firms specialize in providing comprehensive information services that facilitate supply chain arrangements. Such fourth-party service providers arrange services, often integrating third-party asset operators on behalf of their customers.

The 2007 third-party contract logistics market was estimated to be $122 billion.[7] The growth of integrated service providers makes both the formation and dismantling of supply chain arrangements easier. Thus, supply chain participants have the opportunity to engage the capabilities of what amounts to a virtual logistics network. Such outsourcing helps facilitate process-focused integrative management.

As discussed, the advent of collaboration, extended enterprise visioning, and the increased availability of integrated service providers combined to drive radically new supply chain solutions. The notion of shared and synergistic benefits served to solidify the importance of relationships between firms collaborating in a supply chain. The extended enterprise logic stimulated visions of increased efficiency, effectiveness, and relevance as a result of sharing information, planning, and operational specialization between supply chain participants. The deregulation of transportation served as a catalyst for the development of integrated service providers. This development served to redefine and expand the scope of specialized services available to facilitate supply chain operations. In combination, these three drivers helped create integrated supply chain management. They served to identify and solidify the strategic benefits of integrated management. They combined to reinforce the value of core-competence specialization and cast the challenges and opportunity of creating virtual supply chains.

Responsiveness

One could argue that the challenges and benefits of integrative management offered sufficient reason for the supply chain revolution. However, other basic drivers continue to make supply chain arrangements even more appealing. A fundamental paradigm shift in

---

[7] "U.S. 3PL/Contract Logistics Market," Armstrong & Associates, Inc., 2008.

strategic thinking occurred as a direct impact of information technology. Information connectivity created the potential for developing responsive business models. To elaborate the far-reaching implications of this major development, it is useful to contrast traditional or **anticipatory** business practice to the emerging time-based **responsive**[8] (or **pull**) business model. Strategies related to incorporation of postponement are also developed. Postponement is a major strategy in contemporary supply chain management.

Anticipatory Business Model

Since the industrial revolution, the dominant business model has required anticipation of what customers will demand in the future. Because information concerning purchase behavior was not readily available and firms loosely linked together in a channel of distribution did not feel compelled to share their plans, business operations were driven by forecasts. The typical manufacturer produced products based upon a market forecast. Likewise, wholesalers, distributors, and retailers purchased inventory based on their unique forecasts and promotional plans. Since the forecast results were more often than not wrong, considerable discontinuities existed between what firms planned to do and what they, in fact, ended up doing. Such discontinuity typically resulted in unplanned inventory. Because of high cost and risk associated with conducting business on an anticipatory basis, the prevailing relationship between trading partners was adversarial; each firm needed to protect its own interest.

Figure 1.2 illustrates the typical stages in the anticipatory business model: forecast, purchase materials, manufacture, warehouse, sell, and then deliver. In nonmanufacturing firms, operations involved anticipatory purchase of inventory assortments to accommodate expected sales. The key point is that almost all essential work has been traditionally performed in anticipation of future requirements. The likelihood of misgauging customer requirements rendered the anticipatory business model highly risky. In addition, each firm in the distribution channel duplicated the anticipatory process.

Responsive Business Model

The fundamental difference in anticipatory and responsive supply chain arrangements is timing. The responsive business model seeks to reduce or eliminate forecast reliance by joint planning and rapid exchange of information between supply chain participants.

The availability of low-cost information has created **time-based competition.** Managers are increasingly sharing information to improve both the speed and accuracy of supply chain logistics. To illustrate, managers may share information to improve forecasting accuracy or even eliminate forecasts in an effort to reduce anticipatory inventory deployment. This transformation from anticipatory toward responsive business is possible because today's managers have the information technology to rapidly obtain and share

[8] Donald J. Bowersox and Nicholas J. Lahowchic, *Start Pulling Your Chain! Leading Responsive Supply Chain Transformation* (Port St. Lucie, FL: OGI Enterprises LLC, 2008).

FIGURE 1.2 **Anticipatory Business Model**

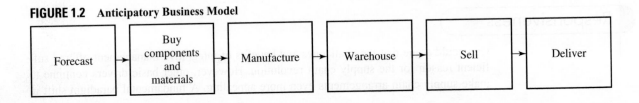

FIGURE 1.3
Responsive Business Model

accurate sales data and exercise improved operational control. When all members of the supply chain synchronize their operations, opportunities exist to reduce overall inventory and eliminate costly duplicate practices. More important, customers can be provided with products they want, fast.

Figure 1.3 illustrates a responsive business model that manufactures or assembles products to customer order. The fundamental difference in responsive models is the sequence of events that drive business practice. Also notable, in comparison to Figure 1.2, are the fewer steps required to complete the responsive process. Fewer steps typically equate to less cost and less elapsed time from order commitment to delivery. The responsive sequence is initiated by a sale followed by a sequence of material purchase, custom manufacturing, and direct customer delivery.

In many ways, the responsive business model is similar to the traditional build-to-order manufacturing. The primary differences between modern responsive operations and traditional build-to-order are the time to execute and the degree of potential customization. While response-based examples are observable in many different industries, a high degree of attention has focused on the operational model developed by Dell Corporation. In 2004 Dell perfected a responsive distribution model wherein computers sold in the United States were built to order in China and delivered to United States consumers within a five-day order-to-delivery cycle.

In terms of time to execute the order to delivery, the contemporary responsive system is substantially faster than the traditional build-to-order manufacturing. It is becoming common practice to replenish retail store inventories of consumer products on a daily basis. Custom-built automobiles are being promised for delivery within 10 working days, with the goal to even further reduce the order-to-delivery cycle. Such compressed order-to-delivery cycles were not even imaginable a few years ago.

Perhaps an even more appealing attribute of responsive supply chains is their potential to uniquely customize products on smaller orders than was typical of traditional build-to-order lot size manufacturing. Direct connectivity with customers via Internet-based customer connectivity is accelerating customization. In most traditional anticipatory distribution systems, the customer is a passive participant. About the only power the customer has in the traditional process is the decision to buy or not buy. Direct connectivity of customers in a responsive process has at least three benefits. First, involvement provides comprehensive search capabilities that serve to expand the range of sources and choices a customer can consider when selecting a product or service. Second, customers can be better informed about prices and, in some situations, are able to drive price advantage by virtue of bids and/or auctions. Finally, information-intense responsive systems provide innovation such as a **customer choice-board** wherein customers design or customize their own product configuration.[9]

[9] Adrian J. Slywotzky, "The Age of the Choiceboard," *Harvard Business Review* (January/February 2000), pp. 40–41; and Jarrus D. Pagh and Martha C. Cooper, "Supply Chain Postponement and Speculation Strategies: How to Choose the Right Strategy," *Journal of Business Logistics* 19, no. 2 (1998), pp. 13–28.

Postponement

At the heart of time-based competition is the capability to postpone customization and the timing of logistical fulfillment. The concept of **postponement** has long been discussed in business literature.[10] However, practical examples involving postponement are directly related to advancements in information technology. Postponement strategies and practices serve to reduce the anticipatory risk of supply chain performance. As noted earlier, anticipatory arrangements require most inventory to be produced to final product state and deployed on the basis of forecasts or planned requirements. Working arrangements, which allow postponement of final manufacturing, customization, or distribution of a product until receipt of a customer order, reduce the incidence of wrong manufacturing or incorrect inventory deployment. Two types of postponement are common in highly responsive supply chain operations: (1) manufacturing, or **form postponement;** and (2) geographic, or **logistics postponement.**

Manufacturing Postponement

The global competitive climate of the 21st century is facilitating the development of new manufacturing techniques designed to increase flexibility and responsiveness while maintaining unit cost and quality. Traditional practice has focused on achieving economy of scale by planning extensive manufacturing runs. In contrast, flexible manufacturing logic is typically driven by a desire to increase responsiveness to customer requirements.

The vision of **manufacturing, or form, postponement** is one of products being manufactured one order at a time with no preparatory work or component procurement until exact customer specifications are fully known and purchase confirmation is received. This dream of building to customer order is not new. What is new is the expectation that flexible manufacturing can achieve such responsiveness without sacrificing efficiency. To the degree technology can support market-paced flexible manufacturing strategies, firms are freed from forecast-driven anticipatory operations.

In practice, manufacturing lot size economics cannot be ignored. The challenge is to quantify cost trade-offs between procurement, manufacturing, and logistics. At this point, it is sufficient to understand that the trade-off is between the cost and risk associated with anticipatory manufacturing and the loss of economy of scale resulting from introducing flexible procedures. Manufacturing lot size reduction requires a trade-off between line setup, switchover, and associated procurement expense balanced against cost and risk associated with stockpiling finished inventory. In the traditional functional style of management, manufacturing schedules were established to realize the lowest unit cost of production. From an integrative management perspective, the goal is to achieve desired customer satisfaction at the lowest total cost. This may require manufacturing postponement at some per-unit-cost sacrifice to achieve overall supply chain efficiency.

The operative goal of manufacturing postponement is to maintain products in a neutral or noncommitted status as long as possible. The ideal application of form postponement is to manufacture a standard or base product in sufficient quantities to realize economy of scale while deferring finalization of features, such as color or accessories, until customer commitment is received. Given a postponement-driven manufacturing scenario, economy of scope is introduced into the logistics equation by producing a standard or base product to accommodate a wide range of different customers. One of the first commercially viable examples of manufacturing postponement was mixing paint color at retail stores

---

[10] Wroe Alderson, *Marketing Behavior and Executive Action* (Homewood, IL: Richard D. Irwin, Inc., 1957), p. 426. For a more contemporary discussion of postponement, see B. Joseph Pine II, Bart Victor, and Andrew C. Boynton, "Making Mass Customization Work," *Harvard Business Review* (September/October 1993), pp. 108–19.

to accommodate individual customer request. Perfecting the in-store mixing process dramatically reduced the number of stockkeeping units required at retail paint stores. Instead of trying to maintain inventories of premixed color paint, retail stores stock a base paint and customize the color to accommodate specific orders.

In other industries, manufacturing practice is to process and store product in bulk, postponing final packaging configuration until customer orders are received. In some situations products are processed and packed in cans with brand identification labeling being postponed until specific customer orders are received. Other examples of manufacturing postponement include the increased practice of installing accessories at automobile, appliance, and motorcycle dealerships, thereby customizing products to customer request at the time of purchase.

These manufacturing postponement examples have one thing in common: They reduce the number of stockkeeping units in logistical inventory while supporting a broad-line marketing effort and retaining mass manufacturing economies of scale. Until the product is customized, it has the potential to serve many different customers.

The impact of manufacturing postponement is twofold. First, the variety of differentiated products, moved in anticipation of sale, can be reduced, and therefore the risk of logistics malfunction is lower. The second and perhaps the more important impact is the increased use of logistical facilities to perform light manufacturing and final assembly. To the extent that a degree of specialized talent or highly restrictive economy of scale does not exist in manufacturing, product customization may be best delegated and performed near the customer destination market. This form of manufacturing postponement is often called **late customization.** The traditional mission of logistical warehouses in some industries has changed significantly to accommodate manufacturing postponement.

Geographic Postponement

In many ways **geographic,** or **logistics, postponement** is the exact opposite of manufacturing postponement. The basic notion of geographic postponement is to build and stock a full-line inventory at one or a limited number of strategic locations. Forward deployment of inventory is postponed until customer orders are received. Once the logistical process is initiated, every effort is made to accelerate the economic movement of products directly to customers. Under the concept of geographic postponement, the anticipatory risk of inventory deployment is partially eliminated while manufacturing economy of scale is retained.

Many applications of geographic postponement involve service supply parts. Critical and high-cost parts are maintained in a central inventory to assure availability for all potential users. When demand occurs, orders are electronically transmitted to the central service center and expedited shipments are made direct to the forward service center, using fast, reliable transportation. The end result is highly reliable customer service with reduced overall inventory investment.

The potential for geographic postponement has been facilitated by increased logistical system capability to process, transmit, and deliver precise order requirements with a high degree of accuracy and speed. Geographic postponement substitutes accelerated delivery of precise order requirements for the anticipatory deployment of inventory to local market warehouses. Unlike manufacturing postponement, systems utilizing geographic postponement retain manufacturing economies of scale while meeting customer service requirements by accelerating direct shipments.

In combination, manufacturing and geographic postponement offer alternative ways to refrain from anticipatory distribution by waiting until customer commitments are received. The factors favoring one or the other form of postponement hinge on volume, value, competitive initiatives, economies of scale, and desired customer delivery speed and consistency. In a growing number of supply chains, both types of postponement are combined to create a highly flexible strategy.

Barriers to Implementing Responsive Systems

In reality, today's best supply chain practices do not reflect either extreme anticipatory or responsive design. Most established firms remain, to a significant degree, committed to anticipatory practices. However, responsive strategies are rapidly emerging. Perhaps the greatest barrier to adopting responsive arrangements is the need for publicly held corporations to maintain planned quarterly profits. This accountability creates expectations concerning continued sales and financial results. Such expectations often drive promotional and pricing strategies to "load the channel" with inventory to create timely sales. Conversely, it is never timely to make a major reduction in channel inventory. Efforts to lean or deload inventory to implement a more responsive operating posture require the ability to absorb a one-time sale reduction among supply chain partners. Start-up ventures are ideally positioned to implement responsive fulfillment systems because they do not face the channel deload challenge.

A second barrier to implementing responsive operations is the need to establish collaborative relationships. Most business managers simply do not have training or experience in development of collaborative arrangements designed to share benefits and risks. While managers generally express a high degree of belief in the long-term potential for responsive alliances, they typically confront considerable frustration concerning how to implement such supply chain arrangements.

For the foreseeable future, most firms will continue to implement strategies that combine anticipatory and responsive supply chain arrangements. The trend toward increased involvement in responsive arrangements with specific customers and suppliers will continue to expand as the full advantage of Web-based operations materializes.

Financial Sophistication

Few managers question the benefits of applying the time-based strategies discussed above to supply chain operations. However, a valid question is, How fast is fast enough? Speed simply for the sake of being fast has little, if any, enduring value.[11] The answer concerning how much speed is desirable is found in the financial impact. The process of creating value dictates that faster, more flexible, and more precise ways of servicing customers are justified as long as they can be provided at competitive prices. A third force driving competitive supply chain strategy is the ability to manage in a more timely manner to achieve financially attractive working arrangements.

The financial benefits of timely response are straightforward. Fast delivery translates to less inventory and reduced need for distribution facilities. Faster to customers means less working capital is required to support supply chain operations. Three aspects of financial sophistication are cash-to-cash conversion, dwell time minimization, and cash spin.

Cash-to-Cash Conversion

The time required to convert raw material or inventory purchases into sales revenue is referred to as **cash-to-cash conversion.** Cash conversion is generally related to inventory turn: The higher the inventory turn, the quicker the cash conversion. A goal of supply chain design is to reduce and control order receipt-to-delivery time in an effort to accelerate inventory turns.

---

[11] George Stalk Jr. and Alan M. Webber, "Japan's Dark Side of Time," *Harvard Business Review* (July/August 1993), pp. 93–102.

In traditional business arrangements, benefits related to cash-to-cash conversion have typically been enjoyed at the expense of business partners. Given typical purchase discounts and invoicing practices, it is operationally possible for firms to rapidly sell merchandise and still qualify for prompt payment discounts. To illustrate, terms of sale offering a 2 percent discount net 10-day payment (2% net 10) means that a prompt payment discount is earned if the invoice is paid within 10 days from confirmed time of delivery. Thus, if the invoice is $1000, a payment made within 10 days will earn a $20 discount. If the firm sells the product for cash before the invoice payment date, it, in effect, enjoys free inventory and may even earn interest by investing cash while awaiting the payment date.

In responsive systems, cash-to-cash conversion benefits can be shared by managing inventory velocity across the supply chain. This ability to manage inventory velocity from origin to final destination has the potential to achieve greater overall efficiencies than are attainable by a single firm. Coordinated operations may require that a designated firm in the supply chain serve as the principal inventory stocking location. Such practice means that risk and benefits related to inventory need to be shared by participating firms. To facilitate such arrangements, supply chain members often replace the discounts with **dead net pricing.**[12]

Dead net pricing means that all discounts and allowances are factored in the selling price. Thus, incentives for timely payment are replaced by detailed performance commitments at a specified net price. Invoice payment, based on negotiated net price, is completed upon verification of physical receipt. Such payment is typically in the form of Electronic Funds Transfer (EFT), thereby streamlining both the flow of physical goods and cash among supply chain partners. Managing supply chain logistics as a continuous synchronized process also serves to reduce dwell time.

Dwell Time Minimization

Traditional distribution arrangements typically involve independent business units loosely linked together on a transaction-to-transaction basis. Such traditional business operations are driven by a series of **independent** transactions buffered by inventory. In contrast, a supply chain has the potential to function as a synchronized series of **interdependent** business units.

At the heart of supply chain operating leverage is the willingness to transfer inventory on an as-needed basis, taking advantage of as much collaboration and information as possible. Such collaboration and information can be focused on maintaining the continued flow and velocity of inventory moving throughout the supply chain. The potential of such synchronization is a key benefit of supply chain connectivity.

A significant measure of supply chain productivity is **dwell time.** Dwell time is the ratio of time that an asset sits idle to the time required to satisfy its designated supply chain mission. For example, dwell time would be the ratio of the time a unit of inventory is in storage compared to the time that it is moving or otherwise contributing to achieving sales or operational objectives.

To reduce dwell time, firms collaborating in a supply chain need to be willing to eliminate duplicate and non-value-added work. For example, if three different firms perform identical processes as a product flows along a supply chain, dwell times will accumulate. Designating a specific firm to perform and be accountable for the value-added work can serve to reduce overall dwell.

Likewise, timely arrival and continuous inventory flow between supply chain partners reduces dwell. When a product flows from a supplier through a retailer's cross-dock sortation process without coming to rest or being diverted to warehouse storage, overall dwell

---

[12] Logistical pricing is discussed in Chapter 9.

time is minimized. A collateral benefit of reducing dwell time and the associated logistics cost is the ability to reduce investment in inventory and related assets.

Cash Spin

A popular term for describing the potential benefits of reducing assets across a supply chain is **cash spin,** sometimes referred to as **free cash spin.**[13] The concept is to reduce overall assets committed to supply chain performance. Thus, a dollar of inventory or the investment in a warehouse, if eliminated by a reengineered supply chain, spins cash for redeployment. Such free capital can be reinvested in projects that might otherwise have been considered too risky.

Naturally, cash spin opportunity is not unique to the supply chain. The potential to spin cash applies to all areas of a firm. What makes the potential of supply chain cash spin so attractive is the opportunity to collaborate between firms.

The benefits flowing from fast cash-to-cash conversion, reduced dwell time, and cash spin combine to increase the financial attractiveness of effective collaboration. Another major force driving expansion of supply chain management is the growing involvement of most firms in international operations.

Globalization

A conservative estimate is that as much as 90 percent of global demand is not fully satisfied by local supply. Current demand coupled with a world population projected to increase by an average of over 200,000 persons per day for the next decade equates to substantial market opportunity. The range of product/service growth potential varies greatly between industrialized and emerging economies. In industrialized sectors of the global economy, opportunities focus on upscale consumer products. These more advanced economies offer substantial opportunities for the sale of products combined with value-added services. While it is true that consumers in developing nations enjoy relatively less purchasing power than those in their industrialized counterparts, demand in such economies for basic products and necessities is huge. Consumers in developing nations are more interested in quality of basic life than in fashion or technology. For example, the growing populations of India and China offer huge market opportunities for basic products like food, clothing, and consumer durables such as refrigerators, washing machines, and automobiles. Firms with aggressive growth goals cannot neglect the commercialization of the global marketplace.

In addition to sales potential, involvement in global business is being driven by significant opportunities to increase operating efficiency. Such operational efficiencies are attainable in at least three areas. First, the global marketplace offers significant opportunity to strategically source raw material and components. Second, significant labor advantages can be gained by locating manufacturing and distribution facilities in developing nations. Third, favorable tax laws can make the performance of value-adding operations in specific countries highly attractive.

The decision to engage in global operations to achieve market growth and enjoy operational efficiency follows a natural path of business expansion. Typically, firms enter the global marketplace by conducting import and export operations. Such import and export transactions constitute a significant portion of global international business. The second stage of internationalization involves a firm's establishment of local presence in foreign nations and trading areas. Such presence can range from franchise and licensing of local businesses to the establishment of manufacturing and distribution facilities. The important

---

[13] Gene Tyndall et al., *Supercharging Supply Chains* (New York: John Wiley & Sons, 1988), p. 1.

distinction between import/export involvement and establishment of local presence is the degree of investment and managerial involvement characteristic of stage 2. The third stage of internationalization is the full-fledged conduct of business operations within and across international boundaries. This most advanced phase of international engagement is typically referred to as **globalization.**

The logistics of internationalization involves four significant differences in comparison to national or even regional operations. First, the **distance** of typical order-to-delivery operations is significantly longer in international as contrasted to domestic business. Second, to accommodate the laws and regulations of all governing bodies, the required **documentation** of business transactions is significantly more complex. Third, international logistics operations must be designed to deal with significant **diversity** in work practices and local operating environment. Fourth, accommodation of cultural variations in how consumers **demand** products and services is essential for successful logistical operations.

Finally, 21st-century commerce is conducted within a constant threat of terrorism, which requires increased security. The intensity and severity of terrorist disruption involves both the shipment itself and the exposure to using the logistics infrastructure as a means to deliver explosive and chemical devices. The security aspects of global logistics are further discussed in Chapter 17. It is important to understand that successfully going supply chain global requires mastering the associated logistical challenges.

While logistics principles and the ideals of supply chain integration are essentially the same globally as they are domestically, the above characteristics make operating environments more complex and costly. The cost of logistics on a global basis is estimated to exceed $8 trillion a year.[14] Such expenditure is justified in terms of potential market expansion and operating efficiencies. However, risk exposure related to capitalizing on international supply chain management and its logistical components requires integrated operating strategies and tactics.

Summary

The development of integrated management skill is critical to continued productivity improvement. Such integrative management must focus on quality improvement at both functional and process levels. In terms of functions, critical work must be performed to the highest degree of efficiency. Processes that create value occur both within individual firms and between firms linked together in collaborative supply chains. Each type of process must be continuously improved.

The idea that all or even most firms will link together to form highly collaborative end-to-end supply chain initiatives at any time in the foreseeable future is quite unlikely. The dynamics of a free competitive market system will serve to harness such an end state. However, initiatives aimed at cross-enterprise integration along the supply chain are increasingly occurring and, to the extent successfully implemented, offer new and exciting business models for gaining competitive advantage. Once achieved, such supply chain integration is hard to maintain and is subject to continuous redefinition. What works today may not work tomorrow. Conversely, what won't work today may work tomorrow.

Thus, supply chain collaborations must be viewed as highly dynamic. Such collaborations are attractive because they offer new horizons for achieving market position and operating efficiency. Supply chain opportunities are challenges that 21st-century logistics managers must explore and exploit. However, supply chain integration is a means to increased profitability and growth and not an end in itself.

[14] Donald J. Bowersox, Roger J. Calantone, and Alexandre M. Rodrigues, "Estimation of Global Logistics Expenditures Using Neural Networks," *Journal of Business Logistics* 26, no. 2 (2005), pp. 1–16.

From the perspective of integrated logistics management, supply chain strategies define the relevant operating framework. What must be logistically accomplished is directly linked to supply chain structure and strategy. When such structure and strategy are internationally positioned, logistics performance must embrace challenges related to globalization. In short, the supply chain strategy or lack of strategy and its related structure serve to shape the framework for logistical requirements. Chapter 2 presents logistics in greater detail.

Challenge Questions

1. Why can the current movement toward the establishment of supply chains be characterized as a revolution?

2. Compare and contrast economic, market, and relevency value.

3. Compare the concept of a modern supply chain with more traditional distribution channels. Be specific regarding similarities and differences.

4. What specific role does logistics play in supply chain operations?

5. Describe integrative management. Be specific concerning the relationship between function and process.

6. In terms of enterprise extension, describe the importance of the information sharing and process specialization paradigms.

7. Describe and illustrate an integrated service provider. How does the concept of integrated service provider differ from traditional service providers, such as for-hire transportation and warehousing?

8. Compare and contrast anticipatory and responsive business models. Why has responsiveness become popular in supply chain strategy and collaboration?

9. Compare and contrast manufacturing and geographic postponement.

10. Define and illustrate cash-to-cash conversion, dwell time minimization, and cash spin. How do supply chain strategy and structure impact each?

Logistics

Chapter Outline

No other area of business operations involves the complexity or spans the geography of logistics. All around the globe, 24 hours of every day, 7 days a week, during 52 weeks a year, logistics is concerned with getting products and services where they are needed at the precise time desired. It is difficult to visualize accomplishing any marketing, manufacturing, or international commerce without logistics. Most consumers in highly developed industrial nations take a high level of logistical competency for granted. When they purchase goods—at a retail store, over the telephone, or via the Internet—they expect product delivery will be performed as promised. In fact, their expectation is for timely, error-free logistics every time they order, even during the busiest periods. They have little or no tolerance for failure to perform.

Although logistics has been performed since the beginning of civilization, implementing 21st-century best practices is one of the most exciting and challenging operational areas of supply chain management. Because logistics is both old and new, we choose to characterize the rapid change taking place in best practice as a **renaissance.**

Logistics involves the management of order processing, inventory, transportation, and the combination of warehousing, materials handling, and packaging, all integrated throughout a network of facilities. The goal of logistics is to support procurement, manufacturing, and customer accommodation supply chain operational requirements. Within a firm the challenge is to coordinate functional competency into an integrated supply chain focused on servicing customers. In the broader supply chain context, operational synchronization is essential with customers as well as material and service suppliers to link internal and external operations as one integrated process.

Logistics refers to the responsibility to **design and administer systems to control movement and geographical positioning of raw materials, work-in-process, and finished inventories at the lowest total cost.** To achieve lowest total cost means that financial and human assets committed to logistics must be held to an absolute minimum. It is also necessary to hold operational expenditures as low as possible. The combinations of resources, skills, and systems required to achieve superior logistics are challenging to integrate, but once achieved, such integrated competency is difficult for competitors to replicate.

This chapter focuses on the contribution of logistics to integrated supply chain management. First, cost and service are emphasized. Next, the logistics value proposition is developed. Then traditional business functions that combine to create the logistical process are reviewed. Next, the objectives of integrated logistics are reviewed. Finally, the importance of logistical synchronization to supply chain integration is highlighted in terms of performance cycle structure and dynamics.

The Logistics of Business Is Big and Important

It is through the logistical process that materials flow into the manufacturing capacity of an industrial nation and finished products are distributed to consumers. The recent growth in global commerce has expanded the size and complexity of logistical operations.

Logistics adds value to the supply chain process when inventory is strategically positioned to achieve sales. Creating logistics value is costly. Although difficult to measure, most experts agree that the annual expenditure to perform logistics in the United States in 2007 was approximately 10.1 percent of the $13.84 billion Gross Domestic Product (GDP), or $1,398 billion.[1] Expenditure for transportation in 2007 was $857 billion, which represented 61.3 percent of total logistics cost. As further illustrated in Table 2.1, the logistics of business is truly big business!

Despite the sheer size of logistical expenditure, the excitement about logistics is not cost containment or reduction. The excitement generates from understanding how select firms use logistical competency to help achieve competitive advantage. Firms having world-class logistical competency enjoy competitive advantage as a result of providing their most important customers superior service. Leading performers typically utilize information

[1] Rosalyn Wilson, 19th Annual "State of Logistics Report," Council of Supply Chain Management Professionals, Oak Brook, IL, June 2008.

TABLE 2.1   U.S. Logistics Cost, 1980–2007 ($ Billion except GDP)

Source: Adapted from Rosalyn Wilson, 19th Annual "State of Logistics Report," Council of Supply Chain Management Professionals. Oak Brook, IL, 2008.

Year	Nominal GDP ($ trillion)	Values of All Business Inventory	Percent of Inventory Carrying Rate	Inventory Carrying Costs	Transportation Costs	Administrative Costs	Total U.S. Logistics Cost	Logistics (% of GDP)
1980	$ 2.80	692	31.8	220	214	17	451	16.1
1981	3.13	747	34.7	259	228	19	506	16.2
1982	3.26	760	30.8	234	222	18	474	14.5
1983	3.54	758	27.9	211	243	18	472	13.3
1984	3.93	826	29.1	240	268	20	528	13.4
1985	4.22	847	26.8	227	274	20	521	12.3
1986	4.45	843	25.7	217	281	20	518	11.6
1987	4.74	875	25.7	225	294	21	540	11.4
1988	5.10	944	26.6	251	313	23	587	11.5
1989	5.48	1005	28.1	282	329	24	635	11.6
1990	5.80	1041	27.2	283	351	25	659	11.4
1991	5.99	1030	24.9	256	355	24	635	10.6
1992	6.34	1043	22.7	237	375	24	636	10.0
1993	6.64	1076	22.2	239	396	25	660	9.9
1994	7.05	1127	23.5	265	420	27	712	10.1
1995	7.40	1211	24.9	302	441	30	773	10.4
1996	7.81	1240	24.4	303	467	31	801	10.3
1997	8.32	1280	24.5	314	503	33	850	10.2
1998	8.70	1317	24.4	321	529	34	884	10.1
1999	9.27	1381	24.1	333	554	35	922	9.9
2000	9.82	1478	25.3	374	594	39	1007	10.3
2001	10.13	1403	22.8	320	609	37	966	9.5
2002	10.46	1451	20.7	300	582	35	917	8.8
2003	10.96	1508	20.1	304	607	36	947	8.6
2004	11.69	1650	20.4	337	652	39	1028	8.8
2005	12.43	1773	22.3	395	739	46	1180	9.5
2006	13.19	1863	24.0	447	809	50	1306	9.9
2007	13.84	2026	24.1	487	857	54	1398	10.1

technology capable of monitoring global logistical activity on a real-time basis. Such technology identifies potential operational breakdowns and facilitates corrective action prior to delivery service failure. In situations where timely corrective action is not possible, customers can be provided advance notification of developing problems, thereby eliminating the surprise of an unavoidable service failure. In many situations, working in collaboration with customers and suppliers, corrective action can be taken to prevent operational shutdowns or costly customer service failures. By performing at above industry average with respect to inventory availability, speed and consistency of delivery, and operational efficiencies, logistically sophisticated firms are ideal supply chain partners.

The Logistical Value Proposition

Thus far it has been established that logistics should be managed as an integrated effort to achieve customer satisfaction at the lowest total cost. Logistics performed in this manner creates **value.** In this section, the elements of the logistical value proposition—service and cost minimization—are discussed in greater detail.

Service Benefits

Almost any level of logistical service can be achieved if a firm is willing to commit the required resources. In today's operating environment, the limiting factor is economics, not technology. For example, a dedicated inventory can be maintained in close geographical proximity to a major customer. A fleet of trucks can be held in a constant state of delivery readiness. To facilitate order processing, dedicated communications can be maintained on a real-time basis between a customer and a supplier's logistical operation. Given this high state of logistical readiness, a product or component could be delivered within minutes of identifying a customer requirement. Availability can be even faster when a supplier agrees to consign inventory on site at a customer's facility, eliminating the need to perform logistical operations when a product is required. The logistics to support consignment is completed in advance of the customer's need for the product. While such extreme service commitment might constitute a sales manager's dream, it is costly and typically not necessary to support most customer expectations and manufacturing operations.

The key strategic issue is how to outperform competitors in a cost-effective manner. If a specific material is not available when required for manufacturing, it may force a plant shutdown resulting in significant cost, potential lost sales, and even the loss of a major customer's business. The profit impact of such failures can be significant. In contrast, the profit impact of an unexpected 1- or 2-day delay in delivering products to replenish warehouse inventory could be minimal or even insignificant in terms of impact on overall operational performance. In most situations, the cost/benefit impact of logistical failure is directly related to the importance of service to the customer. The more significant the service failure impact upon a customer's business, the greater is the priority placed on error-free logistical performance.

Creation and basic logistical performance is measured in terms of inventory availability, operational performance, and service reliability. The term **basic logistics service** describes the level of service a firm provides all established customers.

Availability involves having inventory to consistently meet customer material or product requirements. The traditional paradigm has been the greater the desired availability, the larger the required inventory amount and cost. Information technology that facilitates system flexibility is providing new ways to achieve high availability for customers without correspondingly high capital investment in inventory. Information that facilitates flexibility with respect to inventory availability is critical to achieving high-level logistics performance.

Operational performance deals with the time required to deliver a customer's order. Operational performance involves delivery **speed** and **consistency.** Naturally, most customers want fast delivery. However, fast delivery is of limited value if inconsistent from one order to the next. A customer gains little benefit when a supplier promises next-day delivery but frequently delivers late. To achieve smooth operations, firms typically focus on delivery consistency first and then seek to improve delivery speed. Other aspects of operational performance are also important. A firm's operational performance can be viewed in terms of its **flexibility** to accommodate unusual and unexpected customer requests. Another aspect of operational performance is frequency of malfunction and, when such malfunction occurs, the typical recovery time. Few firms can perform perfectly all the time. It is important to estimate the likelihood of something going wrong. **Malfunction** is concerned with the probability of logistical performance failure, such as damaged products, incorrect assortment, or inaccurate documentation. When such malfunction occurs, a firm's logistical competency can be measured in terms of **recovery time.** Operational performance is concerned with how a firm handles all aspects of customer requirements, including service failure, on a day-in and day-out basis.

Service reliability involves the **quality** attributes of logistics. The key to quality is accurate measurement of availability and operational performance. Only through comprehensive performance measurement is it possible to determine if overall logistical operations are achieving desired service goals. To achieve service reliability, it is essential to identify and implement inventory availability and operational performance measurements. For logistics performance to continuously meet customer expectations, it is essential that management be committed to continuous improvement. Logistical quality does not come easy; it's the product of careful planning supported by employee training, operational dedication, comprehensive measurement, and continuous improvement. To improve service performance, goals need to be established on a selective basis. Some products are more critical than others because of their importance to the customer and their relative profit contribution.

The level of basic logistical service should be realistic in terms of customer expectations and requirements. In most cases, firms confront situations wherein customers have significantly different purchase potential. Some customers require unique or special value-added services. Thus, managers must realize that customers are different and that services provided must be matched to accommodate unique requirements and purchase potential. In general, firms tend to be overly optimistic when committing to basic customer service performance. Inability to consistently meet an unrealistically high basic service target might result in more operating and customer relationship problems than if less ambitious goals had been attempted from the outset. Unrealistic across-the-board service commitments can also dilute a firm's capability to satisfy special requirements of high-potential customers.

Cost Minimization

The focus of logistics can be traced to relatively recent developments of total costing theory and practice. In 1956, a classic monograph describing potential airfreight economics provided a new perspective concerning logistical total cost.[2] In an effort to explain conditions under which high-cost air transport could be justified, Lewis, Culliton, and Steele conceptualized the total cost logistics model. Total cost was positioned to include all expenditures necessary to perform logistical requirements. The authors illustrated an electronic parts distribution strategy wherein the high variable cost of direct factory-to-customer air transport was more than offset by reductions in inventory and field warehouse costs. They concluded that the least total cost logistical way to provide the desired customer service was to centralize inventory in one warehouse and make deliveries using air transportation.

This concept of total cost had not previously been applied to logistical operations. Probably because of the economic climate of the times and the radical departure to traditional practice, the total cost proposition generated a great deal of debate. The prevailing managerial practice, reinforced by accounting and financial control, was to focus attention on achieving the lowest possible cost for each individual function of logistics with little or no attention to integrated total cost trade-offs. Managers had traditionally focused on minimizing functional cost, such as transportation, with the expectation that such effort would achieve the lowest combined costs. Development of the total cost concept opened the door to examining how functional costs interrelate and impact each other. Subsequent refinements provided a more comprehensive understanding of logistical cost components and identified the critical need for developing functional cost analysis and activity-based costing capabilities. However, the implementation of effective logistical process costing

[2] Howard T. Lewis, James W. Culliton, and Jack D. Steele, *The Role of Air Freight in Physical Distribution* (Boston: Harvard University Press, 1956).

remains a 21st-century challenge. Many long-standing practices of accounting continue to serve as barriers to fully implementing total cost logistical solutions.

Logistics Value Generation

The key to achieving logistical leadership is to master the art of matching operating competency and commitment to key customer expectations and requirements. This customer commitment, in an exacting cost framework, is the **logistics value proposition.** It is a unique commitment of a firm to an individual or selected customer groups.

The typical enterprise seeks to develop and implement an overall logistical competency that satisfies customer expectations at a realistic total cost expenditure. Very seldom will either the lowest total cost or the highest attainable customer service constitute the appropriate logistics strategy. Likewise, the desired combination will be different for different customers. A well-designed logistical effort must provide high customer impact while controlling operational variance and minimizing inventory commitment. And, most of all, it must have relevancy to specific customers.

Significant advances have been made in the development of tools to aid management in the measurement of cost/service trade-offs. Formulation of a sound strategy requires a capability to estimate operating cost required to achieve alternative service levels. Likewise, alternative levels of system performance are meaningless unless viewed in terms of overall business unit customer accommodation, manufacturing, and procurement strategies. Supply chain design is the focus of Part Three.

Leading firms realize that a well-designed logistical system can help achieve competitive advantage. In fact, as a general rule, firms that obtain a strategic advantage based on logistical competency establish the nature of their industry's competition.

The Work of Logistics

In the context of supply chain management, logistics exists to move and position inventory to achieve desired time, place, and possession benefits at the lowest total cost. Inventory has limited value until it is positioned at the right time and at the right location to support ownership transfer or value-added creation. If a firm does not consistently satisfy time and location requirements, it has nothing to sell. For a supply chain to realize the maximum strategic benefit from logistics, the full range of functional work must be integrated. Decisions in one functional area will impact cost of all others. It is this interrelation of functions that challenges the successful implementation of integrated logistical management. Figure 2.1 provides a visual representation of the interrelated nature of the five areas of logistical work: (1) order processing; (2) inventory; (3) transportation; (4) warehousing, materials handling, and packaging; and (5) facility network. Integrated work related to these functional areas creates the capabilities needed to achieve logistical value.

Order Processing

The importance of accurate information to achieving superior logistical performance has historically been underappreciated. While many aspects of information are critical to logistics operations, the processing of orders is of primary importance. Failure to fully comprehend this importance resulted from not fully understanding how distortion and operational failures in order processing impact logistical operations.

Current information technology is capable of handling the most demanding customer requirements. When desired, order information can be exchanged between trading partners.

FIGURE 2.1
Integrated Logistics

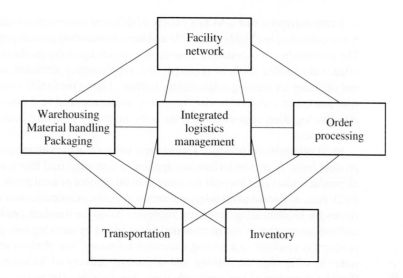

The benefit of fast information flow is directly related to work balancing. It makes little sense for a firm to accumulate orders at a local sales office for a week, mail them to a regional office, process the orders in a batch, assign them to a distribution warehouse, and then ship them via air to achieve fast delivery. In contrast, Internet communication of orders direct from the customer, combined with slower, less costly surface transportation, may achieve even faster and more constant delivery service at a lower total cost. The key objective is to balance components of the logistical system.

Forecasting and communication of customer requirements are the two areas of logistical work driven by information. The relative importance of each facet of operational information is directly related to the degree to which the supply chain is positioned to function on a responsive or anticipatory basis. This balance between responsiveness and anticipatory driven operations constitutes the basic paradigm shift taking place in 21st-century supply chain design. The more responsive the supply chain design, the greater the importance is of accurate and timely information regarding customer purchase behavior.

In most supply chains, customer requirements are transmitted in the form of orders. The processing of these orders involves all aspects of managing customer requirements, including initial order receipt, delivery, invoicing, and collection. The logistics capabilities of a firm can only be as good as its order processing competency.

Inventory

The inventory requirements of a firm are directly linked to the facility network and the desired level of customer service. Theoretically, a firm could stock every item sold in every facility dedicated to servicing each customer. Few business operations can afford such a luxurious inventory strategy because the risk and total cost are prohibitive. The objective of an inventory strategy is to achieve desired customer service with the minimum inventory commitment. Excessive inventories may compensate for deficiencies in basic design of a logistics system but will ultimately result in higher-than-necessary total logistics cost.

Logistical strategies should be designed to maintain the lowest possible financial investment in inventory. The basic goal is to achieve maximum inventory turn while satisfying service commitments. A sound inventory strategy is based on a combination of five aspects of selective deployment: (1) core customer segmentation, (2) product profitability, (3) transportation integration, (4) time-based performance, and (5) competitive performance.

Every enterprise that sells to a variety of different customers confronts uneven demand. Some customers are highly profitable and have outstanding growth potential; others do not. The profitability of a customer's business depends upon the products purchased, volume, price, value-added services required, and supplemental activities necessary to develop and maintain an ongoing relationship. Because highly profitable customers constitute the core market of every enterprise, inventory strategies need to focus on them. The key to effective logistical segmentation rests in the inventory priorities dedicated to support core customers.

Most enterprises experience a substantial variance in the volume and profitability across product lines. If no restrictions are applied, a firm may find that less than 20 percent of all products marketed account for more than 80 percent of total profit. While the so-called 80/20 rule, or **Pareto principle,** is common in business, management must avoid such outcomes by implementing inventory strategies based on fine-line product classification. A realistic assessment of the incremental value added by stocking low-profit or low-volume products is essential to avoiding excessive inventory. For obvious reasons, an enterprise wants to offer high availability and consistent delivery of its most profitable products. High-level support of less profitable items, however, may be necessary to provide full-line service to core customers. The trap to avoid is high service performance on less profitable items that are typically purchased by fringe or noncore customers. Therefore, product line profitability analysis is essential in developing a selective inventory policy.

The product stocking plan at a specific facility has a direct impact upon transportation performance. Most transportation rates are based on the volume and shipment size. Thus, it may be sound strategy to stock a sufficient range or assortment of products at a warehouse to be able to arrange consolidated shipments. The corresponding savings in transportation may more than offset the increased cost of holding the inventory.

A firm's degree of commitment to deliver products rapidly to meet a customer's inventory requirement is a major competitive factor. If products and materials can be delivered quickly, it may not be necessary for customers to maintain large inventories. Likewise, if retail stores can be replenished rapidly, less safety stock is required. The alternative to stockpiling and holding safety stock is to receive exact and timely inventory replenishment. While such time-based programs reduce customer inventory to absolute minimums, the savings must be balanced against other supply chain costs incurred as a result of the time-sensitive logistical process.

Finally, inventory strategies cannot be created in a competitive vacuum. A firm is typically more desirable to do business with than competitors if it can promise and perform rapid and consistent delivery. Therefore, it may be necessary to position inventory in a specific warehouse to gain competitive advantage even if such commitment increases total cost. Selective inventory deployment policies may be essential to gain a customer service advantage or to neutralize a strength that a competitor currently enjoys.

Material and component inventories exist in a logistical system for reasons other than finished product inventory. Each type of inventory and the level of commitment must be viewed from a total cost perspective. Understanding the interrelationship between order processing, inventory, transportation, and facility network decisions is fundamental to integrated logistics.

Transportation

Transportation is the operational area of logistics that geographically moves and positions inventory. Because of its fundamental importance and visible cost, transportation has traditionally received considerable managerial attention. Almost all enterprises, big and small, have managers responsible for transportation.

Transportation requirements can be satisfied in three basic ways. First, a private fleet of equipment may be operated. Second, contracts may be arranged with dedicated transport specialists. Third, an enterprise may engage the services of a wide variety of carriers that provide different transportation services as needed on a per shipment basis. From the logistical system viewpoint, three factors are fundamental to transportation performance: (1) cost, (2) speed, and (3) consistency.

The **cost of transport** is the payment for shipment between two geographical locations and the expenses related to maintaining in-transit inventory. Logistical systems should utilize transportation that minimizes **total system cost.** This may mean that the least expensive method of transportation may not result in the lowest total cost of logistics.

Speed of transportation is the time required to complete a specific movement. Speed and cost of transportation are related in two ways. First, transport firms capable of offering faster service typically charge higher rates. Second, the faster the transportation service is, the shorter the time interval during which inventory is in transit and unavailable. Thus, a critical aspect of selecting the most desirable method of transportation is to balance speed and cost of service.

Transportation consistency refers to variations in time required to perform a specific movement over a number of shipments. Consistency reflects the dependability of transportation. For years, transportation managers have identified consistency as the most important attribute of quality transportation. If a shipment between two locations takes 3 days one time and 6 the next, the unexpected variance can create serious supply chain operational problems. When transportation lacks consistency, inventory safety stocks are required to protect against service breakdowns, impacting both the seller's and buyer's overall inventory commitment. With the advent of advanced information technology to control and report shipment status, logistics managers have begun to seek faster movement while maintaining consistency. Speed and consistency combine to create the quality aspect of transportation.

In designing a logistical system, a delicate balance must be maintained between transportation cost and service quality. In some circumstances low-cost, slow transportation is satisfactory. In other situations, faster service may be essential to achieving operating goals. Finding and managing the desired transportation mix across the supply chain is a primary responsibility of logistics.

Warehousing, Materials Handling, and Packaging

The first three functional areas of logistics—order processing, inventory, and transportation—can be engineered into a variety of different operational arrangements. Each arrangement has the potential to contribute to a specified level of customer service with an associated total cost. In essence, these functions combine to create a system solution for integrated logistics. The fourth functionality of logistics—warehousing, materials handling, and packaging—also represents an integral part of a logistics operating solution. However, these functions do not have the independent status of those previously discussed. Warehousing, materials handling, and packaging are an integral part of other logistics areas. For example, inventory typically needs to be warehoused at selected times during the logistics process. Transportation vehicles require materials handling for efficient loading and unloading. Finally, the individual products are most efficiently handled when packaged together into shipping cartons or other unit loads.

When distribution facilities are required in a logistical system, a firm can choose between the services of a warehouse specialist or operating its own facility. The decision is broader than simply selecting a facility to store inventory, since many value-adding activities may be performed during the time products are warehoused. Examples of such activities are sorting, sequencing, order selection, transportation consolidation, and, in some cases, product modification and assembly related to postponement strategies.

Within the warehouse, materials handling is an important activity. Products must be received, moved, stored, sorted, and assembled to meet customer order requirements. The direct labor and capital invested in materials handling equipment is a significant element of total logistics cost. When performed in an inferior manner, materials handling can result in substantial product damage. It stands to reason that the fewer the times a product is handled, the less potential exists for product damage. A variety of mechanized and automated devices exist to assist materials handling. In essence, each warehouse and its materials handling capability represent a minisystem within the overall logistical process.

To facilitate handling efficiency, products in the form of cans, bottles, or boxes are typically combined into larger units. This larger unit, typically called the **master carton,** provides two important features. First, it serves to protect the product during the logistical process. Second, the master carton facilitates ease of handling, by creating one large package rather than a multitude of small, individual products. For efficient handling and transport, master cartons are typically consolidated into larger unit loads.

When effectively integrated into an enterprise's logistical operations, warehousing, materials handling, and packaging facilitate the speed and overall ease of product flow throughout the logistical system. In fact, several firms have developed processes to move product assortments from manufacturing plants directly to retail stores with limited intermediate handling and storage.

Facility Network Design

Classical economics neglected the importance of facility location and overall network design to efficient business operations. When economists originally discussed supply-and-demand relationships, facility location and transportation cost differentials were assumed either nonexistent or equal among competitors.[3] In business operations, however, the number, size, and geographical relationship of facilities used to perform logistical operations directly impacts customer service capability and cost. Facility network design is a primary responsibility of logistical management, since a firm's facility structure is used to ship products and materials to customers. Typical logistics facilities are manufacturing plants, warehouses, cross-dock operations, and retail stores.

Facility network design is concerned with determining the number and location of all types of facilities required to perform logistics work. It is also necessary to determine what inventory and how much to stock at each facility as well as the assignment of customers. The facility network creates a structure from which logistical operations are performed. Thus, the network integrates information and transportation capabilities. Specific work tasks related to processing customer orders, warehousing inventory, and materials handling are all performed within the facility network.

The design of a facility network requires careful analysis of geographical variation. The fact that a great deal of difference exists between geographical markets is easy to illustrate. The 50 largest U.S. metropolitan markets in terms of population account for the majority of retail sales. Therefore, an enterprise marketing consumer products on a national scale

---

[3] Alfred Weber, *Theory of the Location of Industries,* translated by Carl J. Friedrich (Chicago: University of Chicago Press, 1928); August Lösch, *Die Rümliche Ordnung der Wirtschaft* (Jena: Gustav Fischer Verlag, 1940); Edgar M. Hoover, *The Location of Economic Activity* (New York: McGraw-Hill Book Company, 1938); Melvin L. Greenhut, *Plant Location in Theory and Practice* (Chapel Hill, NC: University of North Carolina Press, 1956); Walter Isard et al., *Methods of Regional Analysis: An Introduction to Regional Science* (New York: John Wiley & Sons, 1960); Walter Isard, *Location and Space Economy* (Cambridge, MA: The MIT Press, 1968); and Michael J. Webber, *Impact of Uncertainty on Location* (Cambridge, MA: The MIT Press, 1972).

must establish a logistical network capable of servicing prime markets. A similar geographic disparity exists in typical material and component part source locations. When a firm is involved in global logistics, issues related to network design become increasingly complex.

The importance of continuously modifying the facility network to accommodate change in demand and supply infrastructures cannot be overemphasized. Product assortments, customers, suppliers, and manufacturing requirements are constantly changing in a dynamic competitive environment. The selection of a superior locational network can provide a significant step toward achieving competitive advantage.

Logistical Operations

The internal operational scope of integrated logistics operations is illustrated by the shaded area of Figure 2.2. Information from and about customers flows through the enterprise in the form of sales activity, forecasts, and orders. Vital information is refined into specific manufacturing, merchandising, and purchasing actions. As products and materials are procured, a value-added inventory flow is initiated, which ultimately results in ownership transfer of finished products to customers. Thus, the logistical process is viewed in terms of two interrelated flows: inventory and information. While internal process integration is important to success, the firm must also align and integrate across the supply chain. To be fully effective in today's competitive environment, firms must extend their enterprise integration to incorporate customers and suppliers. This extension reflects the position of logistics in the broader perspective of supply chain management. Supply chain integration is discussed later in this chapter (see Supply Chain Synchronization).

Inventory Flow

The operational management of logistics is concerned with movement and storage of inventory in the form of materials, work-in-process, and finished products. Logistical operations start with the initial shipment of a material or component part from a supplier and are finalized when a manufactured or processed product is delivered to a customer.

FIGURE 2.2 **Logistical Integration**

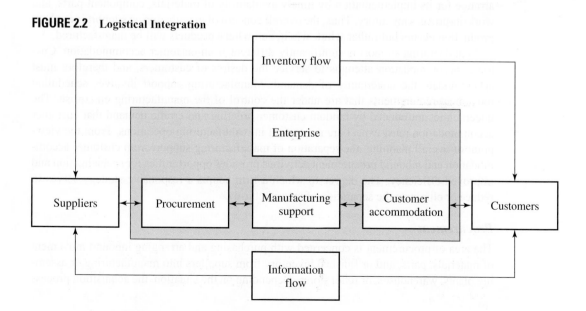

From the initial purchase of a material or component, the logistics process adds value by moving inventory when and where needed. Providing all goes well, materials and components gain value at each step of their transformation into finished inventory. In other words, an individual part has greater value after it is incorporated into a machine than it had as a part. Likewise, the machine has greater value once it is delivered to a customer.

To support manufacturing, work-in-process inventory must be properly positioned. The cost of each component and its movement becomes part of the value-added process. For better understanding, it is useful to divide logistical operations into three areas: (1) customer accommodation, (2) manufacturing support, and (3) procurement. These components are illustrated in the shaded area of Figure 2.2 as the combined logistics operational units of an enterprise.

Customer Accommodation

The movement of finished product to customers is customer accommodation. In customer accommodation, the customer's ship-to location represents the final destination. The availability of product is a vital part of each channel participant's marketing effort. Unless a proper assortment of products is efficiently delivered when and where needed, a great deal of overall marketing effort will be jeopardized. Dealing with the varied aspects of customer accommodation is typically called **customer relationship management** (CRM). It is through the customer relationship management process that the timing and geographical placement of inventory become an integral part of marketing. To support the wide variety of marketing systems that exist in a highly commercialized nation, many different customer relationship strategies are available. All customer relationship systems have one common feature: They align manufacturers, wholesalers, and retailers into supply chain arrangements to provide customers product availability.

Manufacturing Support

The area of manufacturing support concentrates on managing work-in-process inventory as it flows between stages of manufacturing. The primary logistical responsibility in manufacturing is to participate in formulating a master production schedule and to arrange for its implementation by timely availability of materials, component parts, and work-in-process inventory. Thus, the overall concern of manufacturing support is not how production occurs but rather **what, when,** and **where** products will be manufactured.

Manufacturing support is significantly different from customer accommodation. Customer accommodation attempts to service the desires of customers, and therefore must accommodate the uncertainty of demand. Manufacturing support involves scheduling movement requirements that are under the control of the manufacturing enterprise. The uncertainties introduced by random customer ordering and erratic demand that customer accommodation must expect are not typical in manufacturing operations. From the viewpoint of overall planning, the separation of manufacturing support from customer accommodation and inbound procurement activities provides opportunities for specialization and improved efficiency. The degree to which a firm adopts a responsive strategy serves to reduce or eliminate the separation of manufacturing.

Procurement

The area of procurement is concerned with purchasing and arranging inbound movement of materials, parts, and/or finished inventory from suppliers into manufacturing or assembly plants, warehouses, or retail stores. Depending on the situation, the acquisition process is commonly identified by different names. In manufacturing, the process of acquisition is typically called **purchasing.** In government circles, acquisition has traditionally been referred to as **procurement.** In retailing and wholesaling, **buying** is the most widely used term. In many circles, the process is referred to as **supply management.** For the purposes of this text, the term **procurement** will include all types of purchasing. The term **material** is used to identify inventory moving inbound to an enterprise, regardless of its degree of readiness for resale. The term **product** is used to identify value-added inventory that is sold to customers. In other words, materials are involved in the process of adding value through manufacturing whereas products are ready for consumption. The fundamental distinction is that products result from the value added to material during manufacture, sortation, or assembly.

Within a typical enterprise, the three logistics operating areas overlap. Viewing each as an integral part of the overall value-adding process creates an opportunity to specialize performance and capitalize on the unique attributes of each within the overall process. Table 2.2 provides a more exacting definition of the day-to-day work involved in each subprocess of logistics. The overall challenge of a supply chain is to integrate the logistical processes of participating firms in a manner that facilitates overall efficiency.

Information Flow

Information flow identifies specific locations within a logistical system that have requirements. Information also integrates the three operating areas. Within individual logistics areas, different movement requirements exist with respect to size of order, availability of inventory, and urgency. The primary objective of information flow management is to reconcile these differentials to improve overall supply chain performance. It is important to stress that information requirements parallel the actual work performed in customer accommodation, manufacturing support, and procurement. Whereas these areas contain the actual logistics work, information facilitates coordination of planning and control of day-to-day operations. Without accurate information, the effort involved in the logistical system can be misdirected.

TABLE 2.2
Specific Operating
Concerns of
Customer
Accommodation,
Manufacturing
Support, and
Procurement
in Logistics
Performance

Customer Accommodation

Activities related to providing customer relationship management. Requires performing order receipt and processing, deploying inventories, storage and handling, and outbound transportation within a supply chain. Includes the responsibility to coordinate with marketing planning in such areas as pricing, promotional support, customer service levels, credit delivery standards, handling return merchandise, and life cycle support. The primary market distribution objective is to assist in revenue generation by providing strategically desired customer service delivery levels at the lowest total cost.

Manufacturing Support

Activities related to planning, scheduling, and supporting manufacturing operations. Requires master schedule planning and performing work-in-process storage, handling, transportation, and sortation, kilting, sequencing, and time phasing of components. Includes the responsibility for storage of inventory at manufacturing sites and maximum flexibility in the coordination of geographic and assembly postponement between manufacturing and customer accommodation operations.

Procurement

Activities related to obtaining products and materials from outside suppliers. Requires performing resource planning, supply sourcing, negotiation, order placement, inbound transportation, receiving and inspection, storage and handling, and quality assurance. Includes the responsibility to coordinate with suppliers in such areas as scheduling, supply continuity, hedging, and speculation, as well as research leading to new sources or programs. The primary procurement objective is to support manufacturing or resale organizations by providing timely purchasing at the lowest total cost.

Logistical information has two major components: planning/coordination and operations. In-depth discussion of information technology is reserved for Chapter 5 in which the architecture of logistical information systems is developed in detail. Logistical integration objectives are discussed next.

Logistical Integration Objectives

To achieve logistical integration within a supply chain context, six operational objectives must be simultaneously achieved: (1) responsiveness, (2) variance reduction, (3) inventory reduction, (4) shipment consolidation, (5) quality, and (6) life cycle support. The relative importance of each is directly related to a firm's logistical strategy.

Responsiveness

A firm's ability to satisfy customer requirements in a timely manner is referred to as **responsiveness.** As noted earlier, information technology is facilitating response-based strategies that permit operational commitment to be postponed to the last possible time, followed by accelerated delivery. The implementation of responsive strategies serves to reduce inventories committed or deployed in anticipation of customer requirements. Responsiveness serves to shift operational emphasis from forecasting future requirements to accommodating customers on a rapid order-to-shipment basis. Ideally, in a responsive system, inventory is not deployed until a customer commits. To support such commitment, a firm must have the logistical attributes of inventory availability and timely delivery once a customer order is received.

Variance Reduction

All operating areas of a logistical system are susceptible to variance. Variance results from failure to perform any expected facet of logistical operations as anticipated. For example, delay in customer order processing, an unexpected disruption in order selection, goods arriving damaged at a customer's location, and/or failure to deliver at the right location on time all create unplanned variance in the order-to-delivery cycle. A common solution to safeguard against detrimental variance is to use inventory safety stocks to buffer operations. It is also common to use premium transportation to overcome unexpected variance that delays planned delivery. Such practices, given their associated high cost, can be minimized by using information technology to maintain positive logistics control. To the extent that variance is minimized, logistical productivity will improve. Thus, **variance reduction,** the elimination of system disruptions, is one basic objective of integrated logistics management.

Inventory Reduction

To achieve the objective of **inventory reduction,** an integrated logistics system must control asset commitment and turn velocity. Asset commitment is the financial value of deployed inventory. Turn velocity reflects the rate at which inventory is replenished over time. High turn rates, coupled with desired inventory availability, mean assets devoted to inventory are being efficiently and effectively utilized; that is, overall assets committed to support an integrated operation are minimized.

It is important to keep in mind that inventory can and does facilitate desirable benefits. Inventories are critical to achieving economies of scale in manufacturing and procurement. The objective is to reduce and manage inventory to the lowest possible level while simultaneously achieving overall supply chain performance objectives.

Shipment Consolidation

One of the most significant logistical costs is transportation. Over 60 cents of each logistics dollar is expended for transportation. Transportation cost is directly related to the type of product, size of shipment, and movement distance. Many logistical systems that feature direct fulfillment depend on high-speed, small-shipment transportation, which is costly. A system objective is to achieve **shipment consolidation** in an effort to reduce transportation cost. As a general rule, the larger a shipment and the longer the distance it is transported, the lower is the cost per unit. Consolidation requires innovative programs to combine small shipments for timely consolidated movement. Such programs require multifirm coordination because they transcend the supply chain. Successful e-commerce fulfillment direct-to-consumers requires innovative ways to achieve effective consolidation.

Quality

A fundamental operational objective is continuous **quality** improvement. Total Quality Management (TQM) is a major initiative throughout most facets of industry. If a product becomes defective or if service promises are not kept, little if any value can be added by the logistics process. Logistical costs, once expended, cannot be reversed or recovered. In fact, when product quality fails after customer delivery and replacement is necessary, logistical costs rapidly accumulate. In addition to the initial logistics cost, products must be returned and replaced. Such unplanned movements typically cost more than original distribution. For this reason, commitment to zero-defect order-to-delivery performance is a major goal of leading-edge logistics.

Logistics itself is performed under challenging conditions. The difficulty of achieving zero-defect logistics is magnified by the fact that logistical operations typically are performed across a vast geographical area during all times of day and night and without direct supervision.

Life Cycle Support

The final integration design objective is **life cycle support.** Few items are sold without some guarantee that the product will perform as advertised. In some situations, the initial value-added inventory flow to customers must be reversed. Product return is common as a result of increasingly rigid quality standards, product expiration dating, and responsibility for hazardous consequences. Reverse logistics also results from the increasing number of laws encouraging recycling of beverage containers and packaging materials. The significant point concerning reverse logistics is the need to maintain maximum control when a potential health liability exists, such as a contaminated product. The operational requirements for reverse logistics range from lowest total cost, such as returning bottles for recycling, to maximum control in situations involving defective products. Firms that design efficient reverse logistics often are able to reclaim value by reducing the quantity of products that might otherwise be scrapped or sold at a discount. Sound integrative strategy cannot be formulated without careful review of reverse logistical requirements.

For some products, such as copying equipment and printers, primary profit lies in the sale of supplies and aftermarket service. The importance of life cycle support is significantly different in situations wherein a majority of profits are achieved in the aftermarket. For firms marketing consumer durables or industrial equipment, the commitment to life cycle support constitutes a versatile and demanding marketing opportunity as well as one of the largest costs of logistical operations. Life cycle support requires **cradle-to-cradle** logistics. Cradle-to-cradle logistical support goes beyond reverse logistics and recycling to include the possibility of aftermarket service, product recall, and product disposal. The structure and dynamics of supply chain logistics are discussed next.

Logistical Operating Arrangements

The potential for logistical services to favorably impact customers is directly related to operating system design. The many different facets of logistical performance requirements make operational design a complex task, as an operating structure must offer a balance of performance, cost, and flexibility. When one considers the variety of logistical systems used throughout the world to service widely diverse markets, it is astonishing that any structural similarity exists. But keep in mind that all logistical arrangements have two common characteristics. First, they are designed to manage inventory. Second, the range of logistics alternatives is limited by available technology. These two characteristics tend to create commonly observed operating arrangements. Three widely utilized structures are echelon, direct, and combined.

Echelon

Classification of a logistical system as having an echeloned structure means that the flow of products typically proceeds through a common arrangement of firms and facilities as it moves from origin to final destination. The use of echelons usually implies that total cost analysis justifies stocking some level of inventory or performing specific activities at consecutive levels of a supply chain.

Echelon systems utilize warehouses to create inventory assortments and achieve consolidation economies associated with large-volume transportation shipments. Inventories positioned in warehouses are available for rapid deployment to meet customer requirements. Figure 2.3 illustrates the typical echeloned value chain.

Typical echelon systems utilize either break-bulk or consolidation warehouses. A break-bulk facility typically receives large-volume shipments from a variety of suppliers. Inventory is sorted and stored in anticipation of future customer requirements. Food distribution centers operated by major grocery chains and wholesalers are examples of break-bulk warehouses. A consolidation warehouse operates in a reverse profile. Consolidation is typically required by manufacturing firms that have plants at different geographical locations. Products manufactured at different plants are consolidated at a central warehouse facility to allow the firm to ship full-line assortments to customers. Major consumer product manufacturers are prime examples of enterprises using echeloned systems for full-line consolidation.

Direct

In contrast to inventory echeloning are logistical systems designed to ship products direct to customer's destination from one or a limited number of centrally located inventories. Direct distribution typically uses the expedited services of premium transport combined with information technology to rapidly process customer orders and achieve delivery

FIGURE 2.3   Echelon-Structured Logistics

performance. This combination of capabilities, designed into the order delivery cycle, reduces time delays and overcomes geographical separation from customers. Examples of direct shipments are plant-to-customer truckload shipments, direct store delivery, and various forms of direct-to-consumer fulfillment required to support Internet shopping. Direct logistical structures are also commonly used for inbound components and materials to manufacturing plants because the average shipment size is typically large.

When the economics permit, logistic executives desire direct alternatives because they reduce anticipatory inventories and intermediate product handling. The deployment of direct logistics is limited by high transportation cost and potential loss of control. In general, most firms do not operate the number of warehouses today that were common a few years ago and have been able to modify echelon structures to include direct logistics capabilities. Figure 2.4 illustrates direct logistics capability being added to an echeloned logistics structure.

Combined

The ideal logistical arrangement is a situation wherein the inherent benefits of echeloned and direct logistics structures are combined. As noted in Chapter 1, anticipatory commitment of inventory should ideally be postponed as long as possible. Inventory strategies often position fast-moving products or materials in forward warehouses, while other, more risky or costly items are stocked at a central location for direct delivery to customers. The basic service commitment and order size economics determine the most desirable and economical structure to service a specific customer.

To illustrate, automobile replacement parts are typically distributed to customers by utilizing a combined logistics strategy. Specific parts are inventoried in warehouses located at various distances from dealers and retail outlets on the basis of pattern and density of demand. As a general rule, the slower the part turnover is, the more erratic the demand is, and therefore the greater the benefit of centralized inventory. The slowest or least-demanded parts may be stocked at only one location that services customers throughout the world. Fast-moving parts that have more predictable demand are stocked in forward warehouses close to dealers to facilitate fast, low-cost delivery.

A contrasting example is an enterprise that sells machine parts to industrial firms. The nature of this business supports a completely opposite combined distribution strategy. To offer superior service to customers who experience machine failure and unexpected downtime, the firm stocks slow movers in all local warehouses. In contrast to the automotive firm, high-demand, fast-turnover parts in this industry can be more accurately forecasted

FIGURE 2.4 **Combined Echeloned and Direct Delivery**

because of routine preventive maintenance. The least-cost logistical methods for these fast movers are to ship direct from a centralized warehouse located adjacent to the parts manufacturing plant.

These alternative strategies, both of which use different logistical capabilities, are justified on the basis of unique customer requirements, total cost to service, and intensity of competition confronted. The automotive manufacturer is the sole supplier of parts during the new-car warranty period and must provide dealers rapid delivery of parts to promptly repair customer cars. Dealers require fast replenishment of parts inventory to satisfy customers while minimizing inventory investment. As cars become older and the demand for replacement parts increases, alternative suppliers enter the replacement parts market. During this highly competitive stage of the model's life cycle, rapid logistical response is required to be competitive. As a model ages, competition drops out of the shrinking aftermarket, leaving the original manufacturer as the sole supplier.

The industrial component supplier, in contrast to the automotive company, offers standard machine parts having a high degree of competitive substitutability. Whereas products used on a regular basis can be forecasted, slow- or erratic-demand products are impossible to forecast. This enterprise forces a situation wherein customers measure suppliers in terms of how fast unexpected machine breakdowns can be remedied. Failure to perform to the level of customer expectation can open the door for a competitor to prove its capability.

Each enterprise faces a unique customer situation and can be expected to use a different logistics strategy to achieve competitive superiority. The strategy that satisfies customer expectations at lowest attainable total cost typically utilizes a combination of echeloned and direct capabilities.

Beyond the basic channel structure, flexible capabilities can be designed into a logistical system by developing a program to service customers by using alternative facilities.

Flexible Structure

Flexible operations are preplanned contingency strategies to prevent logistical failures. A typical emergency occurs when an assigned shipping facility is out of stock or for some other reason cannot complete a customer's order. For example, a warehouse may be out of an item with no replenishment inventory scheduled to arrive until after the customer's specified order delivery date. To prevent back-ordering or delivery cancellation, a contingency operating policy may assign the total order, or at least those items not available, for shipment from an alternative warehouse. The use of flexible operations is typically based on the importance of the specific customer or the critical nature of the product being ordered.

A flexible logistics capability that has gained popularity as a result of improved communications involves procedures for serving specified situations as part of the basic logistical strategy. The flexible logistics rule and decision scenarios specify alternative ways to meet specific service requirements, such as assignment of different shipping facilities. A strategy that utilizes flexible operations is common practice in four different situations.

First, the customer-specified delivery facility might be near a point of equal logistics cost or equal delivery time from two different logistics facilities. Customers located at such indifference points offer the supplying firm an opportunity to fully utilize available inventory and logistical capacity. Orders can be serviced from the facility having the best inventory position or the available transportation capacity to achieve timely delivery. This form of flexible logistics offers a way to fully utilize system capacity by balancing workloads between facilities while protecting customer service commitments. The benefit is operating efficiency, which is transparent to the customer, who experiences no service deterioration.

A second situation justifying flexible distribution is when the size of a customer's order creates an opportunity to improve logistical efficiency if serviced through an alternative channel arrangement. For example, the lowest-total-cost method to provide small shipment delivery may be through a distributor. In contrast, larger shipments may have the lowest total logistical cost when shipped factory direct to customers. Provided that alternative methods of shipment meet delivery expectations, total logistical cost may be reduced by implementing flexible policies.

A third type of flexible operation may result from a selective inventory stocking strategy. The cost and risk associated with stocking inventory require careful analysis to determine which items to place in each warehouse. With replacement parts, a common strategy mentioned earlier is to stock selected items in specific warehouses with the total line being stocked only at a central facility. In general-merchandise retailing, a store or distribution center located in a small community may stock only a limited or restricted version of a firm's total line. When customers desire nonstocked items, orders must be satisfied from an alternative facility. The term **master facilities** is often used to describe inventory strategies that designate larger facilities for backup support of smaller restricted facilities. Selective inventory stocking by echelon level is a common strategy used to reduce overall inventory risk. The reasons for selective echelon stocking range from low product profit contribution to high per-unit cost of inventory maintenance. One way to operationalize a fine-line inventory classification strategy is to differentiate stocking policy by system echelons. In situations following such classified stocking strategies, it may be necessary to obtain advanced customer approval for split-order delivery. However, in some situations firms that use differentiated inventory stocking strategies are able to consolidate customer orders for same-time delivery, thereby making the arrangement customer transparent.

The fourth type of flexible operations results from agreements between firms to move selected shipments outside the established echeloned or direct logistics arrangements. Two special arrangements gaining popularity are flow through **cross-docks** and **service supplier** arrangements. A cross-dock operation involves multiple suppliers arriving at a designated time at the handling facility and is typically deployed in situations where storage and materials handling can be avoided. Inventory receipts are sorted across the dock and consolidated into outbound trailers for direct destination delivery. Cross-dock operations are growing in popularity in the retail industry for building store-specific assortments and are common methods of continuous inventory replenishment for mass merchants.

Another form of flexible operations is to use **integrated service providers** to consolidate products for delivery. This is similar to consolidation for transportation purposes discussed in the previous section of this chapter. However, as a form of flexible logistics, specialists are used to avoid storage and handling of slow-moving products through the mainstream of the echeloned logistics structure. Such service providers can also provide important value-added services. For example, Smurfit-Stone builds in-store point-of-sale displays for direct store delivery.

Figure 2.5 introduces flexibility to the logistical operating structures previously illustrated. A prerequisite to effective flexible operations is the use of information technology to monitor inventory status throughout the logistical network and provide the capability

FIGURE 2.5 **Flexible Echeloned and Direct Delivery**
Arrows reflect information flows facilitating a specific service profile.

to rapidly switch methods for servicing customer orders. The use of flexible operations in emergency situations has a well-established track record. The overall improvement in information technology is resulting in flexible operations becoming a part of basic logistics strategy.

Supply Chain Synchronization

The previous discussion positioned logistics as an integrated management process within an individual firm. A challenge of supply chain management is to integrate operations across multiple firms. In an effort to facilitate logistical operations, supply chain participants must jointly plan and implement operations. Multifirm operational integration across a supply chain is referred to as **supply chain synchronization.**

Supply chain synchronization seeks to coordinate the flow of materials, products, and information between supply chain partners to reduce duplication and unwanted redundancy. It also seeks to reengineer internal operations of individual firms to leverage overall supply chain capability. Leveraged operations require a joint plan concerning the logistics work that each participating firm in a supply chain will perform and be held accountable for. At the heart of supply chain integration is the goal of leveraging member core competencies to achieve overall reduction of **inventory dwell time.**

As defined in Chapter 1, dwell time is the ratio of time inventory sits idle in comparison to the amount of time it is being productively moved to a desired location in the supply chain. To illustrate, a product or component stored in a warehouse is dwelling. In contrast, the same part moving in a transportation vehicle on the way to a customer is being productively deployed. Ideally, the shipment will arrive in a timely manner to be immediately used by the customer in a value-added process. The desire is to directly integrate inventory into the customer's value-adding process without product being placed in storage or otherwise restricting continuous movement. The benefits of synchronization serve to support the generalization that speed of performing a specific service or product movement is secondary to synchronizing the timing of supply with demand requirements.

Performance Cycle Structure

The **performance cycle** represents the elements of work necessary to complete the logistics related to customer accommodation, manufacturing, or procurement. It consists of specific work ranging from identification of requirements to product delivery. Because it integrates various aspects of work, the performance cycle is the primary unit of analysis for logistical design and synchronization. At a basic level, information and transportation must link all firms functioning in a supply chain. The operational locations that are linked by information and transportation are referred to as **nodes.**

In addition to supply chain nodes and links, performance cycles involve inventory assets. Inventory is measured in terms of the asset investment level allocated to support operations at a node or while a product or material is in transit. Inventory committed to supply chain nodes consists of **base stock** and **safety stock.** Base stock is inventory held at a node and is typically one-half of the average shipment size received. Safety stock exists to protect against variance in demand or operational lead time. It is at and between supply chain nodes that work related to logistics is performed. Inventory is stocked and flows through nodes, necessitating a variety of different types of materials handling and, when necessary, storage. While a degree of handling and in-transit storage takes place within transportation, such activity is minor in comparison to that typically performed within a supply chain node, such as a warehouse.

Performance cycles become dynamic as they accommodate **input/output requirements.** The **input** to a performance cycle is demand, typically an order that specifies requirements for a product or material. A high-volume supply chain will typically require a different and wider variety of performance cycles than a chain having fewer throughputs. When operating requirements are highly predictable or relatively low-volume throughput, the performance cycle structure required to provide supply chain logistical support can be simplified. The performance cycle structures required to support a large retail enterprise like Target or WalMart* supply chains are far more complex than the operating structure requirements of a catalog fulfillment company.

Supply chain **output** is the level of performance expected from the combined logistical operations. To the extent that operational requirements are satisfied, the combined logistical performance cycle structure of the supply chain is **effective** in accomplishing its mission. **Efficiency** of a supply chain is a measure of resource expenditure necessary to achieve such logistical effectiveness. The effectiveness and efficiency of logistical performance cycles are key concerns in supply chain management.

Depending on the operational mission of a particular performance cycle in a supply chain structure, the associated work may be under the complete control of a single enterprise or may involve multiple firms. For example, manufacturing support cycles are often under the operational control of a single enterprise. In contrast, performance cycles related to customer accommodation and procurement typically involve multiple firms.

It is important to realize that transaction frequency and intensity will vary between performance cycles. Some performance cycles are established to facilitate a one-time purchase or sale. In such a case, the associated supply chain is designed, implemented, and abolished once the transaction is complete. Other performance cycles represent long-standing operating arrangements. A complicating fact is that any operation or facility in one supply chain may simultaneously be participating in a number of other arrangements.

For example, the warehouse facility of a hardware wholesaler might regularly receive merchandise from multiple manufacturers and service competing retailers. Likewise, a motor carrier may participate in numerous different supply chains, spanning a wide variety of industries.

When one considers a supply chain of national or multinational scope that is involved in marketing a broad product line to numerous customers, engaging in basic manufacturing and assembly, and procuring materials and components on a global basis, the notion of individual performance cycles linking all participating firms' operations is difficult to comprehend. It is almost mind-boggling to estimate how many performance cycles exist in the supply chain structure of General Motors or IBM.

Regardless of the number and different missions of performance cycles a specific supply chain deploys to satisfy its logistical requirements, each must be individually designed and operationally managed. The fundamental importance of performance cycle design and operation cannot be overemphasized: **The logistics performance cycle is the basic unit of supply chain design and operational control. In essence, the performance cycle structure is the framework for implementation of integrated logistics across the supply chain.**

Figure 2.6 portrays an echeloned supply chain structure illustrating basic logistics performance cycles. Figure 2.7 illustrates a network of flexible performance cycles integrated in a multiecheloned structure.

Three points are important to understanding the architecture of integrated supply chain logistical systems. First, as noted earlier, the performance cycles are the fundamental unit for integrated logistics across the supply chain. Second, the performance cycle structure

FIGURE 2.6
Logistical
Performance Cycles

FIGURE 2.7   **Multi-echeloned Flexible Logistical Network**

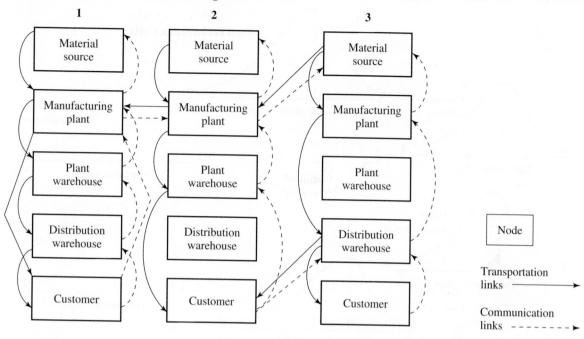

of a supply chain, in terms of link and nodal arrangement, is basically the same whether one is concerned with customer accommodation, manufacturing support, or procurement. However, considerable differences exist in the degree of control that an individual firm can exercise over a specific type of performance cycle. Third, regardless of how vast and complex the overall supply chain structure, essential interfaces and control processes must be identified and evaluated in terms of individual performance cycle arrangements and associated managerial accountability.

Performance Cycle Uncertainty

A major objective of logistics in all operating areas is to reduce performance cycle uncertainty. The dilemma is that the structure of the performance cycle itself, operating conditions, and the quality of logistical operations all randomly introduce operational variance.

Figure 2.8 illustrates the type and magnitude of variance that can develop in performance cycle operations. The performance cycle illustration is based on finished goods inventory delivery. The time distributions, as illustrated, statistically reflect operational history for each task of the performance cycle. The diagram illustrates the minimum to maximum time historically required to complete each task and the resultant time distribution for the overall performance cycle. The vertical dashed line reflects the average time for performing each task.

In terms of specific tasks, the variance results from the nature of the work involved. Order transmission is highly reliable when electronic transfer (EDI) or Internet communications are used and more erratic when telephone or routine mail is used. Regardless of the level of technology deployed, operational variance will occur as a result of daily changes in workload and resolution of unexpected events.

FIGURE 2.8   **Performance Cycle Uncertainty**

Time and variance related to order processing are a function of workload, degree of automation, and policies related to credit approval. Order selection, speed, and associated delay are directly related to capacity, materials handling sophistication, and human resource availability. When a product is out of stock, the time to complete order selection may include manufacturing scheduling or inventory purchase. The required transportation time is a function of distance, shipment size, type of transport, and operating conditions. Final delivery to customers can vary, depending on authorized receiving times, delivery appointments, workforce availability, and specialized unloading and equipment requirements.

In Figure 2.8 the history of total order-to-delivery time performance ranges from 5 to 40 days. The 5-day cycle reflects the unlikely event that each task will be performed at the minimum possible time. The 40-day cycle represents the equally unlikely opposite extreme wherein each task requires maximum time. The planned or target order-to-delivery cycle performance is to control combined variance so that actual operations are 10 days as often as possible. Whenever actual performance is more or less than 10 days, managerial action may be necessary to satisfy customer requirements. Such expediting and de-expediting require extra resources and reduce overall logistical efficiency.

The goal of performance cycle synchronization is to achieve the planned time performance. Delayed performance at any point along the supply chain results in potential disruption of operations. Such delays require that safety stocks be established to cover variances. When performance occurs faster than expected, unplanned work will be required to handle and store inventory that arrives early. Given the inconvenience and expense of either early or late delivery, it is no wonder that logistics managers place a premium on operational consistency. Once consistent operations are achieved, every effort should be made to reduce the time required to complete the performance cycle to a minimum. In other words, shorter cycles are desirable because they reduce total assets deployed. However, the importance of speed is directly related to performance consistency. Given consistency as the primary goal, faster order cycles reduce inventory risk and improve turn performance.

Summary

Logistics is the process that links supply chain participants into integrated operations. The cost of performing logistics is a major expenditure for most businesses and supply chain arrangements.

Logistical service is measured in terms of availability, operational performance, and service reliability. Each aspect of service is framed in terms of customer expectations and requirements. Logistics is all about providing the essential customer service attributes at the lowest possible total cost. Such customer accommodation, in an exacting cost framework, is the logistics value proposition.

The actual work of logistics is functional in nature. Facility locations must be established to form a network, information must be formulated and shared, transportation must be arranged, inventory must be deployed, and, to the extent required, warehousing, materials handling, and packaging activities must be performed. The traditional orientation was to perform each functional task as well as possible with limited consideration given to how one work area impacted another. Because the work of logistics is extremely detailed and complex, there is a natural tendency to focus on functional performance. While functional excellence is important, it must be supportive of overall logistical competency. Thus, the integrated performance of all logistical functions is of primary importance.

The functions of logistics combine into the three primary operational processes of customer accommodation, manufacturing support, and procurement. To achieve internal integration, the inventory and information flows between these areas must be coordinated.

In supply chain synchronization, the operational focus becomes the logistics performance cycle. The performance cycle is also the primary unit of analysis in logistical design. The performance cycle structure provides the logic for combining the nodes, levels, links, and allocation of assets essential to performing customer accommodation, manufacturing support, and procurement operations. Many similarities and a number of critical differences exist between performance cycles dedicated to these logistics operating areas. Fully understanding these similarities and differences is vital to planning and controlling overall supply chain integration. The basic proposition is that regardless of size and complexity, logistical integration is best understood and evaluated by the structure and dynamics of performance cycles.

The primary goal is to achieve consistant service at the lowest possible total cost. The challenge is to design a supply chain capable of performing the required logistical work as rapidly but, even more important, as consistently as possible. Unexpected delays, as well as faster than expected performance, can combine to increase or decrease the elapsed time required to complete a performance cycle. Both early and late delivery are undesirable and unacceptable from an operational perspective.

Chapter 2 has developed some important foundations of the logistical discipline and how it creates value in a supply chain context. These insights regarding the nature of logistics work, the importance of achieving internal operational integration through managing inventory and information flow, viewing the performance cycle structure as the basic unit of analysis, and the management of operational uncertainty combine to form a logically consistent set of concepts essential to supporting supply chain management. Logistics and supply chain are not one and the same concepts. Supply chain is a strategy that integrates all aspects of satisfying customer requirements. Logistics is the process of positioning and managing inventory throughout the supply chain. Chapter 3 focuses on customer accommodation and relationship management, which are the primary forces driving supply chain performance.

Challenge Questions

1. Illustrate a common trade-off that occurs between the work areas of logistics.

2. Discuss and elaborate on the following statement: "The selection of a superior location network can create substantial competitive advantage."

3. Why are customer accommodation operations typically more erratic than manufacturing support and procurement operations?

4. How has transportation cost, as a percentage of total logistics cost, tracked since 1980?

5. Describe the logistics value proposition. Be specific regarding specific customer accommodation and cost.

6. Describe the fundamental similarities and differences between procurement, manufacturing support, and customer accommodation performance cycles as they relate to logistical control.

7. Compare and contrast a performance cycle node and a link. Give an example of each.

8. Discuss uncertainty as it relates to the overall logistical performance cycle. Discuss and illustrate how performance cycle variance can be controlled.

9. What is the logic of designing echeloned logistical structures? Can echeloned and direct structures be combined?

10. Discuss and illustrate the statement "logistics and supply chain are not one in the same concepts."

Customer Accommodation

Chapter Outline

While in some ways it's an insight into the obvious, it is important to establish initially that logistics contributes to an organization's success by accommodating customers' delivery and inventory availability expectations and requirements. What is not so obvious, however, is what exactly is meant by the term *customer*. The supply chain management concept requires careful consideration of just what is meant by the term and realization that there are many different perspectives.

From the perspective of the total supply chain, the ultimate customer is the end user of the product or service whose needs or requirements must be accommodated. It has historically been useful to distinguish between two types of end users. The first is a consumer, an individual or a household that purchases products and services to satisfy personal needs. When a family purchases an automobile to be used for personal transportation, that family is the consumer of the supply chain. The second type is an organizational end user. Purchases are made by organizations or institutions to allow an end user to perform a task or job in the organization. When a company buys an automobile for a salesperson or buys tools to be used by an assembly worker in a manufacturing plant, the company is considered to be a customer and the salesperson or assembly worker is the end user of the supply chain's products. A supply chain management perspective demands that all firms in the supply chain focus on meeting the needs and requirements of end users, whether they are consumers or organizational users.

Another perspective of customer exists for a specific firm within the supply chain. This perspective recognizes that intermediate organizations often exist between the firm and end users. Common terminology generally recognizes these organizations as intermediate customers. Thus, in the Procter & Gamble (P&G) supply chain that provides Tide laundry detergent to ultimate consumers, Kroger and Safeway supermarkets are intermediate customers; they purchase Tide from P&G for the purpose of reselling to consumers.

Finally, for a logistician, a customer is any delivery location. Typical destinations range from consumers' homes to retail and wholesale businesses to the receiving docks of manufacturing plants and warehouses. In some cases the customer is a different organization or individual who is taking ownership of the product or service being delivered. In many other situations the customer is a different facility of the same firm or a business partner at some other location in the supply chain. For example, it is common for the logistics manager of a retail warehouse to think of the individual stores to be served as warehouse customers, even though the stores are part of the same organization.

Regardless of the motivation and delivery purpose, the customer being served is the focal point and driving force in establishing logistical performance requirements. It is critical to fully understand customer needs that must be accommodated in establishing logistical strategy. This chapter details various approaches to accommodating customer requirements. The first section presents the fundamental concepts that underlie customer-focused marketing, with consideration of how logistics supports a firm's overall marketing strategy. The second section describes how supply chain outputs impact end users and how such outputs must be structured to meet their requirements. The sections that follow expand upon increasing levels of sophistication in accommodating customers. These levels range from traditional notions of logistics customer service to satisfaction of customers by meeting their expectations to the ultimate in accommodation, helping customers be successful by meeting their business requirements. The chapter concludes with the presentation of a framework for developing customer accommodation strategy.

Customer-Focused Marketing

The basic principles of customer-focused marketing have their roots in the **marketing concept,** a business philosophy that suggests that the focal point of a business's strategy must be the customers it intends to serve. It holds that for an organization to achieve its goals, it must be more effective than competitors in identifying specific customer needs and focusing resources and activities on accommodating these customer requirements. Clearly, many aspects of a firm's strategy must be integrated to accommodate customers, and logistics is only one of these. The marketing concept builds on four fundamental ideas: Customer needs and requirements are more basic than products or services; different customers have different needs and requirements; products and services become meaningful only when available and positioned from the customer's perspective, which is the focus of logistics strategy; and volume is secondary to profit.

The belief that customer needs are more basic than products or services places a priority on fully understanding what drives market opportunities. The key is to understand and develop the combination of products and services that will meet those requirements. For example, if customers require a choice of only three different colored appliances, it makes little sense to offer six colors. It also makes little sense to try to market only white appliances if color selection is important from a customer's perspective. The idea is to develop sufficient insight into basic customer needs so that products and services can be matched to these opportunities. Successful marketing begins with in-depth study of customers to identify product and service requirements.

The second fundamental aspect of the marketing concept is that there is no single market for any given product or service. All markets are composed of different segments, each of which has somewhat different requirements. Effective market segmentation requires that firms clearly identify segments and select specific targets. While a comprehensive discussion of market segmentation is beyond the scope of this text, it is important to note that customers' logistical requirements frequently offer an effective basis for classification. For example, a contractor building new homes may place an order for appliances several weeks before needed for installation, while a consumer buying a replacement for a broken appliance may require immediate availability and delivery. It is unlikely that a company can operate in every market segment or profitably fulfill every possible combination of customer requirements; thus careful matching of capabilities with specific segments is an essential aspect of the marketing concept.

For marketing to be successful, products and services must be available to customers. In other words, the third fundamental aspect of marketing is that customers must be readily able to obtain the products they desire. To facilitate purchase action, the selling firm's resources need to be focused on customers and product positioning. Four economic utilities add value to customers: **form, possession, time,** and **place.** The product's form is for the most part generated during the manufacturing process. For example, form utility results from the assembly of parts and components for a dishwasher. Marketing creates possession by informing potential customers of product/service availability and enabling ownership exchange. Thus, marketing serves to identify and convey the attributes of the product or service and to develop mechanisms for buyer-seller exchange. Logistics provides time and place utility. Essentially, this means that logistics must ensure that the product is available when and where desired by customers. The achievement of time and place requires significant effort and is expensive. Profitable transactions materialize only when all four utilities are combined in a manner relevant to customers.

The fourth aspect of the marketing concept is the focus on profitability as contrasted to sales volume. An important dimension of success is the degree of profitability resulting from relationships with customers, not the volume sold. Therefore, variations in all four basic utilities, form, possession, time, and place, are justified if a customer or segment of customers values and is willing to pay for the modification. In the appliance example, if a customer requests a unique color option and is willing to pay extra, then the request can and should be accommodated, providing a positive contribution margin can be earned. A final refinement of marketing strategy is based on an acknowledgment that all aspects of a product/service offering are subject to modification when justifiable on the basis of profitability.

Transactional versus Relationship Marketing

Traditional marketing strategies focus on obtaining successful exchanges, or transactions, with customers to drive increases in revenue and profit. In this approach, termed **transactional marketing,** companies are generally oriented toward short-term interaction with their customers. The traditional marketing concept emphasizes accommodating customers' needs and requirements, something few business organizations would argue with. However, as practiced in many firms, the result is a focus on creating successful individual transactions between a supplier and its customers.

Paralleling the development of the supply chain management concept, there has been a shift in philosophy regarding the nature of marketing strategy. This shift has generally been acknowledged as **relationship marketing.** Relationship marketing focuses on the development of long-term relations with key supply chain participants such as consumers, intermediate customers, and suppliers in an effort to develop and retain long-term preference and loyalty. Relationship marketing is based on the realization that in many industries it is as important to retain current customers and gain a larger share of their purchases as it is to attract new customers.[1]

The ultimate in market segmentation and relationship marketing is to focus on the individual customer. This approach, referred to as **micromarketing** or **one-to-one marketing,** recognizes that each individual customer may indeed have unique requirements. For example, although WalMart* and Target are both mass merchandisers, their requirements in terms of how they desire to interact logistically with suppliers differ significantly. A manufacturer who wants to do business with both of these major retailers must adapt its logistical operations to the unique needs of each. The best way to ensure long-term organizational success is to intensely research and then accommodate the requirements of individual customers.[2] Such relationships may not be feasible with every customer. It is also true that many customers may not desire this close relationship with all suppliers. However, one-to-one relationships can significantly reduce transaction costs, better accommodate customer requirements, and move individual transactions into a matter of routine.

Supply Chain Service Outputs

Imagine a society in which every individual is totally self-sufficient: Each individual would produce and consume all of the products and services necessary for survival so there would be no need for any economic activity related to the exchange of goods and services between individuals. No such society can be found today. In reality, as individuals begin to specialize in the production of specific goods or services, a mechanism must arise for the exchange of those goods and services to satisfy the consumption needs of individuals. To do so efficiently and effectively, firms must overcome three discrepancies: discrepancy in **space,** discrepancy in **time,** and discrepancy in **quantity and assortment.**

Discrepancy in space refers to the fact that the location of production activities and the location of consumption are seldom the same. Consider, for example, the household furniture industry. Most household furniture in the United States is manufactured in a small geographic area in North Carolina and a great deal of office furniture is manufactured in western Michigan. Yet, where is furniture demanded? All over the United States! This difference between the location of production and the location of consumption is a fundamental transportation challenge that must be overcome to accomplish exchange.

Discrepancy in time refers to the difference in timing between production and consumption. Some products, agricultural commodities, for example, are produced during short time periods but are demanded by customers continuously. On the other hand, many products are manufactured in anticipation of future customer demand. Since manufacturing

---

[1] Don Peppers and Martha Rogers, "Return on Customer: A New Metric of Value Creation," *Journal of Direct, Data, and Digital Marketing Practice* (April–June 2006), pp. 318–321.

[2] For a comprehensive discussion of the one-to-one approach, see Don Peppers and Martha Rogers, *The One-to-One Manager: Real World Lessons in Customer Relationship Management* (New York: Doubleday, 1999).

often does not occur at the same time products are demanded, inventory and warehousing are required. It should be noted that much of the discussion in this text is devoted to the challenges firms face in more closely matching the rate of production with market consumption.

Discrepancy in quantity and assortment refers to the fact that manufacturing firms typically specialize in producing large quantities of a limited variety of items. Customers, on the other hand, typically demand small quantities of numerous items. This difference between the production and consumption sectors of the economy must somehow be reconciled to deliver the required product variety and assortment to customers.

To eliminate these discrepancies, Bucklin developed a longstanding theory that specifies four generic service outputs necessary to accommodate customer requirements: (1) spatial convenience, (2) lot size, (3) waiting or delivery time, and (4) product variety and assortment.[3] As discussed above, different customers may have different requirements regarding such services. It follows that different supply chain structures may be required to accommodate such differences.

Spatial Convenience

Spatial convenience, the first service output, refers to the amount of shopping time and effort that will be required on the part of the customer. Higher levels of spatial convenience are achieved in a supply chain by providing customers with access to its products in a larger number of places, thus reducing shopping effort. Consider, for example, the household furniture industry. Some manufacturers utilize a structure that includes department stores, mass merchandisers, and numerous chain and independent furniture specialty stores. Ethan Allen, on the other hand, restricts brand availability to a limited number of authorized Ethan Allen retail stores. This difference in the level of spatial convenience has major implications for the overall supply chain structure and for the logistics cost incurred in the supply chain. It is also clear that some customers are willing to expend greater time and effort than others as they search for a desired product or brand.

Lot Size

The second service output is lot size, which refers to the number of units to be purchased in each transaction. When customers are required to purchase in large quantities, they must incur costs of product storage and maintenance. When the supply chain allows them to purchase in small lot sizes, they can more easily match their consumption requirements with their purchasing. In developed economies, alternative supply chains frequently offer customers a choice of the level of lot-size service output. For example, consumers who are willing to purchase paper towels in a 12- or 24-roll package may buy at Sam's Club or Costco. As an alternative, they may buy single rolls at the local grocery or convenience store. Of course, the supply chain that allows customers to purchase in small quantities normally experiences higher cost and therefore demands higher unit prices from customers.

Waiting Time

Waiting time is the third generic service output. Waiting time is defined as the amount of time the customer must wait between ordering and receiving products: the lower the waiting time, the higher the level of supply chain service. Alternative supply chains offer consumers and end users choices in terms of the amount of waiting time required. In the personal computer industry, a consumer may visit an electronics or computer specialty store, make a purchase, and carry home a computer with literally no waiting time. Alternatively, the

---

[3] Louis P. Bucklin, *A Theory of Distribution Channel Structure* (Berkeley, CA: IBER Special Publications, 1966).

customer may order from a catalog or via the Internet and wait for delivery to the home or office. In a general sense, the longer the waiting time required, the more inconvenient for the customer. However, such supply chains generally incur lower costs and customers are rewarded in the form of lower prices for their willingness to wait.

Product Variety and Assortment

Product variety and assortment are the fourth service output. Different supply chains offer differing levels of variety and assortment to consumers and end users. Typical supermarkets are involved in supply chains that provide a broad variety of many different types of products and an assortment of brands, sizes, etc., of each type. In fact, supermarkets may have over 35,000 different items on the shelves. Warehouse stores, on the other hand, offer much less product variety or assortment, generally stocking in the range of 8000 to 10,000 items, and usually offer only one brand and size of an item. Convenience stores may stock only a few hundred items, offering little variety or assortment compared to supermarkets.

Supply chains provide additional service outputs to their customers. In addition to the four generic service outputs discussed above, other researchers have identified services related to information, product customization, and after-sales support as critical to selected customers.[4] The point to keep in mind is that there is no such thing as a homogeneous market where all consumers desire the same services presented in the same way. They may differ in terms of which services are most important and in terms of the level of each of the services desired to accommodate their needs. For example, some consumers may require immediate availability of a personal computer while others feel that waiting 3 days for a computer configured to their exact requirements is preferable. Additionally, customers differ in terms of how much they are willing to pay for services. Since higher levels of service generally involve higher market distribution costs, organizations must carefully assess customer sensitivity to prices relative to their desire for reduced waiting time, convenience, and other service outputs. Accommodating customer requirements for service outputs has important implications for how supply chains are ultimately configured, what types of participating companies may be included to satisfy service requirements, and the costs that are incurred in the process. Attention is now focused on more specific considerations of customer accommodation in a logistical context. Three levels of customer accommodation are discussed: customer service, customer satisfaction, and customer success.

Customer Service

The primary value of logistics is to accommodate customer requirements in a cost-effective manner. Although most senior managers agree that customer service is important, they sometimes find it extremely difficult to explain what it is and what it does. While common expressions of customer service include "easy to do business with" and "responsive to customers," to develop a full understanding of customer service, a more thorough framework is required.

Philosophically, customer service represents logistics' role in fulfilling the marketing concept. A customer service program must identify and prioritize all activities required to accommodate customers' logistical requirements as well as, or better than, competitors. In establishing a customer service program, it is imperative to identify clear standards of performance for each of the activities and measurements relative to those standards. In basic

---

[4] For further discussion of service outputs see Ann T. Coughan, Erin Anderson, Louis W. Stern, and Adel I. El-Ansary, *Marketing Channels*, 7th ed. (Upper Saddle River, NJ: Pearson Prentice Hall, 2006), chapter 2.

customer service programs, the focus is typically on the operational aspects of logistics and ensuring that the organization is capable of providing the seven rights to its customer: the right amount of the right product at the right time at the right place in the right condition at the right price with the right information.

It is clear that outstanding customer service adds value throughout a supply chain. The critical concern in developing a service strategy is: **Does the cost associated with achieving specified service performance represent a sound investment?** Careful analysis of competitive performance and customer sensitivity to service attributes is required to formulate a basic service strategy. In Chapter 2, the fundamental attributes of basic customer service were identified as availability, operational performance, and service reliability. These attributes are now discussed in greater detail.

Availability

Availability is the capacity to have inventory when desired by a customer. As simple as this may seem, it is not at all uncommon for an organization to expend considerable time, money, and effort to generate customer demand and then fail to have product available to meet customer requirements. The traditional practice in many organizations is to stock inventory in anticipation of customer orders. Typically an inventory stocking plan is based on forecasted demand for products and may include differential stocking policies for specific items as a result of sales popularity, profitability, and importance of an item to the overall product line and the value of the merchandise.

While the detail of establishing inventory stocking policies is covered in Chapter 7, it should be clear that achieving high levels of inventory availability requires a great deal of planning. In fact, the key is achieving these high levels of availability while minimizing overall investment in inventory and facilities. Exacting programs of inventory availability are not conceived or managed on average; availability is based on three performance measures: stockout frequency, fill rate, and orders shipped complete.

Stockout Frequency

A stockout, as the term suggests, occurs when a firm has no product available to fulfill customer demand. Stockout frequency refers to the probability that a firm will not have inventory available to meet a customer order. For example, studies of retail stores across many industries consistently find that stockouts average about 8 percent. For items that are specifically being promoted, stockouts average about 16 percent![5] It is important to note, however, that a stockout does not actually occur until a customer desires a product. The aggregation of all stockouts across all products is an indicator of how well a firm is positioned to provide basic service commitments in product availability. While it does not consider that some products may be more critical in terms of availability than others, it is the starting point in thinking about inventory availability.

Fill Rate

Fill rate measures the magnitude or impact of stockouts over time. Being out of stock does not affect service performance until a customer demands a product. Then it is important to determine that the product is not available and how many units the customer wanted. While there are several approaches to measuring fill rates discussed in Chapters 7 and 16, item fill rate is a common approach. For example, if a customer wants 100 units of an item and only 97 are available, the fill rate is 97 percent. To effectively consider fill rate, the typical

[5] Tom Gruen and Daniel Corsten, "Improve Out-of-Stock Methods at the Shelf," *Chain Store Age* (July 2006), p. 35.

procedure is to evaluate performance over time to include multiple customer orders. Thus, fill rate performance can be evaluated for a specific customer, product, or any combination of customers, products, or business segments.

Fill rate can be used to differentiate the level of service to be offered on specific products. In the earlier example, if all 100 products ordered were critical to a customer, then a fill rate of 97 percent could result in a stockout at the customer's plant or warehouse and severely disrupt the customer's operations. Imagine an assembly line scheduled to produce 100 automobiles that receives only 97 of its required brake assemblies. In situations where some of the items are not critical to performance, a fill rate of 97 percent may be acceptable. The customer may accept a back order or be willing to reorder the short items at a later time. Fill rate strategies need to consider customer requirements for products.

Orders Shipped Complete

The most exacting measure of performance in product availability is orders shipped complete. It views having everything that a customer orders as the standard of acceptable performance. Failure to provide even one item on a customer's order results in that order being recorded as zero in terms of complete shipment.

These three measures of availability combine to establish the extent to which a firm's inventory strategy is accommodating customer demand. They also form the basis to evaluate the appropriate level of availability to incorporate into a firm's basic logistical service program. High levels of inventory have typically been viewed as the means to increasing availability; however, new strategies that use information technology to identify customer demand in advance of actual customer orders have allowed some organizations to reach very high levels of basic service performance without corresponding increases in inventory.

Operational Performance

Operational performance deals with the time required to deliver a customer's order. Whether the performance cycle in question is customer accommodation, manufacturing support, or procurement, operational performance is specified in terms of speed of performance, consistency, flexibility, and malfunction recovery.

Speed

Performance cycle speed is the elapsed time from when a customer establishes a need to order until the product is delivered and is ready for customer use. The elapsed time required for total performance cycle completion depends on logistical system design and operations strategy. Given today's high level of communication and transportation technology, order cycles can be as short as a few hours or may take several weeks or months.

Naturally, most customers want fast order cycle performance. Speed is an essential ingredient in many just-in-time and quick-response logistical strategies, as fast performance cycles reduce customer inventory requirements. The counterbalance is that speed of service is typically costly: Not all customers need or want maximum speed if it means increased total cost. The justification for speed must be found in the positive trade-offs; that is, the only relevant framework for estimating the value of service speed is the customer's perceived benefits.

Consistency

Order cycle consistency is measured by the number of times that actual cycles meet the time planned for completion. While speed of service is important, most logistical managers place greater value on consistency because it directly impacts a customer's ability to plan and perform its own activities. For example, if order cycles vary, then a customer must carry safety stock to protect against potential late delivery; the degree of variability translates directly into safety stock requirements. Given the numerous activities involved in order cycle execution, there are many potential sources of inconsistency in performance (review Figure 2.8).[6]

The issue of consistency is fundamental to effective logistics operations, as it is becoming increasingly common for customers to actually specify a desired date and even specify a delivery appointment when placing orders. Such a precise specification may be made, taking into consideration a supplier's performance cycle, but that is not always the case. In fact, customers frequently place orders far in advance of their need for product replenishment. In such situations, it is very difficult for customers to understand why failure to deliver as specified occurs. Their viewpoint of supplier consistency in operational performance is whether the supplier delivered at the specified date and time. In such situations the definition of consistency must be modified. It is no longer sufficient to evaluate in terms of planned time, such as 4 days to complete the cycle. It is essential to determine whether the performance cycle was completed according to the customer's specification. Thus, in today's logistical environment, consistency is frequently viewed as a firm's performance in terms of on-time delivery.

Flexibility

Flexibility involves a firm's ability to accommodate special situations and unusual or unexpected customer requests. For example, the standard pattern for servicing a customer may be to ship full-trailer quantities to a customer's warehouse. However, from time to time, the customer may desire to have shipments of smaller quantities made direct to individual retail locations. A firm's logistical competency is directly related to how well it is able to accommodate such unexpected circumstances. Typical events requiring flexible operations are: (1) modification to basic service agreements such as a change in ship-to location; (2) support of unique sales or marketing programs; (3) new-product introduction; (4) product recall; (5) disruption in supply; (6) one-time customization of basic service for specific customers or segments; and (7) product modification or customization performed while in the logistics system, such as pricemarking, mixing, or packaging. In many ways the essence of logistical excellence rests in the ability to be flexible.

Malfunction Recovery

Regardless of how fine-tuned a firm's logistical operations, malfunctions will occur. The continuous performance of service commitments on a day-in, day-out basis is a difficult task. Ideally, adjustments can be implemented to prevent or accommodate special situations, thereby preventing malfunctions. For example, if a stockout of an essential item occurs at a warehouse that normally services a customer, the item may be obtained from an alternative facility by utilizing some form of expedited transportation. In such situations the malfunction may actually be transparent to the customer. While such transparent recoveries are not always possible, effective customer service programs anticipate that malfunctions and service breakdowns will occur and have in place contingency plans to accomplish recovery and measure compliance.

Service Reliability

Service reliability involves the combined attributes of logistics and concerns a firm's ability to perform all order-related activities, as well as provide customers with critical information regarding logistical operations and status. Beyond availability and operational

[6] See Figure 2.8, p. 43

performance, attributes of reliability may mean that shipments arrive damage-free; invoices are correct and error-free; shipments are made to the correct locations; and the exact amount of product ordered is included in the shipment. While these and numerous other aspects of overall reliability are difficult to enumerate, the point is that customers demand that a wide variety of business details be handled routinely by suppliers. Additionally, service reliability involves a capability and a willingness to provide accurate information to customers regarding operations and order status. Research indicates that the ability of a firm to provide accurate information is one of the most significant attributes of a good service program.[7] Increasingly, customers indicate that advanced notification of problems such as incomplete orders is more critical than the complete order itself. Customers hate surprises! More often than not, customers can adjust to an incomplete or late delivery if they have advanced notification.

The Perfect Order

The ultimate in logistics service is to do everything right and to do it right the first time. It is not sufficient to deliver a complete order but to deliver it late. Nor is it sufficient to deliver a complete order on time but to have an incorrect invoice or to incur product damage during the handling and transportation process. In the past, most logistics managers evaluated customer service performance in terms of several independent measures: fill rates were evaluated against a standard for fill; on-time delivery was evaluated in terms of a percentage of deliveries made on time relative to a standard; damage rates were evaluated relative to a standard for damage; etc. When each of these separate measures was acceptable relative to standard, overall service performance was considered acceptable.

Recently, however, logistics and supply chain executives have begun to focus attention on zero-defect or six-sigma performance. As an extension of Total Quality Management (TQM) efforts within organizations, logistics processes have been subjected to the same scrutiny as manufacturing and other processes in the firm. It was realized that if standards are established independently for customer service components, even if performance met standard on each independent measure, a substantial number of customers may have order-related failures. For example, if orders shipped complete, average on-time delivery, average damage-free delivery, and average correct documentation are each 97 percent, the probability that any order will be delivered with no defects is approximately 88.5 percent. This is so because the potential occurrence of any one failure combined with any other failure is $.97 \times .97 \times .97 \times .97$. The converse of this, of course, is that some type of problem will exist on as much as 11.5 percent of all orders.

The notion of the perfect order is that an order should be delivered complete, delivered on time, at the right location, in perfect condition, with complete and accurate documentation.[8] Table 3.1 lists some of the most typical failures that arise in the attempt to provide perfect order performance. Each of these individual elements must comply with customer specifications. Thus, complete delivery means all product the customer originally requested, on time means at the customer's specified date and time, etc. In other words, total order cycle performance must be executed with zero defects, availability and operational performance must be perfectly executed, and all support activities must be completed exactly as promised to the customer. While it may not be possible to offer zero defects as a basic service strategy across the board to all customers, such high-level performance may be an option on a selective basis.

[7] Donald J. Bowersox, David J. Closs, and Theodore P. Stank, *21st Century Logistics: Making Supply Chain Integration a Reality* (Oak Brook, IL: Council of Logistics Management, 1999).
[8] Robert A. Novack and Douglas J. Thomas, "The Challenges of Implementing the Perfect Order Concept," *Transportation Journal* 43, no. 1 (Winter 2004), pp. 5–16.

TABLE 3.1
Typical Perfect
Order Failures

- Wrong quantities (over or short)
- Wrong items
- Late or early delivery
- Missing or incorrect information (e.g., price or promotion codes)
- Wrong transportation mode
- Wrong destination
- Incorrect documentation (e.g., bill of lading, invoice)
- Damaged items
- Incorrect loading/sequencing of shipment
- Incorrect payment processing

It is clear that the resources required to implement a perfect order platform are substantial. Extremely high fill rates require high inventory levels to meet all potential order requirements and variations. However, such complete service cannot be achieved totally on the basis of inventory. One way of elevating logistics performance to at least near zero defects is to utilize a combination of customer alliances, information technology, postponement strategies, inventory stocking strategies, premium transportation, and selectivity programs to match logistical resources to core customer requirements. Each of these topics is the subject of detailed discussion in subsequent chapters. Suffice it to say at this time that firms achieving superior logistical customer service are well aware of the challenge related to achieving zero defects. By having a low tolerance for errors, coupled with a commitment to resolve whatever discrepancies occur, such firms can achieve strategic advantage over their competitors.

Basic Service Platforms

To implement a basic service platform, it is necessary to specify commitment level to all customers in terms of availability, operational performance, and reliability. The fundamental question, "How much basic service should the system provide?" is not easy to answer. The fact is that many firms establish their basic service platforms on the basis of two factors. The first factor is competitor or industry-acceptable practice. In most industries, levels of minimum and average service performance have emerged. These acceptable levels are generally well known by both the suppliers and the customers throughout the industry. It is not uncommon to hear logistics and supply chain executives speak of customer service commitments in terms of doing as well as competition or beating major competitors' performance. The second factor derives from the firm's overall marketing strategy. If a firm desires to differentiate from competitors on the basis of logistics competency, then high levels of basic service are required. If the firm differentiates on price, then it likely will commit to lower levels of logistical service because of the resources required and costs related to high-level commitment.

The fact is that even firms with a high level of basic customer service commitment generally do not take a total zero-defect approach across the board for all customers. The common service commitment is to establish internal performance standards for each service component. These standards typically reflect prevailing industry practice in combination with careful consideration of cost and resource commitments.[9]

Typical service standards such as 97 percent fill rate or delivery within 3 days may be established, and then performance would be monitored relative to these internal standards. While it is generally assumed that this strategic approach results in accommodating

[9] For an excellent discussion of cost and service, see Mariah M. Jeffery, Renee J. Butler, and Linda C. Malone, "Determining a Cost-Effective Customer Service Level," *Supply Chain Management* (March 2008), p. 225.

customers as well as or better than competitors, it does not assure that customers are, in fact, satisfied with either the overall industry performance or even the performance of an organization that performs above industry standard. In fact, there is only one way to be sure customers are satisfied: ask them.

Customer Satisfaction

Customer satisfaction has long been a fundamental concept in marketing and business strategy. In building a customer satisfaction program, however, the first question that must be answered is, "What does it mean to say that a customer is satisfied?" The simplest and most widely accepted method of defining customer satisfaction is known as **expectancy disconfirmation.** Simply stated, if a customer's expectations of a supplier's performance are met or exceeded, the customer will be satisfied. Conversely, if perceived performance is less than what the customer expected, then the customer is dissatisfied. A number of companies have adopted this framework for customer satisfaction and follow a commitment to meet or exceed customers' expectations. In fact, many organizations have gone further by speaking in terms of delighting their customers through performance that exceeds expectations.

While this framework for customer satisfaction is relatively straightforward, the implications for building a customer service platform in logistics are not. To build this platform it is necessary to explore more fully the nature of customer expectations. What do customers expect? How do customers form these expectations? What is the relationship between customer satisfaction and customer perceptions of overall logistics service quality? Why do many companies fail to satisfy customers, and why are so many companies perceived as providing poor logistics quality? If a company satisfies its customers, is that sufficient? The following sections provide some insights to these critical questions.

Customer Expectations

It is clear that when customers transact business with a supplier they have numerous expectations, many of which revolve around the supplier's basic logistical service platform; that is, they have expectations regarding availability, operational performance, and service reliability. Frequently, they have in place formal programs to monitor supplier performance with respect to each of these dimensions of logistical performance. In a pioneering study Parasuraman, Zeithaml, and Berry identified 10 customer expectations that form a useful framework for evaluating logistical impact.[10] Table 3.2 uses their framework to conceptualize specific logistics-based expectations.

In a logistical and supply chain context, the notion of customer expectations is particularly complex because customers are usually business organizations made up of numerous functions and individuals. Different personnel in a customer organization may prioritize the criteria of performance differently, or they may have different levels of expectation for the criteria. For example, some personnel may be most concerned with responsiveness and rapid handling of an inquiry regarding order status, while others may be more concerned with order completeness or meeting a delivery appointment. Meeting customer expectations requires an understanding of how these expectations are formed and the reasons many companies fail to meet those expectations.

---

[10] A. Parasuraman, Valerie Zeithaml, and Leonard L. Berry, "A Conceptual Model of Service Quality and Its Implications for Future Research," Report No. 84-106 (Cambridge, MA: Marketing Science Institute, 1984).

TABLE 3.2 Customer Expectations Related to Logistical Performance

Reliability: Reliability is one of the aspects of the firm's basic service platform. In this context, however, reliability refers to performance of *all* activities as promised by the supplier. If the supplier promises next-day delivery and delivery takes 2 days, it is perceived as unreliable. If the supplier accepts an order for 100 cases of a product, it implicitly promises that 100 cases will be delivered. The customer expects and is only satisfied with the supplier if all 100 are received. Customers judge reliability in terms of all aspects of the basic service platform. Thus, customers have expectations concerning damage, documentation accuracy, etc.

Responsiveness: Responsiveness refers to customers' expectations of the willingness and ability of supplier personnel to provide prompt service. This extends beyond mere delivery to include issues related to quick handling of inquiries and resolution of problems. Responsiveness is clearly a time-oriented concept and customers have expectations regarding suppliers' timely handling of all interactions.

Access: Access involves customer expectations of the ease of contact and approachability of the supplier. For example, is it easy to place orders, to obtain information regarding inventory or order status?

Communication: Communication means proactively keeping customers informed. Rather than waiting for customer inquiries concerning order status, customers have expectations regarding suppliers' notification of status, particularly if problems with delivery or availability arise. Customers do not like to be surprised, and advance notice is essential.

Credibility: Credibility refers to customer expectations that communications from the supplier are in fact believable and honest. While it is doubtful that many suppliers intentionally mislead customers, credibility also includes the notion of completeness in required communications.

Security: Security deals with customers' feelings of risk or of doubt in doing business with a supplier. Customers make plans based on their anticipation of supplier performance. For example, they take risks when they schedule production and undertake machine and line setups in anticipation of delivery. If orders are late or incomplete, their plans must be changed. Another aspect of security deals with customer expectations that their dealings with a supplier will be confidential. This is particularly important in supply chain arrangements when a customer has a unique operating agreement with a supplier who also services competitors.

Courtesy: Courtesy involves politeness, friendliness, and respect of contact personnel. This can be a particularly vexing problem considering that customers may have contact with numerous individuals in the organization ranging from sales representatives to customer service personnel to truck drivers. Failure by one individual may destroy the best efforts of all the others.

Competency: Competence is judged by customers in every interaction with a supplier and, like courtesy, can be problematic because it is perceived in every interaction. In other words, customers judge the competence of truck drivers when deliveries are made, warehouse personnel when orders are checked, customer service personnel when phone calls are made, and so forth. Failure by any individual to demonstrate competence affects customer perceptions of the entire organization.

Tangibles: Customers have expectations regarding the physical appearance of facilities, equipment, and personnel. Consider, for example, a delivery truck that is old, damaged, or in poor condition. Such tangible features are additional cues used by customers as indicators of a firm's overall performance.

Knowing the Customer: While suppliers may think in terms of groups of customers and market segments, customers perceive themselves as unique. They have expectations regarding suppliers' understanding their uniqueness and supplier willingness to adapt to their specific requirements.

A Model of Customer Satisfaction

Figure 3.1 provides a framework for understanding the process by which customers actually form their expectations of supplier performance. It also suggests that frequently a number of gaps exist that a supplier must overcome in order to develop customer satisfaction.

There are several factors that influence customer expectations, both in terms of a prioritization of the criteria discussed above, as well as the level of expectation relative to each of the criteria. The first of these factors is very simply the customers' needs or requirements. At the heart of their own business strategies, customers have requirements that depend on the performance of their suppliers. To a major extent, customers expect that these needs can and will be met by suppliers. Interestingly, however, customers' expectations are frequently not the same as their real requirements or needs. Previous supplier performance is a major factor influencing customer expectations. A supplier who consistently delivers on time will most likely be expected to deliver on time in the future. Similarly, a supplier with a poor record concerning performance will be expected to perform poorly in the future. It is important to note that previous performance experienced with one supplier may also influence the customers' expectation regarding other

FIGURE 3.1 **Satisfaction and Quality Model**

Source: Adapted from A. Parasuraman, Valerie Zeithaml, and Leonard L. Berry, "A Conceptual Model of Service Quality and Its Implications for
Future Research," Report No. 84-106 (Cambridge, MA: Marketing Science Institute, 1984).

suppliers. For example, when Federal Express demonstrated the ability to deliver small
packages on a next-day basis, many customers began to expect a similar performance
capability from other suppliers.

Related to a customer's perception of past performance is word-of-mouth. In other
words, customers frequently communicate with one another concerning their experiences
with specific suppliers. At trade and professional association meetings, the subject of suppliers is a common topic of discussion among executives. Much of the discussion may
revolve around supplier performance capabilities. Such discussions help form individual
customer expectations. Perhaps the most important factor influencing customer expectations is the communications coming from the supplier itself. Promises and commitments
made by sales personnel or customer service representatives, statements contained in marketing and promotional messages, even the printed policies and procedures of an organization represent communications that customers depend upon. These communications
become a critical basis on which they form their expectations. The promise of meeting
a delivery appointment or having full product availability becomes an expectation in the

customer's mind. Indeed many suppliers may be guilty of setting themselves up for failure by overcommitting in an attempt to influence customer expectations. Figure 3.1 also provides a framework for understanding what must be done by an organization to deliver customer satisfaction. The failure of many firms to satisfy their customers can be traced to the existence of one or more of the gaps identified in the framework.

Gap 1: Knowledge

The first and the most fundamental gap that may exist is between customers' real expectations and managers' perception of those expectations. This gap reflects management's lack of knowledge or understanding of customers. While there may be many reasons for this lack of understanding, it is clear that no beneficial customer satisfaction platform can be established without a thorough understanding of customer expectations, how they are prioritized, and how they are formed. Since sales typically has the major responsibility for customer interactions, knowledge regarding logistics expectations is often difficult to obtain.

Gap 2: Standards

Even if full understanding of customer expectations exists, it is still necessary to establish standards of performance for the organization. The standards gap exists when internal performance standards do not adequately or accurately reflect customer expectations. This is precisely the case in many organizations that develop their basic service platform from an examination of internal operating capabilities or a superficial examination of competitive service performance.

Gap 3: Performance

The performance gap is the difference between standard and actual performance. If the standard is a fill rate of 98 percent, based on research with customers regarding their expectations, and the firm actually performs at 97 percent, a performance gap exists. It should be pointed out that many firms focus their efforts to improve satisfaction by eliminating the performance gap. It may be, however, that the dissatisfaction exists as a result of a poor understanding of customer expectations in the first place.

Gap 4: Communications

The role of communications in customer satisfaction cannot be overemphasized. As discussed previously, overcommitment, or promising higher levels of performance than can actually be provided, is a major cause of customer dissatisfaction. There should be no gap between what a firm is capable of doing and what customers are told about those capabilities.

Gap 5: Perception

It is true that customers sometimes perceive performance to be lower or higher than actually achieved. In logistics, many managers frequently lament, "We're only as good as the last order." Thus, although performance over a long time period has been very good, a late or incomplete or otherwise subpar delivery may result in a customer's expression of extreme dissatisfaction.

Gap 6: Satisfaction/Quality

The existence of any one or more of the above gaps leads to customer perception that performance is not as good as expected. In other words, these gaps result in customer dissatisfaction. When building a platform for delivering customer satisfaction, a firm must ensure that these gaps do not exist.

Increasing Customer Expectations

As an important component of TQM the notion of continuous improvement has been accepted by most organizations. As a corollary of continuous improvement, there has been a continued escalation of customers' expectations concerning supplier capabilities. Performance that meets customer expectations one year may result in extreme dissatisfaction next year, as customers increase their expectations regarding acceptable performance levels.

To some extent, the increase in expectations can be traced to the dynamics of competition. As discussed previously, most industries traditionally have had explicit or implied levels of performance, which were considered to be adequate. If a firm wanted to be a serious competitor, it generally had to achieve these minimum industry service expectations. However, when one firm in the industry focuses on logistics as a core competency and provides higher performance levels, customers come to expect other suppliers to follow. Consider, for example, that after Federal Express introduced real-time tracking of shipment status, UPS and other parcel delivery firms shortly followed suit.

Does achieving perfect order performance ensure that customers are satisfied? On the surface it would seem so. After all, if all orders are delivered with no defects, what basis exists for customers to be dissatisfied? Part of the answer to this question lies in the fact that perfect orders, as important as they are, deal with the execution of individual transactions and deliveries. Customer satisfaction is a much broader concept, dealing with many other aspects of the overall relationship between suppliers and customers. For example, a customer may continuously receive perfect orders but be dissatisfied with such aspects of the relationship as difficulty in obtaining information, long delays in response to inquiries, or even the perception that some supplier personnel do not treat the customer with proper courtesy and respect. Thus, satisfaction transcends operational performance to include aspects of personal and interpersonal relationships.

Limitations of Customer Satisfaction

Because of its explicit focus on customers, a commitment to satisfaction represents a step beyond a basic service platform in an organization's efforts to accommodate its customers. It is realistic to think that a firm satisfying customer expectations better than competitors will gain some competitive advantage in the marketplace. Nevertheless, it is important to realize some of the shortcomings and limitations of the customer satisfaction emphasis.

The first limitation is that many executives make a fundamental, yet understandable, mistake in their interpretation of satisfaction. In many organizations it is assumed that customers who are satisfied are also happy, maybe even delighted, with the supplier's performance. That may or may not be the actual situation. It must be remembered that satisfaction is the customers' perception of actual performance in relation to expectation, not their requirements. Examination of Figure 3.2 may help explain this difference between satisfaction and happiness. The fact is that customers may have an expectation that a firm will not perform at a high level. If the customer has an expectation of a low level of

FIGURE 3.2
Satisfaction Is Not the Same as Happiness

		Expectation		
		LO	**MED**	**HI**
	HI	Very Satisfied	Very Satisfied	Satisfied
Performance	**MED**	Very Satisfied	Satisfied	Dissatisfied
	LO	Satisfied	Dissatisfied	Dissatisfied

performance and indeed perceives that the firm performs at this low level, it is clear that performance and expectation match. By definition, the customer is satisfied. The same is true at midlevel expectations and perceptions as well as high levels of each.

This notion that low levels of performance may be considered satisfactory can best be illustrated by example. Suppose a customer expects a supplier to provide, over time, a fill rate of 95 percent, or late deliveries 10 percent of the time, or damage of 2 percent. If the supplier in fact provides this level of performance, as perceived by the customer, the customer is satisfied. Performance perceived to be poorer than the expectation level results in dissatisfaction. Is the satisfied customer necessarily happy about the supplier's fill rate or late deliveries? Of course not. While expectations may be met, indeed may be met as well as or better than competition, there is still no assurance that the customer will be happy. Even performance higher than that expected, while satisfying to customers, may not actually result in happiness. The focus on customer expectations ignores the fact that expectations are not the same as needs or requirements.

The second limitation to consider is actually related to the first: Satisfied customers are not necessarily loyal customers. Even though their expectations are being met, satisfied customers may choose to do business with competitors. This can occur because they expect a competitor to perform at a higher level or at least as well as the organization in question. For many years, marketing and supply chain executives have assumed that satisfied customers are also loyal customers. Yet research has frequently shown that many customers who report being satisfied that their expectations have been met are likely to patronize and do business with competitors.[11] A third limitation to customer satisfaction is that firms frequently forget satisfaction lies in the expectations and perceptions of individual customers. Thus, there is a tendency to aggregate expectations across customers and neglect the basic tenets of marketing strategy related to differences among customer segments as well as individual customers. Simply stated, what satisfies one customer may not satisfy other, much less all, customers.

Despite these limitations, customer satisfaction does represent a commitment beyond basic service to accommodate customers. It provides explicit recognition that the only way to ensure that customers are being accommodated is to focus on customers themselves. Firms that focus primarily on industry and competitor standards of basic service performance are much less likely to find that their customers are very satisfied or highly satisfied with their performance.

Customer Success

In recent years, some firms have discovered that there is another commitment that can be made to gain true competitive advantage through logistical performance. This commitment is based on recognition that a firm's ability to grow and expand market share depends on its ability to attract and hold the industry's most successful customers. The real key, then, to customer-focused marketing lies in the organization's using its performance capabilities to enhance the success of those customers. This focus on customer success represents major commitment toward accommodating customers. Table 3.3 summarizes the evolution that customer-focused organizations have experienced. Notice that a customer service focus is oriented toward establishment of internal standards for basic service performance. Firms typically assess their customer service performance relative to how well these internal standards are accomplished. The customer satisfaction platform is built

[11] Michael J. Ryan, Robert Raynor, and Andy Morgan, "Diagnosing Customer Loyalty Drivers," *Marketing Research* 11, no. 2 (Summer 1999), pp. 18–26.

TABLE 3.3
Evolution of Management Thought

Philosophy	Focus
Customer service	Meet internal standards
Customer satisfaction	Meet expectations
Customer success	Meet customer requirements

on the recognition that customers have expectations regarding performance and the only way to ensure that customers are satisfied is to assess their perceptions of performance relative to those expectations.

Customer success shifts the focus from expectations to the customer's real requirements. Recall from the previous discussion that customer requirements, while forming the basis for expectations, are not the same as expectations. Requirements are frequently downgraded into expectations because of perceptions of previous performance, word-of-mouth, or communications from the firm itself. This explains why simply meeting expectations may not result in happy customers. For example, a customer may be satisfied with a 98 percent fill rate, but for the customer to be successful in executing its own strategy, a 100 percent fill rate on certain products or components may be necessary.

Achieving Customer Success

Clearly, a customer success program involves a thorough understanding of individual customer requirements and a commitment to focus on long-term business relationships having high potential for growth and profitability. Such commitment most likely cannot be made to all potential customers. It requires that firms work intensively with customers to understand requirements, internal processes, competitive environment, and whatever else it takes for the customer to be successful in its own competitive arena. Further, it requires that an organization develop an understanding of how it can utilize its own capabilities to enhance customer performance. As an example, one major manufacturer of electronic components adopted as its logistics slogan, "We take pride in helping our customers become more profitable."

In many ways a customer success program requires a comprehensive supply chain perspective on the part of logistics executives. This is most easily explained by examining the relations depicted in Figure 3.3. The typical focus in basic service and satisfaction programs is that the firm attempts to meet standards and expectations of next-destination customers, whether they are consumers, industrial end users, or intermediate or even internal customers. How those customers deal with their customer is typically not considered to

FIGURE 3.3
Moving toward Customer Success

Us

We'll do whatever they tell us they want

How can we help our customers win?

Our customer

This is not our problem (WRONG)

Our customer's customer

be a problem. A supply chain perspective and a customer success program explicitly recognize that logistics executives must alter this focus. They must understand the entire supply chain, the different levels of customer within that supply chain, and develop programs to ensure that next-destination customers are successful in meeting the requirements of customers down the supply chain. If all supply chain members adopt this perspective, then all members share in the success.

To ensure that a customer is successful may require a firm to reinvent the way a product is produced, distributed, or offered for sale. In fact, collaboration between suppliers and customers to find potential avenues for success may result in the greatest breakthroughs in terms of redefining supply chain processes. The general topic of collaborative relationships and alliances is further developed in Chapter 15. It is enough to say here that such arrangements are not possible without significant amounts of information exchange between the involved businesses to facilitate an in-depth understanding of requirements and capabilities. However, one important way that many firms have responded to the challenges of customer success is through the development of value-added services.

Value-Added Services

The notion of value-added service is a significant development in the evolution to customer success. By definition, value-added services refer to unique or specific activities that firms can jointly develop to enhance their efficiency, effectiveness, and relevancy. Value-added services help foster customer success. Because they tend to be customer specific, it is difficult to generalize all possible value-added services.

When a firm becomes committed to value-added solutions for major customers, it rapidly becomes involved in customized or tailored logistics. It is doing unique things to enable specific customers to achieve their objectives. IBM's ability to produce and deliver customized personal computers and networks to individual customers is one example of adding value to a rather standard product. In a logistical context, firms can provide unique product packages, create customized unit loads, place prices on products, offer unique information services, provide vendor-managed inventory service, make special shipping arrangements, and so forth, to enhance customer success.

In reality, some of the value-added services that buyers and sellers agree to involve integrated service providers that are positioned to provide such services. Transportation carriers, warehouse firms, and other specialists may become intimately involved in the supply chain to make such value-adding activities a reality. At this point, a few specific examples of how they may work within a specific supply chain to provide value-added services are sufficient. Warehouses, whether private or third-party, can be utilized to perform a number of customization activities. For example, a retail customer may desire a unique palletization alternative to support its cross-dock activities and meet the unique product requirements of its individual store units. Each store requires different quantities of specific product to maintain in-stock performance with minimum inventory commitment. In another situation, first-aid kits consisting of many different items are actually assembled in the warehouse as orders are received to meet the unique configuration of kit desired by specific customers. It is also common for warehouses to provide pick-price-repack services for manufacturers to accommodate the unique product configurations required by different retailers.

Another form of value-added service involves the proper sorting and sequencing of products to meet specific customer requirements. For example, an auto assembly plant may require that components not only be received on time but also be sorted and sequenced in a particular manner to meet the needs of specific automobiles on the assembly line. The objective is to reduce assembly plant handling and inspection of incoming components. Meeting such exacting requirements for delivery is far beyond the basic service capability of many component suppliers. The use of third-party specialists is a necessity, especially when subcomponents from multiple suppliers must be integrated and then properly sequenced.

Value-added services can be performed directly by participants in a business relationship or may involve specialists. It has become more common in recent years to turn to specialists because of their flexibility and ability to concentrate on providing the required services. Nevertheless, regardless of how the specifics are organized and implemented, it is clear that logistics value-added services are a critical aspect of customer success programs.

Developing Customer Accommodation Strategy

It follows from the earlier discussion of the marketing concept and relationship marketing that different customers are likely to require different approaches and strategies for customer accommodation. Basic customer service may be appropriate for some customers, customer satisfaction for others, while a success focus may be in order for others. In fact, a basic principle of supply chain logistics is that customers should be segmented based on their service needs, and the supply chain must be adapted to serve those segments.[12]

For example, Unilever has a presence in 150 countries around the world with some 179,000 employees, and offers a product portfolio that spans grocery store shelves with well-known trademarked brand names in categories such as spreads (I Can't Believe It's Not Butter), sauces (Ragu), dressings (Hellmann's and Wish-Bone), beverages (Lipton teas), ice cream (Good Humor and Breyers), frozen food (Bertolli dinners), and personal care products (Dove, Suave, and Axe). As one part of the company's Supply Chain 2010 initiative, Unilever fielded a customer survey to develop a complete understanding of future requirements and anticipated trends. Topics touched upon included ordering and inventory management practices and techniques to reduce retail out-of-stock situations, outsourcing, distribution models and service differentiation, order profiles and frequency trends, collaborative planning through POS data and other means, and product customization needs. Among other findings, these data-gathering efforts made it clear that retailers had increased expectations around the performance of the 2010 inbound supply chain. The vast majority of retailers favored 24- to 48-hour order lead times, with more than half expressing a need for daily order delivery. Nearly two-thirds of respondents expected significant order or product customization. The data was examined by channel and customer to avoid potential fallacies of relying on aggregated data. A major conclusion was that Unilever U.S. should strongly focus on customer-specific strategic supply chain initiatives.[13] To accomplish this, companies such as Unilever need both a framework for choosing the appropriate customer-specific strategies as well as programs for customer relationship management. Each of these is discussed below.

Framework for Strategic Choice

It is clear that customer success approaches are extremely time consuming and resource intensive. No company is likely to be able to implement such approaches with every potential customer. In fact, it is likely that many customers themselves may not desire

[12] David L. Anderson, Frank F. Britt, and Donovan J. Favre, "The Best of Supply Chain Management Review: The Seven Principles of Supply Chain Success," *Supply Chain Management Review* (April 2007), p. 57.
[13] Adapted from Sean Monahan and Robert Nardone, "How Unilever Aligned Its Supply Chain and Business Strategies," *Supply Chain Management Review* (November 2007), p. 44.

such relationships with all (or any) suppliers. From a strategic point of view, then, a company must determine which type of accommodation approach is appropriate for which customers.

There is no easy answer to that question, but one approach relies on the well established Pareto Principle (also known as the 80/20 Principle). This states simply that a large percentage (perhaps 80 percent) of a company's revenue and profit typically is derived from a small percentage of its customers (as few as 20 percent). There is no absolute concerning these percentages, but the concept is very clear. This principle can also be applied to the products a company sells; a few products account for a large percentage of sales revenue and profits. The combination of these facts leads to the diagram presented in Figure 3.4.[14] In the diagram customers are classified as A, B, C, or D on the basis of profitability and products as 1, 2, 3, or 4 on the same basis. For example, A customers are those who are extremely profitable; B customers, very profitable; C customers, somewhat profitable; and D customers, unprofitable. Similarly, products 1 through 4 exhibit similar profitability characteristics.[15] Methodologies for determining specific customer and product profitability are discussed in Chapter 16.

It is likely that only a small number of customer/product combinations are extremely profitable. Those situations are naturally the most likely candidates for a customer success relationship, as depicted in the upper left-hand corner of Table 3.4. It is also likely that even "A" customers may not desire or require the same intensity of development for all products. Thus, satisfaction or even basic service may be acceptable in those situations.

Those customer/product combinations that fall in the lower right-hand corner should be carefully reviewed as to whether or not it is reasonable to maintain them. In many instances there may be good reason to continue. For example, they may be new customers or may be small but rapidly growing companies. Likewise there may be characteristics of the products that must be reviewed. However, in some instances it may simply be a wiser decision to stop doing business with a particular customer and/or eliminate a specific product from the overall assortment.

The above discussion is meant to be suggestive of strategic choice and not necessarily the only approach. For example, it may be necessary to maintain customer success through the entire product range for an A customer. Or it may be desirable to establish a customer success focus with a customer who is currently of limited profitability in order to convert that customer to extremely high profitability. The most important point to remember is that customer success typically must be reserved for a limited number of situations due to the resource constraints. Other situations may require a satisfaction approach. It is clear,

---

[14] This discussion is adapted from and based on Robert Sabbath and Judith M. Whipple, "Integrating Marketing and Supply Chain Management to Improve Profitability," *CSCMP Explores* 4 (Summer 2007), pp. 1–15.
[15] Ibid.

TABLE 3.4 **Choosing Customer Accommodation Strategy**

Source: Adapted from Robert Sabbath and Judith M. Whipple, "Integrating Marketing and Supply Chain Management to Improve Profitability," *CSCMP Explores* 4 (Summer 2007), p. 8.

Customer Category	Product Category			
	1	2	3	4
A	Success	Success	Success/satisfaction	Basic service
B	Success/satisfaction	Success/satisfaction	Basic service	Basic service
C	Basic service	Basic service	Basic service	Basic service/cull
D	Basic service/cull	Basic service/cull	Basic service/cull	Basic service/cull

however, that if a company chooses to do business with a customer, adequate basic service is a minimum requirement.

Customer Relationship Management

The term **customer relationship management (CRM)** has been used by many firms to describe their efforts to accommodate better the needs and requirements of individual customers. However, there is confusion concerning the specific meaning of CRM since different companies have adopted it to describe quite different activities. In many companies CRM is used primarily to describe technology and software that is used to manage and analyze data from numerous sources within an organization to gain greater insight into customer buying behavior (sales calls, call centers, actual purchases, etc.). In fact, numerous software vendors offer packages they describe as CRM software to accomplish this purpose. The technology used for CRM is discussed in Chapter 5. In other companies, CRM not only describes the technology employed for data analysis, but also all forms of communication and information sharing that lead to development of the appropriate relationships with customers.

The objective of customer relationship management is to develop a customer-centered organization. While CRM certainly involves the science of gathering and analyzing data about individual customer needs and purchasing habits, it extends to the process of developing capabilities that enable the organization to meet those individual needs more completely. CRM has grown rapidly over recent years as a process for improving the overall performance of a business by better understanding and anticipating the wants and needs of customers

Companies that have embraced CRM are committed to the notion customers are the sole driver for the entire business. In addition to technology, other efforts are made to build deeper understanding of customer requirements and develop lasting relationships with critical customers. For example, it is becoming increasingly common for suppliers to have their own personnel maintain an office very near, or even inside, the facilities of key customers. In this way, the supplier gains critical knowledge of the customer's needs and plans and can anticipate the customer's actions with a high degree of certainty. As one example, Procter & Gamble has a number of employees who live and work in Bentonville, Arkansas, the headquarters of its largest customer, WalMart*.

CRM's relevance to logistics lies in its need for cross-functional transparency. Logistics has primary responsibility for many of the processes that drive value and customer success. A CRM program provides a business with the platform necessary for the development and management of the appropriate relationships with customers. A much deeper discussion of the actual process for developing and maintaining relationships in logistics is deferred to Chapter 15.

Summary

The fundamental rationale for logistics is the need to accommodate customers, whether those customers are end users, intermediate, or even internal. The marketing concept provides the foundation for customer accommodation with its fundamental focus on customer needs rather than on products or services, the requirement to view and position products and services in a customer context, identification of market segments that differ in needs, and commitment that volume is secondary to profit.

Contemporary implementation of the marketing concept suggests that it is more important to focus on the development of relationships with customers than to perfect individual transactions. This interpretation focuses on the needs and requirements of individual customers as the core ingredient of one-to-one marketing. In a supply chain context, customer requirements related to spatial convenience, lot size, waiting time, and variety and assortment must be supported by logistical performance.

Organizations build their platform for customer accommodation on three levels of increasing commitment. The first of these is basic logistics customer service. To be competitive, a firm needs a basic service capability that balances availability, operational performance, and reliability for all customers. The level of commitment to each dimension of service requires careful consideration of competitive performance and cost/benefit analysis. The highest level of commitment is perfect order performance, which requires zero defects logistics operations. Such high-level commitment is generally reserved for a firm's key customers.

Going beyond basic service to create customer satisfaction represents the second level of customer accommodation. Where basic service focuses on the organization's internal operational performance, customer satisfaction focuses on customers, their expectations, and their perceptions of supplier performance. Customer expectations extend beyond typical logistical considerations and include factors related to communication, credibility access, responsiveness, and customer-specific knowledge as well as reliability and responsiveness of operations. A firm can provide logistics service that is equal to or even better than competitors' but still have dissatisfied customers. Failure to satisfy customers can arise from lack of knowledge about customer expectations, improper standards of performance, performance failure, poor communication, or incorrect customer or firm perception of performance. As customer expectations escalate, logistics executives must continuously monitor customer satisfaction and logistics performance.

The highest level of customer accommodation is known as customer success. Where satisfaction programs seek to meet or exceed expectations, a success platform focuses on customer needs and requirements. Customer expectations are frequently different from needs and requirements. Achieving success requires intimate knowledge of customers' needs and their operational requirements and a commitment by the service provider to enhance a customer's ability to compete more successfully in the marketplace. Value-added services represent one way logistics can contribute to customer success.

A customer accommodation strategy requires in-depth knowledge of the logistical requirements of different customer segments. Customer and product profitability must also be examined to determine when customer success, satisfaction, or basic service is appropriate.

Challenge Questions

1. Explain the differences between transactional and relationship marketing. How do these differences lead to increasing emphasis on logistical performance in supply chain management?

2. Why are the four primary service outputs of spatial convenience, lot size, waiting time, and product variety important to logistics management? Provide examples of competing firms that differ in the level of each service output provided to customers.

3. Using the 10 categories of customer expectations in Table 3.2, develop your own examples of how customers might evaluate performance of a supplier.

4. Compare and contrast the customer service, customer satisfaction, and customer success philosophies of supply chain management.

5. What is meant by value-added services? Why are these services considered essential in a customer success program?

6. Explain the difference between stockouts and fill rates.

7. Why is performance cycle consistency more important than speed?

8. Which of the "gaps" in Figure 3.1 do you think is the most critical gap?

9. Suppose a company provides very high perfect order performance to customers. Does this assure that customers are satisfied? Why or why not?

10. What dimensions other than customer and product profitability could be applied in determing a customer accommodation strategy?

CHAPTER FOUR

Procurement and Manufacturing

Chapter Outline

In Chapter 2, performance cycles were presented as the framework for integrated logistics across the supply chain. Three performance cycles were identified that must be linked through effective logistics. The **procurement cycle** links an organization with its suppliers, the **manufacturing support cycle** involves the logistics of supporting production, and the **customer accommodation cycle** links a firm with its markets. As will be seen later in this chapter, manufacturing firms differ in their manufacturing strategies; thus, alternative approaches to procurement may be implemented to support specific manufacturing requirements. Of course, all of this performance must meet customer requirements for quality products. This chapter begins with a discussion of product quality from a customer's perspective and Total Quality Management programs. Procurement and manufacturing are then each discussed with a focus on alternative strategies. The chapter concludes with a discussion of logistical interfaces necessary to support an organization's chosen procurement and manufacturing strategies.

The Quality Imperative

An overriding concern of all organizations is quality. In a competitive marketplace, no company dares fall behind in providing quality to its customers. Yet quality remains an elusive concept. In the end, quality is in the eyes of customers and how they perceive an organization, its products, and its services. Customer service quality was introduced in Chapter 3 in terms of customer expectations and requirements. Much of the focus in supply chain logistics is on helping ensure products are delivered on time, damage-free, and with all the service attributes necessary to meet customer requirements. In this chapter, dealing with procurement of materials and manufacturing processes, critical issues of **product quality** are addressed.

Dimensions of Product Quality

In the context of physical product form, quality is not as simple as it may first appear. In fact, the term *quality* means different things to different people. While everyone wants a quality product, not all may agree that a particular item or brand has all of the quality attributes desired. Quality is traditionally viewed in terms of eight different competitive dimensions.[1]

Performance

Perhaps the most obvious aspect of quality from a customer's viewpoint is performance, or how well the product actually performs in comparison to how it was designed to perform. For example, personal computers may be judged with respect to their processing speed; audio components, in terms of sound clarity and lack of noise; or dishwashers, relative to how clean and spotless the dishes. Superior performance in a product is generally an objective attribute, which can be compared between items and brands. Of course, an item may actually have several performance dimensions, which complicates comparison. The personal computer is judged not only in terms of processing speed but also by such characteristics as internal memory, hard disk capacity, and numerous other performance features.

Reliability

Reliability refers to the likelihood that a product will perform throughout its expected life. It is also concerned with the number of breakdowns or repairs that a customer experiences after purchase. Consider, for example, Maytag's slogan "The Dependability People" and long-running advertising campaign featuring a company repairman as "the loneliest person in town." Maytag stresses its products are more reliable than those of competitors by showing that the Maytag repairman is never needed to fix a broken appliance. Like performance, reliability is a characteristic of quality that can be objectively measured.

Durability

While related to reliability, durability is a somewhat different attribute. It refers to the actual life expectancy of a product. An automobile with a life expectancy of 10 years may be judged by many consumers to be of higher durability than one with a projected 5-year

---

[1] David A. Garvin, "Competing on the Eight Dimensions of Quality," *Harvard Business Review* (November/December 1987), pp. 101–10.

life. Of course, life span may be extended through repair or preventive maintenance. Thus, durability and reliability are distinct but interrelated aspects of quality.

Conformance

Conformance refers to whether a firm's products actually meet the precise description or specifications as designed. It is frequently measured by looking at an organization's scrap, rework, or rate of defects. Conformance quality measurement is usually internal in an organization. For example, if 95 percent of a firm's products meet the specifications as designed, it has a 5 percent defect rate. Defective products may be scrapped or reworked to bring them into conformance.

Features

Customers frequently judge quality of specific products on the basis of the number of functions or tasks that they perform independent of reliability or durability. For example, a television receiver with features such as remote control, picture-in-picture, and on-screen programming is typically perceived to be of higher quality than a basic model. But, in general, the more features a product contains, the greater is the likelihood that another quality attribute may be lacking, such as reliability.

Aesthetics

Aesthetics, the styling and specific materials used in a product, is used by many consumers to judge quality. In clothing, cashmere sweaters are considered of higher quality than polyester fabrics. In automobiles, the use of leather rather than cloth for seats, wood or metal rather than plastic, is an aesthetic that implies quality. Included in aesthetics is the notion of fit and finish such as high-gloss paint on an automobile or seams having no overlap. Product designs that are unique or innovative are frequently regarded by customers to be of higher quality.

Serviceability

Serviceability, the ease of fixing or repairing a product that fails, is an important aspect of quality for some customers. Consider, for example, how some new appliances contain diagnostic capability, which alerts users or service technicians that a failure is about to occur. Ideally, serviceability would allow the customer to fix the product with little or no cost or time lost. In the absence of such serviceability, customers generally consider those items or brands that can be repaired quickest at least cost to have superior quality.

Perceived Quality

As noted earlier, customers are the ultimate judges of product quality through their perception of how well the product meets their requirements. Perceived quality is based on customers' experience before, during, and after they purchase a product. Total product quality is a combination of the eight dimensions, how they are blended by an organization, and how that blend is perceived by the customer. It is perfectly plausible that two different customers may perceive two different brands as each having best quality, depending upon which blend of elements each considers most critical.

Total Quality Management

Interestingly, quality is not always clearly defined within some firms. Moreover, different functional managers tend to emphasize different aspects of quality. Marketing managers, for example, care a lot about aesthetics and features, whereas manufacturing executives often focus on conformance. Of specific concern in logistics are the quality dimensions related to service, satisfaction, and success. From the customer's perspective, not only does the physical product incorporate the desired elements, but also the product must be available in a timely and suitable manner.

Total Quality Management (TQM) is a philosophy supported by a managerial system focused on meeting customer expectations with respect to all needs, from all departments or functions of an organization, whether the customer is internal or external, a supply chain partner, or a consumer. While the specific tools and methodologies employed in TQM are beyond the scope of logistics, the basic conceptual elements are: (1) top management commitment and support; (2) maintaining a customer focus in product, service, and process performance; (3) integrated operations within and between organizations; and (4) commitment to continuous improvement.

Quality Standards

Establishing global quality standards is extremely difficult as a result of different circumstances, practices, and procedures around the world. As a simple example, engineering tolerances in one country might be measured in millimeters, while in another, they are measured in tenths of an inch. Nevertheless, a set of standards has emerged from the **International Organization for Standardization (ISO)** and has gained worldwide acceptance.

A series of quality standards have been issued under the name ISO 9000. Incorporating several subsets (ISO 9001, 9002, etc.), these standards provide basic definitions for quality assurance and quality management. ISO 9001, for example, deals with the quality system in place for product design, development, production, installation, and service. Several organizations around the world are authorized to perform audits of companies and their practices and procedures for TQM. A company that conforms to the ISO guidelines can receive certification. In 1998, another set of guidelines, ISO 14000, was released. ISO 14000 deals with guidelines and procedures for managing a firm's environmental impact. Certification in both ISO 9000 and ISO 14000 indicates a company conforms to both quality and environmental standards. Most major countries today have accepted the ISO standards, and, in many instances, companies will not purchase from a supplier who has not received ISO certification.

Procurement[2]

Every organization, whether it is a manufacturer, wholesaler, or retailer, buys materials, services, and supplies to support operations. Historically, purchasing has been perceived as a clerical or low-level managerial activity charged with responsibility to execute and process orders initiated elsewhere in the organization. The role of purchasing was to obtain the desired resource at the lowest possible purchase price from a supplier. This traditional view of purchasing has changed substantially in the past several decades. The modern focus is on total cost and the development of relationships between buyers and sellers. As a result, procurement has been elevated to a strategic activity.

The increasing importance of procurement can be attributed to several factors. The most basic of these factors has been the recognition of the substantial dollar spend for purchases of a typical organization and the potential dollar savings from a viable procurement strategy. The simple fact is that purchased goods and services are among the largest cost elements for most firms. In the average manufacturing firm in North America, purchased

---

[2] This section draws on Robert Monczka, Robert Trent, and Robert Handfield, *Purchasing and Supply Chain Management* (Mason, OH: Thomson South-Western, 2005).

goods and services account for approximately 55 cents of every sales dollar.[3] By way of contrast, the average expense of direct labor in the manufacturing process accounts for about 10 cents of each sales dollar. While the percentage spent on purchased inputs varies considerably across manufacturing industries, it is clear that the potential savings from strategic management of procurement can be substantial.

Related to the cost of purchased inputs is a growing emphasis on outsourcing. The result is that the amount spent on procurement has increased significantly in many organizations. Firms today purchase not only raw materials and basic supplies but also complex fabricated components with very high value-added content. They spin off functions to suppliers to focus internal resources on core competencies. The result is that more managerial attention must then be focused on how the organization interfaces and effectively manages its supply base. For example, General Motors uses its first-tier supplier network and third-party logistics providers to complete subassemblies and deliver finished components as needed to their automotive assembly lines. Many of these activities were once performed internally by the General Motors organization. Developing and coordinating these relationships represent critical aspects of an effective procurement strategy. The logistical requirements related to effective procurement strategy are identified later in the chapter.

Procurement Perspectives

The evolving focus on procurement as a key organizational capability has stimulated a new perspective regarding its role in supply chain management. The emphasis has shifted from adversarial, transaction-focused negotiation with suppliers to ensuring that the firm is positioned to implement its manufacturing and marketing strategies with support from its supply base. In particular, considerable focus is placed on ensuring continuous supply, inventory minimization, quality improvement, supplier development, and lowest total cost of ownership.

Continuous Supply

Stockouts of raw materials or component parts can shut down or force a change in production plans, resulting in unexpected cost. Downtime due to production stoppage increases operating costs and may result in an inability to provide finished goods as promised to customers. Imagine the chaos that would result if an automobile assembly line had all parts available but tires. Assembly of automobiles would have to be halted until tires become available. Thus, one of the core objectives of procurement is to ensure that a continuous supply of materials, parts, and components is available to certain manufacturing operations.

Minimize Inventory Investment

In the past, downtime due to material shortages was minimized by maintaining large inventories of materials and components to protect against potential disruption in supply. However, maintaining inventory is expensive and requires scarce capital. One goal of procurement is to maintain supply continuity with the minimum inventory investment possible. This requires balancing the costs of carrying material against the possibility of a production stoppage. The ideal, of course, is to have needed materials arrive just at the moment they are scheduled to be used in the production process, in other words, **just-in-time (JIT).**

[3] Shawn Tulley, "Purchasing: New Muscle," *Fortune*, February 20, 1995, p. 75.

Quality Improvement

Procurement is critical to the quality requirements discussed earlier in this chapter. The quality of finished goods and services is dependent upon the quality of the materials and components used. If poor-quality components and materials are used, then the final product likely will not meet customer quality standards. Thus, both a firm and its suppliers need to be jointly committed to a continuous quality improvement initiative.

Supplier Development

In the final analysis, successful procurement depends on locating or developing suppliers, analyzing their capabilities, and selecting and working with those suppliers to achieve continuous improvement. Developing good supply relationships with firms that are committed to the buying organization's success is critical in supplier development. It is important to develop close relationships with those suppliers in order to share information and resources to achieve better results. For example, a manufacturer might share a production schedule with key suppliers, which in turn allows them to better meet the buyer's delivery requirements. A retailer might share point-of-sale information and promotional plans to help suppliers meet quantity requirements at specific times. This perspective on effective procurement stands in stark contrast to the traditional focus on price alone, which inherently created adversarial relationships between a firm and its suppliers.

Lowest Total Cost of Ownership

Ultimately, the difference in perspective between a traditional adversarial and more contemporary collaborative procurement strategy can be summarized as a focus on **Total Cost of Ownership (TCO)** as contrasted to a focus on purchase price. Procurement professionals recognize that, although the purchase price of a material or item remains important, it is only one part of the total cost for their organization.[4] Service costs and life cycle costs must also be considered.

Whether established through competitive bidding, buyer-seller negotiation, or simply from a seller's published price schedule, the purchase price and discounts of an item are obviously a concern in procurement. No one wants to pay a higher price than necessary. Related to the price quote is normally a schedule of one or more possible discounts a buyer may receive. For example, quantity discounts may be offered as an inducement to encourage buyers to purchase larger quantities or cash discounts may be offered for prompt payment of invoices.

Consideration of supplier's discounts immediately takes the buyer beyond simple quoted purchase price. Other costs associated with purchasing must be considered. For the benefits of quantity discounts to be factored into the total cost, the buyer must quantify inventory holding costs. Larger purchase quantities increase average inventory of materials or supplies. Size of purchase also impacts administrative costs associated with purchasing. Lot-size techniques such as Economic Order Quantity (EOQ), discussed fully in Chapter 7, can help quantify these cost trade-offs.

Supplier terms of sale and cash discount structures also impact the total cost of ownership. A supplier offering more favorable credit terms is, in effect, impacting the purchase price from the buyer's perspective. For example, a discount for prompt

[4] Zeger Degraeve and Filip Roodhooft, "Effectively Selecting Suppliers Using Total Cost of Ownership," *Journal of Supply Chain Management* (Winter 1999), pp. 5–10. See also Lisa M. Ellram, "Total Cost of Ownership," *International Journal of Physical Distribution and Logistics Management* (August 1995), pp. 4–23.

payment of an invoice offered by one supplier must be compared with the offers of other suppliers.

What normally is not considered in traditional purchasing practice is the impact of pricing and discount structures on logistics operations and costs. For example, while traditional EOQ does consider inventory carrying costs, it generally does not include such factors as the impact of order quantity on transportation costs or the costs associated with receiving and handling different size shipments. Many of these logistical considerations are ignored or given cursory consideration as buyers attempt to achieve the lowest purchase price. Today there is increasing recognition of the importance of these logistics costs to the TCO.

Sellers typically offer a number of standard services that must be considered in procurement. Additionally, available value-added services must be evaluated as organizations seek to identify the lowest TCO. Many of these services involve logistical operations and the logistical interface between buyers and sellers.

The simplest of these services is delivery. How delivery will be accomplished, when, and at what location all impact cost structures. In many industries it is standard practice to quote a price that includes delivery. Alternatively, the seller may offer the buyer an allowance if the item being purchased is picked up at the seller's location. The buyer may be able to reduce total costs, not only through taking advantage of such allowances, but also by more fully utilizing its own transportation equipment.

In Chapter 3, value-added services were discussed, ranging from special packaging to preparation of promotional displays. Performance of subassembly operations in a supplier's plant or at an integrated service provider warehouse represents an extension of potential value-added service. The point is that each potential service has a cost to the supplier and a price to the buyer. A key aspect of determining the TCO for purchased requirements is to consider the trade-offs involved in terms of value added versus cost and price of each service. To do so, the purchase price of an item must be **debundled** from the price of services under consideration. Each of the related available services should be priced on an independent basis so that appropriate analysis can be performed. In Chapter 9, this practice will be referred to as **menu pricing.** Where traditional purchasing might overlook value-added services in seeking lowest possible price, effective procurement executives consider whether such services should be performed internally, by suppliers, or at all. Debundling allows the buyer to make the most appropriate procurement decision.

The final aspect of lowest TCO includes numerous elements known as life cycle costs. The total cost of materials, items, or other inputs extends beyond the purchase price and value-added service to include the lifetime costs of such items. Some of these costs are incurred before actual receipt of the items, others are incurred while the item is being used, and some occur long after the buyer has actually used the item.

One aspect of life cycle costs involves the administrative expense associated with procurement. Expenses related to screening potential suppliers, negotiation, order preparation, and transmission are just a few procurement administrative costs. Receiving, inspecting, and payment are also important. The costs related to defective finished goods, scrap, and rework associated with poor supplier quality must also be considered, as well as related warranty administration and repair. Even the costs associated with recycling or recovery of materials after the useful life of a finished product may have an impact on TCO.

Figure 4.1 presents a model of the various elements that TCO comprises. When each of these elements is considered in procurement, it is clear that numerous opportunities for improvement exist in most companies. Many of these opportunities arise from

FIGURE 4.1 **Major Categories for the Components of Total Cost of Ownership**

Source: Reprinted with permission from Michiel Leenders and Harold Fearon, *Purchasing and Supply Management,* 11th ed. (New York: McGraw-Hill Irwin, 1997), p. 334.

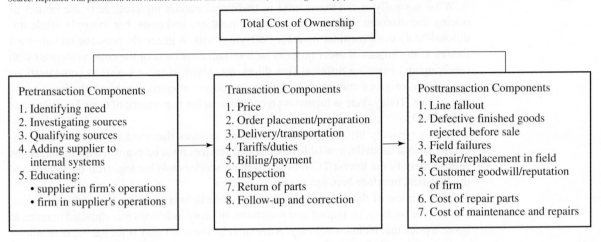

Total Cost of Ownership

Pretransaction Components
1. Identifying need
2. Investigating sources
3. Qualifying sources
4. Adding supplier to internal systems
5. Educating:
   • supplier in firm's operations
   • firm in supplier's operations

Transaction Components
1. Price
2. Order placement/preparation
3. Delivery/transportation
4. Tariffs/duties
5. Billing/payment
6. Inspection
7. Return of parts
8. Follow-up and correction

Posttransaction Components
1. Line fallout
2. Defective finished goods rejected before sale
3. Field failures
4. Repair/replacement in field
5. Customer goodwill/reputation of firm
6. Cost of repair parts
7. Cost of maintenance and repairs

closer working relationships with suppliers than would be possible if adversarial price negotiation dominated the buyer-seller relationship. When buyers work cooperatively with suppliers, several strategies may be employed to reduce both the buyers' and the sellers' costs, making the total supply chain more efficient and allowing it to more effectively meet the requirements of downstream partners. Such strategies are discussed next.

Procurement Strategies

Effective procurement strategy to support supply chain operations requires a much closer working relationship between buyers and sellers than was traditionally practiced. Specifically, three strategies have emerged: volume consolidation, supplier operational integration, and value management. Each of these strategies requires substantial collaboration between supply chain partners and should be considered as stages of continuous improvement.

Volume Consolidation

An important step in developing an effective procurement strategy is volume consolidation through reduction in the number of suppliers. Beginning in the 1980s many firms faced the reality that they dealt with a large number of suppliers for almost every material or input used. In fact, purchasing literature prior to that time emphasized that multiple sources of supply constituted best procurement practice. First, potential suppliers were continually bidding for a buyer's business, ensuring constant pressure to quote low prices. Second, maintaining multiple sources reduced the buyer's dependence on any one supplier. This in turn served to reduce the buyer's risk should a specific supplier encounter supply disruptions such as a strike, a fire, or internal quality problems.

By consolidating volumes with a limited number of suppliers, procurement is also positioned to leverage its share of a supplier's business. At the very least, it increases the buyer's negotiating strength in relationship to the supplier. More important, volume consolidation with a reduced number of suppliers provides a number of advantages for those suppliers. The most obvious advantage of concentrating a larger volume of purchases with a supplier is that it allows the supplier to improve economies of scale by spreading fixed cost over a larger volume of output. Additionally, assured of a volume of purchases, a supplier is more likely to make investments in capacity or processes to improve customer service. When a buyer is constantly switching suppliers, no one firm has an incentive to make such investment.

Clearly, when a single source of supply is used, risk increases. For this reason, supply base reduction programs are almost always accompanied by rigorous supplier screening, selection, and certification programs. In many instances, procurement executives work closely with others in their organization to develop preferred or certified suppliers. It should be noted that volume consolidation does not necessarily mean that a single source of supply is utilized for every, or any, purchased input. It does mean that a substantially smaller number of suppliers are used than was traditionally the case in most organizations. Even when a single source is chosen, it is essential to have a contingency plan.

The savings potential from volume consolidation is not trivial. One consulting firm has estimated that savings in purchase price and other elements of cost can range from 5 to 15 percent of purchases.[5] If the typical manufacturing firm spends 55 percent of its revenue on purchased items and can save 10 percent through volume consolidation, the potential exists to deliver a $5.5 million improvement on revenue of $100 million to the bottom line.

Supplier Operational Integration

The next stage of development occurs when buyers and sellers begin to integrate their processes and activities in an attempt to achieve substantial performance improvement. Such integration typically involves alliances or partnerships with selected suppliers to reduce total cost and improve operational integration.

Such integration takes many different forms. For example, the buyer may allow the supplier to have access to sales and ordering information, thereby giving the supplier continuous knowledge of which products are selling. Detailed sales information allows the supplier to be better positioned to effectively meet buyer requirements at a reduced cost. Cost reduction occurs because the supplier has more information to plan and can reduce reliance on cost-inefficient practices, such as forecasting and expediting.

Further operational integration can result for buyers and suppliers working together to identify processes involved in maintaining supply and searching for ways to redesign those processes. Establishing direct communication linkages to reduce order time and eliminate communication errors is a common benefit of such integration. More sophisticated integrative efforts may involve eliminating redundant activities that both parties perform. For example, in some sophisticated relationships, activities such as buyer counting and inspection of incoming deliveries have been eliminated as greater reliance and responsibility are assumed by suppliers. Many firms have achieved operational integration focused on logistical arrangements, such as continuous replenishment programs and vendor-managed inventory.[6] Such integration has considerable potential for reducing TCO.

Some of the efforts in operational integration strive to reduce total cost through two-way learning. For example, Honda of America works closely with its suppliers to improve their quality management. Honda visits supplier facilities and helps identify ways to increase quality. Such improvements ultimately benefit Honda by reducing the supplier's costs of rework and by providing Honda with higher levels of quality materials.

The primary objective of operational integration is to cut waste, reduce cost, and develop a relationship that allows both buyer and seller to achieve mutual improvements. Combined creativity across organizations can create synergy that one firm, operating in

[5] Matthew Anderson, Les Artman, and Paul B. Katz, "Procurement Pathways," *Logistics* (Spring/Summer 1997), p. 10.
[6] These concepts are discussed in Chapter 7.

isolation, would be unable to achieve. It has been estimated that operational integration with a supplier can provide incremental savings of 5 to 25 percent over and above the benefits of volume consolidation.[7]

Value Management

Achieving operational integration with suppliers creates the opportunity for value management. Value management is an even more intense aspect of supplier integration, going beyond a focus on buyer-seller operations to a more comprehensive and sustainable relationship. Value engineering, reduced complexity, and early supplier involvement in new product design represent some of the ways a company can work with suppliers to reduce TCO.

Value engineering is a concept that involves closely examining material and component requirements at the early stage of product design to ensure that a balance of lowest total cost and quality is incorporated into new product design. Figure 4.2 shows how early supplier involvement can be critical in achieving cost reductions. As a firm's new product development process proceeds from idea generation through the various stages to commercialization, the company's flexibility in making design changes decreases. Design changes are easily accommodated in the early stages, but by the time prototypes have been developed, a design change becomes difficult and expensive. The earlier a supplier is involved in the design process, the more likely an organization is to capitalize on that supplier's knowledge and capabilities.

An example from an automobile manufacturer demonstrates the benefit of early supplier involvement. In designing the front bumper for a new model, the design engineer was completing design of the bracket assembly for the bumper. During the process, an engineer from the assembly supplier, which had already been identified even though actual production was in the future, asked if the bracket location could be moved by about ½ inch. The design engineer, after some consideration, replied that it could be done with no impact on the final product. The design engineer was interested to know why

---

[7] Anderson, Artman, and Katz, "Procurement Pathways," p. 10.

FIGURE 4.2
Flexibility and Cost of Design Changes

Source: Reprinted with permission from Robert M. Monczka et al., *New Product Development; Strategies for Supplier Integration* (Milwaukee: ASQ Quality Press, 2000), p. 6.

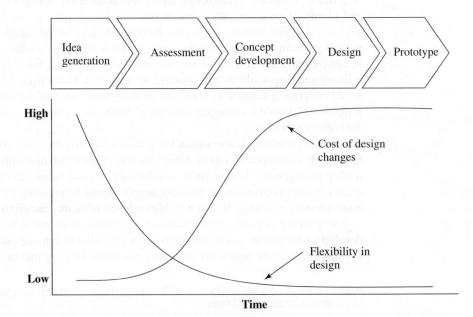

the supplier requested the change. The answer was that by moving the bracket, the supplier would be able to use existing tools and dies to manufacture the bracket. Under the original design, major capital investment would have been required for new tooling. The result was approximately a 25 to 30 percent reduction in cost of the bracket.

Clearly, value management extends beyond procurement in an organization and requires cooperation between numerous participants, both internal and external. Teams representing procurement, engineering, manufacturing, marketing, and logistics as well as key supplier personnel jointly seek solutions to lower total cost, improve performance, or improved accomodation of customer requirements.

Purchase Requirement Segmentation

The Pareto effect applies in procurement just as it applies in almost every facet of business activity. In procurement, it can be stated simply: A small percentage of the materials, items, and services acquired account for a large percentage of the dollars spent. The point is that all procured inputs are not equal. However, many organizations use the same approach and procedures for procuring small-volume items that they do for acquiring their most strategic purchases. As a result, they spend as much in acquiring a $10,000 order of raw materials as they do for a $100 order of copy paper. Since all purchased inputs are not equal, many firms have begun to pay attention to segmented purchase requirements and prioritizing resources and expertise to handle those requirements.

It would be a mistake, though, to simply use dollar expenditure as the basis for segmenting requirements. Some inputs are strategic materials. Others are not. Some inputs have potential for high impact on the business success. Others do not. Some purchases are very complex and high risk. Others are not. For example, failure to have seat assemblies delivered to an auto assembly line on time could be catastrophic, while failure to have cleaning supplies might constitute a nuisance. The key is for an organization to apply a segmented approach to procurement similar to that discussed for customers in Chapter 3. Volume consolidation and supply base reduction most likely can be justified for almost every material and service. The benefits described earlier can be enjoyed for office supplies as well as raw materials. Operational integration and value management may be reserved for more strategic purchase requirements.

E-Commerce and Procurement

The explosion in technology and information systems is having a major impact on the procurement activity of most organizations. Much of the actual day-to-day work in procurement has traditionally been accomplished manually with significant amounts of paperwork, resulting in slow processes subject to considerable human error. Applying technology to procurement has considerable potential to speed the process, reduce errors, and lower acquisition cost.

Probably the most common technology used in procurement is **Electronic Data Interchange (EDI).** EDI involves the electronic transmission of data between a firm and its suppliers. This allows two or more companies to obtain and provide timely and accurate information. Using EDI there are many types of data being directly transmitted, including purchase requisitions, purchase orders, purchase order acknowledgment, order status, advanced shipment notification, and tracking and tracing information. The explosion in EDI usage is a direct recognition of associated benefits, including standardization of data, more accurate information, more timely information, shortening of lead times with associated reductions in inventories, and reduced TCOs. More specifics related to EDI and related information technologies are provided in Chapter 5.

Another procurement application of electronic commerce is the development of electronic catalogs. In fact, making information available about products and who can supply them is a natural application for **Internet-based** communications. Electronic catalogs allow buyers to gain rapid access to product information, specifications, and pricing, allowing buyers to quickly identify products and place orders. Many companies have developed their own online electronic catalogs and efforts have also been devoted to developing catalogs containing products from multiple suppliers, which permits buyers to rapidly compare features, specifications, and prices.

Buying exchanges are another technology-based purchasing development. Typically, buying exchanges allow users to look for sellers or buyers of specific goods or services. Depending on the approach, a buyer may post a request for proposal, post a request for quotation, or invite bids for specified products and services. Transactions can be initiated and completed electronically.

The potential volume of procurement activity through buying exchanges is enormous. Exchanges have been developed in the aircraft parts industry, chemicals, steel building products, food distribution, and even retailing. However, there is a potential downside. Many suppliers fear that the exchanges will become a mechanism that ultimately will reinforce past practice of buyers to focus strictly on purchase price. If buyers post their requirements and needs on the Internet primarily for the purpose of soliciting bids from alternative suppliers, or use the technology to have suppliers enter into an auctioning process, some fear many of the advances in supplier integration and value management will suffer.

In a supply chain management context, the link between a company and its external suppliers is critical. It provides for the integration of materials and resources from outside the organization into internal operations. Procurement is charged with the responsibility of ensuring that this transition is accomplished as efficiently and as effectively as possible. Much of the concern in procurement is focused on the logistical interface between the organization and its supply base. Ultimately, the purpose of procurement is to integrate material flow in accordance with requirements. It's the job of logistics to efficiently move purchases to the desired location. In the next section, alternative manufacturing strategies are discussed with a focus on identifying their logistical requirements.

Manufacturing[8]

A substantial number of firms in the supply chain are involved in manufacturing products. Manufacturers add value by converting raw materials into consumer or industrial products. They create value by producing product/service bundles for either customers or intermediate members in the supply chain. For example, retailers purchase a wide range of products from varied manufacturers to create an appealing assortment for consumers. This section reviews supply chain structure and strategy from a manufacturing perspective. As in the previous section that discussed procurement, the objective is to highlight logistics requirements and challenges necessary to integrate and support manufacturing supply chain operations.

Manufacturing Perspectives

The range of products a firm manufactures is based on its technological capability and marketing strategy. Firms perfect manufacturing competencies on the basis of market opportunity and willingness to take innovative risk. At the outset, a manufacturing firm creates or

---

[8] This section draws on Steven A. Melnyk and Morgan Swink, *Value-Driven Operations Management: An Integrated Modular Approach* (New York: McGraw-Hill, 2003).

invents a new product assortment as its entry point as a value-added supply chain participant. Initial market success serves to define and clarify a firm's competency as perceived
by customers and suppliers. A firm initiating manufacturing operations to produce automotive parts will be viewed by trading partners as being distinctly different from one that
produces garments. While the products produced are clearly different, the real differentiator between firms is found in competencies related to knowledge, technology, process,
and strategy. Once established, a manufacturing firm's image and focus are continuously
modified in the eyes of supply chain partners as it conducts business, researches and develops new products, and performs agreed-to value-added services. Thus, the combinations
of capabilities and competencies that are exhibited by a manufacturing firm are dynamic.
In terms of supply chain participation, the combination of products, services, capabilities,
and competencies represents a firm's value proposition and provides dimension to its supply chain opportunities. A firm's manufacturing competency is based on brand power,
volume, variety, constraints, and leadtime requirements.

Brand Power

Many manufacturers spend a great deal of promotional money to create brand awareness
and acceptance among prospective buyers. As a result, they are typically identified by their
product brands. The measure of a customer's purchase preference based on a manufacturer's reputation, product quality, and supply chain capabilities is known as **brand power.**

Buyers across a supply chain range from consumers to industrial purchasing agents.
Under market conditions wherein a brand has high customer awareness, acceptance, and
preference, manufacturers can be expected to have a great deal of influence. As a general rule, the stronger a firm's product brand image among buyers, the more leverage the
manufacturing organization will have in determining supply chain structure and strategy.
For instance, Deere & Company dominates how farm machinery is sold, distributed, and
maintained.

Independent of customer acceptance is the reality that a firm that brands and markets a
particular line of products may not, in fact, be engaged in either the actual manufacturing/
assembly or in the performance of associated logistics services. It is common practice
for an organization to outsource some or even all manufacturing and logistics operations
required to market a specific product. The nature of the manufacturing process, cost, and
final destination in the supply chain go a long way to determine the attractiveness of such
outsourcing. Logistical requirements are created by the geographical network linking
locations of manufacturing operations and those of suppliers and customers. However,
the power to determine the range of value-added services, physical product movement
requirements, timing, and characteristics of flow along the supply chain is directly related
to brand power.

Volume

Manufacturing processes can be classified in terms of the relationship of cost per unit
to volume of output. The traditional perspective is to treat volume in terms of the well-
established principle of **economy of scale.** The scale principle defines a relationship
wherein the average cost of producing a product declines as its manufacturing volume
increases. In terms of economy of scale, product quantity should be increased as long as
increases in volume decrease the average cost per unit manufactured. Economy of scale
results from efficiencies generated by specialization of process, workforce, fixed asset
utilization, procurement economies, and reduced need for process changeover.

Economy of scale is extremely important when high-fixed-cost machinery is used
to convert raw material into finished products. Typical examples are the paper, steel,
and refining industries. In fact, some petroleum processing firms have decoupled their

refineries from their supply chain marketing structure and positioned them as independent external suppliers. The refineries are then able to sell in the open market to all potential buyers and fully exploit economy-of-scale advantage.

In volume-sensitive industries, high capital investment coupled with high cost of changeover tends to encourage extremely long production runs. In terms of logistical support, two considerations related to volume influence supply chain design. First, supply chain logistics must accommodate the number of times a product is manufactured during a planning period. Such manufacturing frequency has a direct impact on both inbound and outbound logistical requirements. Second, the quantity or lot size typically produced during a manufacturing run determines the subsequent volume that must be handled and warehoused in a supply chain logistics structure.

Variety

In contrast to manufacturing situations dominated by scale, other production technologies feature flexibility. These manufacturing processes are characterized by relatively frequent product runs and high repetition of small lot sizes. As contrasted to economy of scale, manufacturing processes that feature variety rapidly switching production from one product to another while retaining efficiency are referred to as having **economy of scope.** Scope means that a manufacturing process can use varied combinations of overhead support, materials, equipment, and labor to produce a variety of different products.

Variety also refers to the **range** of product variations that are capable of being manufactured by using a given process. Range may result from the sequence of routing products through a manufacturing plant as well as the use of general as contrasted to specialized equipment. The achievement of economy of scope is also directly related to the speed and cost of changeover from one product to another. In terms of logistical support, high variety translates to relatively small manufacturing lot sizes, flexible material requirements, and a broad range of product outputs. High manufacturing variety directly impacts the type of logistical transportation and warehousing services required to support flexible manufacturing.

Constraints

All manufacturing processes reflect a balance between economy of scale and economy of scope. Volume and variety drive logistical support requirements. Constraints interact with volume and variety to create realistic manufacturing plans. The three primary constraints that influence manufacturing operations are **capacity, equipment, and setup/changeover.** Each of these constraints drives compromise regarding ideal manufacturing operations. Such compromise planned in the context of forecasted sales and planned promotions creates the production plan.

Capacity, as the name implies, is a measure of how much product can be produced per unit of time. Of particular interest is a firm's demonstrated capacity of quality production. Whereas a factory, process, or machine may have a rated capacity, the relevant measure is a firm's demonstrated ability to reach and maintain a specific level of quality output in a predictable time period. A measure of manufacturing competency is the speed to which a particular process reaches demonstrated capacity, given an unplanned change in requirements.[9] Such **scalability** is achieved by a combination of manufacturing, procurement, and logistical agility.

Equipment constraints are related to flexibility concerning the use and sequencing of specific machines to perform multiple manufacturing tasks. The variety a factory can

[9] Thomas G. Gunn, *21st Century Manufacturing* (Essex Junction, VT: OM NEO, 1992), Chapter 8.

produce is constrained by the range of available equipment and the required sequence of work. However, some manufacturing requirements are more easily accommodated across a family of machines and by using variable work sequences than are others. In many situations, a specific machine or work task tends to constrain or act as a bottleneck to the overall manufacturing process. Likewise, logistical capability to accommodate different patterns of equipment utilization may serve to enhance or constrain flexibility of the manufacturing process. Manufacturing executives devote substantial time and resources to eliminating bottlenecks that serve to constrain operations. The structure for focusing managerial attention is captured in **theory of constraint** methodology.[10]

Setup/changeover constraints are directly related to the need for variety. Substantial progress has been made in manufacturing management to speed up both process changeover time and the time required to reach demonstrated capacity. Whereas several hours and even days were once required for changeover, today the tasks are being performed in hours. For example, modular-manufacturing units, such as paint sprayers, are being set up and calibrated offline and then being inserted ready to spray paint into assembly lines. Of course all efforts to increase setup/changeover speed are directly dependent upon supply chain logistical support.

Leadtime

Manufacturing leadtime is a measure of the elapsed time between release of a work order to the shop floor and the completion of all work necessary to achieve ready-to-ship product status. Any given manufacturing process consumes operational and interoperational time.[11]

Operational time is the combination of setup/changeover and running or actual production time. In any manufacturing situation, the greater the amount of total leadtime accounted for by actual production, the inherently more efficient is the conversion process. Efficient operational time must be traded off against the issues discussed earlier concerning volume and variety.

Manufacturing processes also encounter unexpected delays or **inoperational time.** During periods that a process, line, or machine is idle because of queuing, waiting, breakdown, or failure in logistical support, manufacturing efficiency is negatively impacted. All forms of unexpected delay represent serious bottleneck issues. For example, it is estimated that between 75 and 95 percent of all nonproductive delays result from unplanned queuing in manufacturing processes.[12] Needless to say, most senior managers have little or no tolerance for unexpected production delays that result from late or damaged arrival of critical materials or components. Logistical delay on the part of a supplier who provides parts or materials can result in manufacturing failure to meet planned output. A firm's strategic impact is directly affected by leadtime performance. As a general rule, firms that compress manufacturing leadtimes and control or eliminate unexpected performance variance exhibit greater flexibility to accommodate customer requirements while simultaneously enjoying low-cost manufacturing.

Logistical operations commitments to supporting manufacturing can impact operating efficiency in a variety of ways. The potential benefits of brand power are based on a firm's track record regarding timely accommodation of customer order-to-delivery requirements. Lot-size efficiencies related to manufacturing frequency and repetition depend on reliable

---

[10] For origins of this logic, see Eliyahu M. Goldratt and J. Cox, *The Goal* (Croton on Hudson, NY: North River Press, 1984); and Eliyahu M. Goldratt and Robert E. Fox, *The Race* (Croton on Hudson, NY: North River Press, 1986).
[11] Steven A. Melnyk and R. T. Christensen, *Back to Basics: Your Guide to Manufacturing* Excellence (Boca Raton: St. Lucie Press, 2000), pp. 15–17.
[12] Ibid., p. 17.

logistical support. The decision to produce large manufacturing lot sizes directly creates need for logistical support. Economy of scale drives procurement best practice and average inventory investment across the supply chain. The decision to focus on variety in manufacturing impacts the logistics requirements by adding the complexity of frequent changeover. Logistical performance is also a key variable in managing constraints. Such constraints can be created or resolved on the basis of logistical flexibility. Finally, logistics is critical to achieving manufacturing leadtime. In particular, logistical failure can increase manufacturing leadtime by introducing unexpected delays.

Logistics, as well as all other factors that impact manufacturing performance predictability, serves to create uncertainty requiring inventory. Inventory safety stocks are required when the timing of customer demand exceeds a firm's, or a supplier's, ability to deliver the correct assortment of products to the right place at the right time.

Manufacturing Strategies

The unique nature of each manufacturing process and customer requirements limit the practical range of alternative manufacturing strategies. Manufacturing strategic range is constrained by both marketing and technological forces. Prevailing marketing practices serve to ground manufacturing strategy in terms of customer acceptability. Technology drives strategy to a manufacturing model that is competitive. For example, a manufacturer having a process dominated by economy of scale may desire to improve process flexibility. However, significant investment will typically be required to increase frequency and repetition.

Over time, the changing nature of the market and available technology serve to alter a firm's strategic posture. Consider, for example, the steel industry, which was long dominated by processes highly dependent on economy of scale. Recent years have witnessed market acceptance of a wide range of new steel-based materials combined with value-added services. The Steel Service Center introduced cutting and shaping postponement to steel distribution as a way to increase customer accommodation. The nature of basic steel production has also undergone dramatic change. New process methods are being perfected that reduce long-time dependence on high-scale manufacturing processes. The combined impact of these changes in market and process has shifted the strategic posture of steel producers.

Manufacturing Processes

Manufacturers must design processes based on the work that needs to be done. Since different processes provide different capabilities, a firm's process structures must be appropriate for the volume and variety of the products it produces. There are four common types of manufacturing process structures.

In a **job shop** products are typically customized for a specific customer. Each order or "job" can involve different materials and inputs. A tool and die shop that makes customized equipment for an automobile manufacturer is an example of a job shop. A more familiar example is a tailor who makes customized suits and other clothes for consumers.

A **batch** process typically is used to manufacture a small quantity of an item in a single production run before changing over to produce another item. John Deere and Caterpillar tend to use batch processes in manufacturing construction and agricultural equipment. A local bakery that produces cookies, cakes, and pies uses a batch process. A batch process structure works well when there is a high variety of products but each has a relatively low volume.

When there are many customers who want a similar product such as automobiles, appliances, and cell phones, a **line flow** process structure is typically used. In line flow processes standard products with a limited number of variations typically move on an assembly line through various stages of production, where pieces or components are added at each stage.

A **continuous** process is typically used to manufacture such items as gasoline, chemicals, laundry detergent, and aluminum soda cans. Many food products such as pasta and cereal are made using continuous processes. These products offer customers very little variety and are often referred to as commodities.

These four general process structures can be modified to create more options. For example, changes in management practices and technology have led to the cost advantages of high-volume continuous and line flow processes while increasing variety through **mass customization,** where a product is produced quickly and at a low cost using a high-volume production process. Dell Computers is an example of mass customization. Selecting from a range of components and warranty options, customers can design a computer system that best meets their needs at the price they want to pay and have delivery within about a week. Standardizing parts, using modular designs, and postponing product differentiation are practices used with mass customization.[13]

Matching Manufacturing Strategy to Market Requirements

In Chapter 3, typical marketing strategies were classified as being mass, segmental and focused, or one-on-one. These strategies are differentiated, in part, in terms of the desired degree of product and service accommodation. Mass marketing requires limited product/service differentiation. In contrast, one-on-one marketing strategy builds on unique or customized product/service offerings for each and every customer. A firm's strategic marketing posture concerning flexibility and agility to accommodate specific customer requirements is directly related to manufacturing capability. To a significant degree, a firm's manufacturing capability drives the feasible range of effective marketing strategy. For a manufacturing firm to effectively compete, it must be able to integrate manufacturing capability into a meaningful marketing value proposition.

Alternative Manufacturing Strategies

The most common manufacturing strategies are **make-to-plan (MTP), make-to-order (MTO),** and **assemble-to-order (ATO).** It is also common to refer to MTP as **make-to-stock (MTS).**

As a general rule, MTP strategies are characteristic of industries exploiting economy of scale gained from long production runs. Significant finished goods inventory is typically manufactured in anticipation of future customer requirements. The logistical requirement to support MTP is warehousing capacity to store finished product and to facilitate product assortment to meet specific customer requirements. When flexible manufacturing is introduced to speed up switchover, the inventory lots produced are typically smaller in quantity. However, warehouses are still required for temporary storage and to facilitate product assortment.

In contrast, MTO manufacturing strategies seek to manufacture to customer specification. While MTO may not be as limited as the traditional job shop, exact quantities and configurations are produced in relatively small quantities. Logistical capacity may be required for temporary storage and to achieve outbound transportation consolidation, but most product produced in an MTO environment is shipped direct to customers.

In ATO situations, base products and components are partially manufactured in anticipation of future customer orders; however, the products are not fully assembled or customized until a customer's order is received. Such final assembly reflects implementation of the

---

[13] Various aspects of postponement and mass customization were discussed in Chapter 1.

principle of manufacturing or form postponement. The need for logistical capacity is critical in ATO operations. In fact, an increasing amount of ATO product finalization is being performed in supply chain logistics warehouses. The attractiveness of an ATO manufacturing strategy is that it has the potential to combine some facets of economy of scale typical of MTP with a degree of flexibility characteristic of MTO. Full implementation of an ATO strategy requires that warehouse operations be integrated in the value creation process to perform customizing and assembly operations.

Manufacturing strategy clearly has a significant impact on the leadtime experienced by customers. The choice of MTO, ATO, or MTP determines whether a customer will bear the cost of waiting for completion of one or more of the three performance cycles discussed in Chapter 2. For MTP items such as most fast-moving consumer goods, customers essentially only experience the customer accommodation cycle, the time from placing an order until the product is received from the supplier. An ATO strategy choice by a manufacturer requires that customers also wait during the time that the product is actually configured to their requirements. Generally, an MTO strategy requires that customers incur the additional time of the manufacturer purchasing the needed components and materials to make the product.

Table 4.1 summarizes the essential characteristics of manufacturing processes and strategies. Each process is associated with the product variety and volume generally produced as well as the strategy generally employed and the resulting impact on customers in terms of their expected total leadtimes. Keep in mind, however, that creative organizations implementing mass customization are exploiting ways to blend different process and strategy combinations.

Total Cost of Manufacturing

The marketing and manufacturing strategies of a firm drive logistical service requirements. For example, MTO manufacturing strategies typically require less finished goods inventory than MTP and ATO strategies. However, MTO strategies typically require significant component inventory and may result in high-cost customer accommodation. In

FIGURE 4.3
Manufacturing Strategy and Performance Cycles

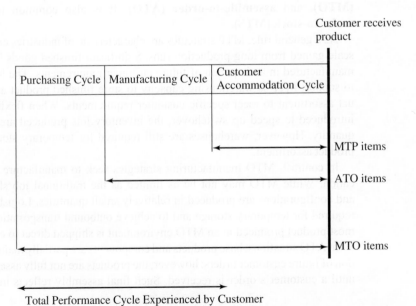

Total Performance Cycle Experienced by Customer

TABLE 4.1
Manufacturing
Process
Characteristics

	Product Variety	Volume	Strategy	Customer Leadtime
Job Shop	Very high	Very low	MTO	Very long
Batch	High	Low	MTO/ATO	Long
Line Flow	Limited	High	ATO/MTP	Short
Continuous Flow	Very limited	Very high	MTP	Very short

light of such cost trade-offs, the design of a logistics support system should be based on the **Total Cost of Manufacturing (TCM).**

Total cost of manufacturing consists of production/procurement, inventory/warehousing, and transportation. All of the above costs are impacted by manufacturing strategy. As such, TCM represents the foundation for formulating a customer accommodation strategy. Figure 4.4 represents a generalized model of the TCM **per unit** ranging across strategic alternatives from MTO to ATO to MTP. Naturally, exact cost relationships will depend upon specifics related to individual business situations. The design objective is to identify the manufacturing strategy that best fits the marketing opportunity confronted.

In Figure 4.4, the per unit cost of manufacturing and procurement declines as quantity increases, reflecting economy of scale associated with MTP. Inventory and warehousing costs increase, reflecting the impact of larger manufacturing lot sizes. Transportation cost per unit decreases as a result of shipment consolidation. In contrast, MTO strategies reflect high per unit manufacturing and procurement costs which are, in part, offset by lower inventory and warehousing costs. In the MTO strategy, transportation cost per unit is higher, reflecting small shipment and/or premium transportation. The value of Figure 4.4 is to generalize relationships and visualize important cross-functional trade-offs. The TCM results from functional integration of manufacturing, procurement, and logistics. From a perspective of integrated management it is important for manufacturing firms to design a supply chain strategy that achieves lowest total cost of manufacturing across the entire process.

FIGURE 4.4
Total Cost of
Manufacturing

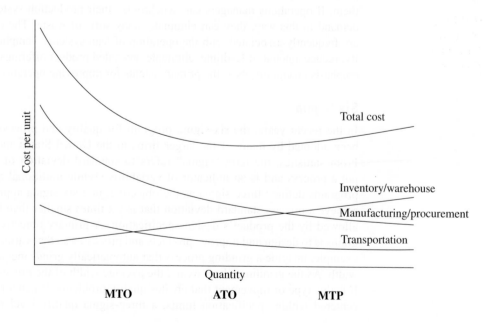

Lean and Six Sigma

Two significant developments in recent years have had a significant impact on supply chain operations. The first is the development of lean principles in manufacturing. The second is development of six-sigma quality initiatives, which have been applied in manufacturing as well as logistics operations. Each is discussed below.

Lean Systems

Lean has been defined in several different ways, but, in general, it is a philosophy of manufacturing that emphasizes the minimization of the amount of all the resources (including time) used in the operations of a company. Operational processes are considered to be lean when they are very efficient and have few wasted resources. The elimination of "waste" is actually the defining principle of lean.

By eliminating wastes of all sorts in the system, the lean approach lowers labor, materials, and energy costs of production. Lean also emphasizes building exactly the products customers want, exactly when they need them. When lean capabilities are introduced in a firm it can produce smaller quantities, and it can change outputs more quickly in response to changes in customer demand.

The primary objectives of lean systems are to

1. Produce only the products (goods or services) that customers want.
2. Produce products only as quickly as customers want to use them.
3. Produce products with perfect quality.
4. Produce in the minimum possible leadtimes.
5. Produce products with features that customers want, and no others.
6. Produce with no waste of labor, materials, or equipment; designate a purpose for every movement to leave zero idle inventory.
7. Produce with methods that reinforce the occupational development of workers.

Note that the first two objectives emphasize producing "just-in-time," that is, building products only when customers want them and at the same rate that customers demand them. If operations managers can synchronize their production systems with the rate of demand in this way, they can eliminate many sorts of waste. The other five objectives are frequently associated with the operation of lean systems—emphasis on perfect quality, reduce amount of leadtime, eliminate unwanted product offerings, and place a greater emphasis on employees as the primary agents for improving operations.

Six Sigma

In the recent years, the **six-sigma** program for quality and process improvements has been adopted by many of the larger firms in the United States and around the world. From statistics, the term "sigma" refers to standard deviation of values for the output a process and is an indicator of variability. While traditional quality management programs defined three sigma as the objective, in a six-sigma approach, the goal is to achieve a process standard deviation that is six times smaller than the range of outputs allowed by the product's design specification. A primary objective of six-sigma programs is to design and improve products and processes so that variability is reduced. For example, imagine a grinding process that automatically grinds metal parts to a specified width. As the grinding wheel wears, the average width of the processed parts increases. It is this type of movement that creates quality problems. When a process is stable and centered within specification limits, a three-sigma quality level means that the firm produces defect-free product 99.74 percent of the time. A six-sigma process that is centered produces defect-free product 99.99966 percent of the time. Thus, a six-sigma process produces only 3.4 defects per million parts, while a three-sigma process produces 66,807 defects per million parts.

The six-sigma approach is actually a structured process for first identifying sources of variability and then reducing them. Early developers of the six-sigma approach at Motorola originally chose six standard deviations as an appropriate goal given the nature of their manufacturing processes. In truth, very few business operations ever attain a six-sigma level of quality. More important than the absolute goal are the quality improvement processes that comprise a six-sigma program.

Logistical Interfaces

The efficient and effective coordination of manufacturing strategy with the procurement of materials and components ultimately depends on logistics. Resources must be procured and positioned as needed to support manufacturing operations. Whether the manufacturing strategy is MTO, ATO, or MTP, logistics links suppliers and customers with manufacturing processes. Clearly, the more seamless the interface, the better the opportunity is for achieving lowest total cost of ownership and, ultimately, lowest total cost of manufacturing. Such operations only emerge when there is high-level supplier integration in both operations and design. Just-in-time, materials requirements planning, design for logistics, and performance-based logistics represent four approaches to achieving desired coordination.

Just-in-Time

Just-in-Time (JIT) techniques have received considerable attention and discussion in recent years in all areas related to supply chain management. Sometimes referred to as just-in-time purchasing, and frequently referred to as just-in-time delivery, the goal of JIT is to time-phase activities so that purchased materials and components arrive at the manufacturing or assembly point just at the time they are required for the transformation process. Ideally, raw material and work-in-process inventories are minimized as a result of reducing or eliminating reserve stocks. The key to JIT operations is that demand for components and materials depends on the finalized production schedule. Requirements can be determined by focusing on the finished product being manufactured. Once the production schedule is established, just-in-time arrival of components and materials can be planned to coincide with those requirements, resulting in reduced handling and minimal inventories.

The implications of JIT are numerous. Obviously, it is necessary to deal with suppliers who have high and consistent levels of quality, as their components will go directly into the finished product. Absolutely reliable logistical performance is required and eliminates, or at least reduces, the need for buffer stocks of materials. JIT generally requires more frequent deliveries of smaller quantities of purchased inputs, which may require modification of inbound transportation. Clearly, to make JIT work, there must be very close cooperation and communication between a manufacturer's purchasing organization and suppliers. In JIT operations, companies attempt to gain the benefits of backward vertical integration but avoid the formal tie of ownership. They achieve many of the same ends through coordination and process integration with suppliers.

Originally, JIT was applied to manufacturing processes characterized as MTP, since the effective functioning of the system is dependent upon a finalized production schedule. However, as manufacturing strategies have evolved with more emphasis on flexibility, reduced lot-size production quantities, and quick changeovers, JIT concepts have evolved to accommodate ATO and MTO manufacturing as well and in manufacturing is now refered to as *lean,* as discussed above. In many situations, lead suppliers are used by manufacturers to sort, segregate, and sequence materials as they flow into assembly operations. The goal is to reduce handling and facilitate continuous JIT.

Some organizations, seeing the benefits of JIT systems and recognizing the benefits of supplier integration, have gone so far as to bring their suppliers' personnel into their production plants. The supplier personnel are empowered to use the customer's purchase orders, have full access to production schedules, and have responsibility for scheduling arrival of materials. Originally introduced by the Bose Corporation, the term **JIT II** has been applied to these efforts to reduce leadtimes and cost.

Requirements Planning

In complex manufacturing organizations a process known as **materials requirements planning (MRP)** is frequently used to aid in the interface between purchaser and supplier. MRP systems attempt to gain benefits similar to those of JIT, minimize inventory, maintain high utilization of manufacturing capacity, and coordinate delivery with procurement and manufacturing activities. Implementation of MRP systems, discussed in Chapter 5, requires a high level of technological sophistication. Software applications such as advanced planning and scheduling systems deal with the complexity of information required, such as leadtimes, quantities on-hand and on-order, and machine capacities for literally thousands of materials across multiple manufacturing locations.

Design for Logistics

The logistics interface with procurement and manufacturing, as well as with engineering and marketing, can be greatly enhanced by incorporating a concept known as **design for logistics** into the early phases of product development. Recall that the objectives of JIT and MRP are to minimize inventories and handling, with materials and components being ready for assembly or transformation as they are needed. How a product is designed and the design of the components and materials themselves can have a significant impact on this process. In particular, product packaging and transportation requirements need to be incorporated into the design process. For example, if inbound components are packaged in containers with a standard quantity of 50 but only 30 components are needed to meet production requirements, then waste will occur. Additionally, product and component design must have consideration of transportation and internal materials handling methods to ensure that cost-efficient, damage-free logistics performance can be achieved. Similar design considerations must be made for the finished product itself.

Performance-Based Logistics[14]

Initiated by the U. S. Department of Defense (**DoD**), a new approach to dealing with suppliers called *performance-based logistics* has recently emerged. PBL is used to buy what the military has traditionally referred to as logistics support. The most interesting aspect of PBL is that the military buys performance outcomes instead of what has historically been individual transactions defined by product specifications.

Historically, the DoD told contractors what products to produce, when to produce them, and what activities to perform, and then paid them upon completion. In this

[14] This section is based on Kate Vitasek and Steve Geary, "Performance Based Logistics," *World Trade* (June 2008), pp. 62–65.

traditional arrangement, the more the contractor produced, the more money it made. With PBL, the government simply tells the contractor what the desired outcomes are and lets the supplier determine the best way to meet those requirements. The government has found PBL to be an effective means for obtaining higher quality while simultaneously achieving lower cost. While PBL has been limited thus far to government purchasing, it is expected that business organizations may begin to adopt the practice in the future.

Table 4.2 summarizes the critical relationships between customer accommodation, manufacturing/procurement, and logistical requirements. The framework is useful in positioning how logistical requirements flow from the customer accommodation, manufacturing, and procurement strategies.

Summary

Managing logistics in the supply chain requires an interface between logistics, procurement, and manufacturing strategies.

A primary concern of procurement and manufacturing is product quality, a prerequisite for any firm that desires to be a global competitor. In fact, product quality has several different dimensions. It can mean reliability, durability, product performance, and conformance to engineered specifications. From a customer's perspective it may also include aspects of product features, aesthetics, or serviceability. World-class companies have implemented Total Quality Management programs in all their activities in an effort to achieve quality from their customer's perspective.

Procurement in an organization is charged with responsibility for obtaining the inputs required to support manufacturing operations. The focus is multidimensional, attempting to maintain continuous supply, minimize leadtimes from suppliers and inventory of materials and components, and develop suppliers capable of helping the organization achieve operating goals. Procurement professionals are focused on the Total Cost of Ownership as contrasted solely on purchase price. This requires careful consideration of trade-offs between purchase price, supplier services and logistical capability, quality of material, and how the material impacts costs over the life cycle of the finished product. Procurement strategies

TABLE 4.2 **Strategic Integration Framework**

Customer Accommodation	Manufacturing	Procurement	Logistics
Focused:	Make-to-Order (MTO):	B2B	Direct Fulfillment:
One-on-one strategies	Maximum variety	Discrete quantities	Time postponement
Unique product/service offerings	Unique configuration	Supplier-managed inventory	Small shipment
Response-based	Flexible manufacturing		
	High variety		
Segmental:	Assemble-to-Order (ATO):	B2B	Form and Time
Limited size	Wide variety	JIT	Postponement:
Customer groups	Quick changeover		Warehouse ATO
Differentiated products	Product customization		Combination direct and warehouse fulfillment
Mixed response and anticipatory	High variety and volume		Consolidated shipment
Mass Marketing:	Make-to-Plan (MTP):	B2B	Warehouse Fulfillment:
Anticipatory	Long product runs	Commodity	Full stocking strategy
Little product differentiation	Focus low cost	Auction	Assortment mixing
	High volume/low variety	E-procurement	Volume shipment

require consolidation of purchase volumes into a small number of reliable suppliers. Such strategies include efforts to integrate supplier and buyer operations to achieve better and lower-cost overall performance.

Manufacturers balance product volumes, varieties, and capacity with customer requirements and constraints. The processes employed reflect alternative strategies related to MTP, ATO, or MTO. In turn, the strategic choice impacts customers in terms of total experienced leadtime. Lean principles focus on eliminating waste and more closely matching manufacturing capabilities with customer demand.

In Chapters 3 and 4, strategic considerations related to customer accommodation, procurement, and manufacturing have been discussed in terms of their combined impact on logistical requirements. A number of important trade-offs were identified. The fundamental point is that isolated optimization of any specific functional area without considering cross-functional impact and requirements is not likely to result in integrated performance. Information technology is the focus of Chapter 5.

Challenge Questions

1. Using television receivers as an example, how could three different brands be perceived by different consumers as being the best quality brand in the market?
2. Why does the contemporary view of procurement as a strategic activity differ from the more traditional view of "purchasing"?
3. How can strategic procurement contribute to the quality of products produced by a manufacturing organization?
4. Explain the rationale underlying volume consolidation. What are the risks associated with using a single supplier for an item?
5. How does lowest TCO differ from lowest purchase price?
6. What is the underlying rationale that explains why firms should segment their purchase requirements?
7. Explain how constraints in manufacturing are interrelated with a company's decisions regarding volume and variety.
8. Why would a company's cost of manufacturing and procurement tend to increase as the firm changes from an MTP to an MTO strategy? Why would inventory costs tend to decrease?
9. How does a firm's marketing strategy impact its decisions regarding the appropriate manufacturing strategy?
10. Explain how logistics performance is crucial to JIT.

Information Technology

Chapter Outline

Supply chain technology systems initiate activities and track information regarding processes, facilitate information sharing both within the firm and between supply chain partners, and assist in management decision making. This chapter describes comprehensive information systems as a combination of transaction, decision support, and communication systems. The chapter begins by describing the role of information systems functionality in supply chain competitiveness. Then the chapter describes the major modules and external interfaces of supply chain information systems. The remaining sections discuss enterprise integration and administration, enterprise operations, enterprise planning and monitoring, and communication technology applications respectively. The final chapter section discusses the movement to offering **software as a service (SaaS)** rather than requiring each firm to have their own copy of each application.

Information System Functionality

From its inception, logistics focuses on product storage and flow through the supply chain. Information flow and accuracy was often overlooked because it was not viewed as being critical to customers. In addition, information transfer rates were limited to manual processes. There are four reasons why timely and accurate information has become more critical in logistics system design and operations. First, customers perceive information regarding order status, product availability, delivery tracking, and invoices as necessary dimensions of customer accommodation. Customers demand real-time information. Second, with the goal of reducing total supply chain assets, managers realize that information can be used to reduce inventory and human resource requirements. In particular, requirements planning based on current information can reduce inventory by minimizing demand uncertainty. Third, information increases flexibility with regard to how, when, and where resources may be utilized to achieve competitive advantage. Fourth, enhanced information transfer and exchange utilizing the Internet is facilitating collaboration and redefining supply chain relationships.

Supply chain information systems (SCIS) are the thread linking logistics activities into an integrated process. The integration builds on four levels of functionality: (1) transaction systems, (2) management control, (3) decision analysis, and (4) strategic planning. Figure 5.1 illustrates logistics activities and decisions at each level of information functionality. As the pyramid shape suggests, management control, decision analysis, and strategic planning enhancements require a strong transaction system foundation.

A **transaction system** is characterized by formalized rules, procedures, and standardized communications; a large volume of transactions; and an operational, day-to-day focus. The combination of structured processes and large transaction volume places a major emphasis on information system efficiency. At the most basic level, transaction systems initiate and record individual logistics activities and their outcomes. Typical transaction functionality includes order entry, inventory assignment, order selection, shipping, pricing, invoicing, and customer inquiry. For example, the customer order entry transaction enters a customer request for products into the information system. The order entry transaction initiates a second transaction as inventory is assigned to the order. A third transaction is then generated to direct warehouse operations to accumulate the order. A fourth transaction initiates order shipment to the customer. The final transaction creates the invoice and a corresponding account receivable. Throughout the process, the firm and customer expect real-time information regarding order status. Thus, the customer order performance cycle is completed through a series of information system transactions.[1]

The second SCIS level, **management control,** focuses on performance measurement and reporting. Performance measurement is necessary to provide feedback regarding supply chain performance and resource utilization. Common performance dimensions include cost, customer service, productivity, quality, and asset management measures. As an example, specific performance measures include transportation and warehousing cost per hundredweight, inventory turnover, case fill rate, cases per labor hour, and customer service perception.

---

[1] For a review of performance cycle structure and dynamics, see Chapter 2.

FIGURE 5.1   **Information Functionality**

While it is necessary that SCIS report historical system performance, it is also necessary for the system to identify operational exceptions. Exception information is useful to highlight potential customer or operational problems. For example, proactive SCIS should be capable of identifying future inventory shortages based on forecast requirements and planned inventory. Exception reporting should also identify potential transportation, warehouse, or labor constraints. While some control measures, such as cost, are well defined, other measures, such as service and quality, are less specific. For example, customer service can be measured internally, from the enterprise's perspective, or externally, from the customer's perspective. While internal measures are relatively easy to track, information concerning external measures is more difficult to obtain, since it involves the customer or other external partners.

The third SCIS level, **decision analysis,** focuses on software tools to assist managers in identifying, evaluating, and comparing strategic and tactical alternatives to improve effectiveness. Typical analyses include supply chain design, inventory management, resource allocation, transportation routing, and segmental profitability. Decision analysis SCIS should ideally include database maintenance, modeling, analysis, and reporting. Like management control, decision analysis may include operational considerations such as vehicle routing and warehouse planning. Decision analysis is also being used to manage customer relationships by determining the trade-offs associated with having satisfied and successful customers.

Strategic planning, the final SCIS level, organizes and synthesizes transaction data into a relational database that assists in strategy evaluation. Essentially, strategic planning focuses on information to evaluate and refine supply chain and logistics strategy. Examples of strategic planning include the desirability of strategic alliances, development and refinement of manufacturing capabilities, and opportunities related to customer responsiveness.

The relative shape of Figure 5.2 illustrates SCIS development characteristics and justification. Development and maintenance costs include hardware, software, communications, and human resources. In the past, most systems development focused on improving transaction system efficiency. While these investments originally offered returns in terms of speed and lower operating costs, there are now fewer improvement opportunities. Most SCIS development and implementation is now focused on enhanced supply chain system integration and improved decision making.

Supply Chain Information System Modules

A comprehensive SCIS initiates, monitors, assists in decision making, and reports on activities required for completion of logistics operations and planning. The major system modules and their interfaces as illustrated in Figure 5.3 are: (1) Enterprise Resource Planning **(ERP)**, (2) communication systems, (3) execution systems, and (4) planning systems. While Figure 5.3 provides a software-oriented perspective, Figure 5.4 illustrates a more application-oriented perspective. This application perspective is used to discuss each module's specific characteristics and functionality.

The ERP systems in Figure 5.4 are the backbone of most firms' logistics information system. This backbone maintains current and historical data and processes to initiate and monitor performance. During the 1990s, many firms began to replace legacy systems with ERP systems designed as integrated transaction modules and processes with a common and consistent database. The database includes information storage capability for both operations (i.e., product and activity based) and financial (i.e., monetary based) transactions. ERP systems facilitate integrated operations and reporting to initiate, monitor, and track critical activities such as order fulfillment and replenishment. ERP systems

FIGURE 5.2 **SCIS Usage, Decision Characteristics, and Justification**

FIGURE 5.3
SCIS: Integrated Modules

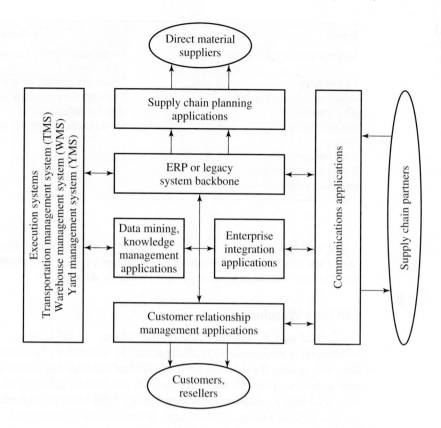

also incorporate an integrated corporatewide database, sometimes referred to as a data warehouse, along with appropriate transactions to facilitate logistics and supply chain planning and operations. Supply chain transactions facilitated by ERP systems include order entry and management, inventory assignment, and shipping. Beyond these supply chain applications, ERP systems typically include financial, accounting, and human resource capability. Table 5.1 lists the traditional and emerging capabilities of ERP systems. Data mining, knowledge management, and other enterprise integration applications operate using the ERP backbone to develop and organize insight regarding customers, products, and operations.

FIGURE 5.4
Application-Oriented SCIS Framework

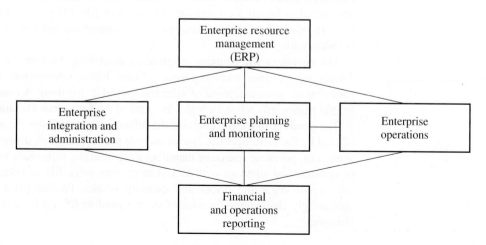

TABLE 5.1
ERP System Capability

Typical	Advanced
Accounts payable and receivable	Collaborative planning, forecasting, and replenishment
General ledger	Customer relationship management
Human resource management	Supply chain event management
Bill of materials	Web-enabled applications
Inventory control	Advanced planning and scheduling
Routings	
Order management	
Project requirements planning	
Execution systems	

The application-oriented modules include: (1) ERP data warehouse, (2) enterprise integration and administration, (3) enterprise operations, (4) enterprise planning and monitoring, and (5) communications technology. Each is briefly described.

ERP Data Warehouse

The core of an ERP system is the central database or information warehouse where all information is maintained to facilitate access to common and consistent data by all modules. Surrounding the database are the functional modules that initiate and coordinate business activities. Although total ERP benefits can best be achieved when all functions are integrated into a common application, many firms elect to implement systems using a modular approach to spread resource requirements and minimize risk, so a limited number of firm functions are in transition at any time.

The **central database** is the relational information repository for the entire ERP system. The central database is described as **relational** because it relates or links information regarding operational entities so that there is minimal information redundancy. Over time, information redundancy usually leads to inaccuracy because one reference to a data item is eventually changed without a comparable change in the other reference. For example, if a customer address is contained in two different locations in the database, it is likely that eventually one reference will be changed if the customer moves but the second reference may be forgotten. At that point, the database would no longer be consistent and all references to the second address would be incorrect. Although the central database is extensive and can contain millions of data items in numerous files, eight major data files are critical to logistics operations: (1) customer file, (2) product-price file, (3) supplier file, (4) order file, (5) bill-of-materials file, (6) purchase order file, (7) inventory file, and (8) history file.

The **customer file** contains information describing the firm's customers. Each entry defines one customer, including name, address, billing information, ship-to location, company contact, price list, terms of sale, and special instructions. A common customer file is helpful particularly when multiple divisions of the firm serve the same customer.

The **product-price file** contains the information describing the products and services offered by the firm. Specific entries include product number, description, physical characteristics, purchase source or manufacturing location, references to equivalent products or updates, and standard cost data. The product-price file or related file also contains information regarding prices and quantity breaks. Product-price file maintenance is increasingly challenging because of shorter product life cycles and more frequent price changes.

The **supplier file** lists the firm's suppliers for materials and services. Specific entries include supplier number, supplier name, address, transportation and receiving information, and payables instructions. A common supplier file is critical to achieve purchasing economies through supplier rationalization and consolidation.

The **order file** contains the information regarding all open orders in some stage of processing or fulfillment by the firm. Each order represents a current or potential request by a customer to ship product. The order file contains the customer number and name, requested receipt date, and the list of products and quantities that are being ordered. The order file is increasingly being required to include special shipping and packaging requests for unique customers. The system must also increasingly accept orders from multiple sources, including EDI and the Internet, as well as by internal order entry.

The **bill-of-materials file** describes how raw materials are combined for finished products. For example, a simple bill-of-materials for an automobile would indicate that one car requires one body, one chassis, four seats, one engine, one transaxle, and four tires. Although these product relationships are typically used in manufacturing, it is becoming increasingly important for logistics as well. Logistics operations are beginning to use bills of materials to facilitate packaging, customization, and kitting in distribution center operations.

The **purchase order (PO) file** is similar to the order file except that it contains the records of purchase orders that have been placed on suppliers. The purchase order may be for raw material to support product or for MRO (Maintenance, Repair, and Operating) supplies necessary to support operations and administration. MRO items are not directly included as finished products sold by the firm. Specific purchase order file information includes purchase order number, supplier number and name, request date, ship-to location, transportation mode and carrier, and a list of the items to be purchased and the corresponding quantity. Other critical requirements of the PO file are the product specifications, delivery requirements, and contracted price.

The **inventory file** records the physical inventory or quantity of product that the firm has available or may be available in the future according to current production schedules. The file also tracks the physical location of the product within the material storage system and facility; the product status in terms of available to ship, damaged, quality hold, or on-hold for a key customer; and lot numbers for products that must be tracked. Specific inventory file information includes product number, facility location, storage location, and inventory quantity for each product status.

The **history file** documents the firm's order and purchase order history to facilitate management reporting, budget and decision analyses, and forecasting. In essence, this file contains summaries of the customer orders that have been filled and the purchase orders that have been received.

Enterprise Integration and Administration

Enterprise integration and administration applications are the ERP modules that are not specifically supply chain applications but do have substantial interactions. Figure 5.5 illustrates the major enterprise integration and administration components. The specific components include (1) general administration, (2) accounts receivable and payable, (3) financial inventory accounting, (4) general ledger, and (5) human resources.

General administration includes the various transactions to structure the firm and define firm process flows. Supply chain operations use these modules to define reporting, functional, and organizational structures as well as to define process flows such as customer and replenishment order fulfillment. Accounts receivable and payable represent the functions for invoice collection from customers and invoice payment to suppliers. While these

FIGURE 5.5
Enterprise
Integration and
Administration
Components

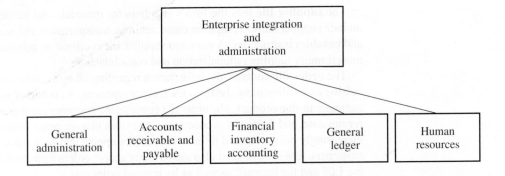

are typically acknowledged as accounting functions, there is a significant interaction with supply chain operations since accounts payable is influenced by materials and services acquisition and accounts receivable is influenced by delivery and invoicing of complete orders. Financial inventory accounting relates to the tracking of value-added processes through the supply chain to facilitate financial and tax reporting. The timing and location of supply chain value-added processes (e.g., production, inventory control, and packaging) can have a significant influence regarding what can be reported to the treasury (for taxation purposes) and the financial markets (for stock valuation purposes). General ledger relates to the structure of the detailed accounts for monitoring and reporting revenues and accounts. Since supply chain involves substantial interaction with firm and external processes, the structure of the general ledger accounts significantly influences the supply chain's ability to measure, monitor, and report cost related to delivering product or serving customers. The human resource module of the ERP systems tracks personnel profiles and their activity levels. Since most firms have a large number of individuals involved in supply chain operations (e.g., manufacturing, distribution, and purchasing) and often in different global environments, the ability to track pay scales and activity levels is critical to make effective supply chain personnel decisions.

Enterprise Operations

Enterprise operations include the SCIS modules required to support day-to-day supply chain operations. Figure 5.6 illustrates the specific modules including: (1) customer accommodation, (2) logistics, (3) manufacturing, (4) purchasing, and (5) inventory deployment. Enterprise operations systems work in conjunction with the firm's ERP system to provide specific functionality to support supply chain operations. While some ERP systems support required supply chain functionality, others lack some functionality such as that required to support warehouse and transportation operations.

Customer accommodation systems, also known as **customer relationship management (CRM)** systems, are relatively new applications designed to facilitate information sharing between customers, sales force, and operations management. The logistics

FIGURE 5.6
Enterprise
Operations Modules

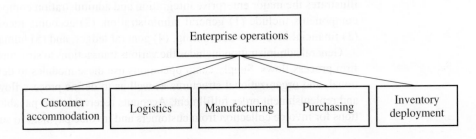

module directs and monitors logistics activities including finished goods inventory management, warehouse management, transportation management, and yard management. The manufacturing module schedules and allocates production resources and determines component requirements. The purchasing module initiates and tracks procurement activities including purchase order initiation, expediting, and supplier management. The inventory deployment system module schedules and monitors material flows to meet production and deployment requirements. Each module is discussed in more detail later in this chapter.

Enterprise Planning and Monitoring

Enterprise planning and monitoring are the processes and technologies that facilitate exchange of planning and coordinating information both within the firm and between supply chain partners. Figure 5.7 illustrates the major enterprise planning and monitoring components. The specific modules include (1) sales and operations planning, (2) supply chain visibility and event management, and (3) supply chain compliance. Since many of these activities involve interaction with other members of the supply chain, effective applications require substantial standardization with other firm functions and supply chain partners.

Sales and operations planning (S&OP), which is discussed further in Chapter 6, describes the process used to balance demand requirements and supply capabilities of the firm and its supply chain partners. While S&OP itself is a process requiring functional coordination and integration, it requires information technology to evaluate the demand, supply, and resource trade-offs. This technology is generally characterized as planning and scheduling applications. Supply chain visibility and event management tracks shipments while they are in-transit and are increasingly capable of proactively suggesting changes in supply chain flows to minimize the potential of manufacturing shutdowns or service failures. Supply chain compliance systems monitor component and product flow information to make sure they comply with government and regulatory requirements for label, taxation, and security restrictions.

Communication Technology

Communication technology is the hardware and technical software that facilitates information exchange between the systems and physical infrastructure within the firm and between supply chain partners. The real-time information interchange between

FIGURE 5.7
Enterprise Planning and Monitoring Modules

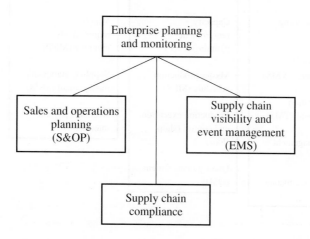

functions and supply chain partners facilitate coordination of inbound material, production, inventory, customer orders, and customer shipment. From a supply chain perspective, the availability of common and consistent requirements, activity, and performance information between supply chain partners enhances both effectiveness and efficiency. These technologies include electronic bar coding and scanning, exchange portals, product codes, radio frequency, and XML. Each is discussed in detail later in the chapter.

Enterprise Operations

Enterprise operations include customer accommodation, logistics, manufacturing, purchasing, and inventory deployment modules. Figure 5.8 lists the major elements of each module, which are discussed in detail below.

Customer Accommodation

Customer accommodation systems facilitate the synthesis and exchange of relevant and accurate information regarding order history, status, and demand generation information between a firm and its customers. The major system components include (1) customer relationship management (CRM), (2) forecasting, and (3) order management.

FIGURE 5.8 Enterprise Operations Modules

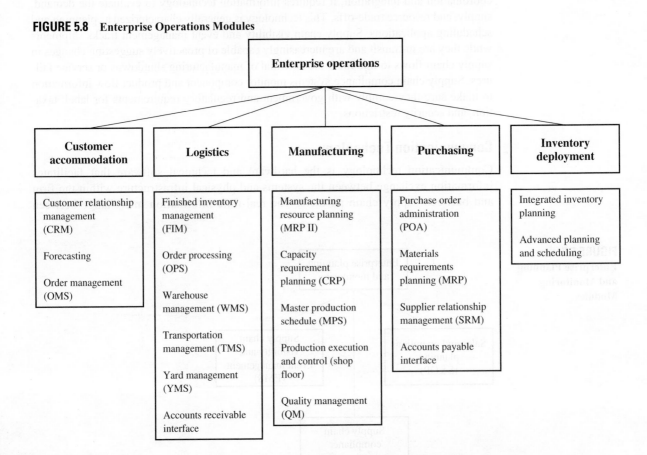

Customer Relationship Management

CRM is designed to extend the functionality of the ERP sales and delivery applications. CRM provides sales representatives and customers with current information regarding sales history, shipment history, order status, promotional summaries, and shipment information. The history and current status information, combined with product development, pricing, and promotion information, allow firms to better create and manage customer orders. Such timely and accurate information exchange between a firm and its customers increases the likelihood that the product sales and promotion plans will be supported with required product. Figure 5.9 illustrates the flow and elements of a CRM system.

While traditional ERP applications focus on efficiently taking customer orders, firms are finding it necessary to transition from treating customers as income sources to be exploited to treating customers as assets to be nurtured. While the traditional sales and delivery technology is configured to accept customer orders in a wide range of formats and allow those orders to be managed throughout the fulfillment process, a broader range of capabilities is necessary to manage the overall customer relationship. An integrated CRM system includes a combination of a server-based common database, remote PCs carried by

FIGURE 5.9
**Typical Customer
Relationship
Management
Extension System**

sales representatives, and a global synchronization process to ensure that both corporate and sales representative data are timely and consistent. Beyond this base functionality, CRM today requires sales tracking, sales history analysis, pricing management, promotion management, product mix management, and category management. In some cases, customers expect their supplier's sales force to manage the entire category of products at the customer's facility. For example, it is becoming more common for grocers to expect their suppliers to manage both the product mix and shelf quantities for major product categories such as beverages and specialty products. This practice, termed **category management,** requires substantial information support from the manufacturer but also facilitates information sharing.

Forecasting

While the CRM system facilitates collaboration between the firm and its customers, the other customer accommodation modules focus on synthesizing the available information into a forecast that best reflects the combined information of the firm and its customers. While all these elements generate forecasts to drive supply chain activity, they represent increasing degrees of sophistication. Using primarily historical data, a basic forecast system projects anticipated demand using the formulae discussed in Chapter 6 with minimal information exchange with the customer. Demand management systems use the historical data but also work proactively with the customer to shift demand timing or product requirements to develop a plan that is achievable within the firm's constraints. CPFR is even more interactive and proactive as the firm and its key customers develop a joint plan that meets their combined objectives within their operating constraints.

Order Management

Once the individual or joint forecast is developed and the planned orders are created, the order management system (OMS) places the orders in the ERP system and allows for their maintenance, processing, and tracking. An effective OMS allows both the firm and its customers to have the most up-to-date status of current orders.

Logistics

Coordinated, integrated logistics operations are essential for supply chain competitiveness. Coordination and integration facilitate smooth and consistent customer and replenishment order information flow throughout the firm and offer current order status visibility. Integrated information sharing reduces delays, errors, and resource requirements. The logistics processes required for customer order fulfillment and to coordinate receipt of purchase orders are (1) order processing, (2) order assignment, (3) warehouse operations, (4) transportation, (5) yard management, and (6) purchasing.

Order Processing

Order processing is the entry point for customer orders and inquiries. It allows entry and maintenance of customer orders by using communication technologies such as mail, phone, fax, EDI, and the Internet. As orders or inquiries are received, order processing enters and retrieves required information, edits for appropriate values, and retains acceptable orders for assignment. Order processing can also offer information regarding inventory availability and delivery dates to establish and confirm customer expectations. Order processing, in conjunction with customer service representatives, forms the primary interface between the customer and the ERP or legacy system.

Table 5.2 lists primary order processing functionality. It includes entry for blanket, electronic, and manual orders. Blanket orders are large orders that reflect demand over an extended time period such as a quarter or year. Future shipments against blanket orders are triggered by individual order releases. Order processing creates and maintains the customer and replenishment order base that initiates remaining operations components.

Order Assignment

Order assignment allocates available inventory to open customer and replenishment orders. Assignment may take place in real time, as orders are received, or in a batch mode. Batch mode means that orders are grouped for periodic processing such as by day or shift. While real-time allocation is more responsive, a batch process provides the firm with more control over situations when inventory is low. For example, in a batch process, order assignment can be designed to allocate stock from current inventory only or from scheduled production capacity. The operational system is more responsive if it allows inventory assignment from scheduled production quantities or capacity. However, there is a trade-off, since assigning

TABLE 5.2   Operations System Functionality

Order Processing	Order Assignment	Inventory Management	Warehouse Operations	Transportation and Shipping	Yard Management	Purchasing
Order entry (manual, electronic, blanket)	Create blanket order	Forecast analysis and modeling	Assign and track storage locations	Carrier selection	Initiate trailer movement to and from docks	Match and pay
Credit check	Generate invoice	Forecast data maintenance and updates	Inventory cycle counting	Carrier scheduling	Initiate trailer movement to and from other yards	Open order review
Inventory availability	Generate order selection documents	Forecast parameter selection	Labor scheduling	Dispatching	Yard control and trailer tracking	Purchase order entry
Order acknowledgement	Inventory allocation	Forecast technique selection	Equipment scheduling	Document preparation	Appointment scheduling	Purchase order maintenance
Order modification	Process blanket order	Inventory parameter selection	Lot control	Freight payment	Carrier performance tracking	Purchase order receipt
Order pricing	Release reserved inventory	Inventory simulation and testing	Order selection, location, replenishment	Performance measurement		Purchase order status
Order status inquiry	Reassign order source	Inventory requirements planning	Receiving	Shipment consolidation and routing		Quote request
Price and discount extension	Release blanket order	Promotion data integration	Putaway	Shipment rating		Requirements communication
Promotion check	Verify shipment	Replenishment order build, release, and scheduling	Storage	Shipment scheduling		Schedule receipt appointment
Returns processing		Define service objectives	Performance measurement	Shipment tracing and expediting		Supplier history
Service management				Vehicle loading		

scheduled production capacity reduces the firm's ability to reschedule production. The best order assignment applications operate interactively in conjunction with order processing to generate an order solution that satisfies customer requirements within enterprise resource constraints. In this type of operational environment, the customer service representative and the customer interact to determine the combination of products, quantities, and performance cycle length that is acceptable for both parties. Possible solutions when there is conflict in order assignment include delivery date adjustments, product substitutions, or shipment from an alternative source.

Table 5.2 lists typical order assignment functionality, including inventory allocation, back-order creation and processing, order selection document generation, and order verification. Order selection documents, in paper or electronic form, direct distribution operations to select an order from the distribution center or warehouse and pack it for shipment. The customer or replenishment order, with its allocated inventory and corresponding order selection material, links order assignment with distribution center physical operations.

Warehouse Operations

Warehouse operations, also known as Warehouse Management Systems (WMS), incorporate processes to guide physical activities, including product receipt, material movement and storage, and order selection. For this reason, they are often termed inventory control or warehouse management systems and sometimes warehouse locator systems, referring to the capability to track inventory storage locations in warehouses. Warehouse operations direct all material handling activities using a combination of batch and real-time assignments. In a batch environment, the warehouse operations system develops a "to do" list of instructions or tasks to guide each material handler in the warehouse. Material handlers are the individuals who operate equipment such as forklifts. In a real-time environment, information-directed technologies such as bar coding, radio-frequency communication, and automated handling equipment operate interactively to reduce the elapsed time between decision and action. The real-time information-directed materials handling technologies, discussed in detail in Chapter 11, also must interface directly with the warehouse operations process to provide operational flexibility and reduce internal performance cycle time requirements.

Table 5.2 lists typical warehouse operation functionality. In addition to directing warehouse operations and activities, the functionality must also plan operating requirements and measure performance. Operations planning includes personnel and resource scheduling, including staff, equipment, and facility. Performance measurement includes developing personnel and equipment productivity reports.

Transportation and Shipping

A Transportation Management System (TMS) plans, executes, and manages transport and movement functions. The TMS includes shipment planning and scheduling, shipment consolidation, shipment notification, transport documentation generation, and carrier management. These processes facilitate efficient transport resource utilization as well as effective carrier management.

Table 5.2 lists transportation and shipping functionality. The TMS generates the documentation to release the order for shipment and measures the firm's ability to satisfactorily deliver the order. Historically, the TMS focused on document generation and rate tracking. Transport documents include manifests and bills of lading, specifically discussed in Chapter 9, and the carrier charges incurred for product movement. The large numbers of shipments made by most enterprises require an automated and exception-driven TMS that can reduce errors and report performance. With the increased opportunity to enhance performance through better transport management, contemporary TMS functionality emphasizes performance monitoring, rate auditing, routing and scheduling, invoicing, reporting, and decision analyses. Advanced TMS applications incorporate increased planning and performance measurement capability and are being termed enterprise execution systems.

A unique characteristic of the TMS is that it often involves three parties—shipper, carrier, and consignee (recipient). To effectively manage the process, a basic level of information integration must exist. Information sharing requires standardized data formats for transport documents.

Yard Management System

A yard management system (YMS) manages full and empty trailers in the parking lot or yard at manufacturing plants and distribution centers. In many operations, there may be hundreds or more trailers in the yard and they move in and out daily. The trailers and containers may represent inbound receipts, outbound orders, or may be empty. For the trailers that are full, the contents may represent a single shipment or a combination of orders. It is clear that the accuracy of a manual system would quickly decline, resulting in lost trailers and inventory.

The objective of a YMS is to make the yard an extension of the plant, distribution center, or warehouse by being able to quickly find a specific trailer and its contents. The system should also be able to sequence receipts, unloads, and loads to replenish desired inventory and to meet customer shipping requirements. Thus, the YMS enhances service by accessing the necessary inventory, even if it is on a trailer in the yard, and makes sure that customer shipments are loaded and dispatched in time to meet the delivery schedule. Table 5.2 lists specific YMS functionality.

Manufacturing

Manufacturing systems form the information system foundation to plan and control manufacturing planning and operation. These components define core activities that guide enterprise resource allocation and performance from procurement to product delivery. The Manufacturing module includes (1) Manufacturing Resource Planning II (MRP II), (2) Capacity requirement planning, (3) Master production scheduling (MPS), (4) Shop floor control, and (5) Quality management.

MRP II is the system that time-phases manufacturing schedules with procurement requirements. The MRP system (discussed below under Purchasing) explodes the bill of materials of the scheduled products to the required raw materials and communicates the requirements to the appropriate suppliers. For example, if an automotive assembly plant is scheduled to make 1,000 cars in the next week, the MRP system would communicate to the tire supplier that 4,000 regular tires would be required next week (assuming that the spares would not be regular tires). The MRP II system extends that capability by coordinating demand management with procurement scheduling. The MRP II system typically operates in more aggregate time buckets such as weeks.

Capacity requirement planning (CRP) maps the schedule developed by the MRP II system to a daily production schedule while considering equipment and personnel capacity constraints. The result is a day-to-day schedule that fits within the capacity constraints of the manufacturing process.

The **master production schedule (MPS)** further maps the capacity constrained schedule developed by CRP to specific equipment sequences and timing. The result is a production thread or sequence that defines precisely how a production order is to flow through the manufacturing process while minimizing waste, delays, and capacity. An integrated MRP II, CRP, and MPS is critical to operating a lean manufacturing system.

The production shop floor control and quality systems control the production equipment and processes to monitor equipment operations for effective operations and quality.

Purchasing

Purchasing manages **purchase order (PO)** preparation, modification, and release and tracks vendor performance and compliance. The specific elements of the purchasing system include administering purchase orders, sharing materials requirements with suppliers, and managing the overall supplier relationship. Although purchasing systems have not traditionally been considered part of logistics systems, the importance of integrating purchasing with logistics schedules is critical to facilitate the coordination of material receipt, facility capacity, and transportation backhaul.

For integrated supply chain management, purchasing must track and coordinate receiving and shipping activities to optimize facility, transport, and personnel scheduling. For example, since loading and unloading docks are often a critical facility resource, an effective purchasing system should coordinate the use of the same carrier for both deliveries and shipments. This capability requires the enterprise system to have both receipt and shipment visibility. Supply chain system integration can be further enhanced through electronic integration with suppliers. Table 5.2 lists purchasing functionality. A state-of-the-art purchasing system provides plans, directs activities, and measures performance, coordinating inbound and outbound activity movement.

Inventory Deployment

Inventory deployment represents one of the major enterprise integrators of sales, marketing, and financial goals. The inventory deployment activity can be completed independently by individual supply chain functions, in an integrated manner by supply chain overall, or in a coordinated manner by the entire firm. When it is done in a coordinated manner by the entire firm, it is often referred to as **Sales & Operations Planning (S&OP)**.

These strategic objectives are typically developed for a multiyear planning horizon that often includes quarterly updates. Sales and marketing's strategic objectives define target markets, product development, promotions, other marketing mix plans, and the role of logistics value-added activities such as service levels or capabilities. The objectives include customer scope, breadth of products and services, planned promotions, and desired performance levels. Sales and marketing goals are the customer service policies and objectives that define logistics and supply chain activity and performance targets. The performance targets include service availability, capability, and quality elements discussed earlier. Financial strategic objectives define revenue, financial and activity levels, and corresponding expenses, as well as capital and human resource constraints.

The combination of sales, marketing, and financial objectives defines the scope of markets, products, services, and activity levels that logistics and supply chain managers must accommodate during the planning horizon. Specific goals include projected annual or quarterly activity levels such as revenue, shipments, and case volume. Events that must be considered include product promotions, new product introductions, market rollouts, and acquisitions. Ideally, the marketing and financial plans should be integrated and consistent, as inconsistencies result in poor service, excess inventory, or failure to meet financial goals.

The inventory deployment process must include both long- and short-term elements. The long-term element focuses on annual and quarterly plans with the objective of coordinating the marketing and financial plans to achieve enterprise goals. While supply chain and logistics operations are not the major focus, they do merit some consideration, as planners must ensure that there is enough aggregate production, storage, and movement capacity available. The short-term element focuses on weekly and daily plans with the objective of coordinating supply chain and logistics resources to ensure that specific customer requests can be satisfied. The key objective of an inventory deployment system is an integrated inventory plan through what is increasingly being termed an **Advanced Planning and Scheduling (APS)** system.

APS System Overview

To correspond with the planning and execution of effective logistics and supply chain strategies, supply chain planning systems incorporate both spatial and temporal considerations. The spatial considerations include movement between raw material providers, manufacturing plants, warehouses, distributors, retailers, and the end customer. The temporal considerations include moving timing and scheduling.

The APS system in Figure 5.10 is a network including plants, warehouses, and customers as well as transportation flows. This network reflects the resource status and allocation at a point in time, for example, on the first day of the month. Effective planning requires a process that can time-phase and coordinate resource requirements and constraints through time. For example, if product X is needed by the customer in period 3, its movement through the supply chain must be time-phased for arrival by period 3. Assuming a one-period performance cycle between each stage in the supply chain, this means that the APS must plan for the shipment of X from the plant during period 1 and shipment from the distribution center during period 2.

More specifically, suppose a firm is facing the situation summarized in Table 5.3. Customers require 200 units of product during each of the next five periods with the exception of period 4, when a special promotion increases demand to 600 units. The firm's production

FIGURE 5.10
Advanced Planning and Scheduling Overview

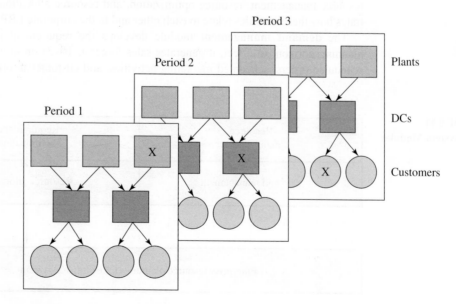

TABLE 5.3
Sample APS
Planning Situation

	Time Period				
	1	2	3	4	5
Requirement	200	200	200	600	200
Production Capacity	300	300	300	300	300
Alternative 1 (overtime):					
Production	200	200	200	600	200
Inventory Carryover	—	—	—	—	—
Alternative 2 (build ahead):					
Production	300	300	300	300	200
Inventory Carryover	100	200	300	—	—

capacity is 300 units per week. On the extremes, the firm can select between two approaches to satisfy customer requirements given the production constraints. Alternative 1 is to wait until the fourth time period and then run production overtime to meet customer requirements. This alternative results in higher production cost but no cost to carry or store inventory. Alternative 2 is to build ahead using the extra 100-unit capacity in the time prior to period 4. With this alternative, an extra 100 units is built and added to inventory each period until it is required during period 4. This alternative does not require overtime production but does require increased inventory carrying and storage costs. There are, of course, intermediate alternatives to these two extremes. The ideal option is to select the combination resulting in the lowest combined cost of manufacturing and storage. Using linear optimization techniques, APS identifies the most cost-effective trade-offs considering all relevant costs. While firms have wanted to consider these trade-offs previously, analysis capabilities only allowed for evaluation of two or three major trade-offs to minimize problem complexity. Supply chain planning tools like APS offer the ability to thoroughly evaluate complex trade-offs involving a large number of alternatives.

APS System Components

While there are many conceptual approaches to designing supply chain planning applications like APS, the major components are fundamentally the same: demand management, resource management, resource optimization, and resource allocation. Figure 5.11 illustrates how these modules relate to each other and to the corporate ERP or legacy system.

The **demand management** module develops the requirement projections for the planning horizon. In effect, it generates sales forecasts based on sales history, currently scheduled orders, scheduled marketing activities, and customer information. In the case

FIGURE 5.11
APS System Modules

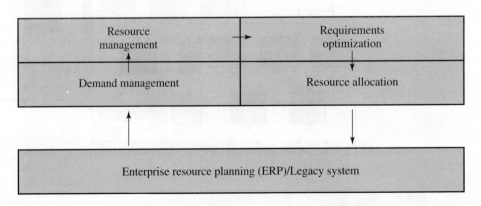

of requirements planning, the forecasts are in terms of orders while it would be shipments in the case of transportation planning. Ideally, demand management works collaboratively and interactively both internally across the firm's functional components and externally with supply chain partners to develop a common and consistent forecast for each time period, location, and item. The forecast must also incorporate feedback from customers to integrate the influence of combined demand generation activities such as advertising and promotion.

The **resource management** component defines and coordinates supply chain system resources and constraints. Since APS systems use the resource and constraint information to evaluate the trade-offs associated with supply chain decisions, information accuracy and integrity are critical to provide optimal decisions and enhance planning system credibility. Obviously, incorrect planning decisions not only suboptimize supply chain performance but also severely reduce management credibility in the planning system itself. In addition to the requirements definition developed by the demand management module, APS requires four other types of information: product and customer definitions, resource definitions and costs, system limitations, and planning objective.

The product and customer definitions provide constants regarding the firm's products and customers to support the planning process. The product definitions provide the product descriptions and physical characteristics, such as weight and cube, standard costs, and bill of material. The customer definitions provide the ship-to location and distribution assignments, along with special service requirements. The combination of both defines what is being manufactured, what is being distributed, where it is being delivered, and the performance cycles involved in distribution.

The resource definitions specify the physical resources used to accomplish supply chain activities such as manufacturing, storage, and movement. The resources include manufacturing equipment and process rates, storage facilities, and transportation equipment and availability. In addition to defining the existence of specific resources, the database must include the cost and performance characteristics and costs associated with resource usage.

System limitations define major supply chain activity constraints. These include the capacity limitations associated with production, storage, and movement. Production capacity defines how much product can be produced within a specific time period and what are the trade-offs associated with making various mixes of products. Storage capacity defines the amount of product that can be stored in a specific facility. Movement capacity defines the volume of product that can be transported between facilities or to customers within a given time frame.

The planning function defines criteria for developing a solution. Typical objective functions include minimizing total cost or any of its subcomponents, meeting all customer requirements, or minimizing the number of instances when capacity is exceeded.

This combination of demand management and resource management information provides the basis for the APS evaluation of alternative supply chain strategies. The module includes the databases to store the definitions, resources, constraints, and objectives as well as the processes to validate and maintain it. Users are finding that one of the major challenges to effective supply chain planning systems is the ability to develop and maintain accurate and consistent data.

The **resource optimization** module is the computational engine or "black box" of the supply chain planning system. Using the requirements from the demand management module and the definitions, resources, limitations, and objectives from the resource management module, resource optimization uses a combination of mathematical programming and heuristics to determine how to most effectively meet customer requirements while optimizing resource utilization. Mathematical programming is a combination of linear programming and mixed-integer programming, which is used to minimize the specified objective function; heuristics are computational rules of thumb or shortcuts that reduce the time or computational resources required to develop an integrated plan. In effect, the resource optimization module evaluates multiple planning alternatives and systematically completes the trade-offs to identify the best alternatives until a near-optimal result is achieved. The resource optimization module also determines when requirements cannot be met and which resources are the most constraining on supply chain performance. The resource optimization module results are supply chain plans projected into future time periods that minimize overall costs while attempting to operate within major resource constraints. The plan specifies which products should be produced when and determines movement and storage requirements across the supply chain.

The resource optimization module can also be used to conduct sensitivity or what-if analyses to determine the impact of changes in market requirements or constraints. These analyses allow the supply chain planner to isolate the impact of demand and performance uncertainty on supply chain capabilities and operations. Using the insight regarding the trade-offs and the impact of uncertainty, the supply chain planning resource optimization module guides the planner in establishing the most effective sourcing, production, movement, and storage strategy.

Following planner review and evaluation of the resource optimization module results, the **resource allocation** module specifies the resource assignments and communicates them to the ERP system to initiate appropriate transactions. The results include requirements for procurement, production, storage, and transport. The specific requests can be communicated to the ERP system in the form of transactions or instructions to complete a specific activity. Each transaction includes detailed instructions regarding type of supply chain activity, suppliers, customer, products involved, and required timing, along with a list of relevant products and quantities. The resource allocation module also provides information regarding when product is available to promise (ATP) or capable to promise (CTP). ATP is used to designate that even though actual inventory is not currently available, it will be available for shipment or promise at a specific date in the future. In effect, the ATP designation allows firms to commit scheduled production to customers. CTP is used to designate when requested product can be promised for future delivery. CTP requires a much broader analysis, as it determines whether there is future specific capacity or capability, given current and projected supply chain demands. ATP and CTP can dramatically enhance supply chain performance and effectiveness by allowing commitments against future production and capacity. The result is more rapid commitments to customers, fewer customer surprises, and enhanced resource utilization.

Supply Chain Planning Benefits

While some supply chain planning system benefits were discussed earlier, there are three broad benefits that accrue from planning system utilization. These are responsiveness to changes, comprehensive perspective, and resource utilization.

First, logistics and supply chain managers have used extended lead times and schedule freezes to plan for future supply chain activity. For example, production would be scheduled three to four weeks into the future and then frozen to minimize uncertainty and allow for effective resource utilization. Long lead times and freeze periods were necessary since the planning process was complex and required substantial analyses. While this approach reduced uncertainty, it also substantially reduced flexibility and responsiveness. Today's customer requires more responsiveness to market needs, and demand for lower inventory levels rules out long cycle times. Marketplace and firm changes can be quickly made in the demand management and resource management modules, allowing for the planning process to use the most current and accurate information. The requirements optimization module then solves the allocation, allowing daily and single week planning cycles rather than multiple weeks or months. Supply chain planning thus results in a process that can be much more responsive to marketplace or firm changes.

Second, effective supply chain management requires planning and coordination across firm functions and between supply chain partners. The process must consider the trade-offs associated with shifting activities and resources across functions and organizations. Such a comprehensive perspective increases planning process complexity substantially. The complexity follows from the number of organizations, facilities, products, and assets that must be considered when coordinating activities and resources across an entire supply chain. Supply chain planning systems offer the capability to consider the extended supply chain and make the appropriate trade-offs to achieve optimal performance.

Third, supply chain planning typically results in substantial performance improvements. While more comprehensive planning and reduced uncertainty usually result in improved customer service, another major planning system benefit is enhanced resource utilization.

More effective and responsive planning allows a more level assignment of resources for existing sourcing, production, storage, and transportation capacity. The result is that existing capacity is used more effectively. Firms also report that supply chain planning systems have significantly reduced asset requirements by smoothing resource demands. The decreases include estimates of 20 to 25 percent reductions in plant, equipment, facilities, and inventory.

Supply Chain Planning Considerations

While comprehensive supply chain planning is a relatively new capability, the future outlook is bright as the technology and capacity to effectively evaluate and manage integrated supply chains are developed. Supply chain planning can take a comprehensive and dynamic perspective of the entire supply chain and focus on reducing the supply chain asset requirements as demanded by financial markets. Prior to the actual implementation, there are many considerations for supply chain planning system adoption. Managers cite their major considerations to be (1) integrated versus bolt-on application, (2) data integrity, and (3) application education.

The first consideration concerns the level of integration with other supply chain applications. Technically, there are three options for acquiring and implementing planning applications. The first is development using internal firm resources. This is not very common, as planning system development requires substantial expertise and most firms without substantial software competency could not effectively design, develop, or maintain such complex planning systems. In addition, the planning process of individual industries or firms is not usually different enough to be able to achieve any significant competitive advantage. Options two and three are to use a supply chain planning application that is integrated with the firm's ERP system or one from a third-party that **bolts on** to the firm's ERP system. Some ERP providers, such as SAP, offer an APS that is designed to be closely integrated with their ERP system. The obvious benefits of such integration include data consistency and integrity, as well as reduced need to transfer data between applications, which results in delays and potential errors. The alternative is to use a **bolt-on** or **best-of-breed** approach that seeks to identify the best supply chain planning system for the firm on the basis of features and functionality and then attach it to the firm's ERP system. The result is a planning system that better meets the firm's specific requirements or offers improved performance but at a probable cost of reduced integration. While providers of both integrated and bolt-on supply chain planning applications are attempting to enhance their integration with ERP system providers, operational integration between execution and planning systems remains a challenge.

Data integrity is a second major consideration for supply chain planning system implementation. Planning systems rely on absolute data integrity for effective decision making. While data integrity has always been important, it is more critical for planning systems since missing and inaccurate data can dramatically impact decision reliability and stability. One often-cited data integrity problem concerns product level detail such as cube and weight. While this is basic data, accuracy is not easy to maintain when there are a large number of products with constant changes and new product introductions. Managers cite that in the process of implementing supply chain planning applications, it is not uncommon to find a few hundred products with incorrect or missing physical characteristics. While it may not be a large percentage of products in number, the inaccuracy can substantially impact planning system decision making. For example, missing or inaccurate cube can result in a transportation planning system making a recommendation to overload a transportation vehicle. Specifically, the planning system will think that a large amount of product can be loaded into a truck when the product data contains an incorrect or zero cube. While the decision errors resulting from data integrity problems can be significant, the larger problem is that such errors substantially reduce the credibility of planning systems in general. A few highly visible errors such as overloading transportation vehicles or storage facilities cause management and planners to question the integrity of the entire planning system and process. The result is that management and operations personnel don't trust the results and prefer to return to the old tried and true methods of planning and scheduling. Thus, the potential for improved planning is reduced until the trust can be redeveloped. A strong focus on developing and maintaining data integrity is critical to effective planning system implementation.

Education regarding planning system application is a third major consideration. User training for supply chain execution and planning systems has usually focused on the mechanics to initiate the transactions. So, the user would be trained in data or parameter entry where the system would provide quick feedback regarding the acceptability of the entry. Supply chain planning systems are relatively more complex, as the feedback is not immediate and the impact may be extensive. For example, changing the requirements or forecast for one item in a time period may shift production schedules for related items on the other side of the world. Understanding planning system dynamics is critical to successful application. Such understanding requires thorough knowledge of APS system mechanics and system interactions. Although such knowledge can be initiated through training, it must be refined and extended through education and experience. Planning system education must focus on the characteristics and relationships between supply chain management activities and processes both internal and external to the firm. The education process must be much broader than existing training approaches. Planning system experience can be developed by using job shadowing experience and simulations. The shadowing environment provides actual on-the-job experience in a real-time environment. The simulated environment provides a laboratory where inexperienced planners can see or observe the results of their planning environment at low risk to the firm. The combination of these two educational experiences provides a solid foundation for implementing successful supply chain planning applications.

Supply Chain Planning Summary

The major objective of an integrated inventory deployment or APS system is integrated and coordinated capacity management of relevant supply chain resources including manufacturing plants, distribution centers, and transportation resources. Capacity management planning balances the market demands with the production resources. On the basis of the activity levels defined by the forecasting system, these constraints determine material bottlenecks and guide resource allocation to meet market demands. For each product, capacity constraints influence the where, when, and how much for production, storage, and movement. The constraints consider aggregate limitations such as periodic production, movement, and storage capacities.

Capacity problems can be resolved by resource acquisition or speculation/postponement of production or delivery. Capacity adjustments can be made by acquisition or alliances such as contract manufacturing or facility leasing. Speculation reduces bottlenecks by anticipating production capacity requirements through prior scheduling or contract manufacturing. Postponement delays production and shipment until specific requirements are known and capacity can be allocated. It may be necessary to offer customer incentives such as discounts or allowances to postpone customer delivery. The capacity limitations time-phase the enterprise's S&OP by taking into account facility, financial, and human resource limitations. These constraints have a major influence on logistics, manufacturing, and procurement schedules.

Enterprise Planning and Monitoring

As described previously, the enterprise planning and monitoring modules facilitate the collaboration and exchange of plans and performance data both across firm functions and between supply chain partners. The three modules are (1) sales and operations planning, (2) supply chain visibility and event management, and (3) supply chain compliance. The function and features of each are discussed.

Sales and Operations Planning

As further discussed in Chapter 6, S&OP is a process that coordinates demand and supply plans across the organization. The process includes information sharing and accountability to systematically develop a common and consistent plan. While S&OP is an organizational process, it also requires substantial information technology support. The technology support can range from something as simple as a few linked spreadsheets to a sophisticated APS system discussed previously.

In general, the S&OP technology integrates the firm's information regarding forecasts, inventory availability, production resources, and other resource constraints.

Requirements include time-phased facility, equipment, labor, and inventory resources necessary to accomplish the logistics mission. For example, the logistics requirement component schedules shipments of finished product from manufacturing plants to warehouses and ultimately to customers. The shipment quantity is calculated as the difference between customer requirements and inventory level. Future requirements are based on forecasts, customer orders, and promotions. Forecasts are based on sales and marketing input in conjunction with historical activity levels. Customer orders include current orders, future committed orders, and contracts. Consideration of promotional activity is particularly important in planning logistics requirements, since it often represents a large percentage of variation in volume and has a large impact on capacity. Current inventory status is product available to ship. Figure 5.12 illustrates the computation for determining periodic logistics requirements.

Specifically, for each planning period, day, week, or month, the sum of forecast plus future customer orders plus promotional volume represents period demand. It is not easy to determine the percentage of the forecasted volume that is accounted for by known customer orders, so some judgment is necessary. Typically, period demand is actually a combination of the three, since current forecasts may incorporate some future orders and promotional volume. In determining period demand, it is important that the overlap between forecast, future customer orders, and promotions be considered. Period logistics requirements are then determined as

FIGURE 5.12
Logistics
Requirements

+ Forecasts (sales, marketing, input, histories, accounts)

+ Customer orders (current orders, future committed orders, contracts)

+ Promotions (promotion, advertising plans)

= Period demand

− Inventory-on-hand

− Planned receipts

Period logistics requirements

the period demand less inventory-on-hand plus planned receipts. Using this form, each period would ideally end with zero inventory available, so planned receipts would exactly equal period demand. While perfect coordination of demand and supply is desirable from an inventory management perspective, it may not be possible or the best strategy for the firm.

Supply Chain Visibility and Event Management

Supply chain visibility and event management systems are more sophisticated versions of what are typically termed "track and trace" systems. Over the last decade, customers ordering mail order increasingly expect the ability to "track and trace" their shipments online using the FedEx, Postal Service, or United Parcel Service Web sites. As such systems became more widely available, logistics managers now desire that similar track and trace capabilities be available from their carriers.

The specific capabilities desired include (1) track and trace, (2) notification, (3) reporting, (4) rerouting, and (5) simulation. Track and trace is the ability to determine where a shipment is currently and which carrier or firm is currently responsible for it. Notification is the capability to provide information to the shipper or customer regarding the status of the shipment. While the notification can be provided when the shipment is on time, it is particularly important to provide information when it is delayed and when it hasn't reached an expected waypoint. The notification capability should provide information in the form of an e-mail, voice-mail, or contact with a personal digital assistant. The reporting capability allows the logistics manager to measure the performance of individual carriers based on their history with actual shipments. The rerouting capability allows logistics managers to change the mode or flow of a shipment if it were to get delayed. For example, if a shipment is delayed arriving at a port, management may want to shift the final delivery mode to air rather than ground to reduce the possibility of shutting down the manufacturing process. The simulation capability allows management to complete "what if" analyses using various routes and shipment modes. For example, this capability would allow a manager to proactively compare a shipment routed through two different ports to determine which is more likely to arrive on time based on recent shipping history.

Given the capabilities that individuals experience with consumer track and trace systems, it may seem that this would be trivial for major corporations. However, most firms don't have the resources or time for event management for each shipment. They want to be notified when there is a problem or an exception rather than have to monitor the hundreds or thousands of shipments that they have in process at any point in time. A second problem is that many shipments, particularly internationally, use multiple carriers and even multiple modes. Major problems in global supply chain event management occur at the interfaces between carriers where there may be system or timing inconsistencies. The major global carriers such as FedEx and UPS have begun to make such a capability a critical dimension of their offerings.

Supply Chain Compliance

Since most firms either source or market globally, if not both, there is increasing need to track transactions from a legal and security perspective as well as to facilitate adequate reporting to relevant governmental agencies. Supply chain compliance systems provide these capabilities so that firms can meet the reporting requirements of local governments and so that the firm doesn't break any import or export laws. In some cases, failure to provide necessary information may result in criminal charges against firm executives.

Supply chain compliance systems include some combination of the following capabilities: (1) global classification, (2) authorized economic operator automation, (3) advance security filing, (4) processing under customs control, (5) C-TPAT compliance, (6) free trade agreements, and (7) export compliance. Global classification defines the nature of the goods for global reporting. For monitoring and reporting purposes, it ensures that the same or essentially similar item from two different suppliers or countries is classified the same for reporting and customs purposes. The authorized economic operator (AEO) automation function ensures that the firms involved in a transaction are authorized to engage in commercial exchanges. The major objective of AEO automation is to ensure that none of the firms involved have a history with illegal, black market, or gray market transactions. Advance security filing capability provides the required shipment documentation to the relevant customs organization with the appropriate leadtime. For example, U.S. Customs requires notification regarding shipment arrival at least 2 to 24 hours prior to arrival depending on transportation method. Processing under customs control provides the information support to track and monitor goods when supply chain value-added processes are completed under customs control. Firms sometimes complete final manufacturing or packing under customs control prior to formal arrival from an international source to reduce duty or to meet local content requirements. C-TPAT (Customs-Trade Partnership against Terrorism) compliance tracks the security authorizations of firms involved in a trade transaction. C-TPAT is further discussed in Chapter 17. Free trade agreement capability is to track and monitor international transactions between countries that have free trade agreements for the items involved. For example, for the North American Free Trade Act (NAFTA) and the European Union (EU) relationships, many transactions are treated as though they are domestic even though the goods cross international borders. Finally, the export compliance capability ensures that goods involved in a transaction can be traded between the countries involved. For example, for security reasons, there are many limitations on the trade of U.S. technology with firms in foreign countries. Failure to follow these restrictions could be embarrassing for the firm involved and in some cases even criminal for the firm's officers.

The increasing volume of international supply chain transactions along with a combination of agreements to motivate trade and restrictions on what can be traded results in an increasing need for information technology capability to monitor and track such transactions. Supply chain compliance systems are evolving to meet that requirement.

Communication Technology

Information-sharing technology is critical to facilitate logistics and supply chain planning and operations. Historically, logistics coordination has been difficult since essential work is typically performed at locations remote from information technology hardware. As a result, information was not available at the work location in terms of both time and content. The past decade has witnessed remarkable advances in logistical communication systems capability, including bar code and scanning, global data synchronization, the Internet, extensible markup language, satellite technology, and image processing.

Bar Code and Scanning

Auto identification (ID) systems such as bar coding and electronic scanning were developed to facilitate logistics information collection and exchange. Typical applications include tracking warehouse receipts and retail sales. These ID systems require significant capital investment but replace error-prone and time-consuming paper-based information collection and exchange processes. In fact, increased domestic and international competition is driving shippers, carriers, warehouses, wholesalers, and retailers to develop and utilize auto ID capability to compete in today's marketplace.

Auto ID allows supply chain members to quickly track and communicate movement details with high accuracy and timeliness, so it is fast becoming a fundamental service requirement for freight tracking by carriers. Both consumers and B2B customers expect to be able to track the progress of their shipment using the Web-based system offered by carriers such as United Parcel Service and FedEx.

Bar coding is the placement of computer-readable codes on items, cartons, containers, pallets, and even rail cars. Bar code development and applications are increasing at a very rapid rate. Table 5.4 summarizes the benefits of auto ID technologies. While the benefits are obvious, it is not clear which symbologies will be adopted as industry standards. Standardization and flexibility are desirable to accommodate the needs of a wide range of industries, but they also increase cost, making it more difficult for small- and medium-size shippers, carriers, and receivers to implement standardized technologies. Finally, while continued convergence to common standards is likely, surveys indicate that select industries and major shippers will continue to use proprietary codes to maximize their competitive position.

Another key component of auto ID technology is the scanning process, which represents the eyes of a bar code system. A scanner optically collects bar code data and converts it to usable information. There are two types of scanners: handheld and fixed position. Each type can utilize contact or noncontact technology. Handheld scanners are either laser guns (noncontact) or wands (contact). Fixed-position scanners are either automatic scanners (noncontact) or card readers (contact). Contact technologies require the reading device to actually touch the bar code. A contact technology reduces scanning errors but decreases flexibility. Laser gun technology is the most popular scanner technology currently in use, outpacing wands as the most widely installed technology.

TABLE 5.4
Benefits of Automatic Identification Technologies

Shippers	Warehousing
Improve order preparation and processing	Improved order preparation, processing, and shipment
Eliminate shipping errors	Provide accurate inventory control
Reduce labor time	Customer access to real-time information
Improve record keeping	Access considerations of information security
Reduce physical inventory time	Reduced labor costs
Carriers	**Wholesalers/Retailers**
Freight bill information integrity	Unit inventory precision
Customer access to real-time information	Price accuracy at point-of-sale
Improved record keeping of customer shipment activity	Improved register checkout productivity
	Reduced physical inventory time
Shipment traceability	Increased system flexibility
Simplified container processing	
Monitor incompatible products in vehicles	
Reduced information transfer time	

Scanner technology has two major applications in logistics. The first is point-of-sale (POS) in retail stores. In addition to ringing up receipts for consumers, retail POS applications provide accurate inventory control at the store level. POS allows precise tracking of each stockkeeping unit (SKU) sold and can be used to facilitate inventory replenishment. In addition to providing accurate resupply and marketing research data, POS can provide more timely strategic benefits to all channel members.

The second logistics scanner application is for materials handling, vehicle identification, and tracking. Through the use of scanner guns, materials handlers and gate operators can track product and vehicle movement, storage location, shipments, and receipts. While this information can be tracked manually, it is very time-consuming and subject to error. Wider usage of scanners in logistical applications will increase productivity and reduce errors. The demand for faster and less-error-prone scanning technology drives rapid changes in the marketplace for applications and technology.

Global Data Synchronization

While the phone, fax, and direct computer connection have enabled information exchange in the past, EDI and the Internet are quickly becoming the standards for effective, accurate, and low-cost information exchange. EDI is defined as direct computer-to-computer exchange of business documents in standard formats to facilitate high-volume transactions. It involves both the capability and practice of communicating information between two organizations electronically instead of via the traditional forms of mail, courier, or even fax.

Communication and information standards are essential for EDI. Communication standards specify technical characteristics necessary for the computer hardware to correctly accomplish the interchange. Communication standards deal with character sets, transmission priority, and speed. Information standards dictate the structure and content of the message. Standards organizations have developed and refined two general standards as well as numerous industry-specific standards in an effort to standardize both communication and information interchange.

EDI Transaction Sets

Communication standards are implemented using transaction sets. A transaction set provides a common standard to facilitate information interchange between partners in a specific industry and country. Table 5.5 lists the common logistics-related industry transaction standards. For each industry, the transaction set defines the documents that can be transmitted. Documents typically cover common logistics activities such as ordering, warehouse operations, and transportation. Table 5.6 lists the transaction set usage matrix. The transaction set consists of a transaction code (or ID) and is followed by the data. The transaction code, for example, indicates whether the electronic communication is a warehouse shipping order (code 940) or a warehouse stock transfer receipt (code 944). In addition to the transaction code, a transaction contains warehouse number, item number, and quantity.

TABLE 5.5
Primary Logistics Industry EDI Standards

UCS (Uniform Communication Standards): grocery
VICS (Voluntary Interindustry Communication Standards Committee): mass merchandisers
WINS (Warehouse Information Network Standards): warehouse operators
TDCC (Transportation Data Coordinating Committee): transportation operators
AIAG (Automotive Industry Action Group): automotive industry

TABLE 5.6
Transaction Set
Usage Matrix

Source: Adapted from materials
provided by Deborah Faragher,
Uniform Code Council, Inc.

TS ID	Transaction Set Name	UCS	VICS EDI
102	Associated Data		√
180	Return Merchandise Authorization and Notification	√	√
204	Motor Carrier Load Tender	√	
210	Motor Carrier Freight Details and Invoice	√	
214	Transportation Carrier Shipment Status Message	√	
753	Request for Routing Instructions		√
754	Routing Instructions		√
810	Invoice	√	√
812	Credit/Debit Adjustment	√	√
816	Organizational Relationships	√	√
818	Commission Sales Report	√	
820	Payment Order/Remittance Advice	√	√
824	Application Advice	√	√
830	Planning Schedule with Release Capability	√	√
831	Application Control Totals	√	√
832	Price/Sales Catalog		√
846	Inventory Inquiry/Advice	√	√
850	Purchase Order	√	√
852	Product Activity Data	√	√
853	Routing and Carrier Instructions		√
855	Purchase Order Acknowledgment	√	√
856	Ship Notice/Manifest	√	√
857	Shipment and Billing Notice	√	
860	Purchase Order Change Request—Buyer Initiated		√
861	Receiving Advice/Acceptance Certificate		√
864	Text Message	√	√
867	Product Transfer and Resale Report	√	
869	Order Status Inquiry		√
870	Order Status Report		√
875	Grocery Products Purchase Order	√	
876	Grocery Products Purchase Order Change	√	
877	Manufacturer Coupon Family Code Structure	√	
878	Product Authorization/De-Authorization	√	
879	Price Information	√	
880	Grocery Products Invoice	√	
881	Manufacturer Coupon Redemption Detail	√	
882	Direct Store Delivery Summary Information	√	√
883	Market Development Fund Allocation	√	
884	Market Development Fund Settlement	√	
885	Store Characteristics	√	
886	Customer Call Reporting	√	
887	Coupon Notification	√	
888	Item Maintenance	√	
889	Promotion Announcement	√	√
891	Deduction Research Report	√	
893	Item Information Request	√	√
894	Delivery/Return Base Record	√	
895	Delivery/Return Acknowledgment and/or Adjustment	√	
896	Product Dimension Maintenance	√	
940	Warehouse Shipping Order	√	√
944	Warehouse Stock Transfer Receipt Advice	√	
945	Warehouse Shipping Advice	√	
947	Warehouse Inventory Adjustment Advice	√	√
997	Functional Acknowledgment	√	√

While applications are migrating toward common standards, there is still conflict regarding the ultimate goal. A single common standard facilitates information interchange between partners in any industry and country, but many firms believe that strategic advantage can be achieved only with proprietary EDI capabilities. Proprietary capabilities allow a firm to offer customized transactions that efficiently meet their unique information requirements.

Many firms resolve this dilemma through the use of value-added networks (VANs). A VAN, illustrated in Figure 5.13, is a common interface between sending and receiving systems. The VAN adds value by managing transactions, translating communication standards, and reducing the number of communication linkages. Transaction management includes broadcast of messages to subsets of suppliers, carriers, or customers and receipt of messages from customers using different communication standards.

The Uniform Code Council (UCC), in partnership with **European Article Numbering (EAN)** International, is the organization responsible for international numbering standards and is committed to developing common global standards for products and transaction sets. Information regarding the status of the council's current initiatives can be found on its Web site at **www.uc-council.org.** Another source documenting the evolving commercial standards is the Voluntary Interindustry Commerce Standards (VICS) at **www.vics.org.**

Electronic Product Code

EPC (electronic product code) is an emerging form of product identification. The Auto-ID Center at Massachusetts Institute of Technology, with support from both manufacturers and retailers, collaborated to develop an "intelligent tracking infrastructure" for supply chains. The two standards organizations EAN (European Article Number) and UCC (Uniform Code Council), which were developers of previous bar code standards, formed an organization called EPCglobal Inc., which is driving the adoption and implementation of the "EPCglobal Network."

As opposed to the widely used UPC bar codes, which contain only the product make (manufacturer) and model, the EPC contains a number that can be linked to an individual SKU in the form of a serial number. Each EPC is 96 bits in length and has the capability to represent all products now and into the reasonable future. In addition, EPC accommodates all existing EAN.UCC keys such as Serial Shipping Container Code (SSCC) and GTIN (Global Trade Identification Number).[2]

---

[2] For a more detailed vision regarding the future of EPC, see Sean Campbell and Sachin Shah, "EPC: A Shared Vision for Transforming Business Processes," in *Reshaping Supply Chain Management Vision and Reality* (IBM Global Business Services, 2007), pp. 252–285.

FIGURE 5.13
Value-Added Networks (VANs)
The VAN collects transaction messages and information from a manufacturer and then translates those messages and information into appropriate industry-specific communication standards.

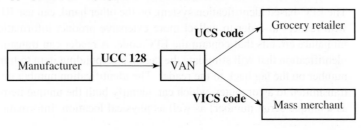

Radio-Frequency Exchange

Radio-frequency data communication (RFDC) technology is used within relatively small areas, such as distribution centers, to facilitate two-way information exchange. A major application is real-time communication with mobile operators such as forklift drivers and order selectors. RFDC allows drivers to have instructions and priorities updated on a real-time basis instead of using a hard copy of instructions printed hours earlier. Real-time or Wi-Fi transmissions guide work flow, offer increased flexibility and responsiveness, and can improve service using fewer resources. Logistics RFDC applications also include two-way communication for warehouse picking, cycle counts, verification, and label printing.

Advanced RFDC capabilities in the form of two-way voice communication are finding their way into logistics warehouse applications. Instead of requiring warehouse operations personnel to interface with a mobile or handheld computer, voice RFDC prompts operators through tasks with audible commands and waits for verbal responses or requests. United Parcel Service uses speech-based RFDC to read zip codes from incoming packages and print routing tickets to guide packages through their sortation facilities. The voice recognition systems are based on keywords and voice patterns of each operator. The primary benefit of voice-based RFDC is an easier operator interface; since keyboard data entry is not required, two hands are available for order picking.

Radio-frequency identification (RFID) is a second form of radio-frequency technology. RFID can be used to identify a container or its contents as it moves through facilities or on transportation equipment. RFID places a coded electronic chip in the container or box. RFID chips can be either active or passive. Active chips continuously emanate radio waves so that product can be located in a warehouse or a retail store, using receivers located throughout the store. Active chip technology is good for locating product in a facility as well as for identifying when it is moving in and out of the facility. Passive chips respond only when they are electronically stimulated by having the product pass through a relatively small gateway or portal that has scanners built in. Since the product must be passed through a gateway for passive chips to operate, these can be used only for tracking product movement in, out, and around a facility. With current technology, the cost of active chips (GEN II) is approximately 10 times that of passive chips because of the need for a battery and larger antenna. As the container or box moves through the supply chain, it can be scanned for an identifying code or even for the list of contents. Retailers are beginning to use RFID to allow entire cartloads of merchandise to be scanned simultaneously. WalMart* and other major retailers began initiatives to require their major suppliers place RFID tags on their cases to facilitate processing in distribution warehouses, receipt at stores, and shelf restocking. While the benefits were apparent for the retailers, they were not so evident for the manufacturers, particularly since the retailers were not generally willing to pay for the chip and the technologies to employ it. While the initiatives to use RFID to track activity for consumer products have declined, there is significant activity investigating the use of RFID to enhance security and minimize counterfeiting. For example, there is increasing use of RFID for pharmaceuticals and expensive technology to reduce counterfeiting and enhance security. It is anticipated that the lessons learned through these applications will reduce the price of RFID and will lead to future logistics applications.

Typically, information on a bar code is captured via a fixed or handheld scanner device. The EPC-based identification system, on the other hand, can use RFID tags in conjunction with readers in order to collect more extensive product information. The RFID tags are miniature circuits that contain the EPC code. A reader can transmit a request for product identification that will stimulate the tag on a responding item to transmit the identification number on the tag back to the reader. The identification number on the reader can then be transmitted to a computer, which can identify both the unique item (SKU number as well as a unique serial number) as well as physical location. Information about a product in a warehouse, store, or any place within transmission range can then be shared and updated in real time across a network. EPC read speed and lack of requiring line-of-sight reading are major advantages over bar code scanners.

Internet

Widespread availability of the Internet and standardized communication interfaces offered through browsers such as Internet Explorer have substantially expanded the opportunities and capability to exchange information between firms of all sizes. The Internet is quickly becoming the supply chain information transmission device of choice for exchanging forecasts, orders, inventory status, product updates, and shipment information. In conjunction with a server and a browser, the Internet offers a standard approach for order entry, order status inquiry, and shipment tracking. An Ohio State University survey predicts the Internet will carry 5 percent of customer orders by the year 2010.[3]

The availability of the Internet has also enabled the development of the exchange portal, a communication medium that has significant supply chain implications. An exchange portal is an infomediary that facilitates horizontal and vertical information exchange between supply chain partners. Figure 5.14 illustrates an exchange portal designed to facilitate communication between supply chain participants. The facilitating firm can provide information regarding raw material requirements, product availability, and price changes and allow the marketplace to react by placing bids or orders.

A second type of exchange portal is industry based. It facilitates communication between all participants within an industry and can substantially reduce transaction costs. Figure 5.15 illustrates the exchange portal that the electronics industry has developed to facilitate communication between the original equipment manufacturers and their multiple tiers of suppliers. This portal offers a common framework for exchanging information, including design information, proposal requests, commodity availability, bids, and schedules. While the information can be made available to all interested parties, it is also possible to restrict information availability. There is increasing fear that industry portal collaborations might increase the potential for monopolistic practices and trade restraints.

[3] The Ohio State University, "Careers Patterns Survey," 2008; available under "careers" at the Council of Supply Chain Management Professionals Web site, **www.cscmp.org.**

FIGURE 5.14
Single-Firm
Exchange Portal

FIGURE 5.15 **Electronics Industry Exchange Portal**

Source: Reprinted with permission from e2open.

Integrating critical information from each tier and providing exception
visibility across the demand-driven supply network

The Federal Trade Commission (FTC) can be expected to play an increasing role in the evolution of the exchange portals, particularly for B2B activities.[4]

A third type of exchange portal is cross-industry-based and is designed to facilitate communication between firms that have common interests in commodities and services. Figure 5.16 illustrates a cross-industry exchange portal for manufacturers, suppliers, service providers, and customers. When one of the member firms has a need for raw material, product, or service, it can access the exchange portal to determine availability and potential price. Similarly, when one of the member firms has excess product or service capacity, such availability can be posted on the portal to solicit interest or a possible bid by one of the exchange members. Reverse auctions can be used most effectively with cross-industry-based portals.

The Internet and the exchange portal have advanced supply chain communication from one-to-one or limited capability to a one-to-many environment capable of being extended to a many-to-many capability. The result is that extended Internet communication is a reality that offers substantial challenge in terms of exploiting widely available information.

One of the major challenges to the wide adoption of exchange portals is the definition and acceptance of online catalogs. Much like the paper version, an online catalog contains a listing of the products and services offered along with their descriptions and specifications. A catalog that is consistent across participating firms is critical to facilitate effective comparison of products and services across firms. For example, a firm desiring to purchase a simple T-shirt from a portal would like all the T-shirt suppliers on that portal to have a similarly formatted entry describing the shirt, its coloring, its content, as well as other minute details so that the customer can make an effective comparison. While customers prefer consistent catalogs, suppliers prefer to use a catalog as a differentiator and are thus reluctant to deviate from their proprietary format. To facilitate information sharing and exchange, the Voluntary Interindustry

---

[4] Kim S. Nash, "Really Check," *Computerworld,* June 5, 2000, pp. 58–59.

FIGURE 5.16
Cross-Industry
Exchange Portal

Commerce Standards (VICS) and Collaborative Planning, Forecasting, and Replenishment (CPFR) are actively promoting common and consistent catalog definitions and standards.

Extensible Markup Language

Extensible Markup Language (XML) is a flexible computer language that facilitates information transfer between a wide range of applications and is readily interpretable by humans. It was published in 1998 by the World Wide Web Consortium to facilitate information transfer between systems, databases, and Web browsers. Since EDI is very structured, the setup cost and required expertise are relatively high, limiting applications to situations involving high transaction volumes. XML is emerging as the information transfer medium between firms and service providers that do not have transaction volumes to justify EDI. XML facilitates communication by breaking down many information technology barriers that have constrained EDI adoption.

A basic XML message consists of three components: the actual information being transmitted, data tags, and a document type definition (DTD). The data tag is a key feature, as it defines the data being transmitted. For example, in a shipment XML, the tag for address would be address and might appear <address> 123 Main St.<address>. The tags indicate to all computer applications what the data between the brackets are and where the data should go in a database or Web page. The use of common terms and the lack of sequencing requirements make XML transactions much easier to use than EDI. The XML DTD tells the computer what document format to refer to when decoding a message. A DTD is essentially a template that maps out a standard form, its tags, and their relation in a database. For example, there would be separate schema for customer orders, advanced shipping notifications, or transportation documentation.

In situations characterized by low volume, XML is superior to EDI for three reasons. First, it is not expensive to install. It is easy to design an application and requires much less time to implement. Second, XML is easy to maintain because it can be easily converted to HyperText Markup Language (HTML), the language of Web browsers. This makes it much easier to modify and share data between applications. Finally, XML is more flexible, allowing for broad applications and quick definition and extension of standards.[5]

[5] For more detail, see Gordon Forsyth,"XML: Breaking Down IT Barriers in Logistics," *American Shipper*, June 2000, pp. 20–26.

Satellite

Satellite technology allows communication across an expansive geographic area such as a region or even the world. The technology is similar to that of microwave dishes used for home television in areas outside the reach of cable. Figure 5.17 illustrates two-way communication between corporate headquarters, vehicles, and remote operational locations.

Satellite communication provides a fast and high-volume channel for information movement. Schneider National, a nationwide truckload carrier, uses communication dishes mounted on its trucks to enable two-way communication between drivers and their dispatchers. Such real-time interaction provides up-to-date information regarding location and delivery information, allowing dispatchers to redirect trucks according to need or congestion. Retail chains also use satellite communication to quickly transmit sales information back to headquarters. WalMart* uses daily sales figures to drive store replenishment and to provide input to marketing regarding local sales patterns.

Image Processing

Image processing utilizes facsimile (fax) and optical-scanning technology to transmit and store freight bill information, as well as other supporting documents such as proof of delivery receipts (POD) or bills of lading (BOL). The rationale for this service is that timely customer shipment information is almost as important as delivering the goods on time. As freight is delivered to customers, support documentation is sent to image processing locations, electronically scanned, and logged into the system.

Electronic images of the documents are then transmitted to a central database where they are stored. By the next day, customers can access the documents through computer linkages or a phone call to their service representative. Customer requests for a hard copy of a document can be filled within minutes by a facsimile transmission. Customer benefits include more accurate billing, faster response from carrier personnel, and easy access to documentation. The carrier also benefits because the system eliminates the need to file paper documents, reduces the chance of loss, and provides improved credibility with customers.

FIGURE 5.17
Logistics Satellite Communication Applications

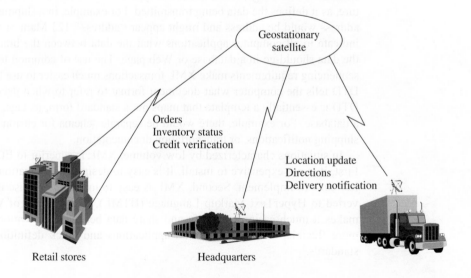

Geostationary satellite

Orders
Inventory status
Credit verification

Location update
Directions
Delivery notification

Retail stores   Headquarters

Satellite technology, RF, and image processing require substantial capital investment prior to achieving significant returns. Experience has shown, however, the primary benefit of these communication technologies is not always lower cost but improved customer service. Improved service is provided in the form of more timely and accurate order entry, quicker shipment tracing, and faster transfer of sales and inventory information. There will be increased demand for these communication technology applications as customers observe the competitive benefits of real-time information transfer.

Software as a Service

Supply chain application software has traditionally been purchased by the firm using it or on behalf of the individual firm by a firm managing their information resources. This was comparable to the arrangement for other firm technology. Recently, some firms are effectively shifting toward software rental in what is being termed as **software as a service (SaaS).** SaaS is offered by a third-party information technology provider and is typically operated on the provider's hardware. This relieves the supply chain firm of the requirement to acquire and maintain either the software or hardware as well as the need to be trained on its internal integration and operation. Table 5.7 summarizes the primary benefits and considerations of SaaS relative to the firm purchasing and operating its own information technology.

Supply chain planning and operations is applying increasingly more sophisticated software and technology. Just as in the case of other logistics services such as transportation and warehousing, some firms are realizing that developing and maintaining a high level of competency in specific information applications is not core to their competitiveness. As a result, they are looking for SaaS providers to meet their technical and operating requirements. The applications that are particularly appropriate for SaaS include those that have significant potential for cross-firm synergies such as TMS and applications requiring a very high level of expertise such as APS.

TABLE 5.7
Benefits and Considerations Related to Software as a Service

Benefits	Considerations[6]
• Shifts much of the software and related hardware cost from fixed to variable based on time or number of transactions.	• Who is providing the service? How long have they been providing it? And what guarentees are there that they will continue to provide it?
• Reduces the need of the firm to develop and maintain specialized expertise.	• Are the servers and other hardware wholly owned or are they subcontracted to another supplier?
• Allows the firm to take advantage of economies of scale in software and hardware acquisition since costs can be shared across a number of user firms.	• If hosting is outsourced, how secure is the data?
	• Are backups made regularly and where are they stored?
• Since information is shared across firms, SaaS opens up the opportunity to share supply chain operations activities.	• Who owns the data and who has access to it?
	• Does the supplier guarantee service and availability levels?
• Access to the application can generally be from anywhere there is a personal computer with access to the Internet	• Who are the reference sites?

[6] Adapted from Alan Stevens, "Before You Sign up to a SaaS Solution," *Personal Computer World* (August 2008).

Summary

Supply chain information systems link logistics activities in an integrated process based on four levels of functionality. The transaction system provides the foundation by electronically taking the order, initiating order selection and shipment, and completing appropriate financial transactions. Management control systems record functional and firm operating performance and provide appropriate management reporting. Decision analysis systems assist management in the identification and evaluation of logistics alternatives. Strategic planning systems provide top management with insight regarding the impact of strategic changes such as mergers, acquisitions, and competitive actions. While the transaction system provides the foundation, management control, decision analysis, and strategic planning systems are becoming critical for high-performance supply chain management.

ERP or legacy systems are the backbone of most SCIS because of their integrated database capabilities and modular transactions. The communication systems facilitate information exchange internally within the firm's functions as well as externally across global sites and with other supply chain partners. The execution systems are becoming more critical for controlling warehouse and transportation operations. The visibility systems monitor product and information flow to reduce supply chain uncertainty and provide government reporting information. Supply chain planning systems will likely become the critical competitive differentiator for the future as firms strive to improve their asset productivity through reduced inventory and physical assets.

The foundation of any firm's supply chain information system is the ERP and execution systems that provide the database and transaction systems to initiate and track supply chain activities. Firms continue to place a strong emphasis on ERP system implementation to achieve information consistency, economies of scale, and integration. These characteristics are becoming basic requirements for global commerce. A broad-based ERP system design includes an integrated database along with modules to support supply chain, service, and financial operations, and for human resource management. The supply chain execution system includes modules for customer accommodation, logistics, manufacturing, purchasing, and inventory deployment.

Remarkable advances have been made to facilitate logistical communication both within a given firm and among its supply chain partners. EDI, satellite, and more recently XML continue to enable quicker and more consistent communication between supply chain partners. Other technologies, such as bar coding, scanning, and radio frequency, are substantially enhancing the communication effectiveness between logistics information systems and the physical environment in which they must operate.

The increasing accessibility and capabilities of these information and communication systems substantially increase the availability and accuracy of supply chain information. Communication technology advances have dramatically reduced the uncertainty between large firms, but substantial opportunities remain for improved communications between smaller firms, which make up the majority of supply chain participants. While further communication system improvement will continue to reduce uncertainty, it is likely that major opportunities for future performance enhancers will be through supply chain analysis and strategic planning systems.

While firms still typically acquire and operate their own information technology applications, there is a trend toward application rental **(SaaS)** to reduce software and hardware assets and lower the cost of maintaining expertise. It is likely that this trend will continue as supply chain software continues to become more specialized and critical to support operations.

Challenge Questions

1. Compare and contrast the role of ERP systems and planning systems in enhancing firm performance and competitiveness.

2. Compare and contrast the role of ERP systems and logistics execution systems.

3. Discuss the rationalization for ERP implementation by firms involved in supply chain management.

4. Discuss the major challenges a firm should expect when implementing an integrated ERP system, including financial, supply chain, service, and human resource applications.

5. Discuss the applications, benefits, and challenges related to the use of RFID to enhance supply chain performance.

6. Compare and contrast how enterprise operations systems differ for MTO and MTP firms.

7. Compare and contrast the role of enterprise operations applications in improving firm competitiveness.

8. Discuss the rationale and risks associated with using a common forecast to drive the firm's planning/coordination flow.

9. Discuss the role of the CRM system in enhancing the firm's competitiveness.

10. Discuss the trade-offs between information technology usage through acquisition versus access through SaaS.

CHAPTER SIX

Integrated Operations Planning

Chapter Outline

The dominant theme of supply chain management is achievement of operational integration. The benefits available from operational integration are directly related to capturing efficiencies between functions within an enterprise as well as across enterprises that constitute a domestic or international supply chain. This chapter focuses on the challenges of supply chain operational planning by examining how and why such planning creates value and by detailing the challenges related to developing an effective plan. The Sales and Operating Planning **(S&OP)** process is discussed from the perspective of effective cross-functional and cross-organizational collaboration. Following a brief discussion of collaborative planning, forecasting, and replenishment **(CPFR)**, the chapter is concluded with a comprehensive discussion of forecasting. Building on the technology discussion of Chapter 5, this final chapter of Part 1 serves to set the framework for the operational discussion presented in Part 2.

Supply Chain Planning

Supply chain operational planning requires the coordination of the processes identified in Chapter 1. Demand planning responsiveness, customer relationship collaboration, order fulfillment/service delivery, manufacturing customization, supplier relationship collaboration, life-cycle support, and reverse logistics must be coordinated to satisfy customers and effectively deploy resources. The framework to provide this coordination is supply chain planning.

The supply chain planning system and supportive information systems seek to integrate information and coordinate overall logistics and supply chain decisions while recognizing the dynamics between other firm functions and processes. The three factors driving effective planning are (1) supply chain visibility, (2) simultaneous resource consideration, and (3) resource utilization.

Supply Chain Visibility

The first reason for planning system development is the need for **visibility** regarding location and status of supply chain inventory and resources. Visibility implies not only being able to track supply chain inventory and resources but also that information regarding available resources can be effectively evaluated and managed. For example, at any given point in time, manufacturers may have thousands of shipments in-transit and inventory being held at hundreds of locations around the globe. Simply being able to identify shipments and inventory is not sufficient; supply chain visibility requires exception management to highlight the need for resource or activity plans to minimize or prevent potential problems.

While the United States and its allies demonstrated the benefits of effective military planning and technology deployment during the Gulf Wars, the Defense Department learned that its logistics and supply chain systems did not perform to the same standard. A major reason cited for poor logistical performance was lack of supply chain visibility. For deployment and security, the Defense Department and its key suppliers did not have integrated information systems capable of documenting or identifying inventory status or location. There was minimal integration between each military service (Army, Navy, and Air Force) and their logistics service providers, such as the Defense Logistics Agency. Such logistics integration had not historically received major attention. This lack of integration coupled with the fear that potential foes could gain an advantage by breaking into the tracking system or monitoring movements resulted in performance that was not reflective of modern supply chain management.

Limited visibility regarding inventory in-transit and expected arrival times resulted in significant uncertainty regarding product availability. The lack of certainty in a situation where product availability is critical resulted in additional inventory and requisitions to reduce the chance of stockouts. While it is clear that no military force can tolerate short supply, excessive inventories are expensive and typically wasteful of critical resources.

Simultaneous Resource Consideration

If planning system visibility determines resource status and availability, the second reason for a planning system is the need to consider combined supply chain demand, capacity, material requirements, and constraints. Supply chain design reflects customer demand for product quantity, delivery timing, and location. While some of these customer requirements may be negotiable, logistics must execute to the agreed-to requirements and standards.

The constraints to meeting customer requirements are materials, production, storage, and transportation capacity, which represent the physical limitations of processes and facilities. Traditional planning methods have typically considered these capacity constraints in a sequential manner. For example, an initial plan is made that operates within production constraints. The initial plan is then adjusted to reflect material and sourcing constraints. This second plan is then revised to consider storage and transportation constraints. While the processes and sequences may be different, sequential decision making results in suboptimal and inferior planning and capacity utilization.

Achieving desired supply chain performance requires simultaneous consideration of relevant requirements and capacity constraints to identify trade-offs where increased functional costs, such as in manufacturing or storage, might lead to lower total system costs. A planning system needs to quantitatively evaluate the trade-offs and identify plans to achieve desired overall performance.

Resource Utilization

Logistics and supply chain management decisions influence many enterprise resources, including production, distribution facilities and equipment, transportation equipment, and inventories. These resources consume a substantial proportion of a typical firm's fixed and working assets. Functional management must focus on resource utilization within its scope of responsibility. For example, production management is focused on minimizing plant and equipment required for manufacturing. The typical result is long production runs requiring minimum setups and changeovers. However, longer production runs invariably result in more finished inventory, as substantial quantities are manufactured in anticipation of projected demand. Any excess inventory increases working capital requirements and space requirements. Extended production runs also require longer-term and more accurate forecasts.

With functional resource trade-offs in mind, the final reason driving planning system development is the need for a coordinated approach that considers service requirements while minimizing combined supply chain resources. This is a critical capability when supply chain and firm performance place a strong emphasis on overall asset utilization.

Supply Chain Planning Applications

Supply chain planning is increasing in frequency and scope. Such applications are evolving to facilitate consideration of a broader range of activities and resources within the scope of supply chain plans. There are, however, some applications common for most planning environments. These include demand planning, production planning, and logistics planning.

Demand Planning

The increasing complexity of product offerings and marketing tactics in conjunction with shorter product life cycles requires increased accuracy, flexibility, and consistency in determining inventory requirements. Demand management systems seek to provide such capabilities.

Demand management develops the forecast that drives anticipatory supply chain processes. The forecasts are the projections of monthly, weekly, or daily demand that determine production and inventory requirements. Each projected quantity might include some portion of future orders placed in anticipation of customer demand along with some portion of forecasted demand based on history. Essentially, the demand management process integrates historically based forecasts with other information regarding events that could influence future sales activity, such as promotional plans, pricing changes, and new product introductions, to obtain the best possible integrated statement of requirements. Forecast techniques and procedures are discussed later in this chapter.

Another aspect of the demand management process focuses on creating forecast consistency across multiple products and warehouse facilities. Effective integrated management requires a single accurate forecast for each item and facility. The aggregate and combined requirements must reflect a plan that is consistent with divisional and overall firm sales and financial projections. The demand management system is the information technology component of the sales and operations planning **(S&OP)** process to develop the unconstrained marketing plan. The demand management system begins with a base forecast and then incorporates such factors as product life cycle, changes in distribution channels, pricing and promotional tactics, and product mix variations. The demand management system also rationalizes the detailed logistics plans, unique forecasts for each warehouse and product, with the aggregate product group and national plans. For example, the sum of individual warehouse facility sales should be consistent with national sales projections. Similarly, item level requirements need to be adjusted to reflect the activity level for related items. For instance, requirements for existing products may have to be reduced to reflect the market's reaction to a new product introduction or one item's requirements may need to be adjusted during the promotion of a substitutable item.

Production Planning

Production planning uses the statement of requirements obtained from demand management in conjunction with manufacturing resources and constraints to develop a workable manufacturing plan. The statement of requirements defines what items are needed and when. Although there has been a definite trend toward make-to-order **(MTO)** and assemble-to-order **(ATO)** manufacturing, such response-based practices are not always possible because of production technology, capacity, or resource constraints. The limitations occur in the form of facility, equipment, and labor availability.

Production planning systems match the requirements plan with the production constraints. The objective is to satisfy the necessary requirements at the minimum total production cost while not violating any constraints. Effective production planning results in a time-sequenced plan to manufacture the correct items in a timely manner while operating within facility, equipment, and labor constraints. Production planning identifies the items that should be produced in anticipation of need to remain within production constraints and yet minimize inventory.

Logistics Planning

Logistics planning coordinates transportation, warehousing, and inventory within the firm and between supply chain partners. Historically, purchasing and finished goods transportation both attempted to minimize their freight cost individually. Procurement minimized the expense of raw material movements by working with suppliers and inbound carriers. Logistics focused on minimizing outbound freight expense by working with customers and their transportation carriers. There is also often a third managerial focus related to international shipments. The individual perspectives of transportation often result in limited economies of scale, limited information sharing, and excessive transportation expense.

Logistics planning integrates overall movement demand, vehicle availability, and relevant movement cost into a common decision support system that seeks to minimize overall freight expense. The analysis suggests ways that freight can be shifted among carriers or consolidated to achieve scale economies. It also facilitates information sharing with carriers and other service providers to enable better asset utilization.

Logistics planning is essential for effective resource utilization. Lack of accurate and comprehensive logistics and supply chain planning tools historically resulted in poor utilization of production, storage, and transportation capacity. The increasingly strong focus on improved asset utilization in conjunction with improved information management and decision analysis capabilities and techniques has brought comprehensive planning systems to reality.

Effective planning requires a combination of information systems to provide the data and managers to make decisions. The following section illustrates some of the specific conflicts associated with S&OP and describes the major process and system components.

Sales and Operations Planning (S&OP)

An integrated S&OP process is increasingly necessary for effective supply chain operations. The S&OP process collaboratively establishes a coordinated plan for responding to customer requirements within the resource constraints of the enterprise. Traditionally, firms have sequentially and often independently developed financial, sales, and operations plans. First, finance develops revenue plans often designed to meet the expectations of Wall Street. Second, sales develops marketing plans and tactics that meet the revenue targets for the firm's product groups. This includes establishing specific product innovation, pricing, and promotion plans to achieve the desired results. Finally, supply chain operations develop materials, manufacturing, and logistics plans that can meet customer demands within the operating constraints of the firm and its supply chain partners. Figure 6.1 illustrates some of the conflicts involved. Sales would like to sell a wide variation of products, rapidly responding to customers, and with short lead times. In effect, the sales goal is to maximize revenue by providing the customers whatever they want and when they want it. Supply chain operations would prefer to minimize the product variations and production changeovers, constrain schedule variations, and extend lead times to take advantage of economies of scale. In effect, a major focus of supply chain operations is to take advantage of manufacturing, transportation, and handling economies of scale. Since there is significant potential for conflict in these objectives, meeting unique customer requests versus operations economies of scale, it is necessary

FIGURE 6.1
Planning Process Conflicts

Balancing Objectives

Operations		Sales
• Detailed forecasts • Few products • Long runs • Stable schedules • Long lead times • Maximize production	• High working capital (inventories) • Lower service levels • Lower quality • Lower margins	• Aggregate forecasts • Many product variations • Rapid response • High service • Maximize revenue

Traditional functional approach to planning leads to differing interests, suboptimal actions, and slower improvement to systematically consider the trade-offs and collaboratively create consistent plans. This includes developing and agreeing to forecasts, product introduction, marketing tactics, and operating plans that can meet financial and customer commitments within the constraints of the enterprise.

While S&OP has significant information technology considerations, it is not just an information technology application. It is a combination of information systems, with significant elements of financial, marketing, and supply chain planning elements, integrated with organizational processes, responsibility, and accountability to develop consensus and execute collaborative plans. Thus, an effective S&OP requires a blending of process and technology within a collaborative organization. Figure 6.2 illustrates the S&OP process. The first component of the S&OP process is a business plan in terms of a financial forecast and a corresponding budget. This plan is used to guide activity levels and determine aggregate volume and resource requirements. The second component of the S&OP is the sales plan, which is developed from the unconstrained marketing plan. The unconstrained marketing plan determines the maximum sales and profitability level that could be achieved if there were no supply chain operating constraints. As Figure 6.2 indicates, the unconstrained marketing plan synthesizes the information regarding orders on hand, current customers, new customers, competition, selling margins, new product potential, pricing, and the overall economy to project what sales could be if there were no supply chain or operations constraints. The final component of the S&OP is the resource plan, which is developed from the firm's internal and partner resource constraints. The operations plan synthesizes the resource demands and constraints to identify and evaluate potential trade-offs.

The business, unconstrained marketing, and resource plans are integrated and synchronized through the S&OP process. The process requires a combination of technology to identify and evaluate the binding constraints as well as managerial input to determine which constraints might be released in the form of prioritizing customer shipments, changes in marketing plans, overtime operations, or outsourcing production. Once the S&OP process

FIGURE 6.2   **S&OP Process**

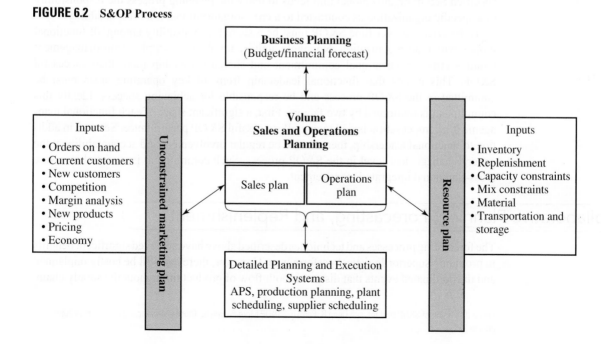

is completed for current and future time periods, the result is a common and consistent plan that synthesizes the firm's financial and marketing plans with its resource capabilities. Once this aggregate plan is approved, it becomes the basis of more detailed supply chain planning application systems. The next section discusses some of these applications in detail.[1]

While not every firm uses an integrated and coordinated S&OP process, virtually all firms develop business, marketing, and operational plans. When the S&OP process is not integrated and collaborative, there are no feedback loops or synchronization. The result is a high probability that they will not be consistent and conflicts will arise. As indicated in Figure 6.1, such conflicts will often result in unsatisfied customer and/or poor resource utilization. It is important to note that the arrows in Figure 6.2 are bidirectional, indicating that an effective S&OP process requires two-way information flow and collaboration. Firms are becoming increasingly interested in a more formal and collaborative S&OP process to facilitate meeting the precise requirements of increasingly demanding customers within the constraints that are being imposed by firms that are increasingly asset conscious.

Making S&OP Work

Positioning S&OP as a core business planning process requires a well-understood operational framework. Successful S&OP requires collaborative analysis of available information, shared operational metrics, and senior leadership. The keys to successful S&OP implementation are presented in Table 6.1.

Senior Leadership Involvement

A common question concerning S&OP is organizational positioning. It is critical to understand that S&OP is a cross-functional process and not a specific job. A great deal of work is required to execute successful S&OP. The S&OP process is required to be performed and monitored on a continuous basis to assure successful execution. At a minimum a new or updated plan is necessary for each successive operating period. Given the repetitive aadetailed work required for successful S&OP, senior management might justify creating an organizational unit to undertake the continuous planning. While logical, creation of a specified S&OP organizational unit tends to make the planning process the responsibility of a specific organization as contrasted to a cross-organizational joint responsibility.

To be effective over time S&OP must be a shared responsibility among all functional groups within an organization. No single activity involved in supply chain management requires cross-organizational commitment and shared ownership more than successful S&OP. This means that functional leadership from all key operating areas must be committed to the S&OP process and be responsible for achieving success. Ideally this commitment is reinforced by two factors. First, a significant share of each functional management's compensation is tied to overall successful S&OP performance. Second, in addition to functional leadership, there should be regular involvement and accountability at the general management level in the S&OP process. Such commitment is essential to assure cross-functional integrated management.

Collaborative Planning, Forecasting, and Replenishment

The forecasting processes and techniques described above have achieved significant benefits in providing superior logistical performance. However, there can still be costly unplanned and uncoordinated events that distort smooth flow of product throughout the supply chain.

[1] For a discussion of S&OP content, see Deep R. Parekh, "S&OP More Prevalent, Global," *American Shipper*, June 2008, pp. 28–33.

TABLE 6.1
**Eight Keys
to Achieving
Superior Business
Performance Using
S&OP**

Reprinted with permission
from Stephen P. Crane, *CVCR
Newsletter*, 3, no.1, 2008
(Winter).

Executing the Process Every Month

While the details of a good S&OP process, like any routine, can seem to be a bit of a grind, reducing the frequency of monthly meetings is only possible in best-case scenarios—for those businesses that experience little change in their markets, channels, supply lines, or product offerings. These businesses would have to operate with small deviations to their plan and have best-in-class key performance indicators (KPIs). Most do not, so they need to meet monthly.

Process Ownership and Clarity of Roles and Responsibilities

S&OP requires a process champion, someone to drive the entire process so that functional managers can direct operations that align with your business's long-term strategic plans. The ideal S&OP leader should be a process facilitator and manager who has direct involvement in determining the strategic direction for the business.

Organizational Commitment to Achieving High Forecast Accuracy

A business needs to have a long-term commitment and view to taking whatever actions are necessary to achieve high forecast accuracy. The Demand Plan drives the entire supply chain from the supply plan, production plan, inventory plan, sourcing plan, and the financial plan. If you don't have a good handle on what you expect customers to buy, it is then difficult to make good supply chain decisions.

Focus Should Be on the Next 3 to 12 Months

While it is important to understand where a business stands relative to the budget, the focus should not be on past results. It should be on looking forward, examining what the next 3 to 12 months are projected to look like. A proper S&OP process should really have an 18-month planning horizon. Companies that have a longer-term view have a better grasp of the demand drivers influencing their business; as a result their demand plans are much more reliable, predictable, and actionable.

One Integrated Plan That Integrates the Actions of the Entire Organization

The fundamental purpose of an integrated S&OP process is to review deviations in operational forecasts, new product plans, budgets, capital plans, and plans as they relate to achieving the goals of the business or company. Every step in your S&OP process should be governed by an overarching focus on executing the strategic plans of the business.

Senior Management Decision Making

In a best-in-class Sales and Operations planning process the endgame is decision making. If senior management is not willing to take action, the result will just be a lot of hand waving and will not have any benefit to the business. This problem is typical where the Executive S&OP Meeting serves more as a "reporting" session, from which few decisions are made and even fewer action items are assigned.

Measuring End-to-End Supply Chain Performance

Many leaders do not like the prospect of having their work conspicuously evaluated on a monthly basis and in public. Companies that embrace measurement as a starting point for continuous improvement are far better served by S&OP than those that resist measurement. In any S&OP process, the metrics are vital to ensuring success. They provide indicators of how well the business is performing, and they clearly illustrate progress that has been made to drive improvement.

S&OP Forecast versus Operating Plan or Budget

The majority of the time the S&OP forecast will not match a company's operating plan target or budget for a given year. It's alright that these two plans are not the same at any point in time. Companies should never artificially adjust the S&OP forecast to match the budget. Since the S&OP forecast should be driving all the other supply chain decisions, artificially adjusting a forecast will just increase costs and will not help to meet the budget. The greatest business value is realized when companies are willing to analyze the gaps between the forecast and budget and take the time to identify the actions that need to be taken to close the gaps.

These distortions occur because individual businesses frequently fail to coordinate their individual forecasts of final consumer demand and marketing events designed to stimulate demand. Imagine, for example, that at the beginning of the month, the manufacturer forecasts sales of 100,000 cases to a particular retail customer with planned advertising and sales promotions to support that level of sales. Meanwhile, that same retailer forecasts sales of 150,000 and plans specific promotional events to achieve that forecast. Clearly, joint planning and information sharing concerning such events would increase the likelihood of a successful relationship.

Collaborative planning, forecasting, and replenishment **(CPFR)** is a process initiated by the consumer products industry to achieve such coordination. It does not replace replenishment strategies but supplements them by a cooperative process. In essence, CPFR coordinates the requirements planning process between supply chain partners for demand creation and demand fulfillment activities. Figure 6.3 illustrates the base CPFR relationships. The CPFR solution shares information involving promotions, forecasts, item data, and orders, using either EDI or the Internet. The collaboratively developed information is then used jointly and iteratively by planners to generate demand, determine replenishment requirements, and match production to demands.

The first step in the CPFR process is joint business planning, wherein a customer and supplier share, discuss, coordinate, and rationalize their own individual strategies to create a joint plan. The joint plan offers a common and consistent vision of what is expected to be sold, how it will be merchandised and promoted, in which marketplace, and during what time period. A joint calendar is created to share information determining product flow. A common sales forecast is created and shared between retailer and supplier based on shared knowledge of each trading partner's plan. CPFR includes an iterative process where the forecast and requirements plan is exchanged and refined between the partners until a consensus is developed. Using this consensus forecast, production, replenishment, and shipment plans are developed. Ideally, the collaborative forecast becomes a commitment between the two firms.

Relational distribution channels hold great promise for superior logistical performance. Conventional channels are primarily adversarial in nature, fail to acknowledge dependency, and are driven by information hoarding rather than sharing, so they cannot achieve the sophisticated logistical interfaces required by CPFR. Alliances and partnerships create long-term relationships between supply chain partnerships. When problems occur, as they inevitably will, they can be quickly resolved. Ultimately, the close-working arrangements reduce the cost of doing business for all channel members. Issues and concepts related to effective supply chain collaboration are discussed in greater detail in Chapter 15.

FIGURE 6.3
CPFR in the Retail Information Technology Environment

Source: Reprinted with permission from Matt Johnson, "Collaboration Data Modeling: CPFR Implementation Guidelines," *Proceedings of the 1999 Annual Conference of the Council of Supply Chain Management Professionals,* Oak Brook, IL, p. 17.

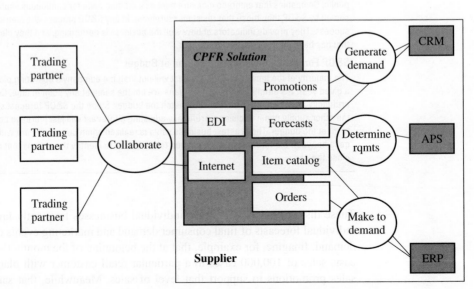

Forecasting

Accommodating customer requirements in most supply chain arrangements requires a forecast to drive the process. The forecast is the specific definition of what is projected to be sold, when, and where. The forecast identities requirements for which the supply chain must schedule inventory and operational resources. Since there are many logistics and supply chain activities that must be completed in anticipation of a sale, forecasting is a critical capability.

Table 6.2 illustrates how the need for forecasting is influenced by replenishment response time and economies of scale. Accurate forecasting should be a major focus for situations where there are long replenishment lead times and large economies of scale. On the other hand, accurate forecasts are not as critical when there are shorter lead times or lesser economies of scale. The variables in Table 6.2 can be applied two different ways. First, one could consider the product characteristics as requiring long lead time and high economies of scale and decide to place emphasis on forecasting. Alternatively, one could evaluate the potential for developing accurate forecasts, given short life cycle and high number of variations, and decide to place primary focus for this item on reduced lead time. These situations illustrate that, while improved forecasts are often desirable, there are other ways to achieve the objectives of enhanced service or reduced inventory. One is to forecast at a higher level of aggregation. The second is to develop a responsive supply chain capable of manufacturing to order, even further reducing inventory. While firms are using these methods to reduce their reliance on forecasting, there are still many situations where forecasting is necessary to achieve service objectives or take advantage of scale economies.

With the above considerations in mind, this section focuses on forecasting needs, benefits, methods, techniques, applications, and measures. It provides background to understand logistics applications of forecasting, forecast components, forecasting process, forecasting techniques, software applications, and forecasting error.

Forecasting Requirements

Effective logistics requires matching the product requirements of customers with the capacity capabilities of the enterprise and supply chain. Although consumer demands in terms of service level and product variations are increasing, the focus on reduced supply

TABLE 6.2
How Product Characteristics Influence the Need to Forecast

Source: Reprinted with permission from David J. Closs, *Forecasting and Its Use in Logistics,* Council of Supply Chain Management Professionals, Oak Brook, IL.

	Low Economies of Scale	High Economies of Scale
Long response time experienced in replenishing product	Detailed accurate forecasting is not as critical, as the firm has more production flexibility. For example, final product customization could be postponed so that it's only necessary to forecast the base units (i.e, at a higher level of aggregation) with final customization much nearer time of demand.	Accurate forecasting is critical in this case as it's necessary to forecast an extended time into the future to allow for production or transportation economies.
Short response time experienced in replenishing product	When it's possible to obtain product quickly and there are limited scale economies, the focus should shift from forecasting to the design of a responsive and flexible process.	Focus on developing an accurate short-term forecast with strong consideration of marketing and competitive tactics and less consideration of history.

chain assets simultaneously requires more timely and accurate forecasts. Logistics forecasts are necessary (1) to support collaborative planning, (2) to drive requirements planning, and (3) to improved resource management.

Collaborative Planning

Without collaboration, each partner tries to plan the level and timing of demand for its customers, both individually and collectively. The result is speculative inventory positioned in anticipation of independently forecasted demand resulting in a never-ending cycle of inventory excesses and out-of-stocks. Historically, manufacturers have scheduled their promotions, price changes, new product introductions, and special events, either independently or without collaboration with their major retailers. When no single retailer accounted for a substantial proportion of a firm's sales volume, such collaboration was not critical. However, when a single major customer can approach 25 percent of a firm's sales,which is the case of WalMart* with many of its suppliers, such coordination becomes essential.Without a collaborative plan, the supplier-customer combination typically results in either inventory excess or shortage. A collaborative forecast, jointly agreed to by supply chain partners, provides a common goal that can be the basis for developing effective operating plans. CPFR was discussed earlier in this chapter.

Requirements Planning

Once a collaborative forecast is developed, logisticians use the forecasts to drive requirements planning. The plan determines inventory projections and resulting replenishment or production requirements for the planning horizon. Sales and operations planning **(S&OP)**, discussed earlier in this chapter, integrates forecasts, open orders, available inventory, and production plans into a definition of periodic inventory availability and requirements. Ideally, the requirements planning process operates collaboratively and interactively both internally across the firm's operations and externally with supply chain partners to develop a common and consistent plan for each time period, location, and item.

Resource Management

Once the plan is completed, it can be used to manage critical supply chain processes such as production, inventory, and transportation. Accurate forecasts collaboratively developed by supply chain partners along with a consistent definition of supply chain resources and constraints enable effective evaluation of trade-offs associated with supply chain decisions. The trade-offs consider the relative costs of supply chain strategies such as maintaining extra production or storage capacity, speculative production or product movement, or outsourcing. Timely identification and evaluation of these trade-offs enable a better match of requirements to resources and better resource utilization.

Forecasting Components

The forecast is generally a monthly or weekly figure for each stockkeeping unit **(SKU)** and distribution location. The forecast components include: (1) base demand, (2) seasonal, (3) trend, (4) cyclic, (5) promotion, and (6) irregular. Assuming the base demand as the average sales level, the other components, except for irregular, are multiplicative factors of the base level available to support positive or negative adjustments. The resulting forecast model is:

$$F_t = (B_t \times S_t \times T \times C_t \times P_t) + I$$

where

F_t = forecast quantity for period t

B_t = base level demand for period t

S_t = seasonality factor for period t

T = trend component index reflecting increase or decrease per time period

C_t = cyclical factor for period t

P_t = promotional factor for period t

I = irregular or random quantity.

While some forecasts may not include all components, it is useful to understand the behavior of each so that each component can be tracked and incorporated appropriately. For example, some forecasting techniques cannot effectively address seasonality whereas others can.

The **base demand** represents the long-term average demand after the remaining components have been removed. The base demand is the average over an extended time. The base demand is the forecast for items having no seasonality, trend, cyclic, or promotional components.

The **seasonal** component is an annually recurring upward and downward movement in demand. An example is the annual demand for toys, which reflects low demand for three-fourths of the year and then increased demand just before Christmas. It should be noted that the seasonality discussed above refers to consumer retail seasonality. Seasonality at the wholesale level precedes consumer demand by approximately one quarter of a year.

The **trend** component is the long-range shift in periodic sales. Trend may be positive, negative, or neutral in direction. A positive trend means that sales are increasing over time. For example, the trend for personal computer sales during the decade of the 1990s was increasing. Over the product life cycle, trend direction may change a number of times. For example, beer consumption changed from a neutral to an increasing trend during the past decade. Increases or decreases result from changes in overall population or consumption patterns. Knowledge of which factor is primarily influencing sales is important in making such projections. For example, a reduction in the birth rate implies that a reduction in the demand for disposable diapers will follow. However, a trend toward usage of disposable as contrasted to cloth diapers may result in increased demand of a specific product category even though overall market size is decreasing. The above are obvious examples of forecast trend. While the impact of trend on short-range logistics forecasts is subtle, it still must be considered. Unlike the other forecast components, the trend component influences base demand in the successive time periods. The specific relationship is

$$\mathrm{B}_{t+1} = \mathrm{B}_t \times \mathrm{T}$$

where

B_{t+1} = base demand in period $t + 1$

B_t = base demand in period t

T = periodic trend index.

The trend index with a value greater than 1.0 indicates that periodic demand is increasing, while a value less than 1.0 indicates a declining trend.

The **cyclic** component is characterized by periodic shifts in demand lasting more than a year. These cycles may be either upward or downward. An example is the business cycle in which the economy typically swings from recession to growth cycles every 3 to 5 years. The demand for housing, as well as the resulting demand for major appliances, is typically tied to this business cycle.

The **promotional** component characterizes demand swings initiated by a firm's marketing activities, such as advertising, deals, or promotions. These swings can often be characterized by sales increases during the promotion followed by sales declines as customers sell or use inventory purchased to take advantage of the promotion. Promotions can be deals offered to consumers or trade promotions offered only to wholesalers and retailers. The promotion can be regular and thus take place at the same time each year. From a forecasting perspective, a regular promotion component resembles a seasonal component. An irregular promotion component does not necessarily occur during the same time period, so it must be tracked and considered separately. The promotional component is particularly important to track, especially for consumer industries, since it has a major influence on sales variation. In some industries, promotional activity explains 50 to 80 percent of volume variations. Thus, promotion results in demand that is more lumpy than would otherwise be the case. The promotional component is different from the other forecasting components in that its timing and magnitude are controlled, to a large extent, by the firm. Thus, it should be possible to input information from the firm's sales or marketing departments regarding the timing and likely impact of scheduled promotional plans. The benefits of coordinating such promotional offerings among channel partners provide the rationale for collaborative forecasting practices.

The **irregular** component includes the random or unpredictable quantities that do not fit within the other categories. Because of its random nature, this component is impossible to predict. In developing a forecast process, the objective is to minimize the magnitude of the random component by tracking and predicting the other components.

Forecasting Process

Logistics planning and coordination require the best possible estimate of SKU/location demand. Although forecasting is far from an exact science, the forecast management process should incorporate input from multiple sources, appropriate mathematical and statistical techniques, decision support capability, and trained and motivated individuals.

Supply chain operational forecasts are normally developed for daily, weekly, or monthly periods. An effective forecast management process requires a number of components, as illustrated in Figure 6.4. The process foundation is the forecast database, including open orders, demand history, and the tactics used to stimulate demand, such as promotions, special deals, or product changes. The forecast database is ideally part of an enterprise resource planning system **(ERP)** central data warehouse, although some firms maintain independent forecast databases. Other environmental data, such as the state of the economy and competitive action, are often included in this database. To support effective forecasting, this database must include timely historical and planning information in a manner facilitating its manipulation, summarization, analysis, and reporting.

Finally, the development of an effective forecast requires a process that integrates three components: forecast technique, forecast support system, and forecast administration. The box on the right side of Figure 6.4 illustrates that it would be ideal if a firm could use a common and consistent forecast for all planning functions.

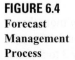

FIGURE 6.4
Forecast
Management
Process

Technique

The technique component is the mathematical or statistical computation used to combine base, seasonal, and cyclical components and elements of promotion history into a forecast quantity. Techniques include time series modeling, in which sales history is a major factor, and correlation modeling, in which relationships with other independent variables are the major forecast drivers. Specific techniques are discussed in the forecast technique section of this chapter. While techniques can easily connect historical patterns into future forecasts, they do not do as well at incorporating the input of anticipated future events. As a result, it is increasingly apparent that accuracy requires integration of the forecast techniques with appropriate support and administrative systems.

Support System

The forecast support system includes the supply chain intelligence to gather and analyze data, develop the forecast, and communicate the forecast to relevant personnel and planning systems. This component allows consideration of external factors such as the impact of promotions, strikes, price changes, product line changes, competitive activity, and economic conditions. For example, if the firm plans to promote 12-packs of a beverage, it is reasonable to assume 2-liter sales will decrease. The system must be designed not only to allow the consideration of these factors but also to encourage them. As another example, the marketing manager may know that the promotion scheduled for next month is likely to increase sales by 15 percent. However, if the forecast support system makes it difficult to adjust the forecast figures for next month, the forecast adjustments may not occur. Similarly, when a package size change is announced, it is likely that forecast history should be changed to reflect the new package size so that future forecasts will reflect correct sizes and volumes. If this is difficult to accomplish within the system constraints, the individual completing the forecast will probably not consider the adjustments. It is thus very important that an effective forecasting process include a support system to facilitate the maintenance, update, and manipulation of the historical database and the forecast.

Administration

Forecast administration includes the organizational, procedural, motivational, and personnel aspects of forecasting and its integration into the other firm functions. The organizational aspect concerns individual roles and responsibilities. It is important these impacts be specified in detail in defining the forecast administration function. If an integrated forecast is desirable, it is necessary to specifically define each organization's forecasting responsibility and then hold it accountable with specific measurements. Effective forecast administration requires that organizational responsibility and procedural guidelines are documented and measured. Effective administration also requires that forecast analysts be trained in both the process and the input of forecasts on supply chain logistics operations.

Dynamic simulation illustrates the impact of forecast inconsistency across multiple members of the supply chain. From initial stimulant to feedback, the cost of direct communication of sales or forecasts is overshadowed by the cost of a faulty message. Since a great deal of supply chain action is initiated in anticipation of future transactions, communications containing overly optimistic predictions or projections may stimulate a fever of ultimately useless work. Analysis of communications between channel members suggests that anticipation has a tendency to amplify as it proceeds between supply chain participants, particularly as the information gets further from the ultimate consumer. Each error in the interpretation of transaction requirements creates a disturbance for the total logistical channel. In a classic work, Forrester simulated channel interrelationships to demonstrate how the total channel may enter into an oscillating corrective pattern, resulting in a series of over-and-under adjustments to real market requirements.[2] Figure 6.5 illustrates the channel inventory oscillations that are stimulated when the retailer increases demand by 10 percent but does not directly inform the other members of the channel.

Figure 6.5 illustrates that an increase of retail demand by 10 percent without clear communication back to other members of the supply chain results in inventory swings of 16 percent for the distributor, 28 percent for the factory warehouse, and 40 percent for factory production. These swings, commonly referred to as the bullwhip effect, obviously increase supply chain variance, which increases costs and diminishes asset utilization.

By the very nature of its mission, a distribution channel must respond to transaction requirements. The system must stand ready to initiate logistical action upon receipt of a message. Extreme care must be taken to structure the communication function with a high degree of reliability while retaining the flexibility required for change and adaptation.

It is important to realize that a meaningful forecast process requires an integrated and consistent combination of components. Historically, it was thought that intensive effort in one of the individual components such as technique could overcome problems in the other components. For example, it was thought that a "perfect" forecast technique could be identified that would overcome the need for systems support and a consistent process. There is increasing realization that all three components must work together. The design process must adequately consider the strengths and weaknesses of each individual component, and design for the optimal performance of the integrated system.

Even though the forecast technique is only one component of the overall demand management process, it is useful to understand the breadth of techniques available and the measures to evaluate them.

[2] Jay W. Forrester, *Industrial Dynamics* (Cambridge, MA: The MIT Press, 1961).

FIGURE 6.5
Response of a Simulated Production/ Distribution System to a Sudden 10 Percent Increase in Sales at the Retail Level

Source: Reprinted with permission from Jay W. Forrester, *Industrial Dynamics* (Waltham, MA: Pegasus Communications, 1961), www.pegasuscom.com.

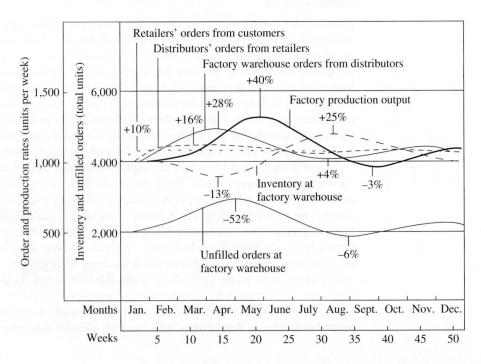

Forecasting Techniques

Demand forecasting requires the selection of appropriate mathematical or statistical techniques to generate periodic forecasts. The effective use of a technique requires matching the characteristics of the situation with the abilities of the technique. Some criteria for evaluating the applicability of a technique include: (1) accuracy, (2) forecast time horizon, (3) the value of forecasting, (4) data availability, (5) type of data pattern, and (6) experience of the forecaster.[3] Each alternative forecast technique must be evaluated both qualitatively and quantitatively with respect to these six criteria.

There are three categories of forecast techniques: (1) qualitative, (2) time series, and (3) causal. A qualitative technique uses data such as expert opinion and special information to forecast the future. A qualitative technique may or may not consider the past. A time series technique focuses entirely on historical patterns and pattern changes to generate forecasts. A causal technique, such as regression, uses refined and specific information regarding variables to develop a relationship between a lead event and forecasted activity.

Qualitative

Qualitative techniques rely heavily on expertise and are quite costly and time-consuming. They are ideal for situations where little historical data and much managerial judgment are required. Using input from the sales force as the basis of the forecast for a new region or a new product is an example of a supply chain application of a qualitative forecast technique. However, qualitative methods are generally not appropriate for supply chain forecasting because of the time required to generate the detailed SKU forecasts necessary. Qualitative forecasts are developed by using surveys, panels, and consensus meetings.

Time Series

Time series techniques are statistical methods utilized when historical sales data containing relatively clear and stable relationships and trends are available. Using historical sales data, time series analysis is used to identify seasonality, cyclical patterns, and trends. Once individual forecast components are identified, time series techniques assume the future will reflect the past. This implies that past demand patterns will continue into the future. This assumption is often reasonably correct in the short term, so these techniques are most appropriate for short-range forecasting.

When the rate of growth or trend changes significantly, the demand pattern experiences a turning point. Since time series techniques use historical demand patterns and weighted averages of data points, they are typically not sensitive to turning points. As a result, other approaches must be integrated with time series techniques to determine when turning points will likely occur.

Time series techniques include a variety of methods that analyze the pattern and movement of historical data to establish recurring characteristics. On the basis of specific characteristics, techniques of varying sophistication can be used to develop time series forecasts. Four time series techniques in order of increasing complexity are (1) moving averages, (2) exponential smoothing, (3) extended smoothing, and (4) adaptive smoothing.

Moving average forecasting uses an average of the most recent period's sales. The average may use any number of previous time periods, although 1-, 3-, 4-, and 12-period averages are common. A 1-period moving average results in next period's forecast being projected by last period's sales. A 12-period moving average, such as monthly, uses the average of the last 12 periods. Each time a new period of actual data becomes available,

---

[3] Spyros Makridakis, Steven Wheelright, and Robert Hyndman, *Forecasting, Methods and Applications,* 3rd ed. (New York: John Wiley & Sons, 1997).

it replaces the oldest time period's data; thus, the number of time periods included in the average is held constant.

Although moving averages are easy to calculate, there are several limitations. Most significantly, they are unresponsive or sluggish to change and a great amount of historical data must be maintained and updated to calculate forecasts. If the historical sales variations are large, average or mean value cannot be relied upon to render useful forecasts. Other than the base component, moving averages do not consider the forecast components discussed earlier.

Mathematically, moving average is expressed as

$$F_t = \frac{\sum_{i=1}^{n} S_{t-i}}{n}$$

where

F_t = moving average forecast for time period t

S_{t-i} = sales for time period i

n = total number of time periods

For example, an April moving forecast based on sales of 120, 150, and 90 for the previous 3 months is calculated as follows:

$$F_{April} = \frac{120 + 150 + 90}{3}$$

$$= 120.$$

To partially overcome these deficiencies, weighted moving averages have been introduced as refinements. The weight places more emphasis on recent observations. Exponential smoothing is a form of weighted moving average. **Exponential smoothing** bases the estimate of future sales on the weighted average of the previous demand and forecast levels. The new forecast is a function of the old forecast incremented by some fraction of the differential between the old forecast and actual sales realized. The increment of adjustment is called the **alpha factor.** The basic format of the model is

$$F_t = D_{t-1} + (1 -)F_{t-1}$$

where

F_t = forecasted sales for a time period t

F_{t-1} = forecast for time period $t - 1$

D_{t-1} = actual demand for time period $t - 1$

α = alpha factor or smoothing constant ($0 \le \alpha \le 1.0$)

To illustrate, assume that the forecasts for the most recent time period were 100 and actual sales experience was 110 units. Further, assume that the alpha factor being employed is 0.2. Then, by substitution,

$$F_t = \alpha D_{t-1} + (1 - \alpha)F_{t-1}$$

$$= (0.2)(110) + (1 - 0.2)(100)$$

$$= 22 + 80$$

$$= 102$$

So the forecast for period t is for product sales of 102 units.

The prime advantage of exponential smoothing is that it permits a rapid calculation of a new forecast without substantial historical records and updating. Thus, exponential smoothing is highly adaptable to computerized forecasting. Depending on the value of the smoothing constant, it is also possible to monitor and change technique sensitivity.

The major decision when using exponential smoothing is selecting the alpha factor. If a factor of 1 is employed, the net effect is to use the most recent period's sales as the forecast for next period. A very low value, such as .01, has the net effect of reducing the forecast to almost a simple moving average. Large alpha factors make the forecast very sensitive to change and therefore highly reactive. Low alpha factors tend to react slowly to change and therefore minimize response to random fluctuations. However, the technique cannot tell the difference between seasonality and random fluctuation. Thus, exponential smoothing does not eliminate the need for judgment. In selecting the value of the alpha factor, the forecaster is faced with a trade-off between eliminating random fluctuations or having the forecast fully respond to demand changes.

Extended exponential smoothing incorporates the influence of trend and seasonality when specific values for these components can be identified. The extended smoothing calculation is similar to that of the basic smoothing model except that there are three components and three smoothing constants to represent the base, trend, and seasonal components.

Like basic exponential smoothing, extended smoothing allows rapid calculation of new forecasts with minimal data. The technique's ability to respond depends on the smoothing constant values. Higher smoothing constant values provide quick responsiveness but may lead to overreaction and forecast accuracy problems.

Adaptive smoothing provides a regular review of alpha factor validity. The alpha value is reviewed at the conclusion of each forecast period to determine the exact value that would have resulted in a perfect forecast for the previous period. Once determined, the alpha factor used to generate the subsequent forecast is adjusted to a value that would have produced a perfect forecast. Thus, managerial judgment is partially replaced by a systematic and consistent method of updating alpha. Most forecast software packages include the capability to systematically evaluate alternative smoothing constants to identify the one that would have given the best performance in the most recent time periods.

More sophisticated forms of adaptive smoothing include an automatic tracking signal to monitor error. When the signal is tripped because of excessive error, the constant is automatically increased to make the forecast more responsive to smoothing recent periods. If the recent-period sales demonstrate substantial change, increased responsiveness should decrease forecast error. As the forecast error is reduced, the tracking signal automatically returns the smoothing constant to its original value. While adaptive techniques are designed to systematically adjust for error, their weakness is that they sometimes overreact by interpreting random error as trend or seasonality. This misinterpretation leads to increased errors in the future.

Causal

Forecasting by regression estimates sales for an SKU on the basis of values of other independent factors. If a good relationship can be identified, such as between expected price and consumption, the information can be used to effectively predict requirements. Causal or regression forecasting works well when a leading variable such as price can be identified. However, such situations are not particularly common for supply chain applications. If the SKU forecast is based upon a single factor, it is referred to as **simple regression.** The use of more than one forecast factor is **multiple regression.** Regression forecasts use the correlation between a leading or predictable event and the dependent demand SKU's sales. No cause/effect relationship need exist between the product's sale and the independent event if a high degree of correlation is consistently present. A correlation assumes that the forecasted sales are preceded by some leading independent factor such as the sale of a related product. However, the most reliable use of regression forecasting of sales is based on a cause/effect relationship. Since regression can effectively consider external factors and events, causal techniques are more appropriate for long-term or aggregate forecasting. For example, causal techniques are commonly used to generate annual or national sales forecasts. From the preceding discussion, it should be clear that forecasting software offers a wide range of capabilities in terms of both techniques and sophistication. Table 6.3 provides a summary of applications and limitations of available forecast techniques.

Forecasting Accuracy

Forecast accuracy refers to the difference between forecasts and corresponding actual sales. Forecast accuracy improvement requires error measurement and analysis. While forecast error can be defined generally as the difference between actual demand and

TABLE 6.3
Forecast Technique Summary

Source: Reprinted with permission from David J. Closs, *Forecasting and Its Use in Logistics,* Council of Supply Chain Management Professionals, Oak Brook, IL.

Forecast Technique	Description	Application	Limitations
Moving average	An unweighted average of the previous periods of sales	Useful when there are only base and irregular demand components	Not useful when there is significant seasonality or trend
Exponential smoothing	An exponentially weighted moving average using smoothing constants to place greater weights on more recent demands	Useful when necessary to maintain data and generate forecasts for a large number of items that incorporate individual trend and seasonality components	Not as useful when there are other factors influencing demand, such as promotions, price changes, or competitive actions not regularly scheduled
Time series	Uses time period as the independent variable to predict future demand patterns	Useful when demand patterns repeat with some cyclic, seasonal, or trend components	Not particularly responsive to change, as it takes numerous periods for the model to identify changes in patterns and for the forecast to respond to the pattern changes; also requires judgment in selecting variables that should be included
Regression	Uses other independent variables, such as price, promotion plans, or related product volumes, to predict sales	Useful when there's a strong linear or nonlinear relationship between independent variables and demand	Not particularly responsive to change, as it takes numerous periods for the model to identify changes in patterns and for the forecasts to respond to the pattern changes; also requires judgment in selecting which variables should be included
Multivariate	Uses more complex statistical techniques to identify more complex demand history relationships; techniques include spectral analysis, Fourier analysis, transfer functions, and neural networks	Useful when there's a complex, generally nonlinear relationship between historical patterns and demand. The analyses identify and evaluate alternative sets of parameters to determine the best fit and use it to predict future demand. These techniques are often more useful for predicting macro forecasts, such as energy consumption, economic growth, or aggregate transportation.	While there are quantitative factors for selecting the best model, there is often substantial judgment involved as well, so these techniques are often nonsuited for detailed item–location –time period forecasts.

TABLE 6.4
Monthly Personal Computer Demand and Forecast

(1) Month	(2) Demand	(3) Forecast	(4) Error	(5) Absolute Error
January	100	110	−10	10
February	110	90	20	20
March	90	90	0	0
April	130	120	10	10
May	70	90	−20	20
June	110	120	−10	10
July	120	120	0	0
August	90	110	−20	20
September	120	70	50	50
October	90	130	−40	40
November	80	90	−10	10
December	90	100	−10	10
Sum	1200	1240	−40	200
Mean	100	103.3	−3.3	16.7 [a]
Percent (error/mean)				17.1% [b]

a = Mean absolute deviation (MAD).
b = Mean of (Monthly forecast error/monthly demand).

forecast, a more precise definition is needed for calculation and comparison. Table 6.4 provides monthly unit demand and forecast for a specific personal computer model at a regional distribution center. This example illustrates alternative forecast error measures.

One approach for error measurement is to sum up the errors over time, as illustrated in column 4. With this approach, errors are summed over the year and a simple average is calculated. As illustrated, the average error is very near zero even though there are some months with significant error. The concern with this approach is that the positive errors cancel negative errors, masking a significant forecasting problem. To avoid this problem, an alternative approach is to ignore the "sign" and evaluate absolute error. Column 5 illustrates the computation of the absolute error and the resulting Mean Absolute Deviation **(MAD)**. To compare forecasts, error percentages are usually calculated. Mean absolute percentage error **(MAPE)** is calculated by dividing mean absolute error by mean demand.

Another consideration is the measurement level or aggregation. Assuming that individual SKU detail is recorded, forecast error can be calculated for individual SKU location combinations, groups of SKUs or locations, and nationally. Generally, more aggregation results in lower relative forecast errors. For example, Figure 6.6 illustrates comparative forecast errors at the national, brand for groups of SKUs, and SKU location level. The figure illustrates the minimum, maximum, and mean relative forecast error for a sample of firms marketing consumer products. As Figure 6.6 illustrates, while a relative error of 40 percent is average for a SKU/location level of aggregation, it would reflect very poor forecasting if measured at the national level.

Summary

Effective supply chain management requires both cross-functional and cross enterprise planning and collaboration. Successful supply chain planning requires (1) supply chain visibility, (2) simultaneous resource consideration, and (3) joint resource utilization. Successful achievement of all three of these requirements depends on collaboration.

FIGURE 6.6
Comparative
Forecast Errors

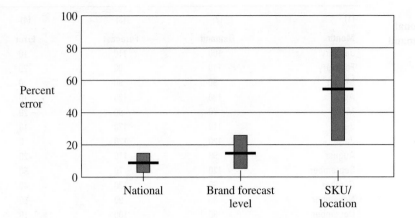

The synchronized execution of demand planning, production planning, and logistics planning is necessary to achieve an integrated overall plan. Most firms have implemented an S&OP process to drive successful integrated planning. To be successful, S&OP requires continuous senior leader attention and guidance. While there is much work and coordination required for successful S&OP, it is important to keep foremost in mind that it is a process and not an individual's or organization's job. It has become common practice for supply chain participants from multiple organizations to jointly develop and implement CPFR processes.

In most supply chains, customer requirements must be anticipated by using forecasts. Forecasts include a number of components with the major ones being level, trend, and seasonality. While these external components are significant, demand variation also results from operational actions such as promotions, price changes, and new product introductions. The forecasting process must incorporate a combination of techniques, support systems, and administration. Forecasting techniques provide a quantitative starting point, the support system refines the data in consideration of changes in the market, and forecast administration provides a management process to guide and monitor the overall effort. There are qualitative and causal forecasting techniques, but most logistics and supply chain forecasts are developed by using time series methods. While there have been some advancements in forecasting techniques and methods, the most substantial forecast improvements have been achieved through the use of collaborative techniques such as CPFR, involving multiple supply chain partners.

Challenge Questions

1. How does improved supply chain visibility improve the planning process?
2. How are demand management and production planning linked to logistics planning?
3. What factors other than transportation are important to logistics planning?
4. In your words, what is the primary goal of the S&OP process?
5. Why is senior leadership ownership essential to successful S&OP?
6. How are CPFR and S&OP related?
7. Identify and discuss the major forecast components. Why is it important to decompose demand into these components when developing new forecasts?

8. Compare and contrast the basic logic differentiator of time series and causal forecast techniques. Under what conditions would each be appropriate?

9. Discuss how error accountability can be a major factor in improving forecast performance.

10. Discuss how a minor change in demand at the retail level can significantly impact supply chain variation at distributors, manufacturers, and suppliers.

PART TWO

Supply Chain Logistics Operations

Part 2 consists of five chapters describing detailed logistics activities and functions. Chapter 7 focuses on inventory management, including the rationale for inventory, costs associated with carrying inventory, procedures for setting and monitoring appropriate inventory levels, and a framework for managing overall inventory resources. Chapter 8 describes the transportation infrastructure, including role, functionality, and principles. The chapter continues with a description of the transportation regulatory environment, characteristics of transportation modes and the range of services provided. Chapter 9 focuses on the more managerial aspects of transportation operations such as economics, pricing, and administration. Together, costs related to inventory and transportation represent a significant majority of total logistics expense. Chapter 10 discusses the economic and service justification for warehousing and the activities required for facility design and operations. Chapter 11 focuses inside the four walls of a warehouse by reviewing packaging and materials handling technologies. The chapter discusses requirements for packaging materials and efficiency followed by a discussion of materials handling equipment capabilities and trade-offs. It is from the integrated performance of individual activities that the power of supply chain logistics is realized.

Inventory

Chapter Outline

Inventory decisions are both high risk and high impact throughout the supply chain. Inventory committed to support future sales drives a number of anticipatory supply chain activities. Without the proper inventory assortment, lost sales and customer dissatisfaction may occur. Likewise, inventory planning is critical to manufacturing. Material or component shortages can shut down manufacturing or force production schedule modification, added cost and potential finished goods shortages. Just as shortages can disrupt marketing and manufacturing plans, inventory overstocks also create operating problems. Overstocks increase cost and reduce profitability as a result of added warehousing, working capital, insurance, taxes, and obsolescence. Management of inventory resources requires an understanding of functionality, principles, cost, impact, and dynamics.

Inventory Functionality and Definitions

Inventory management involves risk which varies depending upon a firm's position in the distribution channel. The typical measures of inventory exposure are time duration, depth, and width of commitment.

For a manufacturer, inventory risk is long-term. The manufacturer's inventory commitment begins with raw material and component parts purchase, includes work-in-process, and ends with finished goods. In addition, finished goods are often positioned in warehouses in anticipation of customer demand. In some situations, manufacturers are required to consign inventory to customer facilities. In effect, this practice shifts all inventory risk to the manufacturer. Although a manufacturer typically has a narrower product line than a retailer or wholesaler, the manufacturer's inventory commitment is deep and of long duration.

A wholesaler purchases large quantities from manufacturers and sells smaller quantities to retailers. The economic justification of a wholesaler is the capability to provide customers an assortment of merchandise from different manufacturers in specific quantities. When products are seasonal, the wholesaler may be required to take an inventory position far in advance of the selling season, thus increasing depth and duration of risk. One of the greatest challenges of wholesaling is product-line expansion to the point where the width of inventory risk approaches that of the retailer while depth and duration of risk remain characteristic of traditional wholesaling. In recent years, powerful retailers have driven a substantial increase in depth and duration by shifting inventory responsibility back to wholesalers.

For a retailer, inventory management is about the velocity of buying and selling. Retailers purchase a wide variety of products and assume substantial risk in the marketing process. Retail inventory risk can be viewed as wide but not deep. Because of the high cost of store location, retailers place prime emphasis on inventory turnover. Inventory turnover is a measure of inventory velocity and is calculated as the ratio of sales for a time period divided by average inventory.

Although retailers assume a position of risk on a wide variety of products, their position on any one product is not deep. Risk is spread across more than 30,000 stockkeeping units (SKUs) in a typical supermarket. A mass retailer offering general merchandise and food often exceeds 50,000 SKUs. Faced with this width of inventory, retailers attempt to reduce risk by pressing manufacturers and wholesalers to assume greater and greater inventory responsibility. Pushing inventory back up the channel has resulted in retailer demand for fast delivery of mixed-product shipments from wholesalers and manufacturers. Specialty retailers, in contrast to mass merchandisers, normally experience less width of inventory risk as a result of handling narrower assortments. However, they must assume greater risk with respect to depth and duration of inventory holding.

If a business plans to operate at more than one level of the distribution channel, it must be prepared to assume the associated inventory risk. For example, a food chain that operates a regional warehouse assumes risk related to wholesale functionality over and above normal retail operations. To the extent that an enterprise becomes vertically integrated, inventory must be managed at multiple supply chain levels.

Inventory Functionality

From an inventory perspective, the ideal situation would be a response-based supply chain. At various points in early chapters, the practicality of implementing a fully response-based supply chain was discussed in terms of the total costs and timeliness of customer support. While a zero-inventory supply chain is typically not attainable, it is important to remember that each dollar invested in inventory is a trade-off to an alternative use of assets.

Inventory is a current asset that should provide return on the capital invested. The return on inventory investments is the marginal profit on sales that would not occur without inventory. Accounting experts have long recognized that measuring the true cost and benefits of inventory on the corporate profit-and-loss is difficult.[1] Lack of measurement sophistication makes it difficult to evaluate the trade-offs between service levels, operating efficiencies, and inventory levels. While aggregate inventory levels throughout sectors of the economy have decreased, many enterprises still carry more inventory than needed to support actual business requirements. The forces driving this generalization are understood better through a review of the four prime functions of inventory. Table 7.1 summarizes inventory functionality.

These four functions, **geographical specialization, decoupling, balancing supply and demand, and buffering uncertainty,** require inventory investment to achieve operating objectives. While logistics, as discussed in Chapter 2, has made significant progress in reducing overall supply chain inventory, inventory properly deployed creates value and reduces total cost. Given a specific manufacturing/marketing strategy, inventories planned and committed to operations can only be reduced to a level consistent with performing the four inventory functions. All inventory exceeding the minimum level represents excess commitments.

At the minimum level, inventory invested to achieve geographical specialization and decoupling can be modified only by changes in network facility location and operational processes of the enterprise. The minimum level of inventory required to balance supply and demand depends on ability to estimate seasonal requirements. With increased experience over a number of seasonal periods, the inventory required to achieve marginal sales during periods of high demand can be projected fairly well. A seasonal inventory plan can be formulated on the basis of this experience.

[1] Douglas M. Lambert, *The Development of an Inventory Costing Methodology* (Chicago: National Council of Physical Distribution Management, 1976), p. 3; and *Inventory Carrying Cost, Memorandum 611* (Chicago: Drake Sheahan/Stewart Dougall, Inc., 1974).

TABLE 7.1
Inventory
Functionality

Geographical Specialization	Allows geographical positioning across multiple manufacturing and distributive units of an enterprise. Inventory maintained at different locations and stages of the value-creation process allows specialization.
Decoupling	Allows economy of scale within a single facility and permits each process to operate at maximum efficiency rather than having the speed of the entire process constrained by the slowest.
Supply/Demand Balancing	Accommodates elapsed time between inventory availability (manufacturing, growing, or extraction) and consumption.
Buffering Uncertainty	Accommodates uncertainty related to demand in excess of forecast or unexpected delays in order receipt and order processing in delivery and is typically referred to as safety stock.

Inventories committed to safety stocks represent the greatest potential for improved logistical performance. These commitments are operational in nature and can be adjusted rapidly in the event of an error or policy change. A variety of techniques are available to assist management in planning safety stock commitments. The focus of this chapter is the analysis of safety stock relationships and inventory policy development.

Inventory Definitions

In designing inventory policy, specific inventory relationships must be considered. Management must understand these relationships to determine inventory policy with respect to when and how much to order. The inventory policy drives desired inventory performance. The two key indicators of inventory performance are **service level** and **average inventory.**

Inventory Policy

Inventory policy consists of guidelines concerning what to purchase or manufacture, when to take action, and in what quantity. It also includes decisions regarding geographical inventory positioning. For example, some firms may decide to postpone inventory positioning by maintaining stock at the plant. Other firms may use a more speculative strategy of positioning product in local markets or regional warehouses. The development of sound inventory policy is the most difficult dimension of inventory management.

A second aspect of policy concerns inventory management practice. One approach is to independently manage inventory at each stocking facility. At the other extreme is central inventory management of all stocking locations. Centralized inventory management requires effective communication and coordination. The increased availability of information technology and integrated planning systems allows more firms to implement centralized inventory planning. Centralized inventory planning systems can reduce demand uncertainty between distribution locations.

Service Level

Service level is a performance target specified by management. It defines inventory performance objectives. Service level is often measured in terms of an order cycle time, case fill rate, line fill rate, order fill rate, or any combination of these. The **performance cycle** is the elapsed time between the release of a purchase order by a buyer to the receipt of shipment. A **case fill rate** is the percent of cases or units ordered that are shipped as requested. For example, a 95 percent case fill rate indicates that, on average, 95 cases out of 100 are filled from available stock. The remaining five cases are back-ordered or deleted. The **line fill rate** is the percent of order lines filled completely. **Order fill** is the percent of customer orders filled completely.

Inventory management is a major element of supply chain logistics strategy that must be integrated to achieve overall service objectives. While one strategy to achieve a high service level is to increase inventory, an alternative approach may be the use of faster or more reliable transportation and collaboration with customers and service providers to reduce uncertainty.

Average Inventory

The materials, components, work-in-process, and finished product typically stocked in the logistical system are referred to as **inventory** and the typical amount across time is referred to as **average inventory.** From a policy viewpoint, target inventory levels must be planned for each facility. Figure 7.1 illustrates the performance cycles for one item at one location. At the maximum, the facility has in stock during the normal performance cycle $70,000 and a minimum of $30,000. The difference between these two levels, $40,000 ($70,000 − $30,000), is the order quantity, resulting in a cycle inventory of $20,000. Cycle inventory or base stock

FIGURE 7.1
Inventory Cycle for Typical Product

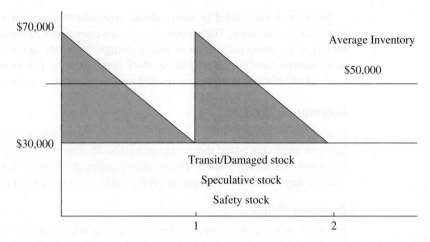

is the portion of average inventory that results from replenishment. Stock level is at a maximum following stock receipt from the supplier. Customers deplete inventory until the stock level reaches its minimum. Prior to the stock level reaching the minimum, a replenishment order is initiated so that inventory will arrive before an out-of-stock occurs. The replenishment order must be initiated when the available inventory is less than or equal to forecasted demand during the performance cycle time. The amount ordered for replenishment is termed the **order quantity.** Given this basic order formulation, average cycle inventory or base stock equals one-half order quantity.

The **transit inventory** represents the amount typically in transit between facilities or on order but not received. The **obsolete inventory** is the stock that is out-of-date or that has not experienced recent demand. Eventually, it is donated, destroyed, or sold at a loss. **Speculative inventory** is bought prior to need to hedge a currency exchange or to take advantage of a discount.

The remainder of inventory in the typical logistics system is **safety stock.** Safety stock is maintained in a logistical system to protect against demand and performance cycle uncertainty. Safety stock is used only near the end of replenishment cycles when uncertainty has caused higher-than-expected demand or longer-than-expected performance cycle times. Thus, typical average inventory is **one-half order quantity plus safety stock and in-transit stock.**

Average Inventory across Multiple Performance Cycles

In initial policy formulation, it is necessary to determine how much inventory to order at a specified time. To illustrate, assume the replenishment performance cycle is a constant 10 days and daily sales rate is 10 units per day. Also assume the order quantity is 200 units.

Figure 7.2 illustrates this relationship. This type of chart is referred to as a **sawtooth diagram** because of the series of right triangles. Since complete certainty exists with

FIGURE 7.2
Inventory Relationship for Constant Sales and Performance Cycle

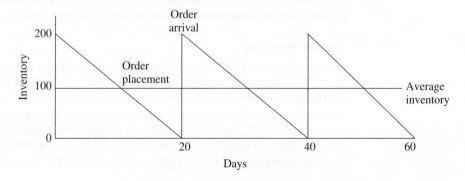

respect to usage and performance cycle, orders are scheduled to arrive just as the last unit is sold. Thus, no safety stock is necessary. Since the rate of sale in the example is 10 units per day and it takes 10 days to complete inventory replenishment, a sound reorder policy might be to order 200 units every 20 days. Given these conditions, common terminology related to policy formulation can be specified.

First, the **reorder point** is specified as 100 units on hand. The reorder point defines when a replenishment order is initiated. In this example, whenever the quantity on hand drops below 100, an additional order for 200 units is placed. The result of this policy is that daily inventory level ranges from a maximum of 200 to a minimum of zero over the performance cycle.

Second, average inventory is 100 units, since stock on hand exceeds 100 units one-half of the time, or for 10 days, and is less than 100 units one-half of the time. In fact, average inventory is equal to one-half the 200-unit order quantity.

Third, assuming a work year of 240 days, 12 purchases will be required during the year. Therefore, over a period of 1 year, 200 units will be purchased 12 times for a total of 2400 units. Sales are expected to equal 10 units per/day over 240 days for a total of 2400 units. As discussed above, average inventory is 100 units. Thus, **inventory turns** will be 24 (2400 total sales/100 units of average inventory).

In time, the sheer boredom of such routine operations would lead management to ask some questions concerning the arrangement. What would happen if orders were placed more frequently than once every 20 days? Why not order 100 units every 10 days? Why order as frequently as every 20 days? Why not reorder 600 units once every 60 days? Assuming that the inventory performance cycle remains a constant 10 days, what would be the impact of each of these alternative ordering policies on reorder point, average base inventory, and inventory turnover?

The policy of ordering a smaller volume of 100 units every 10 days means that two orders would always be outstanding. Thus, the reorder point would remain 100 units on hand or on order to service average daily sales of 10 units over the 20-day inventory cycle. However, average inventory on hand would drop to 50 units, and inventory turnover would increase to 48 times per year. The policy of ordering 600 units every 60 days would result in an average base inventory of 300 units and a turnover of approximately eight times per year. These alternative ordering policies are illustrated in Figure 7.3.

The figure illustrates that average inventory is a function of the reorder quantity. Smaller replenishment order quantities do result in lower average inventory, but there are other factors such as performance cycle uncertainty, purchasing discounts, and transportation economies that are important when determining order quantity.

FIGURE 7.3   **Alternative Order Quantity and Average Inventory**

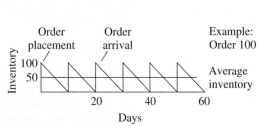

An exact order quantity policy can be determined by balancing the cost of ordering and the cost of maintaining average inventory. The **Economic Order Quantity (EOQ)** model provides a specific quantity balancing of these two critical cost components. By determining the EOQ and dividing it into annual demand, the frequency and size of replenishment orders minimizing the total cost of cycle inventory are identified. Prior to reviewing EOQ, it is necessary to identify costs typically associated with ordering and maintaining inventory.

Inventory Carrying Cost

Inventory carrying cost is the expense associated with maintaining inventory. Inventory expense is calculated by multiplying annual inventory carrying cost percent by average inventory value. Standard accounting practice is to value inventory at purchase or standard manufacturing cost rather than at selling price.

Assuming an annual inventory carrying cost percentage of 20 percent, the annual inventory expense for an enterprise with $1 million in average inventory would be $200,000 (20% × $1,000,000). While the calculation of inventory carrying expense is basic, determining the appropriate carrying cost percent is less obvious.

Determining carrying cost percent requires assignment of inventory-related costs. Financial accounts relevant to inventory carrying cost percent are capital, insurance, obsolescence, storage, and taxes. While cost of capital is typically based on managerial policy, expense-related taxes, insurance, obsolescence, and storage varies depending on the specific attributes of individual products.

Capital

The appropriate charge to place on capital invested in inventory varies widely. Capital assessments range from the prime interest rate to a higher managerially determined percent. The logic for using the prime interest rate or a specified rate pegged to the prime rate is that cash to replace capital invested in inventory can be obtained in the money markets at that rate. Higher managerially specified capital costs are based on expected or target return on investment for capital deployed. Such target rates are typically termed **hurdle** rates.

The cost of capital may vary significantly by firm and industry. Firms that are aggressive in uses of cash will typically employ a higher cost of capital percentage. Similarly, industries with high value or short life cycle product will employ a higher cost of capital to drive lower inventories.

Confusion often results from the fact that senior management frequently does not establish a clear-cut capital cost policy. For supply chain logistics planning, the cost of capital must be clearly specified since it has significant impact on system design and performance.

Taxes

Local taxing authorities in many areas assess taxes on inventory held in warehouses. The tax rate and means of assessment vary by location. The tax expense is usually a direct levy based on inventory level on a specific day of the year or average inventory level over a period of time.

Insurance

Insurance cost is an expense based upon estimated risk or loss over time. Loss risk depends on the product and the facility storing the product. For example, high-value products that are easily stolen and hazardous products result in high insurance cost. Insurance cost is also influenced by facility characteristics such as security cameras and sprinkler systems that might help reduce risk. Since September 11, 2001, issues related to terrorist risk have become of greater concern in supply chain design.

Obsolescence

Obsolescence cost results from deterioration of product during storage. A prime example of obsolescence is product that ages beyond recommended sell-by date, such as food and pharmaceuticals. Obsolescence also includes financial loss when a product no longer has fashion appeal or no longer has any demand. Obsolescence costs are typically estimated on the basis of past experience concerning markdowns, donations, or quantity destroyed. This expense is the percent of average inventory value declared obsolete each year.

Storage

Storage cost is facility expense related to product holding rather than product handling. Storage cost must be allocated on the requirements of specific products since it is not related directly to inventory value. In public or contract warehouses, storage charges are billed on an individual basis. The cost of total annual occupancy for a given product can then be assigned by multiplying the average daily physical space occupied by the standard cost factor for a specified time. This figure can then be divided by the total number of units of merchandise processed through the facility to determine average storage cost per merchandise unit.

Table 7.2 illustrates the components of annual inventory carrying cost and typical range of component costs. It should be clear that the final carrying cost percent used by a firm is a matter of managerial policy. Decisions regarding inventory cost are important because they trade off against other logistics cost components in system design and operating decisions.

Planning Inventory

Inventory planning consists of determining when and how much to order. When to order is determined by average and variation in demand and replenishment. How much to order is determined by the order quantity. Inventory control is the process of monitoring inventory status.

When to Order

As discussed earlier, the reorder point defines when a replenishment shipment should be initiated. A reorder point can be specified in terms of units or days' supply. This discussion focuses on determining reorder points under conditions of demand and performance cycle certainty.

TABLE 7.2
Inventory Carrying Cost Components

Element	Average Percent	Percent Ranges
Cost of capital	10.00%	4–40%
Taxes	1.00	.5–2
Insurance	.05	0–2
Obsolescence	1.20	.5–2
Storage	2.00	0–4
Totals	14.25%	5–50%

The basic reorder point formula is:

$$R = D \times T,$$

where

R = Reorder point in units;

D = Average daily demand in units; and

T = Average performance cycle length in days.

To illustrate this calculation, assume demand of 20 units/day and a 10-day performance cycle. In this case,

$$R = D \times T$$
$$= 20 \text{ units/day} \times 10 \text{ days}$$
$$= 200 \text{ units.}$$

An alternative form is to define reorder point in terms of days of supply. For the above example, the days of supply reorder point is 10 days.

The use of reorder point formulations implies that the replenishment shipment will arrive as scheduled. When uncertainty exists in either demand or performance cycle length, safety stock is required. When safety stock is necessary to accommodate uncertainty, the reorder point formula is:

$$R = D \times T + SS,$$

where

R = Reorder point in units;

D = Average daily demand in units;

T = Average performance cycle length in days; and

SS = Safety stock in units.

Computation of safety stock under conditions of uncertainty is discussed later in this chapter.

How Much to Order

Lot sizing balances inventory carrying cost with the cost of ordering. The key to understanding the relationship is to remember that average inventory is equal to one-half the order quantity. Therefore, the greater the order quantity, the larger the average inventory and, consequently, the greater the annual carrying cost. However, the larger the order quantity, the fewer orders required per planning period and, consequently, the lower the total ordering cost. Lot quantity formulations identify the precise quantities at which the annual combined total inventory carrying and ordering cost is lowest for a given sales volume. Figure 7.4 illustrates the relationships. The point at which the sum of ordering and carrying cost is minimized represents the lowest total cost. The objective is to identify the ordering quantity that minimizes the total inventory carrying and ordering cost.

Economic Order Quantity

The EOQ is the replenishment practice that minimizes the combined inventory carrying and ordering cost. Identification of such a quantity assumes that demand and costs are relatively stable throughout the year. Since EOQ is calculated on an individual product basis, the basic formulation does not consider the impact of joint ordering of multiple products.

FIGURE 7.4
Economic Order Quantity

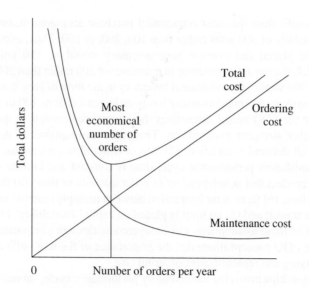

The most efficient method for calculating EOQ is mathematical. Earlier in this chapter a policy dilemma regarding whether to order 100, 200, or 600 units was presented. The answer can be found by calculating the applicable EOQ for the situation. Table 7.3 contains the necessary information.

To make the appropriate calculations, the standard formulation for EOQ is:

$$EOQ = \sqrt{\frac{2C_oD}{C_iU}}$$

where

EOQ = Economic order quantity;

C_o = Cost per order;

C_i = Annual inventory carrying cost;

D = Annual sales volume, units; and

U = Cost per unit.

Substituting from Table 7.3,

$$EOQ = \sqrt{\frac{2 \times 19 \times 2400}{0.20 \times 5.00}}$$
$$= \sqrt{91,200}$$
$$= 302 \text{ (round to 300)}.$$

Total ordering cost would amount to $152 (2400/300 × $19.00), and inventory carrying cost to $150 [300/2 × (5 × 0.20)]. Thus, rounding to allow ordering in multiples of 100 units, annual reordering, and inventory carrying cost have been equated.

TABLE 7.3
Factors for Determining EOQ

Annual demand volume	2400 units
Unit value at cost	$5.00
Inventory carrying cost percent	20% annually
Ordering cost	$19.00 per order

To benefit from the most economical purchase arrangement, orders should be placed in the quantity of 300 units rather than 100, 200, or 600. Thus, over the year, eight orders would be placed and average base inventory would be 150 units. Referring back to Figure 7.4, the impact of ordering in quantities of 300 rather than 200 can be identified. An EOQ of 300 implies that additional inventory in the form of base stock has been introduced into the system. Average inventory has been increased from 100 to 150 units on hand.

While the EOQ model determines the optimal replenishment quantity, it does require some rather stringent assumptions. The major assumptions of the simple EOQ model are: (1) all demand is satisfied; (2) rate of demand is continuous, constant, and known; (3) replenishment performance cycle time is constant and known; (4) there is a constant price of product that is independent of order quantity or time; (5) there is an infinite planning horizon; (6) there is no interaction between multiple items of inventory; (7) no inventory is in transit; and (8) no limit is placed on capital availability. The constraints imposed by some of these assumptions can be overcome through computational extensions; however, the EOQ concept illustrates the importance of the trade-offs associated with inventory carrying and replenishment ordering cost.

Relationships involving the inventory performance cycle, inventory cost, and economic order formulations are useful for guiding inventory planning. First, the EOQ is found at the point where annualized order placement cost and inventory carrying cost are equal. Second, average base inventory equals one-half order quantity. Third, the value of the inventory unit, all other things being equal, will have a direct relationship with replenishment order frequency. In effect, the higher the product value, the more frequently it will be ordered.

While the EOQ formulation is relatively straightforward, there are other factors that must be considered in actual application. These factors refer to various adjustments necessary to take advantage of special purchase situations and unitization characteristics. Three typical adjustments are volume transportation rates, quantity discounts, and other EOQ adjustments.

Volume Transportation Rates

In the EOQ formulation, no consideration was given to the impact of transportation cost upon order quantity. Regardless of whether product is sold on a delivered basis or ownership is transferred at origin, the cost of transportation must be paid by supply chain participants. Collaborative efforts to order in quantities that minimize total cost are essential to sound logistical arrangements.

As a general rule, the greater the weight of an order, the lower the cost per pound of transportation from any origin to destination.[2] A freight-rate discount for larger shipments is common across all transportation modes. Thus, all other things being equal, supply chain arrangements should facilitate quantities that offer maximum transportation economies. Such quantities may be larger than the EOQ purchase quantity. Increasing order size has a twofold impact upon inventory cost. Assume for purposes of illustration that the most desirable transportation rate is obtained when a quantity of 480 is ordered, as compared to the EOQ-recommended order of 300 calculated earlier. The first impact of the larger order is to increase the average base inventory from 150 to 240 units. Thus, ordering in larger quantities increases inventory carrying cost.

The second impact is a decrease in the number of orders required to satisfy annual requirements. Decreased number of orders increases the shipment size, facilitating lower per-unit transportation cost.

To complete the analysis it is necessary to formulate the total cost with and without transportation savings. While this calculation can be directly made by modification of the EOQ formulation, direct comparison provides a more insightful answer. The only additional data

---

[2] To determine transportation rates, the unit quantity must be converted to weight.

TABLE 7.4
EOQ Data
Requirements for
Consideration of
Transportation
Economies

Annual demand volume	2400 units
Unit value at cost	$5.00
Inventory carrying cost percentage	20% annually
Ordering cost	$19.00 per order
Small shipment rate	$1.00 per unit
Large shipment rate	$0.75 per unit

required are the applicable freight rate for ordering in quantities of 300 and 480. Table 7.4 provides the data necessary to complete the analysis.

Table 7.5 illustrates total cost analysis. Reducing total annual cost by purchasing 480 units five times per year rather than the original EOQ solution of 300 units eight times per year results in approximately a $570 savings.

The impact of volume transportation rates upon total cost of procurement cannot be neglected. In the example above, the equivalent rate per unit dropped from $1 to $0.75, or by 25 percent. Thus, any EOQ must be tested for transportation cost sensitivity across a range of weight breaks.

Another point illustrated in the data in Table 7.5 is the fact that rather substantial changes in the size of an order and the number of orders placed per year result in only a modest change in the total ordering and inventory carrying cost. The EOQ quantity of 300 had a total annual cost of $302, whereas the revised order quantity had a comparative cost of $335.

EOQ formulations are much more sensitive to significant changes in order cycle or frequency. Likewise, substantial changes in cost factors are necessary to significantly change the economic order quantity.

Finally, two factors regarding inventory cost under conditions of origin purchase are noteworthy. FOB (Free On Board) origin purchase means that the buyer is responsible for freight cost and risk while the product is in transit. It follows that any change in weight break leading to a shipment method with a different transit time should be considered, using the added cost or savings as appropriate in a total cost analysis.

Second, the transportation cost must be added to the purchase price to determine the value of goods tied up in inventory. Once the inventory has been received, the cost of the product must be increased to reflect the inbound transportation.[3]

Quantity Discounts

Purchase quantity discounts represent an EOQ extension analogous to volume transportation rates. Table 7.6 illustrates a sample schedule of discounts. Quantity discounts can be handled directly with the basic EOQ formulation by calculating total cost at any given volume-related purchase price, as in the process used in calculating transportation rate impact, to determine associated EOQs. If the discount at any associated quantity is sufficient to offset the added inventory carrying cost less the reduced cost of ordering, then the quantity discount is a viable choice. It should be noted that quantity discounts and volume

[3] Pricing is discussed in greater detail in Chapter 9.

TABLE 7.5
Volume
Transportation Rate
Modified EOQ

	Alternative 1: $EOQ_1 = 300$	Alternative 2: $EOQ_2 = 480$
Inventory Carrying Cost	$150	$240
Ordering Cost	$152	$95
Transportation Cost	$2,400	$1,800
Total Cost	$2,702	$2,135

TABLE 7.6
Example of Quantity Discounts

Cost	Quantity Purchased
$5.00	1–99
4.50	100–200
4.00	201–300
3.50	301–400
3.00	401–500

transportation rates each drive larger purchase quantities. This does not necessarily mean that the lowest total cost purchase will always be a larger quantity than would otherwise be the case under basic EOQ.

Other EOQ Adjustments

A variety of other special situations may justify adjustments to the basic EOQ. Examples are (1) production lot size, (2) multiple-item purchase, (3) limited capital, (4) dedicated trucking, and (5) unitization. Production lot size refers to the most economical quantities from a manufacturing perspective. Multiple-item purchase refers to situations when more than one product are bought concurrently, so quantity and transportation discounts must consider the impact of product combinations. Limited capital describes situations with budget limitations for total inventory investment. Since the multiple product order must be made within the budget limitations, order quantities must recognize the need to allocate the inventory investment across the product line. Dedicated trucking can influence order quantity since the truck has a fixed cost consideration.[4] Once it is decided to use a dedicated fleet to transport replenishment product, the enterprise should try to purchase in quantities that fully use available capacity. Back haul capacity availability may justify purchasing products earlier than otherwise determined by EOQ considerations.

Another consideration when determining replenishment order quantity is unitization. Many products are stored and moved in standard units such as cases or pallets. Since these standardized units are often designed to fit transportation vehicles, there may be significant diseconomies when the EOQ does not reflect standard units. As an example, suppose that a full pallet quantity is 200 units of a specified product. Using an EOQ of 300 units would require shipments of 1.5 pallets. From a handling or transportation utilization perspective, it is probably more effective to order either one or two pallets alternately or permanently.

Managing Uncertainty

To understand basic principles, it is useful to understand inventory relationships under conditions of certainty. Formulation of inventory policy must consider uncertainty. Two types of uncertainty directly impact inventory policy. **Demand uncertainty** is rate of sale during inventory replenishment. **Performance cycle uncertainty** involves inventory replenishment time variation.

Demand Uncertainty

Sales forecasting estimates unit demand during the inventory replenishment cycle. Even with good forecasting, demand during replenishment cycle typically exceeds or falls short of what is planned. To protect against a stockout when demand exceeds forecast, safety

---

[4] See Chapter 9. In such situations, the cost of money invested in inventory should be appropriately charged when the goods are paid for at the origin.

FIGURE 7.5
Inventory
Relationship,
Demand Uncertainty,
and Constant
Performance Cycle

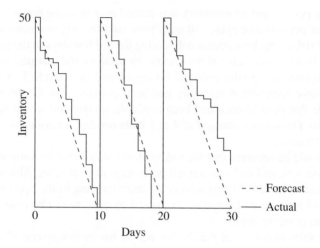

stock is added to base inventory. Under conditions of demand uncertainty, average inventory represents one-half order quantity plus safety stock. Figure 7.5 illustrates the inventory performance cycle under conditions of demand uncertainty. The dashed line represents the forecast. The solid line illustrates inventory on hand across multiple performance cycles. The task of planning safety stock requires three steps. First, the likelihood of stockout must be gauged. Second, demand during a stockout period must be estimated. Finally, a policy decision is required concerning the desired level of stockout protection.

Assume for purposes of illustration that the inventory performance cycle is 10 days. History indicates daily sales range from 0 to 10 units with average daily sales of 5 units. The economic order is assumed to be 50, the reorder point is 50, the planned average inventory is 25, and sales during the performance cycle are forecasted to be 50 units.

During the first cycle, although daily demand experienced variation, the average of 5 units per day was maintained. Total demand during cycle 1 was 50 units, as expected. During cycle 2, demand totaled 50 units in the first 8 days, resulting in a stockout. Thus, no sales were possible on days 9 and 10. During cycle 3, demand reached a total of 39 units. The third performance cycle ended with 11 units remaining in stock. Over the 30-day period total sales were 139 units, for average daily sale of 4.6 units.

From the history recorded in Table 7.7, it is observed that stockouts occurred on 2 of 30 total days. Since sales never exceed 10 units per day, no possibility of stockout exists on the first 5 days of the replenishment cycle. Stockouts were possible on days 6 through 10 on the remote possibility that demand during the first 5 days of the cycle averaged

TABLE 7.7
Typical Demand
Experience during
Three Replenishment
Cycles

Day	Forecast Cycle 1		Stockout Cycle 2		Overstock Cycle 3	
	Demand	**Accumulated**	**Demand**	**Accumulated**	**Demand**	**Accumulated**
1	9	9	0	0	5	5
2	2	11	6	6	5	10
3	1	12	5	11	4	14
4	3	15	7	18	3	17
5	7	22	10	28	4	21
6	5	27	7	35	1	22
7	4	31	6	41	2	24
8	8	39	9	50	8	32
9	6	45	Stockout	50	3	35
10	5	50	Stockout	50	4	39

10 units per day and no inventory was carried over from the previous period. Since during the three performance cycles 10 units were sold on only one occasion, it is apparent that the real risk of stockout occurs only during the last few days of the performance cycle, and then only when sales exceed the average by a substantial margin.[5] Some approximation is possible concerning sales potential for days 9 and 10 of cycle 2. A maximum of 20 units might have been sold if inventory had been available. On the other hand, it is remotely possible that even if stock had been available, no demand would have occurred on days 9 and 10. For average demand of 4 to 5 units per day, a reasonable appraisal of lost sales is 8 to 10 units.

It should be apparent that the risk of stockouts created by variations in sales is limited to a short time and includes a small percentage of total sales. Although the sales analysis presented in Table 7.7 helps achieve an understanding of the opportunity, the appropriate course of action is still not clear. Statistical probability can be used to assist management in planning safety stock.

The sales history over the 30-day period has been aggregated in Table 7.8 as a frequency distribution. The main purpose of a frequency distribution is to observe variations around the average daily demand. Given an expected average of 5 units per day, demand exceeded average on 11 days and was less than average on 12 days. An alternative way of illustrating a frequency distribution is by a bar chart, as in Figure 7.6.

Given the historical frequency of demand, it is possible to calculate the safety stock necessary to provide a specified degree of stockout protection. Probability theory is based on the random chance of a specific occurrence within a large number of occurrences. The situation illustrated uses a 28-day sample. In actual application, a larger sample size would be desirable.

The probability of occurrences assumes a pattern around a measure of central tendency, which is the average value of all occurrences. While a number of frequency distributions can be used in inventory management, the most common is the **normal distribution.**

A normal distribution is characterized by a symmetrical bell-shaped curve, illustrated in Figure 7.7. The essential characteristic of a normal distribution is that the three measures of central tendency have equal value. The **mean** (average) value, the **median** (middle) observation, and the **mode** (most frequently observed) all have the same value. When these three measures are nearly identical, the frequency distribution is **normal.**

[5] In this example, daily statistics are used. An alternative, which is technically more correct from a statistical viewpoint, is to utilize demand over multiple performance cycles. The major limitation of order cycles is the length of time and difficulty required to collect the necessary data

TABLE 7.8
Frequency of Demand

Daily Demand (in units)	Frequency (days)
Stockout	2
0	1
1	2
2	2
3	3
4	4
5	5
6	3
7	3
8	2
9	2
10	1

FIGURE 7.6
Historical Analysis of
Demand History

The basis for predicting demand during a performance cycle using a normal distribution is the **standard deviation** of observations around the three measures of central tendency. The standard deviation is the dispersion of observations within specified areas under the normal curve. For the inventory management application, the observation is unit sales per day and the dispersion is the variation in daily sales. Within 1 standard deviation, 68.27 percent of all events occur. This means that 68.27 percent of the days during a performance cycle will experience daily sales within ± 1 standard deviation of the average daily sales. Within ± 2 standard deviations, 95.45 percent of all observations occur. At ± 3 standard deviations, 99.73 percent of all observations are included. In terms of inventory policy, the standard deviation provides a method of estimating the safety stock required to achieve a specified degree of out-of-stock protection.

The first step in setting safety stock is to calculate the standard deviation. Most calculators and spreadsheets calculate standard deviation, but if one of these aids is not available, another method to compute the standard deviation is:

$$\sigma = \sqrt{\frac{\sum F_i D_i^2}{n}}$$

FIGURE 7.7
Normal Distribution

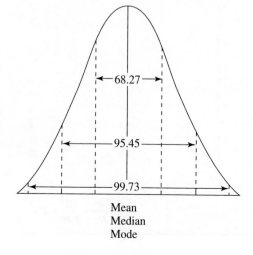

where

σ = Standard deviation;

F_i = Frequency of observation i;

D_i = Deviation of observation from mean for observation i; and

n = Total observations available.

The necessary data to determine standard deviation are contained in Table 7.9.

The standard deviation of the data in Table 7.9 is rounded to 3 units. When setting safety stocks, 2 standard deviations of protection, or 6 units, would protect against 95.45 percent of all observations included in the distribution. However, the only situations of concern in determining safety stock requirements are observations that exceed the mean value. No problem exists concerning inventory to satisfy demand equal to or below the average. Thus, on 50 percent of the days, no safety stock is required. Safety stock protection at the 95 percent level will, in fact, protect against 97.72 percent of all possible observations. The 95 percent coverage will cover all situations when daily demand is ± 2 standard deviations of the average plus the 2.72 percent of the time when demand is more than 2 standard deviations below the mean. This added benefit results from what is typically called a **one-tail** statistical application.

The above example illustrates how statistical probability can assist with the quantification of demand uncertainty, but demand conditions are not the only source of uncertainty. Performance cycles can also vary.

Performance Cycle Uncertainty

Performance cycle uncertainty means operations cannot assume consistent delivery. The planner should expect that actual performance cycle experience will cluster near the expected value and be skewed toward delayed delivery.

Table 7.10 presents a sample frequency distribution across multiple performance cycles. Although 10 days is the most frequent, replenishment experience ranges from 6 to 14 days. If the performance cycle follows a normal distribution, an individual performance cycle would be expected to fall between 8 and 12 days 68.27 percent of the time.

TABLE 7.9
Calculation of Standard Deviation of Daily Demand

Units	Frequency (F)	Deviation from Mean (D_i)	Deviation Squared (D_i^2)	F_iD_i^2
0	1	−5	25	25
1	2	−4	16	32
2	2	−3	9	18
3	3	−2	4	12
4	4	−1	1	4
5	5	0	0	0
6	3	+1	1	3
7	3	+2	4	12
8	2	+3	9	18
9	2	+4	16	32
10	1	+5	25	25
$n = 28$	$\bar{s} = 5$			$\sum F_iD_i^2 = 181$

$$\sigma = \sqrt{\frac{F_iD_i^2}{N}} = \sqrt{\frac{181}{28}} = 2.54$$

TABLE 7.10
Calculation of
Standard Deviation
of Replenishment
Cycle Duration

Performance Cycle (days)	Frequency (F_i)	Deviation from Mean (D_i)	Deviation Squared (D_i^2)	$F_iD_i^2$
6	2	−4	16	32
7	4	−3	9	36
8	6	−2	4	24
9	8	−1	1	8
10	10	0	0	0
11	8	+1	1	8
12	6	+2	4	24
13	4	+3	9	36
14	2	+4	16	32

$$\sum F_iD_i^2 = 200$$

$$N = 50 \quad t = 10$$

$$\sigma = \sqrt{\frac{F_iD_i^2}{N}} = \sqrt{\frac{200}{50}} = \sqrt{4} = 2 \text{ days}$$

From a practical viewpoint, when cycle days drop below 10, there is not any need for safety stock. If the performance cycle were consistently below the planned performance cycle, then adjustment of expected duration would be in order. The situation of most immediate concern occurs when the duration of the performance cycle exceeds 10 days.

From the viewpoint of the probability of exceeding 10 days, the frequency of such occurrences, from the data in Table 7.10, can be restated in terms of performance cycles greater than 10 days and equal to or less than 10 days. In the example data, the standard deviation would not change because the distribution is normal. However, if the actual experience has been skewed in excess of the expected cycle duration, then a **Poisson distribution** may have been more appropriate. In Poisson frequency distributions, the standard deviation is equal to the square root of the mean. As a general rule, the smaller the mean, the greater the degree of skewness.

Safety Stock with Combined Uncertainty

The typical situation confronting the inventory planner is illustrated in Figure 7.8, where both demand and performance cycle uncertainties exist. Planning for both demand and performance cycle uncertainty requires combining two independent variables. The duration of the cycle is, at least in the short run, independent of the daily demand. However, in setting safety stocks, the joint impact of the probability of both demand and performance cycle variation must be determined. Table 7.11 presents a summary of sales and replenishment cycle performance. The key to understanding the potential relationships of the data in Table 7.11 is the 10-day performance cycle. Total demand during the 10 days potentially ranges from 0 to 100 units. On each day of the cycle, the demand probability is independent of the previous day for the entire 10-day duration. Assuming the full range of potential situations illustrated in Table 7.11, total sales during a performance cycle could range from 0 to 140 units. With this basic relationship between the two types of uncertainty in mind, safety stock requirements can be determined by either numerical or convolution procedures.

The **numerical compounding** of two independent variables involves multinominal expansion. This type of procedure requires extensive calculation. A direct method is to

FIGURE 7.8
Combined Demand and Performance Cycle Uncertainty

Duration: *Cycle 1.* 10 days
Cycle 2. 14 days
Cycle 3. 10 days

determine the standard deviations of demand and performance cycle uncertainty and then to approximate the combined standard deviation using the convolution formula:

$$\sigma_c = \sqrt{TS_s^2 + D^2 S_t^2},$$

TABLE 7.11
Frequency Distribution— Demand and Replenishment Uncertainty

Demand Distribution		Replenishment Cycle Distribution	
Daily Sales	**Frequency**	**Days**	**Frequency**
0	1	6	2
1	2	7	4
2	2	8	6
3	3	9	8
4	4	10	10
5	5	11	8
6	3	12	6
7	3	13	4
8	2	14	2
9	2		
10	1		
	$n = 28$	$n = 50$	
	$D = 5$	$T = 10$	
	$S_s = 2.54$	$S_t = 2$	

where

σ_c = Standard deviation of combined probabilities;

T = Average performance cycle time;

S_t = Standard deviation of the performance cycle;

D = Average daily sales; and

S_s = Standard deviation of daily sales.

Substituting from Table 7.11,

$$\sigma_c = \sqrt{10.00(2.54)^2 + (5.00)^2(2)^2}$$
$$= \sqrt{64.52 + 100} = \sqrt{164.52}$$
$$= 12.83 \text{ (round to 13)}.$$

This formulation estimates the convoluted or combined standard deviation of T days with an average demand of D per day when the individual standard deviations are S_t and S_s, respectively. The average for the combined distribution is the product of T and D, or 50.00 (10.00 × 5.00).

Thus, given a frequency distribution of daily sales from 0 to 10 units per day and a range in replenishment cycle duration of 6 to 14 days, 13 units (1 standard deviation multiplied by 13 units) of safety stock is required to protect 84.14 percent of all performance cycles. To protect at the 97.72 percent level, a 26-unit safety stock is necessary. These levels assume a one-tail distribution since it is not necessary to protect against leadtime demand below average.

It is important to note that the specific event being protected against is a stockout during the performance cycle. The 84.14 and 97.72 percent levels are not product availability levels. These percentages reflect the probability of a stockout during a given order cycle. For example, with a 13-unit safety stock, stockouts would be expected to occur during 15.86 (100 − 84.14) percent of the performance cycles. Although this percentage provides the probability of a stockout, it does not estimate magnitude. The relative stockout magnitude indicates the percentage of units stocked out relative to overall demand.

Still assuming the replenishment order quantity of 50 units, average inventory requirements would be 25 units if no safety stock were desired. The average inventory with 2 standard deviations of safety stock is 51 units [25 + (2 × 13)]. This inventory level would protect against a stockout during 97.72 percent of the performance cycles. Table 7.12 summarizes the alternatives confronting the planner in terms of assumptions and corresponding impact on average inventory.

TABLE 7.12

Average Inventory Impact Resulting from Changes in EOQ

	Order Quantity	Safety Stock	Average Inventory
Assume constant S sales and constant T performance cycle	50	0	25
Assume demand protection $+2\sigma$ and constant T performance cycle	50	6	31
Assume constant S demand and $+2\sigma$ performance cycle protection	50	20	45
Assume joint $+2\sigma$ for demand and performance cycle	50	26	51

FIGURE 7.9 **Impact of Order Quantity on Stockout Magnitude**

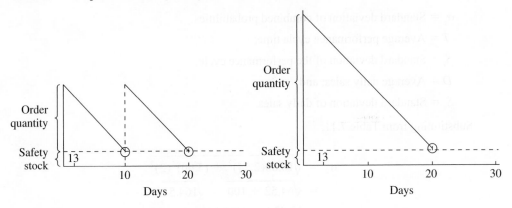

Estimating Fill Rate

The fill rate is the magnitude rather than the probability of a stockout. The case fill rate is the percentage of units that can be filled when requested from available inventory. Figure 7.9 graphically illustrates the difference between stockout probability and stockout magnitude. Both illustrations in Figure 7.9 have a safety stock of 1 standard deviation or 13 units. For both situations, given any performance cycle, the probability of a stockout is 31.73 percent. However, during a 20-day period, the figure illustrates two instances where the stock may be depleted. These instances are at the ends of the cycle. If the order quantity is doubled, the system has the possibility of stocking out only once during the 20-day cycle. So, while both situations face the same demand pattern, the first one has more stockout opportunities and potential. In general, for a given safety stock level, increasing the replenishment order quantity decreases the relative magnitude of potential stockouts and conversely increases customer service availability.

The mathematical formulation of the relationship is:

$$SL = 1 - \frac{f(k)\sigma_c}{Q},$$

where

SL = The stockout magnitude (the product availability level);

$f(k)$ = A function of the normal loss curve which provides the area in a right tail of a normal distribution;

σ_c = The combined standard deviation considering both demand and replenishment cycle uncertainty; and

Q = The replenishment order quantity.

To complete the example, suppose a firm desired 99 percent product availability or case fill rate. Assume the Q was calculated to be 300 units. Table 7.13 summarizes the required information.

TABLE 7.13
Information for Determining Required Safety Stock

Desired Service Level	99%
σ_c	13
Q	300

Since $f(k)$ is the term used to calculate safety stock requirements, the above equation must be solved for $f(k)$ using algebraic manipulation. The result is:

$$f(k) = (1 - SL) \times (Q/\sigma_c).$$

Substituting from Table 7.13,

$$f(k) = (1 - 0.99) \times (300/13)$$
$$= 0.01 \times 23.08 = .2308.$$

The calculated value of $f(k)$ is then compared against the values in Table 7.14 to find the one that most closely approximates the calculated value. For this example, the value of k that fits the condition is 0.4. The required safety stock level is:

$$SS = k \times \sigma_c,$$

where

SS = Safety stock in units;

k = The k factor that corresponds with $f(k)$;

σ_c = The combined standard deviation.

So, substituting in for the example,

$$SS = k \times \sigma_c$$
$$= .04 \times 13 = 5.2 \text{ units.}$$

The safety stock required to provide a 99 percent product fill rate when the order quantity is 300 units is approximately 5 units. Table 7.15 shows how the calculated safety stock and average inventory levels vary for other order quantities. An increased order size can be used to compensate for decreasing the safety stock levels, or vice versa. The existence of such a trade-off implies that there is a combination of replenishment order quantities that will result in desired customer service at the minimum cost.

TABLE 7.14
Loss Integral for Standardized Normal Distribution

k	f(k)	k	f(k)
0.0	.3989	1.6	.0232
0.1	.3509	1.7	.0182
0.2	.3068	1.8	.0143
0.3	.2667	1.9	.0111
0.4	.2304	2.0	.0085
0.5	.1977	2.1	.0065
0.6	.1686	2.2	.0049
0.7	.1428	2.3	.0037
0.8	.1202	2.4	.0027
0.9	.1004	2.5	.0020
1.0	.0833	2.6	.0015
1.1	.0686	2.7	.0011
1.2	.0561	2.8	.0008
1.3	.0455	2.9	.0005
1.4	.0366	3.0	.0004
1.5	.0293	3.1	.0003

TABLE 7.15
Impact of Order Quantity on Safety Stock

Order Quantity (Q)	k	Safety Stock	Average Inventory
300	0.40	5	155
200	0.70	8	108
100	1.05	14	64
50	1.40	18	43
25	1.70	22	34

Dependent Demand Replenishment

With respect to dependent demand replenishment, inventory requirements are a function of known events that are not generally random. Therefore, dependent demand does not require forecasting because there is no uncertainty. It follows that no specific safety stock should be necessary to support a time-phased procurement program such as materials requirements planning **(MRP).**[6] The basic notion of time phasing is that parts and subassemblies need not be carried in inventory as long as they arrive when needed or just-in-time.

The case for carrying no safety stocks under conditions of dependent demand rests on two assumptions. First, procurement replenishment to support planning is predictable and constant. Second, vendors and suppliers maintain adequate inventories to satisfy 100 percent of purchase requirements. The second assumption may be operationally attained by use of volume-oriented purchase contracts that assure vendors and suppliers of eventual purchase. In such cases the safety stock requirement still exists for the overall supply chain, although the primary responsibility rests with the supplier.

The assumption of performance cycle certainty is more difficult to achieve. Even in situations where dedicated transportation is used, an element of uncertainty is always present. The practical result is that safety stocks do exist in most dependent demand situations.

Three basic approaches have been used to introduce safety stocks into dependent demand situations. First, a common practice is to put **safety time** into the requirements plan. For example, a component is ordered earlier than needed to assure timely arrival. A second approach is to increase the requisition by a quantity specified by some estimate of expected plan error. For example, assume that plan error will not exceed 5 percent. This procedure is referred to as **over-planning top-level demand.** The net result is to increase procurement of all components in a ratio to their expected usage plus a cushion to cover plan error. Components common to different end products or subassemblies covered by the overplanning will naturally experience greater quantity buildups than single-purpose components and parts. The third method is to utilize the previously discussed statistical techniques for setting safety stocks directly to the component rather than to the item of top-level demand.

Inventory Management Policies

Inventory management implements inventory policy. The reactive or pull inventory approach uses customer demand to pull product through the distribution channel. An alternative philosophy is a planning approach that proactively allocates inventory on the basis of forecasted demand and product availability. A third, or hybrid, logic uses a combination of push and pull.

---

[6] These concepts are discussed later in this chapter under Requirements Planning.

Inventory Control

The managerial procedure for implementing an inventory policy is **inventory control.** The accountability of control measures units on hand at a specific location and tracks additions and deletions. Accountability and tracking can be performed on a manual or computerized basis.

Inventory control defines how often inventory levels are reviewed to determine when and how much to order. It is performed on either a perpetual or a periodic basis.

Perpetual Review

A perpetual inventory control process continuously reviews inventory levels to determine inventory replenishment needs. To utilize perpetual review, accurate tracking of all SKUs is necessary. Perpetual review is implemented through a reorder point and order quantity.

As discussed earlier,

$$\text{ROP} = D \times T + \text{SS},$$

where

ROP = Reorder point in units;

D = Average daily demand in units;

T = Average performance cycle length in days; and

SS = Safety or buffer stock in units.

The order quantity is determined using the EOQ.

For purposes of illustration, assume no uncertainty so no safety stock is necessary. Table 7.16 summarizes demand, performance cycle, and order quantity characteristics. For this example,

$$\text{ROP} = D \times T + \text{SS}$$
$$= 20 \text{ units/day} \times 10 \text{ days} + 0 = 200 \text{ units}.$$

The perpetual review compares on-hand and on-order inventory to the item's reorder point. If the on-hand plus on-order quantity is less than the established reorder point, a replenishment order is initiated.

Mathematically, the process is:

$$\text{If } I + Q_{\text{O}} \leq \text{ROP, then order } Q,$$

where

I = Inventory on hand;

Q_{o} = Inventory on order from suppliers;

ROP = Reorder point in units; and

Q = Order quantity in units.

TABLE 7.16
Sample Demand, Performance Cycle, and Order Quantity Characteristics

Average daily demand	20 units
Performance cycle	10 days
Order quantity	200 units

For the previous example, a replenishment order of 200 is placed whenever the sum of on-hand and on-order inventory is less than or equal to 200 units. Since the reorder point equals the order quantity, the previous replenishment shipment would arrive just as the next replenishment is initiated. The average inventory level for a perpetual review system is:

$$I_{avg} = Q/2 + SS,$$

where

I_{avg} = Average inventory in units;

Q = Order quantity units; and

SS = Safety stock units.

Average inventory for the previous example is calculated as:

$$I_{avg} = Q/2 + SS$$
$$= 300/2 + 0 = 150 \text{ units.}$$

Most illustrations throughout this text are based on a perpetual review system with a fixed reorder point. The reorder formulation assumes purchase orders will be placed when the reorder point is reached, and the method of control provides a perpetual monitoring of inventory status. If these two assumptions are not satisfied, the control parameters **(ROP and Q)** determining the perpetual review must be refined.

Periodic Review

Periodic inventory control reviews the inventory status of an item at regular intervals such as weekly or monthly. For periodic review, the basic reorder point must be adjusted to consider the intervals between review. The formula for calculating the periodic review reorder point is:

$$ROP = D(T + P/2) + SS,$$

where

ROP = Reorder point;

D = Average daily demand;

T = Average performance cycle length;

P = Review period in days; and

SS = Safety stock.

Since inventory counts occur periodically, any item could fall below the desired reorder point prior to the review period. Therefore, the assumption is made that the inventory will fall below ideal reorder status prior to the periodic count approximately one-half of the review times. Assuming a review period of 7 days and using conditions similar to those of the perpetual example, the ROP then would be as follows:

$$ROP = D(T + P/2) + SS$$
$$= 20(10 + 7/2) + 0 = 20(10 + 3.5) = 270 \text{ units.}$$

The average inventory formulation for the case of periodic review is:

$$I_{avg} = Q/2 + (P \times D)/2 + SS,$$

where

I_{avg} = Average inventory in units;

Q = Order quantity in units;

P = Review period in days;

D = Average daily demand in units;

SS = Safety stock in units.

For the preceding example, the average inventory is calculated as:

$$I_{avg} = Q/2 + (P \times D)/2 + SS$$
$$= 300/2 + (7 \times 10)/2 + 0 = 150 + 35 = 185 \text{ units.}$$

Because of the time interval introduced by periodic review, periodic control systems generally require larger average inventories than perpetual systems.

Reactive Methods

The **reactive** or **pull inventory system,** as the name implies, responds to a channel member's inventory needs by drawing the product through the distribution channel. Replenishment shipments are initiated when available warehouse stock levels fall below a predetermined minimum or order point. The amount ordered is usually based on some lot-sizing formulation, although it may be some variable quantity that is a function of current stock levels and a predetermined maximum level.

The basic perpetual or periodic review process discussed earlier exemplifies a typical reactive system. Figure 7.10 illustrates a reactive inventory environment for a warehouse serving two wholesalers. The figure shows the current inventory (I), reorder point (ROP), order quantity (Q), and average daily demand (D) for each wholesaler. A review of the wholesaler inventory indicates that a resupply order for 200 units should be placed by wholesaler A from the warehouse. Since current inventory is above ROP for wholesaler B, no resupply action is necessary at this time. However, more thorough analysis illustrates that the independent actions by wholesaler A will likely cause a stockout at wholesaler B within a few days. Wholesaler B will likely stock out because inventory level is close to the reorder point and the supplying warehouse center will not have enough inventory to replenish wholesaler B.

FIGURE 7.10

A Reactive Inventory Environment

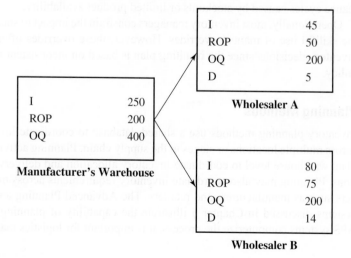

I	45
ROP	50
OQ	200
D	5

Wholesaler A

I	250
ROP	200
OQ	400

Manufacturer's Warehouse

I	80
ROP	75
OQ	200
D	14

Wholesaler B

Classical reactive inventory logic is rooted in the following assumptions. First, the system is founded on the basic assumption that all customers, market areas, and products contribute equally to profits.

Second, a reactive system assumes infinite capacity at the source. This assumption implies that product can be produced as desired and stored at the production facility until required throughout the supply chain.

Third, reactive inventory logic assumes infinite inventory availability at the supply location. The combination of assumptions 2 and 3 implies relative replenishment certainty. The reactive inventory logic provides for no back orders or stockouts in processing replenishment orders.

Fourth, reactive decision rules assume that performance cycle time can be predicted and that cycle lengths are independent. This means that each performance cycle is a random event and that extended cycles don't generally occur for subsequent replenishment orders. Although reactive logic assumes no control over cycle times, many managers are, in fact, able to influence performance cycle length through expediting and alternative sourcing strategies.

Fifth, reactive inventory logic operates best when customer demand patterns are relatively stable and consistent. Ideally, demand patterns should be stable over the relevant planning cycle for statistically developed inventory parameters to operate correctly. Most reactive system decision rules assume demand patterns based on standard normal, gamma, or Poisson distributions. When the actual demand function does not resemble one of the above functions, the statistical inventory decision rules based on these assumptions will not operate correctly.

Sixth, reactive inventory systems determine each distribution warehouse's timing and quantity of replenishment orders independently of all other sites, including the supply source. Thus, there is little potential to effectively coordinate inventory requirements across multiple distribution warehouses. The ability to take advantage of inventory information is not utilized—a serious defect when information and its communication are among the few resources that are decreasing in cost in the supply chain.

The final assumption characteristic of reactive inventory systems is that performance cycle length cannot be correlated with demand. The assumption is necessary to develop an accurate approximation of the variance of the demand over the performance cycle. For many situations higher demand levels create longer replenishment performance cycles since they also increase the demands on inventory and transportation resources. This implies that periods of high demand should not necessarily correspond to extended performance cycles caused by stockouts or limited product availability.

Operationally, most inventory managers constrain the impact of such limitations through the skillful use of manual overrides. However, these overrides often lead to ineffective inventory decisions since the resulting plan is based on inconsistent rules and managerial policy.

Planning Methods

Inventory planning methods use a shared database to coordinate inventory requirements across multiple locations or stages in the supply chain. Planning activities may occur at the plant warehouse level to coordinate inventory allocation and delivery to multiple destinations. Planning may also coordinate inventory requirements across multiple channel partners such as manufacturers and retailers. The Advanced Planning and Scheduling **(APS)** systems discussed in Chapter 5 illustrate the capability of planning applications. While APS systems computerize the process, it is important for logistics managers to understand the underlying logic and assumptions. Two inventory planning methods are fair share allocation and Distribution Requirements Planning **(DRP).**

Fair Share Allocation

A simplified inventory management planning method that provides each distribution facility with an equitable distributor of available inventory is called **fair share allocation.** Figure 7.11 illustrates the network structure, current inventory level, and daily requirements for three warehouses served by a single plant warehouse.

Using fair share allocation, the inventory planner determines the amount of inventory that can be allocated to each warehouse from the available inventory at the plant. For this example, assume that it is desirable to retain 100 units at the plant warehouse; therefore, 500 units are available for allocation. The calculation to determine the common days supply is:

$$DS = \frac{AQ + \sum_{j=1}^{n} I_j}{\sum_{j=1}^{n} D_j}.$$

where

DS = Common days supply for warehouse inventories;

AQ = Inventory units to be allocated from plant warehouse;

I_j = Inventory in units for warehouse j; and

D_j = Daily demand for warehouse j.

In this example,

$$DS = \frac{500 + (50 + 100 + 75)}{10 + 50 + 15}$$

$$= \frac{500 + 225}{75} = 9.67 \text{ days.}$$

FIGURE 7.11
Fair Share Allocation
Example

The fair share allocation dictates that each warehouse should be stocked to 9.67 days of inventory. The amount to be allocated to each warehouse is determined by:

$$A_j = (\text{DS} - I_j/D_j) \times D_j,$$

where

A_j = Amount allocated to warehouse j;

DS = Days supply that each warehouse is brought up to;

I_j = Inventory in units for warehouse j; and

D_j = Daily demand for warehouse j.

The amount allocated to warehouse 1 for this example is:

$$A_1 = (9.67 - 50/10) \times 10$$
$$= (9.67 - 5) \times 10$$
$$= 4.67 \times 10 = 46.7 \text{ (round to 47 units)}.$$

The allocation for warehouses 2 and 3 can be determined similarly and is 383 and 70 units, respectively.

While fair share allocation coordinates inventory levels across multiple sites, it does not consider specific factors such as differences in performance cycle time, EOQ, or safety stock requirements. Fair share allocation methods are therefore limited in their ability to manage multistage inventories.

Requirements Planning

Requirements planning is an approach that integrates across the supply chain, taking into consideration unique requirements. Requirements planning is typically classified as Materials Requirements Planning (MRP) or Distribution Requirements Planning (DRP). There is one fundamental difference between the two techniques. MRP is driven by a production schedule. In contrast, DRP is driven by supply chain demand. So, while MRP generally operates in a dependent demand situation, DRP is applicable to an independent demand environment where uncertain customer requirements drive inventory requirements. MRP coordinates scheduling and integration of materials into finished goods, and so controls inventory until manufacturing or assembly is completed. DRP takes coordination responsibility once finished goods are received in the plant warehouse.

Figure 7.12 illustrates the conceptual design of a combined MRP/DRP system that integrates finished goods, work-in-process, and materials planning. The top half of the figure illustrates an MRP system that time-phases raw material arrivals to support the production schedule. The result of MRP execution is finished goods inventory at the manufacturing site. The bottom half of the figure illustrates the DRP system that allocates finished inventory from the manufacturing site to distribution warehouses and ultimately to customers. DRP time-phases the movements to coordinate inventory arrivals to meet customer requirements and commitments. The MRP and DRP systems interface at the manufacturing site. Close coordination between the two systems results in minimal need for safety stock. DRP coordinates inventory levels, schedules, and when necessary, reschedules inventory movement between levels.

The fundamental DRP planning tool is the schedule, which coordinates requirements across the planning horizon. There is a schedule for each SKU at each warehouse. Schedules for the same SKU are integrated to determine the overall requirements for replenishment facilities such as a plant warehouse.

Figure 7.13 illustrates DRP planning schedules for two warehouses and a central supply facility. The schedules are developed using weekly time increments known as **time buckets.**

FIGURE 7.12
Conceptual Design of Integrated MRP/ DRP System

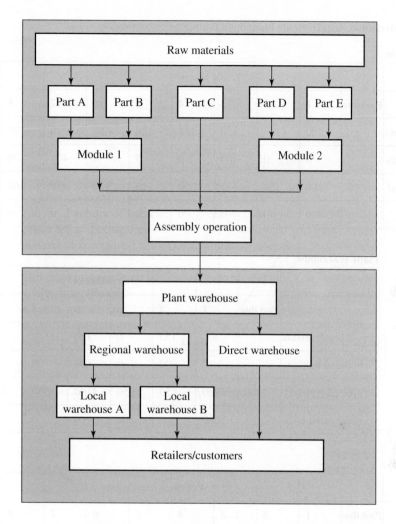

Each bucket projects one period of activity. Although weekly increments are most common, daily or monthly increments can be used. For each site and SKU, the schedule reports current on-hand balance, safety stock, performance cycle length, and order quantity. In addition, for each planning period, the schedule reports gross requirements, scheduled receipts, and projected inventory on hand. Using the combination of requirements and projected availability, DRP determines the planned orders necessary to meet anticipated requirements. Gross requirements reflect customer demand and other distribution facilities supplied by the site under review. For Figure 7.13, the gross requirements of the central supply facility reflect the cascading demands of the Eastern and Western warehouses. Scheduled receipts are the replenishment shipments planned for arrival at the distribution warehouse. Projected on-hand inventory refers to the anticipated week-ending level. It is equal to the prior week's on-hand inventory level less the current week's gross requirements plus any scheduled receipts. While planning approaches to inventory management offer significant benefits, they have some constraints.

First, inventory planning systems require accurate and coordinated forecasts for each warehouse. The forecast is necessary to direct the flow of goods through the supply chain. Ideally, the system does not maintain excess inventory at any location, so little room for error exists in a lean inventory system. To the extent this level of forecast accuracy is possible, inventory planning systems operate well.

FIGURE 7.13 **Distribution Requirements Planning Example**

Eastern Warehouse

					Weeks				
	Past due	1	2	3	4	5	6	7	8
Gross requirements		100	120	150	130	100	80	70	90
Scheduled receipts		0	0	400	0	0	0	400	0
Projected on hand	400	300	180	430	300	200	120	450	360
Planned orders		400	0	0	0	400	0	0	0

Safety stock: 100
Order quantity: 400
Leadtime: 2 weeks

Plant Warehouse

						Weeks				
		Past due	1	2	3	4	5	6	7	8
Gross requirements			400	150	0	150	550	0	0	0
Scheduled receipts			0	600	0	600	0	0	0	0
Projected on hand		600	200	650	650	1100	550	550	550	550
Planned production			600	0	600	0	0	0	0	0

Safety stock: 100
Batch size: 600
Leadtime: 1 week

Western Warehouse

					Weeks				
	Past due	1	2	3	4	5	6	7	8
Gross requirements		40	50	60	90	70	100	40	30
Scheduled receipts		0	0	150	0	150	150	0	0
Projected on hand	200	160	110	200	110	190	240	200	170
Planned orders		0	150	0	150	150	0	0	0

Safety stock: 50
Order quantity: 150
Leadtime: 1 week

Requirement
- - - - - - - - ->

Shipment
————————>

Second, inventory planning requires consistent and reliable product movement between warehouse facilities. While variable performance cycles can be accommodated through safety leadtimes, such uncertainty reduces planning system effectiveness.

Third, integrated planning systems are subject to system nervousness, or frequent rescheduling, because of production breakdowns or delivery delays. System nervousness leads to fluctuation in capacity utilization, rescheduling cost, and confusion in deliveries. This is intensified by the volatile operating environment characteristic of supply chain logistics. Uncertainties such as transportation and vendor delivery reliability can cause an extreme DRP nervousness.

Collaborative Inventory Replenishment

In Chapters 5 and 6 CPFR was introduced and discussed as a major collaborative effort between supply chain trading partners. Several collaborative initiatives focus only on inventory replenishment. Replenishment programs are designed to streamline the flow of goods within the supply chain. There are several specific techniques for collaborative replenishment, all of which build on supply chain relationships to rapidly replenish inventory on the basis of joint planning or actual sales experience. The intent is to reduce reliance on forecasting when and where inventory will need to be positioned to demand on a just-in-time basis. Effective collaborative replenishment programs require extensive cooperation and information sharing among supply chain partners. Specific techniques for collaborative inventory replenishment are quick response, vendor-managed inventory, and profile replenishment.

Quick Response

A technology-driven cooperative effort between retailers and suppliers to improve inventory velocity while providing merchandise supply closely matched to consumer buying patterns is quick response **(QR).** QR is implemented by sharing retail sales for specific products between supply chain participants to facilitate right product assortment availability when and where it is required. Instead of operating on a 15- to 30-day order cycle, QR arrangements can replenish retail inventories in a few days. Continuous information exchange regarding availability and delivery reduces uncertainty for the total supply chain and creates the opportunity for maximum flexibility. With fast, dependable order response, inventory can be committed as required, resulting in increased turnover and improved availability. WalMart*'s system is a prime example of the power of sharing sales to facilitate QR.

Vendor-Managed Inventory

Vendor-managed inventory **(VMI)** is a modification of quick response that eliminates the need for replenishment orders. The goal is to establish a supply chain arrangement so flexible and efficient that retail inventory is continuously replenished. The distinguishing factor between QR and VMI is who takes responsibility for setting target inventory levels and making restocking decisions. In QR, the customer makes the decisions. In VMI, the supplier assumes more responsibility and actually manages a category of inventory for the customer. By receiving daily transmission of retail sales or warehouse shipments, the supplier assumes responsibility for replenishing retail inventory in the required quantities, colors, sizes, and styles. The supplier commits to keeping the customer in stock and to maintaining inventory velocity. In some situations, replenishment involves cross-docking or direct store delivery **(DSD)** designed to eliminate the need for warehousing between the supplier and customer.

Profile Replenishment

Some manufacturers, wholesalers, and retailers are experimenting with an even more sophisticated collaboration known as profile replenishment **(PR).** The PR strategy extends QR and VMI by giving suppliers the right to anticipate future requirements according to their overall knowledge of a merchandise category. A category profile details the combination of sizes, colors, and associated products that usually sell in a particular type of retail outlet. Given PR responsibility, the supplier can simplify retailer involvement by eliminating the need to track unit sales and inventory level for fast-moving products.

Many firms, particularly manufacturers, are using DRP and even APS logic to coordinate inventory planning with major customers. The manufacturers are extending their planning framework to include customer warehouses and, in some cases, their retail stores. Such integrated planning capabilities facilitate manufacturer coordination and management of customer inventories.

TABLE 7.17
Comparative Service and Inventory Characteristics for Anticipatory versus Responsive Inventory Systems

Source: Adapted from David J. Closs et al., "An Empirical Comparison of Anticipatory and Response-Based Supply Chain Strategies," *The International Journal of Logistics Management* 9, no. 2 (1998), pp. 21–34. Used with permission.

	Low Uncertainty Anticipatory	Low Uncertainty Responsive	High Uncertainty Anticipatory	High Uncertainty Responsive
Customer Service				
Fill rate percent	97.69	99.66	96.44	99.29
Inventories				
Supplier inventory	12.88	13.24	14.82	13.61
Manufacturer inventory	6.05	6.12	7.03	6.09
Distributor inventory	5.38	5.86	5.04	5.63
Retailer inventory	30.84	15.79	32.86	20.30
System inventory	55.15	41.01	59.76	45.83

Collaborative planning effectively shares inventory requirements and availability between supply chain partners, thus reducing uncertainty. Table 7.17 illustrates the service and inventory impact in a simulated environment under conditions of low and high uncertainty.[7] Table 7.18 illustrates managerial considerations that drive adaptations of control logic.

Inventory Management Practices

An integrated inventory management strategy defines the policies and process used to determine where to place inventory and when to initiate replenishment shipments, as well as how much to allocate. The strategy development process employs three steps to classify products and markets, define segment strategies, and operationalize policies and parameters.

Product/Market Classification

The objective of product/market classification is to focus and refine inventory management efforts. Product/market classification, which is also called **fine-line** or **ABC classification,** groups products, markets, or customers with similar characteristics to facilitate inventory management. The classification process recognizes that not all products and markets have the same characteristics or degree of importance. Sound inventory management requires that classification be consistent with enterprise strategy and service objectives.

Classification can be based on a variety of measures. The most common are sales, profit contribution, inventory value, usage rate, and item category. The typical classification process sequences products or markets so that entries with similar characteristics are grouped together. Table 7.19 illustrates product classification using sales. The products are classified in descending order by sales volume so that the high-volume products are

[7]David J. Closs et al., "An Empirical Comparison of Anticipatory and Response-Based Supply Chain Strategies," *The International Journal of Logistics Management* 9, no. 2 (1998), pp. 21–34.

TABLE 7.18
Suggested Inventory Management Logic

Use Planning Logic under Conditions of	Use Reactive Logic under Conditions of
Highly profitable segments	Cycle time uncertainty
Dependent demand	Demand uncertainty
Economies of scale	Destination capacity limitations
Supply uncertainty	
Source capacity limitations	
Seasonal supply buildup	

TABLE 7.19
Product Market
Classification (Sales)

Product Identification	Annual Sales (in 000s)	Percent Total Sales	Accumulated Sales (%)	Products (%)	Classification Category
1	$45,000	30.0%	30.0%	5%	A
2	35,000	23.3	53.3	10	A
3	25,000	16.7	70.0	15	A
4	15,000	10.0	80.0	20	A
5	8,000	5.3	85.3	25	B
6	5,000	3.3	88.6	30	B
7	4,000	2.7	91.3	35	B
8	3,000	2.0	93.3	40	B
9	2,000	1.3	94.6	45	B
10	1,000	0.7	95.3	50	B
11	1,000	0.7	96.0	55	C
12	1,000	0.7	96.7	60	C
13	1,000	0.7	97.4	65	C
14	750	0.5	97.9	70	C
15	750	0.5	98.4	75	C
16	750	0.5	98.9	80	C
17	500	0.3	99.2	85	C
18	500	0.3	99.5	90	C
19	500	0.3	99.8	95	C
20	250	0.2	100.0	100	C
	$150,000				

listed first, followed by slower movers. Classification by sales volume is one of the oldest methods used to establish selective inventory policies. For most marketing or logistics applications, a small percentage of the entities account for a large percentage of the volume. This operationalization is often called the **80/20 rule** or **Pareto's law.** The 80/20 rule, which is based on widespread observations, states that for a typical enterprise 80 percent of the sales volume is typically accounted for by 20 percent of the products. A corollary to the rule is that 80 percent of enterprise sales are accounted for by 20 percent of the customers. The reverse perspective of the rule would state that the remaining 20 percent of sales are obtained from 80 percent of the products, customers, etc. In general terms, the 80/20 rule implies that a majority of sales result from a relatively few products or customers.

Once items are classified or grouped, it is common to label each category with a character or description. High-volume, fast-moving products are often described as A items. The moderate-volume items are termed the B items, and the low-volume or slow movers are known as Cs. These character labels indicate why this process is often termed ABC analysis. While fine-line classification often uses three categories, some firms use four or five categories to further refine classifications. Grouping of similar products facilitates management efforts to establish focused inventory strategies for specific product segments. For example, high-volume or fast-moving products are typically targeted for higher service levels. This often requires that fast-moving items have relatively more safety stock. Conversely, to reduce overall inventory levels, slower-moving items may be allowed relatively less safety stock, resulting in lower service levels.

In special situations, classification systems may be based on multiple factors. For example, item gross margin and importance to customers can be weighted to develop a combined index instead of simply using sales volume. The weighted rank would then group items that have similar profitability and importance characteristics. The inventory policy, including safety stock levels, is then established using the weighted rank.

TABLE 7.20
Integrated Strategy

Fine-Line Classification	Service Objective	Forecasting Procedure	Review Period	Inventory Management	Replenishment Monitoring
A (Promotional)	99%	CPFR	Perpetual	Planning—DRP	Daily
A (Regular)	98	Sales history	Perpetual	Planning—DRP	Daily
B	95	Sales history	Weekly	Planning—DRP	Weekly
C	90	Sales history	Biweekly	Reorder point	Biweekly

The classification array defines product or market groups to be assigned similar inventory strategies. The use of item groups facilitates the identification and specification of inventory strategies without requiring tedious development of individual item strategies. It is much easier to track and manage 3 to 10 groups instead of hundreds of individual items.

Segment Strategy Definition

The second step is to define the inventory strategy for each product/market group or segment. The strategy includes specification for all aspects of the inventory management process, including service objectives, forecasting method, management technique, and review cycle.

The key to establishing selective management strategies is the realization that product segments have different degrees of importance with respect to achieving the enterprise mission. Important differences in inventory responsiveness should be designed into the policies and procedures used for inventory management.

Table 7.20 illustrates a sample integrated strategy for four item categories. In this case, the items are grouped by ABC sales volume and as a promotional or regular stock item. Promotional items are those commonly sold in special marketing efforts that result in considerable demand lumpiness. Lumpy demand patterns are characteristic of promotional periods with high volume followed by postpromotion periods with relatively low demand.

Table 7.20 illustrates a management segmentation scheme based on service objectives, forecasting process, review period, inventory management approach, and replenishment monitoring frequency. Additional or fewer characteristics of the inventory management process may be appropriate for some enterprises. Although this table is not presented as a comprehensive inventory strategy framework, it illustrates the issues that must be considered. The rationale behind each element is presented on the basis of the full-line classification.

Policies and Parameters

The final step in implementing a focused inventory management strategy is to define detailed procedures and parameters. The procedures define data requirements, software applications, performance objectives, and decision guidelines. The parameters delineate values such as review period length, service objectives, inventory carrying cost percentage, order quantities, and reorder points. The combination of parameters either determines or can be used to calculate the precise quantities necessary to make inventory management decisions.

Summary

Inventory typically represents the second largest component of logistics cost next to transportation. The risks associated with holding inventory increase as products move down the supply chain closer to the customer because the potential of having the product in the wrong place or form increases and costs have been incurred to distribute the product. In addition to the risk of lost sales due to stockouts because adequate inventory is not available, other risks include obsolescence, pilferage, and damage. Further, the cost of carrying inventory is significantly influenced by the cost of the capital tied up in the inventory. Geographic specialization, decoupling, supply/demand balancing, and buffering uncertainty provide the basic rationale for maintaining inventory. While there is substantial interest in reducing overall supply chain inventory, inventory does add value and can result in lower overall supply chain costs with appropriate trade-offs.

From a supply chain logistics perspective, the major controllable inventory elements are replenishment cycle stock, safety stock, and in-transit stock. The appropriate replenishment cycle stock can be determined using an EOQ formula to reflect the trade-off between storage and ordering cost. Safety stock depends on the mean and variance of demand and the replenishment cycle. In-transit stock depends on the transport mode.

Inventory management uses a combination of reactive and planning logics. Reactive logic is most appropriate for items with low volume, high demand, and high performance cycle uncertainty because it postpones the risk of inventory speculation. Inventory planning logic is appropriate for high-volume items with relatively stable demand. Inventory planning methods offer the potential for effective inventory management because they take advantage of improved information and economies of scale. Adaptive logic combines the two alternatives depending on product and market conditions. Collaboration offers a way for parties in the supply chain to jointly gain inventory efficiency and effectiveness.

Challenge Questions

1. How does the cost of carrying inventory impact the traditional earnings statement of the enterprise?
2. Discuss the relationship between service level, uncertainty, safety stock, and order quantity. How can trade-offs between these elements be made?
3. Discuss the disproportionate risk of holding inventory by retailers, wholesalers, and manufacturers. Why has there been a trend to push inventory back up the channel of distribution?
4. What is the difference between the probability of a stockout and the magnitude of a stockout?
5. Data suggest that while overall average inventory levels are declining, the relative percentage being held by manufacturers is increasing. Explain why you think this observation is either true or false. Describe how such a shift could benefit the operations of the entire channel and how manufacturers could take advantage of the shift.
6. Discuss the differences between reactive and planning inventory logics. What are the advantages of each? What are the major implications of each?
7. Illustrate how fine-line inventory classification can be used with product and market segments. What are the benefits and considerations when classifying inventory by product, market, and product/market?
8. What advantage does DRP have over a fair share method of inventory deployment?
9. Discuss the importance of collaboration in the developing of supply chain inventory strategies. Provide an example.
10. Customer-based inventory management strategies allow the use of different availability levels for specific customers. Discuss the rationale for such a strategy. Are such strategies discriminatory? Justify your position.

CHAPTER EIGHT

Transportation Infrastructure

Chapter Outline

The role of transportation in logistics has changed dramatically over the last four decades. Prior to transportation deregulation, the purchase of transportation could be likened to buying a commodity such as coal or grain. There was very little difference between transport suppliers in terms of product, service, or price. Transportation deregulation in 1980 introduced pricing flexibility and significantly increased the range of services transportation companies could provide customers.

Today a wide range of transportation alternatives are available to support supply chain logistics. For example, logistics managers may integrate private with for-hire transportation to reduce total logistics costs. Many for-hire carriers offer a wide variety of value-added services such as product sortation, sequencing, and customized freight delivery and presentation. Technology has enhanced real-time visibility of the location of freight throughout the supply chain and advanced information concerning delivery. Precise product delivery reduces inventory, storage, and materials handling. As a result, the value of transportation has become greater than simply moving product from one location to another. This chapter provides an overview of the transportation infrastructure and its current regulatory framework.[1]

Transport Functionality, Principles, and Participants

Transportation is a very visible element of logistics. Consumers are accustomed to seeing trucks and trains transporting product or parked at business facilities. Few consumers fully understand just how dependent our economic system is upon economical and dependable transportation. This section provides a foundation by reviewing transportation functionality and the underlying principles of transport operation.

Transport Functionality

Transportation enterprises provide two major services: product movement and product storage.

Product Movement

Whether in the form of materials, components, work-in-process, or finished goods, the basic value provided by transportation is to move inventory to specified destinations. The primary transportation value proposition is product movement throughout the supply chain. The performance of transportation is vital to procurement, manufacturing, and customer accommodation. Transportation also plays a key role in the performance of reverse logistics. Without reliable transportation, most commercial activity could not function. Transportation consumes time, financial, and environmental resources.

Transportation has a restrictive element because inventory is generally inaccessible during the transportation process. Inventory captive in the transport system is referred to as **in-transit inventory.** Naturally, when designing logistical systems, managers strive to reduce in-transit inventory to a minimum. Advancements in information technology have significantly improved access to in-transit inventory and arrival status of shipments by providing exact location and arrival times.

Transportation also uses financial resources. In the United States more than 60 percent of total logistics cost is related to transportation services.[2] Transportation cost results from driver labor, vehicle operation, capital invested in equipment, and administration. In addition, product loss and damage are significant costs.

Transportation impacts environmental resources both directly and indirectly. In direct terms, transportation represents one of the largest consumers of fuel and oil in the U.S. economy. Although the level of fuel and oil consumption has improved as a result of more fuel-efficient vehicles, total consumption remains high. Indirectly, transportation impacts the environment through congestion, air pollution, and noise pollution.

Product Storage

A less visible aspect of transportation is the performance of product storage. While a product is in a transportation vehicle, it is being stored. Transport vehicles can also be used for product storage at shipment origin or destination, but they are comparatively expensive storage facilities. Since the main value proposition of transportation is movement, a vehicle committed to storage is not otherwise available for transport. A trade-off exists between using a transportation vehicle versus temporarily placing products in a

---

[1] Transportation operations are discussed in Chapter 9.
[2] For a component breakdown of total logistics cost see Chapter 2.

warehouse. If the inventory involved is scheduled to be shipped within a few days to a different location, the cost of unloading, warehousing, and reloading the product may exceed the temporary cost of using the transportation vehicle for storage.[3]

Another transport service having storage implications is **diversion.** Diversion occurs when a shipment destination is changed after a product is in transit. For example, the destination of a product initially shipped from Chicago to Los Angeles may be changed to Seattle while in transit. Traditionally, the telephone was used to implement diversion strategies. Today, Internet communication between shippers, carriers' headquarters, and vehicles facilitates more efficient diversion. While diversion is primarily used to improve logistical responsiveness, it also impacts the duration of in-transit storage.

So although costly, product storage in transportation vehicles may be justified from a total cost or performance perspective when loading or unloading costs, capacity constraints, and ability to extend leadtimes are taken into consideration.

Transport Principles

There are two fundamental economic principles that impact transportation efficiency: **economy of scale** and **economy of distance.**

Economy of scale in transportation is the cost per unit of weight decreases as the size of a shipment increases. For example, truckload shipments utilizing an entire trailer's capacity have a lower cost per pound than smaller shipments that utilize a limited portion of vehicle capacity. It is also generally true that larger-capacity transportation vehicles, such as rail and water vehicles, are less costly per unit of weight than smaller-capacity vehicles such as trucks and airplanes. Transportation economies of scale exist because fixed cost associated with transporting a load is allocated over the increased weight. Fixed costs include administration related to scheduling, cost of equipment, time to position vehicles for loading or unloading, and invoicing. Such costs are considered fixed because they do not vary with shipment size. In other words, it costs as much to administer a 100-pound shipment as one weighing 1000-pounds.

Economy of distance refers to decreased transportation cost per unit of weight as distance increases. For example, a shipment of 800 miles will cost less to perform than two shipments of the same weight each moving 400 miles. Transportation economy of distance is often referred to as the **tapering principle.** The rationale for distance economies is similar to economies of scale. Specifically, longer distances allow fixed cost to be spread over more miles, resulting in lower per mile charges.

These principles are important when evaluating transportation alternatives. The goal from a transportation perspective is to maximize the size of the load and the distance being shipped while still meeting customer service expectations.[4]

Transport Participants

The transportation environment impacts the range of decisions that can be implemented in a logistical system. Unlike most commercial transactions, transportation decisions are influenced by six parties: (1) shipper, sometimes referred to as the **consignor;** (2) destination party, traditionally called the **consignee;** (3) carriers and agents; (4) government; (5) Internet; and (6) the public. Figure 8.1 illustrates the relationship among the involved parties. To understand the complexity of the transportation environment it is useful to review the role and perspective of each party.

[3] The technical terms for charges related to using transportation vehicles for storage are *demurrage* for rail cars and *detention* for trucks. See Chapter 9.
[4] For more detailed discussion, see Chapter 9.

FIGURE 8.1
**Relationship among
Transportation
Participants**

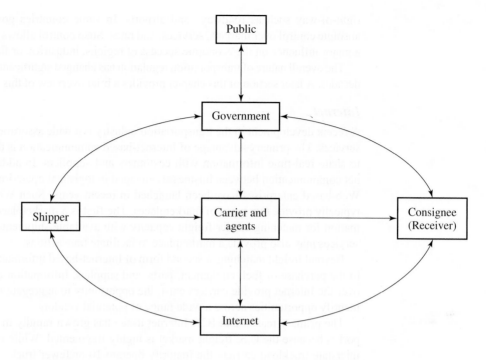

Shipper and Consignee

The shipper and consignee have a common interest in moving goods from origin to destination within a given time at the lowest cost. Services related to transportation include specified pickup and delivery times, predictable transit time, and zero loss and damage, as well as accurate and timely exchange of information and invoicing.

Carrier and Agents

The carrier, a business that performs a transportation service, desires to maximize its revenue for movement while minimizing associated costs. As a service business, carriers want to charge their customers the highest rate possible while minimizing labor, fuel, and vehicle costs required to complete the movement. To achieve this objective, the carrier seeks to coordinate pickup and delivery times to group or consolidate many different shippers' freight into movements that achieve economy of scale and distance. Brokers and freight forwarders are transport agents that facilitate carrier and customer matching. A more recent development has been the emergence of Internet or online brokers that match carrier capacity and shipper requirements.

Government

The government has a vested interest in transportation because of the critical importance of reliable service to economic and social well-being. Government desires a stable and efficient transportation environment to support economic growth.

A stable and efficient transportation environment requires that carriers provide essential services at reasonable cost. Because of the direct impact of transportation on economic success, governments have traditionally been very involved in oversight of carrier practices. In one situation, the United States Postal Service (**USPS**), government is directly involved in providing the transportation service. Government historically regulated carriers by restricting markets they could service and approving prices they could charge. Governments also promote carrier development by supporting research and providing right-of-way such as roadways and airports. In some countries government maintains absolute control over markets, services, and rates. Such control allows government to have a major influence on the economic success of regions, industries, or firms.

The overall nature of transportation regulation has changed significantly over the past three decades. A later section of this chapter provides a brief overview of this regulatory change.

Internet

A recent development in the transportation industry is a wide assortment of Internet-based services. The primary advantage of Internet-based communication is the ability of carriers to share real-time information with customers and suppliers. In addition to direct Internet communication between businesses engaged in logistical operations, a wide variety of Web-based enterprises have been launched in recent years. Such Web-based enterprises typically provide two types of marketplaces. The first is a marketplace to exchange information for matching carrier freight capacity with available shipments. These Web-based services may also provide a marketplace to facilitate transactions.

Beyond freight matching, a second form of Internet-based information exchange relates to the purchase of fuel, equipment, parts, and supplies. Information exchanges operating over the Internet provide carriers exist, the opportunity to aggregate their purchasing and identify opportunities across a wide range of potential vendors.

The primary reason that B2B Internet usage has grown rapidly in motor carrier transport is because the U.S. freight market is highly fragmented. While in excess of 750,000 interstate truckload carriers the majority operate 10 or fewer truck.[5] The use of Internet services to share information in such a fragmented operating environment is attractive for both carriers and shippers.

Finally, the use of the Internet as a communication backbone is rapidly changing the nature of transportation operations. The availability of real-time information is improving shipment visibility to the point where tracing and tracking are no longer a major challenge. In addition to real-time visibility, the Internet can be used to share information concerning scheduling and capacity planning.

Public

The final transportation system participant, the public, is concerned with transportation accessibility, expense, and effectiveness as well as environmental, security, and safety standards. The public indirectly creates transportation demand by purchasing goods. While minimizing transportation cost is important to consumers, concerns also involve environmental impact and safety. The effect of air pollution and oil spillage is a significant transportation-related social issue. The cost of environmental impact and safety is ultimately paid by consumers.

Transportation policy formation is complex because of interaction between these six participants. Such complexity results in frequent conflict between shippers, consignees, and carriers. The concern to protect public interest served as the historical justification for government involvement in economic and social regulation. The next section provides a brief review of how government regulation has changed over the years.

Transportation Regulation

Since transportation has a major impact on both domestic and international commerce, government has historically taken special interest in both controlling and promoting transportation. Control takes the form of federal and state government regulation as well as a

---

[5] *American Trucking Trends, 2007–2008* (Alexandria, VA: American Trucking Association Inc., Press Release, January 25, 2008).

wide range of administration and judicial administration. With the passage of the Act to Regulate Interstate Commerce on February 4, 1887, the federal government became active in protecting the public interest with respect to performance and provision of transportation services.

Types of Regulation

Government transportation regulation can be grouped into two categories: economic regulation and social regulation. Regulatory initiatives have historically focused on economic issues; however, recent regulatory initiatives have increasingly been directed toward safety and social issues.

Economic

Regulation of business practices is the oldest form of government control. To provide dependable transportation service and to foster economic development, both federal and state governments have actively engaged in economic regulation. For over 100 years, government regulation sought to make transportation equally accessible and economical to all without discrimination. To encourage economical and widespread transportation supply, government invested in public infrastructure such as highways, airports, waterways, and deepwater ports. However, to actually provide transportation service, the government supported and regulated a system of privately owned for-hire carriers.

Because of transportation's importance to economic growth, government believed that carriers needed to be regulated to ensure service availability, stability, and fair prices. Availability means that carrier services would be accessible to all business enterprises. Stability means that carriers would be guaranteed sufficient profits to ensure viable long-term operation. Fair prices mean that carriers could not take advantage of shippers by controlling or restricting supply.

Economic regulation generally sought to achieve its goals by controlling entry, rates, and services. In addition, economic regulatory practice treated each type of transport independently. This practice limited carrier ability to develop intermodal relationships and offerings. By 1970, federal economic regulation had reached the point where it provided oversight on 100 percent of rail and air ton-miles, 80 percent of pipeline, 43.1 percent of trucking, and 6.7 percent of domestic water carriers.[6] The degree of direct government economic regulation began to decline during the 1970s and took a dramatic turn in 1980 with the passage of major deregulatory legislation. The contemporary economic regulatory environment is dominated by free market competition more or less regulated by antitrust laws.

Social

In direct contrast to reduced transportation regulation, another trend in the 1970s and 1980s was expanded safety and social regulation. Since its inception in 1966, the federal Department of Transportation **(DOT)** has taken an active role in controlling the transport and handling of hazardous material and rules related to maximum driver hours and safety. The form of regulation was institutionalized by the passage of the Transportation Safety Act of 1974, which formally established safety and social regulation as a governmental initiative. Substantial legislation impacting logistical performance was passed during the next three decades. The Hazardous Materials Transportation Uniform Safety Act of 1990, which provided federal government control over equipment design, hazardous material classification, packaging, and handling, took precedence over state and local environmental regulations.

---

[6] Derived from Department of Transportation, *1972 National Transportation Report* (Washington, DC: U.S. Government Printing Office, 1972), pp. 2–44.

Additional emphasis on transportation safety has increased as a result of environmental and related liability lawsuits.

History of Regulation

The following discussion is divided into time periods reflecting dominant regulatory posture. The early period regulation discussion serves to provide future logistics managers insight into the legislative, administrative, and judicial foundations of today's transportation industry.

Pre-1920: Establishing Government Control

The original purpose of interstate regulation was to scrutinize the activities of for-hire carriers for the public interest. Railroads dominated early transportation, enjoying a near monopoly. Individual states maintained the legal right to regulate discriminatory practices within their borders, but no federal regulation existed to provide consistent interstate controls. In 1887, the Act to Regulate Commerce was passed by Congress and became the foundation of U.S. transportation regulation.[7] The act also created the Interstate Commerce Commission **(ICC).**

Federal regulatory power over carriers evolved from legislation and judicial decisions from 1900 through 1920. At the turn of the century, destructive competitive practices were common as a result of independent pricing by carriers. Although the ICC had the authority to review groups of rates with respect to their just and reasonable nature once published by individual carriers, no regulation existed over rate making. Attempts at joint rate making by railroads had been declared illegal. In 1903, the railroads supported the passage of the Elkins Act. This legislation eliminated secret rebates and special concessions while increasing the penalty for secret agreements to charge different from published rates. It did not, however, eliminate independent and nonregulated pricing which was the primary cause of discrimination.

The passage of the Hepburn Act of 1906 began to establish federal regulatory power over pricing. The just-and-reasonable-review authorization of the 1887 act was expanded to include examination of maximum rates. However, the regulatory posture remained **expost,** or after the fact, until passage of the Mann-Elkins Act in 1910. This act permitted the ICC to rule on the reasonableness of proposed rates **prior** to their effective date and to suspend rates when they appeared discriminatory.

The framework for rate regulation was completed with the passage of the Transportation Act of 1920. The review power of the ICC was expanded to prescribe reasonableness of minimum as well as maximum rates. The ICC was instructed to assume a more aggressive nature concerning proposed rates. The original Act to Regulate Commerce was modified to instruct the commission to initiate, modify, and adjust rates as necessary in the public interest. The 1920 act also changed the name of the 1887 act to the Interstate Commerce Act.

1920–1940: Regulatory Formalization

Several additional transportation laws were enacted during these two decades. With some exceptions, their primary objective was to clarify issues related to the basic acts of 1887 and 1920. In 1935 the Emergency Transportation Act further instructed the ICC to set standards with respect to reasonable rate levels. By the 1930s motor carriers had become important transportation providers. In 1935 the Motor-Carrier Act placed regulation of

---

[7] For an early history of legislative attempts prior to 1887, see L. H. Hanley, *A Congressional History of Railroads in the United States, 1850–1887,* Bulletin 342 (Madison: University of Wisconsin, 1910).

common carrier highway transportation under the jurisdiction of the ICC. This act, which became Part II of the Interstate Commerce Act, defined the basic nature of the legal forms of for-hire and motor carriers.

In 1938 the Civil Aeronautics Act established the Civil Aeronautics Authority **(CAA)** as the ICC's counterpart for regulating air transport. The powers and charges of the CAA were somewhat different from those of the ICC, in that the act specified that the CAA would promote and actively develop the growth and safety of the airline industry. In 1940 the functions of the original CAA were reorganized into the Civil Aeronautics Board **(CAB)** and the Civil Aeronautics Administration, later known as the Federal Aeronautics Administration **(FAA)**. In addition, the National Advisory Committee on Aeronautics was formed in the mid-1930s and in 1951 became known as the National Aeronautics and Space Administration **(NASA)**. Starting in the 1960s, NASA concentrated attention on exploration of outer space. However, NASA was specifically charged with the responsibility for increasing aviation safety, utility, and basic knowledge through the deployment of science and technology. Thus, in the regulatory structure that resulted, the CAB regulated rate making; the FAA administered the airway system; and NASA was concerned with scientific development of aerospace, commercial, and private aviation.

The regulation of pipelines was not as clear-cut as that of railroads, motor carriers, and air transport. In 1906 the Hepburn Act declared that oil pipelines were common carriers. The need for regulation developed from the early market dominance that the Standard Oil Company gained by developing crude oil pipelines to compete with rail transport. In 1912 the ICC ruled, subsequently upheld by the Supreme Court, that private pipelines could be regulated as common carriers. While there are substantial differences between pipeline and other forms of regulation, for all effective purposes the ICC regulated pipeline traffic. Interestingly, a significant difference regarding pipeline regulation is that this type of common carrier was allowed to transport goods owned by the carrier.

1940–1970: Status Quo

Regulation of water transport prior to 1940 was extremely fragmented. Some standards existed under both the ICC and the Federal Maritime Commission **(FMC)**. In addition, a series of acts placed regulation of various aspects of the domestic water transport under specific agencies. For example, the Transportation Act of 1940 put domestic water transport under ICC jurisdiction and gave the FMC authority over water transport in foreign commerce and between Alaska and Hawaii and other U.S. ports.

It is important to understand that the ICC did not actually set or establish carrier prices. Rather, the ICC reviewed and either approved or disapproved rates. Carriers under federal regulation were allowed to jointly set prices because they were exempt from the antitrust provisions of the Sherman, Clayton, and Robinson-Patman acts. This exemption was provided by the Reed-Bulwinkle Act of 1948, which permitted carriers to collaborate in rate-making bureaus. Collaborative pricing was a common feature among for-hire carriers. In particular, for-hire transportation carriers in motor and rail organized freight bureaus that standardized prices and published price lists, called tariffs, for specific geographical areas.

From 1970 until 1973 several acts were passed to aid the rapidly deteriorating rail industry of the United States. In 1970 the Rail Passenger Service Act established the National Railroad Passenger Cooperation **(AMTRAK)**. The Regional Rail Reorganization Act of 1973 **(3-R)** was passed to provide economic aid to seven major northeastern railroads facing bankruptcy. As a result of 3-R Act provisions, the Consolidated Rail Corporation **(CONRAIL)** began to operate portions of the seven lines on April 1, 1976.

The establishment of AMTRAK and CONRAIL represented, with the exception of the United States Postal Service, the first modern attempt of the federal government to own and operate transportation. While the subsequent passage of the Railroad Revitalization and Regulatory Reform Act of 1976 (4-R) and the Rail Transportation Improvement Act of 1976 provided financial support for AMTRAK and CONRAIL, these acts also began to reverse the trend of regulatory expansion that had prevailed for nine decades.

1970–1980: Prelude to Deregulation

In the early 1970s, a movement was gaining momentum to review and modify economic regulation to better meet the requirements of contemporary society. A Presidential Advisory Committee recommended that increased transportation competition would be in the general public's interest. The committee's recommendations were published in a 1960 report issued by the Commerce Department.[8] A Senate Committee in 1961 produced a revised National Transportation Policy. Among other recommendations the 1961 report advocated formation of a Department of Transportation **(DOT).**[9] After its formation in 1966, DOT became a dominant force seeking regulatory modification. From 1972 to 1980 DOT introduced or significantly influenced legislation at two-year intervals to modify the regulatory scope of for-hire carriers.

The initial success in regulatory reform was administrative in nature. From 1977 to 1978 CAB Chairman Alfred Kahn forced de facto deregulation of the Civil Aeronautics Board by virtue of administrative rulings that encouraged air carrier price competition and eased the establishment of new airlines. In 1977, the Federal Aviation Act was amended to deregulate domestic cargo airlines, freight forwarders, and shipper's associations with respect to pricing and entry. The standard for entry into the air cargo industry was modified to require that a new competitor be judged **fit, willing,** and **able** to carry out the proposed service. The traditional regulatory criteria of judging entry applications on the basis of **public convenience necessity** were eliminated. On October 24, 1978, the Airline Deregulation Act was passed, extending free market competition to all forms of passenger air transport. The CAB was closed November 30, 1984.

1980–2000: Deregulation

The drive for economic regulatory change in trucking and the railroads became official with the passage of the Motor Carrier Act of 1980 **(MC 80)** and the Staggers Rail Act (Staggers Act).[10]

MC 80 was a formal effort to stimulate competition and promote efficiency in trucking. Entry restrictions or right to conduct operations were relaxed, allowing firms to offer trucking services if they were judged fit, willing, and able. Restrictions relating to the types of freight carriers could legally haul and the range of services carriers could provide were abolished. While the ICC retained the right to protect the public against discriminatory practices and predatory pricing, individual carriers were given the right to price their services. The trucking industry's collective rate-making practices were restricted and soon would be abolished. The structural impact of MC 80 on the for-hire motor carrier industry was dramatic. Overnight the industry was transformed from a highly regulated to a highly competitive structure.

On October 14, 1980, the railroad industry was deregulated by enactment of the Staggers Rail Act. This act was a continuation of a trend initiated in the 3-R and 4-R acts and supplemented the Rail Transportation Improvement Act of 1976. The dominant philosophy

---

[8] Department of Commerce, *Federal Transportation Policy and Program* (Washington, DC: U.S. Government Printing Office, 1960).
[9] Senate Committee on Commerce, 87th Congress, *National Transportation Policy* (Washington, DC: U.S. Government Printing Office, 1961). The Department of Transportation was established by Public Law 86-670 in 1966 and initiated operation on April 1, 1967.
[10] Motor Carrier Act of 1980 (Public Law 96-296) and the Staggers Rail Act of 1980 (Public Law 96-488).

of the Staggers Act was to provide railroad management with the freedom necessary to revitalize the industry. In that respect, the most significant provision of the Staggers Act was increased pricing freedom. Railroads were authorized to selectively reduce rates to meet competition while increasing other rates to cover operating cost. Carriers were also given increased flexibility with respect to surcharges. Contract rate agreements between individual shippers and carriers were specifically legalized. In addition to price flexibility, railroad management was given liberalized authority to proceed with abandonment of poorly performing rail service. The act also provided the framework for a liberalized attitude toward mergers and increased the ability of railroads to be involved in motor carrier service.

Since the passage of the landmark legislation of 1980, several major legislative acts have further defined pricing practice and structure. The trend toward a competitive transportation marketplace was reinforced by key administrative and judicial rulings. For instance, until the passage of the 1993 Negotiated Rate Act **(NRA),** a regulatory loophole interfered with competitive pricing. Competition led many motor carriers to negotiate lower rates with shippers than those filed with the ICC. Eventually, the motor carrier trustees sued shippers for the difference between the ICC filed rate and the lower negotiated rate—a total of $27 billion in claims.[11] In Maislin Industries versus Primary Steel (1990), the Supreme Court found that the undercharge claims were generally valid. In response, the 1993 NRA act provided a framework for motor carriers to settle undercharge claims. However, in the final undercharge case, 2001 Willig Freight Lines Incorporated versus Shuford Mills Incorporated, the Court found that seeking undercharge restitution was an unreasonable practice.

The authority of the ICC to regulate transportation was generally weakened following passage of the Trucking Industry Regulatory Reform Act of 1994.[12] This act eliminated the need for motor carriers to file rates with the ICC and consequently eliminated undercharges. Effective January 1, 1996, the ICC was abolished by passage of the ICC Termination Act of 1995. This act further deregulated transportation and established a three-person Surface Transportation Board **(STB)** within the DOT to administer remaining economic regulation issues across the industry.[13] The authority of the STB includes all transportation modes and incorporates freight forwarders and brokers.

Over the decades, considerable conflict existed between the federal government and state governments concerning legal right to regulate commerce. Both levels of government claimed inherent rights to regulate. State government clearly had the right to regulate intrastate shipments in terms of vehicle size, entry, rates, and routes. At the height of the regulatory era, 42 states were actively engaged in some form of regulation.[14] The issues of the state's right to regulate were not as clear-cut with respect to freight moving in interstate commerce.

In an effort to increase intrastate regulatory consistency across states, the ICC attempted to clarify and expand interstate transportation. Interstate commerce was traditionally defined as product movement across state lines. In a 1993 ruling, the ICC concluded that shipments from warehouses to markets in the same state could be deemed interstate movements if the commodity had originally been shipped from out of state. The ICC argued that such shipments are part of a continuing movement and that interstate regulation should apply. In an effort to gain more direct control over intrastate regulation, the Federal

[11] Thomas Gale Moore, "Clearing the Track, The Remaining Transportation Regulations," *The CATO Review of Business and Movement,* 1995.
[12] Trucking Industry Regulatory Reform Act of 1994 (Public Law 103-111).
[13] ICC Termination Act of 1995 (Public Law 104-88).
[14] Cassandra Chrones Moore, "Interstate Trucking: Stronghold of the Regulations," *Policy Analysis 204,* February 16, 1994, p. 6.

Aviation Administration Authorization Act and the Reauthorization Act of 1996 essentially preempted economic regulation of intrastate transportation.[15] The preemption was placed in the act because Congress found that state regulation of intrastate transport had (1) imposed an unreasonable cost on interstate commerce; (2) impeded the free flow of trade, traffic, and transportation of interstate commerce; and (3) placed unreasonable cost on consumers.

This legislation preempted state regulation of prices, routes, and services for direct air carriers and related motor carrier pickup and delivery. The purpose was to level the playing field between air and motor carriers with respect to intrastate economic trucking regulation. The net effect was to remove intrastate regulation of transportation.

In 1998 the Ocean Shipping Reform Act revised and updated a previous act passed in 1984. This act served to greatly reduce the regulatory authority of the Federal Maritime Commission. While the FMC continues to regulate ocean liner shipping, carriers no longer are required to file tariffs with the FMC. The act gave carriers substantially more freedom to negotiate rates and contracts with shippers.

2000–Present: Technology, Safety and Security

The new millennium delivered some significant changes to transportation industry. Technology adoption stimulated many of these changes. The Electronic Signatures in Global and National Commerce Act of 2000 gave electronic documents signed by digital signature the same legal status as paper documents. In addition, in July 2004 the U.S. Department of Defense mandated that its 45,000 suppliers attach Radio Frequency Identification (**RFID**) tags to any goods sold to the military. Safety regulations also dominated in the 2000s as significant changes were made to limit truck drivers' hours of service. The most significant changes, however, were due to terrorism and the heightened transportation security of the United States following 9–11. The USA PATRIOT Act, signed into law October 26, 2001, increased inspections at ports, regulated airport screening, and heightened security at land-based border crossings. This act resulted in a widespread implementation of voluntary initiatives between the U.S. customs and private industry known as Customs-Trade Partnership against Terrorism (**C-TPAT**).

Other legislation in the new millenium has been the result of globalization. The Continued Dumping and Subsidy Act of 2000, known as the Byrd Amendment, was passed in response to artificial underpricing and dumping of foreign goods in U.S. markets. The law gives fines collected from foreign companies involved in dumping to U.S. companies filing the dumping complaints. Critics of this law contend that the law has discouraged world trade and violated World Trade Organization (**WTO**) rules. In fact, other nations have retaliated by imposing duties as high as 100% on U.S. goods.[16]

Another example of the impact of globalization on regulation is recent efforts to reframe the Jones Act.[17] The Jones Act mandates that only United States–built ships operating under a U.S. flag and with a U.S. crew can ship goods directly from a U.S. port to another U.S. port. Commonly referred to as short sea shipping (**SSS**), this form of water movement is projected to grow as a result of plans to expand the capacity of the Panama Canal by 2010. Similar regulations are frequently called cabotage laws. Opponents of this law argued that the Jones Act unfairly limited global competition in U.S. domestic

---

[15] Federal Aviation Administration Authorization Act of 1994 (Public Law 103-305) and Federal Aviation Reauthorization Act of 1996 (Public Law 104-164).
[16] "Byrd Amendment Repeal Urged," The National Industrial Transportation League, December 3, 2004.
[17] Maritime Act of 1920, Section 27

TABLE 8.1
The Nations' Freight Bill ($ billions)

Source: Adapted from Rosalyn Wilson, *16th Annual State of Logistics Report,* Council of Supply Chain Management Professionals. Oak Brook, IL, 2005.

	1960	1970	1980	1990	2000	2007
Truck	32.3	62.5	155.3	270.1	481.0	671.0
Railroad	9.0	11.9	27.9	30.0	36.0	58.0
Water	3.4	5.3	15.3	20.1	26.0	38.0
Pipeline	0.9	1.4	7.6	8.3	9.0	10.0
Air	0.4	1.2	4.0	13.7	27.0	41.0
Other carriers	0.4	0.4	1.1	4.0	10.0	31.0
Other shipper costs	1.3	1.4	2.4	3.7	5.0	8.0
Grand total	47.8	83.9	213.7	350.8	594.0	857.0
GNP (trillions)	0.5	1,046	2,831	5,832	9,960	13,840
Grand total of GNP	9.00%	8.03%	7.55%	6.02%	5.92%	6.20%

shipping. However, because of the need to enforce laws regarding domestic trade, most countries continue to have cabotage laws.

Transportation Structure

The freight transportation structure consists of the rights-of-way, vehicles, and carriers that operate within five basic transportation modes. A **mode** identifies a basic transportation method or form. The five basic transportation modes are rail, highway, water, pipeline, and air.

The relative importance of each transportation mode in the United States is measured in terms of system mileage, traffic volume, revenue, and nature of freight transported. Table 8.1 provides a summary of transportation expenditure by mode from 1960 to 2007. Tables 8.2 and 8.3 provide tonnage and revenue share by mode in 2003 and as projected to 2015. These data confirm that the truck share of the domestic freight market far exceeds that of all other modes combined. The 2006 tonnage share was 65.3 percent, and revenue share of truck transportation was 87.7 percent. While all transport modes are vital to a sound national transportation structure, it is clear that the U.S. economy, current and projected, depends on trucks. The following discussion provides a brief overview of the essential operating characteristics of each mode.

Rail

Historically, railroads have handled the largest number of ton-miles within the continental United States. A ton-mile is a standard measure of freight activity that combines weight and distance. As a result of early development of a comprehensive rail network connecting almost

TABLE 8.2
Domestic Shipments by Mode and Volume

Source: Adapted from *United States Freight Transportation Forecast to 2015,* American Transportation Association.

	Freight Volumes (millions of tons)		Mode Share Percent		2003–2015
	2003	2015	2003	2015	Percent Change
Truck	9,062	12,141	68.9%	69.8%	34.0%
Rail	1,700	2,166	12.9%	12.5%	27.4%
Rail intermodal	122	205	0.9%	1.2%	67.7%
Air	18	31	0.1%	0.2%	70.4%
Water	1,018	1,296	7.7%	7.4%	27.2%
Pipeline	1,238	1,556	9.4%	8.9%	25.7%

TABLE 8.3
Domestic Shipments
by Mode and
Revenue

Source: Adapted from *United States Freight Transportation Forecast to 2015,* American Transportation Association.

	Freight Revenue ($ billions)		Mode Share Percent		2003–2015
	2003	2015	2003	2015	Percent Change
Truck	610.1	1,049.1	86.9%	87.3%	72.0%
Rail	36.0	51.5	5.1%	4.3%	43.1%
Rail intermodal	7.6	15.7	1.1%	1.3%	106.6%
Air	13.1	27.8	1.9%	2.3%	112.2%
Water	7.8	12.5	1.1%	1.0%	60.3%
Pipeline	27.3	44.9	3.9%	3.7%	64.5%

all cities and towns, railroads dominated intercity freight tonnage until after World War II. This early superiority resulted from the capability to economically transport large shipments and to offer frequent service, which gave railroads a near monopolistic position. However, with technology advancements, serious motor carrier competition began to develop following World War II and railroads' share of revenues and ton-miles began to decline.

Railroads once ranked first among all modes in terms of the number of miles in service. The extensive development of roads and highways to support the growth of automobiles and trucks after World War II soon changed this ranking. In 1970 there were 206,265 miles of rail track in the United States. By 2005, track mileage had declined to 95,830 miles as a result of significant abandonment.[18]

The capability to efficiently transport large tonnage over long distances is the main reason railroads continue to handle significant intercity tonnage. Railroad operations have high fixed costs because of expensive equipment, right-of-way and tracks, switching yards, and terminals. However, rail enjoys relatively low variable operating costs. The development of diesel power reduced railroad variable cost per ton-mile, and electrification has provided further cost reductions. Modified labor agreements have reduced human resource requirements, resulting in variable cost reductions.

As a result of deregulation and focused business development, rail traffic has shifted from transporting a broad range of commodities to hauling specific freight. Core railroad tonnage comes from material-extractive industries located a considerable distance from improved waterways and heavy items such as automobiles, farm equipment, and machinery. The rail fixed-variable cost structure offers competitive advantages for long-haul moves. Starting in the mid-1970s, railroads began to segment their transportation market by focusing on carload, intermodal, and container traffic. Marketing emphasis became even more segmented following passage of the Staggers Rail Act. Railroads became more responsive to specific customer needs by emphasizing bulk industries and heavy manufacturing, as contrasted to freight boxcar service. Intermodal operations were expanded by forming alliances with motor carriers. For example, United Parcel Service, primarily a multifaceted motor carrier, is the largest user of rail service to transport trailers in the United States.

To provide improved service to major customers, progressive railroads have concentrated on the development of specialized equipment, such as enclosed trilevel automotive railcars, cushioned appliance railcars, unit trains, articulated cars, and double-stack container flatcars. These technologies are being applied by railroads to reduce weight, increase carrying capacity, and facilitate interchange. The last three innovations are explained in greater detail.

[18] U.S. Department of Transportation, Bureau of Transportation Statistics, *Pocket Guide to Transportation* (Washington, DC: U.S. Government Printing Office, 2006).

On a unit train, all capacity is committed to transporting a single product. Typically, the product is a bulk commodity such as coal or grain. Unit trains have also been used to support assembly operations for the automobile industry. The unit train is faster and less expensive to operate than traditional trains, since it can be routed direct and nonstop from origin to destination.

Articulated cars have an extended rail chassis that can haul up to 10 containers on a single flexible unit. The concept is to reduce time required to formulate trains at railyards.

Double-stack railcars, as the name implies, are designed to transport two levels of containers on a single flatcar, thereby doubling the capacity of each railcar. Containers, discussed later in this chapter, are essentially truck trailers without wheels.

The above examples are by no means a comprehensive review of recent railroad innovations. They are representative of attempts to retain and grow railroad market share. It is clear that significant change continues to occur in traditional railroading. The 1970s challenges of survival and potential nationalization have been replaced by a revitalized rail network. Railroads currently perform a highly focused and important role in the transportation structure as the intermodal leaders of the 21st century. Many observers feel the growing level of congestion and rising fuel costs will serve to energize the overall rail industry.

Truck

Highway transportation has expanded rapidly since the end of World War II. To a significant degree the rapid growth of the motor carrier industry has resulted from speed coupled with the ability to operate door-to-door.

Trucks have flexibility because they are able to operate on a variety of roadways. Over one million miles of highway are available to trucks, which is more mileage than all other surface modes combined. The national fleet of over-the-road trucks exceeds 1.7 million tractors and 4.9 million trailers.[19]

In comparison to railroads, trucks have relatively small fixed investment in terminal facilities and operate on publicly financed and maintained roads. Although the cost of license fees, user fees, and tolls is considerable, these expenses are directly related to the number of trucks and miles operated. The variable cost per mile for motor carriers is high because a separate power unit and driver are required for each trailer or combination of tandem trailers. Labor requirements are also high because of driver safety restrictions and need for substantial dock labor. Truck operations are characterized by low fixed and high variable costs. In comparison to railroads, motor carriers more efficiently handle small shipments moving short distances.

Truck capabilities favor manufacturing and distributive trades, at distances up to 500 miles for high-value products. Trucks have made significant inroads into rail for medium and light manufacturing. As a result of delivery flexibility, motor carriers dominate freight moving from wholesalers and warehouses to retail stores. The future prospect for trucking remains bright. Today, with the exception of small package goods moving in premium air service, almost all less-than-15,000-pound intercity shipments are transported intercity by truck.

The trucking industry is not without problems. The primary difficulties relate to increasing cost to replace equipment, maintenance, safety, driver shortages, driver hours-of-service regulations, dock wages and fuel cost. Although accelerating labor rates influence all modes of transport, trucking is labor-intensive, causing high wages to be a major concern. To counteract this trend, carriers have placed a great deal of attention

[19] U.S. Department of Transportation, Bureau of Transportation Statistics, "Highway Statistics, 2006," Washington, DC, 2006.

on improved line-haul scheduling, computerized billing systems, mechanized terminals, tandem operations that haul two or three trailers with a single power unit, and participation in coordinated intermodal transport systems.

An alternative to for-hire truck service is shipper-owned trucks or trucks operated by integrated logistics service providers **(ISPs)** that are under contract to perform transport services for specific shippers.

Approximately 55 percent of all intercity truck tonnage is hauled by shipper-owned or shipper-controlled trucks. Following deregulation, this ratio reached a high of 66 percent by 1987.[20] The decline to 55 percent resulted from shippers realizing the numerous complexities and problems of operating a private fleet. The growth of Integrated Service Providers operated trucking offers a service that combines the flexibility of private with the consolidation potential of for-hire operators. An ISP may perform services for multiple shippers and thus gain both economies of scale and distance.

Since 1980, deregulation has dramatically changed the nature of the for-hire trucking. The industry segments, which have become more defined since deregulation, include truckload **(TL)**, less-than-truckload **(LTL)**, and specialty. The dramatic change is related to the type of carriers operating in each category.

The TL segment includes loads over 15,000 pounds that generally do not require intermediate stops between origin and destination. Although large firms such as Schneider National and J. B. Hunt provide nationwide TL service, the segment is characterized by a large number of relatively small carriers and is generally very price competitive.

The LTL segment involves shipments less than 15,000 pounds that generally must be consolidated to achieve trailer capacity. As a result of origin and destination terminal costs and relatively higher marketing expenses, LTL experiences a higher percentage of fixed costs than TL. The operating characteristics of the LTL freight segment have caused extensive industry consolidation, resulting in a few relatively large national carriers and a strong regional network of smaller carriers. Some major nationwide LTL carriers are Yellow Roadway, USF Corp., FedEx Freight, Con Way Transportation, and Arkansas Best.

Specialty carriers include bulk and package haulers such as Waste Management and United Parcel Service **(UPS).** Specialty firms focus on specific transport requirements of a market or product. Specialty carriers are not generally direct competitors with the other two segments.

On the basis of the sheer size of the trucking industry and the services provided, it is quite apparent that highway transportation will continue to function as the backbone of logistical operations for the foreseeable future.

Water

Water is the oldest mode of transport. The original sailing vessels were replaced by steam-powered boats in the early 1800s and by diesel in the 1920s. A distinction is generally made between deepwater and navigable inland water transport.

Domestic water transport, which involves the Great Lakes, canals, and intracoastal waterways, has maintained a relatively constant annual ton-mile share of between 19 and 30 percent over the past four decades. While the share has remained relatively constant, the mix has changed dramatically. The percentage of river and canal ton-miles has increased by more than 183 million ton-miles between 1965 and 2006, while the Great Lakes ton-miles decreased by more than 22 million ton-miles during this same period. These figures reflect both a shift of bulk product transportation from rail and highway to lower-cost

[20] U.S. Department of Transportation, Bureau of Transportation Statistics, "National Transportation Statistics, 2004," Table 1-46, Washington, DC, 2004.

water movements on rivers and coastal canals as well as a shift from lakeside shipping to motor carrier transport.

In 2006, 26,000 miles of inland waterways were available, not including the Great Lakes or coastal shipping.[21] This network size has been stable over the past decade and is expected to remain for the foreseeable future. Fewer system miles exist for inland water than for any other transportation mode.

The main advantage of water transport is the capacity to transport extremely large shipments. Water transport employs two types of vessels for movement: Deepwater vessels are generally designed for coastal, ocean, and Great Lakes transport; diesel-towed barges generally operate on rivers and canals and have considerably more flexibility.

Water transport ranks between rail and motor carrier in terms of fixed cost. Although water carriers must develop and operate their own terminals, the right-of-way is developed and maintained by the government and results in moderate fixed costs compared to rail. The main disadvantages of water transport are the limited range of operation and slow speed. Unless the origin and destination of the movement are adjacent to a waterway, supplemental haul by rail or truck is required. The capability of water to transport large tonnage at low variable cost places this mode of transport in demand when low freight rates are desired and speed of transit is a secondary consideration.

Water transport will continue to be a viable transportation option in future supply chain logistics. The slow transit time of river transport provides a form of product storage in transit that can benefit logistics system design. In addition, the North American Free Trade Agreement **(NAFTA)** continues to offer the potential for increased utilization of the St. Lawrence Seaway to link new producer and consumer markets in Mexico, the Midwest, and the Canadian port cities. The passage of the Central America Free Trade Act **(CAFTA)** in 2005 is projected to have a significant impact on the use of water transport. Finally, water remains the primary mode of transport for global logistics.

Pipeline

Pipelines are a significant part of the U.S. transportation system. Pipelines accounted for approximately 67.8 percent of all crude and petroleum ton-mile movements. In 2005, 159,512 miles of oil pipeline were operational in the United States.[22]

In addition to petroleum products, the other important product transported by pipeline is natural gas. Like petroleum pipelines, natural gas pipelines in the United States are privately owned and operated, and many gas companies act as both gas distribution and contract transportation providers.

The basic nature of a pipeline is unique in comparison to any other mode of transport. Pipelines operate on a 24-hour basis, 7 days per week, and are limited only by commodity changeover and maintenance. Unlike other modes, there is no empty container or vehicle that must be returned. Pipelines have the highest fixed cost and lowest variable cost among transport modes. High fixed costs result from the right-of-way for pipeline, construction and requirements for control stations, and pumping capacity. Since pipelines are not labor-intensive, the variable operating cost is extremely low once the pipeline has been constructed. An obvious disadvantage is that pipelines are not flexible and are limited with respect to commodities that can be transported, as only products in the forms of gas, liquid, or slurry can be handled.

Experiments regarding potential movement of solid products in the form of slurry or hydraulic suspension continue. Coal slurry pipelines have proved to be an efficient

---

[21] U.S. Department of Transportation, Bureau of Transportation Statistics, "National Transportation Statistics, 2006," Washington, DC, 2006.
[22] Association of Oil Pipelines, "Annual Report Comparisons from 1982–2006," Washington, DC, June 2006.

and economical mode of transporting coal over long distances. Coal slurry lines require massive quantities of water, which is a significant concern among environmentalists.

Air

The newest but least utilized mode of transportation is airfreight. The significant advantage of airfreight lies in the speed with which a shipment can be transported. A coast-to-coast shipment via air requires only hours contrasted to days with other modes of transport. While costly, the speed of air transport allows other aspects of logistics such as warehousing and inventory to be reduced or eliminated.

Air transport, despite its high profile, still remains more of a potential than a reality. Airfreight accounts for 1 percent of intercity ton-miles.[23] Air transport capability is limited by load size, weight lift capacity, and aircraft availability. Traditionally, intercity airfreight was transported on scheduled passenger flights. While the practice was economical, it resulted in a limited capacity and flexibility of freight operations. The high cost of jet aircraft, coupled with the erratic nature of freight demand, served to limit the economic commitment of dedicated aircraft to all-freight operations.

However, the advent of premium air carriers such as Federal Express and United Parcel Air introduced scheduled global airfreight service. While such premium service was originally targeted at high-priority documents, it has expanded to include package freight. For example, premium carriers have integrated their service to include overnight parts delivery from centralized distribution centers located near their air hubs. Overnight air delivery from a centralized warehouse is attractive to firms with a large number of high-value products and time-sensitive service requirements.

The fixed cost of air transport is low compared to rail, water, and pipeline. In fact, air transport ranks second only to highway with respect to low fixed cost. Airways and airports are generally developed and maintained by government. The fixed costs of airfreight are associated with aircraft purchase and the requirement for specialized handling systems and cargo containers. On the other hand, air freight variable cost is extremely high as a result of fuel, user fees, maintenance, and the labor intensity of both in-flight and ground crews.

Since airports require significant real estate, they are generally limited with respect to integration with other transport modes. However, there is substantial interest in integrating air transport with other modes and developing all-freight airports to eliminate conflict with passenger service. For example, Alliance Airport, located near Fort Worth, Texas, was designed to integrate air, rail, and truck distribution from a single location.

No particular commodity dominates the traffic carried by airfreight operations. Perhaps the best distinction is that most freight has high value and priority. Businesses tend to utilize scheduled or nonscheduled air cargo movements when the service proposition justifies high cost. Products with the greatest potential for regular air movement are those having high value or extreme perishability. When the marketing period for a product is extremely limited, such as Christmas gifts, high-fashion clothing, fresh fish, or cut flowers, air may be the only practical transportation method to support global operations. Routine logistics of products such as computers, repair parts, and medical supplies also utilize airfreight.

Modal Classification

Table 8.4 compares the fixed-variable cost structure of each mode. Table 8.5 ranks modal operating characteristics with respect to speed, availability, dependability, capability, and frequency.

---

[23] U.S. Department of Transportation, Bureau of Transportation Statistics, "National Transportation Statistics 2006," Washington, DC, 2006.

TABLE 8.4
Cost Structure for Each Mode

- *Rail.* High fixed cost in equipment, terminals, tracks, etc. Low variable cost.
- *Truck.* Low fixed cost (highways in place and provided by public support). Medium variable cost (fuel, maintenance, etc.).
- *Water.* Medium fixed cost (ships and equipment). Low variable cost (capability to transport large amount of tonnage).
- *Pipeline.* Highest fixed cost (rights-of-way, construction, requirements for control stations, and pumping capacity). Lowest variable cost (no labor cost of any significance).
- *Air.* Low fixed cost (aircraft and handling and cargo systems). High variable cost (fuel, labor, maintenance, etc.).

Speed refers to elapsed movement time. Airfreight is the fastest of all modes. **Availability** refers to the ability of a mode to service any given pair of locations. Highway carriers have the greatest availability since they can drive directly to origin and destination points. **Dependability** refers to potential variance from expected or published delivery schedules. Pipelines, because of their continuous service and limited interference due to weather and congestion, rank highest in dependability. **Capability** is the ability of a mode to handle any transport requirement, such as load size. Water transport is the most capable. The final classification is **frequency,** which relates to the quantity of scheduled movements. Pipelines, again because of their continuous service between two points, lead all modes in frequency.

As Table 8.5 illustrates, the appeal of highway transport is in part explained by its high relative ranking across the five operating characteristics. Motor carriers rank first or second in all categories except capability. Although substantial improvements in motor capability resulted from relaxed size and weight limitations on interstate highways and approval to use tandem trailers, it is not realistic to assume motor transport will surpass rail or water capability.

Infrastructure in Crisis

Following World War II the United States embarked on an aggressive development program that by 2004 resulted in construction of 46,837 miles of interstate highways. In 2006 this federal highway system supported the movement of 10.7 billion tons of freight, which equaled 69 percent of all freight moved in the United States.[24] However, by 2008 this highway system was in need of expansion and widespread repair to sustain the safe movement of over 26 million trucks.[25]

[24] *American Trucking Trends, 2007–2008* (American Trucking Association Business Wire, January 25, 2008).
[25] Ibid.

TABLE 8.5
Relative Operating Characteristics by Mode*

Operating Characteristics	Rail	Truck	Water	Pipeline	Air
Speed	3	2	4	5	1
Availability	2	1	4	5	3
Dependability	3	2	4	1	5
Capability	2	3	1	5	4
Frequency	4	2	5	1	3
Composite Score	14	10	18	17	16

*Lowest rank is best.

On August 1, 2007, the collapse of a major span of interstate highway 1-35W bridging the Mississippi River in downtown Minneapolis vividly called to public attention the nation's crumbling network of bridges, tunnels, and roads. Investigation revealed that in 2007 out of 600,000 public road bridges listed in the National Bridge Inventory, roughly 12 percent, or 79,000, were classified as structurally deficient.[26]

Participants in the transportation system are deeply concerned about these and other growing issues related to safety, congestion, and inadequate system capacity across all five transportation modes. Most transportation professionals agree the United States is in need of a far-reaching National Transportation Plan to facilitate both the repair and reinvention of transportation infrastructure.[27] In January 2009, the Obama Administration made infrastructure renovation a high priority item.

Transportation Service

Transportation service is achieved by combining modes. Prior to deregulation, government policy limited carriers to operating in a single mode. Such restrictive ownership sought to promote competition between modes and limit the potential for monopoly practices. Following deregulation carriers were free to develop integrated modal services in efforts to more efficiently and effectively meet the needs of customers. The following section reviews the current range of services offered by different carriers.

Traditional Carriers

The most basic carrier type is a transportation firm that provides service utilizing only one of the five basic transport modes. Focus on a single operational mode permits a carrier to become highly specialized.

Although single-mode operators are able to offer extremely efficient transport, such specialization creates difficulties for a shipper who desires intermodal transport solutions because it requires negotiation and business planning with multiple carriers. Airlines are an example of a single-mode carrier for both freight and passenger service that traditionally limits service from airport to airport. Since deregulation most carriers are developing services that facilitate multimodal integration.

Package Service

Over the past several decades a serious problem existed in the availability of small-shipment transportation. It was difficult for common carriers to provide reasonably priced small-shipment service because of overhead cost associated with terminal and line-haul operations. This overhead forced motor carriers to implement a **minimum charge.** The minimum applies to all shipments regardless of shipment size or distance. As a result of the minimum charge and lack of alternatives, an opportunity existed for companies offering specialized service to enter the small-shipment or package-service market.

Package services represent an important part of logistics, and the influence of carriers in this segment is increasing because of their size and intermodal capabilities. The advent of e-commerce and the need for consumer-direct last-mile fulfillment have significantly increased demand for package delivery. While package services are expanding,

[26] Robert S. Kirk and William J. Mallett, "Highway Bridges: Conditions and the Federal/State Role," *CRS Report for Congress: August 10,* 2007, p. 2.
[27] Robert J. Bowman, "A Road to Ruin? U.S. Transportation Infrastructure Is a System in Crisis," *Global Logistics and Supply Chain Strategies,* October 2007, pp. 28–35.

the services required do not fall neatly into the traditional modal classification scheme. Packages are regularly transported by using the line-haul services of rail, motor, and air. Package service provides both regular and premium services.

Ground Package Service

Numerous carriers offer delivery services within metropolitan areas. Other carriers offer package delivery service on a national and global basis. The most recognizable carriers are United Parcel Service **(UPS),** the United States Postal Service **(USPS),** and Federal Express Ground.

The original service offered by UPS was contract delivery of local shipments for department stores. Today, UPS offers a diverse range of package services. In fact, UPS has expanded its scope of overall operating authority by shipping packages that conform to specialized size and weight restrictions nationwide and globally for consumers and business enterprises. While UPS provides logistical services related to all types of products, specialization in small packages enables a cost-effective overnight service between most cities within 300 miles.

TABLE 8.6
Examples of Integrated Parcel Carrier Services

Source: Modified and condensed from United Parcel Service Web site, www.ups.com.

	Freight Services
Same Day Air	Guaranteed same day delivery for letters and packages.
Next Day Delivery	Guaranteed weekday (Saturday available), next day delivery. Ranges from early morning (8:00 A.M.) delivery to air saver (3:00–4:30 P.M.) delivery.
Second Day Delivery	Guaranteed delivery on the second business day. Services offered range from noon delivery to end of business day delivery.
3 Day Select	Guaranteed 3 day delivery to and from every U.S. address.
Ground	Low-cost ground delivery with guaranteed delivery date.
Worldwide Express	Guaranteed delivery to and from the U.S., Canada, and Europe with next day, 2 day, and time-definite deliveries.
Standard to/from Canada	Guaranteed, fully tracked, door-to-door ground delivery from the 48 contiguous states to/from all addresses in the 10 Canadian provinces. Many time-definite delivery options available.
World Ease	A worldwide consolidated clearance service that groups several shipments destined for one country into a single shipment.
	Optional, Value-Added Services
Collect on Delivery (COD)	Payment collected immediately upon delivery and delivered promptly to customer. Will exchange international monies.
Delivery Confirmation	Confirms delivery with the recipient's signature. Additional service shows digital signature of person receiving package, proof of delivery, and telephone confirmation of delivery.
Hazardous Materials	Transport hazardous materials and international dangerous goods within the continental U.S.
Hold for Pickup	Packages are delivered to the facility of choice and carrier calls the consignee by telephone for pickup.
Saturday Pickup/Delivery	Packages shipped and picked up on Saturdays.
10KG and 23KG Boxes	A fixed-rate shipping solution for express shipments up to 10 kg (22 lb) and 25 kg (55 lb).
Hundredweight Service	Contract service for multipackage shipments less than 1000 lb that are less than a pallet load sent to a single address.
Returns	Includes labels (preprinted, on demand, and mailed), and authorized return services.
Excess Value Insurance	Third-party insurance provides protection for shipments valued between $100 and $50,000.

UPS has various capabilities and offers a range of services, including ground and premium air. Table 8.6, based on UPS promotional materials, summarizes the integrated services offered by package carriers. It is interesting to note that ground service frequently involves intermodal movement by a combination of truck and train capacity.

The United States Postal Service **(USPS)** operates ground and air parcel service. Charges for parcel post are based on weight and distance. Generally, parcels must be delivered to a post office for shipment origination. However, in the case of large users and when it is convenient for the Postal Service, pickup is provided at the shipper's location. Intercity transport is accomplished by purchasing air, highway, rail, and even water service from for-hire carriers. Delivery is provided to the destination by the Postal Service.

In 2006 the range of services provided by the USPS were significantly expanded as a result of the passage of the Postal Accountability and Enhancement Act **(PAEA).** The USPS has a last-mile advantage over all other package carriers in that it is structured to facilitate delivery to every household in the United States every day. Under provision of the PAEA the USPS was given flexibility in pricing. The traditional practice of charging the same price per unit of freight was modified to include commercial volume pricing, minimum value rebates, and online price breaks. Table 8.7 provides examples of the expanded USPS product offerings. To view the full range of the new pricing structure visit *www.usps.com/prices.*

The importance of parcel service to the logistical system cannot be overemphasized. One of the expanding forms of marketing in the United States is nonstore retailing, in which orders are placed via the Internet, telephone, or mail for subsequent home delivery. Firms that specialize in consumer fulfillment are one of the fastest growing forms of logistics service providers.

Air Package Service

Several carriers, such as Federal Express and UPS, have entered the package or premium transportation market over the past two decades. Most organizations that provide routine package service also offer premium service. UPS, for example, offers next-day and second-day service, while the United States Postal Service provides a variety of priority services.

The first widely recognized premium package service was initiated by Federal Express **(FedEx)** in 1973. FedEx provides overnight service, utilizing a fleet of dedicated cargo aircraft. The original FedEx service attracted attention because of the innovative line-haul plan in which all packages were flown overnight to a terminal hub located in Memphis, Tennessee, for sorting and redistribution. Federal Express original service has been considerably expanded by offering larger package size and weight restrictions and adding global connectivity.

The demand for parcel delivery service has attracted many competitors into overnight premium package service. In addition to specialized firms like FedEx and UPS, major

TABLE 8.7
United States Postal Service Expanded Services

- Express Mail, premium overnight delivery, is switching to an industry standard, zone-based pricing system, resulting in lower prices for closer destinations. Customers will enjoy a 3 percent price reduction by purchasing Express Mail on line or through corporate accounts. Up to an additional 7 percent price reduction is available for those who meet quarterly volume minimums.

- Priority Mail, expedited delivery at economical prices, will be available at an average 3.5 percent savings to customers who use electronic postage or meet other requirements.

- Parcel Select, the Postal Service's "last mile" advantage of delivery to every door, will feature pricing and volume incentives for large- and medium-sized shippers.

- Parcel Return Service, an easy and convenient way for customers to return items to businesses, will move entirely to a weight-based pricing system, resulting in significant price reductions for lighter packages.

motor carriers and airlines have begun to offer competitive service. Many services appeal to commercial business because they satisfy demand for rapid delivery.

Intermodal Transportation

Intermodal transportation combines two or more modes to take advantage of the inherent economies of each and thus provide an integrated service at lower total cost. Many efforts have been made over the years to integrate different transportation modes. Initial attempts at modal coordination trace back to the early 1920s, but during the regulatory years, cooperation was restrained by restrictions designed to limit monopoly practices. Intermodal offerings began to develop more successfully during the 1950s with the advent of integrated rail and motor service commonly termed **piggyback service.** This common intermodal arrangement combines the flexibility of motor for short distances with the low line-haul cost associated with rail for longer distances. The popularity of such offerings has increased significantly as a means to achieve more efficient and effective transportation.[28]

Technically, coordinated or intermodal transportation could be arranged among all basic modes. Descriptive jargon such as fishyback, trainship, and airtruck have become standard transportation terms.

Piggyback/TOFC/COFC

The best known and most widely used intermodal systems are the trailer on a flatcar **(TOFC)** and container on a flatcar **(COFC).** Containers are the boxes utilized for intermodal product storage and movement between motor freight, railroads, and water transportation. Containers are typically 8 feet wide, 8 feet high, and 20 or 40 feet long, and do not have highway wheels. Trailers, on the other hand, are of similar width and height but can be as long as 53 feet and have highway wheels. As the name implies, a trailer or container is placed on a railroad flatcar for some portion of the intercity line-haul and pulled by a truck at origin and destination. Line-haul cost is the expense to move railcars or trucks between cities. Since the original development of TOFC, various combinations of trailer or container on flatcar—double-stack, for instance—have increased significantly.

A variety of coordinated service plans have been developed. Each plan defines the railroad or motor carrier responsibility. Table 8.8 illustrates traditional operating plans. The plans differ by responsibility for equipment, pickup, and delivery.

While the TOFC concept facilitates direct transfer between rail and motor carriage, it also has several technical limitations. The placement of a trailer with highway wheels attached, transferred to a railcar, can lead to wind resistance, damage, and weight problems. The use of containers reduces these potential problems, as they can be double stacked and are easily transferred to water carriers. However, they require special equipment for over-the-road delivery or pickup.

Containerships

Fishyback, trainship, and containership are examples of the oldest form of intermodal transport. They utilize waterways, which are one of the least expensive modes for line-haul movement. A 2004 comparison done by the Maritime Adminstration **(MARAD)** showed that one 15-barge tow has the equivalent capacity of 225 railcars or 900 trucks.[29]

---

[28] For a comprehensive discussion of contemporary intermodel operations, see John C. Taylor and George C. Jackson, "Conflict, Power and Evolution in the Intermodal Transportation Industry's Channel of Distribution," *Transportation Journal,* Spring 2000, pp. 5–17.

[29] U.S. Waterborne Foreign Trade Containerized Cargo, Top 25 U.S. Ports, January–June 2004, Port Import Export Reporting Services. MARAD waterborne traffic statistics, http://www.marad.dot.gov/MARAD.

TABLE 8.8
Traditional Rail–Truck Coordination Plans

- *Plan 250.* Rail transportation of a shipment loaded in a carrier vehicle from terminal at origin to terminal at destination. Shipper is responsible for pickup and delivery services beyond the terminal.
- *Plan 300.* Rail transportation of a shipment loaded in a shipper vehicle from terminal at origin to terminal at destination. Shipper is responsible for pickup and delivery beyond the terminal.
- *Plan 310.* Rail transportation of an empty shipper vehicle having an immediate prior or subsequent loaded domestic movement via mail. Shipper is responsible for pickup and delivery beyond the terminal.
- *Plans 400 to 470.* These services apply only to domestic container shipments involving carrier containers or the repositioning of international containers owned or controlled by steamship companies. They include, where indicated, truck pickup at origin and/or delivery at destination.
  - Plan 400: Door at origin, door at destination.
  - Plan 420: Door at origin, ramp at destination.
  - Plan 450: Ramp at origin, ramp at destination.
  - Plan 470: Ramp at origin, door at destination.
- *Plans 600 to 625 or Service Code 20 to 67.* Their services apply to shipments involving carrier vehicles and shipper vehicles. They include truck pickup at origin and/or delivery at destination.
  - Plan 600: Door at origin, door at destination (carrier vehicle).
  - Plan 605: Door at origin, door at destination (shipper vehicle).
  - Plan 610: Door at origin, ramp at destination (carrier vehicle).
  - Plan 615: Door at origin, ramp at destination (shipper vehicle).
  - Plan 620: Ramp at origin, door at destination (carrier vehicle).
  - Plan 625: Ramp at origin, door at destination (shipper vehicle).
- *Plan 800.* Rail transportation of a loaded shipper vehicle from the terminal at origin to the terminal at destination where the shipment has had/will have an immediate prior or subsequent movement via water transport in international commerce without transfer of cargo. Shipper is responsible for pickup and delivery beyond the terminal.
- *Plan 810.* Rail transportation of an empty shipper vehicle from the terminal at origin to the terminal at destination having an immediate prior or subsequent loaded movement via rail in conjunction with water transport in international commerce. Shipper is responsible for pickup and delivery beyond the terminal.

The fishyback, trainship, and containership concept loads a truck trailer, railcar, or container onto a barge or ship for the line-haul movement on inland navigable waterways. Such services are provided in coastal waters between Atlantic and Gulf ports, and between the Great Lakes and coastal points. Because of the low costs and efficiency of coastal barges, MARAD is advocating expanding **short sea shipping** to ease traffic congestion and alleviate air pollution.

A variant of this intermodal option is the **land bridge** concept that moves containers in a combination of sea and rail transport. The land bridge is commonly used for containers moving between Europe and the Pacific Rim to reduce the time and expense of all-water transport. For example, containers are shipped to the West Coast of North America from the Pacific Rim, loaded onto railcars for movement to the East Coast, and then reloaded onto ships for movement to Europe. The land bridge concept is based on the benefit of ocean and rail combinations that utilize a single tariff, which is lower than the combined total cost of two separate rates.

The transfer of freight between modes often requires the handling of containers and the imposition of duties. Ports are used to make this transfer as seamless and as fast as possible. Water ports on the U.S. coasts and inland waterways provide 3,214 berths for deep draft ships and transfer cargo and passengers through 1,941 public and private marine terminals.[30] While inbound and outbound container traffic continues to grow on a year-over-year basis, berth and terminal capacity is not significantly expanding.

---

[30] American Association of Port Authorities 2004, www.aapa-ports.org.

Port throughput is a big concern to supply chain managers and although there are many ports in the United States, three ocean ports, Los Angeles, Long Beach, and New York account for almost half of all imports and exports in the United States. In 2002, striking terminal workers at Long Beach and Los Angeles ports caused long delays in the transfer of freight. In 2004, the continued increase in the volume of imported containers again congested West Coast ports, causing some logistics companies to inform companies to expect seven-day delays in clearing ports. In July 2005 the ports of Los Angeles and Long Beach implemented a program called PierPass. Designed to reduce prime-time congestion Pier-Pass introduced a Traffic Mitigation Fee during peak hours of $40 per 20-foot equivalent container and for all larger than 20 foot a fee of $80. Firms willing to move freight in off-peak hours were able to register to be exempt from the fee.

Coordinated Air-Truck

Another form of intermodal transport combines air and truck. Local cartage is a vital part of every air movement because airfreight must eventually move from the airport to the final delivery destination. Air-truck movements usually provide service and flexibility comparable to straight motor freight.

Air-truck is commonly used to provide premium package services, such as those offered by UPS and FedEx, but can also be used for more standard freight applications for several reasons. First, there is a lack of airfreight service to smaller cities in the United States. Smaller cities are often served by narrow-body aircraft and commuter planes that are not equipped to handle freight. Thus, motor carriage into small cities from metropolitan airports provides a needed service at a competitive cost. Second, package carriers, while suited to serve small cities, have limited ability to handle heavy freight. Package carriers that are focused on smaller parcels and materials handling systems are limited in ability to handle heavy freight. As a result, many air carriers have extended their motor freight range to provide service to expanded geographical areas.

The concept of intermodalism appeals to both shippers and carriers because of the economic leverage of linking two modes. In fact, many authorities believe the only way to maintain a strong national transportation network is to encourage and foster intermodalism. Efforts to increase intermodalism are of prime interest to logistical planners because such development expands options available in logistical system design.

During the past decade, intermodal innovations have increasingly switched from technology improvements toward collaborate arrangements. The North American Super Coalition **(NASCO)** and the Heartland Corridor are two examples of railroads, deep-water ports, distribution parks, and highway transportation being linked to exploit multimodal capability.

The NASCO corridor is a 2500-mile-long multimodal transportation network linking Mexico, the United States, and Canada. A collaboration of inland port facilities, the North American Inland Port Network **(NAIPN),** is devoted to supporting NASCO by providing U.S. Customs Clearance at strategically located terminal facilities. This inland port capability allows freight to rapidly clear customs, thereby alleviating congestion and delays at maritime ports and U.S. borders.[31]

The Heartland Corridor plans to link Norfolk and Chicago with the Rickenbacker Intermodal Rail Center in Columbus, Ohio. When completed in 2010 freight will move between East Coast ports and Columbus, traveling 200 fewer miles and at least a full day faster than today's movements. The Rickenbacker Intermodal Rail Center will provide access to highway and air transport.[32]

[31] NASCO, *Inbound Logistics,* November 2007, pp. 67–80.
[32] Roger Morton, "Placing the Pieces for the Heartland Corridor," *Logistics Today,* December 2007, pp. 20–21.

These two examples serve to illustrate how infrastructure is being developed to provide an integrated multimodal transportation future. Such integration also serves to improve security and reduced risk.

Nonoperating Intermediaries

The overall transportation industry also includes several business types that do not own or operate equipment. These nonoperating intermediaries broker services of other firms. A transportation broker is somewhat analogous to a wholesaler in a marketing channel.

Nonoperating intermediaries find economic justification by offering shippers lower rates for movement between two locations than would be possible by direct shipment via common carrier. Because of peculiarities in the common-carrier rate structure, such as minimum freight charges, surcharges, and less-than-volume rates, conditions exist whereby nonoperating intermediaries can facilitate savings for shippers. Interestingly, there are cases where nonoperating intermediaries charge higher rates than those offered by carriers. The justification for the higher charges is based on ability to arrange faster delivery and/or more value-added services. The primary intermediaries are freight forwarders, shipper associations, and brokers.

Freight Forwarders

Freight forwarders are for-profit businesses that consolidate small shipments from various customers into a bulk shipment and then utilize a common surface or air carrier for transport. At destination, the freight forwarder splits the consolidated shipment into the original smaller shipments. Local delivery may or may not be arranged by the forwarder. The main advantage of the forwarder is a lower rate per hundredweight obtained from large shipment and, in most cases, faster transport of small shipments than would be experienced if the individual customer dealt directly with the common carrier. Freight forwarders accept full responsibility for shipment performance.

Shipper Association/Cooperatives and Agents

Shipper associations are operationally similar to freight forwarders in that they consolidate small shipments into large movements to gain cost economies. Shipper associations are voluntary nonprofit entities where members, operating in a specific industry, collaborate to gain economies related to small-shipment purchases. Typically, members purchase product from common vendors or from sources of supply located in one area. A common practice is to order small quantities at frequent intervals to minimize retail inventory. Participation in a shipper association typically means improved speed of delivery, since a large number of different products may be purchased at one location, such as the garment district in New York City.

The association requires a group of shippers to establish an administrative office or arrange an agent at the location of frequent merchandise purchase. The agent arranges for individual purchases to be delivered to a local facility. When sufficient volume is accumulated, a consolidated shipment is arranged for local delivery. Some associations operate their own intercity transportation. Each member is billed a proportionate share for transportation plus a prorated share of the association's fixed cost.

Brokers

Brokers are intermediaries that coordinate transportation arrangements for shippers, consignees, and carriers. They also arrange shipments for exempt carriers and drivers who own their trucks. Brokers typically operate on a commission basis. Prior to deregulation, brokers played a minor role in logistics because of service restrictions. Today, brokers provide more extensive services such as shipment matching, rate negotiation, billing, and tracing. The entire area of brokerage operations is highly adaptable to Internet-based transactions and is increasing in importance as a result of increased globalization.

Summary

Transportation is a key activity in logistics because it moves product through the various stages of production and ultimately to consumers. This chapter introduced major principles of transportation economies and provided a brief historical summary of government regulation. It is important that logistics managers have appreciation and understanding of regulation history to fully appreciate the logic underlying today's transport system.

The transportation system contains five modes of operation: rail, motor, water, pipeline, and air. Each mode has specific attributes that render it the transportation choice appropriate for a specific freight movement. Traditional transport supply consisted of a large number of specialized carriers, each limiting operations to one specific mode. The original lack of coordinated transportation resulted in inefficiencies and high cost. Deregulation introduced competitive pricing and carrier flexibility. It became common for carriers to combine multimodal services and offer specialized services to individual customers. As a result, a wide range of specialized transport service is now available to satisfy specific customer requirements. Attention in Chapter 9 is focused on transportation operations, followed by a discussion of carrier economics, pricing, and documentation.

Challenge Questions

1. Compare and contrast the transport principles of economy of scale and economy of distance. Illustrate how they combine to create efficient transportation.
2. Describe the five modes of transportation, identifying the most significant characteristic of each.
3. Why is motor carrier freight transportation the most used method of product shipment?
4. What is the economic justification for the rapid growth of premium package services?
5. Why is it important for a logistics manager to have a degree of understanding of transportation regulatory history?
6. Why have railroad miles declined during a period of national growth?
7. Railroads have the largest percentage of intercity freight ton-miles, but motor carriers have the largest revenue. How do you explain this relationship?
8. Discuss the fundamental difference between TOFC and COFC. Why was double stacking considered a major innovation in multimodal transportation?
9. Explain the value proposition offered by freight forwarding. Provide an example that illustrates why shippers would be attracted to using the services of a freight forwarder as contrasted to arranging their own transportation.
10. The five basic modes of transportation have been available for well over 50 years. Is this the way it will always be, or can you identify a sixth mode that may become economically feasible in the foreseeable future.

CHAPTER NINE

Transportation Operations

Chapter Outline

Transportation is the single largest element of logistics cost. The historical view of traffic departments being staffed with individuals wearing green eyeshades and sitting amid bookshelves filled with tariffs and rate tables is a scenario far from reality in today's competitive environment. Traffic departments commit and manage over 60 percent of a typical firm's logistics expenditures. Transportation managers are responsible for arranging for inventory to be positioned in a timely and economical manner. A fundamental responsibility is to determine whether transportation services should be performed by using private or for-hire capacity. Decisions related to internal performance versus outsourcing are not totally different from those faced in many other enterprise areas. What is different about transportation is the critical impact that operations have on logistical performance. As operational expectations become more precise, order-to-delivery performance cycles more compact, and margins for error reduced near zero, successful firms have come to realize that **there is no such thing as cheap transportation.** Unless transportation is managed in an effective and efficient manner, procurement, manufacturing, and customer accommodation performance will not meet expectations. This chapter provides an overview of how transportation is managed within the logistical process. Near the conclusion, the discussion focuses on how transportation operations are directly linked to product pricing decision.

Transportation Economics and Pricing

Transportation economics and pricing are concerned with factors and characteristics that drive cost. To develop effective logistics strategy, it is necessary to understand such factors and characteristics. Successful negotiation requires a full understanding of transportation economics. An overview of transportation economics and pricing consists of four interrelated topics: (1) economic drivers, (2) costing, (3) carrier pricing strategy, and (4) transportation rates and ratings.

Economic Drivers

Transportation economics are driven by seven factors. While not direct components of transport tariffs, each factor influences rates. The factors are: (1) distance, (2) weight, (3) density, (4) stowability, (5) handling, (6) liability, and (7) market. The following discusses the relative importance of each factor from a shipper's perspective. Keep in mind that the precise impact of each factor varies, depending on specific market and product characteristics.

Distance

Distance is a major influence on transportation cost since it directly contributes to variable expense, such as labor, fuel, and maintenance. Figure 9.1 illustrates the general relationship between distance and transportation cost. Two important points are illustrated. First, the cost curve does not begin at zero because there are fixed costs associated with shipment pickup and delivery regardless of distance. Second, the cost curve increases at a decreasing rate as a function of distance. This characteristic is known as the **tapering principle.**[1]

Weight

The second factor is load weight. As with other logistics activities, scale economies exist for most transportation movements. This relationship, illustrated in Figure 9.2, indicates that transport cost per unit of weight decreases as load size increases. This occurs because the fixed costs of pickup, delivery, and administration are spread over

[1] The principles of economy of scale and economy of distance were introduced in Chapter 8.

FIGURE 9.1
Generalized Relationship between Distance and Transportation Cost

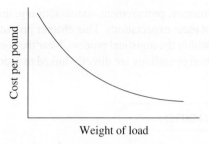

incremental weight. This relationship is limited by the size of the transportation vehicle. Once the vehicle is full, the relationship begins again with each additional vehicle. The managerial implication is that small loads should be consolidated into larger loads to maximize scale economies.

Density

A third factor is product density. Density is the combination of weight and volume. Weight and volume are important since transportation cost for any movement is usually quoted in dollars per unit of weight. Transport charges are commonly quoted per hundredweight (CWT). In terms of weight and volume, vehicles are typically more constrained by cubic capacity than by weight. Since actual vehicle, labor, and fuel expenses are not dramatically influenced by weight, higher-density products allow fixed transport cost to be spread across more weight. As a result, higher density products are typically assessed lower transport cost per unit of weight. Figure 9.3 illustrates the relationship of declining transportation cost per unit of weight as product density increases. In general, traffic managers seek to improve product density so that trailer cubic capacity can be fully utilized.

Stowability

Stowability refers to how product dimensions fit into transportation equipment. Odd package sizes and shapes, as well as excessive size or length, may not fit well in transportation equipment, resulting in wasted cubic capacity. Although density and stowability are similar, it is possible to have items with similar densities that stow very differently. Items having rectangular shapes are much easier to stow than odd-shaped items. For example, while steel blocks and rods may have the same physical density, rods are more difficult to stow than blocks because of their length and shape. Stowability is also influenced by other aspects of size, since large numbers of items may be **nested** in shipments whereas they may be difficult to stow in small quantities. For example, it is possible to accomplish significant nesting for a truckload of trash cans while a single can is difficult to stow.

Handling

Special handling equipment may be required to load and unload trucks, railcars, or ships. In addition to special handling equipment, the manner in which products are physically grouped together in boxes or on pallets for transport and storage will impact handling cost. Chapters 10 and 11 specifically address handling issues related to packaging and storage.

Liability

Liability includes product characteristics that can result in damage. Carriers must either have insurance to protect against potential damage or accept financial responsibility. Shippers can reduce their risk, and ultimately transportation cost, by improved packaging or reducing susceptibility to loss or damage.

Market

Finally, market factors such as lane volume and balance influence transportation cost. A **transport lane** refers to movements between origin and destination points. Since transportation vehicles and drivers typically return to their origin, either they must find a **backhaul** load or the vehicle is returned or **deadheaded** empty. When empty return movements occur, labor, fuel, and maintenance costs must be charged against the original front-haul movement. Thus, the ideal situation is to achieve two-way or balanced movement of loads. However, this is rarely the case because of demand imbalances in manufacturing and consumption locations. For example, many goods are manufactured and processed in the eastern United States and then shipped to consumer markets in the western portion of the country. This results in an imbalance in volume moving between the two geographical areas. Such imbalance causes rates to be generally lower for eastbound moves. Movement balance is also influenced by seasonality, such as the movement of fruits and vegetables to coincide with growing seasons. Demand location and seasonality result in transport rates that change with direction and season. Logistics system design must take such factors into account to achieve back-haul economies whenever possible.

Costing

The second dimension of transport economics and pricing concerns the criteria used to allocate cost. Cost allocation is primarily a carrier concern, but since cost structure influences negotiating ability, the shipper's perspective is important as well. Transportation costs are classified into a number of categories.

Variable

Costs that change in a predictable, direct manner in relation to some level of activity are labeled **variable costs.** Variable costs in transportation can be avoided only by not operating the vehicle. Aside from exceptional circumstances, transport rates must at least cover variable cost. The variable category includes direct carrier cost associated with movement of each load. These expenses are generally measured as a cost per mile or per unit of weight. Typical variable cost components include labor, fuel, and maintenance. The variable cost of operations represents the minimum amount a carrier must charge to pay daily expenses. It is not possible for any carrier to charge customers a rate below its variable cost and expect to remain in business long.

Fixed

Expenses that do not change in the short run and must be paid even when a company is not operating, such as during a holiday or a strike, are **fixed costs.** The fixed category includes costs not directly influenced by shipment volume. For transportation firms, fixed components include vehicles, terminals, rights-of-way, information systems, and support equipment. In the short term, expenses associated with fixed assets must be covered by contribution above variable costs on a per shipment basis.

Joint

Expenses created by the decision to provide a particular service are called **joint costs.** For example, when a carrier elects to haul a truckload from point A to point B, there is an implicit decision to incur a **joint** cost for the back-haul from point B to point A. Either the joint cost must be covered by the original shipper from A to B or a back-haul shipper must be found. Joint costs have significant impact on transportation charges because carrier quotations must include implied joint costs based on assessment of back-haul recovery.

Common

This category includes carrier costs that are incurred on behalf of all or selected shippers. **Common costs,** such as terminal or management expenses, are characterized as overhead. These are often allocated to a shipper according to a level of activity like the number of shipments or delivery appointments handled. However, allocating overhead in this manner may incorrectly assign costs. For example, a shipper may be charged for delivery appointments when not actually using the service.

Carrier Pricing Strategy

When setting rates, carriers typically follow one or a combination of two strategies. Although it is possible to employ a single strategy, the combination approach considers trade-offs between cost of service incurred by the carrier and value of service to the shipper.

Cost-of-Service

The **cost-of-service** strategy is a buildup approach where the carrier establishes a rate based on the cost of providing the service plus a profit margin. For example, if the cost of providing a transportation service is $200 and the profit markup is 10 percent, the carrier would charge the shipper $220. The cost-of-service approach, which represents the base or minimum for transportation charges, is most commonly used as a pricing approach for low-value goods or in highly competitive situations.

Value-of-Service

An alternative strategy that charges a price based on value as perceived by the shipper rather than the carrier cost of actually providing the service is called **value-of-service.** For example, a shipper perceives transporting 1000 pounds of electronics equipment as more critical or valuable than 1000 pounds of coal, since electronics are worth substantially more than the coal. Therefore, a shipper is probably willing to pay more for transportation. Carriers tend to utilize value-of-service pricing for high-value goods or when limited competition exists.

Value-of-service pricing is illustrated in the premium overnight freight market. When FedEx first introduced overnight delivery, there were few competitors that could provide comparable service, so it was perceived by shippers as a high-value alternative. They were willing to pay a premium for overnight delivery of a single package. Once competitors such as UPS, and the United States Postal Service entered the market, overnight rates were discounted to levels reflecting the value and cost of this service.

Combination

A **combination** pricing strategy establishes the transport price at an intermediate level between the cost-of-service minimum and the value-of-service maximum. In practice, most transportation firms use managerially determined midrange pricing. Logistics managers must understand the range of prices and the alternative strategies so they can negotiate appropriately.

Net-Rate

By taking advantage of regulatory freedom generated by the Trucking Industry Regulatory Reform Act (**TIRRA**) of 1994 and the reduced applicability of the filed rate doctrine, a number of common carriers are experimenting with a simplified pricing format termed **net-rate pricing.**[2] Since TIRRA eliminated tariff filing requirements for motor carriers that set rates individually with customers, carriers are now, in effect, able to simplify pricing to fit an individual customer's circumstance and need. Specifically, carriers can replace individual discount sheets and class tariffs with a simplified price sheet. The net-rate pricing approach does away with the complex and administratively burdensome discount pricing structures that became common practice following initial deregulation.

Established discounts and accessorial charges are built into **net rates.** In other words, the net rate is an all-inclusive price. The goal is to drastically reduce a carrier's administrative cost and directly respond to customer demand to simplify the pricing process. Shippers are attracted to such simplification because it promotes billing accuracy and provides a clear understanding of how to generate savings in transportation.

Rates and Rating

The previous discussion introduced key strategies used by carriers to set prices. This section presents the traditional pricing mechanics used by carriers. This discussion applies specifically to common carriers, although contract carriers follow a similar approach.

Class Rates

In transportation terminology, the price in dollars and cents per hundredweight to move a specific product between two locations is referred to as the **rate.** The rate is listed on pricing sheets or on computer files known as **tariffs.** The term **class rate** evolved from the fact that all products transported by common carriers are classified for pricing purposes. Any product legally transported in interstate commerce can be shipped via class rates.

Determination of common carrier class rates is a two-step process. The first step is to determine the **classification** or grouping of the product being transported. The second step is the determination of the precise rate or price based on the classification of the product, weight, and the origin/destination points of the shipment.

Classification

All products transported are typically grouped together into uniform classifications. The classification takes into consideration the characteristics of a product or commodity that will influence the cost of handling or transport. Products with similar density, stowability, handling, liability, and value characteristics are grouped together into a class, thereby reducing the need to deal with each product on an individual basis. The particular class that a given product or commodity is assigned is its **rating,** which is used to determine the freight rate. It is important to understand that the classification does not identify the price or rate charged for movement of a product. Rating refers to a product's transportation characteristics in comparison to other commodities.

[2] See Chapter 8.

Truck and rail carriers each have independent classification systems. The trucking system uses the *National Motor Freight Classification,* while rail classifications are published in the *Uniform Freight Classification.* The truck classification system has 18 classes of freight, and the rail system has 31. In local or regional areas, individual groups of carriers may publish additional classification lists.

In May 2007, the Surface Transportation Board **(STB)** issued a ruling that abolished the antitrust immunity of the National Motor Freight Traffic Association **(NMFTA)** effective December 2007. The NMFTA is a nonprofit organization comprised of more than 1000 motor carriers that collaborate to publish the Nation Motor Freight Classification **(NMFC).** This ruling reversed immunity from legal action, which had prevailed since passage of the Reed-Bulwinkle Act in 1948. Many industry officials and observers feel this administrative ruling represents an effort to encourage simplification of the traditional freight classification practice.

Classification of individual products is based on a relative index of 100. Class 100 is considered the class of an average product, while other classes run as high as 500 and as low as 35. Each product is assigned an item number for listing purposes and then given a classification rating. As a general rule, the higher a class rating, the higher the transportation cost for the product. Historically, a product classified as 200 would be approximately twice as expensive to transport as a product rated 100. While the actual current multiple may not be two, a class 200 rating will still result in substantially higher freight costs than a class 100 rating. Products are also assigned classifications on the basis of the quantity shipped. Less-than-truckload **(LTL)** shipments of identical products will have higher ratings than truckload **(TL)** shipments.

Table 9.1 illustrates a page from the *National Motor Freight Classification.* It contains general product grouping 86750, which is **glass, leaded.** Notice that the leaded glass category is further subdivided into specific types of glass such as *glass, microscopical slide or cover, in boxes* (item 86770). For LTL shipments, item 86770 is assigned a 70 rating. TL shipments of leaded glass are assigned a class 40 rating, provided a minimum of 360 hundredweight is shipped.

Products are also assigned different ratings on the basis of packaging. Glass may be rated differently when shipped loose, in crates, or in boxes than when shipped in wrapped protective packing. It should be noted that packaging differences influence product density, stowability, and damage, illustrating that cost factors discussed earlier enter into the rate-determined process. Thus, a number of different classifications may apply to the same product depending on shipment size, transport mode, and product packaging.

One of the major responsibilities of transportation managers is to obtain the best possible rating for all goods shipped, so it is useful for members of a traffic department to have a thorough understanding of the classification systems. Although there are differences in rail and truck classifications, each system is guided by similar rules.

It is possible to have a product reclassified by written application to the appropriate classification board. The classification board reviews proposals for change or additions with respect to minimum weights, commodity descriptions, packaging requirements, and general rules and regulations. An alert traffic department will take an active role in classification. Significant savings may be realized by finding the correct classification for a product or by recommending a change in packaging or shipment quantity that will reduce a product's rating.

Rate Determination

Once a classification rating is obtained for a product, the rate must be determined. The rate per hundredweight is usually based on the shipment origin and destination, although the actual price charged for a particular shipment is normally subject to a minimum charge and

TABLE 9.1   National Motor Freight Classification 100-S

Source: Reprinted with permission from the American Trucking Association.

Item	Articles	Classes	
		LTL	TL
86750	Glass, leaded, see Note, item 86752:		
Sub 1	With landscape, pictorial, or religious designs, packed in boxes.	200.	70.
Sub 2	With curved, angled, or straight-line patterns, or with designs other than landscape, pictorial, or religious, in boxes.	100.	70.
86752	*Note:* The term "lended glass" means glass either colored or clear, set in lead or in other metal.		
86770	Glass, microscopical slide or cover, in boxes.	70.	40.
86830	Glass, rolled, overlaid with aluminum strips with metal terminals attached, in boxes, crates, or Package 1339.	77.5	45.
86840	Glass, rolled, overlaid with aluminum strips, NOI, in boxes, crates, or Package 1339.	70.	37.5
86900	Glass, silvered for mirrors, not framed, backed, or equipped with hangers or fastening devices:		
Sub 1	Shock (window glass, silvered), in boxes, see Note, item 86902; also TL., in Packages 227 or 300.	86.	40.
Sub 2	Other than shock glass; also TL, in Packages 227 or 300: Bent:		
Sub 3	Not exceeding 15 feet in length or 9 feet in breadth, in boxes.	100.	70.
Sub 4	Exceeding 15 feet in length or 9 feet in breadth, in boxes.	250.	70.
Sub 5	Not bent, see Package 785:		
Sub 6	120 united inches or less, in boxes, crates, or Packages 198,	70.	40.
Sub 7	235, or 1339.		
sub 8	Exceeding 120 united inches but not exceeding 15 feet in length or 9 feet in breadth, in boxes or crates.	100.	40.
Sub 9	Exceeding 15 feet in length or 9 feet in breadth, in boxes or crates.	200.	45.
86902	*Note:* Glass, silvered for mirrors, which has been framed or backed, or equipped with large hangers or fastening devices, is subject to the classes for mirrors, NOI.		
85940	Glass, window, other than plate, with metal edging other than sash or frames, in boxes.	77.5	45.
86960	Glazing units, glass, not in sash, see Note, item 86966, in boxes, crates, or Packages 2133, 2149, or 2281.	70.	45.
86966	*Note:* Applies on units consisting of sheets of glass separated by air or vacuum, sealed at all edges with same or other materials.		
87040	Skylight, roofing, or sidewall construction material consisting of rough rolled glass, wired or not wired, and installation accessories, see Note, item 87042, in boxes or crates.	65.	35.

may also be subject to surcharges. Historically, the origin and destination rates were manually maintained in notebooks that had to be updated and revised regularly. Then rates were provided on diskettes by carriers. Today, options for selecting carriers range from Internet software that examines carrier Web sites and determines the best rates to participation in online auctions.

Origin and destination rates are organized by zip codes. Table 9.2 illustrates rates for all freight classes from Atlanta, Georgia (zip 303), to Lansing, Michigan (zip 489). The table lists rates for shipments ranging in size from the smallest LTL (less than 500 pounds; listed as L5C) to the largest TL (greater than 40,000 pounds; listed as M40M). The rate is quoted in cents per hundredweight. Assuming a shipment of 10,000 pounds, the rate for class 85 between Atlanta and Lansing, using this example tariff, is $12.92 per hundredweight.

Historically, the published rate had to be charged for all shipments of a specific class and origin/destination combination. This required frequent review and maintenance to keep rates current. Following deregulation, carriers offered more flexibility through rate

TABLE 9.2 Example of Rates from Atlanta, Georgia (zip 303), to Lansing, Michigan (zip 489)

					Origin 303: Destination 489: MC: 81.00: RBNO 00775E				
Rate Class	L5C	M5C	M1M	M2M	M5M	M10M	M20M	M30M	M40M
500	233.58	193.89	147.14	119.10	84.05	65.37	40.32	32.25	28.24
400	188.24	156.25	118.58	95.98	67.73	52.69	32.55	26.03	22.79
300	144.11	119.63	90.78	73.48	51.86	40.34	24.94	19.95	17.45
250	126.30	104.84	79.56	64.40	45.45	35.34	21.86	17.48	15.31
200	98.37	81.66	61.97	50.16	35.40	27.53	17.00	13.60	11.91
175	88.65	73.58	55.84	45.20	31.90	24.81	15.30	12.24	10.72
150	76.11	63.18	47.94	38.81	27.38	21.30	13.20	10.56	9.24
125	64.76	53.76	40.80	33.03	23.31	18.12	11.25	9.00	7.88
110	56.27	46.71	35.43	28.69	20.25	15.75	9.88	7.90	6.92
100	52.62	43.68	33.15	26.83	18.94	14.73	9.22	7.38	6.46
92	49.79	41.33	31.37	25.39	17.92	13.94	8.91	7.12	6.24
85	46.15	38.31	29.07	23.53	16.61	12.92	8.58	6.86	6.01
77	42.91	35.62	27.03	21.88	15.44	12.01	8.34	6.67	5.84
70	40.48	33.59	25.50	20.64	14.57	11.33	8.10	6.48	5.67
65	38.46	31.92	24.22	19.61	13.84	10.76	8.02	6.41	5.61
60	36.84	30.58	23.21	18.78	13.26	10.31	7.94	6.35	5.56
55	34.81	28.90	21.93	17.75	12.53	9.74	7.85	6.28	5.50
50	32.79	27.22	20.66	16.71	11.80	9.18	7.77	6.22	5.44
Weight	Under	500–	1000–	2000–	5000–	10,000–	20,000–	30,000–	Over
Limits (lb)	500	1000	2000	5000	10,000	20,000	30,000	40,000	40,000

discounts. Now instead of developing an individual rate table to meet the needs of customer segments, carriers apply a discount from class rates for specific customers. The discount, generally in the range of 30 to 50 percent, depends on the shipper's volume and market competition.

An alternative to the per hundredweight charge is a per mile charge, which is common in TL shipments. As discussed previously, TL shipments are designed to reduce handling and transfer costs. Since the entire vehicle is used in a TL movement and there is no requirement to transfer the shipment at a terminal, a per mile basis offers a more appropriate pricing approach. For a one-way move, charges may range from $1.50 to over $3.00 per mile, depending on the market, the equipment, and the product involved. Although it is negotiable, this charge typically includes loading, unloading, and liability.

In addition to the variable shipment charge applied on either a per hundredweight or per mile basis, two additional charges are common for transportation: **minimum charges** and **surcharges.** The minimum charge represents the amount a shipper must pay to make a shipment, regardless of weight. To illustrate, assume that the applicable class rate is $50/CWT and the shipper wants to transport 100 pounds to a specific location. If no minimum charge exists, the shipper would pay $50. However, if the minimum charge were $250 per shipment, the shipper would be required to pay the minimum. Minimum charges cover fixed costs associated with a shipment.

A surcharge represents an additional charge designed to cover specific carrier costs. Surcharges are used to protect carriers from situations not anticipated when publishing a general rate. The surcharge may be assessed as a flat charge, a percentage, or a sliding scale based on shipment size. A common use of surcharges is to compensate carriers for dramatic changes in fuel cost. The surcharge approach provides a means of immediate relief for the carrier to recover unexpected costs while not including such costs in the long-term rate structure.

Class rates, minimum charges, arbitrary charges, and surcharges form a pricing structure that, in various combinations, is applicable within the continental United States. The tariff indicates the class rate for any rating group between specified origins and destinations. In combination, the classification framework and class rate structure form a generalized pricing mechanism for all participating carriers. Each mode has specific characteristics applicable to its tariffs. In water, specific tariff provisions are made for cargo location within the ship or on the deck. In addition, provisions are made to charter entire vessels. Similar specialized provisions are found in air cargo and pipeline tariffs. Nonoperating intermediaries and package services also publish tariffs specialized to their service.

Cube Rates

Considerable attention has recently focused on development of a simplified method of transportation pricing. Typically called **cube** or **density** rates, the new approach replaces the 18 traditional freight classifications of the NMFC with five cube groupings.[3] Under the cube concept, shippers complete a cube shipping document **(CSD),** which replaces the traditional bill of lading. To further identify freight characteristics, shippers provide the total weight of both stackable **(ST)** and nonstackable **(NST)** freight included in the shipment. Rates are then determined for the weight contained in each category of freight. The CSD offers five weight break groups. Four are weight breaks for shipments under 500 pounds. Rates for shipments over 500 pounds are based on multiples of 500 pounds with no shipment weight limit. While still in development, cube-based rates and the associated cube shipping document offer a promising approach to reducing the complexity of traditional transportation pricing.

Commodity Rates

When a large quantity of a product moves between two locations on a regular basis, it is common practice for carriers to publish a **commodity rate.** Commodity rates are special or specific rates published without regard to classification. The terms and conditions of a commodity rate are usually indicated in a contract between the carrier and shipper. Commodity rates are published on a point-to-point basis and apply only on specified products. Today, most rail freight moves under commodity rates. They are less prevalent in motor carriage. Whenever a commodity rate exists, it supersedes the corresponding class or exception rate.

Exception Rates

Special rates published to provide prices lower than the prevailing class rates are called **exception rates.** The original purpose of the exception rate was to provide a special rate for a specific area, origin/destination, or commodity when justified by either competitive or high-volume movements. Rather than publish a new tariff, an exception to the classification or class rate was established.

Just as the name implies, when an exception rate is published, the classification that normally applies to the product is changed. Such changes may involve assignment of a new class or may be based on a percentage of the original class. Technically, exceptions may be higher or lower, although most are less than original class rates. Unless otherwise noted, all services provided under the class rate remain under an exception rate.

Since deregulation, several new types of exception rates have gained popularity. For example, an **aggregate tender** rate is utilized when a shipper agrees to provide multiple shipments to a carrier in exchange for a discount or exception from the prevailing

---

[3] For an expanded discussion, see Ray Bohman, "New LTL Pricing: Thinking Inside the Cube;" *Logistics Management,* October 2007, pp. 21–24.

class rate. The primary objective is to reduce carrier cost by permitting multiple shipment pickup during one stop at a shipper's facility or to reduce the rate for the shipper because of the carrier's reduced cost. To illustrate, UPS offers customers that tender multiple small package shipments at one time a discount based on aggregate weight and/or cubic volume. Since deregulation, numerous pricing innovations have been introduced by common carriers, based on various aggregation principles.

A **limited service** rate is utilized when a shipper agrees to perform selected services typically performed by the carrier, such as trailer loading, in exchange for a discount. A common example is a **shipper load and count** rate, where the shipper takes responsibility for loading and counting the cases. Not only does this remove the responsibility for loading the shipment from the carrier, but it also implies that the carrier, once the trailer is sealed, is not responsible for guaranteeing case count. Another example of limited service is a **released value rate,** which limits carrier liability in case of loss or damage. Normally, the carrier is responsible for full product value if loss or damage occurs in transit. The quoted rate must include adequate insurance to cover the risk. Often it is more effective for manufacturers of high-value product to self-insure to realize the lowest possible rate. Limited service is used when shippers have confidence in the carrier's capability. Cost can be reduced by eliminating duplication of effort or responsibility.

Under aggregate tender and limited service rates, as well as other innovative exception rates, the basic economic justification is the reduction of carrier cost and subsequent sharing of benefits based on shipper/carrier cooperation.

Special Rates and Services

A number of special rates and services provided by carriers are available for use in logistical operations. Several common examples are discussed.

As indicated earlier, **freight-all-kind (FAK) rates** are important to logistics operations. Under FAK rates, a mixture of different products is transported under a negotiated rating. Rather than determine the classification and applicable freight rate of individual products, an average rating is applied for the total shipment. In essence, FAK rates are line-haul rates since they replace class, exception, or commodity rates. Their purpose is to simplify the paperwork associated with the movement of mixed commodities.

Numerous special rates exist that may offer transportation savings on specific freight movements. When a commodity moves under the tariff of a single carrier, it is referred to as a **local rate** or single-line rate. If more than one carrier is involved in the freight movement, a **joint rate** may be applicable even though multiple carriers are involved in the actual transportation process. Because some motor and rail carriers operate in restricted territory, it may be necessary to utilize the services of more than one carrier to complete a shipment. Utilization of a joint rate can offer substantial savings over the use of two or more local rates.

Special price incentives to utilize a published tariff that applies to only part of the desired route are called **proportional rates.** Proportional provisions of a tariff are most often applicable to origin or destination points outside the normal geographical area of a single-line tariff. If a joint rate does not exist and proportional provisions do, the strategy of moving a shipment under proportional rates provides a discount on the single-line part of the movement, thereby resulting in a lower overall freight charge.

Transit services permit a shipment to be stopped at an intermediate point between initial origin and destination for unloading, storage, and/or processing. The shipment is then reloaded for delivery to the destination. Typical examples of transit services are milling for grain products and processing for sugar beets. When transit privileges exist, the shipment is charged a through rate from origin to destination plus a transit privilege charge.

For a variety of reasons, a shipper or consignee may desire to change routing, destination, or even the consignee after a shipment is in transit. This process is called **diversion and reconsignment.** This flexibility can be extremely important, particularly with regard to food and other perishable products where market demand can quickly change. It is a normal practice among certain types of marketing intermediaries to purchase commodities with the full intention of selling them while they are in transit. **Diversion** consists of changing the destination of a shipment prior to its arrival at the original destination. **Reconsignment** is a change in consignee prior to delivery. Both services are provided by railroads and truck carriers for a specified charge.

A **split delivery** is desired when portions of a shipment need to be delivered to different destinations. Under specified tariff conditions, delivery can involve multiple destinations. The payment is typically structured to reflect a rate as if the shipment were going to the most distant destination. In addition, there typically is a charge for each delivery.

Demurrage and detention are charges assessed for retaining freight cars or truck trailers beyond specified loading or unloading time. The term **demurrage** is used by railroads for holding a railcar beyond 48 hours before unloading the shipment. Trucks use the term **detention** to cover similar delays. In the case of motor carriers, the permitted time is specified in the tariff and is normally limited to a few hours.

In addition to basic transportation, truck and rail carriers offer a wide variety of **special** or **accessorial** services. Table 9.3 provides a list of frequently utilized ancillary services.

Carriers may also offer environmental services and special equipment. **Environmental services** refer to special control of freight while in transit, such as refrigeration, ventilation, and heating. For example, in the summer, Hershey typically transports chocolate confectionery products in refrigerated trailers to protect them from high temperature levels. **Special equipment charges** refer to the use of equipment that the carrier has purchased for a shipper's convenience. For example, specialized sanitation equipment is necessary to clean and prepare trailers for food storage and transit if the trailer has been previously utilized for nonfood products or commodities.

Although the brief coverage of special services is not all-inclusive, it does offer several examples of the range and type of services carriers offer. A carrier's role in a logistical system is most often far greater than providing line-haul transportation.

Transport Administration

Traffic managers administer a wide variety of different activities. Among the most common are: (1) operational management, (2) consolidation, (3) negotiation, (4) control, (5) auditing and claims administration, and (6) logistical integration.

TABLE 9.3
Typical Carrier Ancillary Services

- *COD.* Collect payment on delivery.
- *Change COD.* Change COD recipient.
- *Inside delivery.* Deliver product inside the building.
- *Marking or tagging.* Mark or tag product as it is transported.
- *Notify before delivery.* Make appointment prior to delivery.
- *Reconsignment of delivery.* Redirect shipment to a new destination while in transit.
- *Redeliver.* Attempt second delivery.
- *Residential delivery.* Deliver at a residence without a truck dock.
- *Sorting and segregating.* Sort commodity prior to delivery.
- *Storage.* Store commodity prior to delivery.

Operational Management

The fundamental responsibility of a traffic department is to oversee day-to-day transportation operations. In large-scale organizations, traffic management involves a wide variety of administrative responsibilities. Firms are increasingly implementing Transportation Management Systems **(TMS)** as integral parts of their integration information technology strategies.[4]

In general, a TMS must proactively identify and evaluate alternative transportation strategies and tactics to determine the best methods to move product within the existing constraints. As shown in Table 9.4, this includes capabilities to select modes, plan loads, consolidate loads with other shippers, take advantage of current unbalances in traffic movement, route vehicles, and optimize use of transportation equipment. The principal deliverables of TMS are cost savings and increased functionality to provide credible delivery times.

From an operational perspective, key elements of transportation management are equipment scheduling and yard management, load planning, routing, and carrier administration.

Equipment Scheduling and Yard Management

One major responsibility of the traffic department is equipment scheduling and yard management. Scheduling is an important process in both common carrier and private transportation. A serious and costly operational bottleneck can result from transportation equipment waiting to be loaded or unloaded. Proper yard management requires careful load planning, equipment utilization, and driver scheduling. Additionally, equipment preventive maintenance must be planned, coordinated, and monitored. Finally, any specialized equipment requirements must be planned and implemented.

Closely related to equipment scheduling is the arrangement of delivery and pickup appointments. To avoid extensive waiting time and improve equipment utilization, it is important to preschedule dock positions or slots. It is becoming common practice to establish standing appointments for regular shipments to facilitate loading and unloading. Some firms are implementing the practice of establishing advanced appointments at the time of order commitment. Increasingly, the effective scheduling of equipment is key to implementing time-based logistical arrangements. For example, cross-dock arrangements are totally dependent on precise scheduling of equipment arrival and departure.

Load Planning

How loads are planned directly impacts transportation efficiency. In the case of trucks, capacity is limited in terms of weight and cube. Planning the load sequence of a trailer must consider product physical characteristics and the size of individual shipments, as well

---

[4] The relationship of TMS to overall logistical technology was discussed in Chapter 5.

TABLE 9.4 **Typical Transportation Management System Functionality**	• Order consolidation • Route optimization • Carrier rate management • EDI links with carriers • Internet-based shipment tracking • Integrated claims management • Identify most economical mode: parcel, less-than-truckload, truckload, pool distribution, stops in transit • Calculate best route • Carrier selection based on cost and service including performance • Yard management

as delivery sequence if multiple shipments are loaded on a single trailer. As noted earlier, TMS software is available to help facilitate load planning.

How effectively load planning is performed will directly impact overall logistical efficiency. For example, the load plan drives the work sequence at warehouses. Transportation equipment must be available to maintain an orderly flow of product and material from warehouse or factory to shipment destination.

Routing and Advanced Shipment Notification (ASN)

An important part of achieving transportation efficiency is shipment **routing.** Routing predetermines the geographical path a vehicle will travel. Once again, routing software is an integral part of TMS.

From an administrative viewpoint, the traffic department is responsible for assuring that routing is performed in an efficient manner while meeting key customer service requirements. It is common practice for shippers to electronically provide consignees advanced shipment notification **(ASN).** While the specifics of ASN documents vary, their primary purpose is to allow adequate time to plan arrival, arrange delivery appointments, and plan to redeploy the shipment's content. How deliveries are planned must take into consideration special requirements of customers in terms of time, location, and special unloading services.

Movement Administration

Traffic managers have the basic responsibility of administering the performance of for-hire and private transportation. Effective administration requires continuous carrier performance measurement and evaluation. Until recently, efforts to measure actual carrier service were sporadic and unreliable. A traditional procedure was to include postcards with shipments requesting consignees to record time and condition of arrival. The development of information technology has significantly improved shipment information reliability. The fact that most shippers have reduced their carrier base has greatly simplified administration. Effective administration requires carrier selection, integration, and evaluation.

A basic responsibility of the traffic department is to select carriers to perform for-hire transport. To some degree all firms use the services of for-hire carriers. Even those with commitment to private fleets regularly require the supplemented services of common, contract, and specialized carriers to complete transportation requirements. Most firms that use for-hire transportation have implemented a **core carrier strategy.**

The concept of a core carrier is to build a working relationship with a small number of transportation providers. Historically, shippers followed the practice of spreading their transportation purchases across a wide variety of carriers to assure competitive rates and adequate equipment supply. During the regulated era, few differences in price existed between carriers. As a result, shippers often conducted business with hundreds of different carriers. The concentration of volume in a few core carriers creates a business relationship that standardizes operational and administrative processes. Mutual planning and acknowledged dependency between a shipper and carrier result in dependable equipment supply, customized services, improved scheduling, and more efficient overall administration.

In a number of situations, the core carrier relationships are directly between the shipper and the transportation provider. A recent development is the use of integrated service providers **(ISPs)** to establish and maintain business relationships with core carriers. In such situations, the ISP facilitates administration and consolidates freight across a wide variety of shippers.

The range of relationship models is ever-changing as service providers devise new and better methods of identifying and integrating transportation requirements. However, at the end of the day, it remains a fundamental responsibility of transportation management to assure a firm is supported by reliable and economical transportation. This fundamental responsibility cannot be delegated.

Consolidation

At several different points throughout this text the importance of freight consolidation is discussed. The fact that freight costs are directly related to size of shipment and length of haul places a premium upon freight consolidation. In terms made famous by the late President Truman, *the buck stops here,* meaning traffic management is the business function responsible for achieving freight consolidation.

The traditional approach to freight consolidation was to combine LTL or parcel shipment moving to a general location. The objective of outbound consolidation was straightforward. The transportation savings in moving a single consolidated shipment versus multiple individual, small shipments were typically sufficient to pay for handling and local delivery while achieving total cost reduction.

The shift to response-based logistics has introduced new challenges regarding consolidation. Time-based logistics tends to transpose the impact of unpredictable demand from inventory safety stock to creation of small shipments. All members of the supply chain are seeking to reduce inventory dwell time by more closely synchronizing replenishment with demand. The result is more frequent, small orders. Not only does the increase in small shipments result in higher transportation cost, it also translates to more handling and dock congestion.

To control transportation cost when a time-based strategy is used, managerial attention must be directed to the development of ingenious ways to realize benefits of transportation consolidation. To plan freight consolidation, it is necessary to have reliable information concerning both current and planned inventory status. It is also desirable to be able to reserve or promise scheduled production to achieve planned consolidations. To the extent practical, consolidations should be planned prior to order processing and warehouse order selection to avoid delay. All aspects of consolidation require timely and relevant information concerning planned activity.

From an operational viewpoint, freight consolidation techniques can be grouped as **reactive** and **proactive.** Each type of consolidation is important to achieving transportation efficiency.

Reactive Consolidation

A reactive approach to consolidation does not attempt to influence the composition and timing of transportation movements. The consolidation effort reacts to shipments as they come and seeks to combine individual orders into larger shipments for line-haul movement. Perhaps the most visible example of effective reactive line-haul is United Parcel Service's nightly sortation and consolidation of package freight for intercity movement.

From an operational viewpoint, there are three ways to achieve effective reactive consolidation: (1) market area, (2) scheduled delivery, and (3) pooled delivery.

The most basic method of consolidation is to combine small shipments going to different customers within a geographical **market area.** This procedure does not interrupt the natural freight flow by changing the timing of shipments. Rather, the overall quantity of shipments to a market area provides the consolidation basis.

The difficulty of developing either inbound or outbound market area consolidations is the variation in daily volume. To offset the volume deficiency, three operating arrangements are commonly used. First, consolidated shipments may be sent to an intermediate break-bulk point for purposes of line-haul transportation savings. There, individual shipments are separated and forwarded to their destination. Second, firms may elect to hold consolidated shipments for scheduled delivery on specific days to given destination markets. Third, consolidation of small shipments may be achieved by utilizing the services of a third-party logistics firm to pool delivery. The last two methods require special arrangements, which are discussed in greater detail below.

The limiting of shipments to specific markets to selected days each week is referred to as **scheduled area delivery.** The scheduled delivery plan is normally communicated to customers in a way that highlights the mutual benefits of consolidation. The shipping firm commits to the customer that all orders received prior to a specified cutoff time will be guaranteed for delivery on the scheduled day.

Participation in **pooled delivery** typically means that a freight forwarder, public warehouse, or transportation company arranges consolidation for multiple shippers serving the same geographical market area. Integrated service providers that arrange pooled consolidation services typically have standing delivery appointments at high-volume delivery destinations. It is common, under such arrangements, for the consolidation company to also perform value-added service such as sorting, sequencing, or segregation of inbound freight to accommodate customer requirements.

Proactive Consolidation

While reactive efforts to develop transportation consolidations have been successful, two forces are driving a more proactive approach. First, the impact of response-based logistical systems is creating a larger number of small shipments. This trend toward increased smaller shipments has been intensified by the growth of e-commerce. Second, proactive consolidation reflects the desire for shippers, carriers, and consignees to participate in consolidation savings.

An important step toward achieving proactive consolidation is **preorder planning** of quantity and timing to facilitate consolidated freight movement. Simply stated, the creation of orders should not be restricted to standard buying times or inventory replenishment rules. Buyer participation in order creation can greatly facilitate proactive freight consolidation.[5]

Significant freight consolidation opportunities also may exist if nonrelated firms can be coordinated. Commonly referred to as **multivendor consolidation,** the general idea of grouping different shippers' freight has always been integral to line-haul operations of LTL carriers. The new initiative is jointly planning warehousing and order processing across different companies to facilitate such consolidation. Creating such multivendor consolidation is a value-added service offered by a growing number of ISPs. Likewise, firms are increasingly endorsing pooling arrangements with competitors to achieve logistical efficiency.

Negotiation

Chapter 8 presented a description of basic transportation and associated rate regulation. For any given shipment, it is the responsibility of the traffic department to obtain the lowest possible rate consistent with service required.

The prevailing tariff represents the starting point in transportation negotiation. The key to effective negotiation is to seek win-win agreements wherein both carriers and shippers share productivity gains. As indicated several times throughout this text, the lowest possible cost for transportation may not be the lowest total cost of logistics. The traffic department must seek the lowest rate consistent with service standards. For example, if

---

[5] Carol Casper, "Multi-Vendor Consolidation," *Food Logistics,* January/February 1999, pp. 37–48.

2-day delivery is required, the traffic department seeks to select the method of transport that will consistently meet this standard at the lowest possible cost. Given the special considerations of transportation, several factors discussed throughout this section must guide rate negotiation. However, in the context of building solid carrier relationships, traffic managers must seek fair and equitable rates.

Control

Other important responsibilities under the control of transportation management are tracing, expediting, and driver hours administration. **Tracing** is a procedure to locate lost or late shipments. Shipments committed across a transportation network are bound to be misplaced or delayed from time to time. Most large carriers maintain online tracing to aid shippers in locating a shipment. The tracing action must be initiated by the shipper's traffic department, but once initiated, it is the carrier's responsibility to provide the desired information. **Expediting** involves the shipper notifying a carrier that it needs to have a specific shipment move through the carrier's system as quickly as possible and with no delays.

Driver fatigue concerns prompted the Department of Transportation's Federal Motor Carrier Safety Administration **(FMCSA)** in 2005 to alter the **hours of service (HOS)** that interstate truck drivers could operate. The changes were developed to ensure drivers were getting sufficient off-duty time to rest while at the same time increasing daily driving time for trucking companies. The changes significantly restructured working conditions for truckers. Under the new rules all breaks were counted as on-duty time. Although total driving hours were extended, the impact of the new regulation was to reduce the productive workday and reduce the effectiveness of driver teams. The new rules reduced the time a driver could rest during team movements.

The new regulations lengthened daily driving time; counted rest, unloading, and breaks as driving time; extended the required time off between shifts; and maintained a weekly maximum for on-duty hours. An overview of the rule changes are presented in Table 9.5.

However, there were additional reasons beyond safety for the change; reducing costs for shippers was an HOS goal. The added hour of driving time would help decrease shipping costs. U.S. Transportation Secretary Norman Mineta said, "If we can lower the cost of moving freight by 1 percent, the additional benefit to the economy would be more than $98 billion annually."[6]

The District of Columbia Court of Appeals vacated the new HOS rules on July 16, 2004, citing that the new rules may increase driver fatigue rather than alleviate tiredness. The new rules reflected in Table 9.5 were implemented in 2005. The rules as modified remain under legal review.

[6] U.S. Department of Transportation, "FMCSA 4-03, Revised Hours-of-Service Rule to Help Ensure Truck Drivers Get Adequate Rest," Washington, DC, April 24, 2003.

TABLE 9.5
Hours of Drivers' Service

Source: U.S. Department of Transportation.

Old Hours of Service Rules	New Hours of Service Rules
10 hours' driving	11 hours' driving
15 hours on duty	14 consecutive hours on duty
Breaks do not count as duty time, and extend the day.	Breaks count as on-duty time.
8 cumulative hours off duty	10 consecutive and uninterrupted hours off duty
60/70 hours in 7/8 days	60/70 hours in 7/8 days
	Drivers must take 34 hours off duty before restarting an on-duty period.

HOS regulation is a good example of how government policy can influence transportation. In cases of private transportation, HOS administration is the direct responsibility of the traffic department. In for-hire carriers, oversight is the responsibility of carrier management.

Auditing and Claim Administration

When transportation service or charges are not performed as promised, shippers can make claims for restitution. Claims are typically classified as **loss and damage** or **overcharge/ undercharge.** Loss and damage claims occur when a shipper demands the carrier pay for partial or total financial loss resulting from poor performance. As the name implies, loss and damage claims usually occur when product is lost or damaged while in transit. Overcharge/undercharge claims result when the amount billed is different from that expected and are typically resolved through freight bill audit procedures.

Agreements stipulate the proper procedure for filing claims and help define which parties are responsible. Two factors regarding claim administration are of primary importance. First, detailed attention should be given to claim administration because recoveries are achieved only by aggressive audit programs. Second, large volumes of claims are indicative of carriers that are not performing their service obligations. Regardless of the dollars recovered by claim administration, the breakdown in customer service performance resulting from loss and damage claims impacts a shipper's reputation with its customers.

Auditing freight bills is an important responsibility of the traffic department. The purpose of auditing is to ensure freight bill accuracy. Transport rate complexity results in a higher error probability than in most other purchasing decisions. There are two types of freight audits. A **preaudit** determines proper charges prior to payment of a freight bill. A **postaudit** makes the same determination after payment has been made. Auditing may be either external or internal. If external, specialized freight-auditing companies are employed, utilizing personnel who are experts in specific commodity groupings. This is generally more efficient than the use of internal personnel who may not have the same level of expertise. Payment for external audit is usually based on a percentage of recovered overcharges. It is crucial that a highly ethical firm be employed for this purpose, because valuable marketing and customer information is contained in the freight bill and corporate activities may be adversely affected if sensitive information is not held in confidence.

A combination of internal and external auditing is frequently employed, depending on the value of the freight bill. For example, a bill of $600 with a 10 percent error results in a $60 recovery, but a $50 bill with a 10 percent error results in only a $5 recovery. Therefore, bills with larger recovery potential may be audited internally.

It is common practice for firms to determine and pay freight at the time a shipment is tendered to a carrier. This shifts the audit responsibility to the carrier, which must then file an undercharge claim for recovery from the shipper.

Logistical Integration

For any given operating period, traffic management is expected to provide the required transportation services at budgeted cost. It is also traffic management's responsibility to search for alternative ways to deploy transportation to reduce total logistics cost. For example, a slight change in packaging may create an opportunity for negotiation of a lower freight classification for a product. Although packaging costs may increase, this added expense may be offset by a substantial reduction in transportation cost. Unless such proposals originate from the traffic department, they will likely go undetected in the average firm. As indicated earlier, transportation is the highest single cost area in most logistical systems. This expenditure level combined with the dependence of logistical operations on effective transportation means that the traffic departments must play an active role in supply chain logistics planning.

Documentation

Well-defined documentation is required to perform a transportation service. With the exception of private transfer within the confines of a single firm, products are typically being sold when being transported. Thus, legal title to ownership occurs during the time the transport service is performed. When for-hire carriers are engaged to perform the transportation, the transaction must establish clear legal responsibility for all parties involved. The primary purpose of transportation documentation is to protect all parties involved in the performance of the transaction. Three primary types of transport documentation are bills of lading, freight bills, and shipment manifests.

Bill of Lading

The **bill of lading** is the basic document utilized in purchasing transport services. It serves as a receipt and documents products and quantities shipped. For this reason, accurate product description and count are essential. In case of loss, damage, or delay, the bill of lading is the basis for damage claims. The designated individual or buyer on a bill of lading is the only bona fide recipient of goods. A carrier is responsible for proper delivery according to instructions contained in the document. The information contained on the bill of lading determines all responsibilities related to timing and ownership.

The bill of lading specifies terms and conditions of carrier liability and documents responsibilities for all possible causes of loss or damage except those defined as acts of God. Figure 9.4 provides an example of a Uniform Straight Bill of Lading. Government regulations permit uniform bills of lading to be computerized and electronically transmitted between shippers and carriers.

In addition to the **uniform** bill of lading, other commonly used types are **order-notified, export,** and **government.** It is important to select the correct bill of lading for a specific shipment.

An order-notified or negotiable bill of lading is a credit instrument. It provides that delivery not be made unless the original bill of lading is surrendered to the carrier. The usual procedure is for the seller to send the order-notified bill of lading to a third party, usually a bank or credit institution. Upon customer payment for the product the credit institution releases the bill of lading. The buyer then presents it to the common carrier, which in turn releases the goods. This facilitates international transport where cross-border payment for goods may be a major consideration. An export bill of lading permits a shipper to use export rates, which may be lower than domestic rates. Export rates may reduce total cost when applied to domestic origin or destination line-haul transport. Government bills of lading may be used when the product is owned by the U.S. government.

Freight Bill

The **freight bill** represents a carrier's method of charging for transportation services performed. It is developed by using information contained in the bill of lading. The freight bill may be either **prepaid** or **collect.** A prepaid bill means that transport cost is paid by the shipper prior to performance, whereas a collect shipment shifts payment responsibility to the consignee.

Considerable administration is involved in preparing bills of lading and freight bills. There has been significant effort to automate freight bills and bills of lading through EDI or Internet transactions. Some firms elect to pay their freight bills at the time the bill of lading is created, thereby combining the two documents. Such arrangements are based upon the financial benefits of reduced paperwork cost, and as noted earlier shift the audit responsibility to the carrier.

FIGURE 9.4   **Uniform Straight Bill of Lading**

UNIFORM STRAIGHT BILL OF LADING

Original—Not Negotiable

(To be Printed on "White" Paper)

Shipper's No. . . . .

Agent's No. . . . .

Company

RECEIVED, subject to the classifications and tariffs in effect on the date of the issue of this Bill of Lading,

at . . . . , 19 . . .

from . . . .

the property described below, in apparent good order, except as noted (contents and condition of contents of packages unknown), marked, consigned, and destined as indicated below, which said company (the word company being understood throughout this contract as meaning any person of corporation in possession of the property under the contract) agrees to carry to its usual place (of delivery at mid destination, if on its own road or its own water line, otherwise to deliver to another carrier on the route to said destination. It is mutually agreed, as to each carrier of all or any of said property over all or any portion of said route to destination, and as to each party at any time interested in all or any of said property, that every service to be performed hereunder shall be subject to all the conditions not prohibited by law, whether printed or written, herein contained, including the conditions on back hereof, which are hereby agreed to by the shipper and accepted for himself and his assigns.

(Mail or street address of consignee—For purposes of notification only.)

Consigned to . . . .

Destination . . . . State of . . . . County of . . . .

Route . . . .

Delivering Carrier . . . . Car Initial . . . . Car No. . . . .

No. Pack-ages	Description of Articles, Special Marks, and Exceptions	*Weight (Subject to Correction)	Class or Rate	Check Column	
					Subject to Section 7 of conditions, if this shipment is to be delivered to the consignee without recourse on the consignor, the consignor shall sign the following statement:
					The carrier shall not make delivery of this shipment without payment of freight and all other lawful charges.
					. . . . (Signature of consignor.)
					If charges are to be prepaid, write or stamp here, "To be Prepaid."
					. . . .
					Received $ . . . . to apply in prepayment of the charges on the property described hereon.
					Agent or Cashier.
					Per . . . . (The signature here acknowledges only the amount prepaid.)

* If the shipment moves between two ports by a carrier by water, the law requires that the bill of lading shall state whether it is "carrier's or shipper's weight."

Note.—Where the rate is dependent on value, shippers are required to state specifically in writing the agreed or declared value of the property.

The agreed or declared value of the property is hereby specifically stated by the shipper to be not exceeding

. . . . per . . . .

Charges advanced:

$ . . . .

. . . . Shipper.   . . . . Agent.

Per . . . .   Per . . . .

Permanent postoffice address of shipper . . . .

Shipment Manifest

The **shipment manifest** lists individual stops or consignees when multiple shipments are placed on a single vehicle. Each shipment requires a bill of lading. The manifest lists the stop, bill of lading, weight, and case count for each shipment. The objective of the manifest is to provide a single document that defines the overall contents of the load without requiring review of individual bills of lading. For single-stop shipments, the manifest is the same as the bill of lading.

Pricing

Pricing is an important aspect of marketing strategy that directly impacts logistical operations. The terms and conditions of pricing determine which party has responsibility for performing logistics activities. A major trend in price strategy has been to **debundle** the price of products and materials so that services such as transportation, which were traditionally included in price, become separate and visible items. Pricing practices have a direct impact on the timing and stability of logistical operations. In this section, several basic pricing structures are reviewed, followed by a discussion of pricing impact areas. No attempt is made to review the broad range of economic and psychological issues related to price strategy. The focus is on the relationship between pricing, logistical operations, and transportation decisions.

Pricing Fundamentals

Pricing decisions directly determine which party in the transaction is responsible for performing logistics activities, passage of title, and liability. F.O.B. origin and delivered pricing are the two most common methods.

F.O.B. Pricing

The term F.O.B. technically means **free on board** or **freight on board.** A number of variations of FOB pricing are used in practice. **F.O.B. origin** is the simplest way to quote price. Under F.O.B. origin the seller indicates the price at point of origin and agrees to tender a shipment for transportation loading, but assumes no further responsibility. The buyer selects the mode of transportation, chooses a carrier, pays transportation charges, and takes risk of in-transit loss and/or damage. In **F.O.B. destination pricing,** title does not pass to the buyer until delivery is completed. Under F.O.B. destination pricing, the seller arranges for transportation and the charges are added to the sales invoice.

The range of terms and corresponding responsibilities for pricing are illustrated in Figure 9.5. Review of the various sales terms makes it clear that the firm paying the freight bill does not necessarily assume responsibility for ownership of goods in transit, for the freight burden, or for filing of freight claims. These are issues of negotiation that are critical to supply chain collaboration.

Delivered Pricing

The primary difference between F.O.B. and **delivered pricing** is that in delivered pricing the seller establishes a price that includes transportation. In other words, the transportation cost is not specified as a separate item. There are several variations of delivered pricing.

Under **single-zone delivered pricing,** buyers pay a single price regardless of where they are located. Delivered prices typically reflect the seller's average transportation cost. In actual practice, some customers pay more than their fair share for transportation while

FIGURE 9.5 Terms of Sales and Responsibilities

Source: Reprinted with permission from *The Purchasing Handbook,* McGraw-Hill Publishing Company.

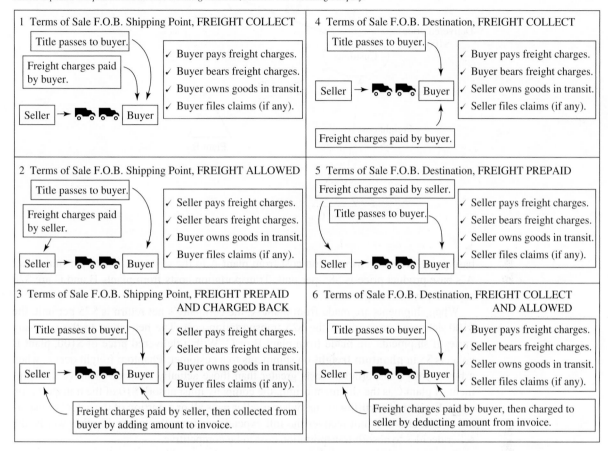

1 Terms of Sale F.O.B. Shipping Point, FREIGHT COLLECT
Title passes to buyer.
Freight charges paid by buyer.
Seller → Buyer
✓ Buyer pays freight charges.
✓ Buyer bears freight charges.
✓ Buyer owns goods in transit.
✓ Buyer files claims (if any).

others are subsidized. The United States Postal Service uses a single-zone pricing policy throughout the United States for first-class letters. The same fee or postage rate is charged for a given size and weight regardless of distance traveled to the destination.

Single-zone delivered pricing is typically used when transportation costs are a relatively small percentage of selling price. The main advantage to the seller is the high degree of logistical control. For the buyer, despite being based on averages, such pricing systems have the advantage of simplicity.

The practice of **multiple-zone pricing** establishes different prices for specific geographic areas. The underlying idea is that logistics cost differentials can be more fairly assigned when two or more zones—typically based on distance—are used to quote delivered pricing. Parcel carriers such as United Parcel Service use multiple-zone pricing.

The most complicated and controversial form of delivered pricing is the use of a **base-point pricing system** in which the final delivered price is determined by the product's list price plus transportation cost from a designated base point, usually the manufacturing location. This designated point is used for computing the delivered price whether or not the shipment actually originates from the base location. Base-point pricing is common in shipping assembled automobiles from manufacturing plants to dealers.

Figure 9.6 illustrates how a base-point pricing system typically generates different net returns to a seller. The customer is quoted a delivered price of $100 per unit. Plant A is the

FIGURE 9.6
Base-Point Pricing

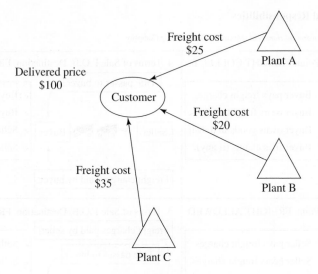

base point. Actual transportation cost from plant A to the customer is $25 per unit. Plant A's base product price is $85 per unit. Transportation costs from plants B and C are $20 and $35 per unit, respectively.

When shipments are made from plant A, the company's net return is $75 per unit, the $100 delivered price minus the $25 transportation cost. The net return to the company varies if shipments are made from plant B or C. With a delivered price of $100, plant B collects $5 in **phantom freight** on shipments to a customer. Phantom freight occurs when a buyer pays transportation costs greater than those actually incurred to move the shipment. If plant C is the shipment origin, the company must absorb $10 of the transportation costs. **Freight absorption** occurs when a seller pays all or a portion of the actual transportation cost and does not recover the full expenditure from the buyer. In other words, the seller decides to absorb transportation cost to be competitive.

Base-point pricing simplifies price quotations but can have a negative impact on customers and supply chain collaboration. For example, dissatisfaction may result if customers discover they are being charged more for transportation than actual freight costs. Such pricing practices may also result in a large amount of freight absorption for sellers.

Pricing Issues

Pricing practices are also integral to logistics operations in at least four other ways: potential discrimination, quantity discounts, pickup allowances, and promotional pricing.

Potential Discrimination

The legality of transportation pricing is an important consideration and must be carefully reviewed and administered to protect against potential discrimination. The Clayton Act of 1914 as amended by the Robinson-Patman Act of 1936 prohibits price discrimination among buyers when the practices **substantially lessen competition.**

Zone pricing has the potential to be discriminatory because some buyers pay more than actual transportation cost while others pay less. Zone pricing systems are illegal when the net result is to charge different delivered prices for identical products to firms that are direct competitors. In recent years, determination of the legality of delivered zone pricing systems has centered around the issue of whether **a seller acts independently and not**

in collusion with competitors. The Federal Trade Commission is unlikely to take action unless there is clear-cut evidence of such conspiracy.

In the past, selected base-point pricing has been found illegal under both the Robinson-Patman Act and the Federal Trade Commission Act. The concern is whether it results in direct competitors having differential margins. To avoid potential legal problems, a majority of firms use either F.O.B. or uniform delivered pricing policies. This strategy is generally preferable compared to defending average costing practices required in zone pricing or contending with the potential legal difficulties associated with base-point pricing. The following guidelines should be considered when establishing geographic pricing: First, a firm should not discriminate between competing buyers in the same region, especially in zone pricing for buyers on either side of a zonal boundary, because such action may violate the Robinson-Patman Act. Second, the firm's strategy should not appear to be predatory, especially in freight absorption pricing, because such a strategy would violate Section 2 of the Sherman Act. Third, in choosing the basing point or zone pricing, the firm should not attempt to fix prices among competitors because such action would violate Section 1 of the Sherman Act.

Quantity Discounts

Quantity discounts are offered by a firm as an inducement to increase order size or overall volume of business. To be nondiscriminatory, an identical discount structure must be available to all buyers. Under the Robinson-Patman Act, it is the responsibility of the seller to prove that the identical, noncumulative discounts are available to all qualified buyers. The quantity discount offered must be justifiable on the basis of direct cost saving.

The Robinson-Patman Act states that cost differences can be justified on the basis of savings in the manufacturing, delivery, or selling of goods. Quantity-related discounts based on reductions in manufacturing or selling cost are difficult to prove. Logistics-related savings are relatively easier to document since many are shipment-specific. Transportation and handling savings are often used to justify quantity discounts. Thus, lower transportation rates for volume shipments are common.

In contrast to noncumulative discounts, cumulative discounts—based on consecutive purchases over some specified time period—are more difficult to justify. Cumulative discounts, by the very nature of their calculation base, favor large-volume purchasers while discriminating against smaller buyers. However, price discrimination can be substantiated only when potential or real injury to competition is determined.

Pickup Allowances

Pickup allowances are equivalent to purchasing merchandise on an F.O.B. origin basis. Buyers are given a reduction from the standard delivered price if they or a representative picks up shipments at the seller's location and performs transportation. A buyer may also use a for-hire carrier or an **integrated service provider (ISP)** to perform merchandise pickup. In the food and grocery industry, which traditionally practiced delivered pricing, firms have realized significant savings by using private and for-hire carriers to pick up rather than purchase merchandise on a delivered basis.

While some confusion exists concerning how to best establish a pickup allowance, a safe rule is that a seller should provide the same allowance to all directly competitive buyers. A uniform pickup allowance is often the price incentive offered to the customer closest to the shipping point. Other common policies offer pickup allowances equivalent to the applicable common carrier rate for the shipment.

Pickup allowances offer potential benefits for both the seller and the buyer. Shippers are required to deal with fewer small shipments, thereby reducing the need for extensive outbound freight consolidation. Buyers gain control over the merchandise earlier and are in a position to achieve greater utilization of transportation equipment and drivers.

Promotional Pricing

An additional aspect of pricing that impacts logistical operations is the use of short-term promotions to provide purchase incentives. Firms that pursue aggressive promotional strategies have a choice of designing their budgets to encourage consumers, via coupons, or wholesalers and retailers, via trade allowances, to purchase their products. For example, Procter & Gamble has an annual advertising and promotional budget that exceeds $2 billion. Marketing management must allocate these funds between media advertising focused on consumers and a combination of coupons and trade promotions. Budget dollars allocated to trade promotion push the purchase of P&G products and cause two results. First, the logistics systems of Procter & Gamble and its customers must handle increased product volume just before, during, and oftentimes immediately after a promotional period. Second, trade promotion spending alters the effective price at which product is being sold. From a logistical perspective, the short-term increase in volume is of primary concern. Thus, while ultimate consumption may not demonstrate seasonal characteristics, logistical operations may have to deal with seasonal-like surges caused by promotional pushes.

The widespread practice of promotional pricing has traditionally been the way to provide trade purchase incentives. Manufacturers establish artificially high list prices with the expectation of reducing the effective price by trade promotion, consumer coupons, and product slotting allowances. **Slotting allowances** are financial incentives provided to retailers by manufacturers in return for their agreement to position products for sale at specific locations in a retail store. Administration of regular price changes usually involves advanced notification to customers, creating the opportunity for them to **forward-buy.** This practice stimulates volume surges, which add excessive costs, and creates practices that in final analyses do not add value. Forward buying involves customers purchasing merchandise beyond their current needs to take advantage of lower prices. Sometimes these customers resell the extra product to others, while retaining some or all of the promotional allowance. This practice of reselling products to other firms is known as **diverting.** In effect, a firm is profiting by taking advantage of purchase incentives available in one area of the country but not others. The product is then resold to other retailers who do not have the purchase incentive available. This practice of diverting creates the opportunity to make a profit by purchasing merchandise for resale to other retailers.

In an effort to stabilize promotional pricing, some firms have begun to develop collaborative programs. Manufacturers and retailers working together agree to **net prices** that are administered over a planned time horizon. The manufacturer and retailer jointly plan the promotion and advertising strategy for a product or merchandising category. A **dead net price** takes into account quantity purchase discounts, prompt payment discounts, and any other applicable price incentives. Finally, an agreement is reached concerning the duration of the negotiated price. These agreements also specify how performance will be measured during the operating period as a basis for future agreements.

The price negotiation framework described above has resulted in what is known as **EveryDay Low Pricing (EDLP).** WalMart* is generally credited with having created EDLP, the strategy around which it seeks to build customer loyalty. Other firms have developed EDLP strategies in collaboration with suppliers while following a promotional pricing in consumer merchandising.

Few firms operate at the extremes of either EDLP or promotional pricing; however, most creative merchandisers develop a combination approach to stimulate consumer purchasing. While price promotion is used to generate consumer traffic and encourage in-store impulse buying, few items are consistently sold as loss leaders, thereby reducing the risk of predatory pricing allegations.

In a more general sense, business in a free market society will and should engage in a wide variety of pricing and advertising activities. The challenge is to fully understand how such promotional efforts impact logistics performance and cost. The timing and magnitude of promotional pricing need to be evaluated in terms of ability to consume and the capacity to efficiently handle volume surges. To a significant degree, **trade loading** practices result from end-of-period or end-of-year earnings pressures. This so-called Wall Street effect goes hand in hand with the use of promotional pricing to stimulate product flow so that sales can be booked during a specific time period. Such practices may offer short-term earnings relief but do little, if anything, to stimulate consumption. They are, however, guaranteed to increase logistics cost. Practices related to end-of-period and end-of-year sales loading are a primary target of Section 404 of the Sarbanes-Oxley (SOX) Act, discussed in Chapter 16.

Menu Pricing

From a seller's perspective, a pricing program must be established to accurately and equitably charge customers for the cost of products and services. Menu pricing is a technique used by many firms to accomplish this objective. An effective menu pricing system has three components: platform service price, value-added service specified costs, and efficiency incentives.

Platform Service Price

The first step in menu pricing is to establish the basic service platform to be offered to all customers and an appropriate price reflecting the costs related to providing that service level. The platform service price is expected to be paid by all customers, whether or not they require or desire the specified services. For example, the basic platform service price might be established for the following service level: "Full trailer of mixed products in unit load quantities on slip sheet from a warehouse for customer unload." The pricing quoted for this combination of delivery specifications, quantity, configuration, and unload requirements is the basis from which any additional charges or discounts are considered. Certain standard discounts may also be quoted as part of the basic service platform. For example, traditional quantity discounts and customer pickup allowances are typically considered in the basic platform price.

Value-Added Service Costs

The second aspect of menu pricing involves specifying upcharges for performing customer-requested value-added services. From the example above, an upcharge would be imposed for customized unit loading requested by a customer, such as layering products on the slip sheet in a specific order or configuring retail-ready unit loads. A separate upcharge would be established for multiple stop-offs during the delivery, and a third upcharge could be charged for using pallets rather than slip sheets. This approach results in each customer paying for the specific combination of services it desires.

Efficiency Incentives

The third step in a comprehensive menu pricing program is the establishment of efficiency incentives. Such incentives may be offered to encourage customers to comply with specified practices that reduce logistics costs. The incentives provide a mechanism for each of the parties to share in the benefits of such cost-reducing efforts. For example, a discount or allowance might be given to encourage Internet ordering, another incentive offered to receivers who guarantee unloading trucks in two hours or less, and a third incentive for using specified pallets.

To introduce costing precision into menu pricing, some industry leaders have begun using **activity-based costing** to help quantify the combined total cost impact of either the buying or selling organization performing a specific task. Armed with precise costs related to performing each aspect of the transaction, both parties are able to quantify value and cost benefits. The result is a **total cost-to-serve model,** which in effect quantifies menu pricing.

Summary

Transportation is usually the largest single cost expenditure in most logistics operations. Prior to deregulation, transportation services were standardized and inflexible, resulting in limited ability to develop a competitive advantage. As a result of deregulation, service offerings have been expanded and restrictions relaxed, allowing transportation resources to be effectively integrated into overall supply chain logistics.

Knowledge of transportation economics and pricing is essential for effective logistics management. The primary drivers of transportation costs are distance, volume, density, stowability, handling, liability, and market factors. These drivers determine transportation prices that are presented to buyers as rates for performing specific services. Logistics managers need to have a working familiarity with the basic rate structure for line-haul and specialized transport-related services.

The fundamental responsibilities of traffic administration are operational management, consolidation, negotiation, control, auditing and claims administration, and logistical integration. All aspects of administration are essential for effective transportation management. The extent to which the administrative responsibilities discussed are performed by an internal traffic department or are provided by an integrated service provider is a matter of managerial preference.

Finally, transportation and pricing decisions are closely related. The growing practice of debundling the price of products and related services, such as transportation, has increased the involvement of logistics managers in general price administration.

Challenge Questions

1. Seven economic drivers that influence transportation cost were presented. Select a specific product and discuss how each factor impacts determination of a freight rate.
2. Compare and contrast variable, fixed, and joint costs.
3. Compare and contrast cost-of-service with value of service as alternative rate-making strategies.
4. Discuss the concept of net pricing. What advantage does net pricing provide for carriers and shippers?
5. What is the purpose of freight classification? Does the concept of classification have relevancy given deregulation of transportation?
6. Describe the difference between a rate and a rating. How do they relate to classification?

7. What is the role of the freight bill and the bill of lading in a transportation transaction?

8. What is the basic concept of multivendor consolidation? How do ISPs help achieve such consolidation?

9. Four aspects of transportation operations management were identified as: (1) equipment scheduling and yard management, (2) load planning, (3) routing and advanced shipment notification, and (4) movement administration. Identify a commercial transportation shipment you are aware of and discuss how each managerial aspect was involved.

10. What is a shipper's responsibility when terms of purchase are F.O.B. origin? F.O.B. destination? Why would a shipper perfer one over the other?

Warehousing

Chapter Outline

Warehousing incorporates many different aspects of logistics operations. Because of the many types of warehouses, the presentation does not fit the neat classification schemes used in areas such as order management, inventory, and transportation. A warehouse has traditionally been viewed as a place to hold or store inventory. However, in contemporary logistical systems, warehouse functionality is more properly viewed as mixing inventory assortments to meet customer requirements. Storage of products is ideally held to a minimum. This chapter provides a foundation for understanding the value warehousing contributes in the logistics process. The discussion is relevant for all types of warehouses, including distribution centers, consolidation terminals, break-bulk facilities, and cross-docks. The objective is to introduce general managerial considerations related to warehousing.

Strategic Warehousing

While effective logistics systems should not be designed to hold inventory for extended times, there are occasions when inventory storage is justified on the basis of cost and service.

Storage has always been an important aspect of economic development. In the preindustrial era, storage was performed by individual households forced to function as self-sufficient economic units. Consumers performed warehousing and accepted the attendant risks.

As transportation capability developed, it became possible to engage in specialization. Product storage shifted from households to retailers, wholesalers, and manufacturers. Warehouses stored inventory in the logistics pipeline, serving to coordinate product supply and consumer demand. Because the value of strategic storage was not well understood, warehouses were often considered necessary evils that added cost to the distribution process. The concept that middlemen simply increase cost follows from that belief. During earlier times the need to deliver product assortments was limited. Labor productivity, materials handling efficiency, and inventory turnover were not major concerns. Because labor was relatively inexpensive, human resources were used freely. Little consideration was given to efficiency in space utilization, work methods, or materials handling. Despite such shortcomings, these initial warehouses provided a necessary bridge between production and marketing.

Following World War II, managerial attention shifted toward strategic storage. Management began to question the need for vast warehouse networks. In the distributive industries such as wholesaling and retailing, it was traditionally considered best practice to dedicate a warehouse containing a full assortment of inventory to every sales territory. As forecasting and production scheduling techniques improved, management questioned such risky inventory deployment. Production planning became more dependable as disruptions and time delays during manufacturing decreased. Seasonal production and consumption still required warehousing, but the overall need for storage to support stable manufacturing and consumption patterns was reduced.

Changing requirements in retailing more than offset any reduction in warehousing obtained as a result of these manufacturing improvements. Retail stores, faced with the challenge of providing consumers an increasing assortment of products, found it more difficult to maintain purchasing and transportation economics when buying direct from suppliers. The cost of transporting small shipments made direct ordering prohibitive. This created an opportunity to establish strategically located warehouses to provide timely and economical inventory replenishment for retailers. Progressive wholesalers and integrated retailers developed state-of-the-art warehouse systems to logistically support retail replenishment. Thus, the focus on warehousing shifted from passive storage to strategic assortment. The term **distribution center** became widely used throughout industry to capture this dynamic aspect of traditional warehousing.

Improvements in retail warehousing efficiency soon were adopted by manufacturing. For manufacturers, strategic warehousing offered a way to reduce holding or dwell time of materials and parts. Warehousing became integral to Just-in-Time **(JIT)** and stockless production strategies. While the basic notion of JIT is to reduce work-in-process inventory, such manufacturing strategies need dependable logistics. Achieving such logistical support across a global market typically requires strategically located warehouses. Utilizing centralized parts inventory at a central warehouse reduces the need for inventory at each assembly plant. Products can be purchased and shipped to the strategically located central warehouse, taking advantage of consolidated transportation. At the warehouse, products are sorted, sequenced, and shipped to specific manufacturing plants as needed.

Where fully integrated, sortation and sequencing facilities become a vital extension of manufacturing.

On the outbound, or market-facing, side of manufacturing, warehouses can be used to create product assortments for customer shipment. The capability to receive mixed product shipments offers customers two specific advantages. First, logistical cost is reduced because an assortment of products can be delivered while taking advantage of consolidated transportation. Second, inventory of slow-moving products can be reduced because of the capability to receive smaller quantities as part of a larger consolidated shipment. Manufacturers that provide sorted and sequenced product shipments on a timely basis are positioned to achieve a competitive advantage.

An important goal in warehousing is to maximize flexibility. Flexibility is facilitated by information technology. Technology has influenced almost every aspect of warehouse operations by creating new and better ways to perform storage and handling. Flexibility is also an essential part of being able to respond to ever-changing customer demand in terms of product assortments, value-added services, and the way shipments are sequenced and presented. Information technology facilitates flexibility by allowing warehouse operators to quickly react to changing customer requirements.[1]

Strategic warehousing serves to satisfy requirements related to **local presence.** While benefits of local presence may not be as obvious as other service benefits, it is often cited by executives as a major advantage of local warehouses. The underlying belief is that a local warehouse can respond faster to customer needs than can a more distant warehouse. It is anticipated that local warehouse presence will increase market share and potentially profitability. While the local-presence factor is a frequently discussed strategy, little solid research exists to confirm or refute its existence. In addition, more reliable transportation and technology-based order processing are closing the response time gap regardless of distance. Unless a warehouse is economically or service justified, it is unlikely that local presence will favorably influence operational results. The fact remains that a network of strategically located warehouses does provide key customers the perception they will be logistically supported.

Benefits realized from strategic warehousing are classified as economic and service. No warehousing should be included in a logistical system unless it is fully justified on some combination of cost and service. Ideally, a warehouse will simultaneously provide both economic and service benefits.

Economic Benefits

Economic benefits of warehousing occur when overall logistics costs are reduced. For example, if adding a warehouse in a logistical system reduces overall transportation cost by an amount greater than required investment and operational cost, then total cost will be reduced. When total cost reductions are achievable, the warehouse is economically justified. Four basic economic benefits are: (1) consolidation and break-bulk, (2) sorting, (3) seasonal storage, and (4) reverse logistics.

Consolidation and Break-Bulk

The economic benefits of consolidation and break-bulk are to reduce transportation cost by using warehouse capability to group shipments.

In consolidation, the warehouse receives materials, from a number of sources, that are combined in exact quantities into a large single shipment to a specific destination. The

---

[1] Arnold Maltz and Nicole De Horatuis, "Warehousing: The Evolution Continues," *WERC* (2004), pp. 1–58.

benefits of consolidations are the realization of the lowest possible freight rate, timely and controlled delivery, and reduced congestion at a customer's receiving dock. The warehouse enables both the inbound movement from origin and the outbound movement to destination to be consolidated into a larger size shipment, which generally results in lower transportation charges per unit and most often quicker delivery.

A break-bulk operation receives a single large shipment and arranges for delivery to multiple destinations. Economy of scale is achieved by transporting the larger consolidated shipment. The break-bulk warehouse or terminal sorts or splits out individual orders and arranges local delivery.

Both consolidation and break-bulk arrangements use warehouse capacity to improve transportation efficiency. Many logistical arrangements involve both consolidation and break-bulk. Figure 10.1 illustrates each activity.

Sorting

The basic benefit of sorting is to reconfigure freight as it flows from origin to destination. Three types of assortment—cross-docking, mixing, and assembly—are widely performed in logistical systems.

The objective of **cross-docking** is to combine inventory from multiple origins into a prespecified assortment for a specific customer. Retailers make extensive use of cross-dock operations to replenish fast-moving store inventories. Cross-docking requires precise on-time delivery from each manufacturer. As product is received and unloaded at the warehouse, it is sorted by destination. In most instances, the customer has communicated precise volume requirements of each product for each destination. The manufacturers, in turn, may have sorted, loaded, and labeled the appropriate quantity by destination. Product is then literally moved across the dock from receiving into a truck dedicated to the delivery destination. Once trucks are loaded with mixed product from multiple manufacturers, they are released for transport to destination. The high degree of precision required for effective cross-docking makes successful operation highly dependent on information technology.

An end result similar to cross-docking is achieved in **mixing.** However, mixing is usually performed at an intermediate location between shipment origin and destination. In a

FIGURE 10.1
Consolidation and Break-Bulk Arrangements

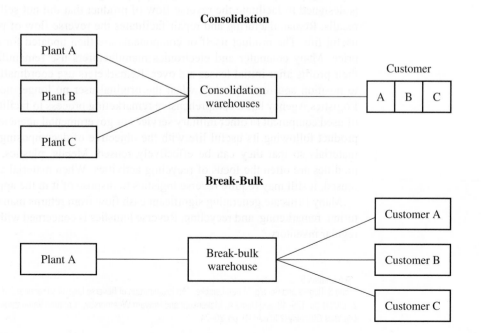

Consolidation

Break-Bulk

typical mixing operation, carloads or truckloads of products are shipped from origin to mixing warehouses. These inbound shipments are planned to minimize inbound transportation cost. Upon arrival at the mixing warehouse, shipments are unloaded and sorted into the combination desired by each customer. In-transit mixing has been traditionally supported by special transportation rates that provide financial incentives to facilitate the process.[2] During the mixing process, inbound products can be combined with others regularly stocked at a warehouse. Warehouses that perform in-transit mixing have the net effect of reducing overall product storage in a logistical system while achieving customer-specific assortments and minimizing transportation cost.

The objective of **assembly** is to support manufacturing operations. Products and components are assembled from a variety of second-tier suppliers by a warehouse, often referred to as **lead suppliers** or **tier one** suppliers, located in close proximity to the manufacturing plant. While manufacturing organizations have traditionally performed assembly, it has become common to utilize value-added services performed by a lead or tier one supplier or an **integrated service provider** (ISP) to sort, sequence, and deliver components when needed in manufacturing. Like cross-docking and mixing, assembly serves to achieve a process grouping of inventory at a precise time and location. Figure 10.2 illustrates these three sorting arrangements.

Seasonal Storage

The direct economic benefit of storage is to accommodate seasonal production or demand. For example, lawn furniture and toys are typically produced year-round but are sold only during a very short marketing period. In contrast, agricultural products are harvested at specific times, with subsequent consumption occurring throughout the year. Both situations require inventory storage to support marketing efforts. Storage provides an inventory buffer, which allows production efficiencies within the constraints imposed by material sources and consumers.

Reverse Logistics Processing

A great deal of the physical work related to reverse logistics is performed at warehouses. Reverse logistics includes the activities to support: (1) returns management, (2) remanufacturing and repair, (3) remarketing, (4) recycling, and (5) disposal. Returns management is designed to facilitate the reverse flow of product that did not sell or to accommodate recalls. Remanufacturing and repair facilitates the reverse flow of product following its useful life. The product itself or components are then updated for sale at a discounted price. Many computer and electronics manufacturers use remanufacturing to enhance their profits after initial leases are over. Remarketers use coordination and reverse flow to position and resell product when the original user no longer needs it. The Defense Logistics Agency has a comprehensive remarketing process to facilitate transfer and sale of used equipment to other military services or governmental agencies. Recycling returns product following its useful life with the objective of decomposing it to its component materials so that they can be effectively reused. Metals, plastics, and precious commodities are often the focus of recycling activities. When material cannot be effectively reused, it still may require reverse logistics to dispose of it in the appropriate landfill.

Many firms are generating significant cash flow from returns management, remanufacturing, remarketing, and recycling. Reverse logistics is concerned with both controlled and regular inventory.[3]

---

[2] See Chapter 9.

[3] Dale S. Rogers and Ronald Tibben-Lembke, "An Examination of Reverse Logistics Practices," *Journal of Business Logistics* 22 (2001), pp. 129–48; and Diane A. Mollenkopf and Howard Weathersby, "Creating Value through Reverse Logistics," *Logistics Quarterly* (2003/2004), pp. 20–24.

FIGURE 10.2
Sorting Arrangements

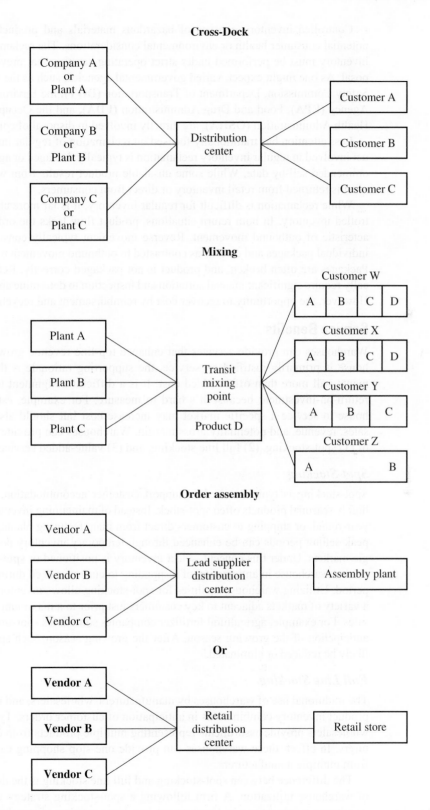

Controlled inventory consists of hazardous materials and product recalls that have potential consumer health or environmental considerations. The reclamation of controlled inventory must be performed under strict operating scrutiny that prevents improper disposal. As one might expect, varied governmental agencies, such as the Consumer Product Safety Commission, Department of Transportation **(DOT),** the Environmental Protection Agency **(EPA),** Food and Drug Administration **(FDA),** and the Occupational Safety and Health Administration **(OSHA),** are directly involved in disposal of controlled inventory.

Less attention has traditionally focused on reclamation of regular inventory. The product involved in regular inventory reclamation is typically damaged or aged beyond the recommended sell-by date. While some unsalable product results from warehouse damage, most is returned from retail inventory or direct from consumers.

While reclamation is difficult for regular inventory, it is far more challenging for controlled inventory. In both return situations, product flow lacks the orderly process characteristic of outbound movement. Reverse movement typically consists of nonuniform individual packages and cartons as contrasted to outbound movement of cases and pallets. Packages are often broken, and product is not packaged correctly. Return products typically require significant manual sortation and inspection to determine appropriate disposal. However, the opportunity to recover cost by reimbursement and recycling is significant.

Service Benefits

Warehouses can provide services that enhance top-line revenue growth. When a warehouse is primarily justified on service, the supporting rationale is that sales improvements will more than offset added cost. It is a difficult assignment to quantify service return-on-investment because it's hard to measure. For example, establishing a warehouse to service a specific market may increase cost but should also increase market sales, revenue, and potentially gross margin. Warehouses can provide service as a result of (1) spot-stocking, (2) full line stocking, and (3) value-added services.

Spot-Stocking

Spot-stocking is typically used to support customer accommodation. Manufacturers of highly seasonal products often spot-stock. Instead of maintaining inventory in a warehouse year-round, or shipping to customers direct from manufacturing plants, responsiveness in peak selling periods can be enhanced through temporary inventory positioning in strategic markets. Under this concept, select inventory is positioned or **spot-stocked** in a local market warehouse in anticipation of responding to customer need during the critical sales period. Utilizing warehouse facilities for spot-stocking allows inventories to be placed in a variety of markets adjacent to key customers just prior to a maximum period of seasonal sales. For example, agricultural fertilizer companies sometimes spot-stock near farmers in anticipation of the growing season. After the growing season, such spot-stocking would likely be reduced or eliminated.

Full Line Stocking

The traditional use of warehouses by manufacturers, wholesalers, and retailers is to stock product inventory combinations in anticipation of customer orders. Typical retailers and wholesalers provide assortments representing multiple products from different manufacturers. In effect, these warehouses can provide one-stop shopping capability for goods from multiple manufacturers.

The difference between spot-stocking and full line stocking is the degree and duration of warehouse utilization. A firm following a spot-stocking strategy would temporarily warehouse a narrow product assortment in a large number of warehouses for a limited time period. The full line stocking warehouse is more often restricted to a few strategic

TABLE 10.1
Value-Added
Services

• Cross-dock/transloading	• Order fulfillment
• Customer returns	• Pick/pack
• Home delivery	• Pool distribution
• In-transit merge	• Repair/refurbish
• Kan Ban	• Returnable container management
• Kitting	• Reverse logistics
• Labeling/preticketing	• RFID tag application
• Lot control	• Sequencing/metering
• Mass customization/postponement	• Specialty packaging
• Manufacturing support	• Store support/direct store delivery (DSD)

locations and operates year-round. Full line stocking warehouses improve service by reducing the number of suppliers that a customer must logistically deal with. The combined assortments also make economical larger shipments possible.

Value-Added Services

The demand for highly customized service has transformed modern distribution warehouses into facilities that specialize in performing **value-added services (VAS).** A value-added service is any work that creates a greater value for customers. Value-added services typically change the physical features or configuration of products so they are presented to customers in a unique or customized manner. Table 10.1 provides a list of typical value-added services.

Warehouses can postpone final product configuration by completing packaging, labeling, and even light manufacturing. For example, vegetables can be processed and canned in **brights** at the processing plants. Brights are cans without labels. Holding inventory as brights means that product is not committed to specific customers or carton configuration during processing. Once a specific customer order is received, the warehouse can complete labeling and finalize packaging. Examples of postponement range from packaging pharmaceuticals to customizing appliances.

Postponement provides two economic benefits. First, risk is minimized because customized packaging is not performed in anticipation of customer orders or to accommodate a forecast. Second, total inventory can be reduced by using inventory of the base product to support multiple customers' labeling and package requirements. The combination of reduced risk and lower inventory can result in reduced total cost to service even if packaging performed at the warehouse is more expensive per unit than if it were completed during manufacturing.

Warehouse Operations

Once a warehouse mission is determined, managerial attention focuses on establishing the operation. A typical warehouse contains materials, parts, and finished goods on the move. Warehouse operations consist of handling and storage. The objective is to efficiently receive inventory, store it as required, assemble it into complete orders, and make customer shipment. This emphasis on product flow renders a modern warehouse as a product mixing facility. As such, a great deal of managerial attention concerns how to design operations to facilitate efficient handling.

Handling

A first consideration is movement continuity and efficiency throughout the warehouse. Movement continuity means that it is better for an employee using handling equipment to perform longer moves than to undertake a number of short handlings to accomplish the same overall inventory move. Exchanging products between handlers or moving goods from one piece of equipment to another wastes time and increases the potential for product damage. Thus, as a general rule, longer warehouse handling movements are preferred. Goods, once in motion, should be continuously moved until arrival at their final destination.

Scale economies justify moving the largest quantities or loads possible. Instead of moving individual cases, handling procedures should be designed to move cases grouped on pallets, slipsheets, or containers.[4] The overall objective of materials handling is to eventually sort inbound shipments into unique customer assortments. The three primary handling activities are receiving, in-storage handling or transfer, and shipping.

Receiving

The majority of products and materials arrive at warehouses in large-quantity truck shipments. The first handling activity is unloading. At most warehouses, unloading is performed mechanically, using a combination of a lift truck, conveyors, and manual processes. When freight is floor stacked in the trailer, the typical procedure is to manually place products on pallets or a conveyor. When inbound product arrives unitized on pallets or in containers, lift trucks are used to move products from the vehicle to the dock. A primary benefit of receiving unitized loads is the ability to rapidly unload and release inbound transportation equipment.

In-Storage Handling

In-storage handling consists of movements that are performed within the warehouse. Following receipt and movement to a staging location, product is often moved within the facility for storage or order selection. Finally, when an order is processed it is necessary to select the required products and move them to a shipping area. These two types of in-storage handling are typically referred to as **transfer** and **selection.**

There are at least two and sometimes three transfer movements in a typical warehouse. The merchandise is initially moved from the receiving area to a storage location. This movement is typically handled by a lift truck when pallets or slipsheets are used or by other mechanical means for other types of unit loads. A second internal movement may be required prior to order assembly, depending upon warehouse operating procedures. When unit loads have to be broken down for order selection, they are usually transferred from storage to an order selection or picking area. When products are large or bulky, such as appliances, this intermediate movement to a picking area may not be necessary. Such product is often selected from the storage area and moved directly to the shipment staging area. The staging area is adjacent to the shipping dock. In order selection warehouses, the assembled customer order is transferred from the selection area to the shipping staging area. Characteristically, in-storage handling involves lower volume movements than receiving, but still relatively similar products.

Order selection is one of the major handling activities within warehouses. The selection process requires that materials, parts, and products be grouped to facilitate order assembly. It is typical for one area of a warehouse to be designated as a selection or picking area to assemble orders. For each order, the combination of products must be selected and packaged to meet specific customer order requirements.

An emerging technology, radio-frequency identificator **(RFID)** holds substantial promise in the area of warehouse layout, receiving, order selection, and shipping. The basic concept of RFID technology was discussed in Chapter 5. Because of the large number of different products processed and handled in a typical distribution center, RFID technology has great potential to improve operational efficiency. The deployment of RFID technology in warehouse design and material handling is discussed in Chapter 11.

---

[4] Specific types of handling equipment, pallets, and unitization are discussed in Chapter 11.

Shipping

Shipping consists of order verification and transportation equipment loading. As in receiving, firms may use conveyors or unit load materials handling equipment such as lift trucks to move products from the staging area into the truck trailer or container. In comparison to receiving, warehouse shipping must accommodate relatively low-volume movements of a mixture of products, thus reducing the potential for economies of scale. Shipping unit loads is becoming increasingly popular because considerable time can be saved in vehicle loading. A unit load consists of unitized or palletized product. To facilitate this loading and subsequent unloading upon delivery, many customers are requesting that suppliers provide mixed combinations of product within a trailer or on a pallet. The alternative is to floor-stack cases in the transportation vehicle. Shipment content verification is typically required when product changes ownership. Verification may be limited to a simple carton count or a piece-by-piece check for proper brand, size, and in some cases serial number to assure shipment accuracy. Over-the-road trailers are typically sealed at the time they are fully loaded and ready for shipment. The seal serves to verify that the content has not been altered during transit. Certification that seals have not been tampered with has become a critical factor in post 9-11 security.[5]

Storage

In planning warehouse layout, it is essential that products be assigned specific locations, called **slots,** on the basis of individual characteristics. The most important product variables to consider in a slotting plan are product velocity, weight, and special storage requirements.

Product velocity is the major factor driving warehouse layout. High-volume product should be positioned in the warehouse to minimize movement distance. For example, high-velocity products should be positioned near doors, primary aisles, and at lower levels in storage racks. Such positioning minimizes warehouse handling and reduces the need for frequent lifting. Conversely, products with low volume are typically assigned locations more distant from primary aisles or higher up in storage racks. Figure 10.3 illustrates a storage plan based on product movement velocity.

[5] See Chapter 17.

FIGURE 10.3
Storage Plan
Based on Product
Movement Velocity

Similarly, the storage plan should take into consideration product weight and special characteristics. Relatively heavy items should be assigned storage locations low to the ground to minimize lifting. Bulky or low-density product requires cubic space. Floor space along outside walls is ideal for such items. On the other hand, smaller items may require storage shelves, bins, or drawers. The integrated storage plan must consider individual product characteristics.

A typical warehouse is engaged in a combination of **active** and **extended** product storage alternatives. Warehouses that directly serve customers typically focus on active short-term storage. In contrast, other warehouses may use extended storage for speculative, seasonal, or obsolete inventory. In controlling and measuring warehouse operations, it is important to differentiate the relative requirements and performance capabilities of active and extended storage.

Active Storage

Regardless of inventory velocity, most goods must be stored for at least a short time. Storage for basic inventory replenishment is referred to as active storage. Active storage must provide sufficient inventory to meet the periodic demands of the service area. The need for active storage is usually related to the capability to achieve transportation or handling economies of scale. For active storage, materials handling processes and technologies need to focus on quick movement and flexibility with minimal consideration for extended and dense storage.

The active storage concept includes **flow-through** or **cross-dock distribution,** which uses warehouses for consolidation and assortment while maintaining minimal or no inventory in storage. The resulting need for reduced inventory favors flow-through and cross-docking techniques that emphasize movement and de-emphasize storage. Flow-through distribution is most appropriate for high-volume, fast-moving products where quantities are reasonably predictable. While flow-through distribution places minimal demands on storage requirements, it does require that product be quickly unloaded, de-unitized, grouped and sequenced into customer assortments, and reloaded into transportation equipment. As a result, the materials handling emphasis is on accurate information-directed quick movement.

Extended Storage

When inventory is held for periods in excess of that required for normal replenishment of customer stocks, it is referred to as **extended storage.** In some special situations, storage may be required for several months prior to customer shipment. Extended storage uses materials handling processes and technologies that focus on maximum space utilization with minimal need for quick access.

A warehouse may be used for extended storage for a variety of reasons. Some products, such as seasonal items, require storage to await demand or to spread supply across time. Other reasons for extended storage include erratic demand items, product conditioning, speculative purchases, and discounts.

Product conditioning sometimes requires extended storage, such as to ripen bananas. Food warehouses typically have ripening rooms to hold products until they reach peak quality. Storage may also be necessary for extended quality checks.

Warehouses may also retain products for an extended basis when they are purchased on a speculative basis. The magnitude of speculative buying depends upon the specific materials and industries involved, but it is very common in marketing of commodities and seasonal items. For example, if a price increase for an item is expected, it is not uncommon for a firm to buy ahead at the current price and warehouse the product for later use. In this case, the discount or savings have to be traded off against extended storage and inventory carrying cost. Commodities such as grains, oil, and lumber may be purchased and stored for speculative reasons.

The warehouse may also be used to realize special discounts. Early purchase or forward-buy discounts may justify extended storage. The purchasing manager may be able to realize a substantial price reduction during a specific time of the year. Under such conditions the warehouse is expected to hold inventory in excess of active storage. Manufacturers of fertilizer, toys, and lawn furniture often attempt to shift the warehousing burden to customers by offering off-season warehouse storage allowances.

Warehouse Ownership Arrangements

Warehouses are typically classified based on ownership. A **private** warehouse is operated by the enterprise that owns the merchandise handled and stored in the facility. A **public** warehouse, in contrast, is operated as an independent business offering a range of for-hire services, such as storage, handling, and transportation. Public warehouse operators generally offer a menu of relatively standardized services to customers. **Contract warehousing,** which is a customized extension of public warehousing, combines the benefits of private and for-hire warehousing. Contract warehousing is a long-term business arrangement that provides unique or tailored logistics services for a limited number of customers. The client and the warehouse operator typically share the risks associated with the operation. The important differences between contract and public warehouse operators are the anticipated length of the relationship, degree of exclusive or customized services, and shared incorporation of benefits and risks.

Private

A private warehouse is typically operated by the firm owning the product. The building, however, may be owned or leased. The decision concerning ownership or lease is essentially financial. Sometimes it is not possible to find a warehouse for lease that fits specialized logistical requirements; for example, the physical nature of an available building may not be conducive for efficient materials handling, such as buildings with inappropriate storage racks or with shipping/receiving dock or support column constraints. The only suitable course of action may then be to design and arrange for new construction.

The major benefits of private warehousing are control, flexibility, cost, and a range of intangibles. Private warehouses offer substantial control since management has authority to prioritize activities. Such control should facilitate integration of warehouse operations with the balance of a firm's logistics operations.

Private warehouses generally offer more flexibility since operating policies, hours, and procedures can be adjusted to meet specific customer and product requirements. Firms with very specialized customers or products are often motivated to own and operate warehouses.

Private warehousing is usually considered less costly than public warehousing because private facilities are not operated for a profit. As a result, both the fixed and variable cost components of a private warehouse may be lower than for-hire counterparts.

Finally, private warehousing may offer intangible benefits. A private warehouse, with the firm's name on its sign, may stimulate customer perceptions of responsiveness and stability. This perception may provide marketing image in comparison to competitors.

Despite the above-noted benefits, the use of private warehousing is declining because of an increasing managerial interest in reducing capital invested in logistical assets. Also, the perceived cost benefit of private warehousing is potentially offset by a public warehouse's ability to gain operational economies of scale and scope as a result of the combined throughput of multiple clients.

Public

Public warehouses are used extensively in logistical systems. Almost any combination of services can be arranged on a for-hire basis for either short or long term. Public warehouses have traditionally been classified based on operational specialization such as (1) general merchandise, (2) refrigerated, (3) special commodity, (4) bonded, and (5) household goods and furniture.

General merchandise warehouses are designed to handle package products such as electronics, paper, food, small appliances, and household supplies. Refrigerated warehouses typically offer frozen or chilled capacity designed to protect food, medical, photographic, and chemical products requiring special temperatures. Special commodity warehouses are designed to handle bulk material or items requiring special handling, such as tires or clothing. Bonded warehouses are licensed by the government to store goods prior to payment of taxes or import/export duties. They exert tight control over movements in and out of the facility, since documents must accompany each move. Finally, household goods or furniture warehouses specialize in handling and storing large, bulky items such as appliances and furniture. Of course, many public warehouses offer a combination of services. Public warehouses provide flexibility and shared services benefits. They have the potential to offer operating and management expertise since warehousing is their core business.

From a financial perspective, public warehousing may be able to achieve lower operating cost than private facilities. Such variable cost differential may result from lower wage scales, better productivity, and shared overhead among clients. Public warehouses typically do not require capital investment on the part of their customers. When management performance is judged according to return on investment, the use of public warehousing can be an attractive alternative. Public warehousing offers flexibility concerning size and number of warehouses, thus allowing users to respond to supplier, customer, and seasonal demands. In comparison, private warehouses are relatively fixed and difficult to change because buildings have to be constructed, expanded, or sold.

Public warehousing can also have the potential to share scale economies since the combined requirements of users can be leveraged. Such leverage spreads fixed costs and may justify investment in state-of-the-art handling equipment. A public warehouse may also leverage transportation by providing consolidation of multiple-client freight. For example, rather than require both supplier A and supplier B to deliver to a retail store from its own warehouse, a public warehouse serving both clients could arrange combined delivery, thus providing reduced transportation cost for the customer.

A great many firms utilize public warehouses for customer accommodation because of the variable cost, scalability, range of services, and flexibility. A public warehouse charges clients a basic fee for in and out handling plus storage. In the case of handling, the charge is assessed on the cases or pounds moved. For storage, the charge is assessed on the cases or weight in storage over a time. Special or value-added services provided by public warehouses are typically priced on a negotiated basis.

Contract

Contract warehousing combines characteristics of private and public operations. A long-term contractual relationship will typically result in lower total cost than a public warehouse. At the same time, contract warehouse operations can provide benefits of expertise, flexibility, scalability, and economies of scale by sharing management, labor, equipment, and information resources across multiple clients.

Contract warehouses typically offer a range of logistical services such as transportation management, inventory control, order processing, customer service, and return merchandise processing. Contract logistics firms, typically called **integrated service providers (ISPs)**, are capable of performing the total logistics responsibility for an enterprise.

For example, Kraft Foods has increasingly utilized contract warehousing as a replacement for private and public frozen and dry grocery facilities. Since the late 1990s, Kraft has used AmeriCold Logistics, an integrated warehousing and distribution services company, to perform storage, handling, and distribution services. The arrangement has multiple benefits for both parties. The long-term contractual arrangement allows Kraft to expand its distribution network without incurring the time or cost of building expansion. Kraft is assured that there will always be space for new products, so its distribution network is protected. AmeriCold doesn't have to be concerned with selling space to Kraft. Moreover, the longer Kraft utilizes AmeriCold's services, the better the contract warehousing firm's capability to understand business needs and provide customized services.

Network Deployment

As would be expected, many firms utilize a combination of private, public, and contract facilities.[6] Full warehouse utilization throughout a year is rare. As a managerial guideline, a typical warehouse will be fully utilized between 75 and 85 percent of the time; so from 15 to 25 percent of the time, space needed to satisfy peak requirements will not be used. In such situations, a deployment strategy may be the use of private or contract warehouses to cover the 75 percent requirement while public facilities are used to accommodate peak demand.

Developing a warehouse network strategy requires answers to two key questions. The first is how many warehouses should be established. The second question focuses on which warehouse ownership types should be used in specific markets. For many firms, the answer is a combination of warehouse alternatives, differentiated by customer and product. Specifically, some customer groups may be served best from a private warehouse, while public or contract warehouses may be appropriate for others. This warehouse segmentation is increasingly popular as key customers are requiring more customized value-added services and capabilities.

Warehouse Decisions

The basic concept that warehouses provide an enclosure for material storage and handling requires detailed analysis before the size, type, and shape of the facility can be determined. This section reviews planning issues that establish the character of the warehouse, which in turn determines attainable handling efficiency.

Site Selection

The first task is to identify both the general and then the specific warehouse location. The general area concerns the broad geography where an active warehouse makes sense from a service, economic, and strategic perspective. The general question focuses on the broader geographic area as illustrated by the need to place a warehouse in the Midwest, which generally implies having a facility in Illinois, Indiana, or Wisconsin. In contrast, a retailer such as Target or Home Depot typically selects a warehouse location that is central to a prerequisite number of retail store locations. Thus, the selection and number of retail outlets drive the support warehouse location.

Once the general warehouse location is determined, a specific building site must be identified. Typical areas in a community for locating warehouses are commercial developments

[6] For a comprehensive discussion of the strategic use of warehousing, see Ken Ackerman, *Warehousing Profitability: A Manager's Guide* (Columbus, OH: Ackerman Publications, 2000).

and outlying or suburban areas. The factors driving site selection are service availability and cost. Land cost is the most important factor. A warehouse need not be located in a major industrial area. In many cities, warehouses are among industrial plants and in areas zoned for light or heavy industry. Most warehouses can operate legally under the restrictions placed upon general commercial property.

Beyond procurement cost, setup, and operating expenses such as transport access, utility hookups, taxes, and insurance rates require evaluation. The cost of essential services may vary extensively between sites. For example, a food-distribution firm recently rejected what otherwise appeared to be a totally satisfactory warehouse site because of projected insurance rates. The site was located near the end of a water main. During most of the day, adequate water pressure was available to handle operational and emergency requirements. However, a water problem was possible during two short periods each day. From 6:30 A.M. to 8:30 A.M. and from 5:00 P.M. to 7:00 P.M. the overall demand for water along the line was so great that a sufficient pressure was not available to handle emergencies. Because of this deficiency, abnormally high insurance rates were required and the site was rejected.

Several other requirements must be satisfied before a site is purchased. The site must offer adequate room for expansion. Necessary utilities must be available. The soil must be capable of supporting the structure. The site must be sufficiently high to afford proper water drainage. Additional requirements may be situationally necessary, depending upon the structure to be constructed. For these reasons and others, the final selection of the site should be preceded by extensive analysis.[7]

Design

Warehouse design must consider product movement characteristics. Three factors to be determined during the design process are the number of floors to include in the facility, a cube utilization plan, and product flow.

The ideal warehouse design is a one-floor building that eliminates the need to move product vertically. The use of vertical handling devices, such as elevators and conveyors, to move product from one floor to the next requires time and energy, and typically creates handling bottlenecks. So, while it is not always possible, particularly in business districts where land is restricted or expensive, as a general rule distribution warehouses should be designed as one-floor operations to facilitate materials handling.

Warehouse design must maximize cubic utilization. Most warehouses are designed with 25- to 30-foot clear ceilings, although selected automated and high-rise handling equipment can effectively use heights over 100 feet. Maximum effective warehouse height is limited by the safe lifting capabilities of materials handling equipment, such as lift trucks, rack design, and fire safety regulations imposed by sprinkler systems.

Warehouse design should facilitate continuous straight product flow through the building. This is true whether the product is moving into storage or is being cross-docked. In general, this means that product should be received at one end of a building, stored as necessary in the middle, and shipped from the other end. Figure 10.4 illustrates straight-line product flow that facilitates velocity while minimizing congestion and redundant handling.

Product-Mix Analysis

An important area of analysis is analysis of products that will be distributed through the warehouse. The design and operation of a warehouse are both dependent on the product mix. Each product should be analyzed in terms of annual sales, demand, weight, cube, and packaging. It is also important to determine the total size, cube, and weight of the average

---

[7] Perry A. Trunlick, "All the Right Moves," *Logistics Today* (November 2003), pp. 38–40.

FIGURE 10.4
Basic Warehouse Design

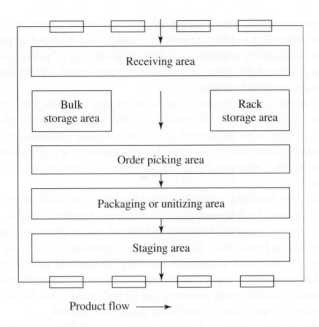

Product flow ⟶

order to be processed through the warehouse. These data provide necessary information for determining warehouse space, design and layout, materials handling equipment, operating procedures, and controls.

Expansion

Because warehouses are increasingly important in supply chain networks, their future expansion should be considered during the initial planning phase. It is common to establish 5- to 10-year expansion plans. Potential expansion may justify purchase or option of a site three to five times larger than required to support initial construction.

Building design should also accommodate future expansion. Some walls may be constructed of semipermanent materials to allow quick removal. Floor areas, designed to support heavy movements, can be extended during initial construction to facilitate expansion.

Materials Handling

A materials handling system is the basic driver of warehouse design. As noted previously, product movement and assortment are the main functions of a warehouse. Consequently, the warehouse is viewed as a structure designed to facilitate efficient product flow. It is important to stress that the materials handling system must be selected early in the warehouse development process. Material handling equipment and technology are discussed in Chapter 11.

Layout

The layout or storage areas of a warehouse should be planned to facilitate product flow. The layout and the material handling system are integral. In addition, special attention must be given to location, number, and design of receiving and loading docks.

It is difficult to generalize warehouse layouts since they are usually customized to accommodate specific product handling requirements. If pallets are utilized, an early step is to determine the appropriate size. A pallet of nonstandard size may be desirable for specialized products. The most common pallet sizes are 40 × 48 inches and 32 × 40 inches. In general, the larger the pallet load, the lower the movement cost per pound or package over a given distance. One lift truck operator can move a large load in the same time and with the same effort required to move a smaller load. Analysis of product cases, stacking patterns, and industry practices will determine the size of pallet best suited to the operation. Regardless of the size finally selected, management should adopt one pallet size for use throughout the warehouse.

The second step in planning warehouse layout involves pallet positioning. The most common practice in positioning pallets is at 90 degree, or square, placement. Square positioning is widely used because of layout ease. Square placement means that the pallet is positioned perpendicular to the aisle. The placement of specific products in selected pallet locations is called **slotting.** Naturally, key to an efficient layout is a well-developed slotting plan.[8]

Finally, the handling equipment must be integrated to finalize layout. The path and tempo of product flow depend upon the materials handling system. To illustrate the relationship between materials handling and layout, two systems and their respective layouts are illustrated in Figure 10.5. These examples represent two of many possible layouts.

Layout A illustrates a materials handling system and layout utilizing lift trucks for inbound and inventory transfer movements and tow tractors with trailer for order selection. This scenario assumes that products can be palletized. This layout is greatly simplified because offices, special areas, and other details are omitted.

The floor plan of layout A is approximately square. The advocates of square design feel that it provides the best framework for overall operating efficiency. As indicated earlier in this chapter, products should be positioned in a specific area of the warehouse for order selection. Such is the case in layout A. This area is labeled the **selection,** or **picking, area.** Its primary purpose is to minimize the distance order pickers must travel when assembling an order.

[8] Helen L. Richardson, "Getting Your Warehouse in Order," *Logistics Today* (October 2003), pp. 38–42.

FIGURE 10.5 **Layouts A and B**

Layout A.

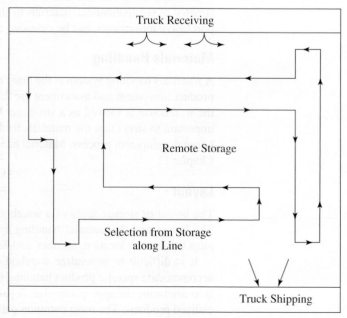

Layout B.

The selection area is supported by a **storage area.** When products are received they are palletized and moved to the storage area. The selection area is replenished from storage as required. Within the selection area, products are positioned according to weight, bulk, and replenishment velocity to minimize outbound movement. Customer orders are assembled by an order selector using a tow tractor pulling trailers through the selection area. The arrows in layout A indicate product selection flow.

Layout B illustrates a materials handling system utilizing lift trucks to move product inbound and for transfer movements. A continuous towline is used for order selection. The floor plan in layout B is rectangular. In a system using a continuous-movement towline, the compact selection area is replaced by order selection directly from storage. Products are moved from receiving areas into storage positions adjacent to the towline. The orders are then selected directly from storage and loaded onto carts, which are pulled around the warehouse by the towline. Merchandise is stored or positioned to minimize inbound movement. The weakness of the fixed towline is that it facilitates selection of all products at an equal speed and frequency and does not consider special needs of high-velocity products. The arrows in layout B indicate major product movements. The line in the center of the layout illustrates the path of the towline.

As indicated, both layouts A and B are greatly simplified. The purpose is to illustrate the extremely different approaches managers have developed to reconcile the relationship between materials handling and warehouse layout.

Sizing

Several techniques are available to help estimate warehouse size. Each method begins with a projection of the total volume expected to move through the warehouse during a given period. The projection is used to estimate base and safety stocks for each product to be stocked in the warehouse. Some techniques consider both normal and peak inventory. Failure to consider utilization rates can result in overbuilding. It is important to note, however, that a major complaint of warehouse managers is underestimation of warehouse size requirements. A good rule of thumb is to allow 10 percent additional space to account for increased volume, new products, and new business opportunities.

Warehouse Management Systems (WMS)

The development of work procedures goes hard in hand with training warehouse personnel. Most firms depend upon a Warehouse Management System **(WMS)** to standardize work procedures and encourage best practice.[9] It is management's responsibility to see that all personnel understand and use these procedures.[10]

One of the main uses of a WMS is to coordinate order selection. Two basic methods of order selection are **discrete selection** and **wave selection,** also known as **batch selection.** In discrete selection, a specific customer's order is selected and prepared for shipment as a specific work assignment. Discrete order selection is often used when order content and handling selection are critical.

Wave selection can be designed and operationalized in a variety of ways. A wave can be coordinated by an area of the warehouse wherein all quantities of all products required to complete all customer orders are selected at one time. Using this type of wave selection, employees are typically assigned responsibility for a specific portion of the warehouse. Waves can also be planned around a specific shipment destination and/or carrier, for example, all UPS shipments to the East Coast. Because each employee has a thorough

---

[9] Christopher R. Barnes, "Warehouse Management," *WERC* (2004), pp. 1–58.
[10] "WMS and Warehouse Productivity," *WERC Watch* (December 2003), pp. 1–7.

knowledge of a specific warehouse selection area or shipping procedure, fewer selection errors typically result using wave picking.

WMS also coordinates work procedures that are important for receiving and shipping. Established procedures for receiving and ensuring product entry into inventory records are critical. If pallets are used, the merchandise must be stacked in appropriate patterns to ensure maximum load stability and consistent case counts. Personnel working in shipping must have knowledge of trailer loading practices. In specific types of operations, particularly when merchandise changes ownership, items must be checked during loading.

Work procedures are not restricted to floor personnel. Procedures must be established for administration and maintenance. Replenishment of warehouse inventory can cause operational problems if proper ordering procedures are lacking. Normally, there is limited interaction between buyers and warehouse personnel, although such communication is improving within integrated supply chain management organizations. Buyers tend to purchase in quantities that afford the best price, and little attention is given to pallet compatible quantities or available warehouse space.

Ideally buyers should coordinate with warehouse personnel before commissioning large orders or introducing new products. The experience of some companies has forced management to require buyers to predetermine warehouse space assignment prior to ordering. Another potential problem is the quantity of cases ordered. The goal is to purchase in pallet-multiple quantities. For example, if a product is ideally stacked on pallets in a 50-case pattern, the buyer should order in multiples of 50. If an order is placed for 120 cases, upon arrival the cases will fill two pallets plus 20 on a third pallet. The extra 20 cases will require the warehouse cubic space typically used for a pallet of 50 and will require the same amount of materials handling capacity to move.

Figure 10.6 illustrates the range of activities coordinated by an advanced WMS. Historical warehouse system functionality focused on receiving replenishment shipments, stock putaway, and order picking. Figure 10.6 illustrates other traditionally standard activities under the category labeled **core functionality.** Warehouses today must offer a broader range of services as they are frequently performing form postponement. They are also

FIGURE 10.6
Warehouse Management System Functionality

Warehouse Management Systems

Core Functionality
Receiving
Put-away
Cycle-count
Pick
Task management
Quality analysis
Replenishment
Pack
Opportunistic cross-dock
Inventory control
Work order management
Ship

Advanced Functionality
Yard management
Labor management
Warehouse optimization
Value-added services
Planned cross-dock
Returns management

Interface systems (middleware)

ERP—TMS—Material handling—Supply chain planning systems

required to manage more inventory on a just-in-time basis. Figure 10.6 illustrates some of these activities indicated as **advanced functionality.** Yard management, sometimes a functionality of a firm's Transportation Management System **(TMS),** refers to the process of managing the vehicles and the inventory within vehicles while in the warehouse yard. Faster inventory turnover requires better visibility of inventory, even when in transportation vehicles. Labor management refers to maximizing the use of warehouse labor. Historically, warehouse labor has been quite specialized, allowing for relatively easy planning. Today, however, warehouse labor is expected to perform a wider range of activities to minimize the number of employees necessary at any given point in time. Warehouse optimization refers to selection of the best location within the warehouse for the storage and retrieval of product to minimize time and movement. **Value-added services** refer to the coordination of warehouse activities to customize product, such as packaging, labeling, kitting, and setting up displays. Planned cross-docking and merging is the integration of two or more parts of a customer order that have been supplied from a different source without maintaining inventory. This strategy is sometimes used in the personal computer industry to merge a processing unit and the display monitor in a warehouse just prior to delivery to the ultimate customer.

Since there is no inventory of either part in the warehouse, the merging activity requires precise timing and coordination. A final execution function is the capability to manage reverse logistics activities such as returns, repair, and recycling. Both customers and environmental interests are increasing their demands that supply chains can accommodate reverse logistics. Table 10.2 summarizes WMS functionality and decision support benefits.

Accuracy and Audits

WMS functionality requires verification of inventory accuracy to maintain operational effectiveness. Inventory accuracy is typically maintained by annual physical inventory counts or by counting specific portions of the inventory on a planned basis. **Cycle counting** is the audit of selected inventory on a cyclic schedule.[11] Selection of individual items to be counted and verified can be based on a specific area of the warehouse, frequency of movement, or turnover. Once counted, discrepancies between physical and WMS inventories are reconciled to assure continued system validity.

Audits related to inventory accuracy are only one type of audit that is typically used to maintain and improve warehouse operating efficiency. Audits are also common to maintain safety, assure compliance to security regulations, drive procedural improvement, and facilitate work changes.[12]

Security

In a broad sense, security in a warehouse involves protection against merchandise pilferage, deterioration, and any form of operational disruption. Each form of security requires management attention.

Pilferage

In warehouse operations it is necessary to protect against theft by employees and thieves as well as from riots and terrorist-related disturbances. Typical security procedures should be strictly enforced at each warehouse. Security begins at the fence. As standard procedure, only authorized personnel should be permitted into the facility and on surrounding

---

[11] Bill Latham, "Cycle Counting: The Best Way to Improve Inventory Accuracy," *Warehousing Forum* 19, no. 12 (November 2004), pp. 1–2.

[12] "The DC Audit," *WERC Sheet* (January 2004), pp. 1–3.

TABLE 10.2
WMS Functionality and Decision Support

Source: Reproduced with permission from Bowersox et al., "RFID Applications within the Four Walls of a Consumer Package Goods Warehouse," from Marketing and Supply Chain Working Paper, Michigan State University, 2005.

Selected Functionality	Decision Support Benefits
Put-away	Improved productivity and cube utilization.
Task interleaving	Routing of fork trucks on demand as contrasted to predetermined assigned tasks, areas, or sequences.
Pick/replenishment	Direct picking from single or multiple locations including pick to assure expiration date compliance. Facilitates replenishment of pick location inventories when appropriate.
Slotting	Variable slot or product placement locator assignment to enhance space utilization.
Cross-docking	Facilitate direct receipt to shipment flow.
Inventory visibility	Tracking specific inventory lots by warehouse location as well as daily visibility of receipts. Date specific lot control.
Work queue resolution	Identification of alternative ways to rapidly or efficiently resolve work constraints or queues.
Picking strategy	Routines to perform selected picking strategies.
Error correction	Ability to identify, resolve, and correct data errors in real time.
	Ability to identify and resolve differences in purchase orders or advanced shipment notifications (ASN) and actual quantities or product received.
Simulations	Performance of real-time decision support scenarios to assist in operational decision making.
Return goods	Facilitate processing and audit compliance for reverse logistics programs.
Cycle counts	Ability to conduct and resolve real-time inventory counts.

grounds. Entry to the warehouse yard should be controlled through a single gate. Without exception, no private automobile, regardless of management rank or customer status, should be allowed to enter the yard or park adjacent to the warehouse.

To illustrate the importance of security guidelines, the following experience may be helpful. A firm adopted the rule that no private vehicles would be permitted in the warehouse yard. Exceptions were made for two office employees with special needs. One night after work, one of these employees discovered a bundle taped under one fender of his car. Subsequent checking revealed that the car was literally a loaded delivery truck. The matter was promptly reported to security, who informed the employee not to alter any packages taped to the car and to continue parking inside the yard. Over the next several days, the situation was fully uncovered, with the ultimate arrest and conviction of seven warehouse employees who confessed to stealing thousands of dollars, worth of company merchandise. The firm would have been far better off had it provided transportation for the two special-needs employees from the regular parking lots to their work locations.

Shortages are always a major concern in warehouse operations. Many are honest mistakes that occur during order selection and shipment, but the purpose of security is to restrict theft from all angles. A majority of thefts occur during normal working hours.

Inventory control and order processing systems help protect merchandise from being carried out of the warehouse unless accompanied by a computer release document. If samples are authorized for salesperson use, such merchandise should be maintained in a separate inventory. Not all pilferage occurs on an individual basis. Organized efforts between warehouse personnel and truck drivers can result in deliberate overpicking or high-for-low-value product substitution in order to move unauthorized merchandise out of the warehouse. Employee work assignment rotation, total case counts, and occasional complete line-item checks can reduce vulnerability to such collaboration.

A final concern is the increased incidence of hijacking over-the-road trailer loads from yards or while in transit. Hijacking is a major logistical concern. Over-the-road hijack prevention is primarily a law-enforcement matter, but in-yard theft can be eliminated by tight security provisions. Such over-the-road theft is a significant problem in developing countries. One beverage company manager reported that he budgeted to lose one truck a week to theft for his South American operation. He instructed his drivers to simply turn over the keys and walk away rather than risk their lives. Procedures and technology related to terrorist-initiated security are discussed in Chapter 17.

Damage

Within the warehouse, a number of factors can reduce a product or material to nonsalable status. The most obvious form of product deterioration is damage from careless materials handling. For example, when pallets of merchandise are stacked in great heights, a marked change in humidity or temperature can cause packages supporting the stack to collapse. The warehouse environment must be carefully controlled and measured to provide proper product protection. Of major concern is warehouse employee carelessness. In this respect, the lift truck may well be management's worst enemy. Regardless of how often lift truck operators are warned against carrying overloads, some still attempt such shortcuts when not properly supervised. In one situation, a stack of four pallets was dropped off a lift truck at the receiving dock of a food warehouse. Standard procedure was to move two pallets per load. The dollar cost of the damaged merchandise exceeded the average daily profit of two retail supermarkets. Product deterioration from careless handling within the warehouse is a form of loss that cannot be insured against or offset with compensating revenue.

Another major form of deterioration is incompatibility of products stored or transported together. For example, care must be taken when storing or shipping chocolate to make sure that it does not absorb odors from products it is being transported with, such as household chemicals.

Safety and Maintenance

Accident prevention is a concern of warehouse management. A comprehensive safety program requires constant examination of work procedures and equipment to locate and take corrective action to eliminate unsafe conditions before accidents result. Accidents occur when workers become careless or are exposed to mechanical or physical hazards. The floors of a warehouse may cause accidents if not properly cleaned. During normal operation, rubber and glass deposits collect on aisles and, from time to time, broken cases will result in product seepage onto the floor. Proper cleaning procedures can reduce the accident risk of such hazards. Environmental safety has become a major concern of government agencies such as OSHA and cannot be neglected by management.

A preventive maintenance program is necessary for materials handling equipment. Unlike production machines, movement equipment is not stationary, so it is more difficult to properly maintain. A preventive maintenance program scheduling periodic checks of all handling equipment should be applied in every warehouse.

Summary

Warehousing exists to contribute to manufacturing and distribution efficiency. While the role of the warehouse has traditionally been to stock inventory, contemporary warehousing provides a broader value proposition in terms of economic and service benefits. Economic benefits include consolidation and break-bulk, sorting, seasonal storage, and reverse logistics. Service benefits include spot-stocking, full line stocking, and value-added services. The perspective of warehousing is changing from a traditional storage mission to one characterized by customization, velocity, and movement.

Distribution centers and warehouses are designed to accommodate the primary activities of inventory handling and storage. Handling includes receiving inbound shipments; in-storage handling to move between different types of storage such as long-term, bulk, and picking; and packing and staging shipments to customers. Active storage facilitates cross-docking, consolidation, break-bulk, and postponement. Extended storage activities facilitate balancing supply and demand and speculation.

Warehouses are usually classified on the basis of ownership. A private warehouse is operated by the enterprise that owns the merchandise in the facility. A public warehouse is operated independently and offers various for-hire value-added services. A contract warehouse is a long-term business arrangement that provides tailored services for a limited number of customers. An integrated warehousing strategy often incorporates a combination of warehouse ownership options.

There are numerous managerial decisions in planning and initiating warehouse operations, including site selection, design, product-mix analysis, expansion, materials handling, layout, sizing, WMS, accuracy and audits, security, safety, and maintenance. Each of these activities requires considerable managerial effort to ensure facilities start up and run smoothly on a day-to-day basis and are able to accommodate change rapidly and successfully, as necessary to meet current business demands.

Challenge Questions

1. Provide a definition and an example of strategic storage from a logistical system you are familiar with.
2. Discuss and illustrate the economic justification for establishing a warehouse.
3. Why could a warehouse be described as a "necessary evil"?
4. How do warehouses perform order sorting?
5. Under what conditions could it make sense to combine private and public warehouses in a logistical system?
6. What role are warehouse operators playing in postponement strategies?
7. What is the concept of local presence? Is local presence growing or declining in importance?
8. Discuss and illustrate the role of warehouses in reverse logistics.
9. Illustrate the relationship between the size and shape of a distribution warehouse and the materials handling system. Why do some warehouses have square design while others are rectangular?
10. Explain the following statement: "A warehouse should merely consist of walls enclosing an efficient handling system."

Packaging and Materials Handling

Chapter Outline

Packaging Perspectives

Packaging for Materials Handling Efficiency
Package Design
Unitization
Communication

Materials Handling
Basic Handling Considerations
Mechanized Systems
Semiautomated Systems
Automated Systems
Information-Directed Systems
Special Handling Considerations

Summary

Within a warehouse and while being transported throughout a logistics system, the package serves to identify and protect products. The package, containing a product, is the entity that must be moved by a firm's materials handling system. For this reason packaging and materials handling are jointly discussed.

Packaging Perspectives[1]

Packaging is typically viewed as being either **consumer,** focused primarily on marketing, or **industrial,** focused on logistics. The primary concern of logistics operations is industrial package design. Individual products or parts are typically grouped into cartons, bags, bins, or barrels for damage protection and handling efficiency. Containers used to group individual products are called **master cartons.** When master cartons are grouped into larger units for handling, the combination is referred to as **containerization** or **unitization.**

Master cartons and unit loads are the basic handling units for logistical operations. The weight, cube, and damage potential of the master carton determines transportation and materials handling requirements. If the package is not designed for efficient logistical processing, overall system performance suffers.

[1] The authors express their appreciation to Professor Diana Tweede from the Michigan State University School of Packaging for assistance provided in preparing this section.

Retail sale quantity or presentation should not be the prime determinant of master carton size. For example, beer, often sold at retail in units of 6, is normally packed in master cartons containing 24 units. The master carton should be large enough to provide handling economies of scale but light enough to facilitate handling by an individual without mechanical assistance. A prime objective in logistics is to design operations to handle a limited assortment of standardized master cartons. Master carton standardization facilitates materials handling and transportation. The importance of standardization can be illustrated by an example adapted from a shoe retailer.

The initial logistical system employed by the retailer to ship shoes from the warehouse to retail stores consisted of reusing vendor cartons. Individual pairs of shoes were grouped as best as possible into available repack cartons. The result was a variety of carton sizes going to each retail store. The method of order selection used to assemble a retail store's order was to work from warehouse-sequenced picking lists that grouped shoes by style and quantity. Shoes were selected in the warehouse, packed into cartons, and then manually stacked on a four-wheel truck for transfer to the shipping dock. The cartons were then loaded into trucks for delivery to stores. While the order picking list provided a summary of all shoes in the total shipment, it was impossible for the retail stores to determine the contents of any given carton.

Viewing materials handling delivery and store operations as an integrated system resulted in a decision to discontinue reusing vendor cartons. The new procedure used a standardized master carton that facilitated order picking and materials handling. The new logistics practice was designed around two concepts. First, standardized master cartons were adopted to permit continuous conveyor movement from point of warehouse order selection to truck loading. Second, the integrated system used a computer process to assure that each standardized master carton was packed to maximum practical cube utilization. Under the new system a picking list was generated for each carton. After the individual pairs of shoes were placed into the carton, the pick list was attached to the carton, providing a summary of contents for retail store personnel.

The advantages of a standardized master carton extended to the retail store's stockroom. Because the contents of each master carton were easily determined, it was not necessary to search through multiple cartons to find a specific style or size of shoe while a customer was waiting. Standard master cartons could be more efficiently stacked, resulting in less backroom congestion. Finally, complete identification of master carton contents facilitated retail inventory management and replenishment.

The new integrated system required purchase of master cartons, since each could be reused only about three times. However, this added cost was more than justified by reduced order picking labor, continuous movement of cartons into over-the-road trailers, and more efficient utilization of transportation trailer capacity. Since each master carton was filled to near cubic capacity, dead space in cartons was reduced. The standardized master carton size was selected to achieve maximum conformity with a high-cube over-the-road trailer, thereby eliminating dead space in stacking. The end result of standardized master carton usage was a substantial reduction in total cost combined with a far more effective materials handling system at both the warehouse and the retail shoe store.

This packaging example illustrates the importance of integrated logistical planning and the principle of lowest total cost. However, the most important point is that master carton standardization facilitated supply chain integration.

Naturally, few organizations can reduce their master carton requirements to a one size fits all. When master cartons of more than one size are required, extreme care should be taken to arrive at an assortment of compatible units. Figure 11.1 illustrates one such concept, utilizing four standard master carton sizes, that achieves modular compatibility.

FIGURE 11.1   Example and Benefits of Modular Packaging

Source: Adapted from materials provided by Walter Frederick Freedman and Company.

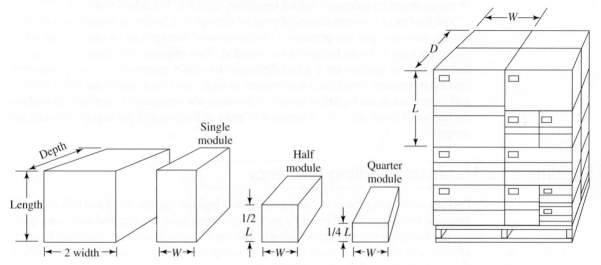

Of course, logistical considerations cannot fully dominate packaging design. The ideal package for materials handling and transportation would be a perfect cube having equal length, depth, and width while achieving maximum possible density. Seldom will such a package exist. The important point is that logistical requirements should be evaluated along with manufacturing, marketing, and product design considerations in finalizing master carton selection.

Another logistical packaging concern is the degree of desired protection. Package design and material must combine to achieve the desired level of protection without incurring the expense of overprotection. It is possible to design a package that has the correct material content but does not provide the necessary protection. Arriving at a satisfactory packaging solution involves defining the degree of allowable damage in terms of expected overall conditions and then isolating a combination of design and materials capable of meeting those specifications. For package design, there are two key principles. First, the cost of absolute protection will, in most cases, be prohibitive. Second, package construction is properly a blend of design and material.

A final logistics packaging concern is the relationship between the master carton size, order quantity, and retail display quantity. From a materials handling perspective, master cartons should be standardized and reasonably large to minimize the number of units handled at the warehouse. For ease of warehouse handling, it is desirable to have retailers purchase in master carton quantities. However, for a slow-moving product, a master carton could contain a substantial overstock for an item that sells only one unit per week but is packed in a case containing 48. Finally, in order to minimize labor, retailers often place trays from master cartons on the retail shelf so that individual products do not have to be unloaded and placed on the store shelf. Master cartons or trays meeting retail requirements for shelf space are preferred.

The determination of final package design requires a great deal of testing to assure that both marketing and logistics concerns are satisfied. While the marketing aspects are generally the focus of consumer research, logistics packaging research is determined from laboratory or experimental testing. Laboratory analysis offers a reliable way to evaluate package design as a result of advancements in testing equipment and measurement techniques. Instrumented recording equipment is available to measure shock severity and characteristics while a package is in transit. To a large degree, care in design has been further encouraged by increased federal regulation regarding hazardous materials.

The four most common causes of product damage in a logistical system are vibration, impact, puncture, and compression. Combinations of damage can be experienced whenever a package is being transported or handled. Test shipment monitoring is expensive and difficult to conduct on a scientific basis. To obtain increased accuracy, computerized environmental simulations can be used to replicate typical conditions that a package will experience in the logistical system. Laboratory test equipment is available to evaluate the impact of shock upon the interaction of product fragility and packaging materials and design.

Packaging for Materials Handling Efficiency

Package utility concerns how packaging impacts logistical productivity and efficiency. All logistical operations are affected by packaging—from truck loading and warehouse picking productivity to transportation vehicle and storage cube utilization. Materials handling efficiency in all of these situations is significantly influenced by package design, unitization, and communication characteristics.

Package Design

Product packaging in standard configurations and order quantities facilitates logistical efficiency. For example, cube utilization can be improved through reduced package size by concentrating products such as orange juice or fabric softener, by eliminating air inside packages, and by shipping items unassembled, nested, and with minimal dunnage. In most cases, dunnage materials, like polystyrene foam peanuts, can be minimized simply by reducing box size. IKEA, the Swedish retailer of unassembled furniture, emphasizes cube minimization to the point that it ships pillows vacuum-packed. IKEA uses a cube minimization packaging strategy to successfully compete in the United States even though the company ships furniture from Sweden. Hewlett-Packard ships computer printers from the United States to Europe using airfreight and minimal packaging.[2] H-P shrink-wraps unit loads of printers to provide stability and reduce damage. In addition to lowering transportation cost, the overall practice reduces import duties since substantial value-added is postponed until the product is finally assembled and sold in Europe.

Cube minimization is most important for lightweight products such as assembled lawn furniture that **cubes out** a transport vehicle before weight limits are reached. On the other hand, heavy products like steel ball bearings or liquid in glass bottles **weigh out** a transport vehicle before its cube capacity is filled. When a vehicle or container weighs out, the firm ends up shipping air in space that can't be filled with product. Total weight can sometimes be reduced by product or package changes. For example, substituting plastic bottles for glass significantly increases the number of bottles that can be loaded in a trailer. The move by Gerber Baby Food toward plastic bottles is partially designed to reduce transportation expenses.

Cube and weight minimization represent a special challenge for mail order and e-commerce operations. These operations tend to use standardized packaging for both purchasing and operating efficiencies. The result is often oversized packages that require excessive dunnage and increased shipping cost. The nature of the products and the breadth

[2] Edward Feitzinger and Hau L. Lee, "Mass Customization at Hewlett-Packard: The Power of Postponement," *Harvard Business Review* (January/February 1999), pp. 116–20.

of e-commerce product lines often require multiple packages to be combined in a single order. This is of great concern for consumers who are becoming more aware of the cost of shipping and handling direct shipments as well as for environmental concerns related to packaging disposal.

Unitization

The process of grouping master cartons into one physical unit for materials handling or transport is referred to as **unitization** or **containerization.** The concept includes all forms of product grouping, from taping two master cartons together to the use of specialized transportation equipment. All types of unitization have the basic objective of increasing handling and transport efficiency. Unit loads provide many benefits over handling individual master cartons. First, unloading time and congestion at destination are minimized. Second, product shipped in unit load quantities facilitates materials handling. Unit loads utilize approximately one-fifth the time required for manual loading or unloading. Inbound shipment verification is also simplified as receipts can be bar coded. Inventory can be positioned rapidly for order selection. Finally, in-transit damage is reduced by unit load shipping and specialized transportation equipment. All these factors reduce logistical cost. The following discussion is limited to unitization methods up to the capacity of transportation equipment.

Rigid Containers

Rigid containers provide a device within which master cartons or loose products are unitized. The premise is that placing products inside a sealed container will both protect them and facilitate handling. The use of containers handled and transported by special equipment and ships is common practice in air and water transport. In domestic distribution, containerization offers substantial transport efficiency and reduced product handling. Approximately one-half the total cost of transporting domestic goods is occurred in shuffling products between vehicles, handling across docks and platforms, packaging, and filing loss and damage claims for pilferage and for insurance. The airlines use rigid containerization both for freight and for passenger baggage. The containers, which are designed to fit in the cargo area of aircraft, facilitate loading and unloading while reducing product damage and pilferage. Table 11.1 summarizes the benefits of rigid containerization.

Returnable containers have traditionally been used to distribute some products. Most reusable packages are steel or plastic, although some firms, as noted earlier, reuse corrugated boxes. Automobile manufacturers use returnable racks for interplant shipment of body parts, and chemical companies reuse steel drums. There is an increasing trend, however, to reusable packaging applications for many small items and parts such as ingredients, grocery perishables, interplant shipments, and retail warehouse-to-store totes.

Returnable containers are particularly appropriate for integrated environments where there is reasonable container security between shippers and customers. The automobile industry uses returnable racking and packaging extensively between component suppliers

TABLE 11.1
Benefits of Rigid Containerization

- Improves overall material movement efficiency.
- Reduces damage in handling and transit.
- Reduces pilferage.
- Reduces protective packaging requirements.
- Provides greater protection from element environment.
- Provides a shipment unit that can be reused a substantial number of times, thereby reducing waste and the need to dispose of the container.

and assembly plants. In a returnable package system, the parties must explicitly cooperate to maximize container usage; otherwise, containers may be lost, misplaced, or forgotten. Alternatively, deposit systems may be necessary in more free-flow supply chains, where members are linked by occasional or nonrepetitive transactions. Deposit systems are frequently used for beverage bottles, kegs, pallets, and steel drums.

The decision to invest in a returnable package system involves explicit consideration of the number of shipment cycles and return transportation costs versus the purchase and disposal cost of expendable containers. Benefits of improved handling and reduced damage should be taken into account, as well as the future costs of sorting, tracking, and cleaning the reusable containers.

Flexible Containers

As the name implies, flexible containers do not protect a product by complete enclosure. The most common type of nonrigid containerization is stacked master cartons on either **pallets** or **slipsheets.** A hardwood pallet is illustrated in Figure 11.2. A slipsheet, which is similar to a pallet in size and purpose, is a flat stocking surface generally made of cardboard or plastic. Because slipsheets lie flat on the floor, special lift trucks are required to handle slipsheet unit loads. The primary advantage of slipsheets in comparison to pallets is cost and weight. Slipsheets are less costly than pallets and are insignificant from a weight and cube perspective.

Most industry associations recommend that a standardized pallet or slipsheet size be used as a unit load platform. The Grocery Manufacturers of America have adopted the 40×48-inch pallet with four-way entry and similar size slipsheets for food distribution. The beverage industry, on the other hand, has standardized on 32×36-inch pallets. Throughout industry, the sizes most frequently used are 40×48, 32×40, and 32×36. It is common practice to first identify the dimension of most frequent entry by handling equipment.

Generally, the larger a platform, the more efficient for materials handling. For instance, the 40×48-inch pallet provides 768 more square inches per stacking tier than the 32×36-inch size. Assuming that master cartons can be stacked as high as 10 tiers, the total added unitization space of the 40×48-inch pallet is 7680 square inches. This is 60 percent larger than the 32×36-inch size. The final determination of size should be based upon load, compatibility with the handling and transport equipment used throughout the logistical system, and standardized industry practice. With modern handling equipment, few restrictions are encountered in weight limitations.

FIGURE 11.2
Example of a Hardwood Pallet

While a variety of different approaches can be used to tier master cartons on slipsheets and pallets, the four most common are block, brick, row, and pinwheel. The block method is used with cartons of equal width and length. With differential widths and lengths, the brick, row, or pinwheel pattern is employed. Figure 11.3 illustrates these four basic patterns. Except for the block method, cartons are placed in the unit load arranged in an interlocking pattern with adjoining tiers placed at 90-degree angles to each other. Load stability is enhanced with interlocking. The block pattern does not have this benefit. While these patterns provide a good starting point when there are limited master carton sizes, most pallet patterns are determined by using computer programs.

The use of flexible unitization can increase damage potential if it is not properly restrained during handling or transport. In most situations, the stability of stacking is insufficient to secure a unit load. Standard methods of improving stability include rope tie, corner posts, steel strapping, taping and antiskid treatment, adhesives, and wrapping. These methods essentially tie the master cartons into the pallet stacking pattern. Increasingly popular methods for securing unit loads are shrink-wrap and stretch-wrap. Both wraps use film similar to that used in a kitchen for food preservation.

Pallet exchange pools have been organized as a way to overcome traditional problems of return and exchange. High-quality pallets are expensive and are difficult to retrieve once they leave the owner's control. When transfer to an external organization occurs, warehouses routinely exchange poor-quality pallets and keep the higher-quality ones. Pallet pools are third-party suppliers that maintain and lease high-quality pallets throughout the country for a variable fee per single cycle. A cycle might be defined as loading of pallets at a manufacturer and transporting to a retailer's warehouse. Pallet pool firms such as CHEP, which is one of the largest, assume responsibility for developing, purchasing, and maintaining pallets as well as providing control and management systems.[3]

Communication

The final logistical packaging functionality is communication or information transfer. This function is becoming increasingly critical to provide content identification, tracking, and handling instructions.

The most obvious communications role is identifying package contents for all channel members. Typical information includes manufacturer, product, container global type, count, and Universal Product Code (**UPC**), Electronic Product Code (**EPC**) and may be

---

[3] For information regarding the products and services offered by a pallet pool organization such as CHEP, see www.chep.com.

FIGURE 11.3
Basic Pallet Master Carton Stacking Patterns

Source: Adapted from palletization guides of the National Wooden Pallet & Container Association, Arlington, VA.

Block   Brick   Row   Pinwheel

communicated using a bar code or RFID technology. The carton information is used to identify product for receiving, order selection, and shipment verification. Visibility is the major content identification consideration as material handlers should be able to observe or electronically read the label from reasonable distances in all directions. The exception for high-visibility packaging are high-value products that often have small or minimal labels to minimize the potential for pilferage.

Ease of package tracking is also important. Effective internal operation and increasingly customers require that product be tracked as it moves through the supply chain. Positive control of all movement reduces product loss and pilferage.

The final role of logistics packaging is to provide handling and damage instruction to materials handlers. The information should note any special product handling considerations such as glass containers, temperature restrictions, stacking considerations, or potential environmental concerns. If the product is potentially dangerous, such as some chemicals, the packaging or accompanying material should provide instructions for dealing with spills and container damage.

Materials Handling

Advancements in materials handling technology and equipment offer the potential to substantially improve logistics productivity. Materials handling processes and technologies impact productivity by influencing personnel, space, and capital equipment requirements. Material handling is a key logistics activity that can't be overlooked. While the technical details of materials handling technology are extensive and beyond the scope of this treatment, the following section introduces basic handling considerations and alternative system solutions.

Basic Handling Considerations

Logistical materials handling occurs throughout the supply chain. A fundamental difference exists in the handling of bulk materials and master cartons. Bulk handling includes situations wherein the product is handled without master cartons. Specialized equipment is required for handling bulk products such as solids and pellets. Bulk handling of such fluids and gaseous materials is generally completed by using pipelines or conveyors. The following discussion focuses on the nonbulk handling wherein products are shipped in master cartons.

There are several basic principles to guide the selection of materials handling processes and technologies. The principles summarized in Table 11.2 offer an initial foundation for evaluating materials handling alternatives.

Handling systems can be classified as **mechanized, semiautomated, automated,** and **information-directed.** A combination of labor and handling equipment is utilized in mechanized systems to facilitate receiving, processing, and/or shipping. Generally, labor constitutes a high percentage of overall cost in mechanized handling. Automated systems,

TABLE 11.2
Principles of Materials Handling

- Equipment for handling and storage should be as standardized as possible.
- When in motion, the system should be designed to provide maximum continuous product flow.
- Investment should be in handling rather than stationary equipment.
- Handling equipment should be utilized to the maximum extent possible.
- In handling equipment selection the ratio of dead weight to payload should be minimized.
- Whenever practical, gravity flow should be incorporated in system design.

in contrast, attempt to minimize labor as much as possible by substituting equipment capital investment. When a combination of mechanical and automated systems is used to handle material, the system is referred to as semiautomated. An information-directed system applies information technology to direct mechanized handling equipment and work effort. Mechanized handling systems are most common, but the use of semiautomated, automated, and information-directed systems is increasing. Each approach to handling is discussed in greater detail.

Mechanized Systems

Mechanized systems employ a wide range of handling equipment. The types of equipment most commonly used are lift trucks, walkie-rider pallet trucks, towlines, tractor-trailer devices, conveyors, and carousels.

Lift Trucks

Lift trucks, also called forklifts, can move loads of master cartons both horizontally and vertically but are limited to handling unit loads. Skids, boxes, or containers may also be transported, depending upon the nature of the product.

Many types of lift trucks are available. High-stacking trucks are capable of up to 40 feet of vertical movement. Palletless or clamp trucks are available for handling products without pallets or slipsheets. Other lift truck variations are available for narrow aisle and side-loading operations. Particular attention to narrow-aisle lift trucks has increased in recent years, as warehouse designers seek to increase rack density and overall storage capacity. The lift truck is not economical for long-distance horizontal movement because of the high ratio of labor per unit of transfer. It is most effectively utilized in shipping and receiving operations and to place merchandise in high cube storage. The two most common power sources for lift trucks are propane gas and battery.

Rider Trucks

Rider trucks provide a low-cost, effective method of general materials handling utility. Typical applications include loading and unloading of transportation equipment, order selection and accumulation, and shuttling loads throughout the warehouse. Rider trucks are widely used in consumer package goods warehouses.

Towlines

Towlines consist of either in-floor or overhead-mounted cable or drag devices. They are utilized to provide continuous power to four-wheel trailers. The main advantage of a towline is continuous movement. However, such handling devices have far less flexibility than lift trucks. The most common application of towlines is for case goods order selection. Order selectors place merchandise on four-wheel trailers that are then towed to the shipping dock. A number of automated decoupling devices are available to route trailers from the main towline to specified shipping docks.

A point of debate is the relative merit of in-floor versus overhead towline installation. In-floor installation is costly to modify and difficult to maintain from a housekeeping viewpoint. Overhead installation is more flexible, but unless the warehouse floor is absolutely level, the line may jerk the front wheels of the trailers off the ground and risk product damage. The overhead line also represents a potential danger to fork truck operations.

Tractor Trailers

Tractor trailers consist of a driver-guided power unit towing a number of individual four-wheel trailers. The typical size of the trailers is 4 × 8 feet. The tractor n combination with trailer, like a towline, is used during order selection. The main advantage of a tow tractor with trailers is flexibility. It is not as economical as the towline because each tow unit requires a driver.

Conveyors

Conveyors are used widely in shipping and receiving operations and serve as the basic handling device for a number of order selection systems. Conveyors are classified according to power, gravity, and roller or belt movement.[4] In power configurations, the conveyor is driven by a chain. Considerable conveyor flexibility is sacrificed in power configurations. Gravity and roller driven applications permit rearrangement with minimum difficulty. Portable gravity-style roller conveyors are often used for loading and unloading and, in some cases, are transported in over-the-road trailers to assist in unloading vehicles. Conveyors are effective in that only the product is moved, eliminating the need for equipment return movements.

Carousels

A carousel operates on a different concept than most other mechanized handling equipment. Rather than require the order selector to go to the inventory storage location, the carousel moves inventory to the order selector. A carousel consists of a series of bins mounted on an oval track or rack. There may be multiple track levels, allowing for very high-density carousel storage. The entire carousel rotates, moving the selection bin to a stationary operator. The typical carousel application is for the selection of packages in such items as pack, repack, and service parts. The rationale behind carousel systems is to shrink order selection labor requirements by reducing walking length and time. Carousels, particularly modern stackable or multitiered systems, also significantly reduce storage space requirements. Some carousel systems also utilize computer-generated pick lists and computer-directed carousel rotation to further increase order selector productivity. These systems are referred to as **paperless picking** because no paperwork exists to slow down employee efforts. A variation of the carousel system is movable racks. Such racks move horizontally to eliminate the permanent aisle between the racks. This system, often used in libraries, provides more storage density but reduces picking efficiency since the racks must be moved to access specific products.

The mechanized materials handling equipment discussion is representative of a wide range of alternatives. Most systems combine different handling devices. For example, lift trucks may be used for vertical movements while tow tractor with trailers or rider trucks are the primary methods of horizontal transfer.

Semiautomated Systems

Mechanized handling is often supplemented by semiautomatic equipment. Typical equipment utilized in semiautomated handling includes automated guided vehicle systems, computerized sortation, robotics, and various forms of live racks.

Automated Guided Vehicles (AGV)

An AGV system typically replaces mechanized tow tractors and trailers. The essential difference is that AGVs are automatically routed and positioned and activated without a driver.

AGV equipment typically relies on an optical, magnetic, or wireless radio guidance system. In the optical application directional lines are placed on the warehouse floor. The AGV is then guided by a light beam focused on the guidepath. Magnetic AGVs follow

---

[4] For a more detailed discussion of conveyor alternatives and characteristics, see David Maloney, "Conveyors," *Modern Materials Handling* 55, no. 1 (January 2000), pp. 490–553.

an energized wire installed within the floor. Wireless radio (Wi-Fi) direction is guided by high-frequency transmission. The primary advantage of an AGV is direct labor reduction. AGVs using wireless guidance systems are not limited to predetermined warehouse flow routes. Lower cost and increased flexibility have enhanced the applicability of AGVs for warehouse movements that are repetitive and frequent or are in very congested areas.

Sortation

Automated sortation devices are typically used in combination with conveyors. As products are selected in the warehouse and placed on a conveyor for movement to the shipping dock, they must be sorted into specific combinations. For example, inventory to satisfy multiple orders may be selected in batches, creating the need for sortation and sequencing into individual shipments. Most sortation controllers can be programmed to permit customized flow and decision logic to meet changing requirements.

Automated sortation provides two primary benefits. The first is a reduction in labor. The second is a significant increase in speed and accuracy of order selection. High-speed sortation systems, such as those used by United Parcel Service, can sort and align packages at rates exceeding one per second.

Robotics

The robot is a machine that can be programmed to perform one or a series of functions. The appeal of robotics lies in the ability to program functionality and decision logic to direct the handling process. The popularity of robotics resulted from its widespread adoption in the automotive industry during the early 1980s in an effort to automate select manual tasks. However, a warehouse provides a far different challenge. In warehousing, the goal is to efficiently accumulate the unique inventory requirements of a customer's order. Thus, requirements can vary extensively from one order to the next, resulting in far less routine than is typical of manufacturing.

A successful application of robotics in warehousing is to build and break down unit loads. In the breakdown process, the robot is programmed to recognize product stacking patterns in unitized loads and place products in a predetermined position on a conveyor belt. The use of robots to build unit loads is essentially the reverse of breakdown. Another use of robotics in warehousing occurs in environments where it is difficult for humans to function. Examples include materials handling in high-noise areas, hazardous materials, and extreme temperature operations, such as frozen foods or heat treatment areas.

Significant potential exists to integrate robots in mechanized warehouses to perform select functions. The capability to incorporate program logic, in addition to robots' speed, dependability, and accuracy, makes robotics an attractive alternative to traditional manual handling in situations that are highly repetitive or unfriendly to humans.

Live Racks

A device commonly used to reduce manual labor in warehouses is storage rack design in which product automatically flows to the desired selection position. The typical live rack contains roller conveyors and is constructed for rear loading. The rear of the rack is elevated higher than the front, causing a gravity flow toward the front. When cartons or unit loads are removed from the front, all other cartons or loads in that specific rack flow forward.

The use of the live rack reduces the need to use lift trucks to transfer unit loads. A significant advantage of live rack storage is the potential for automatic rotation of product as a result of rear loading. Rear loading facilitates **first-in, first-out (FIFO)** inventory management. Applications of gravity flow racks are varied. For example, live racks are utilized to sequence palletized fresh bread for shipping from bakeries.

Automated Systems

For several decades the concept of automated handling has offered great potential and limited accomplishment. Initial automated handling efforts focused on master carton order selection systems. Recently, emphasis has shifted to automated high-rise storage and retrieval systems. While the basic concepts of automation remain valid, the primary barriers are high capital investment and low degree of flexibility.

Potential to Automate

The appeal of automation is that it substitutes capital equipment for labor. In addition to requiring less direct labor, an automated system has the potential to operate faster and more accurately than its mechanized counterpart.

To date, most automated systems have been designed and constructed for specific applications. The guidelines previously noted for selection of mechanized handling systems (Table 11.2) are not applicable to automated systems. For example, storage equipment in an automated system is an integral part of the handling capability and can represent as much as 50 percent of the total investment. The ratio of dead weight to payload has little relevance when handling is automated.

Although information technology plays an important part in all handling systems, it is essential in automated systems. Information technology controls the automated selection equipment and interfaces with the WMS. A major disadvantage of automation is its dependency on proprietary information technology networks. To reduce such dependency, newer automated systems are being linked to the Internet and use standard browsers as the network for controlling warehouse operations. Automated warehouses require integration between the WMS and the material handling operating systems.

Order Selection

Initially, automation was applied to master carton selection or order assembly in the warehouse. Because of high labor intensity in order selection, the basic objective was to integrate mechanized, semiautomated, and automated handling into a system that offers the advantages of high productivity and accuracy while using minimal labor.

The general process begins with an automated order selection device preloaded with product. The device itself consists of a series of flow racks stacked vertically. Merchandise is loaded from the rear and permitted to flow forward in the live rack on gravity conveyors until stopped by a rack door. Between or down the middle of the racks, power conveyors create a merchandise flow line, with several flow lines positioned vertical to each other, one to service each level or height of rack doors.

Upon receipt of an order, the warehouse control system generates sequenced instructions to trip the rack doors and allow merchandise, as required, to flow forward onto the powered conveyors. The conveyors in turn transport merchandise to an order packing area for placement in shipment containers or unitization prior to transfer of products to the shipment staging area. Product is, ideally, selected and loaded sequentially so it can be unloaded in the sequence desired by the customer.

When compared to modern automation, these initial attempts at automated package handling were highly inefficient. A great deal of labor was required to perform merchandise preselection loading into the racks, and the automated selection equipment used was expensive. Early applications were limited to merchandise of extremely high value, with common or standardized master carton size, or situations where working conditions justify such investment. For example, these initial systems were widely tested for frozen food order selection.

Substantial advancements have been made in automated selection of case goods. The handling of fast-moving products in master cartons, typical of cross-docking, can be fully automated from the point of merchandise receipt to placement in over-the-road trailers. Such systems use an integrated network of power and gravity conveyors linking power-motivated live storage. The entire process is computer controlled and coupled with the order and WMS. Upon arrival, merchandise is automatically routed to the live storage position and inventory records are updated. When orders are received, merchandise is precubed to package or vehicle size and scheduled for selection. At the appropriate time, all merchandise is routed in loading sequence and automatically transported by conveyor to the loading dock. In some situations, the first manual handling of the merchandise within the warehouse occurs when it is stacked into the outbound transport vehicle.

Automated Storage/Retrieval

An automated unit-load handling system, or **automated storage and retrieval system (AS/RS),** that uses high-rise storage is a popular form of automation. Figure 11.4 illustrates the concept of a high-rise AS/RS. AS/RSs are particularly appropriate for items such as heavy boxes or those products in controlled environments such as bakeries or frozen food. The high-rise concept of handling is typically automated from receiving to shipping. The four primary AS/RS components include storage racks, storage and retrieval equipment, input/output system, and control system.

The name high-rise derives from the physical appearance of the storage rack. The rack is structured-steel vertical storage, which can be as high as 120 feet. The typical stacking height of palletized cartons in a mechanized handling system is 20 feet, so the potential of high-rise storage is clear. Because humans are not an integral part of AS/RSs, they are often referred to as **lights-out** facilities.

FIGURE 11.4
AS/RS High-Rise Warehouse

Unit load storage rack

Storage and retrieval aisle

Storage and retrieval unit

Unit load Pickup and delivery area

The typical high-rise facility consists of rows of storage racks. The rows of racks are separated by aisles ranging from 120 to over 800 feet in length. Primary storage and retrieval activities occur within these aisles. A storage and retrieval crane travels up and down the aisle alternatively storing and selecting product. A variety of storage and retrieval equipment are available. Most machines require guidance at the top and bottom to provide the vertical stability necessary for high-speed horizontal movement and vertical hoisting. Horizontal speeds range from 300 to 400 feet per minute (fpm) with hoisting speeds of up to 100 fpm or more.

The initial function of the storage and retrieval equipment is to reach the desired storage location rapidly. A second function is to insert or remove merchandise from the rack. For the most part, load insertion and removal are achieved by shuttle tables, which can enter and exit from the rack at speeds up to 100 fpm. Since the shuttle table moves only a few feet, it must accelerate and stop rapidly.

The storage and retrieval machine is essentially a combined lift truck and pallet holder built into a movable crane. The machine moves up and down the aisle to insert or remove a unit load from a storage bin. When the AS/RS operates with unit loads, the process is typically automated. However, the AS/RS often incorporates manual picking when the system selects cases or master cartons. In some installations, the storage and retrieval machine is positioned to service different aisles by transfer cars. Numerous transfer arrangements and layouts are available. Transfer units may be **dedicated** or **nondedicated.** The dedicated transfer car is always stationed at the end of the aisle in which the storage and retrieval equipment is working. The nondedicated transfer car works a number of aisles and retrieval machines on a scheduled basis to achieve maximum equipment utilization. The decision as to whether to include aisle-to-aisle transfer in a high-rise storage system rests with the economics of throughput rate and number of aisles included in the overall system.

The input/output system in high-rise storage is concerned with moving loads to and from the rack area. Two types of movement are involved. First, loads must be transported from receiving docks or production lines to the storage area. Second, within the immediate peripheral area of the racks, loads must be positioned for entry or exit. The greatest potential handling problem is in the peripheral area. A common practice assigns separate stations for pickup and removal capable of staging an adequate supply of loads to each aisle to fully utilize the storage and retrieval equipment. For maximum input/output performance, the normal procedure requires different stations for transfer of inbound and outbound loads assigned to the same aisle. The pickup and discharge **(P/D)** stations are linked to the handling systems that transfer merchandise to and from the high-rise storage area. The control system in high-rise storage is similar to the automated order selection systems described earlier. In addition to scheduling arrivals and location assignments, the control system handles inventory control and stock rotation. The control system also tracks product location within the AS/RS, storage bin utilization, and crane operations. In the case of high-rise storage, system reliability and integrity are critical to achieving productivity and maximum equipment utilization.

In manufacturing applications, product flowing from production is automatically formed into unit loads. The unit load is then transported to the high-rise storage area by power conveyor. When the load arrives, it is assigned to a storage bin and transferred by power conveyor to the appropriate pickup station. At this point, the storage and retrieval equipment takes over and moves the unit load to its planned storage location. When orders are received, the control system directs the retrieval of specified unit loads. From the outbound delivery station, the unit load flows by power and gravity conveyor to the appropriate shipping dock. While retrieval and outbound delivery are being accomplished, all paperwork necessary to initiate product shipment is completed.

AS/RSs seek to increase materials handling productivity by providing maximum storage density per square foot of floor space and to minimize direct labor required in handling. The highly controlled nature of an AS/RS achieves reliable pilferage-free and damage-free handling with extremely accurate control. However, high-rise AS/RSs are generally better as storage than as handling devices, thus reducing their appeal in situations where fast inventory turns are more important than inexpensive storage. The loss of flexibility has caused some firms to rethink the use of automated systems.

Information-Directed Systems

The concept of information-directed handling is relatively new and the subject of a great deal of research and development. The concept is appealing because it combines the control typical of automated handling with the flexibility of mechanized systems. Information-directed systems use mechanized handling controlled by information technology. Three common examples of information-directed materials handling systems are RF wireless **(Wi-Fi)**, Radio-Frequency Identification **(RFID)**, and light-directed operations.

RF Wireless (Wi-Fi) and RFID

RF wireless handling uses standard mechanized materials handling equipment coordinated by information technology to provide operator directions and control in real time. Typical Wi-Fi systems utilize lift trucks. However, the basic use of Wi-Fi to instruct movement of lift trucks is expanded in an information-directed application to become a highly integrated materials handling system. In terms of layout and design, the warehouse facility is often essentially the same as any mechanized facility. The difference is that all lift truck movements are directed and monitored by some combination of computer mounted on the lift truck, handheld computer, or voice-activated communication. The real-time information interchange is designed to achieve flexibility and better utilization.

The main advantage of RF is to improve speed and flexibility of lift truck operations. Instead of following handwritten instructions or computer listings generated in batches, drivers receive work assignments through either handheld or vehicle-mounted RF terminals. Use of RF technology provides real-time communication to central data processing systems. In operation, the WMS in conjunction with the operations control computer plans and initiates all movements, communicates the requirements to the material handlers, and tracks the completion of all tasks. Decision support systems analyze all movement requirements to assign equipment in such a way that direct movement is maximized and deadhead movement is minimized. This process of assigning lift trucks to continuous assignments is called **task interleaving.** In task interleaving, lift trucks are assigned independent of traditional work areas to specific jobs or work areas that need resources such as receiving or shipping.

The use of RFID capabilities creates the opportunity for two-way communication between specific products and lift truck operators. Because the RFID-equipped product can respond to an inquiry from the WMS or the operator, the potential exists to identify the exact location in the warehouse. Such positive identification serves to facilitate information-directed handling.

Information-directed handling offers great potential because selected benefits of automation can be achieved without substantial capital investment. Information-directed systems can also substantially increase productivity by tracking lift truck performance, thereby allowing compensation to be based on performance. The main drawback of information-directed handling is accountability regarding work assignment. As a specific lift truck proceeds during a work period, it may be involved in loading or unloading several different vehicles, selecting items for many orders, and completing several nonrelated handling assignments. The wide variety of work assignments increases the complexity of work direction and can decrease performance accountability. This complexity increases the demands placed on driver capabilities.

Substantial research is being conducted to explore new concepts of warehouse design and layout to fully exploit the potential of information-directed material handling. One concept, referred to as **chatoic design,** builds on the flexibility of using RFID technology to allow a warehouse to be stocked and operated to maximize inbound and outbound movement efficiency. A warehouse operated under chaotic principles would place all merchandise in location as directed by the WMS in an effort to minimize total handling.[5]

Pick-to-Light

A technology referred to as **pick-to-light** is a carousel system variation that is becoming increasingly common. In these systems, order selectors pick designated items directly into cartons or onto conveyors from **lighted** carousel locations or storage bins. A series of lights or a **light tree** in front of each pick location indicates the number of items to pick from each location. A variation of the pick-to-light system is **put-to-light,** where order selectors place product in lighted containers. Each container or tote is assigned to a specific order or customer, so the light is telling which customers are to receive a specific product.

Special Handling Considerations

The primary mission of materials handling is to facilitate merchandise flow in an orderly and efficient manner from manufacturer to point of sale. This section identifies and discusses special considerations important to selection and operation of materials handling equipment.

E-Fulfillment

Satisfaction of Internet fulfillment places some special demands on a firm's warehousing and materials handling. Both e-tailers and brick-and-mortar retailers moving into the e-tail environment have been forced to adapt their processes to meet the specific needs of this marketplace. Four specific considerations that influence warehousing and materials handling in an e-fulfillment environment are order volume, products, people, and tracking.[6] First, to serve end consumers, an e-fulfillment facility typically must process a large number of very small orders. This means that it is difficult to achieve any substantial economies of scale for picking operations. Second, e-fulfillment facilities must generally deal with a wide range of product, which translates to large inventories and the use of flow-through practices to consolidate orders for shipment. Firms electing to consolidate orders must have the capability to effectively receive and merge a large number of very small orders rapidly. Third, an e-fulfillment facility is people-intensive because the required flexibility in picking reduces order selection to manual or limited application of pick-to-light technology. In many cases, e-fulfillment operations are seasonal, increasing the need for ongoing training for new and seasonal employees. Fourth, increased consumer expectations regarding tracking require that many activities within the warehouse and interfacing with the carrier be electronically scanned and tracked. Despite rapid growth in e-tailing, many firms are still trying to resolve the warehousing and materials handling processes most appropriate to support this activity. In many cases, these e-tailers are outsourcing fulfillment to integrated service providers (**ISP**s). In any case, the e-tailing environment will continue

[5] Duncan McFarlane and Yossi Sheffi, "The Impact of Automatic Identification on Supply Chain Operations," *International Journal of Logistics Management* 14, no. 1 (2003), pp. 1–17.
[6] Amy Hardgrove, "Fulfillment: The Last Step in the E-Tail Process," *Grocery Distribution* (July/August 2000), pp. 27–30.

to place increasing demands on a more timely, responsive, and integrated warehouse and materials handling operation.

Environmental Concerns

There is increased concern regarding environmental impact of warehouse operations. In particular, attention has been directed to the impact of materials handling equipment such as lift trucks. Pollution of nonelectric lift trucks is similar to that of automobile engines. There is also increasing interest regarding the handling and disposal of hazardous materials used or stored in warehouse operations. Firms have to ensure that such materials are disposed of properly to avoid pollution liability.

Regulatory Environment

The distribution warehouse is one of the most labor-intensive operations for most firms. It is also one of the most dangerous as approximately 100 deaths and 95,000 injuries occur annually.[7] To reduce these numbers, OSHA is extending its regulatory influence over warehouse operations and technology. In March 1999, OSHA established the Powered Industrial Truck Operator Training **(PITOT)** regulation requiring the training and reevaluation of all lift truck drivers. Drivers failing evaluation and those involved in accidents must undergo refresher training. Another evolving regulation focuses on lift and angle weight. Many of the injuries identified above are back and spinal injuries caused by improper lifting of master cartons or of unitizing equipment. OSHA now places limits on the weight an individual can lift, the angle of lift, and the number of repetitive actions. The recommended weight is calculated, starting at 51 pounds and subtracting for factors relating to how far, how much, and how many. For most repetitive materials handling jobs, the approved weight limits range from 20 to 30 pounds. A third OSHA focus is warehouse cleanliness, particularly for facilities dealing with food and pharmaceuticals. Floors and work areas must be clean to inhibit rodents and to guarantee worker safety from slippage or tripping. Designing warehouse operations to consider these limits is critical, since fines can be substantial and legal liability can result in excessive judgments.

Returns Processing

For a variety of reasons, merchandise may be recalled by or returned to a manufacturer. This is particularly true in an e-tailing environment where up to 30 percent of orders are returned. Normally such reverse logistics is not of sufficient quantity or regularity to justify unitized movement, so the only convenient method for processing reverse flows of merchandise is manual handling. To the degree practical, materials handling design should consider the cost and service impact of reverse logistics. Such flows often involve pallets, cartons, and packaging materials in addition to damaged, dated, or excess merchandise. Many firms are choosing to have returns processed by an integrated service provider to separate flows and reduce the chance for error or contamination.[8]

Summary

Packaging has a significant impact on the cost and productivity of logistics. Purchasing of packaging materials, packaging design, and the subsequent need for material disposal represent the most obvious costs of packaging. Packaging affects the cost of every logistical activity. Inventory control depends upon the accuracy of manual or automatic identification systems keyed by product packaging. Order selection speed, accuracy, and efficiency

[7] Alison Paddock, "Operator Training: Setting the Goals," *Grocery Distribution* (July/August 2000), p. 34.
[8] For an expanded discussion of reverse logistics see Chapter 10.

are influenced by package identification, configuration, and handling ease. Handling cost depends upon unitization capability and techniques. Transportation and storage costs are driven by package size and density. Customer service depends upon packaging to achieve quality control during distribution, to provide customer education and convenience, and to comply with environmental regulations. The concept of packaging postponement to achieve strategic flexibility is particularly important, given the increasing length and complexity of global supply chains and the costs of locating new facilities.

High-performance materials handling is a key to warehouse productivity for several important reasons. First, a significant number of labor hours are devoted to materials handling. Second, materials handling capabilities limit the direct benefits that can be gained by improved information technology. While information technology has introduced new technologies and capabilities, the preponderance of materials handling involves labor. Third, until recently, materials handling has not been managed on an integrated basis with other logistical activities, nor has it received a great deal of senior management attention. Finally, automation technology capable of reducing materials handling labor is only now beginning to reach full potential.

Although discussed separately, packaging, containerization, and materials handling represent integral parts of the logistical operating system. All three must be considered when designing an integrated supply chain.

Challenge Questions

1. Provide an illustration that highlights the differences between consumer and industrial packaging.
2. What is the primary purpose of bar codes or RFID in packaging? Is the role different in materials handling?
3. Discuss the differences between rigid and nonrigid containers. Discuss the importance of load securing in unitization.
4. What benefits do flexible unit-load materials have in contrast to rigid containers?
5. What trade-offs are involved in the use of returnable equipment?
6. In terms of basic materials handling, what is the role of a unit load?
7. Why have automated handling systems failed to meet their expected potential?
8. Compare and contrast order selection and unit load automation.
9. What is the logic of "live racks"?
10. What type of product and logistical applications are most suitable to AS/RS applications?

PART THREE

Supply Chain Logistics Design

One of the two primary responsibilities of a firm's logistics management, as established in Chapters 1 and 2, is to participate in supply chain logistics design. Part 3 contains three chapters devoted to various logistics design issues. Chapter 12 establishes the global perspective of today's business operations. Few firms enjoy the simplicity of conducting business within a single nation. The complexity of globalization has increased as a result of extended operational reach. Given the dynamic nature of contemporary business, it is not unusual for managers to conduct continuous evaluations of their logistics support structure. Chapter 13 focuses on network design. An integrative model is developed and illustrated that combines the temporal and spatial dimensions of logistics into a single theoretical framework. The integration structure provides the basis for process development, trade-off quantification, and integrative measurement. In Chapter 14, network structure is operationalized in terms of methodology and technique to guide logistical systems design. A step-by-step design process provides a guide to deal with channel structure and strategy design and implementation. Chapter 14 also presents an overview of operational planning and analysis tools to assist managers in dealing with logistics operations.

Global Supply Chains

Chapter Outline

Globalization offers many opportunities and challenges for logistics and supply chain operations and strategies. The opportunities include increasing markets and a wider range of manufacturing alternatives with varying absolute and comparative human and material resource advantages. Some regions of the world can provide significant economies of scale because of their low wages, while other regions offer significant flexibility because of their expertise. The challenges encountered when taking advantage of these benefits include more demanding logistics operating environments, security considerations, and more complex total cost analyses. Chapter 12 discusses the rationale for global supply chains, the stages of global supply chain integration, and concludes with guidelines for making global sourcing decisions.

Global Economies

Regardless of size, most firms today include some dimension of global operations. They have materials or products that are sourced globally or they have global customers wanting to purchase from them. In many cases, firms are involved in both global sourcing and delivery. While many believe that firms operate globally, particularly for sourcing and manufacturing, to obtain the lowest cost, there are many other reasons as well. This section identifies some of the primary reasons that firms develop global capabilities.

Table 12.1 lists the primary objectives firms use to justify globalization. While many believe that the primary motivation for shifting manufacturing and supply chain operations is low-cost resources and labor, the rationale in many cases is one of the others cited in the table. For example, although it is believed that many firms moved production to Asia and India to access lower production wages, their primary motivation was often to

TABLE 12.1
Rationale for Globalization

Objective	Rationale
Increase revenue	• Open up more markets • Expand beyond competitors • Obtain accessibility to markets that limit access without local operations
Achieve economies of scale	• Take advantage of available production capacity
Reduce direct cost	• Take advantage of lower labor rates or real estate expense • Reduce energy requirements by reducing distance or changing transportation mode • Take advantage of differences in production requirements
Advance technology	• Obtain access to advanced technology that may not be available from current locations due to historical investments • Obtain access to specialized expertise or language skills
Reduce firm's global tax liability	• Obtain local or regional tax benefits related to property, inventory, or income • Obtain reductions in Value-added-taxes due to localized production or other value-added services (i.e., packaging, inventory management, customization)
Reduce market access uncertainty	• Source product from location that involves less transportation uncertainty • Source product from location that involves fewer security constraints
Enhance sustainability	• Source products or other resources (including human resources) from locations that have ongoing availability of materials and expertise such as energy or trained workers

obtain access to rapidly growing markets. While many have taken advantage of rapidly increasing demand, the increased demand for production employees is driving up wage rates much more rapidly than in the developed world. As a result, the wage differential is declining and firms are beginning to look for the next low-cost production sources which today includes Vietnam and Cambodia. Firms are also beginning to develop supply chain value-added capabilities in South America and Africa to take advantage of market proximity to the developed world and low-cost production.

Global supply chain operations either directly or indirectly are becoming the norm for most firms. Global sourcing and marketing offers many opportunities to enhance the firm's performance, particularly in terms of revenue, volume, and market share. The following sections describe some of the strategies that firms can employ to achieve these benefits along with some of the challenges that firms are likely to encounter.

Global Supply Chain Integration

Whereas an effective logistics system is important for domestic supply chain integration, it is absolutely essential for successful global sourcing, manufacturing, and marketing. Domestic logistics focuses on performing movement and storage activities to support supply chain integration in a relatively controlled environment. Global logistics must support operations in a variety of different national, political, and economic settings while also dealing with increased uncertainty associated with the distance, demand, diversity, and documentation of international commerce.

The operating challenges of global logistics systems vary significantly in each major global region. The North American logistics challenge is one of an open geography with extensive and flexible transportation options and limited need for cross-border documentation. The European logistician, in contrast, is confronted by relatively compact geography involving numerous political, cultural, regulatory, and language situations. The European infrastructure is also quite congested because of population density and the fact that many of the roads date back centuries. The Pacific Rim logistical challenge faces an island-based environment with relative poor infrastructure, requiring extensive water and air shipments to transcend vast distances. These different characteristics require that firms having global operations develop and maintain a wide variety of capabilities and expertise.

In the past, an enterprise could survive by operating with unique North American, European, or Pacific Rim business strategies. While it was easier to create and operate unique regional strategies, the resulting duplication often resulted in loss of economies of scale and poor asset utilization. While regionalization remains viable for some firms, those desiring to grow and prosper must face the challenges of designing and operating a globally integrated enterprise. Strategic business initiatives must change as a firm and its supply chain become progressively more global.

Logistics in a Global Economy

Global operations increase logistics cost and complexity. In 2002, the last available estimate, logistics cost for industrialized nations exceeded $6.7 trillion, or 13.8 percent of estimated global gross domestic product **(GDP)**. Table 12.2 lists GDP and estimated logistics cost by country. In terms of complexity, global operations, in contrast to domestic operations, are characterized by increased uncertainty, increased variability, decreased control, and decreased visibility. Uncertainty results from greater distances, longer leadtimes, and decreased market knowledge. Increased variation results from unique customer and documentation requirements as well as shifting political environments. Decreased control results from the extensive use of international service firms coupled with potential government intervention in such areas as customs requirements and trade restrictions. Decreased visibility results from longer transit and holding times with less ability to track and determine exactly where shipments are located.

These unique challenges complicate development of an efficient and effective global supply chain strategy. Fortunately, there are forces that both drive and facilitate globalization and necessitate borderless logistics operations.

Stages of International Development

The continuum of global trade development ranges from export/import to local presence to the concept of a globally integrated enterprise. The following discussion describes conceptual and managerial implications of strategic development. Table 12.3 lists the product, marketing, supply chain, management, information technology, and human resource strategies characteristic for each stage of globalization.

Export/Import: A National Perspective

The initial stage of international trade is characterized by exporting and importing. A participating organization typically is focused on its domestic operations and views international transactions in terms of supporting domestic business. Specifically, a firm uses

TABLE 12.2
Estimated 2002
National Logistical
Expenditures

Source: Reprinted with permission from Alexandre M. Rodrigues, Donald J. Bowersox, and Roger J. Calantone "Estimation of Global Logistics Expenditures: Current Update," from *Journal of Business Logistics*, Vol. 26, no. 2, 2005, pp. 1–16.

Region	Country	GDP (U.S.$ billion)	Logistics (U.S.$ billion)	Logistics (% GDP)
North America	Canada	925	110	11.9%
	Mexico	905	136	15.0%
	United States	10,308	957	9.3%
	Region	12,137	1,203	9.9%
Europe	Belgium	285	35	12.1%
	Denmark	166	23	13.6%
	France	1,601	186	11.6%
	Germany	2,236	374	16.7%
	Greece	199	26	13.0%
	Ireland	143	21	14.9%
	Italy	1,525	186	12.2%
	Netherlands	470	56	11.8%
	Portugal	186	25	13.4%
	Spain	878	124	14.1%
	United Kingdom	1,549	174	11.3%
	Region	9,238	1,229	13.3%
Pacific Rim	China	5,861	1,052	17.9%
	India	2,800	487	17.4%
	Hong Kong, China	183	24	13.2%
	Japan	3,425	390	11.4%
	Korea, Rep.	807	102	12.7%
	Singapore	100	14	14.3%
	Taiwan, China	406	57	14.1%
	Region	13,582	2,127	15.7%
South America	Brazil	1,355	204	15.0%
	Venezuela, RB	135	16	12.0%
	Argentina	413	52	12.6%
	Region	1,903	272	14.3%
Remaining other countries		11,912	1,902	16.0%
Total		48,771	6,732	13.8%

an export/import strategy to increase the revenues or decrease costs associated with a domestic operation. As Table 12.3 indicates, an export/import strategy typically involves a standardized product manufactured in the firm's home country, focused on a limited customer base, with logistics services required for export/import provided by specialized logistics integrators. The business context is transaction driven, with the common financial statements providing the only level of integration.

A national export/import business orientation influences logistical decisions in three ways. First, sourcing and resource choices are influenced by artificial constraints. These constraints are typically in the form of use restrictions, local content laws, or price surcharges. A **use restriction** is a limitation, usually government imposed, that restricts the level of import sales or purchase. For example, the enterprise may require that internal divisions be used for material sources even though prices or quality is not competitive. **Local content laws** specify the proportion of a product that must be sourced within the local economy. **Price surcharges** involve higher charges for foreign-sourced product imposed by governments to maintain the viability of local suppliers. Price surcharges usually exist in the form of duties or tariffs. In combination, use restrictions, local content laws, and price surcharges limit management's ability to select what otherwise would be the preferred supplier.

TABLE 12.3 Differential Characteristics of Global Development

Three Stages of Development	Product Focus	Marketing Strategy	Supply Chain Strategy	Management	Information and Decision Support	Human Resource Development
Export/import	Domestic production and distribution	Specific customers	Agents and third-party logistics service providers	Transaction driven with integrated financials	Home country focused with limited EDI	Management with "home country" focus and limited international experience
International operations: local presence	Local market customization supported by postponement or local production	Focused specific market areas, which may cross national boundaries	Subsidiaries and local distributors with specific business charters and visible local presence	Decentralized management of local operators and strategic alliances with local profit responsibility	Independent database and decision support	Limited top management with international experience and strong "home country" decision focus
Globalization	Global brands	All economic regions	Worldwide flow of key resources to leverage global sourcing and marketing advantages	Centralized planning with locally flexible distribution supported with common systems	Integrated database and decision support	International training and experience required for all upper-level management with some requirements for midlevel management

Second, logistics to support export/import operations increases planning complexity. A fundamental logistics objective is smooth product flow to facilitate efficient capacity utilization. This objective is sometimes difficult in an export/import operation because of transportation uncertainty, infrastructure constraints, and government restrictions.

Third, an export/import strategy extends domestic logistics systems and operating practices to global origins and destinations. While an export/import strategy doesn't introduce much complexity into domestic operations, it likely increases operational complexity, since exceptions are numerous. Local managers must accommodate exceptions while remaining within corporate policy and procedure guidelines. For example, while bribery is both an illegal and unethical practice in most developed countries, such "facilitating" payments may be the only means of getting product moved or cleared through customs in developing countries. As a result, foreign-based logistics management must often accommodate local, cultural, language, employment, and political environments without full understanding at corporate headquarters.

International Operations: Local Presence

The second stage of international development is characterized by establishment of operations in a foreign country. Internal operations may include varied combinations of marketing, sales, production, and logistics. Establishment of local facilities and operations serves to increase market awareness and sensitivity. This is often referred to as establishing **local presence.** The local presence strategy uses local production and distribution often supported by a postponement strategy to customize products. Firms engaged in local presence often restrict their operations to a limited number of geographic areas. At the outset of a local presence strategy, foreign operations will often depend on parent company management and personnel, values, procedures, and operations. However, over time, business units operating within a foreign market area will have to adopt local business practices.

This adoption typically means developing unique management, marketing, and sales organizations and may include the use of local business systems. As local presence operations expand, the host country philosophy will increasingly emerge; however, the company headquarters' strategic vision remains dominant. Individual country operations are still measured against home country expectations and standards.

Globally Integrated Enterprise

The globally integrated enterprise contrasts sharply to operations guided by either an export/import or international perspective. The original concept of the globally integrated enterprise was popularized in a *BusinessWeek* article two decades ago under the title "The Stateless Corporation."[1] Management of a truely globally integrated enterprise makes market, location, and resource decisions with little or no regard to national boundaries. Globally integrated enterprises maintain operations and develop a headquarters structure to coordinate across area operations. "Unlike the multinational—which creates miniature versions of itself in markets around the world—the globally integrated enterprise locates work, skills, and operations wherever it makes sense, based on access to expertise, on superior economies and on the presence of open environments and technologies. Thus, the enterprise is globally integrated in the sense that no specific home or parent country dominates policy".

IBM offers a good example of an organization that is striving for global integration.[2] Senior management likely represents a combination of nationalities. Denationalized operations function on the basis of local marketing and sales initiatives are typically supported by world-class manufacturing and logistics operations. Product sourcing and marketing decisions can be made across a wide range of geographical alternatives. Systems and procedures are designed to meet individual country requirements and are aggregated as necessary to share knowledge and for financial reporting. A truly global firm employs global brands with limited customization to reflect market sensitivities, operates in most global regions, employs a global resource view in terms of production and logistics, and incorporates integrated reporting systems and planning technologies to achieve global operating synergies. Although limited customization is desirable to minimize product complexity, the globally integrated enterprise can discriminate between features that represent a critical market difference and those that do not.

Consider, for example, an enterprise that has its historical origin in Germany, Japan, or the United States, but with a high percentage of its sales, ownership, and assets maintained and managed in China. China is estimated to be the world's third largest economy, but there are many supply chain aspects such as logistics capabilities and infrastructure that are still quite third-world. China's communications, intermodal transport systems, tracking and tracing, and limited highways outside major cities make it very difficult to employ 21st-century supply chain operating practices. For these reasons, a globally integrated enterprise operating in China needs a combination of local management to facilitate local operations and enterprise management that fully understands the implications of developing business systems, a rapid rate of change, and exploding but unbalanced export/import volume.

Examples of firms that fit the specification of globally integrated enterprises are ABB (Switzerland), Coca Cola (United States), Dow Chemical (United States), Hoechst (Germany),

---

[1] "The Stateless Corporation," *BusinessWeek*, May 14, 1990, p. 98.
[2] Samuel Palmisano, "The Global Consumer Gives Small Companies a Big Reach," *Financial Times*, May 6, 2008, p. 11.

IBM (United States), ICI (Britain), Johnson & Johnson (United States), Nestlé (Switzerland), Novartis (Switzerland), and Philips (Netherlands). These firms are characterized by a combination of global brands produced and marketed globally with integrated systems and management that can synthesize global operations while being sensitive to regional and local considerations.

While most enterprises engaged in international business are operating in stages 1 and 2, to become a global player, a truly international firm must migrate toward global marketing and operations. Such globalization requires a significant level of management trust that transcends countries and cultures. Such trust can grow only as managers increasingly live and work across cultures.

Managing the Global Supply Chain

To enhance a firm's global capabilities, logistics management must consider five major differences between domestic and international operations: (1) performance cycle structure, (2) transportation, (3) operational considerations, (4) information systems integration, and (5) alliances. These considerations must then be incorporated into the firm's global operating strategy.

Performance Cycle Structure

The length of the performance cycle is a major difference between domestic and global operations. Instead of 1- to 5-day transit times and 2- to 10-day total performance cycles, global operational cycles often require weeks or months. For example, it is common for automotive parts from Pacific Rim suppliers to take 60 days from order release until physical delivery at a U.S. manufacturing facility. Similarly, fashion merchandise may take anywhere from 30 to 60 days from the time the manufacturer order is released until it is received at a U.S. distribution warehouse.

The reasons leading to a longer order cycle to delivery cycle are communication delays, financing requirements, special packaging requirements, ocean freight scheduling, slow transit times, and customs clearance. Communication may be delayed by time zone and language differences. Financing delays are caused by the requirements for letters of credit and currency translations. Special packaging may be required to protect products from in-transit damage due to high humidity, temperature, and weather conditions. Once a product is containerized, it must be scheduled for movement to and between ports having appropriate handling capabilities. This scheduling process can require up to 30 days if the origin and destination ports are not located on high-volume traffic lanes or the ships moving to the desired port lack the necessary equipment. Transit time, once the ship is en route, ranges from 10 to 21 days. Port delays are common as ships wait for others to clear harbor facilities. Customs clearance may further extend total time. Although it is increasingly common to utilize electronic messaging to preclear product shipments through customs prior to arrival at international ports, the elapsed performance cycle time is still lengthy. Security issues can create additional delays. Another problem is restricted availability of containers. Movement from Asia to the United States is generally unbalanced as more material is imported into the United States than is exported to Asia. As a result, there is strong demand for containers to move product from Asia to the United States but little motivation to ship the empty containers back. This demonstrates how unbalanced trade, either domestically or internationally, can introduce complexity into logistics operations.

These factors cause international logistics performance cycles to be longer, less consistent, and less flexible than typical in domestic operations. This lack of consistency makes planning and coordination more difficult. Determination of shipment status and anticipation of arrival times also require substantially more effort. The longer performance cycle also results in higher asset commitment because significant inventory is in transit at any point in time.

Transportation

The U.S. initiative to deregulate transportation during the early 1980s has extended globally. Four significant global changes have occurred: (1) intermodal ownership and operation, (2) privatization, (3) cabotage and bilateral agreements, and (4) infrastructure constraints.

Historically, there have been regulatory restrictions regarding international transportation ownership and operating rights. Transport carriers were limited to operating within a single transportation mode with few, if any, joint pricing and operating agreements. Traditionally, steamship lines could not own or manage integrated land-based operations such as motor or rail carriers. Without joint ownership, operations, and pricing agreements, the operation and tracking of international shipping was very complex. International shipments typically required multiple carriers to perform a single freight movement. Specifically, government rather than market forces determined the extent of services foreign-owned carriers could perform. Although some ownership and operating restrictions remain, marketing and alliance arrangements among countries have substantially improved transportation flexibility. The removal of multimodal ownership restrictions in the United States and in most other industrialized nations served to facilitate integrated movement. In response to some of these changes in national ownership requirements, an increasing number of global service providers have been established such as DeutschePost, FedEx, TNT, and United Parcel Service.

A second transportation influence on global operations is increased carrier privatization. Historically, many international carriers were owned and operated by national governments in an effort to promote trade and provide national security. Government-owned carriers are typically subsidized and often place surcharges on foreign enterprises that use these services. Artificially high pricing and poor service often made it costly and unreliable to ship via such government-owned carriers. Inefficiencies and inflexibility also resulted from strong unionization and work rules. The combination of high operating cost and low efficiency caused many government-owned carriers to operate at a loss. A great many such carriers have been privatized and must operate in a competitive environment. Carrier privatization has resulted in increased availability of efficient international carriers.

Changes in cabotage and bilateral service agreements are the third transportation influence impacting international trade. Cabotage laws require passengers or goods moving between two domestic ports to utilize only domestic carriers. For example, water shipment from Los Angeles to New York was required to use a U.S. carrier. Similar cabotage laws restricted Canadian drivers from transporting a backhaul load to Detroit once a shipment originating in Canada was unloaded in Texas. Cabotage laws were designed to protect domestic transportation industries even though they also served to reduce overall transportation equipment utilization and related efficiency. The European Community has relaxed cabotage restrictions to increase trade efficiency. Such reduced cabotage restrictions will save U.S. corporations 10 to 15 percent in intra-European shipping costs. While the United States has not rescinded its cabotage laws relating to Canada and Mexico, some of the restrictions have been reduced to enhance equipment utilization and to reduce the environmental impact.

Many regions, both developed and undeveloped, are experiencing major constraints on their physical infrastructure. Global operations are significantly increasing the demand specifically on port and airport capacities. Since much of the infrastructure in the world was developed over 50 years ago, it was designed for substantially less capacity and without extensive growth capability in terms of surrounding land. Although information and handling technology has facilitated rapid movement of goods through ports and airports, the volume increase still results in substantial congestion.[3] At the same time, tight local, state, and federal budgets have limited the reinvestment that can be made in the existing

---

[3] Christopher Norek and Monica Isbel, "The Infrastructure Squeeze on Global Supply Chains," *Supply Chain Management Review,* October 2005, pp. 18–24.

infrastructure. As a result, logistics managers are being driven to seek out alternative suppliers, carriers, or port locations.

Operational Considerations

There are a number of unique operational considerations to support global supply chains. First, international operations typically require multiple languages for both product and documentation. A technical product such as a computer or a calculator must have local features such as keyboard characters and language on both the product itself and related manuals. From a logistics perspective, language differences dramatically increase complexity since a product is limited to a specific country once it is language-customized. For example, even though Western Europe is much smaller than the United States in a geographic sense, it requires relatively more inventory to support marketing efforts since separate inventories may be required to accommodate various languages. Although product proliferation due to language requirement has been reduced through multilingual packaging and postponement strategies, such practices are not always acceptable. Some consumers are reluctant to accept products not labeled in their native tongue. In addition to product language implications, international operations may require multilingual documentation for each country through which the shipment passes. Although English is the general language of commerce, some countries require that transportation and customs documentation be provided in the local language. This increases the time and effort for international operations, since complex documents must be translated prior to shipment. These communication and documentation difficulties can be somewhat overcome through standardized electronic transactions.

The second global operational consideration is unique national accommodations such as performance features, technical characteristics, environmental considerations, and safety requirements. Performance feature differences include specific product functionality such as speed or process constraints. Technical characteristics include power supplies, documentation, and metrics. Environmental considerations include chemicals that can be used or the types and amount of waste generated. Safety requirements include automatic shutoffs and specialized documentation. While they may not be substantial, the small differences between country requirements may significantly increase required SKUs and subsequent inventory levels.

The third operating consideration is the sheer amount of documentation required for international operations. While domestic operations can generally be completed by using only an invoice and bill of lading, international operations require substantial documentation regarding order contents, transportation, financing, and government control. Table 12.4 lists and describes common forms of international documentation.

The fourth operating consideration is the high incidence of countertrade and duty drawback found in some international situations. While most established firms prefer cash transactions, countertrade is important. Countertrade, in essence, is when a seller agrees to accept products as payment or purchase products from the buyer as part of a sales agreement. While such agreements have financial consequences, they also have major implications for logistics and marketing in terms of disposal of goods received as payment. Duty drawback describes situations when a firm pays a duty to import goods into a foreign country but the duty paid can be drawn back or returned if the items or a comparable designate is exported. For example, Pepsi supplies syrup to the Soviet government, which bottles and markets the soft drink with practically no control from Pepsi. In return, Pepsi is paid for the syrup by receiving exclusive rights to distribute Russian Stolichnaya vodka in the United States. This exclusive right requires marketing and logistics support.

TABLE 12.4
Common Forms of International Logistics Documentation

- *Export irrevocable commercial letter of credit.* A contract between an importer and a bank that transfers liability or paying the exporter from the importer to the (supposedly more creditworthy) importer's bank.
- *Bank draft (or bill of exchange).* A means of payment for an import/export transaction. Two types exist: transaction payable on sight with proper documents (*sight draft*) and transaction payable at some fixed time after acceptance of proper documents (*time draft*). Either type of draft accompanied by instructions and other documents (*but no letter of credit*) is a documentary draft.
- *Bill of lading.* Issued by the shipping company or its agent as evidence of a contract for shipping the merchandise and as a claim to ownership of the goods.
- *Combined transport document.* May replace the bill of lading if goods are shipped by air (*airway bill*) or by more than one mode of transportation.
- *Commercial invoice.* A document written by the exporter to precisely describe the goods and the terms of sale (similar to a shipping invoice used in domestic shipments).
- *Insurance certificate.* Explains what type of coverage is utilized (fire, theft, water), the name of the insurer, and the exporter whose property is being insured.
- *Certificate of origin.* Denotes the country in which the goods were produced to assess tariffs and other government-imposed restrictions on trade.

Information Systems Integration

A major challenge in globalization is information systems integration. Since firms typically globalize by acquisition and merger, the integration of systems typically lags. Operational integration requires the ability to route orders and manage inventory requirements electronically throughout the world. Development of supportive technology integration represents substantial capital investment. As discussed in Chapter 5, two types of system integration are required to support global operations. The first is a global transaction or ERP system. The global ERP system is necessary to provide common data regarding global customers, suppliers, products, and financials. It is also necessary to provide common and consistent information regarding order and inventory status regardless of the location from which a global customer is inquiring or where the shipment is to be delivered. The second system integration requirement is a global planning system that can maximize overall manufacturing and delivery asset utilization while meeting customer service requirements. Few firms have fully integrated global information systems or capability.

Alliances

A final international operations consideration is the growing importance of third-party alliances. While alliances with carriers and specialized service suppliers are important in domestic operations, they are essential for international commerce. Without alliances, it would be necessary for an enterprise operating internationally to maintain contacts with retailers, wholesalers, manufacturers, suppliers, and service providers throughout the world. International alliances provide market access and expertise and reduce the inherent risk of global operations. The number of alternatives, breadth of activities, and complexity of globalization require alliances.

In summary, globalization is an evolving frontier that increasingly demands more extensive supply chain integration. As firms expand their focus toward international markets, demand for logistical competency increases because of longer supply chains, more variation, increased uncertainty, and more documentation. While the forces of change push toward borderless operations, supply chain logistics management still confronts market, financial, and channel barriers. The barriers are exemplified by distance, demand, diversity, and documentation. The challenge is to position an enterprise to take advantage of the benefits of global marketing and manufacturing by developing world-spanning logistical competency.[4]

Global Sourcing

One of today's major business challenges specificly impacting logistical management is the dramatic increase in international sourcing, particularly from low-cost countries such as China and Malaysia. Firms in virtually all durable goods industries are investigating Asia, Eastern Europe, Latin America, and Africa as potential sources for finished goods or, at least, component parts. This section reviews the rationale for international sourcing from low-cost countries, identifies some of the specific challenges, and offers some guidelines regarding sourcing strategy.

Rationale for Low-Cost-Country Sourcing

Increased need for global competitiveness is driving many firms, particularly those in durable and fashion industries, to identify and establish relationships with suppliers in low-cost countries. There are a number of justifications for such sourcing initiatives. First, sourcing from countries with low wage rates typically reduces manufacturing cost. While such strategies may reduce manufacturing cost, some firms do not consider the total cost impact of international sourcing particularly with respect to the logistics cost components of transportation and inventory. Second, seeking out suppliers in low-cost countries can also increase the number of possible sources and thus increase the competitive pressure on domestic suppliers. Third, low-cost-country sourcing can increase the firm's exposure to state-of-the-art product and process technologies. Without pressure from global suppliers, there may be reluctance on the part of domestic suppliers to investigate or invest in new technologies because they have significant assets tied up in older technologies. Conversely, global suppliers may place significant focus on new technologies to establish a competitive position in foreign markets even given the issues discussed earlier regarding extended supply chains. A final rationale for low-cost-country sourcing is to establish a local presence to facilitate sales in the international country. For example, while the U.S. automobile industry is significantly increasing sourcing from low-cost countries to reduce component cost, it is also seeking to facilitate automobile sales in the local country. Because of political or legal constraints, it is often necessary for a firm to have local relationships and production operations to be allowed to sell their product in the local country. The combination of these makes a strong case for sourcing from a low-cost country, but it is necessary to also consider the challenges.

Challenges for Low-Cost-Country Sourcing

While the rationale for low-cost-import sourcing is substantial, there is also a long list of issues and challenges related to such sourcing strategies. These issues and challenges are further complicated by the fact that the benefits and costs related to low-cost-country sourcing accrue to different organizational units. Procurement or manufacturing may receive the benefits through lower-cost materials or components. Many of the costs and the challenges to ship and guarantee delivery of the materials are the responsibility of logistics. Benefits

---

[4] The Council of Supply Chain Management Professionals (CSCMP) has produced a number of *Global Perspectives* reports that describe the logistics characteristics and challenges confronted in over 20 specific countries. The reports are available free to members in paper and electronic form from the Web site at www.cscmp.org. For a more comprehensive discussion, see Greg Cudahy, Narendra Mulani, and Christophe Cases. "Mastering Global Operations in a Multipolar World," *Supply Chain Management Review,* March 2008, pp. 22–29.

and costs must be integrated across the full supply chain process in order to make the correct sourcing decision.

The first challenge is the identification of sources capable of producing the materials in the quality and quantity required. While it is becoming easier to achieve the quality objective, ensuring that the potential supplier has the ability to meet volume and seasonal fluctuation demands in a suitable time frame often remains a challenge.

The second challenge considers the protection of a firm's intellectual property as products or components are produced and transported. The suppliers and countries involved need to have legal constraints in place to protect product designs and related trade secrets.

The third challenge relates to understanding import/export compliance issues. There may be government regulations regarding the volume of a commodity that can be imported before duties or other restrictions are enforced. The percentage of materials that are foreign-sourced may also restrict a firm's ability to sell to select customers. Government contracts may require a specific level of domestically made components. For example, if the contract requires that the product is "Made in the U.S.A.," 95 percent of the material must be of domestic origin.

The fourth challenge relates to communication with suppliers and transportation companies. While the procurement negotiation with low-cost countries is not easy, there is often a greater difficulty in dealing with carriers, freight forwarders, and government customs as a result of time zone, language, and technology differences.

The fifth challenge is the need to guarantee the security of the product while in transit. Not only does supply chain security require that the product is secure, the process must also secure containers and vehicles involved both full and empty.

The sixth challenge concerns the inventory and obsolescence risk associated with extended transit times. With the longer transit times associated with low-cost-country sourcing, it is not uncommon for the firm to have one or two months' supply of product in transit, which must be counted as an asset and incur related inventory carrying cost. Extended leadtimes also increase the potential for obsolescence, as orders have longer leadtimes and there is generally little flexibility for change. Such extended leadtimes also can impact recovery when a quality issue develops. It is not unusual for firms to fly components from offshore suppliers to recover from unexpected quality problems or delayed shipments.

The final challenge, which synthesizes the previous ones, focuses on the need to understand the difference between piece price and total cost. While the piece price may include the material as well as direct and indirect labor, the total cost perspective needs to consider other cost elements, including freight, inventory, obsolescence, duties, taxes, recovery, and other risk considerations.

Guidelines for Sourcing

The decision to source material and components domestically or from a low-cost country is a complex one. While direct and indirect product costs represent one major factor, there are many other factors that must be considered and weighed appropriately. Products and components that have extended times between manufacturing changeovers are ideal for low-cost-country sourcing. A counterexample would be the life cycle for an electronics component, which is typically quite short and so would generally trend toward domestic sourcing. Products and components that have numerous variations should also generally be domestically sourced because the extended leadtimes associated with low-cost-country sourcing make it difficult to forecast the precise mix of product that will be demanded. Products or components with high labor content should take advantage of the typically low labor rates in low-cost counties. Products or components with high intellectual property

TABLE 12.5
Sourcing Guidelines

Criteria	Domestic Sourcing	Low-Cost-Country Sourcing
Product life cycle length	Short	Long
Product variations in size, color, or style	Many	Few
Labor content	Low	High
Intellectual property content	High	Low
Transport cost	High	Low
Product value	High	Low
Security or import constraints	High	Low
Transport uncertainty	High	Low

content should be sourced domestically, as the legal systems in many of the low-cost countries do not provide adequate trade secret protection. Domestic sourcing is generally appropriate for products and components with relatively high transport cost such as those that are bulky or damage easy. Due to increasing energy prices, many firms are beginning to reconsider more localized sourcing. Products or components with relatively low value are ideal for low-cost-country sourcing, as the inventory carrying cost while it is in transit is not significant. Products and components that are constrained for security or other types of import restrictions by a domestic government should tend toward domestic sourcing. For example, there may be customs delays in importing electronic goods when the supplier does not have the trust of the importing government because of the potential for importing contraband. Finally, products or components that have a high degree of transport uncertainty because of relatively low volumes or location on trade lanes with limited service would suggest domestic sourcing.

There is no simple answer regarding which products or components should be domestically sourced, as a number of the criteria are somewhat qualitative. Table 12.5 lists the general sourcing criteria.[5] The final determination depends on the specific item and the firm's expertise. As firms increase their global operations and marketing efforts, logistics managers should be increasingly involved to provide a realistic assessment of the total cost and performance implications.

As a supply chain strategy becomes more global, increased complexities are encountered. These complexities result from longer distances, demand differentials, cultural diversity, and complex documentation. Nevertheless, firms will increasingly confront the need to expand operations into the global arena. Strategies to achieve a share of the rapidly expanding world market range from export/import to local presence to true globalization. Regardless of the strategic focus, success will, to a large extent, be dependent upon a firm's logistical capabilities.

Summary

Global operations are becoming more of the norm for logistics and supply chain executives. Decisions regarding global sourcing and marketing require more complex trade-off analyses than traditionally required for domestic logistics. Both the quantitative and qualitative factors are more complex. While transportation, inventory, and warehousing costs are very substantial for global operations, other cost components, including taxes, tariffs,

[5] For a more detailed discussion regarding sourcing in Asia and China specifically, see Robert Handfield and Kevin McCormack, "What You Need to Know about Sourcing from China," *Supply Chain Management Review,* September 2005, pp. 28–36.

duties, documentation, and import restrictions, can also have a substantial impact on true total cost. However, in addition to the quantitative considerations, international operations introduce a number of other variables that are much more difficult to quantify. Many of these variables relate directly to logistics operations. The major qualitative considerations include relationship management, infrastructure consistency, production and transit reliability, and security. With increased global marketing and manufacturing operations, logistics management needs to be more involved in developing and implementing global strategies.

Challenge Questions

1. Compare and contrast domestic and global logistics operations.
2. Discuss how logistics management must evolve to reflect the differing needs for each stage of international development.
3. Discuss the logistics operational considerations for operating in a global environment.
4. Discuss the role that federal, state, and local government play in supply chain design and operating decisions.
5. Describe the logistics characteristics of a firm moving toward a globally integrated enterprise.
6. Describe some of the strategies that firms can use to overcome the challenges related to transportation infrastructure congestion.
7. Discuss the rationale and challenges related to sourcing from low-cost countries.
8. Describe the factors that should be considered by logistical management in the total cost analysis for global sourcing and marketing
9. Discuss how product variations, security and import constraints, and transportation uncertainty should impact global sourcing and marketing decisions.
10. Compare and contrast export/import operations to local presence. What are the logistics ramifications of each stage of international development?

Network Design

Chapter Outline

For the most part, managers confront a new and challenging assignment when they are asked to participate in logistical network reengineering. Due to the rapid rate of change in almost every facet of logistical operations, managers can expect considerable discontinuity when they try to use previous experience to guide the creation and implementation of new logistical competencies. Therefore, success or failure may depend on how well the planning team is able to quantify the forces at work and rationalize a logical and believable action plan. Having a comprehensive understanding of the theoretical constructs that serve as the foundation of logistical integration provides an important step toward developing an integrated strategy.

In earlier chapters, the essence of logistical strategy was identified as achieving least-total-cost operations while simultaneously maintaining flexibility. Flexibility is the key to providing high-level basic customer accommodation while at the same time maintaining sufficient operating capacity to meet and exceed key customer expectations. To exploit flexibility, an enterprise needs to achieve a high level of logistical process integration. Integration is required at two operating levels. First, the operating areas of logistics must be integrated across a network of warehouse facilities supportive of customer accommodation, manufacturing, and procurement requirements. Such network integration is essential if a firm is using logistical competency to gain competitive advantage. Second, integration must extend beyond a single firm by supporting relationships across the supply chain. This chapter presents a framework to assist managers in achieving such integration.[1]

Enterprise Facility Network

Prior to the availability of low-cost dependable surface transportation, most of the world's commerce relied on product and material movement by water. During this early period, commercial activity concentrated around port cities. Overland transport of goods was costly and slow. For example, the lead time to order designer clothing from across the continental United States could exceed 9 months. Although demand for fast and efficient transport existed, it was not until the invention of the steam locomotive in 1829 that the transportation technology revolution began in the United States. Today, the transportation system in this country is a highly developed network of rail, water, air, highway, and pipeline services. Each transport alternative provides a different type of service for use within a logistical system. This availability of economical transportation creates the opportunity to establish a competitively superior warehouse network to service customers.

The importance of facility location analysis has been recognized since the middle of the 19th century, when the German economist Joachim von Thünen wrote *The Isolated State*.[2] For von Thünen, the primary determinant of economic development was the price of land and the cost to transport products from farm to market. The value of land was viewed as being directly related to the cost of transportation and the ability of a product to command an adequate price to cover all cost and result in profitable operation. Von Thünen's basic principle was that the value of specific produce at the growing location decreases with distance from the primary selling market.

Following von Thünen, Alfred Weber generalized location theory from an agrarian to an industrial society.[3] Weber's theoretical system consisted of numerous consuming locations spread over a geographical area and linked together by linear transportation costs. Weber developed a scheme to classify major materials as either **ubiquitous** or **localized.** Ubiquitous materials were those available at all locations. Localized raw materials consisted of mineral deposits found only at selected areas. On the basis of his analysis, Weber developed a **material index.** The index was the ratio of the localized raw material to the total weight of the finished product. Various types of industry were assigned a **locational weight** based on the material index. Utilizing these two measures, Weber generalized that industries would locate facilities at the point of consumption when the manufacturing process was weight-gaining and near the point of raw material deposit when the manufacturing process was weight-losing. Finally, if the manufacturing process were neither weight-gaining nor weight-losing, firms would select plant locations at an intermediate point.

Several location theorists followed von Thünen and Weber. The most notable contributions toward a general theory of location were developed by August Lösch, Edgar Hoover,

---

[1] The reader is cautioned that this chapter stresses theoretical constructs that determine logistical system design. The material offers a framework to guide trade-off analysis. While theoretical discussions tend to be abstract, the principles presented are logically consistent regardless of the competitive or cultural setting within which logistical reengineering is performed.

[2] Joachim von Thünen, *The Isolated State,* Beziehung auf Landwirtschaft und Nationalökonomie. Hamburg, 1826.

[3] Alfred Weber, *Theory of the Location of Industries,* translated by Carl J. Friedrich (Chicago, IL: University of Chicago Press, 1928).

Melvin Greenhut, Walter Isard, and Michael Webber.[4] In their writings, these five authors highlighted the importance of geographical specialization in industrial location, including quantification of the importance of transportation.

Spectrum of Location Decisions

In terms of logistical planning, transportation offers the potential to link geographically dispersed manufacturing, warehousing, and market locations into an integrated system. Logistical system facilities include all locations at which materials, work-in-process, or finished inventories are handled or stored. Thus, all retail stores, finished goods warehouses, manufacturing plants, and material storage warehouses represent logistical network locations. It follows that selection of individual locations, as well as the composite locational network, represents important competitive and cost-related logistical decisions.

A manufacturing plant location may require several years to fully implement. For example, General Motors' decision to build a new Cadillac assembly plant in Lansing, Michigan, spanned over five years from concept to reality. In contrast, some warehouse arrangements are sufficiently flexible to be used only during specified times. The selection of retail locations is a specialized decision influenced by marketing and competitive conditions. The discussion that follows concentrates on selecting warehouse locations. Among all the location decisions faced by logistical managers, those involving warehouse networks are most frequently reviewed.

Local Presence: An Obsolete Paradigm

A long-standing belief in business is that a firm must have facilities in local markets to successfully conduct business. During economic development of North America, erratic transportation service created serious doubt about a firm's ability to promise delivery in a timely and consistent manner. In short, customers felt that unless a supplier maintained inventory within the local market area it would be difficult, if not impossible, to provide consistent delivery. This perception, commonly referred to as the **local presence paradigm,** resulted in logistical strategies committed to forward deployment of inventory. As recently as the early 1960s it was not uncommon for manufacturers to operate 20 or more warehouses to service the U.S. mainland. Some firms went so far as to have full-line inventory warehouses located near all major sales markets.

When a tradition such as local warehousing is part of a successful strategy, it is difficult to change. However, for the past several decades the cost and risk associated with maintaining local presence have required reexamination. Transportation services have dramatically expanded, and reliability has increased to the point where shipment arrival times are dependable and predictable. Rapid advances in information technology have reduced the time required to identify and communicate customer requirements. Technology is available to track transportation vehicles, thereby providing accurate delivery information. Next-day delivery from a warehouse facility located as far away as 800 to 1000 miles is common practice.

Transportation, information technology, and inventory economics all favor the use of smaller rather than larger numbers of warehouses to service customers within a geographical area. In many situations, customer perceptions concerning local presence continue to

[4] August Lösch, *Die Räumliche Ordnung der Wirtschaft* (Jena: Gustav Fischer Verlag, 1940); Edgar M. Hoover, *The Location of Economic Activity* (New York: McGraw-Hill Book Company, 1938); Melvin L. Greenhut, *Plant Location in Theory and Practice* (Chapel Hill, NC: University of North Carolina Press, 1956); Walter Isard et al., *Methods of Regional Analysis: An Introduction to Regional Science* (New York: John Wiley & Sons, Inc., 1960); Walter Isard, *Location and Space Economy* (Cambridge, MA: The MIT Press, 1968); and Michael J. Webber, *Impact of Uncertainty on Location* (Cambridge, MA: The MIT Press, 1972).

influence decentralization of inventory. The answer to the question "How much local presence is desirable?" is best understood by carefully examining the relationships that drive logistical system design.

Warehouse Requirements

Warehouses are established in a logistical system to lower total cost or to improve customer service. In some situations, the benefits of cost reduction and improved service can be achieved simultaneously.

Warehouses create value for the processes they support. Manufacturing requires warehouses to store, sort, and sequence materials and components. Facilities used for inbound materials and components are often referred to as **supply facing warehouses.** Warehouses are also used to store, sequence, and combine inventory for consolidated shipment to next-destination customers in the supply chain. Warehouses used to support customer accommodation are often referred to as **demand facing warehouses.** Demand facing warehouse requirements are directly related to manufacturing and marketing strategies.

Due to the specialized materials handling and inventory process requirements, warehouses typically specialize in performing either supply or demand facing services. Warehouses committed to supporting manufacturing are typically located close to the factories they support; in contrast, warehouses dedicated to customer accommodation are typically strategically located throughout the geographical market area serviced.

The combinations of information technology, e-procurement fulfillment, and response-based business strategies have combined to radically alter how and why warehouses are used. The economic justification and desired functionality of a warehouse is typically distinctly different for facilities dedicated to procurement, manufacturing, or customer accommodation.

Procurement Drivers

Procurement drivers, as discussed in Chapter 4, center on using warehouses to help purchase materials and components at the lowest total inbound cost. Sophisticated purchasing executives have long realized that a combination of purchase price, quantity discount, payment terms, and logistical support is required to achieve lowest delivered cost. In an effort to develop and support dedicated and customized working relationships, most firms have reduced their overall number of suppliers. The logic is the development of a limited number of relationships with suppliers that can be operationally integrated into a firm's supply chain. The goals of relational buying are to eliminate waste, duplication, and unplanned redundancy.

In an effort to improve overall operating efficiency, life cycle considerations have become prominent in purchase decisions. This relational dynamic of working with limited suppliers is based on a cradle-to-grave philosophy, spanning from new product development to reclamation and disposal of unused materials and unsold inventory. Such a **closed-loop** focus results from buying practices that directly impact the requirements and functionality of supply faced warehousing. Value-added services related to procurement are increasingly being debundled from the purchase price. Such debundling facilitates functional absorption and spin-off between manufacturers and their suppliers. There is also a trend toward more response-based business strategies, which is redefining expectations concerning supplier support and participation in the value-added process. The result is new structural relationships, such as tier one suppliers and lead facilitators. Finally, the seasonality of selected supplies, opportunities to purchase at reduced prices, and the need to rapidly accommodate manufacturing spikes continue to make selected warehousing of materials a sound business decision.

As a result of these trends, the role of supply facing warehouses continues to change. Warehouses were traditionally used to stockpile raw materials and component parts. Today such facilities place greater emphasis on sorting and sequencing materials and components as they flow into manufacturing. The goal is to streamline flow of materials and components by eliminating duplicate handling and storage of identical inventories at multiple locations throughout the material supply network.

Manufacturing Drivers

Warehouses that support manufacturing are used to consolidate finished product for outbound customer shipment. The capability to consolidate a variety of products contrasts to individual product shipment. A primary advantage of a manufacturing demand facing warehouse is the ability to provide customers full-line product assortment on a single invoice at truckload transportation rates. In fact, a manufacturer's capability to provide such consolidation may be the primary reason for selection as a preferred supplier.

Leading examples of demand facing warehouses are the networks used by such firms as General Mills, Johnson & Johnson, Kraft, and Kimberly-Clark. At Johnson & Johnson, warehouses are used to support hospital and consumer business sectors by serving as inventory consolidators for a variety of different business units. As a result, customers can purchase full assortments of products from different business units on a single invoice for shipment on one order. Kimberly-Clark produces a wide variety of individual products on specific manufacturing lines at specialized plants. Such products as Kleenex®, Scott Tissue®, and Huggies® disposable diapers are manufactured at economy-of-scale volume, then temporarily are positioned in demand facing warehouses. Customer-specific truckloads of assorted products are assembled at the warehouse. At the Nabisco Division of Kraft, branch warehouses are located adjacent to individual bakeries. Inventories of all major products are maintained at each branch to facilitate full-service shipments to customers.

The primary determinant of the warehousing required to support manufacturing is the specific production strategy being implemented. In Chapter 4, three basic manufacturing strategies—make to plan (**MTP**), make to order (**MTO**), and assemble to order (**ATO**)—were discussed. The extent of demand facing warehousing can be directly linked to the support requirements of each manufacturing strategy. In a general sense, MTO manufacturing strategies require supply facing warehousing support but little, if any, demand facing storage. Conversely, MTP manufacturing strategies, which focus resources to achieve maximum manufacturing economy of scale, require substantial demand facing warehouse capacity.

Customer Accommodation Drivers

Customer accommodation warehouses create value by providing customized inventory assortments to wholesalers and retailers. A warehouse located geographically close to customers seeks to minimize inbound transportation cost by maximizing consolidation and length of haul from manufacturing plants followed by relatively short outbound movement to customers. The geographic size of a market area served from a support warehouse depends on the number of suppliers, the desired service speed, size of average order, and cost per unit of local delivery. The warehouse facility exists to provide customers inventory assortment and replenishment. A warehouse is justified if it offers a way to achieve a competitive service or cost advantage.

Rapid Replenishment

Customer accommodation warehouses have traditionally provided assortments of products from varied manufacturers and various suppliers for retailers. A retail store typically does not have sufficient demand to order inventory in large quantities directly from wholesalers or manufacturers. A typical retail replenishment order is placed with a wholesaler that sells a variety of different manufacturer products.

Customer accommodation warehouses are common in the food and mass merchandise industries. The modern food warehouse usually is located geographically near the retail stores it services. From this central warehouse, consolidated product assortments can rapidly replenish retail inventories because of the close geographical proximity. Large retail stores may receive multiple truckloads from the warehouse on a daily basis. Location of the warehouse within the market served is justified as the least-cost way to rapidly replenish an assortment of inventory to either an end customer or a retailer.

Market-Based ATO

The design of a customer accommodation warehouse network is directly related to inventory deployment strategy. The establishment of a warehouse is a result of forward inventory deployment in anticipation of future demand. This assumption means that a manufacturing firm utilizing such a distributive network is to some degree dependent upon forecasting inventory requirements to offset response time to meet customer requirements. The preceding discussion indicates that inventories deployed forward after manufacturing are typical in situations where firms are manufacturing to plan or when they are engaged in decentralized assembly to order. In assemble to order **(ATO)** situations, common or undifferentiated components are stocked in warehouse inventory in anticipation of performing customized manufacturing or assembly at the warehouse upon receipt of customer orders.

An increasing amount of ATO operations are performed in warehouses located close to customers, as contrasted to centralized manufacturing locations. Assembly in close proximity to major markets allows the benefits of postponement while avoiding the high cost and time related to long-distance direct shipment.

Warehouse Justification

Warehouses are justified in a logistical system when a service or cost advantage results from their positioning between suppliers, manufacturers, and customers. Competitive advantage generated by establishing a warehouse network can result from lower total cost or faster delivery. From the viewpoint of transportation economies, cost advantage results from using the warehouse to achieve freight consolidation. However, freight consolidation typically requires inventory to support assembly of customized orders. Alternatively, consolidation or assortment may be achieved by establishing flow-through facilities or cross-dock sortation that operates without predetermined inventories. Such continuous movement effectively converts warehouses from inventory storage to mixing facilities. Of course some business situations will justify a combination of inventory storage and continuous flow-through or cross-dock operations to effectively and economically service customers. From the perspective of integrative management, the key logistics system design questions become: How many and what kinds of warehouses should a firm establish? Where should they be located? What services should they provide? What inventories should they stock? Which customers should they service? This sequence of interrelated questions represents the classical logistics network design challenge. For manufacturing firms, network design begins with marketing strategy and continues into manufacturing and procurement planning. In retailing and wholesaling enterprises, the framework spans from purchasing to customer accommodation strategies.

Systems Concept and Analysis

The **systems concept** is an analytical framework that seeks **total** integration of components essential to achieving stated objectives. The components of a logistics system are typically called functions. The logistical functions, as discussed in Chapter 2, were identified as order processing, inventory, transportation, warehousing, materials handling and packaging, and facility network design. **Systems analysis,** applied to logistics, seeks to quantify trade-offs between these five functions. The goal of systems analysis methodology is to create a whole or integrated effort, which is greater than the sum of the individual parts or functions. Such integration creates a synergistic interrelationship between functions in pursuit of higher overall achievement. In systems terminology, functional excellence is defined in terms of contributions a function makes to the overall process as contrasted to isolated performance in a specific area. Until the last few decades of the 20th century, process integration was generally neglected by managers who were trained to pursue functional excellence. Rapid advancement in information technology has increased the ability to identify and understand trade-offs to enhance logistics and supply chain initiatives.

When analyzed from a process perspective, the goal is balanced performance between functional areas within an enterprise and across the supply chain. For example, manufacturing economics are typically minimized by long production runs and low procurement costs. In contrast, integrated process management raises questions concerning the total cost and customer impact of such practices. A traditional financial orientation typically seeks to minimize inventories. While inventory should always be maintained as low as practical, arbitrary reductions below a level required to facilitate integrated operations typically increase total cost. Marketing's basic desire is to have finished goods inventory available in local markets. Inventory stocked in close geographical proximity to customers is believed to facilitate sales. Such anticipatory deployment of inventory is risky and may be in direct conflict with the least total cost process. In fact, Web-based connectivity and fulfillment strategies are driving entirely different inventory stocking and logistics strategies.

In systems analysis, attention is focused on the interaction between components. Each component contributes a specific functionality essential to achieving system objectives. To illustrate, consider a high-fidelity stereo system. Many components are integrated for the single purpose of sound reproduction. The speakers, transistors, amplifier, and other components have purpose only if they contribute to quality sound. However, failure of any component will cause the output of the stereo system to fail.

Some principles can be stated concerning general systems theory. First, the performance of the total system or process is of singular importance. Components are important only if they enhance total system performance. For example, if the stereo system can achieve superior sound with two speakers, then it is unnecessary to include additional speakers. Second, individual components need not have best or optimum design. Emphasis is on the integrated relationship between components that constitute the system. Transistors, as an example, are hidden from view inside the stereo system. As such, they do not need to be aesthetically pleasing. To spend money and time designing an appealing transistor is not necessary in terms of system integration. Third, a functional relationship, called **trade-off,** exists between components that serve to stimulate or hinder total system performance. Suppose a trade-off allows a lower-quality amplifier to be used if an extra transistor is added to the system. The cost of the extra transistor must be justified in terms of savings in amplifier cost. Finally, components linked together as an integrated system may produce end results greater than possible through individual performance. In fact, the desired result may be unattainable without such integrated performance. A stereo system will technically operate without speakers, but audible sound is impossible.

The principles of systems analysis are basic and logically consistent. An integrated process with cross-functional integration can be expected to achieve greater results than one deficient in coordinated performance. In logistical systems, synergistic performance is targeted customer service at the lowest possible total cost. Although logical and indisputable in concept, effective application of systems integration is operationally difficult. In the final analysis, it matters little how much a firm spends to perform any specific function, such as transportation, as long as overall performance goals are realized at the lowest total cost expenditure.

Total Cost Integration

Economic forces such as transportation and inventory should determine a firm's initial network of warehouse facilities. The following discussion identifies cost trade-offs individually related to transportation and inventory, and their integration, to identify the least-total-cost facility network.

Transportation Economics

The key to achieving economical transportation is summarized in two basic principles. The first, often called the **quantity principle,** is that individual shipments should be as large as the involved carrier can legally transport in the equipment being used. The second, often called the **tapering principle,** is that large shipments should be transported distances as long as possible. Both of these principles were developed in detail in Chapter 9. In combination they serve to spread the fixed cost related to transportation over as much weight and as many miles as possible.

Cost-Based Warehouse Justification

The basic economic principle justifying establishment of a warehouse is transportation consolidation. Manufacturers typically sell products over a broad geographical market area. If customer orders tend to be small, then the potential cost savings of consolidated transportation may provide economic justification for establishing a warehouse.

To illustrate, assume a manufacturer's average shipment size is 500 pounds and the applicable freight rate to a customer is $7.28 per hundredweight. Each shipment made direct from the manufacturing location to the market would have a transportation cost of $36.40. The quantity or volume transportation rate for shipments 20,000 pounds or greater is $2.40 per hundredweight. Finally, local delivery within the market area is $1.35 per hundredweight. Under these conditions, products shipped to the market via quantity rates and distributed locally would cost $3.75 per hundredweight, or $18.75 per 500-pound shipment. If a warehouse could be established, stocked with inventory, and operated for a total cost of less than $17.65 per 500-pound shipment ($36.40 − $18.75), or $3.53 per hundredweight, the overall cost of distributing to the market by using a warehouse would be reduced. Given these economic relationships, establishment of a warehouse offers the potential to reduce total logistics cost.

Figure 13.1 illustrates the basic economic principle of warehouse justification. *PL* is identified as the manufacturing location, and *WL* is the warehouse location within a given market area. The vertical line at point *PL* labeled P_c reflects the handling and shipping cost associated with preparation of a 500-pound LTL shipment (*C*) and a 20,000-pound truck-load shipment (*A*). The slope of line *AB* reflects the truckload freight rate from the plant to *WL,* the warehouse, which is assumed for this example to be linear with distance. The vertical line labeled *WC* at point *WL* represents the cost of operating the warehouse

FIGURE 13.1
**Economic
Justification
of a Warehouse
Facility Based on
Transportation Cost**

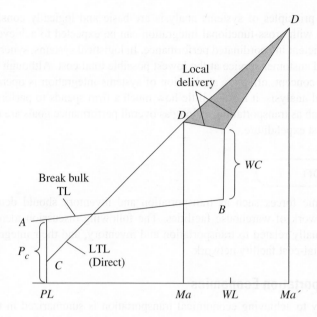

and maintaining inventory. The lines labeled *D* reflect delivery cost from the warehouse to customers within the market area *Ma* to *Ma'*. The slope of line *CD* reflects the LTL rate from the plant to customers located between the plant and the boundary *Ma*. The shaded area represents the locations to which the total cost of a 500-pound customer shipment using a consolidation warehouse would be lower than direct shipment from the manufacturing plant.

From the perspective of cost alone, it would make no difference whether customers located exactly at points *Ma* and *Ma'* were serviced from the manufacturing plant or the warehouse.

Network Transportation Cost Minimization

As a general rule, warehouses would be added to the network in situations where

$$\sum \frac{P_{\bar{v}} + T_{\bar{v}}}{N_{\bar{x}}} + W_{\bar{x}} + L_{\bar{x}} \leq \sum P_{\bar{x}} + T_{\bar{x}},$$

where

$P_{\bar{v}}$ = Processing cost of volume shipment;

$T_{\bar{v}}$ = Transportation cost of volume shipment;

$W_{\bar{x}}$ = Warehousing cost of average shipment;

$L_{\bar{x}}$ = Local delivery of average shipment;

$N_{\bar{x}}$ = Number of average shipments per volume shipment;

$P_{\bar{x}}$ = Processing cost of average shipment; and

$T_{\bar{x}}$ = Direct freight cost of average shipment.

The only limitation to this generalization is that sufficient shipment volume be available to cover the fixed cost of each warehouse facility. As long as the combined cost of warehousing and local delivery is equal to or less than the combined cost of shipping direct

FIGURE 13.2
Transportation Cost as a Function of the Number of Warehouse Locations

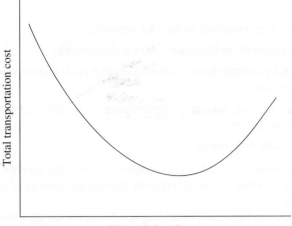

to customers, the establishment and operation of additional warehouse facilities would be economically justified.

The generalized relationship of transportation cost and number of warehouses in a network is illustrated in Figure 13.2. Total transportation cost will initially decline as warehouses are added to the logistical network. In actual operations, a consolidation location can be a warehouse or a cross-dock facility offering transportation break-bulk. It is not necessary to stock inventory in a warehouse to achieve the lowest transportation cost. The reduction in transportation cost results from consolidated volume shipments to the break-bulk location, coupled with short-haul small shipments to final destination. The cost of shipping small orders direct from manufacturing to customers is at the extreme upper left of the cost curve illustrated in Figure 13.2. At the low point near the middle of the transportation cost curve, the number of facilities required to achieve maximum freight consolidation is identified. Transportation cost is minimized at the point of maximum freight consolidation.

If facilities are expanded beyond the maximum consolidation point, total transportation cost will increase because the inbound volume capable of being consolidated to each facility decreases. The increased frequency of smaller inbound shipments results in a higher cost per hundredweight for shipments inbound to the facility. In other words, as the frequency of small inbound shipments increases, total transportation cost increases.

Inventory Economics

Inventory level in a logistical system directly depends on the number of stocking locations. The framework for planning inventory deployment is the performance cycle. Although one element of the performance cycle is transportation, which provides spatial closure, the key driver of inventory economics is time. The forward deployment of inventory in a logistical system potentially improves service response time. Such deployment also increases overall system inventory, resulting in greater cost and risk.

Service-Based Warehouse Justification

The inventory related to a warehouse network consists of **base, safety stock,** and **transit.** For the total logistical network, average inventory commitment is

$$\overline{I} = \sum_{i=j}^{n} \frac{Q_s}{2} + SS_i + IT$$

where

$\bar{I}$ = Average inventory in the total network;

n = Number of performance cycles in the network;

Q_s = Order quantity for a given performance cycle identified by the appropriate subscript;

SS_i = safety stock, for a given performance cycle identified by the appropriate subscript; and

IT = In-transit inventory.

As warehouses are added to a logistics system, the number of performance cycles increases. This added complexity directly impacts the quantity of inventory required across the network.

The impact on base stock by adding warehouses is not significant. The base stock level within a logistical system is determined by manufacturing and transportation lot sizes, which do not change as a function of the number of market facing warehouses. The combination of maintenance and ordering cost, adjusted to take into consideration volume transportation rates and purchase discounts, determines the replenishment EOQ and the resultant base stock. In just-in-time procurement situations, base stock is determined by the order quantity required to support the planned manufacturing run or assembly. In either situation, the base stock determination is independent of the number of market facing warehouses in the logistical system.

Transit stock is inventory captive in transportation vehicles. While in transit, this inventory is **available to promise** but it cannot be physically accessed. Available to promise means it can be committed to customers by use of a reservation or inventory mortgaging capability in the order management system. As more performance cycles are added to a logistical network, the anticipated impact is that existing cycles will experience a reduction in transit inventory. This reduction occurs because the total network transit days and related uncertainty are reduced. To illustrate, assume a single product is being sold in markets A and B and is currently being supplied from warehouse X, as presented in Figure 13.3.

FIGURE 13.3
Logistical Network:
Two Markets, One
Warehouse

FIGURE 13.4
Logistical Network: Two Markets, Two Warehouses

Assume the forecasted average daily sales are 6 units for market A and 7 for market B. The performance cycle duration is 6 days to market A and 10 days to market B.

With other things held constant, what will happen to transit inventory if a second warehouse is added, as in Figure 13.4? Table 13.1 provides a summary of results. The main change is that the performance cycle to market B has been reduced from 10 to 4 days. Thus, the second warehouse reduced average transit inventory for the network from 53 to 32 units. It should be noted that the second warehouse did not create additional performance cycles on the customer accommodation side of the logistics flow. However, on the inbound side, each product stocked in the new warehouse requires a replenishment source. Assuming a full product line at each warehouse, the number of performance cycles required to replenish the network will increase each time a new warehouse is added.

Despite the increased need for inventory replenishment, the average in-transit inventory for the total network dropped as new warehouses were added because of a reduction in days required to service customers. Assume that warehouse X is supplied by four manufacturing plants whose individual performance cycles and forecasted average usage are illustrated in Table 13.2.

TABLE 13.1
Transit Inventory under Different Logistical Networks

Forecasted Average Daily Sales	Market Area	Warehouse X Only	Two-Warehouse Facilities		
			Warehouse X	Warehouse Y	Combined
6	A	36	36	—	36
7	B	70	—	28	28
	$\Sigma A + B$	106			64
	$\bar{I}_a$	18			18
	$\bar{I}_b$	35			14
	$\sum \bar{I}$	53			32

TABLE 13.2
Logistical Structure:
One Warehouse,
Four Plants

	Warehouse X			
Manufacturing Plant	Performance Cycle Duration	Forecasted Average Sales	Transit Inventory	$\bar{I}$
A	10	35	350	175
B	15	200	3,000	1,500
C	12	60	720	360
D	20	80	1,600	800
	57	375	5,670	2,835

For purposes of comparison, assume a unit value of $5 for all warehouse products. Utilizing only warehouse X, the average transit inventory would be 2835 units at $5 each, or $14,175.

Table 13.3 illustrates the addition of warehouse Y. Average transit inventory in the two-warehouse logistical network dropped to 2248 units or, at $5 each, $11,240. Thus, even though four new plant-to-warehouse replenishment cycles were added to the logistical network, the average transit time was reduced because of the reduction in total replenishment days.

The addition of warehouses typically will reduce total in-transit days and, thus, in-transit inventory. This result will vary in accordance with the particulars of each situation. Each network of locations must be carefully analyzed to determine average transit inventory impact. The key to understanding the general nature of the relationship is to remember that total transit days are reduced even though the number of required performance cycles increases. The qualification is that while an increase in the number of performance cycles typically reduces transit days, it may also increase overall lead time uncertainty. As the number of performance cycles increases, the possibility of breakdowns leading to potential service failures also increases. This potential impact is accommodated by safety stock.

Safety stock is added to base and transit stock to provide protection against sales and performance cycle uncertainty. Both aspects of uncertainty are time-related. Sales uncertainty is concerned with customer demand that exceeds forecasted sales during the replenishment time. Performance cycle uncertainty is concerned with variation in the total days required to replenish warehouse inventory. From the viewpoint of safety stock, the

TABLE 13.3
Logistical Structure:
Two Warehouses,
Four Plants

Manufacturing Plant	Performance Cycle Duration	Forecasted Average Sales	Transit Inventory	$\bar{I}$
		Warehouse X		
A	10	20	200	100
B	15	100	1,500	750
C	12	35	420	210
D	20	30	600	300
	57	185	2,720	1,360
		Warehouse Y		
A	5	15	75	38
B	8	100	800	400
C	6	25	150	75
D	15	50	750	375
	34	190	1,775	888
	$\Sigma xy = 91$	$\Sigma xy = 375$	$\Sigma xy = 4,495$	$\overline{\Sigma xxy} = 2.248$

expected result of adding warehouses will be an increase in average system inventory. The purpose of safety stock is to protect against unplanned stockouts during inventory replenishment. Thus, **if safety stock increases as a function of adding warehouses, then the overall network uncertainty must also be increasing.**

The addition of warehouses to the logistical network impacts uncertainty in two ways. First, as performance cycle days are reduced, the variability in sales during replenishment as well as cycle variability are both also reduced. Therefore, reducing the length of the performance cycle relieves, to some degree, the need for safety stock to protect against variability.

Adding locations also has a significant impact on average inventory. Each new performance cycle added to the system creates the need for an additional safety stock. The introduction of an additional warehouse to service a specific market area reduces the size of the statistical distribution used to determine safety stock requirements for each warehouse. In effect, the size of the market area being serviced by any given facility is reduced without a corresponding reduction in uncertainty. To illustrate, when the demand of several markets is combined by using a single warehouse, the variability of demand is averaged across markets. This allows peaks in demand in one market to be offset by low demand in others. In essence, the idle stock of one market can be used to meet safety stock requirements of other markets.

To illustrate, Table 13.4 provides a summary of monthly sales in three markets on a combined and separate basis. Average sales for the three markets combined is 22 units per month, with the greatest variation above the average in month 6, when sales reached 29 units, or 7 units over the average. If the goal is to provide 100 percent protection against stockout and total sales of 29 units have an equal probability of occurring in any month, a safety stock of 7 units would be required.

The average monthly sales for markets A, B, and C are 8, 4, and 10 units (rounded), respectively. The maximum demand in excess of forecast is in market A, with 5 units in month 12; for market B, 3 units in month 8; and for market C, 4 units in month 6. The total of each of these three extreme months equals 11 units. If safety stocks are planned for each market on a separate basis, 11 units of safety stock would be required for the total network while only 7 units of safety stock would be required to service all markets from a single

TABLE 13.4
Summary of Sales in One Combined and Three Separate Markets

Month	Combined Sales, All Markets	Unit Sales per Market		
		A	B	C
1	18	9	0	9
2	22	6	3	13
3	24	7	5	12
4	20	8	4	8
5	17	2	4	11
6	29	10	5	14
7	21	7	6	8
8	26	7	7	12
9	18	5	6	7
10	24	9	5	10
11	23	8	4	11
12	23	12	2	9
Total Sales	265	90	51	124
Average Monthly Sales	21.1	7.5	4.3	10.3
Value Greater Than Average	7	4	3	4

warehouse. An increase in total system safety stock of 4 units is required to provide the same inventory availability when using three warehouses.

This simplified example illustrates the general safety stock impact of adding warehouses to a logistical network. The important point to understand is that increased safety stock results from an inability to aggregate uncertainty across market areas. As a consequence, unique safety stocks are required to accommodate local demand variation.

Network Inventory Cost Minimization

The overall impact upon average inventory of increasing the number of warehouses in a logistical network is generalized in Figure 13.5. A reduction in average transit inventory is assumed as illustrated by the line $\bar{I}_t$. The assumption is that a linear relationship exists between average transit inventory and the number of warehouses in the network. As noted earlier in this section, such a relationship may not be linear, depending upon the characteristics of the particular system under consideration. However, the general tendency is for a linear reduction as performance cycles are increased.

The curve labeled $\bar{I}_{ss}$ (average safety stock) increases as warehouses are added to the network. Inventory increases at a decreasing rate, since the net increase required for each new facility declines. The incremental safety stock is the sum of added inventory to accommodate uncertainty of demand minus the inventory reduction required to accommodate for less lead time uncertainty. Thus, the incremental inventory required to maintain customer service performance diminishes for each new warehouse location added to the system. The average inventory curve, $\bar{I}$, represents the combined impact of safety stock and transit inventory. The significant observation is that the safety stock dominates the impact of transit inventory. For the overall network, the average inventory is the safety stock plus half of the order quantity and transit inventory. Thus, given the same demand and customer service goals, total inventory increases at a decreasing rate as the number of warehouses in a logistical network increases.

FIGURE 13.5
Average Inventory as a Function of Number of Warehouse Locations

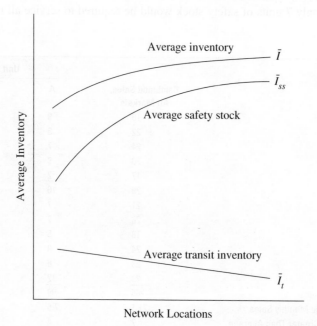

Total Cost Network

As noted earlier, the identification of the least-total-cost-network design is the goal of logistical integration. The basic concept of total cost for the overall logistical system is illustrated in Figure 13.6. The low point on the total transportation cost curve is between seven and eight facilities. Total cost related to average inventory commitment increases with each additional warehouse. For the overall system, the lowest total cost network is six locations. The point of lowest inventory cost would be a single warehouse.

Trade-off Relationships

The identification of the least-total-cost network of six warehouses in Figure 13.6 illustrates the trade-off relationships. Note that the **minimal total cost point for the system is not at the point of least cost for either transportation or inventory.** This trade-off illustrates the hallmark of integrated logistical analysis.

Assumptions and Limitations

In actual practice, it is difficult to identify and measure all aspects of total logistical cost. Many assumptions are required for logistical network analysis. An additional concern is the fact that analysis such as that illustrated in Figure 13.6 does not encompass the complexity of total cost integration.

The two-dimensional display in Figure 13.6 represents projected sales across a single planning period. Transportation requirements are represented by a single average-size shipment. In actual operations, it is likely that neither of these assumptions will represent actual circumstances. First, the nature of logistical network design is not that of a short-term planning problem. When facility decisions are involved, the planning horizon should consider a range of different sales alternatives. Second, actual shipment and order sizes will vary substantially around an average. A realistic approach to planning must incorporate a range of shipment sizes supported by alternative logistical methods to satisfy customer service requirements. In actual operation, alternative modes of transportation are employed, as necessary, to achieve the desired speed of delivery.

FIGURE 13.6
Least-Total-Cost
Network

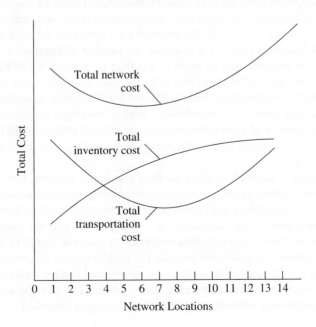

Significant cost trade-offs exist between inventory and transportation. Inventory cost as a function of the number of warehouses is directly related to the desired level of inventory availability. If no safety stock is maintained in the system, total inventory requirement is limited to base and transit stock. Under a no-safety-stock situation, the total least cost for the system would be at or near the point of lowest transportation cost. Thus, assumptions made with respect to the desired inventory availability and fill rate are essential to trade-off analysis and have a significant impact on the least-total-cost-design solution.

The locational selection aspect of logistical network planning is far more complex than simply deciding how many facilities to choose from a single array of locations, as illustrated in Figure 13.6. A firm engaged in nationwide logistics has a wide latitude in choice of where to locate warehouses. Within the United States there are 50 states, within which one or more distribution warehouses could be located. Assume that the total allowable warehouses for a logistical system cannot exceed 50 and locations are limited to a maximum of one in each state. Given this range of options, there still are 1.1259×10^{15} combinations of warehouses to be evaluated in the identification of the least-total-cost network.

To overcome some of these limitations, variations in shipment size and transportation alternatives need to be introduced for the analysis. Extending the analysis to a more complete treatment of variables typically requires the use of planning models and techniques discussed in Chapter 14. Three critical variables are shipment size, transportation mode, and location alternatives. The constants are level of inventory availability, performance cycle time, and the specific warehouse locations being evaluated.

In constructing a more comprehensive analysis, shipment size can be grouped in terms of frequency of occurrence and transportation mode economically justified to handle each shipment size within the specified performance cycle time constraints. For each shipment size, a total cost relationship can be identified. The result is a two-dimensional analysis for each shipment size and appropriate transportation mode. Next, the individual two-dimensional profiles can be linked by joining the points of least-cost by a planning curve. In a technical sense, this is an **envelope curve** that joins the low total-cost points of individual shipment size/transport mode relationships. Figure 13.7 offers a three-dimensional picture of integrated shipment size, transportation mode, and location.

The planning curve joins the point of total least cost for each shipment size. It does not join locational points. For example, the number of locations to support least cost for one size of shipment may be more or less than for another. Further analysis is required to identify the specific locations that offer the least-cost alternative for each shipment size and transport combination. Assume that the locations under consideration consist of a network ranging from 1 to 12 warehouses. Within this range, the planning curve will identify a smaller number of acceptable locations for detailed evaluation. In Figure 13.7, the points of least cost, shipment size, and transportation combinations fall within a range of four to eight locations.

Analysis is required to select the final warehouse network. Initially, the time duration of the performance cycle and inventory availability assumptions should be held constant. The service availability and performance cycle duration serve as parameters to help isolate an initial least-cost approximation. At a later point in strategy formulation, these parameters can be relaxed and subjected to sensitivity analysis. The fit of the least-cost planning curve requires marginal cost analysis for each shipment size/transportation mode combination for networks of four, five, six, seven, and eight warehouse locations. Provided customer service objectives are achieved within the four- to eight-warehouse range, a first-cut least-total-cost network of potential warehouses is identified.

FIGURE 13.7
Three-Dimensional
Total Cost Curve

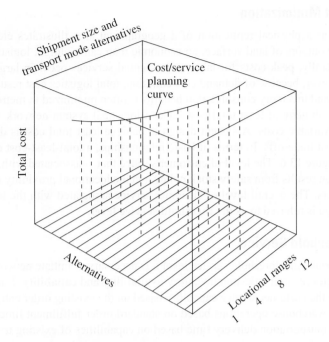

A final refinement involves the evaluation of specific warehouse sites or facilities. In the case of Figure 13.7, which is also the situation in most complex modeling approaches, the best-fit-location network is limited to an array of warehouse locations preselected for analysis. The results may be managerially satisfactory but not cost-superior to a different group of locations. Each warehouse assortment selected for analysis will have a least-cost combination. The final policy may require that the analysis be completed with several different network combinations to identify those most suitable for a given business situation. The final warehouse selection made by using such a trial-and-error methodology will never identify the mathematical optimal solution to minimize total logistical cost. It will, however, help management identify a superior network to the existing operation that will improve service and/or reduce total logistics cost.

To evaluate the wide range of variables in designing a logistical system, complex models have been developed. The assumptions required to support integrated system design are important from the viewpoint of their impact upon strategy formulation. The integrated total cost curve must take into consideration all relevant variables that are critical to logistical system design.

Formulating Logistical Strategy

To finalize logistical strategy, it is necessary to evaluate the relationships between alternative customer service levels and associated cost. While substantial difficulties exist in the measurement of revenue, the comparative evaluation of marginal service performance and related cost offers a way to approximate an ideal logistical system design. The general approach consists of (1) determining a least-total-cost network, (2) measuring service availability and capability associated with the least-total-cost-system design, (3) conducting sensitivity analysis related to incremental service and cost directly with revenue generation, and (4) finalizing the plan.

Cost Minimization

Just as a physical replication of a geographical area illustrates elevations, depressions, and contours of land surface, an economic map can highlight logistical cost differentials. Generally, peak costs for labor and essential services occur in large metropolitan areas. However, because of demand concentration, total logistics cost resulting from transportation and inventory consolidation benefits is often minimized in metropolitan areas.

A strategy of least total cost seeks a logistical system network with the lowest fixed and variable costs. A system design to achieve least total cost is driven purely by cost-to-cost trade-offs. In terms of basic relationships, a total-least-cost design was illustrated in Figure 13.6. The level of customer service that is associated with a least-cost logistical design results from safety stock policy and the locational proximity of warehouses to customers. The overall level of customer service associated with the least-total-cost-system design is referred to as the **threshold service level.**

Threshold Service

To establish a threshold service level it is necessary to initiate network reengineering with policies regarding desired inventory **availability** and **capability.** It is common practice to have the customer service capability based on the existing order entry and processing system, warehouse operations based on standard order fulfillment time at existing facilities, and transportation delivery time based on capabilities of existing transportation methods. Given these assumptions, current performance provides the starting point for evaluating potential service improvement.

The typical starting point for customer service availability analysis is to assume performance at a generally acceptable fill rate. Often the prevailing industry standard is used as a first approximation. For example, if safety stock availability were established at 97.75 percent for combined probability of demand and lead time uncertainty, it would be anticipated that approximately 98 out of 100 items ordered would be delivered as specified.

Given the initial assumptions, each customer is assigned a shipment location on the basis of least total cost. In multiproduct situations, selection of service territories for each facility will depend on the products stocked at each warehouse and the degree of consolidation required by customers. Because costs have significant geographical differentials, the service area for any given facility will vary in size and configuration. Figure 13.8 provides an illustration of the assignment of warehouse service areas based upon equalized total delivered cost. The irregularity of service territories results from outbound transportation cost differentials from the three warehouses.

In Figure 13.8 the warehouses are identified by the letters X, Y, and Z. The hypothetical cost associated with each facility represents all logistical cost for an average order except transportation. The differential of average order cost between facilities reflects local differentials.

Around each facility total cost lines are displayed at intervals of $1.50, $2.50, and $3.50. The cost represented by the line is the total cost of logistics, including transportation to points connected along the line. Customers located within a given area can be serviced at a cost less than that displayed on the line. The overall service area of each warehouse is determined by lowest total cost assignment. The territory boundary line represents the point of equal total cost between two warehouses. Along this line, total cost to service a customer is equal. However, a substantial difference could exist in delivery time.

Two conditions are assumed in Figure 13.8. First, the illustration is based on distribution of an average order. Thus, outbound logistics costs are equated on the average. To the degree that order size varies from the average, alternative territory boundaries would vary according to shipment size. Second, delivery time is estimated on the basis of distance.

FIGURE 13.8
Determination of Service Territories: Three-Point, Least-Cost System

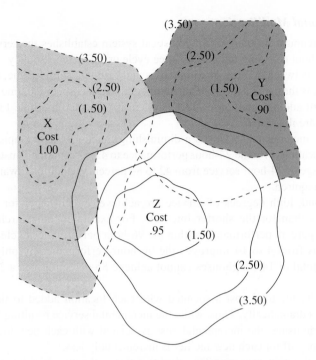

Transit inventory also is estimated based on delivery time. In accordance with this initial analysis of threshold service, it cannot be concluded that delivery times will be consistent within territories or that equal total logistics cost will be experienced within a service area.

The fact that the initial network is designed to achieve least logistics cost does not mean that threshold customer service will be low. The elapsed time from the customer's order placement to product delivery in a least-cost system is expected to be longer on average than would be experienced in alternative networks that have been modified to improve overall service performance. However, customers located near a warehouse facility in all networks have potential to receive rapid delivery. Because the least-cost location tends to favor areas of high demand concentration, a substantial number of customers will have rapid delivery potential.

Given an estimate of expected order cycle time, management is in a position to make basic customer delivery commitments. A service statement policy may be as follows: Order performance for area A will be 5 days from receipt of orders at the warehouse facility. It is our policy to be able to fill 98 percent of all orders within the 5-day period.

The actual performance of a logistical system is measured by the degree to which such service standards are consistently achieved. Given quantification of the variables involved, the threshold service related to the least-total-cost system offers the starting point of developing a firm's basic service platform. The next step in policy formulation is to test the customer suitability of the threshold service level.

Service Sensitivity Analysis

The threshold service resulting from the least-total-cost logistical design provides a basis for **service sensitivity analysis.** The basic service capabilities of a network can be increased or decreased by variation in number of warehouses, change in one or more performance cycles to increase speed or consistency of operations, and/or change in safety stock policy.

Locational Modification

The warehouse structure of the logistical system establishes the service that can be realized without changing the performance cycle or safety stock policy. To illustrate the relationship between number of warehouses and resultant service time, assume an important measure is the percentage of demand satisfied within a specified time interval. The general impact of adding warehouses to the system is presented in Table 13.5. Several points of interest are illustrated.

First, incremental service is a diminishing function. For example, the first five warehouse locations provide 24-hour performance to 42 percent of all customers. To double the percentage of 24-hour service from 42 to 84 percent, 9 additional warehouses, or a total of 14, are required.

Second, high degrees of service are achieved much faster for longer performance intervals than for the shorter intervals. For example, four warehouse locations provide 85 percent performance within the 96-hour performance cycle. Increasing the total locations from 4 to 14 improves the 96-hour performance by only 9 percent. In contrast, a total of 14 warehouses cannot achieve 85 percent given a 24-hour performance cycle.

Finally, the total cost associated with each location added to the logistical network increases dramatically. Thus, while the incremental service resulting from additional locations diminishes, the incremental cost associated with each new location increases. The service payoff for each new facility is incrementally less.

Logistics managers are often asked to estimate the inventory impact of adding or deleting warehouses. This relationship between uncertainty and required inventory is called the **portfolio effect.**[5] The portfolio effect can be estimated using the **square root rule.** The square root rule, originally proposed by Maister, suggests that the safety stock increase as a result of adding a warehouse is equal to the ratio of the square root of the number of

---

[5] For a more detailed discussion of the portfolio effect, see Walter Zinn, Michael Levy, and Donald J. Bowersox, "Measuring the Effect of Inventory Centralization/Decentralization on Aggregate Safety Stock: The Square Root Law Revisited," *Journal of Business Logistics* 10, no. 1 (1989), pp. 1–14; and Philip T. Evers, "Expanding the Square Root Law: An Analysis of Both Safety and Cycle Stocks," *Logistics and Transportation Review* 31, no. 1 (1995), pp. 1–20.

TABLE 13.5
Service Capabilities within Time Intervals as a Function of Number of Locations

Network Locations	Percentage Demand by Performance Cycle Duration (hours)			
	24	48	72	96
1	15	31	53	70
2	23	44	61	76
3	32	49	64	81
4	37	55	70	85
5	42	60	75	87
6	48	65	79	89
7	54	70	83	90
8	60	76	84	90
9	65	80	85	91
10	70	82	86	92
11	74	84	87	92
12	78	84	88	93
13	82	85	88	93
14	84	86	89	94

locations in the newly prepared network divided by the square root of the number of existing locations.[6]

For example, assume that a manager wants to estimate the inventory impact of shifting from a one- to a two-warehouse network. In effect, the network is being doubled. For reasons discussed earlier, demand variability will be increased. Using the square root rule, the firm's aggregate safety stock (SS_j) for a two-warehouse system can be estimated as

$$SS_j = \frac{\sqrt{N_j}}{\sqrt{N_i}} \times SS_i$$

$$= \frac{\sqrt{2}}{\sqrt{1}} \times SS_i$$

$$= 1.41 \times SS_i$$

where

SS_j = Aggregate safety stock for N_j warehouses or product variations;

N_j = Number of warehouse locations or product variations for the new configuration;

N_i = Number of warehouse locations or product variations for the existing configuration; and

SS_i = Aggregate safety stock for N_i warehouses or product variations.

The projected inventory increase resulting from adding a second warehouse is estimated as a 141 percent increase in safety stock. Table 13.6 illustrates the impact of the change for a range of one to five warehouses. Although the square root rule works reasonably well for estimating inventory impact, it requires assumptions regarding demand. The first assumption is that the stocking locations or product variations must have approximately the same level of demand. Specifically, if there are currently two stocking locations, they must have approximately the same demand level for the square root rule to work accurately. Second, the demand levels at each warehouse or for each product variation must not be correlated. This means that demand deviation for each location must be independent. Finally, the square root rule requires that demand for each warehouse approximate a normal distribution. While the appropriateness of these assumptions must be taken into consideration, the square root rule is a useful way to estimate the inventory impact of adding or deleting warehouses to a logistical network.

Performance Cycle Modification

Speed and consistency of service can be varied to a specific market or customer by a modification of some aspect of the performance cycle. To improve service, Web-based ordering and premium transportation can be used. Therefore, geographical proximity and

[6] D. H. Maister, "Centralization of Inventories and the 'Square Root Law,'" *International Journal of Physical Distribution* 6, no. 3 (1976), pp. 124–134.

TABLE 13.6
Inventory Impact of Modified Warehouse Network from a Base of One Warehouse

Network Locations	Safety Stock Level
1	100
2	141
3	173
4	200
5	224

the number of warehouses do not equate directly to fast or consistent delivery. The decision to increase service by adopting a faster performance cycle arrangement will typically increase variable cost. In contrast, service improvement, by virtue of added warehouses, involves a high degree of fixed cost and could result in less overall system flexibility.

No generalizations can be offered regarding the cost/service improvement ratio attainable from performance cycle modification. The typical relationship of premium to lowest cost transportation results in a significant incentive in favor of large shipments. Thus, if order volume is substantial, the economics of logistics can be expected to favor use of a warehouse or consolidation point to service a market area.

The impact of using premium transportation will increase total cost. Adjustments from the least-total-cost logistical system can typically be justified if the improved service results in increased profitability.

Safety Stock Modification

A direct way to change service is to increase or decrease the amount of safety stock held at one or more warehouses. The impact of increasing the safety stock across a total system will shift the average inventory cost curve upward. A goal of increasing customer service availability will result in increased safety stocks at each warehouse. As availability is increased, the safety stocks required to achieve each equal increment of availability increase at an increasing rate.

Finalizing Strategy

Management often falls into the trap of being overly optimistic in terms of service commitments to customers. The result may be excessively high customer expectations followed by erratic performance. In part, such overcommitment results from lack of understanding of the total cost required to support high, zero-defect service.

The final step in establishing a strategy is to evaluate the cost of incremental service in terms of generating offsetting revenue. To illustrate, assume that the current system is geared to service at least 90 percent of all customers at a 95 percent inventory availability within 60 hours of order receipt. Furthermore, assume that the current logistical system is meeting these objectives at lowest total cost by utilizing a network of five warehouses. Marketing, however, is not satisfied and believes that service capability should be increased to the point where 90 percent of all customers would receive 97 percent inventory availability delivered within 24 hours. Logistical management needs to estimate the cost of this strategic commitment.

Figure 13.9 illustrates how the alternative strategies can be evaluated. Assume marketing is requesting a 2 percent improvement in inventory availability combined with a 36-hour improvement in delivery capability. Assume design analysis identifies that 12 warehouse facilities represent the lowest-cost network capable of achieving the new service standards. The total cost of this expanded service capability is measured on the vertical axis of Figure 13.9 by the distance between points *A* and *B*. The total cost of achieving marketing's requested service will require approximately a $400,000 per year increase in logistical cost. Assuming an average before-tax profit margin of 10 percent of sales, it would be necessary to generate $4 million in incremental sales to break even on the cost of providing the added service.

Acceptance or rejection of marketing's proposal for increased service involves strategic positioning. Logistics can provide whichever performance the firm's overall customer service strategy requires. Policy changes, once adopted, will influence the logistical network design. To finalize logistical policy management typically requires considering a range of strategic alternatives.

FIGURE 13.9
Comparative Total Cost for 5- and 12-Distribution-Point Systems

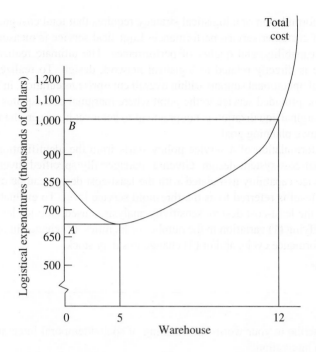

Summary

The primary drivers of logistics network design are requirements resulting from integrated procurement, manufacturing, and customer accommodation strategies. Within the framework of these interlocking strategies, integrated logistics requirements are satisfied by achieving total cost and service trade-offs. These capabilities play out across a network of enterprise facilities. Important to the performance of logistics requirements are warehouse facilities. Such facilities are justified in logistical system design as a result of their contribution to cost reduction, service improvement, or a combination of both.

Transportation and inventory economics are critical network design considerations. In the least-total-cost equation, transportation reflects the spatial aspects of logistics. The ability to consolidate transportation is a primary justification for including warehouses in a network design. Inventory introduces the temporal dimension of logistics. Average inventory increases as the number of warehouses in a system increase in a stable demand situation. Total cost integration provides a framework for simultaneous integration of logistics, manufacturing, and procurement costs. Thus, total cost analysis provides the methodology for logistical network integration.

Accurate total cost analysis is not without practical problems. Foremost is the fact that a great many important costs are not specifically measured or reported by standard accounting systems. A second problem involved in total cost analysis is the need to consider a wide variety of network design alternatives. To develop complete analysis of a planning situation, alternative shipment sizes, modes of shipment, and range of available warehouse locations must be considered.

These problems can be overcome if care is taken in network analysis. The cost format recommended for total cost analysis is to group all functional costs associated with inventory and transportation. The significant contribution of total cost integration is that it provides a simultaneous analysis of time- and space-impacted costs involved in logistical network design.

The formulation of a logistical strategy requires that total cost analysis be evaluated in terms of customer service performance. Logistical service is measured in terms of availability, capability, and quality of performance. The ultimate realization of each service attribute is directly related to logistical network design. To realize the highest level of logistical operational support within overall enterprise integration, in theory each customer should be provided service to the point where marginal cost equates to marginal revenue. Such marginal equalization is not practical to achieve; however, the relationship serves as a normative planning goal.

The formulation of a service policy starts from the identification and analysis of the least-total-cost-system design. Given a managerially specified inventory availability target, service capability associated with the least-cost design can be quantified. This initial service level is referred to as the threshold service level. To evaluate potential modifications to the least-cost design, sensitivity analysis is used. Service levels may be improved by modifying (1) variation in the number of facilities, (2) change in one or more aspects of the performance cycle, and/or (3) change in safety stock.

Challenge Questions

1. Describe in your words the meaning of spatial/temporal integration in logistical system integration.

2. What justification of logic can be presented to support the placement of a warehouse in a logistical system?

3. Why do transportation costs initially decrease as the number of warehouses in a system increases? Why do transportation costs eventually increase as the number of warehouses increase? Why do inventory costs increase as the number of warehouses in a system increases?

4. In your words, what is the locational impact of inventory? How does it differ for transit inventory and safety stock?

5. What is meant by the threshold service level of a least-cost system?

6. Why does customer service not increase proportionately to increases in total cost when a logistical system is being designed?

7. In Table 13.5, why does customer service speed of performance increase faster for customers located greater distances from a warehouse facility? What is the implication of this relationship for system design?

8. Discuss the differences between improving customer service through faster and more consistent transportation, higher inventory levels, and/or expanded numbers of warehouses.

9. Explain the following statement: "The methodology is systems analysis and the theoretical framework is the systems concept."

10. In what ways can customer service performance be improved by incorporating flexible distribution operations into a logistical system design?

CHAPTER FOURTEEN

Network and Operational Planning

Chapter Outline

The supply chain logistics environment is constantly evolving as a result of changes in markets, competitors, suppliers, technology, and relative economics. To develop and focus the enterprise strategy to match this changing environment and effectively evaluate alternatives, a systematic planning and design methodology is necessary. This chapter presents a generalized methodology that includes an overview of techniques used for logistics planning.

Planning Methodology

Even for established industries, a firm's markets, demand, cost, and service requirements change rapidly in response to customer and competitor behavior. To accommodate such change, firms often face questions such as: (1) How many warehouses should our logistics system use and where should they be located? (2) What are the inventory/service trade-offs for each warehouse? (3) What types of transportation equipment should be

FIGURE 14.1
Research Process

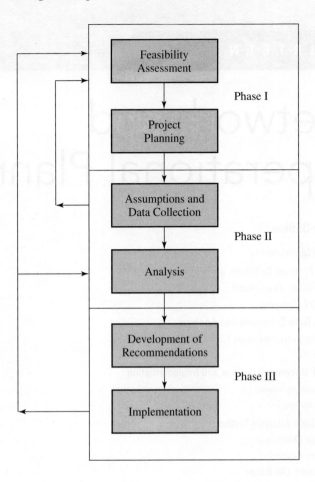

used and how should vehicles be routed? (4) Is investment in a new materials handling technology justified?

The answers to such questions are usually complex and data-intensive. The complexity is due to the large number of factors influencing logistics total cost and the range of alternative solutions. The data-intensiveness is due to the large amount of information required to evaluate logistical alternatives. A typical logistics system design must evaluate a range of service alternatives, cost assumptions, and operating technologies. Such analyses require a structured process and effective analytical tools.

Just as no ideal logistical system is suitable for all enterprises, the method for identifying and evaluating alternative logistics strategies can vary extensively. However, there is a general process applicable to most logistics design and analysis situations. Figure 14.1 illustrates a generalized planning process flow. The process is segmented into three phases: problem definition and planning, data collection and analysis, and recommendation and implementation.

Phase I: Problem Definition and Planning

Phase I of logistics system design and planning provides the foundation for the overall analysis. A thorough and well-documented problem definition and plan are essential to all that follows.

Feasibility Assessment

Logistics design and planning must begin with a comprehensive evaluation of the current operating situation. The objective is to understand the environment, process, and performance characteristics of the current system and to determine what, if any, modifications appear worthy of consideration. The process of evaluating change is referred to as a feasibility assessment, and includes situational analysis, framing the supporting logic, and cost/benefit estimation.

Situation Analysis

The collection of performance measures, characteristics, and information describing the current logistics environment is called the situational analysis. A typical analysis requires internal operational review, a market assessment, and a technology assessment to determine existing capabilities and improvement potential.

The internal operating review focuses on developing a clear understanding of existing logistics practices and processes. It profiles historical performance, data availability, strategies, operations, and tactical policies and practices. The review usually covers the overall process as well as each logistics function. In order to fully understand how logistics supports procurement, manufacturing operations, and customer accommodation, the situational analysis should span the full functionality of the supply chain.

A complete internal review examines all major resources, such as workforce, equipment, facilities, relationships, and information. In particular, the internal review should focus on a comprehensive evaluation of the existing system's capabilities and deficiencies. Each element of the logistics system must be carefully examined with respect to its stated objectives and its capabilities to meet those objectives. For example, is the logistics management information system consistently providing and measuring the agreed-to customer service objectives? Likewise, does the material management process adequately support manufacturing requirements? Does the current network of warehouses effectively support customer service objectives? Finally, how do logistics performance capabilities and measures compare across business units and locations? These and many similar questions form the basis of the self-appraisal required for the internal analysis. The comprehensive review attempts to identify the opportunities that might motivate or justify logistics system redesign or refinement.

Table 14.1 lists some of the topics frequently covered during an internal review. The format highlights the fact that the assessment must consider the processes, decisions, and key measures for each major logistics activity. Process considerations focus on physical and information flows through the supply chain. Decision considerations focus on the logic and criteria currently used for supply chain management. Measurement considerations focus on the key performance indicators and the firm's ability to measure them. Supply chain performance metrics are further developed in Chapter 16.

The specific review content depends on the scope of the analysis. It is unusual that the information desired is readily available. The purpose of the internal review is not detailed data collection but rather a diagnostic look at current logistics processes and procedures as well as a probe to determine what type of data are available. Most significantly, the internal review is directed at the identification of areas where substantial opportunity for improvement exists.

The market assessment is a review of the trends and service demands required by customers. The market assessment objective is to document and formalize customer perceptions and desires with regard to potential changes in the firm's logistics capabilities. The assessment might include interviews with select customers or more substantive customer surveys. Table 14.2 illustrates some typical market assessment topics. The assessment

TABLE 14.1 Selected Internal Review Topics

	Processes	Decisions	Measurements
Customer Service	What is the current information flow? What is the order profile and how is it changing? How are orders received?	How are order sourcing decisions made? What happens when inventory is not available to fill an order? How are manufacturing and warehouse capacity allocation decisions made?	What are the key measures of customer service? How are they measured? What is the current performance level?
Materials Management	What is the current material flow through plants and warehouses? What processes are performed at each manufacturing site and warehouse?	How are production planning and scheduling decisions made?	What are the key manufacturing and warehouse capacity limitations? What are the key measures of materials management performance? How are they measured? What is the current performance level?
Transportation	What modes are currently used? What is the weight profile of orders and shipments and how are they different? What is the flow for requesting, paying, and exchanging information with carriers? What is the information flow for shipment documentation?	How are the mode and carrier choice decisions made for each shipment? How are carriers evaluated?	What are the key transportation performance measures? How are they measured? What is the current performance level? What are the relative economic performance characteristics of each mode and carrier?
Warehousing	What storage and handling facilities are currently used and what functions do they perform? What product lines are maintained in each facility? What are the storage, handling, and other value-added functions that are or may be performed at each facility?	How are shipment consolidation decisions made at each facility? What decisions are made by material handlers and how do they make those decisions? How is product stored in the facility and how are product selection decisions made?	What is the throughput and storage volume of each facility? What are the key warehouse performance measures? How are they measured? What is the current performance level? What are the relative economic performance characteristics of each facility?
Inventory	What value-added functions do current inventory stockpiles play? What inventory is the firm responsible for, and where is it stored?	How are inventory management decisions made? Who makes them and what information is used to support the decisions?	What is the corporate inventory carrying cost? What are the key inventory performance measures? How are they measured? What is the current performance level?

should focus on external relationships with suppliers, customers, and in some situations consumers. The assessment should consider trends in requirements and processes as well as enterprise and competitor capabilities.

Technology assessment focuses on the application and capabilities of key logistics technologies, including transportation, storage, materials handling, packaging, and information processing. The assessment considers the firm's capabilities in terms of current

TABLE 14.2   Sample Market Assessment Topics

	Market Trends	Enterprise Capabilities	Competitive Capabilities
Suppliers	What value-added services are suppliers providing? What are the major bottlenecks with current suppliers?	What are the opportunities to internalize or outsource value-added services? How can processes be changed to reduce bottlenecks?	What actions are competitors taking to refine product and information flow with suppliers? What are competitive benchmarks in terms of number of suppliers, cost characteristics, and performance measures?
Customers	What are the major constraints and bottlenecks when servicing key customers? What are the cost impacts of these constraints and bottlenecks? How are customer ordering patterns changing? What are the primary customers' criteria?	What functions or activities can be shifted to or from customers to enhance logistics system performance? How do customers evaluate our performance on their key measurement criteria?	What services are competitors providing our customers? How do competitors perform on key performance measures as identified by customers?
Consumers	How are consumer purchasing patterns changing with respect to purchase locations, times, and selection criteria? What are the consumer trends with respect to logistics activities such as purchase quantities, packaging, home delivery, and product quality?	How are we able to respond to changes in consumer purchasing patterns and selection criteria?	How are our competitors responding to changes in consumer purchasing patterns and selection criteria?
Risk	What are the specific resources that may be constrained in the future?	What are the options we have in place to avoid, minimize, mitigate, or respond to risk?	What are the critical risks where competitors may have an advantage over our firm?

technology as well as the potential for applying new technologies. For example, can advanced materials-handling capabilities offered through integrated service providers enhance logistics performance? What is the role of advanced information technology, communication, and decision support systems in enabling responsive logistics capabilities? Finally, what can wireless, RFID, satellite, scanning, supply chain event management, or other communication technology contribute to improved logistics system capability? The objective of the technology assessment is to identify technology advancements that facilitate effective trade-offs with other logistics resources such as transportation or inventory. Table 14.3 illustrates typical technology assessment topics across selected logistics functions. Such an assessment should be completed with respect to each component of the logistics system as well as from the perspective of overall integration.

Supporting Logic

The second feasibility assessment task is the development of a supporting logic to integrate the findings of the internal review, market assessment, and technology study. Supporting logic development often constitutes the most difficult part of the strategic planning process. The purpose of the situational analysis is to provide senior management with the best

TABLE 14.3 **Typical Technology Assessment**

	Current Technology	State-of-the Art Technology
Forecasting	What are the current technologies for collecting, maintaining, and developing forecasts?	How are the best firms developing forecasts?
Order Entry	What order entry technologies are used currently?	How are the best firms performing order entry?
	What order entry technology are customers requiring?	What new technologies are available to improve order entry effectiveness?
Order Processing	What is the process to allocate available inventory to customer orders?	How are the best firms performing order processing?
	What are the limitations of the current approach?	What new technologies (hardware and software) are available to improve order processing effectiveness?
Requirements Planning	What decision processes are used to determine production and distribution inventory requirements?	How are the best firms making production and inventory planning decisions?
	How are these processes supported with current information and decision aids?	What new technologies are available to improve equirements planning effectiveness?
Invoicing and EDI	How are invoices, inquiries, advanced shipment notifications, and payments currently transmitted?	How are the best firms using EDI?
		What new communications and data exchange technologies are available to improve invoicing and other forms of customer communication?
Warehouse Operations	How are warehouse personnel and scheduling decisions made?	How are the best firms using information and materials handling technologies in the warehouse?
	How are warehousing operating instructions provided to supervisors and material handlers?	What new information and materials handling technologies are available to improve warehouse operating effectiveness?
	How do warehouse supervisors and material handlers track activities and performance?	
Transportation	How are transportation consolidation, routing, and scheduling decisions made?	How are the best firms using information, packaging, and loading technologies with carriers?
	How is transportation documentation developed and communicated with carriers and customers?	What new information, packaging, loading, and communication technologies are available to improve transportation operating effectiveness?
	How are transportation costs determined, assessed, and monitored?	
	What packaging and loading technologies are used?	
Decision Support	How are logistical, tactical, and strategic planning decisions made?	How are the best companies making similar tactical or strategic decisions?
	What information is used and what analysis is completed?	What information and evaluation technologies are available to enhance decision effectiveness?

possible vision of the strengths and weaknesses of existing logistics system capabilities for both the existing and potential future logistical requirements. Supporting logic development builds on this comprehensive review in three ways.

First, it must identify the value proposition to justify detailed research and analysis. In this sense, the supporting logic development forces a critical view of potential improvement opportunities, including determination of whether the cost/benefit justification provides a solid business case. Supporting logic development utilizes logistics principles, such as the tapering principle, principle of inventory aggregation, and total landed cost principle discussed in previous chapters, to determine the feasibility of conducting a detailed analysis to quantify the potential benefits. While completing the remaining tasks in the managerial planning process does not commit a firm to implementation or even guarantee an improved logistics system design, the potential benefits and risks associated with change should be clearly identified in developing the supporting logic.

Second, supporting logic development critically evaluates current procedures and practices on the basis of a comprehensive factual analysis to remove perceptual biases. Identification of areas with improvement potential, as well as those where operations are satisfactory, provides a foundation to determine the need for strategic change. For example, it may be apparent that excess inventory or obsolete stock represents a serious problem and significant potential exists to reduce cost and improve service. While the appraisal process frequently confirms that many aspects of the existing system are more right than wrong, the decisions to consider change should be based on potential improvement. If supporting logic supports the current number and location of warehouses, subsequent analysis can focus on streamlining inventory levels without serious risk of suboptimization. The deliverables of this evaluation process include classification of planning and evaluation issues prioritized into primary and secondary categories across short- and long-range planning horizons.

Third, the process of developing supporting logic should include clear statements of potential redesign alternatives. The statement should include: (1) definition of current procedures and systems, (2) identification of the most likely system design alternatives based on leading industry competitive practices and the prevailing theories of integrated logistics and supply chains, and (3) suggestion of innovative approaches based on new theory and technologies. The alternatives should challenge existing practices, but they must also be practical. The less frequently a redesign project is conducted to reevaluate current procedures and designs, the more important it is to identify a range of options for consideration. For example, evaluation of a total logistics management system or supply chain structure should consider a wider range of options if done every five years than if completed every two years.

At this point in the planning and design process, it is well worth the effort to construct flow diagrams and/or outlines illustrating the basic concepts and justification associated with each alternative. The illustrations should frame opportunities for flexible logistics practices, clearly outline value-added and information flow requirements, and provide a comprehensive overview of the options. Some refined or segmented logistics practices are difficult to illustrate in a single flow diagram. For example, regional variations, product-mix variations, and differential shipment policies are difficult to depict, although they do form the basis of design alternatives. When segmental strategies are proposed, it is easier to portray each option independently.

A recommended procedure requires the manager responsible for evaluating the logistical strategy to develop a logical statement and justification of potential benefits. Using the customer accommodation concepts discussed in Chapter 3 and logistics integration logic and methodology from Chapter 13, the responsible manager should document and justify the most attractive strategy modifications.

Cost/Benefit Estimate

The final feasibility assessment task, the cost/benefit estimate, projects the potential benefits and risks associated with performing a logistics analysis and implementing the recommendations. Benefits should be categorized in terms of service improvements, cost reduction, and cost prevention. The categories are not mutually exclusive, given that logistics strategy and operations might include some degree of all three benefits simultaneously. The risks represent the potential downside related to the proposed changes. Service improvement includes an estimate of the impact of enhanced availability, quality, or capability. Improved service increases loyalty of existing customers and may also attract new business.

Cost reduction benefits may be observed in two forms. First, benefits may occur as a result of a one-time reduction in financial or managerial resources required to support and operate the logistics system. For example, logistical redesign may allow the sale of warehouses, materials handling equipment, or information technology systems. Reductions in capital deployed for inventory and other logistics-related assets can significantly enhance a firm's performance if ongoing costs are eliminated and free cash spin-off is generated. Second, cost reductions may be found in the form of reduced out-of-pocket or variable expenses. For example, new technologies for materials handling and information processing often reduce variable cost by allowing more efficient processing and operations.

Cost prevention helps eliminate involvement in programs and operations experiencing cost increases. For example, many materials handling and information technology upgrades are at least partially justified through financial analysis regarding the implications of future labor availability and wage levels. Initiatives to reduce energy consumption can also prevent cost in periods of increasing energy prices. Naturally, any cost-prevention justification is based on an estimate of future conditions and therefore is vulnerable to a degree of error. While logistics system redesign may not be approved entirely on the basis of cost prevention because of such uncertainty, these preventive measures are still important to consider.

No rules exist to determine when a planning situation offers adequate cost/benefit potential to justify in-depth analysis. Ideally, some review should be completed on a continuous basis at regular intervals to assure the viability of current and future logistics operations. In the final analysis, the decision to undertake in-depth planning will depend on how convincing the supporting logic is, how believable estimated benefits are, and whether estimated benefits offer sufficient return on investment to justify organizational and operational change. These potential benefits must be balanced against the out-of-pocket cost required to complete the process.

Although they are not always a goal of a planning and design project, immediate improvement opportunities are frequently possible. The rapid capture of "low hanging fruit" can often increase revenue or decrease cost sufficiently to justify the remainder of an analysis. As the project team identifies these opportunities, the responsible executive should evaluate each opportunity to balance the quick return in terms of the implementation risk.

Project Planning

Project planning is the second Phase I activity. Logistics system complexity requires that any effort to identify and evaluate strategic or tactical alternatives must be planned thoroughly to provide a sound basis for implementing change. Project planning involves these specific tasks: statement of objectives, statement of constraints, measurement standards, assumptive logic, analysis techniques, and project work plan.

Statement of Objectives

The statement of objectives documents the cost and service expectations for the logistics system revisions. It is essential that they be stated specifically and in terms of measurable factors. The objectives define market or industry segments, the time frame for change, and specific performance expectations. These requirements typically define specific goals that management is seeking to achieve. For example, the following suggest a combination of measurable objectives that might be used to guide logistics analysis:

A. Provide the 100 most profitable customers with perfect order performance on all orders.
B. For all other customers provide the following performance:
  1. Inventory availability:
     - 99 percent for category A products
     - 95 percent for category B products
     - 90 percent for category C products
  2. Desired delivery of 98 percent of all orders within 48 hours of order placement
  3. Minimize customer shipments from secondary warehouses
  4. Fill mixed commodity orders without back order on a minimum of 85 percent of all orders
  5. Hold back orders for a maximum of five days

Specific definition of these objectives directs system design efforts to achieve explicit customer service performance levels. Total system cost to meet the service objectives can then be determined by using an appropriate analytical method as discussed later in this chapter. To the extent that logistics total cost does not fall within management expectations, alternative customer service performance levels can be tested by using sensitivity analysis to determine impact on overall logistics cost.

Alternatively, performance objectives can establish maximum total cost constraints, and then a system that achieves maximum customer service level attainable within an acceptable logistics budget may be designed. Such cost-driven solutions are practical since recommendations are guaranteed to fit within acceptable budget ranges. However, such cost-constrained design solutions lack sensitivity to service-oriented drivers.

Statement of Constraints

The second project planning consideration concerns design constraints. On the basis of the situational analysis, it is expected that senior management will place some restrictions on the scope of permissible system modifications. The nature of such restrictions depends upon the specific circumstances of individual firms. However, two typical examples are provided to illustrate how constraints can affect the overall planning process.

One restriction common to warehouse network system design concerns the existing manufacturing facilities and their product-mix assortment. To simplify the study, management often holds existing manufacturing facilities and product mix constant during logistical system redesign. Such constraints may be justified on the basis of large financial investments in existing manufacturing plants and the ability of the organization to absorb change.

A second example of constraints concerns customer accommodation activities of separate divisions. In firms with a traditional pattern of decentralized profit responsibility, management may elect to include some divisions in a centralized logistics system while omitting others. Thus, some divisions are managerially identified as candidates for change while others are not.

All design constraints serve to limit the scope of the analysis. However, as one executive stated, "Why study things we don't plan to do anything about?" Unless there is a reasonable chance that management will be inclined to accept recommendations to significantly change logistics strategy or operations, their limitations may best be treated as a study constraint.

The purpose of developing a statement of constraints is to have a well-defined starting point and overall perspective for the planning effort. If quantitative analysis techniques are used, major constraints may be reconsidered later. In contrast to the situation assessment discussed earlier, the statement of constraints defines specific organizational elements, buildings, systems, procedures, and/or practices to be retained from the existing logistical system.

Measurement Standards and Assumptive Logic

The feasibility assessment often highlights a central need for measurement standard development. Such standards direct the analysis by identifying cost assumptions and performance objectives essential to evaluate recommendations. Management must stipulate measurement standards and objectives as a prerequisite for plan formulation. It is important that the standards adequately reflect total system performance rather than a limited, suboptimal focus on logistics functions. Once formulated, such standards must be monitored and tracked throughout system development to allow measurement of change impact. Although considerable managerial discretion exists in the formulation of standards, care must be exercised not to dilute the validity of the analysis and subsequent results by setting impractical or constantly changing goals.

An important requirement is to establish a list of assumptions that provide the logic supporting the standards. These assumptions should receive top-management approval because they can significantly shape the results of the strategic plan. For example, a relatively small variation in the standard cost and procedure for evaluating inventory can create major variations in the resulting strategic plan.[1]

Measurement standards should include definitions of how cost components such as transportation, inventory, and order processing are quantified, including detailed financial account references. The standards must also include specification of relevant customer service measures and method of calculation.

Project Work Plan

On the basis of feasibility assessment, objectives, constraints, standards, and analysis techniques, a project work plan can be developed and the resources and time required for completion identified. The alternatives and opportunities specified during the feasibility assessment provide the basis for determining the scope of the study. In turn, the scope determines the required time to complete the study.

Project management is responsible for the achievement of expected results within time and budget constraints. One of the most common errors in strategic planning is to underestimate the time required to complete a specific assignment. Overruns increase financial expenditures and reduce project credibility. Fortunately, there are a number of PC-based software project management packages available to structure projects, guide resource allocation, and measure progress. Such methodologies identify deliverables and the interrelationship between tasks.[2]

Phase II: Data Collection and Analysis

Once the feasibility assessment and project plan are completed, Phase II of the research process focuses on data collection and analysis. This phase requires assumption definition, data collection, and analysis of alternatives.

---

[1] For a detailed measurement discussion, see Patrick M. Byrne and William J. Markham, *Improving Quality and Productivity in the Logistics Process* (Oak Brook, IL: Council of Logistics Management, 1991), Chap. 10.

[2] An example of such planning software is *Microsoft Project* (Redmond, WA).

Assumptions and Data Collection

This activity extends the feasibility assessment and project plan by developing detailed planning assumptions and identifying data collection requirements by (1) defining analysis approaches and techniques, (2) defining and reviewing assumptions, (3) identifying data sources, (4) collecting data, and (5) collecting validation data.

Defining Analysis Approaches and Techniques

An early Phase II task is the determination of the appropriate analysis technique for the planning situation under consideration. While a wide number of options are available, the most common techniques are analytical, simulation, and optimization. An analytical approach uses numerical tools such as spreadsheets to evaluate each logistical alternative. A typical example of an analytical approach is the determination of inventory/service trade-offs using the formulas discussed in Chapter 7. Spreadsheet availability and capability have increased the use of analytical tools for logistical analysis.

A simulation approach can be likened to a laboratory for testing supply chain logistics alternatives. Simulation is widely used, particularly when significant uncertainty is involved. The testing environment can be physical, such as a model materials handling system that physically illustrates product flow in a scaled-down environment, or numerical, such as a computer model. Current software makes simulation one of the most cost-effective approaches for evaluating dynamic logistics alternatives.[3] For example, a PC-based simulation can model the flows, activity levels, and performance characteristics. Many simulations have the capability to illustrate system characteristics graphically. For example, supply chain dynamic simulation can be used to illustrate the trade-off between inventory allocation strategy and supply chain performance.[4]

Optimization uses linear or mathematical programming to evaluate alternatives and select the best design or alternatives under consideration. While optimization has the benefit of being able to identify the best option, optimizations are often smaller in scope than typical simulation applications.

Defining and Reviewing Assumptions

Assumption definition and review builds on the situation analysis, project objectives, constraints, and measurement standards. For planning purposes, the assumptions define the key operating characteristics, variables, and economics of current and alternative systems. While the format will differ by project, assumptions generally fall into three classes: (1) business assumptions, (2) management assumptions, and (3) analysis assumptions.

Business assumptions define the characteristics of the general business environment, including relevant market, consumer, product trends, resource availability, and competitive actions. The assumptions define the broad environment within which an alternative logistics plan must operate. Business assumptions are generally outside the ability of the firm to change.

Management assumptions define the physical and economic characteristics of the current or alternative logistics environment and are generally within management's ability to change or refine. Typical management assumptions include the alternative warehouse locations to be considered, transport modes and ownership arrangements, logistics processes, and fixed and variable cost.

---

[3] For a comprehensive discussion of simulation alternatives, see John D. Sterman, *Business Dynamics: Systems Thinking and Modeling for a Complex World* (Burr Ridge, IL: McGraw-Hill, 2000).

[4] For a general simulation modeling tool incorporating graphics, see W. David Kelton, Randall P. Sadowski, and David T. Sturrock, *Simulation with Arena,* 4th ed. (New York: McGraw-Hill, 2007). For a more specialized business process modeling tool, see IBM WBI Workbench (Armonk, NY: International Business Machines, 2003).

Analysis assumptions define the constraints and limitations required to fit the problem to the analysis technique. These assumptions frequently focus on problem size, degree of analysis detail, and solution methodology. Table 14.4 offers more detailed descriptions for each assumption category.

Identifying Data Sources

In actual practice, the process of data collection begins with a feasibility assessment. In addition, a fairly detailed specification of data is required to formulate or fit the desired analytical technique. However, at this point in the planning procedure, detailed data must be collected and organized to support the analysis. For situations when data is extremely difficult to collect or when the necessary level of accuracy is unknown, sensitivity analysis can be used to identify data impact. For example, an initial analysis may be completed using transportation costs estimated with distance-based regressions. If analysis indicates that the best answer is very sensitive to the actual freight rates, then additional effort is required to obtain more precise transport rates from carrier quotes. Once a technique is operational, sensitivity analysis can be used to identify the major solution drivers. When these sensitive drivers, such as outbound transportation expense, are identified, additional effort can be directed to increasing transportation replication accuracy.

The first major data category is sales and customer orders. The annual sales forecast and percentage of sales by month, as well as seasonality patterns, are usually necessary to determine logistics volume and activity levels. Historical samples of customer invoices are also necessary to determine shipping patterns by market and shipment size. The combination of aggregate measures of demand and shipment profiles characterizes the logistics requirements that must be met.

Specific customer data are also required to add a spatial dimension to a logistics analysis. The spatial dimension reflects the fact that effective logistics to key customers requires

TABLE 14.4 Assumption Categories Elements

Assumption Classes/Categories	Description
Business Assumptions	
Scope	Definition of business units and product lines to be included.
Alternatives	Range of options that can be considered.
Market trends	Nature and magnitude of change in market preferences and buying patterns. Projected changes in resource availability and cost.
Product trends	Nature and magnitude of change in product buying patterns, particularly with respect to package size and packaging.
Competitive actions	Competitive logistics strengths, weaknesses, and strategies.
Management Assumptions	
Markets	Demand patterns by market area, product, and shipment size.
Distribution facilities	Locations, operating policies, economic characteristics, and performance history of current and potential distribution facilities.
Transportation	Transportation rates for movement between potential and existing distribution facilities and customers.
Inventory	Inventory levels and operating policies for each distribution facility.
Analysis Assumptions	
Product groups	Detailed product information aggregated to fit within scope of analysis technique.
Market areas	Customer demand grouped to aggregate market areas to fit the scope of analysis technique.

that the delivery cost and time associated with precise locations be quantified. In the overall analysis, customers and markets are often aggregated by location, type, size, order frequency, and growth rate to reduce analysis complexity. However, such aggregation is normally not satisfactory for evaluation of key customer service capability.

For supply chain logistics analysis, it is necessary to identify and track the costs associated with manufacturing and purchasing. While manufacturing plant locations may not be a variable component in a logistical system design, it is typically necessary to consider the number and location of plants, product mix, production schedules, and seasonality. Policies and costs associated with inventory transfer, reordering, and warehouse processing must be identified. In particular, inventory control rules and product allocation procedures are important elements. Finally, for each current and potential warehouse, it is necessary to establish operating costs, capacities, product mix, storage levels, and service capabilities.

Transportation data requirements include the number and type of modes utilized, modal selection criteria, rates and transit times, shipping rules, and policies. If private transportation is included in the analysis, then information is required regarding the operating characteristics of the private fleet.

The preceding discussion offers some perspective regarding the necessary data to evaluate logistics alternatives. The primary justification for placing the formal data collection process after the selection of analysis technique is to match the data to the analysis technique requirements.

It is also useful to benchmark competitive logistical capabilities and flows to provide information regarding competitor strategies and capabilities. In most cases, this information is readily available from published material, annual reports, and general knowledge of company executives. The main purpose in collecting such data is to provide competitive benchmarks that compare customer service capabilities, facility networks, and operating capabilities.

Data Collection

Once alternative data sources have been identified, the data collection process can begin. The process includes assembly of required data and conversion to appropriate formats for the analysis tool. This is often a tedious and time-consuming task, so errors are likely. Potential errors include collecting data from a misrepresentative time period and overlooking data that do not reflect major components of logistics activity, such as customer pickup volume. For this reason, the data collection process should be carefully documented to assist in identifying errors that might reduce analysis accuracy and to determine any necessary changes to achieve acceptable accuracy.

Validation Data

In addition to collecting data to support alternative analysis, base case or validation data must also be collected to verify that the results accurately reflect reality. The specific question concerns whether the chosen analytical approach accurately replicates historical logistics practices. The objective of validation is to increase credibility with management regarding the analysis process. If the process does not yield credible results, management will have little confidence in analysis results and resulting recommendations.

Analysis

Analysis involves use of the technique and data to evaluate strategic and tactical logistics alternatives. The analysis process includes: (1) analysis questions, (2) validating baseline analysis, (3) analyses of alternatives, and (4) sensitivity analysis.

Analysis Questions

The first task defines specific analysis questions concerning alternatives and the range of acceptable uncertainty. The specific questions build on research objectives and constraints by identifying specific operating policies and parameters. For example, the questions for a warehouse site analysis must identify the specific location combinations to be evaluated. In the case of an inventory analysis, questions might focus on alternative service and uncertainty levels.

Suppose that a strategic planning effort is focusing on the identification of a network of warehouses to serve the U.S. domestic market. Assume that the current network uses four warehouses located in Newark, New Jersey; Atlanta, Georgia; Chicago, Illinois; and Los Angeles, California. Table 14.5 summarizes the shipment volume, cost, and service characteristics of the existing system. Shipment volume is defined in terms of weight shipped; cost, in terms of transportation and inventory carrying expenses; and service level, in terms of the percentage of sales volume serviced within 2 days' transit time from the warehouse. Likely questions for the analysis might be: (1) What is the performance impact if the Chicago warehouse is closed? (2) What is the performance impact of removing the Los Angeles warehouse? and (3) What is the performance impact of removing the Atlanta warehouse?

These questions represent but a few of the potential analysis alternatives. Other alternatives could include fewer or more warehouse locations or evaluation of different locations or more refined inventory management policies such as stratified inventory stocking based on product volume. It is important to recognize that care must be taken to define the analysis questions so that a wide range of possible options can be evaluated without requiring time-consuming modification of the model or additional data collection.

Validating Baseline Analysis

The second task involves a baseline analysis of the current logistics environment. Results should be compared with the validation data collected previously to determine the degree of fit between historical and analytical findings. The comparison should focus on identifying significant differences and determining sources of possible error. Potential errors may result from incorrect or inaccurate input data, inappropriate or inaccurate analysis procedures, or unrepresentative validation data. As discrepancies are encountered, errors should be identified and corrected. In some cases the error cannot be corrected but can be otherwise explained. Once discrepancies have been removed or explained to within ± 2 percent, the application is generally accepted as a valid representation.

Analyses of Alternatives

Once the approach has been validated, the next step is to complete an evaluation of design alternatives. The analysis should determine the relevant performance characteristics for each alternative design or strategy. The options should quantify the impact of changes in

TABLE 14.5
Summary
Distribution
Performance

Distribution Center	Shipment Volume (000 lbs)	Inbound Transportation	Outbound Transportation	Inventory Carrying Cost ($)	Total Cost
Newark	693,000	317,000	264,000	476,000	1,750,000
Atlanta	136,400	62,000	62,000	92,000	216,000
Chicago	455,540	208,000	284,000	303,000	795,000
Los Angeles	10,020	5,000	5,000	6,000	16,000
Total	1,294,960	592,000	615,000	877,000	2,777,000

management policies and practices involving factors such as the number of warehouses, inventory target levels, or the transportation shipment size profile.

Sensitivity Analysis

Once this analysis is completed, the best-performing alternatives can be targeted for further sensitivity evaluation. Here uncontrollable factors such as demand, resource costs, and competitive actions can be varied to assess each alternative's ability to operate under a variety of conditions. For example, suppose that the alternative analysis indicates that four warehouses provide the ideal cost/service trade-off for the firm's market area assuming the base demand level. Sensitivity analysis would test the appropriateness of this solution under alternative demand or cost scenarios. In other words, would four warehouses still be the correct decision if demand increased or decreased by 10 percent? The current environment requires an assessment regarding the impact of increased energy cost. Sensitivity analysis in conjunction with an assessment of potential scenario probabilities is then used in a decision tree to identify the best alternative to meet managerial expectations.

Phase III: Recommendations and Implementation

Phase III operationalizes planning and design efforts by making specific management recommendations and developing implementation plans.

Recommendations

Alternative and sensitivity analysis results are reviewed to finalize managerial recommendations. This review process includes four tasks: (1) identifying the best alternative, (2) estimating costs and benefits, (3) developing a risk appraisal, and (4) developing a presentation.

Identifying the Best Alternative

The alternatives and sensitivity analyses should identify the best options to consider for implementation. However, multiple alternatives often yield similar or comparable results. Performance characteristics and conditions for each alternative must be compared to identify the two or three best options. Although the concept of best may have different interpretations, it will generally be the alternative that meets desired service objectives at the minimum total cost.

Estimating Costs and Benefits

In the earlier discussion of strategic planning, potential benefits were identified as service improvement, cost reduction, and cost prevention. It was noted that these benefits are not mutually exclusive and that a sound strategy might realize all benefits simultaneously. When evaluating the potential of a particular logistics strategy, an analysis comparing present cost and service capabilities with projected conditions should be completed for each alternative. The ideal cost/benefit analysis compares the alternatives for a base period and then projects comparative operations across some planning horizon. Benefits can thus be projected on the basis of both one-time savings that result from system redesign as well as recurring operating economies.

Evaluating Risk

A second type of justification necessary to support strategic planning recommendations is an assessment of the risk involved. Risk assessment considers the probability that the planning environment will match the assumptions. Additionally, it considers the potential hazards related to system changeover.

Risk related to adoption of a specific alternative can be quantified by using sensitivity analyses. For example, assumptions can be varied and the resulting impact on system performance across alternatives can be determined. To illustrate, sensitivity analysis can be used to identify the system performance for different demand and cost assumptions. If the selected alternative is still best even though demand increases or decreases by 20 percent, management can conclude that there is little risk associated with moderate errors in the demand environment. The end result of a risk appraisal provides a financial evaluation of the downside risk if planning assumptions fail to materialize.

Presentation

The final task is development of a managerial presentation that identifies, quantifies, and justifies suggested changes. The presentation and accompanying report must identify specific operating and strategic changes, provide a qualitative rationale as to why such change is appropriate, and then quantitatively justify the changes in terms of service, expense, asset utilization, and productivity improvements. The presentation should incorporate extensive use of graphs, maps, and flowcharts to illustrate changes in logistics operating practices, flows, and distribution network.

Implementation

The actual plan or design implementation is the final process activity. An adequate implementation plan is critical since putting the plan or design into action is the only means to obtain a return on the planning process. While actual implementation may require a number of events, there are four broad tasks: defining the implementation plan, scheduling implementation, defining acceptance criteria, and implementing the plan.

Defining the Plan

The first task defines the implementation plan in terms of the individual events, their sequence, and dependencies. While the initial plan may be macro level, it must ultimately be refined to provide individual assignment responsibility and accountability. Plan dependencies identify the interrelationships between events and, thus, define the completion sequence.

Scheduling

The second task schedules the implementation and time-phases the assignments identified previously. The schedule must allow adequate time for acquiring facilities and equipment, negotiating agreements, developing procedures, and training. Implementation scheduling, ideally, should employ one of the software scheduling aids discussed earlier.

Acceptance

The third task defines the acceptance criteria for evaluating the success of the plan. Acceptance criteria should focus on service improvements, cost reduction, improved asset utilization, and enhanced quality. If the primary focus is service, acceptance criteria must identify detailed components such as improved product availability or reduced performance cycle time. If the primary focus is cost, the acceptance criteria must define the expected positive and negative changes in all affected cost categories. It is important that the acceptance criteria take a broad perspective so that motivation focuses on total logistics system performance rather than performance of an individual function. It is also important that the acceptance criteria incorporate broad organizational input.

Plan Implementation

The final task is actual implementation of the plan or design. Implementation must include adequate controls to ensure that performance as scheduled and that acceptance criteria are carefully monitored. It is critical that a formalized process be used to guide logistics system design and refinement projects to ensure that the objectives are documented and understood and that the analyses are completed appropriately.

Supply Chain Analysis Methods and Techniques

High-performance supply chain management requires regular comprehensive analyses of supply chain strategies and operations. Supply chain design analysis performs the strategic evaluation of supply chain alternatives such as sourcing, plant location, warehouse location, and market service areas, increasingly important to optimize flows for global supply chains. Dynamic simulation can be used to investigate the dynamics of multiple-stage inventories such as among suppliers, plants, and warehouses, and tactical transportation analysis assists in truck routing and scheduling. Regular freight lane analysis is necessary to respond to rate changes and balance of freight flows; tactical inventory analyses are necessary to identify items with excess inventory and to determine the appropriate inventory target levels. For this range of decisions, the following sections describe the specific questions, alternative analytical techniques, and typical data requirements.

Design Decisions

Logistics and supply chain managers are often faced with decisions regarding the strategic and operational network and process designs. Supply chain networks include the combination of suppliers, manufacturing plants, warehouses, consolidation points, service providers, and retailers to bring product from the raw material stage to the end consumer. The broad decisions include commodity and product flow as well as where specific value-added activities should take place within the supply chain. Increased material sourcing alternatives, production economies of scale, reduced transportation, and integrated service provider alternatives have increased the need to regularly and more comprehensively evaluate supply chain design alternatives. In recent years, supply chain design analysis is extending further to include marketing channel design as a result of global sourcing and marketing considerations. For example, many firms are investigating the use of alternative channels to market such as home delivery. Supply chain design analysis can be used to determine the total costs and trade-offs in considering alternative channel strategies, activity outsourcing, or offshoring. Global operations also dramatically increase supply chain design alternative complexity and the importance of an accurate assessment of supply chain trade-offs. Thus, the importance of regular supply chain design analysis has increased substantially.

Supply chain design decisions focus on selecting the number and location of plants, warehouses, and other supply chain **nodes.** Typical management questions include:

1. Where should the manufacturing plants be located and which products should they produce?
2. How many warehouses should the firm use, and where should they be located?
3. What customers or market areas should be serviced from each warehouse?
4. Which product lines should be produced or stocked at each plant or warehouse?
5. What is the role of master or regional distribution centers relative to field or local warehouses?

6. What sourcing and marketing channels should be used to source material and serve international markets?
7. What combination of public and private warehouse facilities should be used?
8. What service providers and value-added services should be used meet market requirements?

A typical supply chain design requires analyses addressing combinations of the above questions.

Typical supply chain design problems can be characterized as very complex and data-intensive. Complexity is created by the number of sourcing, plant, warehouse, market, and product alternatives that can be considered; data intensity is created because the analysis requires detailed demand and transportation data for existing strategies as well as for potential alternatives. Sophisticated modeling and analysis techniques must be employed to effectively deal with the complexity and data intensity necessary to identify the best alternatives. The decision support systems used to evaluate supply chain design alternatives are generally some form of mathematical optimization. The general logic and data requirements are described below.

Design Logic

Supply chain design techniques typically use some form of optimization to systematically evaluate design alternatives. The design alternatives include combinations of suppliers, plants, warehouses, and product stocking strategies. Linear or mixed integer optimization are common techniques used to select from a number of available options given specific constraints. Mixed integer optimization is the most common, as it can force some variables to be integers that would require warehouses to be open or closed.

Optimization models consider aggregate customer demand, aggregate supply availability (through either purchase or production), the possible product and information flows and intermediary locations, the transportation alternatives and costs, and other variable costs such as warehouse handling and duties. The supply chain network design tools systematically evaluate alternative network combinations while considering relevant constraints. For the relevant problem scope, the analyses include fixed and variable cost resulting from the operation of facilities such as suppliers, manufacturing plants, warehouses, consolidation points, transportation, handling, production, and inventory.

The software tools to perform supply chain network and design analyses are constantly being refined and updated. Therefore, it is difficult for any textbook to provide current data regarding the status and availability of design software. There are, however, numerous professional articles describing the tools and their applications for many organizations.[5] There are also an increasing number of network design tools that go beyond minimizing cost to include considerations such as minimizing carbon footprint.[6] Figure 14.2 illustrates the scope of a typical supply chain design analysis. The major supply chain design constraints include market region demands, plant production capacity, warehouse storage capacity, and product stocking strategy. Notwithstanding the value of optimization, linear programming confronts some major problems when dealing with complex logistical system designs. First, to format a comprehensive design, it is necessary to develop explicit functional relationships for the full range of design options. The functional relationship

---

[5] See "Master of Design," *Supply Chain Management Review* 4, no. 5. (November/December 2000), pp. 74–81, for an interview with Dr. David Simchi-Levi regarding the development and application of supply chain network design tools. Examples of applications of supply chain network design tools include, Paul Bender, "How to Design an Optimum Worldwide Supply Chain," *Supply Chain Management Review* 1. no. 1. (Spring 1997), pp. 70–81, and Brian Cargille and Chris Fry, "Design for Supply Chain: Spreading the Word Across HP," *Supply Chain Management Review*, 10, no. 5. (July/August 2006), pp. 34–41.
[6] Jari Tavi, "The Green Supply Chain: Forcing Corporations to Take Stock," *Supply Chain Management Review*, June 16, 2008.

FIGURE 14.2 Total Cost Analysis Approach

Manufacturing

Warehouses

Dealers

Expense components

Sourcing

+ Production

+ Handling

+ Inbound transport

+ Warehouse handling

+ Inventory

+ Customer transport

_____

Total cost

must consider all possible combinations for suppliers, production locations, distribution locations, wholesalers, markets, and products. The sheer number of alternatives and the associated constraints result in a very large problem. Second, the optimality feature of the technique is relative; that is, it is only as valid as the design problem definition. Too many simplifying assumptions can render a solution mathematically optimal but useless in terms of business practice. Third, the capability of existing linear programming procedures is typically limited by the number of echelons or stages in the supply chain and by the problem size. For example, problems requiring the analysis of flows from production locations to warehouses and then to markets (i.e., three echelons) can be solved easily by most optimizers. However, the size limitations may make it difficult to perform a complete supply chain analysis.

As discussed earlier in the chapter, the analysis phase of the process includes identification of appropriate tools, data requirements, and evaluation of alternatives. Each task is discussed below.

Tool Selection

A supply chain design analysis typically begins with the selection of an appropriate modeling tool. While generalized mixed integer programming packages can be used, supply chain design is unique and common enough that it is advisable to seek out one of the customized tools. There are a number of PC-based packages that can be used to effectively evaluate supply chain alternatives. Ballou and Masters have completed a number of surveys documenting the availability of these tools.[7] These design tools typically differ in their capacity, flexibility, graphics, and solution speed. These analysis tools can be purchased or leased for limited use. In general, the tools try to determine the combination of plant and distribution center alternatives that minimizes the cost while operating within demand and capacity constraints.

_____

[7] Ronald H. Ballou and James M. Masters, "Facility Location Commercial Software Survey," *Journal of Business Logistics* 20, no. 1 (1999), pp. 215–33.

Data Requirements

The primary supply chain design analysis data requirements include market product, network, customer demand, transportation rate, and variable and fixed cost definitions.

Supply chain design analysis requires that demand be classified or assigned to geographic market areas. The combination of geographic areas constitutes a logistics service area. Such an area may be a country or global region. The demand for each customer is assigned to one of the market areas. The selection of a market definition method is an extremely important element of the system design procedure. Figure 14.3 illustrates how the United States might be segmented into market areas for a supply chain analysis. Each dot represents an aggregation of demand. A number of market definition structures have been developed. The most useful structures for supply chain modeling are (1) county, (2) standard metropolitan statistical area (SMSA), and (3) zip or postal codes. Postal codes are the international equivalent of zip codes. The most common structure uses zip or postal codes since company records usually include such information. In addition, extensive government and transportation data are available by zip codes. The major issues for selecting a market definition approach concern the number of areas required to provide accurate results. While more market detail increases accuracy, it also increases analysis effort and time. Research indicates that for North America, approximately 200 markets offer an effective trade-off between accuracy and analysis effort.[8]

Product definition refers to the number of stockkeeping units required to complete the analysis. Although individual SKU flows can be considered in performing supply chain

[8] For original research regarding the number of market areas, see Robert G. House and Kenneth D. Jaime, "Measuring the Impact of an Alternative Method Classification System in Distribution Planning," *Journal of Business Logistics* 2, no. 2 (1981), pp.1–31; and Ronald H. Ballou, "Information Considerations for Logistics Network Planning," *International Journal of Physical Distribution and Materials Management* 17, no. 7 (1987), pp. 3–14.

FIGURE 14.3
Supply Chain Network

Source: Used with permission from Logic Tools, Chicago.

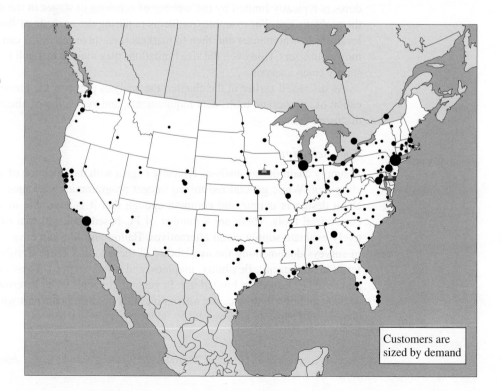

Customers are sized by demand

design analysis, it is usually not necessary to use such detail. Individual items, especially those with similar distribution characteristics, production sites, and channel arrangements, can be grouped or aggregated to simplify the analysis. Typical supply chain analyses are completed at the product family level. SKU aggregation into product families reduces analysis complexity and therefore data collection and optimizer run times.

The network definition specifies the channel members, institutions, and possible locations to be included in the analysis. Specific issues concern the combinations of suppliers, manufacturers, warehouses, wholesalers, and retailers that are to be included. Network definition also includes consideration of new plants, warehouses, or channel member alternatives. Figure 14.4 illustrates a channel for industrial and retail customers. While using a more comprehensive definition reduces the chance of suboptimizing system performance, total channel and supply chain design analysis increases complexity, again resulting in more extensive data collection and longer solution times. Supply chain analysts must evaluate the trade-offs between increasing analysis complexity and improved potential for total supply chain optimization.

Market demand defines shipment volume to each geographic area identified as a market. Specifically, supply chain analysis is based on the relative product volume shipped to each market area. While the volume may pertain to the number of units or cases shipped to each market, most supply chain design analyses are based on weight, since transportation cost is strongly influenced by weight moved. Market demand utilized in the analysis may also be based on historical shipments or anticipated volume if substantial changes are expected. The market demand must be profiled into different shipment sizes, since transportation cost is significantly influenced by shipment size.

Inbound and outbound transportation rates are a major supply chain design data requirement. Rates must be provided for shipments between existing and potential supply chain members and markets. In addition, rates must be developed for each shipment size and for each potential transportation link between existing and alternative warehouses and markets. It is common for supply chain analysis to require in excess of a million individual rates. Because of the large number, rates are commonly developed by using regressions or are retrieved from carrier rate files.

FIGURE 14.4
Channel Network Example

Variable and fixed costs associated with operating manufacturing plants and warehouses are the final major supply chain design factor. Variable cost includes expenses related to labor, energy, utilities, and materials. In general, variable expenses are a function of facility throughput. Fixed costs include expenses related to facilities, equipment, and supervisory management. Within a relevant plant and warehouse facility operating range, fixed costs remain relatively constant. While variable and fixed cost differences by geography are typically not substantial, there are minor geographic considerations, which should be included to ensure analysis accuracy. The major differences result from geographic peculiarities in wage rates, energy cost, land values, and taxes.

Another factor that is increasingly influencing supply chain network design is taxes. Some cities and countries, particularly those involved in international trade, are employing tax incentives to attract firms to locate supply chain activities and their related employment. The tax incentives may be in the form of reduced corporate income tax, property tax, and value-added tax. Countries that have been very successful at such strategies include Ireland, Singapore, and the United Arab Emirates.

Evaluation of Alternatives

Typical supply chain design analysis can lead to evaluation of a large number of alternatives, even for a relatively small analysis where the enterprise wants to consider all possible combinations of just 10 different distribution centers, for example. There are 6.2 million variations ranging from 10 different combinations of 1 distribution center to 1 combination of 10. If it took a single minute to evaluate each alternative, it would take 11 years to investigate all possible options. This emphasizes the importance of the feasibility assessment discussed earlier. This does not even include the possibility of looking at combinations of different suppliers or manufacturing plants.

The baseline analysis is typically first to validate the costs and establish the credibility of the analysis tool. Figure 14.5 illustrates the baseline results of a supply chain system

FIGURE 14.5
Base Supply Chain Network

Source: Used with permission from Logic Tools, Chicago.

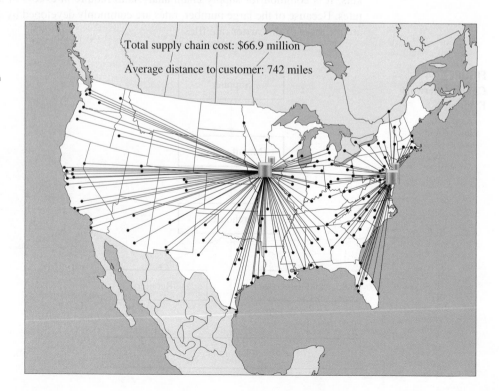

Total supply chain cost: $66.9 million

Average distance to customer: 742 miles

with two plants and two warehouses. The figure illustrates a supply chain with a plant with colocated warehouses in Pennsylvania and Iowa. As noted in the figure, the performance of this scenario is $66.9 million and an average distance of 742 miles. While supply chain design tools provide good performance data in terms of cost, service is typically reported in distance or time to market rather than a measure such as fill rate. The distance is a proxy variable representing transit time from the warehouse to the customer. Prior to investigating other scenarios, these results should be compared with the firm's historical data to determine if the model's costs provide an approximate representation of the firm's actual operation. If the historical and modeled costs are not approximately equal, any differences must be investigated to identify potential errors or provide some explanation. Reasonable accuracy is critical to build managerial credibility.

Other alternatives can be modeled to investigate other supply chain design options. In some cases, supply chain design tools can systematically evaluate a series of alternatives such as determining the optimum number of warehouses between 3 and 10. In other cases, when the number or production mix of plants is under investigation, the analyst must identify and evaluate each option separately. This again emphasizes the need to critically assess each alternative regarding its feasibility so that it is not necessary to complete a detailed evaluation of alternatives with limited feasibility.

Figure 14.6 illustrates a revised supply chain design based on the situation discussed earlier. The results demonstrate that a 3-plant and 4-warehouse supply chain yields substantially better performance than the baseline case. As the figure notes, the total cost is reduced to $61.8 million with an average distance between the warehouse and customer of 428 miles. In this case, the alternative supply chain design can both improve service, in terms of distance to the customer, and reduce total cost.

Although the supply chain design tools are increasingly sophisticated, there are a few issues that must be considered in their application. The first concerns the treatment of inventory carrying cost. As illustrated in Chapter 13, inventory carrying cost should

FIGURE 14.6
Alternative Supply Chain Network

Source: Used with permission from Logic Tools, Chicago.

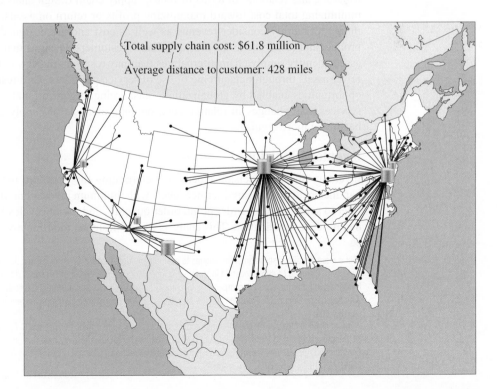

Total supply chain cost: $61.8 million

Average distance to customer: 428 miles

theoretically increase at a decreasing rate as the number of distribution centers increases. While this is generally true, there may be exceptions such as when a regional distribution center is used to provide backup stock for slow-moving items at five warehouses. Even though the total number of warehouses is increased to six, it likely that the total inventory to provide equivalent service would actually decrease because of the pooling of backup inventory. Similarly, many of the supply chain design tools do not have standardized processes to determine the inventory implications of different design alternatives. Since there is no standardized process, it is important to understand and make any appropriate adjustments to the inventory carrying cost computed by supply chain design tools.[9]

The second concerns changes in assumptions regarding shipment sizes. Most of the supply chain design tools use a constant shipment size for each transport lane. While this may be acceptable as long as the number of distribution centers does not change significantly, it is likely that the shipment size would change with a significant change in the number of warehouses. For example, if current shipments between a plant and four warehouses are a truckload, it is likely that shipments would be smaller if the number of warehouses increased to eight. The analysis must consider the impact of such change.

The third concerns the focus of the analyses. In the past, a substantial number of supply chain design analyses focused on warehouse location. Since logistics networks were relatively stable, it was unnecessary for firms to complete logistics system analyses regularly; however, the dynamics of alternative supply chain options, changing cost levels, and availability of integrated service providers requires that supply chain networks be evaluated and refined more frequently today. It is also increasingly necessary to coordinate supply chain design strategy with product and process design, which may require evaluations annually, quarterly, or even monthly.[10]

Over the past decade, there has been an increase in both the scope and focus of supply chain design analyses. In terms of scope, the analyses consider a broader range of supply chain members, including commodity providers, suppliers, manufacturers, distributors, and retailers. In terms of focus, supply chain design analyses are shifting from minimizing total cost toward maximizing profits or return on assets. Designs that maximize profitability consider revenue as well as cost and are designed to assign available product and resources to the most profitable customers. Designs that maximize return on assets identify supply chain alternatives that may result in higher variable costs but utilize fewer assets through outsourcing or use of service providers. As a result of the increasing opportunities enabled by globalization, outsourcing, organizational consolidation, shared services, and changes in relative cost, ongoing analysis of supply chain alternatives is becoming more regular.

Inventory Decisions

Inventory analysis decisions focus on determining the optimum inventory management parameters to meet desired service levels with minimum investment. Inventory parameters refer to safety stock, reorder point, order quantity, and review cycles for a specific facility and product combination. This analysis can be designed to refine inventory parameters on

---

[9] For a more detailed discussion of techniques to evaluate multiple location inventories, see Ronald H. Ballou and Apostolos Burnetas, "Planning Multiple Location Inventories," *Journal of Business Logistics* 24, no. 2 (2003), pp. 65–90; and Pablo Miranda and Rodrigo Garrido, "Incorporating Inventory Control Decisions into a Strategic Distribution Network Design Model with Stochastic Demand," *Transportation Research. Part E, Logistics & Transportation Review* 40E, no. 3. (May 2004), pp. 183–208.

[10] For an example process for coordinating product, process, and supply chain design, see C. Forza, F. Salvador, and M. Rungtusanatham, "Coordinating Product Design, Process Design, and Supply Chain Design Decisions: Part B. Coordinating Approaches, Tradeoffs, and Future Research Direction," *Journal of Operations Management* 23, no. 3. (April 2005), pp. 319.

a periodic or daily basis. Daily refinements make parameters more sensitive to environmental changes such as demand levels or performance cycle length; however, they also result in nervous inventory management systems. System nervousness causes frequent expediting and deexpediting of numerous small shipments.

Inventory analysis focuses on the decisions discussed in Chapter 7. Specific questions include: (1) How much product should be produced during the next production cycle? (2) Which warehouses should maintain inventories of each item? (3) Should slow-moving items be centralized? (4) What is the optimum size of replenishment orders (the order quantity decision)? (5) What is the necessary reorder point for replenishment orders (the safety stock decision)?

There are two types of methods to evaluate and select from inventory management options: analytic and simulation.

Analytic Inventory Techniques

Analytic inventory methods utilize functional relationships such as those discussed in Chapter 7 to determine ideal inventory stocking parameters based on the desired service level. Figure 14.7 illustrates the analytic inventory concept. The technique uses service objectives, demand characteristics, performance cycle characteristics, and the logistics system characteristics as input to calculate optimum inventory parameters. From an inventory management perspective, service objectives are typically defined in terms of case or order fill rates. Demand characteristics describe the periodic average and standard deviation of customer demand. Performance cycle characteristics describe the average and standard deviations for replenishment performance cycles. Logistics system characteristics describe the number of distribution stages or echelons requiring inventory management decisions. The analytical inventory technique is based on assumptions describing the logistics system stocking echelons and the probabilities relating demand and performance cycle characteristics. The probability relationships, along with the service level objectives, determine the optimal inventory management parameters in terms of replenishment order quantities

FIGURE 14.7   Analytic Inventory Overview

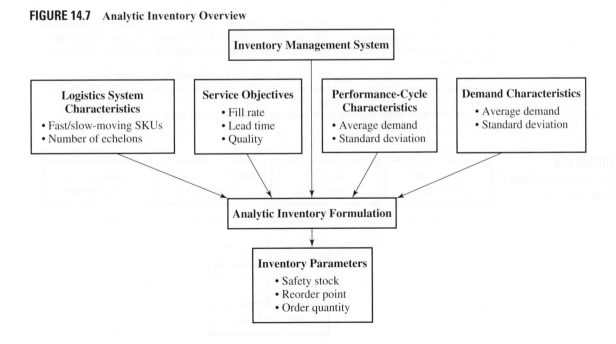

and reorder points. Numerous examples of software applications exist that utilize analytic techniques to determine optimum inventory management parameters.[11]

The advantage of analytic inventory techniques is the ability to directly determine optimum inventory parameters, given certain assumptions regarding operating environment. On the other hand, analytic inventory techniques are limited in terms of accuracy when assumptions are not met. For example, since most analytic inventory techniques assume normally distributed demand and performance cycles, the techniques lose accuracy when the shape of actual demand or performance cycles deviates from the normality assumption.[12] Nevertheless, analytical inventory techniques are often a good place to start when attempting to determine optimum inventory parameters.[13]

Simulation Inventory Techniques

The inventory simulation approach creates a mathematical and probabilistic model of the logistics operating environment as it actually exists. As Figure 14.8 illustrates, the simulation approach is similar to creating a laboratory testing environment for the supply chain network and operating policies. Simulation is similar to the analytic approach except that the roles of the inventory parameters and service levels are reversed.

In simulation, inventory parameters such as the order quantities and reorder points to be tested become the simulation inputs. These inputs define the environment to be tested. The major simulation outputs are the service level and inventory performance characteristics of the testing environment. The simulation, in effect, evaluates the performance of a specific situation. If the reported performance does not achieve desired objectives, the inventory parameters must be changed and a new environment is simulated. It is sometimes necessary to complete a number of simulations to identify the combination of inventory parameters that yields desired performance.

The major benefit of simulation techniques is the ability to model a wide range of supply chain environments without requiring simplifying assumptions. It is possible to accurately simulate virtually any supply chain environment by incorporating network characteristics and operating policies. The major shortfall of simulation techniques is their limited ability to search for and identify optimum solutions. While there are inventory

---

[11] An example of such an inventory management system is *Inventory Analyst* from Logic-Tools (Chicago), which determines the ideal inventory parameters to optimize order quantity and safety stock. Most APS applications, such as i2's *Rhythm*, SAP's *Advanced Planning Optimizer*, and *Manugistics*, incorporate analytic techniques into their advanced planning and scheduling software.

[12] These assumptions regarding normal demand and lead times can be overcome with numerical methods such as those discussed in J. Masters, "Determination of Near Optimal Stock Levels for Multi-Echelon Distribution Inventories," *Journal of Business Logistics* 14, no. 2 (1993), pp. 165–96.

[13] Spreadsheets can be used to develop and apply analytical inventory techniques. For an example, see the "Inventory Calculator" from the supporting material.

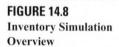

FIGURE 14.8
Inventory Simulation Overview

simulation examples that incorporate search algorithms, they are limited in capability and scope. There are indications that simulation is becoming more popular as firms attempt to understand inventory dynamics in the logistics channel.[14]

Inventory decision support applications are increasing in importance due to the emphasis on streamlining inventory levels to reduce the logistics asset base. The demand for more refined inventory parameters has increased the need for more sophisticated inventory analysis techniques. Software firms have responded by developing both stand-alone and integrated applications.[15]

Transportation Decisions

Transportation analyses focus on routing and scheduling of transportation equipment to improve vehicle and driver utilization while meeting customer service requirements. Transportation decisions can be characterized as strategic or tactical. Strategic transportation decisions concern long-term resource allocation, such as for extended time periods. Thus, strategic routing decisions identify fixed transport routes that may be used for months or years. Tactical transportation decisions concern short-term resource allocations such as daily or weekly routes. The objective of transportation analysis is to minimize the combination of vehicles, hours, and miles required to deliver product. Typical transportation analysis questions include: (1) How should deliveries be grouped to form routes? (2) What is the best delivery sequence for servicing customers? (3) Which routes should be assigned to which vehicle types? (4) What is the best type of vehicle for servicing different customer types? (5) What delivery sequence should be used to accommodate time restrictions imposed by customers? Figure 14.9 illustrates a typical routing or delivery problem. The warehouse represents the central departure site for all delivery vehicles, and each stop represents a customer location, such as a retailer.

Transportation Analysis Techniques

Routing and scheduling analyses have been well researched for supply chain tactical and operational planning. They are particularly important for firms completing partial load delivery activities such as package or beverage distribution. The techniques can generally be classified as heuristic approaches, exact approaches, interactive approaches, and combination approaches.[16]

Heuristic approaches utilize rule-of-thumb clustering or savings techniques to develop routes by sequentially adding and deleting stops. Exact, or optimal, approaches use mathematical (linear) programming to identify the best routes. Historically, optimization solution methods have been too computationally complex for even the fastest computers, but recent mathematical programming advances have enhanced their capabilities. The main difficulties with most exact procedures are (1) the large number of constraints and variables needed to represent even the basic routing and scheduling problem and (2) the impact of this size on computation time and computer storage space.

[14] D. van der Zee and J. van der Vorst. "A Modeling Framework for Supply Chain Simulation: Opportunities for Improved Decision Making," *Decision Sciences* 36, no. 1 (February 2005), pp. 65–95.

[15] Examples include James Aaron Cooke, "Simulate Before You Act," *Logistics Management and Distribution Report* 38, no. 9. (September 1999), pp.77–80; and "IBM Product Analyzes Your Supply Chain," *Industrial Distribution* 88, no. 8. (August 1999), p. 44.

[16] For a further discussion of each of these approaches, see Kevin Bott and Ronald H. Ballou, "Research Perspectives in Vehicle Routing and Scheduling," *Transportation Research* 20A, no. 3 (1986), pp. 239–43. Other examples of such applications are Asvin Goel and Volker Gruhn, "A General Vehicle Routing Problem," *European Journal of Operational Research* 191, no. 3. (December 2008), pp. 650–60; and T. Van Woensel, L. Kerbache, H. Peremans, and N. Vandaele, "Vehicle Routing with Dynamic Travel Times: A Queueing Approach," *European Journal of Operational Research* 186, no. 3. (May 2008), pp. 990–1007.

FIGURE 14.9
Typical Routing or
Delivery Problem

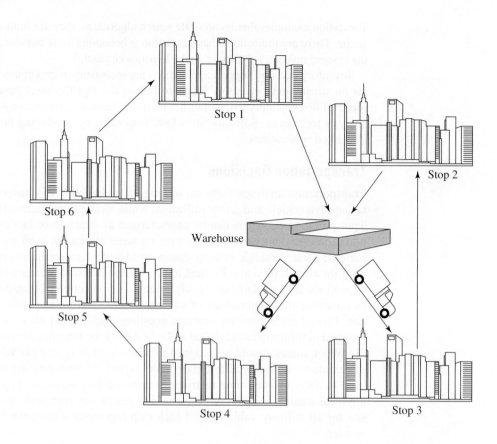

Interactive approaches utilize a combination of simulation, cost calculator, or graphics capability to support an interactive decision process. The decision maker identifies the alternatives for evaluation. The interactive decision support system then determines and plots the routes and calculates the performance characteristics in terms of time and cost. The decision maker then interactively evaluates the performance characteristics of each alternative and refines the strategy until no additional improvement is likely. The obvious drawback of interactive approaches is the dependence on the skill and ability of the decision maker, particularly as the problem size and complexity increase.

Combinations of the three approaches have proved very effective. Two criteria are important in evaluating alternative solution approaches: generalizability and accuracy. Generalizability is the ability to efficiently incorporate extensions for special situations, such as pickups and deliveries, multiple depots, time windows, vehicle capacities, and legal driving times, in an actual setting. Accuracy refers to the ability to closely approximate performance characteristics and the results' proximity to an optimal solution. Accuracy determines the level of and credibility in the possible savings as a result of decreased vehicle operating expense, better customer service, and improved fleet productivity.[17] There are numerous examples of PC- and server-based routing and scheduling packages.[18]

---

[17] For an expanded discussion of alternative analysis approaches, see Bott and Ballou, "Research Perspectives in Vehicle Routing and Scheduling"; Ronald H. Ballou and Yogesh K. Agerwal, "A Performance Comparison of Several Popular Algorithms for Vehicle Routing and Scheduling," *Journal of Business Logistics* 9, no. 1 (1988), pp. 51–64; and Ronald H. Ballou, "A Continued Comparison of Several Popular Algorithms for Vehicle Routing and Scheduling," *Journal of Business Logistics* 11, no. 2 (1990), pp. 111–26. For a discussion of a transport planning success story, see Jonathan Bridle. "Integrated Transport Planning: Supply-Chain Success." *Logistics and Transport Focus* 6, no. 5. (June 2004), pp. 50–53.
[18] Examples of transportation routing and scheduling software include CAPS RoutePro (www.CAPS.com) and Descartes Systems Routing & Scheduling (www.Descartes.com).

Transportation Analysis Data Requirements

Transportation analysis requires three types of data: network, pickup or delivery demand, and operating characteristics. The network defines all possible routes and is the backbone of any transportation routing system. In some cases, a network is defined by using street maps of the delivery area. Each intersection is a node, and the streets become links. The network contains the links between each node, the road distance, the transit time, and any special constraints such as weight limits or tolls. A street-level network is very accurate and precise, particularly when there are constraints such as rivers and mountains. The deficiency of a street-level network is the high cost of development and maintenance. The other approach involves plotting customers on a grid and then computing the possible links between customers, using straight-line distance. Latitude and longitude coordinates are often used. While a grid system is less costly to develop and maintain than a street-level network, it is less accurate and does not consider constraints as well. The use of global positioning satellites (**GPS**) has facilitated determination of network locations and possible routes. GPS are also useful to provide delivery drivers with directions.

Demand data defines periodic customer pickup and delivery requirements. For strategic or long-term analyses, demand is specified in terms of average periodic pickups or deliveries per customer. Routes are then created on the basis of the average demand with a capacity allowance for extremely high-demand periods. For tactical routing analysis, demand typically represents customer orders scheduled for delivery during the period being planned, such as daily. Tactical analysis allows the routes to be precisely designed for delivery requirements with no allowance for uncertainty.

Operating characteristics define the number of vehicles, vehicle limitations, driver constraints, and operating costs. Vehicle limitations include capacity and weight restrictions as well as unloading constraints such as dock requirements. Driver constraints include driving time and unloading restrictions. Operating costs include fixed and variable expenses associated with vehicles and drivers.

Transportation analysis for vehicle routing and scheduling is receiving increased interest because of the effectiveness and availability of low-cost software and increasing fuel prices. Many firms involved in day-to-day transportation operations have reduced transportation expenses by 10 to 15 percent through the use of tactical or strategic transportation analysis. As customers continue to demand smaller orders, transportation analysis will become increasingly important to make effective routing, scheduling, and consolidation decisions.

Freight Lane Analysis

One common logistics analysis concerns transportation movements on specific freight lanes. The analysis can be completed on a very specific basis between facilities or on a broader regional basis. Freight lane analysis focuses on the balance of volume between origin and destination points. To maximize vehicle utilization, movements should be balanced, or roughly equal, in both directions. Lanes may include two or more points, as Figure 14.10 illustrates. Triangular freight lanes attempt to coordinate movement between three points by moving combinations of material and finished product between suppliers, manufacturers, and customers.

Freight lane analysis involves both movement volume and the number of shipments or trips between points. The objective is to identify imbalances that offer opportunities for enhanced logistics productivity. Once lane imbalances are identified, management attempts to identify volume that can be transported in the underutilized direction. This might be accomplished by switching carriers or modes, shifting volume to or from a private fleet, increasing back-haul of raw materials, or creating an alliance with another

FIGURE 14.10
Example of
Triangular Freight
Lane

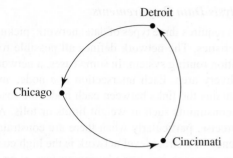

shipper. Conversely, volume in the overutilized direction might be diverted to other carriers or shippers or sourced from an alternative location.

Table 14.6 illustrates a lane analysis that clearly identifies shipment imbalances. The transportation manager should attempt to balance the triangular move by developing additional volume between Cincinnati and Detroit. The volume could be developed either by moving product sources to the Cincinnati area or by creating an alliance with a shipper that moves volume between Cincinnati and Detroit with no back-haul.

Inventory Analysis

Another common logistics analysis focuses on inventory performance and productivity. Typical inventory analysis considers relative product sales volume and inventory turnover and is performed on an ABC basis, as discussed in Chapter 7. For example, by listing the top 10 sales and inventory groupings in decreasing sequence, a logistics manager can quickly determine product groups that have a major influence on volume and inventory levels. As indicated in Chapter 7, 80 percent of sales are typically accounted for by 20 percent of the items. It is also typical that 80 percent of the inventory accounts for only 20 percent of the volume. Knowledge of these characteristics and the items that make up each product group is useful in targeting inventory management efforts. Items that demonstrate a large inventory commitment relative to sales can be selected for intensive management efforts to reduce inventory level and improve performance.

Table 14.7 illustrates a typical inventory analysis report. This example is sorted by item sales, although there is some logic to sequencing the report by decreasing inventory level or inventory turns. Items with relatively high inventories or low turns should be targeted for management attention.

Summary

This chapter provides a comprehensive review of the logistics planning process, decisions, and techniques. It is designed to guide the logistics manager through the overall process of situation analysis, alternative identification, data collection, quantitative evaluation, and development of viable recommendations.

TABLE 14.6
Freight Lane
Analysis of Monthly
Movements

Origin	Destination	Weight (CWT)	Shipments
Detroit	Chicago	8740	23
Chicago	Cincinnati	5100	17
Cincinnati	Detroit	2000	8

TABLE 14.7 Typical Inventory Analysis Report

Product	Total Unit Demand	Standard Cost	Sales at Standard Cost	Percent Sales	Cumulative Sales Percent	Total Inventory	Inventory at Standard Cost	Percent Inventory	Cumulative Inventory Percent	Item	Cumulative Items	Inventory Turns	Class
Part A	3,487	423.76	1,477,656.03	14.35	14.35	453	191,931,32	16.58	16.58	1	4.00	7.70	A
Part B	31,347	43.82	1,373,573.25	13.34	27.68	1,938	84,909.82	7.33	23.91	1	8.00	16.18	A
Part C	21,221	47.49	1,007,770.10	9.79	37.47	1,652	78,447.73	6.78	30.69	1	12.00	12.85	A
Part D	15,077	52.82	796,319.01	7.73	45.20	1,489	78,669.62	6.79	37.48	1	16.00	10.12	A
Part E	14,956	35.22	526,774.13	5.11	50.32	1,767	62,241.97	5.38	42.86	1	20.00	8.46	A
Part F	5,826	80.93	471,481.17	4.58	54.89	272	22,041.74	1.90	44.76	1	24.00	21.39	A
Part G	57,304	8.16	467,868.82	4.54	59.44	3,630	29,637.63	2.56	47.32	1	28.00	15.79	A
Part H	3,591	74.64	267,986.82	2.60	62.04	379	28,303.30	2.44	49.76	1	32.00	9.47	A
Part I	8,139	32.46	264,225.47	2.57	64.60	1,467	47,640.20	4.11	53.88	1	36.00	5.55	A
Part J	19,036	13.50	257,079.87	2.50	67.10	453	6,114.31	0.53	54.41	1	40.00	42.05	A
Part K	8,169	31.38	256,344.63	2.49	69.59	153	4,806.26	0.42	54.82	1	44.00	53.34	A
Part L	33,457	7.60	254,277.51	2.47	72.06	9,022	68,572.76	5.92	60.74	1	48.00	3.71	A
Part M	6,609	38.32	253,245.67	2.46	74.52	1,655	63,401.31	5.48	66.22	1	52.00	3.99	A
Part N	29,394	8.61	252,950.09	2.46	76.97	3,391	29,177.21	2.52	68.74	1	56.00	8.67	A
Part O	17,296	14.45	249,861.10	2.43	79.40	1,414	20,420.37	1.76	70.50	1	60.00	12.24	A
Part P	3,089	76.08	235,029.27	2.28	81.68	921	70,039.66	6.05	76.55	1	64.00	3.36	B
Part Q	1,579	144.08	227,520.08	2.21	83.89	340	48,916.42	4.22	80.78	1	68.00	4.65	B
Part R	6,577	34.41	226,278.06	2.20	86.09	440	15,155.23	1.31	82.09	1	72.00	14.93	B
Part S	6,326	35.02	221,551.81	2.15	88.24	201	7,032.45	0.61	82.69	1	76.00	31.50	B
Part T	5,041	43.11	217,344.77	2.11	90.35	970	41,808.09	3.61	86.30	1	80.00	5.20	B
Part U	8,906	23.74	211,432.08	2.05	92.40	1,473	34,960.94	3.02	89.32	1	84.00	6.05	B
Part V	2,106	99.55	209,613.04	2.04	94.44	314	31,234.67	2.70	92.02	1	88.00	6.71	B
Part W	10,097	19.73	199,176.93	1.93	96.37	705	13,897.74	1.20	93.22	1	92.00	14.33	C
Part X	10,031	19.85	199,145.62	1.93	98.31	2,489	49,412.08	4.27	97.49	1	96.00	4.03	C
Part Y	34,529	5.05	174,510.19	1.69	100.00	5,753	29,077.41	2.51	100.00	1	100.00	6.00	C
TOTAL	363,189		10,299.016	100.00%	100.00%	42,740	1,157,850	100.00	100.00%	25		8.89	

The methodology, which is generic enough for most logistics problem solving, includes three phases: problem definition and planning, data collection and analysis, and recommendations and implementation. The problem definition and planning phase is concerned with the feasibility assessment and project planning. Feasibility assessment includes situation analysis, supporting logic development, and cost/benefit estimation. Project planning requires statements of objectives, constraints, measurement standard, analysis technique specification, and project work plan development.

The data collection and analysis phase develops assumptions, collects data, and completes the quantitative and qualitative analyses. Assumptions development and data collection include tasks to define the analysis approach, formalize assumptions, identify data sources, and collect and validate data. The analysis step involves definition of analysis questions, completion of validation and baseline analyses, and completion of alternative and sensitivity analyses.

The recommendations and implementation phase develops the final plan. The recommendation development step includes identification and evaluation of the best alternatives. The implementation step defines a recommended course of action, schedules development, defines acceptance criteria, and schedules final implementation.

Regular supply chain design analysis is becoming increasingly critical to respond to changes in global material availability, market demands, and production resource availability. In response to this requirement, supply chain design optimization tools are becoming more widely available to support strategic and tactical analyses. More tactical tools such as dynamic simulation and routing and scheduling algorithms can be used to investigate and evaluate inventory and transportation alternatives. The importance of such comprehensive planning and analysis methods and tools is growing as a result of the possible alternatives to and complexity of global supply chains. Ad hoc tactical analyses such as freight lane balancing and ABC inventory analysis must be completed regularly to respond to changes in transportation rates, flows, and product demands.

Challenge Questions

1. What is the basic objective in a logistics design and analysis study? Is it normally a one-time activity?

2. What is sensitivity analysis, and what is its role in systems design and analysis?

3. Why is it important to develop supporting logic to guide the logistical planning process?

4. Both internal and external review assessments must consider a number of measures. What are they and why are they important?

5. Why is a cost/benefit evaluation important to logistical systems design efforts?

6. What is the key objective in freight lane analysis?

7. In a general sense, what are the essential differences between analytic and simulation techniques?

8. What is the main advantage of the typical optimization technique in comparison to simulation?

9. At what point in the typical analysis does the technique give way to the managerial review and evaluation process?

10. Compare and contrast strategic and tactical transportation decisions.

PART FOUR

Administration

This final part deals with the second primary responsibility of a firm's logistical management—administration. Chapter 15 develops principles of organization and relationship management that are essential for realizing integrated operations. Alternative collaborative models are developed and illustrated as a means to facilitate cooperation among customers, material suppliers, service suppliers, and the enterprise orchestrating the supply chain arrangement. Attention is also directed to cross-organizational change management and concepts of human resource organization. The ubiquitous nature of logistical operations creates a unique organizational structure challenge. The dispersion of logistical operations across vast geographical areas serves to place special attention on developing effective management and control processes. Chapter 16 shifts focus to performance assessment and the development of cost measurement to support activity-based management. Particular attention is directed to the development of logistics and supply chain performance metrics. Chapter 17 describes administrative responsibility regarding firm risk management. It specifically focuses on the dimensions of complexity, regulations, resource availability, and security.

CHAPTER FIFTEEN

Relationship Development and Management

Chapter Outline

Among the topics of logistics, few hold more managerial interest than developing and managing organizational relationships. For most of business history, emphasis was devoted to relationships internal to an organization, developing an appropriate organizational structure to efficiently and effectively perform the work of logistics. Additionally, attention today is being devoted to the integration of logistics with other functions in the organization, especially marketing, operations, and procurement. However, the information revolution and the focus on supply chain integration are forcing logistics executives to rethink nearly every aspect of traditional organizational logic and to extend their thinking to relationships with suppliers and customers. In fact, the essence of supply chain management lies in the ability to orchestrate collaborative relationships both internally and with supply chain partners.

Development and Management of Internal Logistics Relationships

Prior to the 1950s, functions now accepted as logistics were generally viewed as facilitating or support work. Organization responsibility for logistics was typically dispersed throughout the firm. Figure 15.1 is a hypothetical organization chart that depicts the fragmentation that was typical at that time. This fragmentation often meant that aspects of logistical work were performed without coordination, often resulting in duplication and waste. Information was frequently distorted or delayed, and lines

FIGURE 15.1
Traditional Organization of Logistically Related Functions

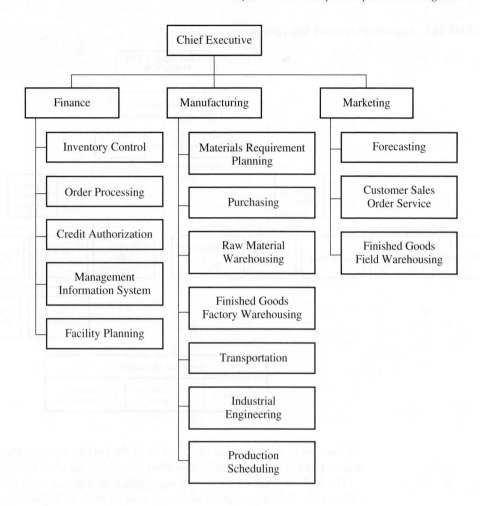

of authority and responsibility were typically blurred. Managers, recognizing the need for total cost control, began to reorganize and combine logistics functions into a single managerial group. Structuring logistics as an integrated organization first appeared in the 1950s.[1]

Functional Aggregation

The motivation driving functional aggregation was a growing belief that grouping logistics functions into a single organization would increase the likelihood of integration and facilitate improved understanding of how decisions and procedures in one operational area impact performance in other areas. The belief was that eventually all functions would begin to work as a single group focused on total system performance. This integration paradigm, based on organizational proximity, prevailed throughout a 35-year period. Many different types and levels of functional integration appeared during this time. For many firms, the

[1] For early articles discussing this initial integration of logistics activities, see Donald J. Bowersox, "Emerging Patterns of Physical Distribution Organization," *Transportation and Distribution Management,* May 1968, pp. 53–59; John F. Stolle, "How to Manage Physical Distribution," *Harvard Business Review,* July/August 1967, pp. 93–100; and Robert E. Weigand, "The Management of Physical Distribution: A Dilemma," *Michigan State University Business Topics,* Summer 1962, pp. 67–72.

FIGURE 15.2 Logistics Functional Aggregation

ink had barely dried on what appeared to be the perfect logistics organization when new and far more pervasive rethinking of what constituted the ideal structure emerged.[2]

The highest level of functional aggregation in logistics organization is depicted in Figure 15.2. This organization structure seeks to unify all logistical functions and operations under a single senior manager. Organizations having the comprehensive nature illustrated in Figure 15.2 were and continue to be rare. However, the trend was clearly to group as many logistical planning and operational functions as practical under single authority and responsibility. The goal was the strategic management of all materials and finished product movement and storage to the maximum benefit of the enterprise.

The rapid development of logistical information systems provided an impetus for functionally integrated organizations. Information technology became available to plan and operate systems that fully integrated logistical operations. Several aspects of the structure presented in Figure 15.2 justify further discussion.

[2] For a review of empirical research related to logistics organization evolution, see A. T. Kearney, *Measuring Productivity in Physical Distribution: The $40 Billion Gold Mine* (Oak Brook, IL: Council of Logistics Management, 1978); A. T. Kearney, "Organizing Physical Distribution to Improve Bottom Line Results," *Annual Proceedings of the Council of Logistics Management,* 1981, pp. 1–14; A. T. Kearney, *Measuring and Improving Productivity in the Logistics Process: Achieving Customer Satisfaction Breakthroughs* (Oak Brook, IL: Council of Logistics Management, 1991). A. T. Kearney completed and published studies in Europe, Asia, and North America in 1993. These studies were distributed by Kearney in captive publications. For a review of Michigan State University research on logistics organization and best practice, see Donald J. Bowersox et al., *Leading Edge Logistics: Competitive Positioning for the 1990s* (Oak Brook, IL: Council of Logistics Management, 1989); Donald J. Bowersox et al., *Logistical Excellence: It's Not Business as Usual* (Burlington, MA: Digital Press, 1992); The Global Logistics Research Team at Michigan State University, *World Class Logistics: The Challenge of Managing Continuous Change* (Oak Brook, IL.: Council of Logistics Management, 1995); Donald J. Bowersox, David J. Closs, and Theodore P. Stank, *21st Century Logistics: Making Supply Chain Integration a Reality* (Oak Brook, IL: Council of Logistics Management, 1999).

First, each area of logistics—purchasing, manufacturing support, and customer accommodation—is structured as a separate line operation. The lines of authority and responsibility directly enable each bundle of supportive services to be performed as part of an overall integrated logistical effort. Since areas of operation responsibility are well defined, it is possible to establish manufacturing support as an operation unit similar to purchasing and customer accommodation. Because each unit is operationally self-sufficient, each can maintain the flexibility to accommodate critical services required by its respective operational area. In addition, since overall logistical activities can be planned and coordinated on an integrated basis, operational synergies between areas can be exploited.

Second, five capabilities grouped under logistical support are positioned as operational services. This shared service orientation is the mechanism to integrate logistical operations. It is important to stress that logistical support is not a staff organization. Rather, the group manages day-to-day logistics work, which is structured with matrix accountability for direct liaison between customer accommodation, manufacturing support, and purchasing operations.

Third, logistical resource planning embraces the full potential of management information to plan and coordinate operations. Order processing triggers the logistical system into operation and generates the integrated database required for control. Logistical resource planning facilitates integration. Logistical resource plans are based on product/market forecasting, order processing, and inventory status to determine overall requirements for any planning period. On the basis of identified requirements, the planning unit operationalizes manufacturing by coordinating production scheduling, capacity planning, and materials requirement planning.

Finally, overall planning and controllership exist at the highest level of the organization. These initiatives serve to facilitate integration. The planning group is concerned with long-range strategic positioning and is responsible for logistical system quality improvement and reengineering. The logistical controller is concerned with measurement of cost and customer service performance and provision of information for managerial decision making. The development of procedures for logistical controllership is one of the most critical areas of integrated logistical administration. The need for accurate measurement is a direct result of increased emphasis placed on continuous improvement in customer service performance.[3] The measurement task is extremely important because of the large operating and capital dollar expenditures involved in logistics.

The functionally integrated logistical organization offers a single logic to guide the efficient application of financial and human resources from material sourcing to final product customer delivery. It therefore positions a firm to manage trade-offs among purchasing, manufacturing support, and customer accommodation.

A Shift in Emphasis from Function to Process

Almost overnight, the emphasis shifted from function to process. Firms began to examine the role logistical competency could play in the overall process of creating customer value. This ushered in new thinking regarding how to best achieve integrated logistical performance. To a significant degree, the focus on process reduced the pressure to aggregate functions into all-encompassing organizational units. The critical question became not how to organize individual functions, but rather how to overcome barriers to integration and best manage the overall logistical process.

[3] Performance measurement is discussed in greater detail in Chapter 16.

Process Integration Barriers

Managers do not attempt to integrate operations in a vacuum. It is important to recognize barriers that serve to inhibit process integration. Barriers to internal integration find their origins in traditional functional practices related to organization, measurement and reward systems, inventory leverage, infocratic structure, and knowledge hoarding.

The organization structure of a business can serve to stifle cross-functional processes. Most business organizations seek to align authority and responsibility on the basis of functional work. In essence, both structure and financial budget closely follow work responsibility. The traditional practice has been to group all persons involved in performing specific work into departments such as purchasing, manufacturing, and logistics. Each of these organizations has an operational responsibility, which is reflected in its functional goals. The traditional managerial belief was that functional excellence would automatically equate to superior performance. In integrated process management, it matters little how much is spent to perform a specific function as long as process performance goals are achieved at the lowest total cost expenditure. Successful integration of processes requires that managers look beyond their organizational structure and achieve cross-functional integration. This may or may not require organizational change. Regardless, successful process integration requires significant traditional management behavioral modification.

Traditional measurement and reward systems also serve to make cross-functional coordination difficult. Measurement systems typically mirror organization structure. Most reward systems are based on functional achievement. To facilitate internal process integration, new measures, increasingly called **balanced scorecards,** must be developed. Managers must be encouraged to view specific functions as contributing to a process rather than their stand-alone performance. A function may, at times, have to absorb increased costs for the sake of achieving lower total process cost. Unless a measurement and reward system is in place that does not penalize managers who absorb cost, integration will remain more theory than practice.

Inventory can also serve as a barrier to process integration because it is a proven fact that inventory can be leveraged to facilitate functional performance. The traditional position is to maintain sufficient inventory to protect against demand and operational uncertainty. Stockpiling both materials and finished inventory leverages maximum manufacturing economy of scale. Such economy of scale can result in low per unit cost of manufacturing. Forward commitment of inventory to local markets can leverage sales. While such practices create benefits, they may be achieved at a cost, which is not typically allocated to that function. The integrative challenge is the cost/benefit balance of such leveraging and risks associated with potential inventory obsolescence.

While information technology is a key enabler of process integration, a significant problem results from the fact that structure and availability of information have traditionally been based on functional organization relationships. As a result, information is typically formatted in terms of functional requirements and accountability. This early practice in formatting information has developed what is referred to as infocratic structure. The content and flow of available information follows long-standing functional organization lines of command and control. When managers attempt to reorganize to enable cross-functional processes, the infocratic structure serves as an invisible force to retain traditional functional information flows. The impact of infocratic structure is one of the driving reasons why Enterprise Resource Planning **(ERP)** systems have great general management appeal. The infocratic structure also helps explain why ERP implementations are so difficult.

In most business situations, knowledge is power, so unwillingness to share and a general lack of understanding regarding how to share knowledge are not uncommon. By enforcing functional specialization and by developing a workforce composed of experts, organizations inherently doom process integration. Consider, for example, the case when an experienced employee retires or for some other reason departs a firm. Replacement personnel must be given sufficient time to learn, but if information is restricted, all the time in the world may not help bring the new employee up to speed. A more serious situation occurs when managers fail or are unable to develop procedures and systems for transferring cross-functional knowledge. Much process work is shared between jobs and is not restricted to a specific functional area, so transfer of knowledge and experience is vital.

The Great Divide

Clearly many obstacles make functional integration difficult. To some extent, the five barriers discussed above have contributed to a common situation in business referred to as the **great divide.** The great divide reflects an organizational condition wherein achieved integration is partial but not complete on an end-to-end basis, as illustrated in Figure 15.3. The most common situation is when a firm achieves only partial integration of distribution/marketing on the outbound side of the enterprise and procurement/manufacturing on the inbound side. The paradox is that firms seem to be capable of achieving highly integrated operations with suppliers from whom they purchase materials and components. Firms also join operations in customer accommodation to service customers. Such initiatives reflect cross-functional integration that, in fact, extends beyond a single business enterprise. Despite these accomplishments, managers report considerable difficulty in linking these two types of external collaboration into an enterprisewide integrative process. In short, managers seem to achieve more successful integration with external business partners than they do with managers and departments within their own firm.[4] Sales and operations planning **(S&OP)**, discussed in Chapter 6, represents one mechanism to achieve this needed internal integration.

The phenomenon of the great divide is interesting and challenging. The fact that such operational discontinuity is common among firms in many different industries supports generalization. First, integration appears to be easier with groups external to a firm, such as suppliers and customers, at least in part because the balance of power is typically clear and integrative objectives such as sales and costs can be quantified. Second, senior managers in most organizations do not have a sufficiently clear vision of internal process requirements and related measures to drive across-the-enterprise integration. Finally, the barriers outlined earlier serve to render end-to-end integration a difficult-to-achieve end state in most organizations.

Most observers of current logistics practice feel significant inroads into improved process performance are being realized as a result of modifying and repositioning functional capabilities. The key is to align, focus, and measure functional performance in terms of process contribution. The goal is to close the great divide by achieving a single strategy, facilitated by well-defined processes, relevant measurement, common forecasting and planning, and a supportive reward system.

[4] Donald J. Bowersox, David J. Closs, and Theodore P. Stank, *21st Century Logistics: Making Supply Chain Integration a Reality* (Oak Brook, IL: Council of Logistics Management, 1999).

FIGURE 15.3 **The Great Divide: The Challenge of Managing across Functional Boundaries**

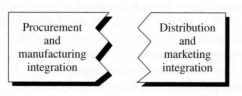

Procurement and manufacturing integration

Distribution and marketing integration

FIGURE 15.4
Process Organization

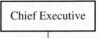

	Chief Executive

Process owner: Demand planning	Process team: Marketing, sales, logistics, manufacturing, finance, information technology
Process owner: Customer relationship management	Process team: Marketing, sales, logistics, information technology
Process owner: Order fulfillment/service delivery	Process team: Sales, order processing, logistics, customer service, accounting
Process owner: Product/service development launch	Process team: New product development, marketing, procurement, manufacturing, logistics
Process owner: Manufacturing customization	Process team: Procurement, manufacturing, logistics
Process owner: Supplier relationship collaboration	Process team: Procurement, manufacturing, information technology
Process owner: Life cycle support	Process team: Procurement, logistics, customer service, finance
Process owner: Reverse logistics	Process team: Logistics, customer service

Process Structure

Figure 15.4 illustrates how the process-oriented organization might be structured around the eight supply chain processes discussed in Chapter 1. Each key process is led by a process owner who manages a team of members drawn from the critical functional areas that impact process performance.

The concept of process organization is envisioned as the result of three factors: (1) the development of a highly involved work environment with self-directed work teams as a vehicle to empower employees to generate maximum performance; (2) improved productivity that results from managing processes rather than functions, a notion that has always rested at the core of integrated logistics; and (3) the rapid sharing of accurate information that allows all facets of the organization to be integrated. Information technology is viewed as the load-bearing structure of the new enterprise, replacing organizational hierarchy.

The essence of the argument for this radical restructuring is that the traditional concept of organization change through functional aggregation is not sufficient to stimulate major breakthroughs in service or productivity. Rather, traditional organization change shifts or realigns functions without serious redesign of the basic work process. Because such restructuring typically assumes that functional organizations will continue to perform basic work, little or no difference in actual practice results. In essence, companies are refocusing old business practices rather than designing new, more efficient processes.

The challenges of managing these processes are threefold. First, all effort must be focused on value added to the customer. An activity exists and is justified only to the extent it contributes customer value. Therefore, a commitment must be motivated by a belief that customers desire a specific activity to be performed. Logistical managers must develop the capacity to think externally. Second, integrating logistics as part of a process requires that all skills necessary to complete the work be available regardless of their functional organization. Organizational grouping on the basis of selected function can artificially separate natural work flows and create bottlenecks. When horizontal structures are put in place, critical skills need to be positioned and made accessible to assure that required work is accomplished. Finally, work performed in a process context should stimulate synergism. With systems integration, the design of work as a process means that overall organizational trade-offs are structured to achieve maximum performance for minimum input investment.

The radical changes proposed by a shift from a functional to a process orientation have mixed messages for managers involved in logistics. On the positive side, general adoption of a process orientation builds upon the basic principles of systems integration. At the core of integrated logistics is a commitment to functional excellence that contributes to process performance. A general shift to managing logistics as a process means that it will be positioned as a central contributor to all initiatives that focus on new product development and customer order generation, fulfillment, and delivery. The overall trend of process integration expands the operational potential and impact of logistics.

Less clear is a full understanding of how processes themselves will be performed and managed. The most advanced logistical solutions observed during the past decade have combined organization form and best-practice performance to manage the overall logistics process using a modified hierarchical structure. The concept of matrix organization has emerged as a common structure to facilitate horizontal management. The availability of superior information to operationalize a matrix approach relaxes dependence on a rigid formal organization structure. In terms of architecture for a logistical organization, the critical questions are: (1) How much formal hierarchical structure can and should be retained in seeking to enable and encourage a process orientation? (2) How can an organization be structured so that it can manage a process as complex as global logistics without becoming overly bureaucratic? To address these questions, managers need to fully understand the potential of virtual organization, which advocates information-driven logistical networks that integrate across organization boundaries.

Virtuality and Organization Transparency

It is highly unlikely that the attention being given to process will end management's quest for ideal logistical organization. While several different scenarios concerning the organization of the future are technologically feasible, one of the most intriguing is speculation that formal hierarchical command and control organization structure will be replaced with an informal electronic network often referred to as a **virtual organization.**[5] The adjective **virtual** implies underlying existence without formal recognition.[6] In other words, a virtual organization, whether it is a total enterprise or a specific core competency, would exist as a provider of integrated performance but not as an identifiable unit of formal organization structure. In the case of logistics, key work teams may be electronically linked to perform critical activities in an integrated fashion. These work teams could be transparent in

[5] For more detail and examples of virtual organizations, see Nicholas G. Carr, "Being Virtual: Character and The New Economy," *Harvard Business Review,* May/June 1999, pp. 181–86; and Kevin P. Gayne and Renee Dye, "The Competitive Dynamics of Network-Based Businesses," *Harvard Business Review,* January/February 1998, pp. 99–109.
[6] Webster's dictionary defines *virtual* as "being such in essence or effect though not formally recognized or admitted."

terms of the formal organization structure of their membership; that is, formal organization charts may not be related to actual work flow. In fact, logistics organizations of the future could be characterized by functional disaggregation throughout the organization to focus on work flow rather than structure.

The concepts of virtuality and transparency have far-reaching implications for long-standing organizational concepts such as centralization and decentralization. To meet customer requirements for speed and response, authority would need to be pushed down the organization. Strategic direction would be expected to originate at headquarters. Operational adaptations would increasingly be made on the front lines. Frontline managers would be increasingly expected to refine strategy and apply it directly to operations. Centralization and decentralization would increasingly become meaningless terms. Organizations of the future would seek to capture the best of centralization and decentralization without commitment to either concept.[7]

The idea behind disaggregation is that the power of information technology would facilitate integrated management and performance of logistics work without grouping or aggregating functions into a formal organization unit. The responsibility for performing logistics work should ideally be organizationally positioned with users. The user, in this sense, is the organization that requires transportation, warehousing, inventory, or any other logistics service to complete its mission. Making those who perform the logistical services an integral part of the user organization has potential to increase relevancy and flexibility. In essence, ultimate empowerment would result. Each organization throughout an enterprise would perform its required logistical services. The disintegration paradigm is based on the belief that logistical functionality need not be organizationally assigned to a special command and control structure to efficiently and effectively coordinate performance.

There are many arguments counter to functional disaggregation. First and foremost is the possibility that disaggregation would create a danger of reverting to a functional fixation or myopia characteristic of fragmented logistics. A second concern is that critical scale and scope in logistical operations would be lost and result in diseconomies. Finally, standardization and simplification of work could decrease if similar types of work are spread throughout user organizations without formal feedback mechanisms.

While the above arguments are not exhaustive, they are characteristic of the concerns managers have about abandoning formal integrated organizations. The key to improved performance is the realization that relevancy and flexibility may be increased by creating an electronic network to facilitate logistical coordination as contrasted to reliance on formal organization structuring. Actually, adequate information technology to facilitate integration did not exist when the paradigm of functional organization grouping was first embraced.

The jury is out concerning if and when the functionally disaggregated information-coordinated network will become a realistic logistics organization solution. Research on best practice indicates that some firms are at the initial stages of linking disparate work electronically rather than physically or organizationally.[8]

Leading Organization Change

A final topic of concern to logistics managers is how to lead change. It is one thing to decide what should be done. It is an entirely different thing to get it done. Once again, logistics managers cannot expect to find a blueprint to guide them. As a general rule, they are involved in three primary types of change.

[7] Donald J. Bowersox et al., *Logistical Excellence: It's Not Business as Usual* (Burlington, MA: Digital Press, 1992), pp. 173–74.
[8] For a comprehensive discussion of research regarding virtual organizations, see Shekhar Sandhya, "Understanding the Virtuality of Virtual Organizations," *Leadership and Organization Development Journal* 20, no. 6 (2006), pp. 465–83.

First, there are issues related to strategic change. Strategic change issues involve the implementation of new and improved ways to service customers. The topic of strategic change management has been dealt with in several different places throughout the text.

The second type of change concerns modifications in a firm's operational structure. On the basis of strategic considerations, logistics executives are constantly engaged in modifying where products are positioned, how customer requirements are handled, and so forth. Such network and operations reengineering represents a great deal of the change that must be managed to keep a firm's capabilities in line with its strategic requirements.

The third type of change concerns human resource structure. As the mission and scope of logistics change, managers have traditionally found it difficult to alter organization structures in a timely manner. Research clearly illustrates that organization change is frequent.

It is critical to avoid a quick-fix mentality. The prevailing command and control organization structure has survived for centuries—it need not all be dismantled overnight. The key is development of a change model that charts a meaningful and believable course of transition. As noted earlier, managers should use caution in trying to accelerate the transition of logistical organization structures. Despite the appeal of changing quickly, real success may be enhanced by proceeding with care.

A final consideration concerning change is an organization's capacity to absorb new and challenging operational practices. While all of the desired change is taking place, the day-to-day business still needs to be run. Though some advocate radical change, it does not appear to fit logistical organizations very well. In the final analysis, the tempo of change a firm can accommodate remains unique to each organization. How much change an organization can absorb requires precise calibration. Typically, it is less than most change managers gauge it to be and actual change takes longer than anticipated.

Development and Management of Supply Chain Relationships

A supply chain perspective shifts the relevant business model from a loosely linked group of independent businesses to a multienterprise coordinated effort focused on supply chain efficiency improvement and increased competitiveness. While not all supply chain collaborative arrangements involve logistics, most do. In such arrangements, attention shifts from firm-based logistical management to the coordination of supply chain performance. Two beliefs facilitate this drive for efficiency and competitiveness.

First, the fundamental belief is that cooperative behavior will reduce risk and greatly improve efficiency of the overall logistical process. To achieve a high degree of cooperation it is necessary for supply chain participants to share strategic information. Such information sharing must not be limited to transaction data. Equally or more important is a willingness to share information concerning future plans so participating firms can jointly develop the best way to satisfy customer requirements. Collaborative information is essential to positioning and coordinating participating firms to jointly do the right things faster and more efficiently.

The second belief is the opportunity to eliminate waste and duplicate effort. As a result of collaboration, substantial inventory deployed in a traditional channel can be eliminated. Supply chain collaboration can also eliminate or reduce risk associated with inventory speculation. The notion of supply chain rationalization is not that inventory is bad and should be totally eliminated; rather, inventory deployment should be driven by economic and service necessities and not tradition and anticipatory practices.

Firms that have increased supply chain competitiveness exhibit several similarities. First, their collaborative practices are technology driven. Second, their business solutions achieve competitive superiority. Finally, most initiatives combine the experience and talents of key supply chain participants blended with a combination of third-party or integrated service providers. At the heart of these firms is a solid commitment to creating and maintaining a unique supply chain culture. Such cultures are forged on a fundamental understanding of risk, power, and leadership.

Risk, Power, and Leadership

Dependency is a primary driver of supply chain solidarity. To the degree that participating enterprises acknowledge mutual dependency, the potential exists to develop collaborative relationships. Dependency drives a willingness to plan functional integration, share key information, and participate in joint operations. The concepts of **risk, power,** and **leadership** are essential to understanding acknowledged dependency and how it makes supply chain integration work.

Risk

Enterprises that participate in supply chain arrangements must acknowledge they have responsibility for performing specific roles. They must also believe that their business will be better off in the long run as a result of collaboration. Each enterprise must be positioned to specialize in an operational area or function based on its unique core competency. The driving force behind supply chain integration is to leverage these core competencies.

As a general rule, a supply chain member whose competency is highly specialized will assume comparatively less risk with respect to overall performance. Conversely, firms that have a great deal at stake will be positioned as the prime facilitators and will confront the most risk in the supply chain arrangement. Firms with unique specialization, more often than not, will participate in multiple supply chains. For example, a wholesaler incurs risk as a result of stocking products for a specific manufacturer. The traditional practice among wholesalers is to hedge such risk by offering customers an assortment of many different manufacturers' products, thereby reducing reliance on any supplier.

In contrast, a manufacturer with a limited product line may be totally captive to a few supply chain arrangements. In essence, the manufacturer may be betting the business that the collaboration will be successful. For manufacturers, commitment to supply chain arrangements can be risky business. The **disproportionate risk** among channel members is of primary importance because it structures dependency relationships and determines how the collaboration will be managed. Some participants have a deeper dependence on supply chain success than others. Therefore, participants with the most risk can be expected to assume active roles and shoulder greater responsibility for facilitating collaboration.

Power

In a practical sense, the prerogative and even the obligation to spearhead collaboration rest with the supply chain participant who enjoys the greatest relative power. In many situations, that participant will also be the firm having the greatest risk. Over the last decade significant power shifts have occurred in business. One of the most significant is the increased power of retailers, which resulted from four somewhat independent developments.

First, the general trend of retail consolidation translated into fewer but more dominant retailers with more extensive market coverage. Second, the proliferation of point-of-sale data, frequent-shopper programs, and credit card use provides retailers with easy access to vital market information. As a result, retailers are positioned to rapidly identify and accommodate consumer trends. Many mass merchants maintain in-store computers and continuous point-of-sale transmission to keep merchandise buyers fully informed of developing market trends. A third factor favoring retailers is the increasing difficulty and high cost manufacturers confront in developing new brands. The fact is that many private-label products owned by retailers have greater market penetration than so-called national brands.[9] For example, the Gap and The Limited almost exclusively distribute private branded merchandise. Finally, as discussed throughout the text, the process of logistical replenishment has shifted toward a response-based posture. The exact timing and sophisticated orchestration of a high-velocity market-paced logistics system are ideally driven from the point of consumer purchase. When consumers purchase products, the final or ultimate value of the supply chain is achieved.

While the above noted forces are a modern reality, not all forces are shifting power forward in the supply chain. Today's scrambled merchandising environments result in products increasingly being cross-channel-distributed to accommodate specific markets that are volatile and rapidly changing. New retail formats, both Internet-based and traditional brick and mortar, are blurring channel arrangements. The result is that manufacturers have a growing range of alternatives for distributing their products.

As a substitute for full reliance on traditional brand power, selected manufacturers have reengineered their operations to become the dominant supplier for selected consumer product or categories. The movement toward category dominance allows manufacturers to offer greater value to their prospective supply chain partners. In addition to superior brands at competitive prices, dominant category position can involve several key operational capabilities that increase a firm's attractiveness as a supply chain participant.

Because both manufacturers and distributors have repositioned traditional operations, the potential exists to leverage collaboration. **As a general rule, powerful firms tend to link together in the development of supply chain arrangements.** For the arrangement to be successful, the dominant parties to the cooperative arrangement need to agree to a leadership model.

Leadership

Just as individual organizations need leaders, so do supply chains. At the present stage of supply chain maturity, no definitive generalization can be made concerning how firms gain leadership responsibility. In many situations, specific firms are thrust into a leadership position purely as a result of their size, economic power, customer patronage, or comprehensive product portfolio. In other arrangements, for less obvious reasons, there is a clear presence of leadership on the part of one enterprise, which is acknowledged in the form of mutual dependency and respect on the part of other participating supply chain members. In other situations leadership appears to gravitate to the firm that initiates the relationship. Regardless of who leads, it has been shown that greater relationship commitment exists in supply chain relationships when leaders exercise power in the form of rewards and expertise. Firms that attempt to lead through coercive practices find that partners are much less committed to the relationship and more likely to seek alternative arrangements.[10]

The Range of Extended Supply Chain Relationships

There are numerous types and forms of interorganizational relationships that tend to be characterized as examples of supply chain integration and collaboration.[11] Figure 15.5 presents a classification framework for these relationships.

---

[9] Janet Grober, "Betting the House on Private Brands," *Stores* 90, no. 2 (2008), p. 26.

[10] X. Zhao, B. Huo, B. B. Flynn, and J. H. Yeung, "The Impact of Power and Relationship Commitment between Manufacturers and Customers in a Supply Chain," *Journal of Operations Management* 26, no. 3. (May 2008), p. 368.

[11] The terminology used to describe types of relations varies widely. For a discussion, see Lloyd Rinehart, James A. Eckert, Robert B. Handfield, Thomas J. Page Jr., and Thomas Atkin, "An Assessment of Supplier Customer Relationships," *Journal of Business Logistics* 25, no. 1 (2004), pp. 25–61.

FIGURE 15.5
Relationship
Classification
Framework

As discussed earlier, the driving force underlying the emergence of collaborative relationships among firms in a supply chain is the recognition of mutual dependence. When a firm acknowledges dependency with its suppliers and/or its customers, the stage is set for collaboration. The degree to which dependence is mutually recognized and acknowledged by all parties in the relationship defines the nature of the resulting relationship.

As seen in Figure 15.5, there are five basic forms of collaboration among supply chain participants. The most elementary of these are contracting and outsourcing. In these relationships, dependency is acknowledged only to a limited extent. Contracting with a supplier or customer introduces a time dimension to traditional buying and selling by framing price, service, and performance expectations over a specified period. A manufacturer may contract with a material or parts supplier to purchase a particular item or items for a specified period at a specified price. In turn, the supplier agrees to deliver the specified item(s) according to negotiated terms and delivery requirements. In outsourcing, the focus shifts from buying or selling a product or material to performing a specific service or activity. Typical outsourced activities range from manufacturing to logistics activities such as transportation or warehousing. It is critical to understand, however, that contracting and outsourcing do not necessarily imply that comprehensive supply chain integration and collaboration take place. The relationships involve a degree of information sharing, primarily operational information, but there is limited joint planning among the firms involved, and there are generally specific periods for rebidding or terminating the relationships. Although firms that outsource functions, or even processes, must maintain cordial relationships with the service suppliers, the service being provided is precisely specified in terms of performance and cost, and the relationship among the firms is clearly based in traditional command-and-control principles, with the buyer as the leader.

In administered relationships, a dominant firm assumes leadership responsibility and seeks collaboration with trading partners and/or service suppliers. In such relationships there is frequently sharing of not only operational information but, to a limited degree, strategic information as well. Additionally, there is limited joint planning, to the extent that independent firms have an understanding that they will be better off if they work together and follow the leader. A distinguishing feature of such relationships is that the expectation is that the relationship will be continuous and there is no specific termination or rebid time frame. However, although the leader must consider all participants' welfare, the relationship is basically governed by command and control based in the leader's power.

Although different terminology may be used, true collaborative relationships among supply chain participants can be described as alliances or, in the extreme, as enterprise extension. The distinguishing feature of these relationships is that they are governed by the participants' desire and willingness to voluntarily work together in an intellectual and operational manner. They voluntarily agree to integration of human, financial, operational, or technical resources to create greater efficiency and greater impact with consumers. Ultimately, through collaboration, participating firms create joint policies and integrate operations. The relationship includes extensive joint planning and is expected to be continuous for at least the intermediate term and potentially the very long term. Enterprise extension represents the extreme of interdependence and information sharing. In such instances, two or more firms willingly integrate to the extent that they essentially can be viewed as a single entity. Alliances and similar arrangements are rapidly increasing in logistics and supply chain management. Some estimates place the growth rate at 25 percent per year and suggest that, for some firms, they account for as much as one-third of revenue.[12] Some examples of such success include the highly publicized WalMart* arrangements with Procter & Gamble, Dell's arrangements with its suppliers, and H.E. Butt's supplier relationships in the food industry.

Supply Chain Integrative Framework[13]

A supply chain integrative framework is required to define the nature of collaboration required in alliances and enterprise extension. Such a framework requires that capabilities and competencies essential to integrating supply chain logistics are identified and implemented. The creation of value related to supply chain integration is best achieved by simultaneous orchestration of the four critical flows shown in Figure 15.6: product/service, market accommodation, information, and cash. In fact, logistics executives view flow coordination as the key to successful alliance performance.[14]

The product/service value flow represents the value-added movement of products and services from the raw material source to the end customers. Product value increases as it flows along the supply chain as a result of physical modification, packaging, market proximity, customization, service support, and related activities that enhance end-consumer desirability of the product.

While the product/service flow generally moves from the resource base to end customers, as noted earlier, supply chain arrangements must also accommodate critical reverse flows such as product recalls, reclamation, and recycling. The market accommodation flow provides a structure to achieve postsales service administration. Market accommodation

FIGURE 15.6
Supply Chain Flows

[12] Jonathon Hughes and Jeff Weiss, "Simple Rules for Making Alliances Work," *Harvard Business Review* 85, no. 11. (November 2007), p. 122.

[13] This section and illustrations are based on Donald J. Bowersox, David J. Closs, and Theodore P. Stank, *21st Century Logistics: Making Supply Chain Integration a Reality,* Council of Supply Chain Management Professionals, Oak Brook, IL, 1999.

[14] Brian Fugate, Fundha Sahin, and John T. Mentzer, "Supply Chain Coordination Mechanisms," *Journal of Business Logistics* 27, no. 2 (2006), pp. 139–62.

also involves information exchange concerning sales patterns and product usage essential for supply chain planning. Examples are product customization requirements, point-of-sale (POS) data, end-customer consumption, and warehouse releases. This information provides supply chain members with channel visibility concerning the timing and location of product consumption. Planning and operations can be better synchronized when all participants share a common understanding of demand and consumption patterns.

The information flow is bidirectional exchange of transactional data, inventory status, and strategic plans between supply chain participants. Typical examples of this aspect of collaboration are forecasts, promotional plans, purchase orders, order acknowledgments, shipping and inventory information, invoices, payments, and replenishment requirements. Information exchange initiates, controls, and records the product/service value flow. Historically paper-based, an increasing amount of the information flow is now being exchanged via EDI and Web-based connectivity.

Cash typically flows in the reverse direction of value-added activities. However, in arrangements involving promotion and rebate, cash flows to facilitate product and service movement. Cash flow velocity and asset utilization are critical to superior supply chain performance.

Naturally, these four flows must occur between firms even when the supply chain is not integrated. However, situations characterized by low coordination and integration between supply chain participants typically result in delay, redundancy, and inefficiency. To facilitate effective and efficient supply chain flows, competencies and their supporting capabilities must be integrated.

Framework Constructs

The supply chain integrative framework illustrated in Figure 15.7 encompasses a broad range of capabilities and competencies. The framework serves to facilitate operations into a supply chain context by integrating basic work, functions, capabilities, and competencies.

A job or basic work, such as order picking or truck driving, is the most visible part of the logistical operations. Jobs are often industry- or firm-specific in content; however, they are usually grouped into organizational units to facilitate control. For example, all the jobs related to warehousing are often grouped. Another common grouping is to organize all jobs related to transport into a transportation department. These functional groupings are significant because they are highly visible elements of an organization. Departments have traditionally been the focal point for financial budgeting, performance measurement, and operational control. Functional work arrangements constitute the drivers of logistical best practice. It is the functions or drivers that combine to create value. The critical shift in operational thinking is to view functional excellence in terms of process performance that enhances *overall* supply chain integration.

To achieve integration, functional value should be focused in terms of universal capabilities. A **capability** is the knowledge and achievement level essential to developing integrated performance. Capabilities relate to why work is being performed as contrasted to a functional perspective concerning how it is performed. The capability reflects the value contribution of the work. Inherent in a capability is the application of integrative principles that allow multiple functions to be synchronized into value-creating competencies. Whereas jobs and functions may be highly relevant to specific industries and work situations, capabilities are universal. Capabilities span the supply chain and are equally applicable to suppliers, manufacturers, wholesalers/distributors, and across the full range of retail formats. Capabilities reflecting best logistics practice are to some degree observable in all firms that participate in a supply chain.

Examples of capabilities include the ability to (1) identify and accommodate the needs of specific customers; (2) work with supply chain partners to achieve integrated

FIGURE 15.7
Supply Chain
Framework

operations; (3) effectively share operating and planning information between supply chain partners; (4) measure and understand overall supply chain performance; and (5) share benefits and risks.

The fusing of capabilities results in universal **competencies.** Table 15.1 details the capabilities related to each of the six integrative competencies grouped in terms of their supply chain context. The operational context includes traditional processes related to procurement, production, and customer accommodation. The planning and control context incorporates information technology and planning systems, as well as measurement competency. The behavioral context relates to how a firm manages internal and external relationships among supply chain entities.

The Operational Context

Operations involve the processes that facilitate order fulfillment and replenishment across the supply chain. To achieve leading performance in an operational context, firms must be customer-focused, must achieve interorganizational coordination, and must excel in functional and process performance.

Customer integration builds on the philosophies and activities that develop intimacy and is the competency that builds lasting competitive advantage. Firms have always paid attention to the needs of customers but only recently have begun to identify and consider their differences in terms of capable operational segmentation. Any firm seeking supply chain integration must also demonstrate strong commitment to the supportive capabilities of segmentation, relevancy, responsiveness, and flexibility.

Internal integration focuses on the joint activities and processes within a firm that coordinate functions related to procurement, manufacture, and customer accommodation. Many firms have attempted to integrate internal functionality but anecdotal and quantitative evidence strongly indicates that the Great Divide still exists in many organizations. The capabilities that support internal integration are cross-functional unification, standardization, simplification, compliance, and structural adaptation.

TABLE 15.1 **Supply Chain Context, Competencies, and Supportive Capabilities**

	Operational Context			Planning and Control Context		Behavioral Context
Competencies	**Customer Integration**	**Internal Integration**	**Material/Service Supplier Integration**	**Technology and Planning Integration**	**Measurement Integration**	**Relationship Integration**
Supportive Capabilities	Segmental focus	Cross-functional unification	Strategic alignment	Information management	Functional assessment	Role specificity
	Relevancy	Standardization	Operational fusion	Internal communication	Activity-based and total cost methodology	Guidelines
	Responsiveness	Simplification	Financial linkage	Connectivity	Comprehensive metrics	Information sharing
	Flexibility	Compliance	Supplier management	Collaborative forecasting and planning	Financial impact	Gain/risk sharing
		Structural adaptation				

Supplier integration focuses on capabilities that create operational linkages with material- and service-providing supply chain partners. While the customer is the overriding focal point or supply chain driver, overall success also will depend on strategic alignment, operational fusion, financial linkage, and supplier management. Competency in supplier integration results from performing the capabilities seamlessly in internal work processes. Firms that desire to excel must blend their operating processes with those of supply partners to meet increasingly broad and demanding customer expectations.

The Planning and Control Context

Operational excellence must be supported by integrated planning and measurement capabilities. This involves joining technology across the supply chain to monitor, control, and facilitate overall supply chain performance.

Planning and control integration concerns the design, application, and coordination of information to enhance purchasing, manufacturing, customer order fulfillment, and resource planning. This competency includes database access to enable sharing of appropriate information among supply chain participants. It also concerns transaction systems to initiate and process replenishment and customer orders. In addition to information management, it is essential that capabilities related to internal communication, connectivity, and collaboration be developed. Collaborative Planning, Forecasting, and Replenishment, discussed in Chapter 6, illustrates this capability.

Measurement integration is the ability to monitor and benchmark functional and process performance, both within the firm and across the supply chain. Because each firm is unique, the collaborative effort must define, operationalize, and monitor standard or common measures. Competency in measurement requires the capabilities of functional assessment and activity-based methodologies, comprehensive metrics, and financial impact assessment.

The Behavioral Context

Effective relationship management is the final competency essential in supply chain engagements. Successful implementation of supply chain strategy rests on the quality of the basic business relationship between partners. In general, managers are far more experienced in competition than they are in collaboration.

Whereas guidelines exist for the development of meaningful and distinctive supply chain relationships, no two situations are identical. No shortcuts or substitutes exist for the detailed commitment necessary to build and develop successful long-term relationships. In dealing with customers, suppliers, and service providers, firms must specify roles, define guidelines, share information, share risk and gains, resolve conflict, and, when necessary, be able to dissolve an unproductive arrangement. The managerial skill sets required for successful supply chain integration require development of an interorganizational culture. This is particularly true since the dynamic environment in which firms compete requires regular review of assumptions, processes, and measures to assure those relationships remain relevant.

Finally, ample evidence suggests that managers must plan for the ultimate dismantling or renovation of supply chains. While some arrangements may encounter a natural death as a result of losing momentum, others may persevere to the point that they no longer embody leading-edge practice. Thus, like most managerial concerns, supply chain integration is a dynamic situation that must be continuously reevaluated.

Initiating Relationships

In an effort to better understand the anatomy of what makes for a successful collaborative relationship, a pioneering research study was completed that involved in-depth interviews with grocery manufacturing firms that are generally recognized as leaders in interorganizational arrangements.[12] The alliances investigated included relationships with material suppliers, logistical service providers, and merchandisers. Guidelines were developed concerning initiating an alliance, implementing an alliance, and maintaining alliance vitality. While the focus was specifically on alliances, the logic can be extended to any successful collaborative relationship.

The alliances studied were typically initiated by the firm that was the customer in the relationship. One potential explanation for this pattern is the exercise of buying power. In a buyer/seller relationship, the seller will often implement reasonable changes at the request of its customer to facilitate interorganizational exchange. Also, when a seller's personnel initially approach a potential customer about forming an alliance, the suggestion does not carry the same weight and impact as when the suggestion is generated within the buying firm's organization.

Some alliances do show some anomalies to this pattern. In some cases the seller actually sparked the initial deal by planting the seed as far as conceptualizing the viability of an alliance. When the customer was ready to form the alliance, it initiated more detailed discussion.

Another critical consideration during the development of a collaborative relationship is the need for the initiating firm to perform an in-depth assessment of its internal practices, policies, and culture. The initiating firm should evaluate its ability to make any necessary internal changes to implement and support a successful relationship.[13] For example, in manufacturer/material supplier alliances, the manufacturers had to examine their ability to redefine the importance of purchase price. Buyers needed a method to incorporate the intangible benefits of an alliance in competitive evaluations. The key for the buyer was the evaluation of total cost of ownership, not strictly purchase price.

Another internal assessment includes the ability to truly empower the key alliance contacts to manage the relationship. For example, manufacturers needed to honestly assess the level of operational and strategic integration they could foster with service suppliers.

[15] This section is adapted from Judith M. Schmitz, Robert Frankel, and David J. Frayer, "ECR Alliances: A Best Practice Model," Joint Industry Project on Efficient Consumer Response, Grocery Manufacturers Association, Washington, DC, 1995.
[16] For an in-depth discussion of internal assessment, see Clifford F. Lynch, *Logistics Outsourcing: A Management Guide* (Oak Brook, IL: Council of Logistics Management, 2000), pp. 37–38.

Integration that generated the type of competitive advantage envisioned at the alliance's initial design, such as increased productivity of rapid response to customer orders, could be achieved only through extensive information sharing. The questions to be addressed concern the level of systems capability, data collection, analysis, performance measurement, and training that was necessary to enable the information to be shared in a timely and accurate manner.

Integration capability also needs to be evaluated if the alliance involves a number of partner plants, warehouses, and/or stores that operate under different conditions, capabilities, or competitive requirements. This is especially important for firms that operate multiple warehouses and/or store locations. A key concern in this situation is the ability for internal units to utilize common operating practices and compatible information systems. The flexibility to adapt to meet specific market-based requirements is important to long-term viability.

Implementing Relationships

The key to a successful implementation is choosing a partner wisely. The partners should have compatible cultures, a common strategic vision, and supportive operating philosophies. It is not necessary that organization cultures be identical. Rather, the strategic intentions and philosophies must be compatible to ensure that core competencies and strengths are complementary.

For example, manufacturers initiated alliances with service suppliers in part to achieve improved warehousing operations, transportation reliability, and/or increased consolidation programs that support their particular strategic competitive advantage in the marketplace. Although the service suppliers are leaders, manufacturers may have a more sophisticated conceptualization and operationalization of quality, performance measurement standards, and expertise. The attraction between the partners is based, to a considerable degree, on the service suppliers' ability and willingness to provide creative, innovative operational and information-based solutions to the manufacturer's problems and on the service suppliers' desire to internalize the quality and performance measurement expertise that are the hallmark of the manufacturer. In this sense, the alliance partners' operating philosophies support and complement each other, in particular by enhancing their common strategic vision of improving systemwide logistics processes.

The alliances should start on a small scale to foster easily achievable successes or early wins. It is important that such early wins be acknowledged to motivate key contacts and build confidence concerning alliance performance. For example, in the manufacturer/ material supplier alliances, starting small meant that investments were not initially made in information technology. Manual communication systems were sufficient and provided the opportunity for key contacts. A critical issue is to implement the alliance in its simplest form and then fine-tune the arrangement with technological sophistication when improvements will add substantial value.

Maintaining Relationships

Long-term continuity is dependent on three key activities: (1) mutual strategic and operational goals, (2) two-way performance measurements, and (3) formal and informal feedback mechanisms.

Strategic and operational goals must be mutually determined when the alliance is implemented. It is perhaps less well understood that these goals must be tracked, reviewed, and updated frequently to gain improvements over the long term. For example, if a manufacturer develops a new product, a mutual goal must be set with customers concerning that product's position, especially its market launch. This goal must include consideration of the merchandiser's critical role in new product introduction and acceptance.

Goals should be translated into specific performance measures that can be continually tracked. The performance measurements used and the measurement frequency should be jointly determined. Also, the measures should be two-way. Oftentimes, performance measures between manufacturers and material suppliers focus specifically on the suppliers' performance attributes, such as on-time delivery and quality. One of the alliances studied developed a joint measure of success—total systems inventory. The manufacturer acknowledged that it was important for both partners to reduce inventory, not just the manufacturer. The measure of total systems inventory includes consideration of both partners to ensure that reductions are real and benefit both parties.

Feedback on performance can be provided through formal and informal methods. Annual reviews are formal assessments of alliance performance. These reviews typically involve top managers and focus primarily on examining and updating strategic goals. Quarterly or monthly reviews are not as formal as annual assessments and usually do not include top managers. They focus on tracking and reviewing strategic goals and operational performance. When used, the reviews enable changes in operating practice to be made to achieve strategic goals and create an avenue for continuous improvement projects to be identified.

Weekly/daily reviews may also occur on an informal basis. These reviews are managed by the key contacts and are intended to solve specific problems and identify potential opportunities for improvement. They are critical to resolving or avoiding conflicts and allow key contacts to develop close working relationships. These informal relationships ultimately result in ever-increasing collaborative behavior.

Developing Trust

It is clear that no real collaboration can exist in supply chain relationships without meaningful trust. While a powerful firm may be able to influence the behavior of a less powerful organization, the change in behavior may be temporary and certainly entered into unwillingly. In fact, while research shows that issues such as technology compatibility, information exchange, and appropriate measurement systems are all key issues to be resolved in collaborative alliances, the human behavior issues related to culture and trust are much more difficult issues to solve.[14] To do so, the complexities of different forms of trust must be understood.

Reliability and Character-Based Trust

It is clear that trust has more than one dimension. While several typologies of trust exist, the most meaningful way to understand trust in supply chain collaboration is to distinguish between reliability-based trust and character-based trust.

Reliability-based trust is grounded in an organization's perception of a potential partner's actual behavior and operating performance. Essentially, it involves a perception that the partner is willing to perform and is capable of performing as promised. If supply chain participants cannot rely on partner performance as promised, all efforts to develop collaborative relationships fail. Simply put, a firm that is perceived as incapable of delivering as promised will also be perceived as being unreliable and therefore unworthy of trust in a relationship.

Character-based trust is based in an organization's culture and philosophy. Essentially, it stems from perceptions that supply chain partners are interested in each other's welfare and will not act without considering the action's impact on the other. When

---

[17] Stanley E. Fawcett, Gregory M. Magnan, and Matthew W. McCarter, "Benefits, Barriers, and Bridges to Effective Supply Chain Management," *Supply Chain Management* 13, no. 1 (2008), p. 35.

this aspect of trust is developed, participants do not feel vulnerable to the actions of one another. Trusting partners believe that each will protect the other's interest. For example, a manufacturer who shares its plans for new product introductions or promotion with a retailer trusts that the retailer will not share that information with a competitive supplier. Likewise, sharing of production schedule information with a supplier of component parts will occur only when a manufacturer has trust that the information will be used appropriately.

It is clear that reliability-based trust is necessary to the formation of collaborative relationships in supply chains, but it is not a sufficient condition. For example, a partner who frequently threatens to punish and consistently follows through with that punishment can be said to have reliability. It is not likely, however, to be trusted in character.

Trust clearly develops over time and repeated interactions among organizations. In particular, character-based trust evolves when partners perceive that each acts fairly and equitably with the others. Notions of character-based trust are especially relevant when one supply chain partner is clearly more powerful than the others are.

Building Trust in Relationships

To build trust first requires that a firm demonstrate reliability in its operations, consistently performing as promised and meeting expectations. As noted above, however, reliability is only one aspect of building trust.

The second key requirement for building trust is full and frank sharing of all information necessary for the effective functioning of the relationship. In fact, information sharing and communication have been stressed throughout the text as the foundation for effective collaboration. Companies that hoard information or fail to disclose vital facts are not likely to be trusted.

Related to information sharing is explanation. Sometimes a company, because of competitive pressures, may be required to undertake actions that its supply chain partners may perceive as threatening. For example, a manufacturer opening new distribution channels might threaten existing retailers. Just such a situation arose when John Deere introduced a second line of lawn tractors and recruited Home Depot and other independent dealers, bypassing its traditional network. In such situations, trust may be maintained through thorough explanation of the rationale and business case that drove such a decision.

In many ways the entire subject of supply chain management is also a discussion of relationship management. The text has focused on issues related to logistical processes in the supply chain and managing these processes across company boundaries. Unique operating relationships among supply chain participants differ significantly in their intensity and extent of real collaboration. Power, leadership, conflict, cooperation, risk, and reward are all critical issues in relationship management. Resolution of these issues, however, ultimately depends upon the development of trust among supply chain participants.

Summary

Logistics is undergoing massive change. New concepts and ideas concerning how the best organizations achieve logistical goals appear daily. The challenge is to sort through the best of time-proven practices and merge them with the most applicable new ideas and concepts.

A careful review of logistics organization development suggests that most advanced firms have evolved through many forms of functional aggregation. The evolution started from a highly fragmented structure in which logistical functions were assigned to a wide variety of different departments. For over four decades firms have been grouping an increasing number of logistical functional responsibilities into single-organization units. The typical format for aggregation was the traditional bureaucratic organization structure. The objective was to aggregate functions in an effort to improve operational integration.

The advent of management focusing on critical processes began to usher in what is referred to as horizontal organizations. Today, leading-edge firms are beginning to experiment with process management as a means for overcoming the divide that exists among internal functions. There is increasing evidence that a new form of organization may be emerging that adopts the use of information technology to implement and manage logistics as a transparent organization structure. While such arrangements remain more conceptual than real, the required information technology is available today. The concept has particular appeal to the management of logistics, which involves substantial challenge in terms of time and geographical scope of operations.

Perhaps the most difficult job of all is managing change in the organization. Whether the change is strategic, involving fundamental new processes, operational, or only in personnel, managers must develop new skills that allow them to implement change without disrupting the focus of the organization.

In addition to managing the internal organization, supply chain executives are intimately involved in managing relationships among organizations. Collaborative relationships provide a mechanism to reduce operating expense, enhance productivity, and meet customer requirements. Successful integration requires cross-organizational programs to facilitate operations, technology and planning, and relationship management. Initiating, implementing, and maintaining relationships with suppliers and customers are highly dependent upon the existence of trust among those firms. While reliability is a critical aspect of trust, ultimate success in relationship management will depend upon evaluation of character as firms make decisions concerning which supply chains they choose to participate in.

Challenge Questions

1. What is the functional aggregation paradigm and why is it important?
2. Discuss the three challenges logistics faces as it manages on a process, rather than a functional, basis. Describe each challenge and give an example of how it may be overcome.
3. How do reward systems serve as barriers to integration?
4. In your own words, describe and illustrate the *great divide*. Do you believe the great divide phenomenon is as widely experienced as the text indicates? Support your position with an illustration.
5. What is a horizontal company and how would this type of company be organized? What are the strengths of this type of organization structure?
6. What creates power in the context of supply chain collaboration? Why do many observers feel power is shifting forward or closer to consumers in many supply chain arrangements?
7. Distinguish among different types of supply chain collaborative arrangements. What drives the differences?
8. Describe the relationship between logistical capabilities and competencies.
9. What are the major considerations in initiating a logistics alliance? In implementation? In maintenance?
10. Distinguish between reliability and character-based trust. Why is character-based trust critical in collaborative relationships?

Operational and Financial Performance Measurement

Chapter Outline

Measurement System Objectives

Operational Assessment

Functional Perspectives

Measuring Customer Accommodation

Determining Appropriate Metrics

Supply Chain Comprehensive Metrics

Benchmarking

Financial Assessment

Cost-Revenue Analysis

Strategic Profit Model

Requirements for Financial Reporting

Summary

Creating competitive advantage through high-performance logistics requires integrated measurement systems. The old adage, "If you don't measure it, you can't manage it," holds true for logistical activities both internal to an organization and externally with supply chain partners. For this reason, a framework for performance assessment must be established.

Measurement System Objectives

Effective measurement systems must be constructed to accomplish the three objectives of monitoring, controlling, and directing logistical operations.

Monitoring is accomplished by the establishment of appropriate metrics to track system performance for reporting to management. For example, typically metrics are developed and data gathered to report basic service performance related to fill rates and on-time deliveries and for logistics costs such as transportation and warehousing. **Controlling** is accomplished by having appropriate standards of performance relative to the established metrics to indicate when the logistics system requires modification or attention. For example, if fill rates fall below standards, logistics managers must identify the causes and make adjustments to bring the process back into compliance. The third objective, **directing,** is related to employee motivation and reward for performance. For example, some companies

FIGURE 16.1
The Balanced Scorecard

Source: Adapted from Robert S. Kaplan and David P. Norton, "The Balanced Scorecard—Measures That Drive Performance," *Harvard Business Review* 70, no. 1 (1992), p. 72.

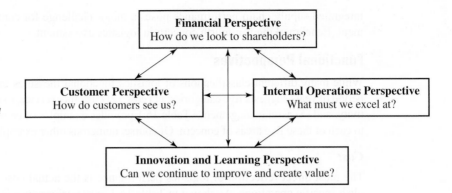

encourage warehouse personnel to achieve high levels of productivity. They must be paid for eight hours of work, on the basis of standard measures of picking or loading. If the tasks are completed in less than eight hours, they may be allowed personal time off.

An overriding objective of superior logistical performance is to improve **shareholder value.** The Balanced Scorecard is a framework for performance measurement developed by Kaplan and Norton.[1] The framework suggests that while improving shareholder value is critical, a comprehensive system for assessing performance must represent a balance between financial and nonfinancial metrics. A balanced scorecard incorporates measures from four different perspectives, as shown in Figure 16.1.

The customer perspective focuses on how customers perceive a company and, therefore, must include customer opinions. In a logistics context, metrics related to this perspective generally include assessment of logistics service, quality, and satisfaction. The internal operations perspective asks what must be done internally and typically incorporates metrics related to process quality (damage rates, errors, etc.) as well as measurement of efficiency and productivity. The innovation and learning perspective is future oriented and focuses on process improvement as well as efforts related to human resources, which are generally considered the driver of improvements in any organization. Benchmarking may also be an aspect of the innovation and learning perspective. Finally, the financial perspective reflects the fact that financial success must be achieved in every organization. Succeeding in the other three perspectives is not adequate if the organization fails to improve profitability and return on investment, thus increasing shareholder value.

It is critical to understand that the balanced scorecard does not offer a specific set of metrics that should be implemented in a company. Specific metrics must be derived from an understanding of the firm's fundamental business strategy. For example, the specific metrics chosen by a firm that has chosen a "low-cost" strategy may be quite different from an organization that follows a "high-service" strategy. The challenge for logistics executives is to define that strategy and select an appropriate balanced set of metrics that guides them in monitoring, controlling, and directing them toward successful implementation.

Operational Assessment

A system for logistics performance assessment first requires a functional perspective. In addition to basic functional performance, improved methods for measurement of customer accommodation are receiving increased attention in many organizations. Measurement of

[1] Robert S. Kaplan and David P. Norton: "The Balanced Scorecard—Measures That Drive Performance," *Harvard Business Review* 70, no. 1 (1992), pp. 71–79.

integrated supply chain performance poses a major challenge for contemporary management. Benchmarking is a fourth concern in logistics assessment.

Functional Perspectives

While many different classifications of logistics functional measures exist, research over a period of years suggests five categories: (1) cost, (2) customer service, (3) quality, (4) productivity, and (5) asset management.[2] Table 16.1 provides examples of common metrics related to each of these five areas of concern. Of course, numerous other examples exist as well.

Cost

The most direct reflection of logistics performance is the actual cost incurred to accomplish specific operations. As shown in Table 16.1, cost performance is typically measured in terms of total dollars spent. Early in the text, the work of integrated logistics was identified as incorporating five interrelated areas: order processing, inventory, transportation, warehousing and materials handling, and facility network.[3] Total logistics cost, sometimes

[2] Donald J. Bowersox et al., *Leading Edge Logistics: Competitive Positioning for the 1990s* (Oak Brook, IL: Council of Logistics Management, 1989); World Class Logistics Research Team at Michigan State University, *World Class Logistics: The Challenge of Managing Continuous Change* (Oak Brook, IL: Council of Logistics Management, 1995); Donald J. Bowersox, David J. Closs, and Theodore P. Stank, *21st Century Logistics: Making Supply Chain Integration a Reality* (Oak Brook, IL: Council of Logistics Management, 1999).
[3] See Chapter 2, p. 26.

TABLE 16.1   Typical Performance Metrics

Cost Management	Customer Service	Quality	Productivity	Asset Management
Total cost	Fill rate	Damage frequency	Units shipped per employee	Inventory turns
Cost per unit	Stockouts	Order entry accuracy	Units per labor dollar	Inventory levels, number of days of supply
Cost as a percentage of sales	Shipping errors	Picking/shipping accuracy	Orders per sales representative	Obsolete inventory
Inbound freight	On-time delivery	Document/invoicing accuracy	Comparison to historical standard	Return on net assets
Outbound freight	Back orders	Information availability	Goal programs	Return on investment
Administrative	Cycle time	Information accuracy	Productivity index	Inventory classification (ABC)
Warehouse order processing	Delivery consistency	Number of credit claims	Equipment downtime	Economic value-added (EVA)
Direct labor	Response time to inquiries	Number of customer returns	Order entry productivity	
Comparison of actual versus budget	Response accuracy		Warehouse labor productivity	
Cost trend analysis	Complete orders		Transportation labor productivity	
Direct product profitability	Customer complaints			
Customer segment profitability	Sales force complaints			
Inventory carrying	Overall reliability			
Cost of returned goods	Overall satisfaction			
Cost of damage				
Cost of service failures				
Cost of back order				

referred to as total landed cost, is the sum of costs related to performance and administration of each of these areas of work Unfortunately, recent research suggests that few organizations have the ability to actually capture the information required to measure total cost. This occurs because different organizations may have different orientations toward which of the areas identified above actually constitute integrated logistics, or because of the lack of readily available data.[4] Nevertheless, at senior management levels of responsibility this total cost should be monitored closely. It is also important to monitor cost data for each of the individual functions so that appropriate diagnosis and control can take place. The functional cost data may be further fine-tuned and measured for individual activities such as order picking and order loading in the warehouse function.

It is also common to monitor and report cost data as a percentage of sales or as a cost per unit of volume. For example, transportation cost is frequently expensed as a percentage of dollar sales volume and as the number of dollars spent per order delivered. Warehouse cost may also be reported as a percentage of sales and cost of individual activities reported such as the picking cost per item or loading cost per order. Such measures, when compared to historical levels or performance standards, provide critical information regarding the potential need to take corrective action. When considering the number of different specific logistics activities, ranging from entering an order to picking an item to unloading a delivery vehicle, and the number of different ways in which volume can be measured, ranging from sales dollars to number of orders to pounds of product, a rather lengthy list of possible cost metrics could be generated. The key is for logistics executives to identify the most appropriate metrics for their organization and consistently apply them over time to control and direct the activities.

Table 16.1 also shows other measures that require measurement of logistics cost, such as direct product profitability, customer profitability, and cost of service failures. In fact, most firms recognize the importance of these measures but currently lack the information necessary to accurately assess these costs. Accurate measurement in these critical dimensions requires a level of sophistication in accounting data that has just recently become available. Activity-based costing is discussed later in this chapter as a means to more accurately assess the cost related directly to customers and products.

Customer Service

In Chapter 3, the elements of basic customer service were identified as availability, operational performance, and service reliability. An effective basic service platform requires specific metrics for assessing performance in each dimension.

Availability is typically reflected by an organization's fill rate. It is critical to note, however, that fill rate may be measured in a variety of ways:

$$\text{Item fill rate} = \frac{\text{Number of items delivered to customers}}{\text{Number of items ordered by customers}}$$

$$\text{Line fill rate} = \frac{\text{Number of purchase order lines delivered complete to customers}}{\text{Number of purchase order lines ordered by customers}}$$

$$\text{Value fill rate} = \frac{\text{Total dollar value delivered to customers}}{\text{Total dollar value of customer orders}}$$

$$\text{Order fill rate} = \frac{\text{Number of orders delivered complete}}{\text{Number of customer orders}}$$

Clearly, the order fill rate, also known as orders shipped complete, is the most stringent measure of a firm's performance relative to product availability. In this metric, an order

---

[4] SC Digest Editorial Staff, "Getting to Accurate Total Landed Costs," *Supply Chain Digest,* June 9, 2008, pp. 1–4.

that is missing only one item on one line is considered to be incomplete. It is also common for companies to track specifically the number of stockouts encountered and number of back orders generated during a time period as indicators of availability.

Operational performance deals with time and is typically measured by average order cycle time, consistency of order cycle time, and/or on-time deliveries. **Average order cycle time** is typically computed as the average number of days, or other units of time, elapsed between order receipt and delivery to customers. **Order cycle consistency** is measured over a large number of order cycles and compares actual with planned performance. For example, suppose average order cycle time is five days. If 20 percent were completed in two days and 30 percent in eight days, there is great inconsistency around the average. In situations where delivery dates or times are specified by customers, the most stringent measure of order cycle capability is **on-time delivery,** the percentage of times the customer's delivery requirements are actually met.

Quality

Performance relative to service reliability is generally reflected in an organization's measurement of logistics quality. As Table 16.1 shows, many of the quality metrics are designed to monitor the effectiveness of individual activities, while others are focused on the overall logistics function. Accuracy of work performance in such activities as order entry, warehouse picking, and document preparation is typically tracked by computing the ratio of the total number of times the activity is performed correctly to the total number of times it is performed. For example, picking accuracy of 99.5 percent indicates that 99.5 out of every 100 times, the correct items were picked in the warehouse.

Overall quality performance can also be measured in a variety of ways. Typical measures include damage frequency, which is computed as the ratio of the number of damaged units to the total number of units. While damage frequency can be measured at several points in the logistics process, such as warehouse damage, loading damage, and transportation damage, it frequently is not detected until customers receive shipments or even some point in time after receipt. Therefore, many organizations also monitor the number of customer returns of damaged or defective goods. It is also common to measure customer claims and refunds on adjustments.

Other important indicators of quality performance relate to information. Many organizations specifically measure their ability to provide information by noting those instances when information is not available on request. It is also common to track instances when inaccurate information is discovered. For example, when physical counts of merchandise inventory differ from the inventory status as reported in the database, the information system must be updated to reflect actual operating status. Additionally, the occurrence of information inaccuracy should be recorded for future action.

Productivity

The relationship between output of goods, work completed, and/or services produced and quantities of inputs or resources utilized to produce the output is productivity. If a system has clearly measurable outputs and identifiable, measurable inputs that can be matched to the appropriate outputs, productivity measurement is quite routine.

Generally, as Table 16.1 shows, logistics executives are very concerned with measuring the productivity of labor. While the labor input can be quantified in many ways, the most typical manner is by labor expense, labor hours, or number of individual employees. Thus, typical labor productivity measures in transportation include units shipped or delivered per employee, labor dollar, and labor hour. Warehouse labor productivity may be measured by units received, picked, and/or stored per employee, dollar, or hour. Similar measures can be developed for other activities, such as order entry and order processing. It is also common for managers to set goals for productivity improvement and compare actual performance to goal, or at the very least to prior year performance.

Asset Management

Utilization of capital investments in facilities and equipment as well as working capital invested in inventory is the concern of asset management. Logistics facilities, equipment, and inventory can represent a substantial segment of a firm's assets. For example, in the case of wholesalers, inventory frequently exceeds 80 percent of total capital. Asset management metrics focus on how well logistics managers utilize the capital invested in operations.

Facilities and equipment are frequently measured in terms of capacity utilization, or the percentage of total capacity used. For example, if a warehouse is capable of shipping 10,000 cases per day, but ships only 8,000, capacity utilization is only 80 percent. It is also common to measure equipment utilization in terms of time. Logistics managers are typically concerned with the number or percentage of hours that equipment is not utilized, which is measured as equipment **downtime.** Downtime can be applied to transportation, warehouse, and materials handling equipment. These measures indicate the effective or ineffective utilization of capital asset investment.

Asset management measurement also focuses on inventory. **Inventory turnover rate** is the most common measure of performance. Throughout the text, improved inventory turnover has been stressed as a critical focus of logistical management. It is important to understand how firms specifically measure inventory turnover rate. In fact, three specific metrics exist, each of which is used by different types of firms:

$$\text{Inventory turnover} = \frac{\text{Cost of goods sold during a time period}}{\text{Average inventory valued at cost during the time period}}$$

$$\text{Inventory turnover} = \frac{\text{Sales revenue during a time period}}{\text{Average inventory valued at selling price during time period}}$$

$$\text{Inventory turnover} = \frac{\text{Units sold during a time period}}{\text{Average unit inventoy during the time period}}$$

The vast majority of firms use the first to calculate inventory turnover rate. However, some retail organizations use the second. In fact, either of the two ratios should yield approximately the same result. Any differences in the two calculations would result from changes in the amount of gross margin (the difference between sales and cost of goods sold) during the time period.

The third approach, using units rather than dollars, is particularly applicable to products whose cost or selling prices change significantly during a relatively short time. For example, inventory turnover of gasoline, which changes in cost and price almost daily, would most appropriately be measured by computing units of gasoline sold and units of inventory rather than dollars of any kind.

As a final note on computation of turnover, it is critical that average inventory be determined by using as many data points as possible. For example, suppose a company had no inventory at the beginning of the year, bought and held a large quantity for 11 months, then sold all inventory before end of year. Using only the beginning and ending inventory positions, average inventory would be zero and turnover infinite. Clearly, this would be misleading to management.

Inventory investment can also be tracked in terms of the amount that is available to meet forecasted sales volume and is expressed as the **days of supply.** For example, if sales are forecast at 100 units per day and 5,000 units are in inventory, the firm has 50 days of supply on hand.

Of major interest to senior executives is **return on assets** and **return on investment.** Rate of return is of such importance that it is discussed in considerable detail later in this chapter.

Most organizations have substantially improved their functional measurement systems over the past 10 years. The number of specific metrics has increased, and the quality of information has improved. Much of the improvement in information quality can be attributed to improved technology. Years ago measurement of on-time delivery typically did not actually monitor delivery receipt by the customer. Most firms had no mechanism to capture information concerning when customers received orders. Instead, they typically measured on-time shipment by discerning if the order was shipped on time. It was assumed that if shipments left the supplier's facility "on time," then they also arrived at customer facilities "on time." Thus, the transportation delivery aspect of the order cycle was ignored. Today, using EDI linkages, satellite, and Internet tracking, many organizations monitor whether orders actually arrive at the customer location on time.

Measuring Customer Accommodation

Chapter 3 presented the conclusion that basic logistical service performance is necessary but is not sufficient for firms that are truly committed to logistical excellence. Today, many firms have focused increased attention on alternative methods of measuring their ability to accommodate customer requirements. As a result, an additional set of metrics is required for companies that strive to move beyond measuring basic customer service. Measurement of perfect orders, absolute performance, and customer satisfaction are three such approaches. The ultimate in accommodation, customer success, has no specific metrics but remains the goal for firms committed to supply chain relationships.

Perfect Orders

The perfect order concept was discussed in Chapter 3 as an indicator of an organization's commitment to zero-defect logistics. Delivery of perfect orders is the ultimate measure of quality in logistics operations. A perfect order measures the effectiveness of the firm's overall integrated logistical performance rather than individual functions. It measures whether an order proceeds flawlessly through every step—order entry, credit clearance, inventory availability, accurate picking, on-time delivery, correct invoicing, and payment without deductions—of the order management process without fault, be it expediting, exception processing, or manual intervention. In fact, as many as 20 different logistic service elements may impact a perfect order. From a measurement perspective, perfect order performance is computed as the ratio of perfect orders during a given time period to the total number of orders completed during that period.

AMR Research has estimated that the return to companies that provide high levels of perfect order fulfillment can be substantial. Improving perfect order performance by 3 percent can result in a 1 percent increase in profits.[5] In reality, measuring perfect order performance is not a simple task. Depending on which items are included in the perfect order, multiple information systems within a firm must be integrated and linked to the original purchase order. Assuming a perfect order includes order fill, on-time delivery, and invoice accuracy, three separate information systems must be linked with the order management system: the warehouse management system, the transportation management system, and the accounts receivable system.[6] Today, with some exceptions, even the best logistics organizations

[5] Reported in Susannah Patton, "The Perfect Order," *CIO* 18, no. 20. (August 1, 2005), p. 1.

[6] Robert A. Novack and Douglas J. Thomas, "The Challenges of Implementing the Perfect Order Concept," *Transportation Journal* 43, no. 1 (Winter 2004), p. 5.

report achieving only 60 to 70 percent perfect order performance. There are simply so many things that can go wrong with an order!

Absolute Performance

Most basic service and quality measures, and even perfect order measures, are aggregated over many orders and over a period of time. The problem some executives report with these on-average, over-time measures is that they tend to disguise the organization's real impact on its customer base. These executives feel that such measures can actually result in a feeling of complacency within the firm and that it is more appropriate to track absolute performance as close to real time as possible. The absolute approach provides a better indication of how a firm's logistical performance really impacts customers. For example, managers may feel that 99.5 percent on-time delivery represents excellent performance. As an executive of a large delivery company said, "To us, 99.5 percent on-time delivery would mean that on a typical day, over 5000 customers received late orders. We can't feel good about having that kind of impact on that many customers." This firm, and many other companies seeking to achieve maximum impact in the market, monitors absolute rates of failure and success as well as the more typical ratio and percentage metrics.

Customer Satisfaction

As mentioned at the beginning of this chapter, measuring customer perceptions and opinions is fundamental in a balanced scorecard. All of the internally generated statistics related to basic service, perfect order, or absolute performance may be internal indicators of customer accommodation, but to quantify satisfaction requires monitoring, measuring, and collecting information from the customer. While a comprehensive discussion of interview and survey research methodology is beyond the scope of this text, typical satisfaction measurement requires careful investigation of customer expectations, requirements, and perceptions of firm performance related to all aspects of logistics operations. For example, the typical survey measures customer expectations and performance perceptions regarding availability, order cycle time, information availability, order accuracy, problem resolution, and other aspects of logistics quality. It is useful to gather information concerning customers' overall feelings of satisfaction in addition to their assessment of specific logistics activities. Additional questions may be included to capture customer perceptions of competitor performance. Only through collecting data from customers can real satisfaction be assessed! Further, efforts to enhance customer success can be measured only from the customer's perspective.

Determining Appropriate Metrics

Thus far, many different performance metrics have been described, but no framework for determining the appropriate metrics or for prioritizing the need for specific metrics has been offered. In fact, several different frameworks have been proposed in the logistics literature.[7] A particularly useful framework has been offered by Griffis, Cooper, Goldsby, and Closs.[8] They propose a framework built on three dimensions: (1) competitive basis, (2) measurement focus, and (3) measurement frequency.

Competitive basis is a dimension reflecting a fundamental strategic choice between responsive logistics and efficient logistics performance. They note that performance

[7] See, for example, John T. Mentzer and John Firman, "Logistics Control Systems in the 21st Century," *Journal of Business Logistics* 15, no. 1 (1994), pp. 215–27; and N. Nanji, John Rigas, and Ip-Shing Fan, "A Framework to Review Performance Measurement Systems, *Business Process Management Journal* 11, no. 2 (2005), pp. 109–22.
[8] Stanley E. Griffis, Thomas J. Goldsby, Martha Cooper, and David J. Closs, "Aligning Logistics Performance Measures to the Information Needs of the Firm," *Journal of Business Logistics* 28, no. 2 (2007), pp. 35–56.

favoring responsiveness likely comes at the expense of efficiency. The measurement focus dimension represents the needs of the organization along a continuum ranging from operational metrics to those that provide strategic direction. The third dimension, measurement frequency, suggests that some metrics are needed frequently to monitor day-to-day performance, while others may be consulted less frequently for the purpose of diagnosing performance problems.

Figure 16.2 provides an illustration of this framework and an example of its application. Suppose a firm is interested in frequent assessment of efficiency in operations (indicated by the star in the diagram). In the figure only two metrics are considered: (1) total logistics cost as a percent of sales and (2) percent error pick rate. The proximity of metric 2 (percent error pick rate) is more closely aligned with fulfilling that assessment need than is metric 1 (total logistics cost as a percent of sales). This is not to suggest that metric 2 would not also be appropriate for an organization, as every organization has many assessment needs. The authors suggest that fully populating the framework with many possible metrics would allow a firm to choose performance metrics best suited to its measurement needs.[9]

Supply Chain Comprehensive Metrics

The contemporary focus on overall supply chain performance and effectiveness demands metrics that provide an integrated perspective. This perspective must be comparable and consistent across both firm functions and supply chain institutions. Without integrated measures, managers in different functions and in different firms may have different perspectives concerning actual logistical performance. Specific measures to consider are cash-to-cash conversion time, supply chain inventory days of supply, dwell time, on-shelf in-stock percentage, total supply chain cost, and supply chain response time.

[9] Ibid. p. 47.

FIGURE 16.2
Illustration of Measurement Framework

Source: Stanley E. Griffis, Thomas J. Goldsby, Martha Cooper, and David J. Closs, "Aligning Logistics Performance Measures to the Information Needs of the Firm," *Journal of Business Logistics* 28, no. 2 (2007), pp. 35–56.

1: Total logistics cost as percent of sales
2: Percent error pick rate
☆ Measurement need

Cash-to-Cash Conversion

The cash-to-cash conversion concept was introduced in Chapter 1. It is a measure of an organization's effective use of cash. While inventory is typically reported as a current asset on the balance sheet, the reported dollar value may not be a valid indicator of the organization's true asset deployment. Some inventory may have been delivered to customers that, because of trade credit terms of sale, have not yet paid for related invoices. Conversely, an organization may owe its suppliers for products or components that are in its possession. Cash-to-cash cycle time is the time required to convert a dollar spent on inventory into a dollar collected from sales revenue. It can be measured by adding a firm's days of supply of inventory and its days of accounts receivable outstanding, subtracting the days of trade accounts payable outstanding. Consider a hypothetical retailer that maintains a 30-day supply of inventory, has 30 days' trade credit from suppliers, and sells to end consumers in cash-only transactions. This firm theoretically has a cash-to-cash cycle time equal to zero because it sells and collects from end customers just as its payment is due to suppliers. More importantly, the firm's actual investment of money in inventory is zero, regardless of what the balance sheet says.

Cash-to-cash cycle time is not solely impacted by logistics, although logistics is an important aspect. It is a measure of internal process because it includes a component of marketing—customer pricing and terms of sale—as well as a component from procurement—supplier pricing and terms. It offers an integrated perspective of the organization's real commitment of financial resources to inventory.

Inventory Days of Supply

Traditional measures of inventory performance, turnover, and days of supply focus on individual firms. From a supply chain perspective, the flaw in these measures is that one firm may improve its performance by simply shifting inventory to its suppliers or to customers. Supply chain inventory days of supply is focused on total inventory at all locations and is typically defined as the total finished goods inventory at all plants, warehouses, wholesalers, and retailers expressed as the calendar days of sales available based on recent sales activity. This measure may be further extended to include raw materials and components held by manufacturing plants and suppliers. These unfinished inventories are converted to equivalent units of finished goods and included as part of the true total supply chain inventory. This measure, when adopted by all members of a supply chain, provides the focus of integrated operations.

Dwell Time

Dwell time is another metric reflecting overall supply chain performance in managing assets. Inventory dwell time is the ratio of the days inventory sits idle in the supply chain to the days it is being productively used or positioned. While it is sometimes necessary for inventory to sit idle for reasons of quality control or to buffer uncertainty, extended dwell time reflects the potential magnitude of nonproductive inventory. Dwell time can also be computed for other assets, especially transportation equipment. For example, railcar utilization can be measured by computing the number of days a rail car sits idle and empty versus the number of days it is loaded with freight. Reducing asset dwell time is a key objective for many logistics executives. Assets that sit idle are not contributing to productivity in the supply chain.

On-Shelf In-Stock Percent

Ultimately, a key objective of all participants in a supply chain is to have products available when and where end customers are ready to buy. Individual firm metrics related to fill rates at warehouses or to retail stores provide little assurance that products are available for consumer selection when a consumer is shopping. For example, a study of catalog retailers found that in-stock levels averaged less than 85 percent.[10] For this reason, in some supply chain relationships, a critical measure of overall performance is the on-shelf in-stock percent, the percentage of time that a product is available on the shelf in a store. The rationale is that consumers typically cannot or will not select and buy an item that is not easily available on the store shelf. Increasing the on-shelf in-stock percent benefits all members of the supply chain, not only the retailer. While it focuses on the retail impact, consider also the impact on suppliers when their products are not on the shelves at the time consumers want to buy.

Supply Chain Total Cost

Much of the discussion of cost thus far has focused on an individual firm's logistics costs. Figure 16.3 illustrates the fact that total supply chain cost is the aggregate of costs across all firms in the supply chain, not an individual organization. This perspective is absolutely critical to effective supply chain management. Focusing on a single firm's cost may lead to suboptimization and attempts by one company to shift cost to another. If the objective in supply chain management is to reduce total cost, it is reasonable to assume that one organization may actually experience increased cost as others in the supply chain experience reductions. As long as the total reductions in cost are larger than the cost increase for one supply chain member, the supply chain as a whole is improved. It is then incumbent upon those companies whose cost is reduced to share benefits to fairly compensate those whose cost is increased. This willingness to share benefits and risks associated with changes in operational integration is the essence of true relationship management discussed in the previous chapter.

Supply Chain Response Time

An interesting and extremely meaningful metric for comprehensive supply chain performance is **supply chain response time (SCRT).** SCRT is computed as the amount of time required for all firms in a supply chain to recognize a fundamental shift in marketplace demand, internalize that finding, replan, and adjust output to meet that demand. For

[10]John C. Taylor and Stanley E. Fawcett, "Catalog Retailer In-Stock Performance: An Assessment of Customer Service Levels," *Journal of Business Logistics* 25, no. 2 (2004), pp. 119–35.

FIGURE 16.3
Total Supply Chain Cost

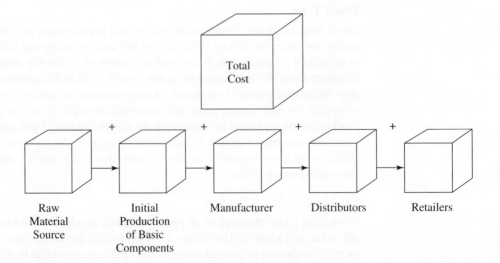

| Raw Material Source | Initial Production of Basic Components | Manufacturer | Distributors | Retailers |

example, in the auto industry, when it was discovered that demand for sport utility vehicles was extremely high, it took several years for the auto companies to develop sufficient production and capacity, rearrange supplier relationships, and meet consumer demand. In most instances, developing an actual metric for SCRT would be a theoretical approximation rather than a real measure. Nevertheless, it is extremely useful for supply chain executives to think in terms of how long it would take for an entire supply chain to ready all activities from raw material sourcing to final distribution when demand for a product is significantly greater (or less) that anticipated.

Benchmarking

Benchmarking is a critical aspect of performance measurement that makes management aware of state-of-the-art business practice. Many firms have adopted benchmarking as a tool to assess their operations in relation to those of leading firms, both competitors and noncompetitors, in related and nonrelated industries. While benchmarking performance metrics has become a fairly standard practice, many firms do not benchmark processes.

An important decision in benchmarking is the choice of organizations to benchmark. Many firms compare performance of internal business units involved in similar operations or located in different regions. For example, Johnson & Johnson, with over 150 different business units, has ample opportunity for internal benchmarking. Since business units in large diversified corporations are often unaware of what occurs in other units, internal benchmarking provides a way to share knowledge as well as improve performance.

Internal benchmarking, however, provides little information concerning performance relative to competition. A firm may be lagging competition and not be aware of it. Information about competitor performance can be used to identify where improvement is most needed; however, it is extremely difficult to capture information about competitors' operational processes.

Nonrestricted benchmarking involves efforts to compare both metrics and processes to best practices, regardless of where the relevant practice is found. It does not restrict sources of information to any particular company or industry. Nonrestricted benchmarking is grounded in the philosophy that it is possible to learn from organizations in unrelated industries that have outstanding performance or use innovative approaches. L. L. Bean, the mail and catalog company, has been benchmarked in order fulfillment processes by firms from such diverse fields as food, personal care, and electronics.

Benchmarking is an important tool in the performance assessment system of an organization. In a study of best-practice supply chain companies referenced in Table 16.2, it was found that those firms that perform at high levels of supply chain capability are much

TABLE 16.2   Performance Benchmarking Differential

Source: Reprinted with permission from Donald J. Bowersox, David J. Closs, and Theodore P. Stank, *21st Century Logistics: Making Supply Chain Integration a Reality,* Oak Brook, IL, Council of Supply Chain Management Professionals, 1999, p. 97.

Performance Dimension	Percent of High Index Achieving Firms	Percent of Average Index Achieving Firms
Customer Service	92.5	56.0
Cost Management	80.0	47.1
Quality	70.0	31.0
Productivity	77.5	38.5
Asset Management	55.0	25.8

Note: All differentials are statistically significant at the .05 level.

more likely to be involved in benchmarking activity than firms that demonstrate average supply chain capability. Table 16.2 shows the results of the research related to benchmarking. In all categories, high-achieving companies are more involved in benchmarking than average-achieving firms. It is clear that benchmarking is considered an essential aspect of measurement by leading organizations.

Financial Assessment

Recall that a balanced scorecard places significant emphasis on improving shareholder value. Thus, logistics executives must be informed and ready to demonstrate how supply chain practices and processes affect the overall financial health of their organization. Measurement systems must enable logistics managers to link supply chain performance directly to financial results. To do so effectively, logistics managers must be well grounded in two critical tools for financial assessment: cost-revenue analysis and the strategic profit model.

Cost-Revenue Analysis

The achievement of logistical integration requires the establishment of a cost-revenue analysis framework. Traditional accounting practices make such a framework difficult for logistics executives. Contribution margin and full-costing methodologies have been supplemented by the use of **activity-based costing (ABC)** as the most promising way to identify and control logistics expenses.

Public Accounting Practice

The two main financial reports of a business enterprise are the **balance sheet** and the **income statement.** The balance sheet reflects the financial position of a firm at a specific point in time. The purpose of a balance sheet is to summarize assets and liabilities and to indicate the net worth of ownership. The income statement reflects the revenues and costs associated with specific operations over a specified period of time. As the name income implies, its purpose is to determine the financial success of operations. Logistical functions are an integral part of both statements; however, the primary deficiency in logistical costing and analysis is the method by which standardized accounting costs are identified, classified, and reported. Unfortunately, the conventional methods of accounting do not fully satisfy logistical costing requirements.

The first problem results from the fact that accounting practice aggregates costs on a standard or natural account basis rather than on an activity basis. The practice of grouping expenses into natural accounts such as salaries, rent, utilities, and depreciation fails to identify or assign operations responsibility. To help overcome the natural account aggregation, it is common for statements to be subdivided by managerial or organizational areas of responsibility within an enterprise. Internal income statements generally classify and group expenses along organization budgetary lines. Thus, costs are detailed by managerial responsibility. However, many expenses associated with logistical performance cut across organization units. For example, efforts to reduce inventory will reduce inventory carrying cost, but they may also lead to more back orders, which would increase total transportation cost. The result is inadequate data for integrated performance measurement.

A somewhat overlapping deficiency of accounting involves the traditional methods of reporting transportation expenditures. It remains standard practice in accounting to deduct inbound freight expense from gross sales as part of the cost of goods to arrive at a gross margin figure. Outbound freight, on the other hand, is generally reported as an operating expense. However, the problem extends beyond where freight is accounted for and reported. In many purchasing situations, freight is not reported as a specific cost. Many products are purchased on a delivered price basis, which includes transportation cost. Most progressive procurement procedures require that expenses for all services, including transportation, be debundled from the total purchase cost for evaluative purposes.

A final deficiency in traditional accounting practice is the failure to specify and assign inventory cost. The deficiency has two aspects. First, full costs associated with the maintenance of inventory, such as insurance and taxes, are not identified, resulting in an understatement or obscurity in reporting inventory cost. Second, the financial burden for assets committed to material, work-in-process, and finished goods inventory is not identified, measured, or separated from other forms of capital expense incurred by the enterprise. In fact, if a firm deploys internal funds to support inventory requirements, it is likely that no capital expenses will be reflected by the profit and loss statement.

To remedy these shortcomings, several modifications to traditional accounting are required to track logistical costs. In particular, the two largest individual expenses in logistics—transportation and inventory—have traditionally been reported in a manner that obscures their importance instead of highlighting them. Although the situation is improving, routine isolation and reporting of logistical costs is not standard practice in most organizations.

To control cost and improve operational efficiency, it is necessary to properly identify and capture all relevant cost information in a manner that is meaningful to decision makers. Logistical costing must also provide those executives with the information to determine whether a specific segment of business such as a customer, order, product, channel, or service is profitable. This requires the matching of specific revenue with specific costs.

Effective costing requires identification of the specific expenses included in an analysis framework. Two frameworks that each have numerous proponents are the **contribution approach** and the **net profit approach.**

Contribution Approach

A pure contribution approach requires that all costs be identified as fixed or variable according to the cost behavior. Fixed costs are those that do not directly change with volume of activity. In the short term those costs would remain even if volume were reduced to zero. For example, the cost of a delivery truck is fixed. If the truck cost $40,000, the firm is charged $40,000 (or the appropriate depreciation) whether the truck is used for 1 or 1,000 deliveries. Variable costs are those costs that do change as a result of volume. The gasoline required to operate a delivery truck is variable: Total gasoline cost depends upon how frequently and how far the truck is driven.

It is also necessary in contribution analysis to specify which are direct costs and which are indirect costs. Direct costs are those that are specifically incurred because of the existence of the product, customer, or other segment under consideration. If that segment were eliminated, the direct cost would no longer exist. All variable costs can be directly traced to specific products, customers, channels, and the like. Some fixed costs may also be direct if they exist to logistically support a specific business segment. For example, a warehouse facility may be constructed specifically to support a specific product line or major customer account. Indirect costs exist because of more than one segment of business and would continue to exist even if one specific segment were eliminated. Thus, a warehouse that maintains multiple product lines would continue to operate even if one product line was discontinued. In this case, the warehouse is indirect to the products.

Income statements in the contribution method of analysis can be prepared that identify profitability for each segment by determination of fixed, variable, direct, and indirect costs. Table 16.3 provides a hypothetical example of such income statements for a firm analyzing profitability of two customers, a hospital and a retailer. Variable costs of goods sold are directly related to the product mix sold in each customer segment; it includes only direct labor, materials, and supplies. All factory overhead costs are treated as indirect costs in the contribution margin approach. Variable direct costs include such items as sales commission, discounts, certain logistics costs related to servicing each customer, and any other expenses that vary directly with volume sold to each customer. Fixed direct costs include any other costs that can be traced directly to the specific customer. Such costs might include certain aspects of sales, salaries and expenses, advertising, transportation, warehousing, order processing, and other logistical activities. The key is that these expenses must be directly attributable to those customers. Indirect fixed costs includes all expenses that cannot easily be traced to a specific segment. Many of these may also be logistics-related costs. For example, shared warehouse, transportation equipment, and other jointly used resources should be specified as indirect costs.

In Table 16.3, both customers are covering direct costs and making a substantial contribution to indirect fixed cost. The hospital, however, has a substantially higher percentage net segment contribution than does the retailer—37 percent versus 26 percent. A large portion of this difference is attributable to the difference in variable gross profit of 58 percent versus 50 percent. This difference suggests that analysis of the product mix for the retailer should be conducted to determine whether emphasis should be placed on a more profitable mix. Elimination of the retailer would be a clear mistake, however, as the hospital customer would then have to bear all of the indirect fixed cost, resulting in a net loss of $4,000.

Net Profit Approach

The net profit approach to financial assessment of segments requires that all operating costs be charged or allocated to an operating segment. Proponents of this approach argue that all of a company's activities exist to support the production and delivery of goods and services to customers. Furthermore, in many firms most costs are, in fact, joint or shared costs. To determine the true profitability of a channel, territory, or product, each segment must be allocated its fair share of these costs. In the previous example, allocating indirect fixed cost on the basis of sales volume would result in the hospital being charged with 40 percent, or $16,400, and the retailer 60 percent, or $24,600. The net profit of serving the hospital would be $20,600. The net profit from the retail customer would be $14,400.

Clearly, significant problems arise in determining how to allocate indirect costs on a fair and equitable basis. Proponents of the contribution margin approach contend that such allocations are necessarily arbitrary and result in misleading financial assessment. They point to the use of sales volume as a typical basis for allocation of expense and the inherent

TABLE 16.3
Contribution Margin Income Statement for Two Customers

	Hospital	Retailer	Total
Revenue	$100,000	$150,000	$250,000
Less: Variable Cost of Goods Sold	42,000	75,000	117,000
Variable Gross Profit	58,000	75,000	133,000
Less: Variable Direct Cost	6,000	15,000	21,000
Gross Segment Contribution	52,000	60,000	112,000
Less: Fixed Direct Costs	15,000	21,000	36,000
Net Segment Contribution	$ 37,000	$ 39,000	76,000
Less: Indirect Fixed Costs			41,000
Net Profit			$ 25,000
Net Segment Contribution Ratio	37%	26%	30.4%

bias in such an approach. For example, the retailer above accounts for 60 percent of total sales volume but does not necessarily account for 60 percent of the expense of advertising, warehousing, order processing, or any other shared activity. It may account for much more or less of each expense category, depending upon circumstances that are not at all related simply to sales volume.

Net profit proponents argue, however, that the traditional notions of fixed and variable cost and direct and indirect cost are too simplistic. Many of the so-called indirect fixed costs are not, in fact, indirect or fixed at all. These expenses rise and fall, depending upon demands placed upon the business by the various operating segments.

Activity-Based Costing

As a partial solution to the problem of arbitrary allocations, **activity-based costing (ABC)** suggests that costs should first be traced to activities performed and then activities should be related to specific product or customer segments of the business. Suppose, for example, the order processing expense is basically a fixed indirect cost in our hypothetical example, amounting to $5,000. Allocating this expense to the two customers on the basis of sales volume results in a charge of $2,000 to the hospital and $3,000 to the retailer. However, it is likely that the hospital places very many orders during the year, each of a small quantity, while the retailer may place only a few large orders. If the hospital placed 80 orders and the retailer placed 20 orders, an ABC approach would charge the hospital with 80 percent, or $4,000, and the retailer with 20 percent, or $1,000, of the order processing expense. Applying similar logic to other indirect fixed costs by identifying the activities and cost drivers could result in further refinement of customer profitability.

Identifying the activities, related expenses, and the drivers of expense represents the biggest challenge in an ABC approach. Order processing cost may be related to the number of orders in one company and to the number of lines on orders in another company. Warehouse picking expense may be related to the number of items picked in one company and to the number of pounds in another. Transportation might be related to number of deliveries for one firm and number of miles driven for another. According to proponents of this activity-based costing method, one cost that should be excluded from allocation to segments is the cost of excess capacity. Thus, if an order processing system could process 5 million orders per year but is only utilized for 4 million orders, the excess capacity should not be charged to any segment. Similarly, if a warehouse and its employees could handle 100,000 shipments but are only used for 80,000, the excess capacity is a cost of the time period rather than a cost attributable to an existing operating segment. All other costs, however, should be traced through an activity-based system.

Much of the distinction between the contribution margin and net profit approaches to segment cost analysis is disappearing as analysts are developing better approaches to identify expense behavior. Advocates of direct costing and contribution margin would probably go along with the tracing of costs to segments based on activities performed, as long as the basis for tracing reflects the real cost of the activity. Historically, their argument has been based on the fairness and appropriateness of the allocation method. Even the most avid proponent of full costing, on the other hand, would not argue in favor of arbitrary allocation of cost. Recent developments such as time-driven activity based costing promise even greater accuracy and may further aid in resolving this controversy.[11]

[11] Patricia Everaert, Werner Bruggeman, Gerrit Sarens, Steven Anderson, and Yves Levant, "Cost Modeling in Logistics Using Time-Driven ABC: Experiences from a Wholesaler," *International Journal of Physical Distribution & Logistics Management* 38, no. 2 (2008), pp. 172–89.

Strategic Profit Model

While costing and profitability assessment are important aspects of financial controllership, the most critical measure of strategic success is **return on investment (ROI).** There are two ways of viewing ROI. The first is **return on net worth (RONW),** which measures the profitability of the funds that the owners of the firm have invested in the firm. The second is **return on assets (ROA),** which measures the profitability generated by managing a firm's operational assets. While owners and investors are most likely interested in RONW, ROA offers a measure of how well management is utilizing assets to earn profits.

Figure 16.4 presents the Strategic Profit Model **(SPM),** with hypothetical data. The SPM is a tool frequently used to analyze ROI in a business firm. In fact, the SPM is a tool that incorporates both income and balance sheet data and demonstrates how these data relate to each other to result in ROA.

One of the primary benefits of the SPM is that it shows very clearly that a key financial objective of the firm is to achieve and increase ROA. Too often, managers focus on more limited objectives. For example, sales management may focus on sales as the primary objective of the business and, therefore, will base decisions on sales volume. Logistics managers may focus on cost minimization or turnover and feel that decisions must be based on reducing expense or increasing the firm's efficient utilization of assets. The SPM

FIGURE 16.4 **Strategic Profit Model**

demonstrates that there are two fundamental ways in which a firm can increase return on assets: managing net profit margin and/or managing asset turnover. Logistics operations have a significant impact on both.

Net Profit Margin

Expressed as a percentage, net profit margin is net profit divided by net sales. Going beyond this simple expression, however, net profit margin actually measures the proportion of each sales dollar that is kept by the firm as net profit. For example, the hypothetical firm has a net profit margin of 5 percent; this simply means that $0.05 out of every $1 represents net profit for the company. It is important to note that net profit margin is also divided into a number of specific components. These components are sales volume, cost of goods sold, and operating expenses. For a full evaluation of whether the firm's net profit margin is adequate, and whether it might be improved, it is necessary to investigate each component to determine whether an increase or decrease in any one component or in any combination of components might lead to improved net profit margin performance.

Asset Turnover

The ratio of total sales divided by total assets is asset turnover, which measures the efficiency of management in utilizing assets. It shows how many dollars in total sales volume are being generated by each dollar that the firm has invested in assets. For example, the hypothetical company with an asset turnover ratio of 2:1 is generating $2.00 in sales volume for each dollar it has invested in assets. As Figure 16.4 illustrates, there are a number of assets used to generate sales. The most important are inventories, accounts receivable, and fixed facilities. Inventory is a particularly important asset to many firms because it is typically one of the largest areas of asset investment. Thus, it is common in logistics to focus specifically on the management of the inventory turnover ratio.

Applications of the SPM

The SPM can be used for many different types of logistical analysis. Two of the most common are the impact of changes in logistical activities or processes on ROA and analysis of segmental ROA.

Figure 16.5 illustrates a recomputation of ROA assuming that the hypothetical firm was able to accomplish an inventory reduction of $100. The most obvious impact of this inventory reduction occurs through the reduction in the inventory asset from $400 to $300. A corresponding change in total assets results in a new asset turnover rate of 2.22 versus the base case of 2.0 times. It is assumed, for explanatory purposes, that sales volume remains the same.

However, a reduction in average inventory also has an impact on operating expenses. Inventory carrying costs, discussed in Chapter 7 should be reduced as well. In this example, assuming an inventory carrying cost of 20 percent, the expense reduction amounts to $20, increasing net profit to $120, and net profit margin to 6 percent. The combined profit margin and asset turnover impact of inventory reduction result in an increase in ROA from 10 percent to over 13.3 percent. No wonder so many organizations are focusing on methods to improve inventory management!

The simplifying assumption of no change in sales could be subjected to further examination by using the SPM. A variety of scenarios regarding potential changes in volume, expenses, and investments can be proposed and analyzed. In fact, the SPM framework is very adaptable to a spreadsheet model, which allows investigation and analysis of many different changes in logistics operations and their projected impact on ROA. Changes in facility structure or methods with projected changes in expenses, asset investment, and sales level can be analyzed to project impact on ROA.

FIGURE 16.5 **Strategic Profit Model (Inventory Reduction)**

The SPM, in conjunction with concepts discussed in the section on cost/revenue analysis, can also be used to examine the return on assets generated by various customer or product segments of a business. Table 16.4 provides a sample calculation of **contribution margin return on inventory investment (CMROI)** for two products. Contribution margin for each product is calculated by using only those expenses directly traced to each product.

No indirect costs are allocated. Similarly, asset investments directly attributable to specific products should be identified. In this case, the only direct asset investment is inventory investment. Notice that product B has lower gross margin and contribution margin but actually provides a substantially higher return because of its low average inventory investment. In other situations, for example, analysis of customer return on assets, accounts receivable, and other direct asset investments attributable to a specific customer should be included.

Other segment profitability and ROI analyses can be conducted by using the SPM framework. It requires careful thought and identification of those costs and asset investments traceable to specific segments. With this approach, the logistics executive has a powerful and useful tool for identifying how logistics process, activities, and decisions impact the financial objectives of the organization.

TABLE 16.4
CMROI for Two
Products

	Product A	Product B
Sales	$100,000	$50,000
Cost of Goods	60,000	35,000
Gross Margin	40,000 (40%)	15,000 (30%)
Direct Expense	25,000	9000
Contribution Margin	15,000 (15%)	6000 (12%)
Average Inventory	40,000	10,000
CMROI	37.5%	60%

One problem faced by logistics executives is that typical approaches to logistics performance assessment are not generally expressed in terms that are meaningful to other senior executives. For example, transportation expense per mile, warehouse picking expense, and cost-related metrics are extremely meaningful in terms of managing those specific activities but are somewhat obscure to executives in finance and marketing. The SPM framework is a very useful tool for relating logistics activities to the overall financial objectives of the organization. It provides a mechanism to trace specifically how changes in logistics' assets or expenses relate directly to measures that are more meaningful to other executives: measures such as profit margin, asset turnover, and return on assets.

Requirements for Financial Reporting

Because of numerous instances of financial mismanagement by major corporations, in 2002 the U.S. Congress passed the Sarbanes-Oxley Act **(SOX)**. Although the focus of the law is on financial reporting by corporations to their shareholders, it became apparent soon after its enactment that it also has important implications for logistics and supply chain management, especially with respect to how performance is measured and reported.

Section 404 of SOX requires that a company file an internal control report at the same time it files its corporate annual report. The SEC will evaluate the internal controls used by the firm to determine its adequacy for ensuring that the financial reports are consistent and accurate. Thus, every firm covered by the act must have internal measurement capabilities that comply with SEC requirements. It is important to note that the SEC does not specify what the internal controls and measures must be, but it does require that the controls ensure the integrity of financial information. In essence, companies must demonstrate that their measurement systems ensure that financial data such as revenue, cost of goods sold, expenses, assets, and liabilities are accurately reported. This has a direct impact on logistics performance measurement.[12]

Table 16.5 provides examples of supply chain and logistics activities, the financial elements affected, and measures that might be used to ensure the accuracy of the financial information. APICS, a professional association, and Protiviti, a consulting firm, suggest that the internal metrics shown in column 5 of the table can be used to validate the financial elements shown in columns 3 and 4. For example, measuring inventory accuracy is critical to ensure that the firm accurately reports cost of sales on its income statement and investment in inventory on the balance sheet. Likewise, other internal measures shown in the table can be linked directly to income statement and balance sheet items. Although the framework suggested in the table is only an example, it demonstrates the fact that companies are required by SOX to have a system of internal measurement that ensures the accuracy of financial information.

[12] Roger Morton, "SOX and the Supply Chain," *Logistics Today* 45, no. 10 (October 2004), p. 27.

TABLE 16.5   **Supply Chain and Logistics Measures Related to Financial Reporting**

Source: Reprinted with permission from Protiviti/APICS, "Capitalizing on Sarbanes-Oxley Compliance to Build Supply Chain Advantage," May 2003, p. 9.

Supply Chain Business Process	Supply Chain Transactions	Financial Reporting Elements (balance sheet)	Financial Reporting Elements (income statement)	Supply Chain Reporting Elements (some examples)
		Activity Level		
Plan	Raw materials are purchased	• Raw materials • Accounts payable • Cash and debt	• Cost of sales	• Supplier delivery performance • Cost and quality • Planned deliveries
Source	Purchase of equipment, direct and indirect material, and services	• Property and equipment (net) • Accounts payable • Cash and debt	• Depreciation • Taxes	• Supplier delivery performance • Cost and quality • Planned deliveries
Produce	Products are manufactured or raw materials are converted	• Raw materials • Work in process • Accounts payable • Accrued expenses • Wages payable • Cash	• Cost of sales • Wages • Utilities	• On-time delivery • Quality and cost • Routing accuracy • Production plan performance • Production schedule performance • Scrap rate • WIP levels • Planned production
Store	Raw materials, work in process, or finished goods are stored	• Raw materials • Work in process • Finished goods • Accounts payable • Accrued expenses • Wages payable • Cash	• Cost of sales • Wages • Utilities	• Inventory accuracy • Queue, buffer, and safety stock levels • Inventory turnover • Scrap rate
Transport	Goods are transported	• Work in process • Finished goods • Accounts payable • Wages payable • Cash	• Cost of sales • Wages	• On-time delivery • Quality and cost • Scrap rate
Sell	Products or services are sold	• Accounts receivable (net) • Finished goods • Warranty reserves • Commissions payable • Cash	• Net revenues • Cost of sales • Selling expenses • Marketing expenses • Commissions	• Sales plan performance • Customer service • Percent sales order changes • Order entry accuracy
Return	Sold goods are returned	• Accounts receivable (net) • Inventory reserves • Accounts payable • Warranty reserves • Commissions payable • Cash	• Net revenues	• Quality and customer service • Planned returns

Of particular importance to logistics and supply chain executives are the requirements of SOX to measure and report all off-balance-sheet liabilities, obligations, or transactions that may have a material effect on the financial reports. Activities such as vendor-managed inventories, long-term purchase agreements, and slotting allowances are examples of such items. Thus, attempts to gain competitive advantage by using these approaches become public knowledge due to the disclosure requirements of SOX.[13]

In addition to reporting transactions, companies are also required to report any event that may have a material effect on financial reports. Consider, for example, shipments of goods that have a long lead time and/or have the potential to be held up for a long time at an international border because of security risks or transportation delays. In many instances, the buyer may be contractually obligated to pay for the goods regardless of when they are received. Thus, the buyer owns inventory but may not receive actual possession for some time.[14] Historically, such situations were essentially unknown to senior executives, but in the current environment this financial commitment, and its impact must be acknowledged. Basically, the requirements for full disclosure of the financial status of the organization have forced senior executives to have a much greater understanding of the details of logistical operations. It also places a premium on having the ability to monitor the location and status of shipments in a timely and accurate manner.

Although many managers feel that the legal requirements of SOX are a burden on the organization, others view it as an opportunity for improvement. The requirements for more detailed knowledge of where finished products and materials are at all times, from their point of origin to arrival at final destination, make it necessary for companies to commit more resources to providing supply chain visibility to management. In turn, by having greater visibility, the opportunity exists to improve decisions by basing them on better and more timely information.

Summary

Effective management of logistics operations and supply chain integration requires establishment of a framework for performance assessment and financial controllership. The balanced scorecard provides the framework to monitor system performance, control activities, and direct personnel to achieve higher levels of productivity.

Comprehensive performance measurement systems include metrics for each of the logistics functions. Five critical dimensions of functional performance must be addressed: cost, customer service, quality, productivity, and asset management. Leading firms extend their functional measurement systems to include metrics focused on their ability to accommodate customer requirements. These include measures of absolute performance rather than average performance, perfect orders, consumer-focused measures, and customer satisfaction. Given the numerous metrics that might be used for assessment of logistics performance, choosing the most appropriate measures for a firm is a difficult task that must be guided by the specific information needs of an organization. To aid in achievement of supply chain integration, leading firms have instituted a set of across-firm metrics such as inventory days of supply, inventory dwell time, cash-to-cash cycle time, and total supply chain cost.

Effective financial assessment requires knowledge of cost-revenue analysis and the strategic profit model. Traditional accounting practices are typically inadequate for logistics costing. Effective decision making requires that management be able to match revenues with expenses incurred to service specific customers, channels, and products. Contribution and net profit approaches represent alternative formats for cost/revenue analysis. Activity-based costing provides management the ability to more specifically trace

---

[13] S. Scott Nadler and John F. Kros, "An Introduction to Sarbanes-Oxley and Its Impact on Supply Chain Management," *Journal of Business Logistics* 29, no.1 (2008), p. 244.

[14] Peter M. Tirshwell, "How to Avoid This," *Journal of Commerce*, November 2, 2004, p. 1.

logistics expenses to the segments that generate revenue. An additional tool for controllership is the strategic profit model. This model provides managers the ability to assess the impact of logistics decisions on profitability, asset utilization, and return on assets. It also provides the ability to more accurately assess segments in terms of profit and return on investment. Sarbanes-Oxley requires that external financial reports include disclosure of significant logistics transactions and events on both the balance sheet and corporate profitability.

Challenge Questions

1. Briefly discuss the three objectives for developing and implementing performance measurement systems.
2. How does the balanced scorecard concept help guide logistics managers in the development of a performance measurement system?
3. Is the ideal of a perfect order a realistic operational goal?
4. Why is it important that a firm measure customer perception as a regular part of performance measurement?
5. Why are comprehensive measures of supply chain performance, such as total supply chain cost, so difficult to develop?
6. Compare and contrast the contribution approach with the net profit approach in cost/revenue analysis.
7. Do you believe that activity-based costing represents an equitable basis for allocating indirect expenses?
8. Suppose you have been asked by a firm to assess the impact on return on assets of outsourcing transportation. Currently the firm uses a private truck fleet and is considering a switch to a for-hire transportation company. Which aspects of the strategic profit model would be affected?
9. How can the strategic profit model be integrated with cost-revenue analysis for the purpose of analyzing the return on assets from servicing a specific customer account?
10. How does the Sarbanes-Oxley Act impact requirements for logistics performance measurement?

Supply Chain Risk

Chapter Outline

The focus of supply chain management is rapidly expanding to include many new dimensions. While these expansions place increasing demands on logistics and supply chain executives in terms of knowledge and skills, they also expand supply chain's importance and role in firm competitiveness. Specifically, supply chain leadership must take a more active and critical role in managing and balancing supply chain and other dimensions of corporate risk management. Chapter 17 begins by characterizing specific risk dimensions. For each of these critical dimensions, the chapter discusses the implications regarding supply chain strategy and operations and suggests some approaches for overcoming them.

Supply Chain Risk Management

As discussed in previous chapters, supply chain and logistics management requires effective evaluation and decision making involving trade-offs between procurement, manufacturing, logistics, and customer accommodation. As illustrated in Figure 17.1, the primary role of supply chain executives has been satisfying customer service objectives while seeking the lowest total cost by trading off the functional activities involved in procurement, manufacturing, logistics, and customer accommodation. As discussed in Chapter 16, increased use of balanced scorecards has expanded performance measures to include return on assets and revenue as illustrated in Figure 17.2. As global financial markets have increased the focus on firm revenue, supply chain executives are increasingly involved with activities such as new product introduction and global expansion. For many firms, new product introductions or reintroductions amount to 25 percent of

FIGURE 17.1
**Extending the Role
of Supply Chain
Management**

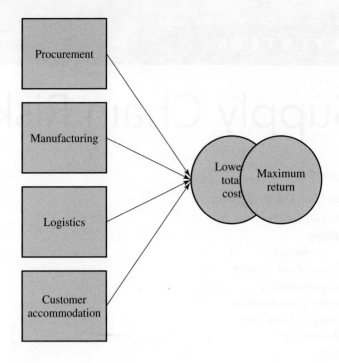

all items and volume shipped each year. Significant new product introduction volume causes significant challenges for logistics and supply chain operations due to the need for surge activity to have the new products manufactured and moved to the field and the activities involved in the recovery of the product that is being superseded. As discussed in Chapter 12, global expansion introduces a number of challenges to logistics and the supply chain as well.

Over the past decade, the challenges have continued to grow with the focus expanding to include sustainability. While least total cost, maximum return on assets, and maximum revenue are still important, events over the past decade require that firms consider long-term sustainability when developing their strategy. A sustainable supply chain reflects the firm's ability to plan for, mitigate, detect, respond to, and recover from likely risks. Risks that have substantial supply chain implications include (1) product complexity, (2) regulatory, (3) resource availability, and (4) security. Figure 17.3 illustrates the impact of this trend with increased focus on these considerations. The following sections discuss each of these considerations.

Product Complexity

Product complexity refers to the number of product design variations that the firm decides to offer and correspondingly support. The required activities include all actions related to product development, sourcing, manufacture, delivery, and aftermarket support. Complexity management is the collective set of decisions, supporting processes, value systems, and initiatives pertaining to the most effective product portfolio such as the mix of product variants, feature sets, and component choices. From a supply chain perspective, it is generally known that increased complexity results in higher cost. The major rationale is that increased product variations result in more inventory and fewer economies of scale, and requires more management attention. However, from a marketing and

FIGURE 17.2
Extending the Role of Supply Chain Management

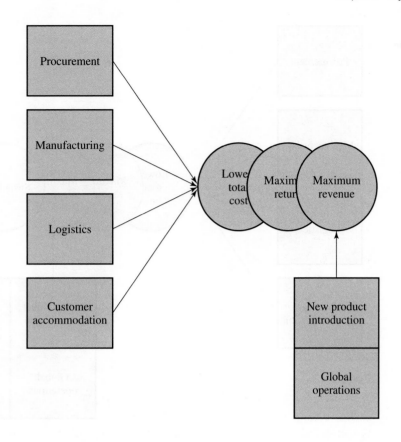

globalization perspective, increased complexity can often result in increased revenue which may improve profitability and asset utilization. The result is the need for effective trade-offs combining both marketing and supply chain perspectives.

In general, less product complexity (also termed as more commonality) reduces supply chain–related costs as listed in Table 17.1. It simplifies product development since less research and testing are required for fewer product variations. Similarly, less complexity results in fewer quality and reliability problems. Toyota has been widely known to focus on reduced product complexity. For example, Toyota is reported to have only two variants of their automobile door latches while other major automotive companies have over 10. Fewer SKUs also allow more accurate forecasting. John Deere's Worldwide Commercial and Consumer Equipment division has focused extensively on reducing component and flow complexity for their garden and lawn tractors and have reduced their finished goods inventory by approximately one-half, or $1 billion.[1] Low complexity also reduces selling and support cost. Fewer product variations mean lower inventory and less training are required to provide customer support. Procter & Gamble has also reported numerous initiatives to reduce distribution center, product line, packaging, and display case complexity.[2]

On the other hand, reduced product variations can reduce the attractiveness of a firm's market offerings. For example, consumers may decide to not purchase a specific item

[1] James Cooke, "Running Inventory Like a Deere," *CSCMP's Supply Chain Quarterly* (Quarter 4, 2007), pp. 46–50.
[2] Jonathan Birchall, and Elizabeth Rigby, "P&G Fights to Keep 3.5 Billion Consumers Happy," *Financial Times* (London, UK), June 27, 2008, p. 16.

FIGURE 17.3
**Extending the Role
of Supply Chain
Management**

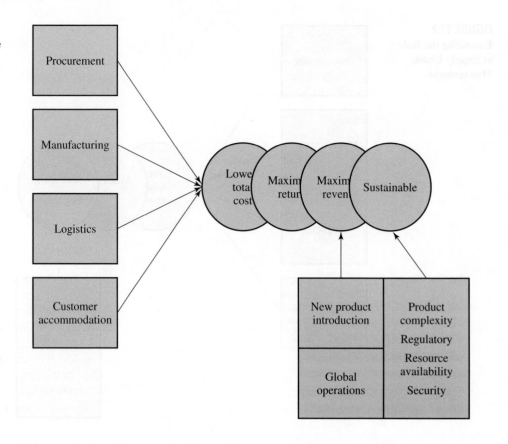

because it doesn't have the precise combination of features or characteristics that they desire. These features and characteristics can include color, technical capabilities, size, quality, and support. Examples of products that tend to have many variants to satisfy consumer needs include automobiles, appliances, cell phones, and electronics. Marketers generally argue that the variants are necessary so the consumer will not defect to another brand. Table 17.2 summarizes the characteristics of increased product complexity. While it is argued that increased complexity can increase revenue and reduce lost sales due to a better fit with consumer desires, variation typically results in higher supply chain cost. More complexity may also reduce the firm's ability to innovate because of the need for consistency, compatibility, and challenges related to retrofitting existing products. More product variations substantially increase the difficulty related to innovation and change.

Since product complexity impacts both market and cost considerations, the firm's goal is to identify the balance that maximizes profit, as Figure 17.4 illustrates. Too few product variations will likely result in lost sales and minimal profit. Too many variations will result

TABLE 17.1
**Benefits of Low
Complexity**

- Better product development
- Improved product quality and reliability
- Improved demand / forecasting / customer service
- Lower sales support costs / resources
- Increased flexibility and reduced lead time

TABLE 17.2
**Characteristics of
High Complexity**

- Increased revenue
- Higher product cost
- Lowered ability to change/innovate
- Other costs/risks
- Lost sales
- Lowered service and support opportunities

in increased revenue but at some point, the cost associated with each variant increases faster than the revenue causing profitability to decline. As illustrated in Figure 17.4, the goal is to build and maintain the most profitable product portfolio.[3]

Regulatory

Supply chain management involves many interactions with external parties such as consumers, suppliers, government, and competitors. As a result, supply chain management is increasingly subject to regulation protecting individuals, commerce, and the environment. Regulations can promote or constrain supply chain activities. A promotional law may provide financial or tax advantages for completing supply chain activity in a specific country or region. A constraint may limit the types of activities and impact permissible in a region. The scope of a specific regulation may cover the globe or be limited to local region. The World Trade Organization **(WTO)** is a global body that promotes many policies that try to simultaneously enhance global trade while limiting widespread impact.[4] In contrast, many regulations are limited to a specific locale. A detailed review of promotional and constraint regulation is beyond the scope of this text. However, the following sections provide specific examples illustrating how regulation impacts supply chain operations. The specific regulatory examples discussed include environmental and financial and taxation.

[3] David Closs, Mark Jacobs, Morgan Swink, and G. Scott Webb, "Toward a Theory of Competencies for the Management of Product Complexity: Six Case Studies," *Journal of Operations Management* 26 (2008), pp. 590–610. For an expanded discussion of complexity and its impact on business operations, see John L. Mariotti, *The Complexity Crisis* (Avon, MA: Platinum Press), 2008.
[4] For a more detailed discussion of The World Trade Organization, see www.wto.org.

FIGURE 17.4
**Complexity and
Profitability**

Goal is to build and maintain the most profitable product portfolio

Complexity within and across products

Environmental

There are many dimensions of environmental regulation that directly affect supply chain activities. There are two that are particularly relevant due to increasing activity by political and consumer groups. These include green initiatives and recycling/returns.

Green initiatives include a wide category of regulations and activities aimed at directly reducing the supply chain's impact on the environment. Examples of these are vehicle emissions, reduced packaging, and supply chain redesign. As discussed in Chapter 8, the federal government has mandated that vehicle manufacturers reduce their harmful emissions. These mandates have resulted in improved diesel technology for both on-road and marine applications.[5] For example, the ports of Long Beach and Los Angeles, California, have restricted the types of diesels and hours that may be used to pick up and deliver freight at the port. A related example is increased regulations restricting pick-up and delivery times in congested areas such as central business districts or ports. Many cities are restricting the time of permissible truck operations and scheduling port operation to reduce the concentration of trucks.

In packaging, some firms have established their own initiatives to reduce waste and transportation expense. Following their focus on RFID discussed in Chapter 5, WalMart* began to work with their top suppliers to reduce packaging waste. Specifically, they have established an online scorecard to guide their suppliers.[6] Their goal is to reduce their packaging by 5 percent by 2013. WalMart* has extended the requirements for reduced packaging to Asia, thus resulting in global implications.

Some firms are redesigning their supply chain to meet regulated or social environmental standards. Supply chain redesign initiatives include plant and distribution center relocation to minimize energy use or carbon footprint, facility "greening" with more environmental lighting and fork trucks, shifting transportation modes, and reduced transport risk. Dow Chemical and Whirlpool have both demonstrated significant efforts to reduce the environmental impact of their supply chains.[7]

Recycling/return initiatives have been underway for many years but are beginning to experience renewed growth. Governments are modifying regulations to encourage firms to accept and promote consumer return of used product and packaging. Numerous U.S. states require consumer beverage container deposits in an effort to motivate returns for recycling. Some states are developing plans to include juice and water containers in such deposit plans to further motivate recycling. The European Union has instigated broader legislation to require the recycling of electronic waste. The Wastes of Electric and Electronic Equipments **(WEEE)** legislation requires manufacturers to take responsibility for end-of-life acceptance and processing of their products.[8] Specifically, firms manufacturing appliances and electronics in Europe are required to enable reverse supply chains that accept end-of-life product, return it to a reprocessing facility, and either recondition it for resale or decompose it to components that can be reused or recycled. Similar initiatives are beginning to develop for the automotive industry. Other developed countries are beginning to consider similar legislation.

There are two issues firms must consider when faced with recycling initiatives. The first concerns how active the firm should be in guiding or promoting the recycling initiative.

---

[5] For more detail, see www.epa.gov/otaq/highway-diesel/index.htm.

[6] Marcus Kabel, "Wal-Mart Goes Online to Cut Packaging Waste," *Transport Topics,* no. 3746 (June 18, 2007), p. S11.

[7] For a more detailed discussing regarding these redesign initiatives, see Esther D'Amico, "Shippers Focus on Safety and Security Link across Supply Chain," *Chemical Week* 170, no. 2. (January 1, 2008), p. 9; and James A. Cooke, "The Greening of Whirlpool's Supply Chain," *CSCMP Quarterly* (Quarter 2, 2008), pp. 46–49.

[8] Rita Gamberini, Elisa Gebennini, Andrea Grassi, Cristina Mora, and Bianca Rimini, "An Innovative Model of WEEE Recovery Network Management in Accordance with the EU Initiatives," *International Journal of Environmental Technology and Management* 8, no. 4 (2008), p. 348.

In many cases, firms want to minimize their involvement or at least their visibility so that they are not labeled as "anti-environmental." However, it is sometimes advantageous for firms to become actively involved to educate policy makers and consumers regarding the trade-offs associated with regulatory and policy alternatives. This is particularly true when there are a number of governmental entities involved. For example, there are a number of U.S. states requiring the recycling of beverage containers, as mentioned previously. While one can argue the relative cost and benefits of such initiatives, the current recycling systems have a number of different variants. In some cases, the consumer returns the recycled product to retailers, in others to recycling centers. In situations where separate political entities implement different policies, national firms are forced to develop recycling systems to accommodate each unique situation. This substantially reduces economies of scale and increases the cost of recycling. More proactive involvement by industry leaders can educate policy makers and consumers regarding the total costs associated with each option and the benefits of consistency.

The second issue concerns the design of the reverse logistics system. In some cases, public policy makers "design" the system by defining the process in the legislation. For example, the State of Michigan beverage container recycling law requires that retailers accept empty beverage containers for all brands they sell. In turn the distributor is required to arrange for empties to be picked up. Other states use different recovery systems. In other industries, such as cameras and electronic goods, the supply chain used in initial product distribution also perform the reverse logistics activity. Others use channels specifically designed to facilitate reverse logistics. The advantage of using the current system is that it is not necessary to maintain a separate system. The disadvantage of using the current system is that reverse flow can hinder the efficiency of the channel. Organizations such as the Reverse Logistics Executive Council work jointly with manufacturers, distributors, and retailers to design reverse logistic systems that are both effective and efficient.[9]

Financial and Taxation

Chapter 13 discussed the concepts and processes regarding supply chain design. While meeting desired service requirements is the major focus, a critical requirement is to minimize total supply chain cost. This includes the combination of procurement, manufacturing, logistics, and customer accommodation related costs. National, regional, and even local tax considerations are becoming increasingly significant for supply chain design.

National, regional, and local taxes can impact supply chain design in multiple ways including property, income, and value-added taxes **(VAT)**. As countries and localities try to maintain or develop jobs, they are increasingly considering tax incentives related to supply chain activities to attract firms. States, provinces, and cities have used property tax incentives and holidays to attract firms to locate manufacturing plants and distribution centers within their areas. In effect, a tax holiday is when they waive taxes on property, equipment, and/or inventory either for a defined time period or permanently. The political entities believe this is good public policy to attract jobs and the resulting housing and income tax base. While firms have traditionally considered taxes when making supply chain and facility location decisions, the relative tax rates between locations have not been decisive factors. However, as taxes have increased, these holidays have caused firms to shift facilities between relatively nearby cities and states. For example, many firms have located warehousing in or near Reno, Nevada, rather than in California to reduce property and inventory taxes.

[9]For more detail regarding reverse logistics best practices, see the Reverse Logistics Executive Council at www.rlec.org.

More recently, countries have begun to use tax abatements to attract supply chain facilities to locations that may not have been otherwise desirable. In such cases, countries have changed their tax policies to reduce VAT, corporate, or individual income taxes. The VAT is based on the value-added in a particular country and may range from 10–40 percent of the value increase. As an example, the European Union allowed Ireland to offer firms in the electronics and pharmaceutical industries a reduced VAT. For those industries, the firms could produce product in Ireland with a VAT of 10–12 percent rather than approximately 20 percent for the remainder of Europe. Since this policy approximated a reduction of 5–10 percent in the taxes on the good, depending on the contribution margin, the differential was often great enough to relocate facilities to Ireland, even though the strategy from an operational perspective may result in higher overall supply chain cost. With corporate income taxes in the range of 30–50 percent, firms are also electing to move major supply chain activities to locales with corporate and personal income tax advantages.

Whether it is property, VAT, or income taxes, many governments are using tax strategies to successfully attract firms to their locations. In some cases, such decisions may improve the firm's overall financial performance by minimizing global taxes. However, the tax-stimulated decision may also introduce supply chain challenges. In the situation cited above, for example, while the tax strategy attracted firms to locate in Ireland, the island location and the dependence on air transport capacity introduced many supply chain operational problems that needed to be resolved. Other locales including Singapore, Asia, South America, the Middle East, and Africa are developing tax-alignment strategies. The result is that supply chain executives must work with their financial counterparts to tax align their supply chain **(TASC)**.[10] TASC aims to help firms achieve a favorable worldwide tax rate.

There are two supply chain strategies that firms can use to tax align their supply chain. The first is a central entrepreneur or principal model that centralizes key functions and business risks in a low-tax country. For example, firms may centralize corporate purchasing or inventory management in a low-tax country and then arrange their intracorporate transfer pricing to realize a substantial proportion of the income in the tax-advantaged location. The second is an incremental strategy that considers the tax implications of incremental supply chain changes such as single facility location. The incremental strategy requires that firms systematically consider the property, VAT, and income tax implications of supply chain decisions.

While such tax strategies have typically been used by countries to attract firm supply chain activities, states, provinces, and cities have begun to use similar strategies to attract firms to their specific locale. This is likely to increase as many regional politicians attempt to maintain local jobs and tax base. However, it is important to recognize that while advantageous tax strategies can be established quickly, they can also be withdrawn. Therefore, the probable duration of the incentives must be carefully evaluated.

Resource Availability

While global supply chain operations can significantly increase firm opportunities in terms of resource availability, technology, and market access, they also substantially increase dependence on critical resources including expertise and transport capability. Significant changes in the availability or cost of these resources can dramatically change supply chain design and operations. This section presents a strategic discussion regarding resource availability.

[10] Maurice Emmer and Dan Lange, "Advantages of Tax-Aligning the Supply Chain," *Financial Executive* 23, no. 8 (October 2007), pp. 56–59.

Supply Chain Expertise

One of the major challenges faced by global supply chain executives is the development and retention of supply chain talent. Without a pool of existing talent and a pipeline of future talent, it becomes increasingly difficult for firms to sustain global competitiveness. Two dimensions of expertise are particularly important for sustainable supply chain management. The first is cross-functional expertise that systematically develops and maintains knowledge regarding the breadth of supply chain functionality including customer accommodation, logistics, manufacturing, and procurement. The second is a broad and deep knowledge regarding both global requirements and individual country operations. While it is generally not possible for individuals to have both, individual firms need to develop an appropriate talent team including combinations of both types of individuals. Guidelines for developing such a team are discussed below.

Most important, a SCM professional should have experience in multiple supply chain functions and must be able to lead or direct the design, implementation, and management of cross-functional supply chain solutions. While these solutions could be completely internal, they generally extend outside of the enterprise and involve multiple tiers of suppliers and customers. These solutions require the integration and coordination of the eight universal processes introduced in Chapter 1.

At a senior level, a supply chain management executive must evaluate and make trade-offs between supply chain functions, other firm functions, and external organizations. To effectively identify and evaluate these trade-offs, it is essential to blend sufficient functional knowledge depth with an understanding of cross-functional integration and cross-organizational collaboration. For example, a supply chain management executive must be able to balance customer service and quality with total supply chain costs across all organizations and functions. To perform this balancing act successfully, the supply chain leader must consider all of the supply chain planning, management, and measurement of activities involved in procurement, manufacturing, logistics, and customer accommodation management. It is important that the assessment include products, services and solutions, and related information. In striking the right balance, the professional also needs to consider coordination and collaboration with customers and suppliers as well as other associated supply chain stakeholders such as sales and marketing.

In addition to identifying the trade-offs, it is essential to develop and implement integrated and comprehensive supply chain solutions. Innovative, end-to-end supply chain solutions need to be implemented on a broad business scale—across the enterprise on a global basis.

The supply chain professional's job also includes disseminating knowledge and experience to help business partners in their supply chain design and execution. To this end, supply chain professionals should be viewed by their peers and senior leadership as supply chain consultants. They should be able to apply the principles and methodologies of supply chain management to other parts of the organization and define enterprise-level architecture for resolution of complex problems. Finally, the professional must also be able to analyze the overall business performance to facilitate sustainable competitive advantage.

The supply chain management executive needs to develop the skills and capabilities to operate effectively as described above. Developing the right skills and knowledge can enhance not only supply chain performance, but also enterprise performance. Supply chain managers can no longer rely solely on the focused functional skills of the past to ensure a bright future. Instead, they need to develop cross-functional management skills, which must be integrated and aligned with the firm's overall business strategy. In many cases, such integrative management requires a redefinition of the skills, roles, and responsibilities of the traditional supply chain professional. It is apparent that a variety of skills are needed to manage the complexity and uncertainty inherent in SCM. Furthermore, supply chain managers need to be open to continual learning as today's supply chain skills may not maintain relevance for the future.

The importance of possessing the right supply chain skills is underscored by Myers et al.[11] Their study demonstrated that a supply chain manager's experience and education does not predict work performance; instead, job skills predict success. Therefore, it is important for aspiring supply chain management executives to be provided with appropriate opportunities and guidance to develop the job skills that will enhance their potential for success.

While researchers and practitioners alike are calling for the development of supply chain management, there is some disagreement regarding how this process will evolve. Most agree that context-independent skills are important for supply chain professionals. These include broader managerial capabilities such as people skills, social skills, coordination, change management, communication, decision-making skills, problem-solving skills, time management, and cultural skills.

Regarding technical and technological skills, however, there is some disagreement. Some researchers have suggested that supply chain management should not include technical skills. Others regard technical skills as fundamental for developing cross-functional, cross-enterprise managerial skills. Some experts have also placed special emphasis on information technology skills and expertise. From the literature, however, it is clear that researchers are not advocating deep technical skills. The consensus seems to be that supply chain professionals not only have to be competent in their technical expertise but must have leadership skills that are context-independent and can cut across boundaries of function and organization.

Dischinger et al. have suggested that a true supply chain management executive must have skills and capabilities in the following five areas: (1) functional, (2) technical, (3) leadership, (4) global management, and (5) experience and credibility.[12]

Functional Skills

A supply chain mangement executive should have established subject-matter expertise and relevant skills in several of the major supply chain functions including procurement, transportation, demand/supply planning, inventory, manufacturing, global operations, and customer fulfillment. As one approaches senior leadership responsibility, ideally they will have worked at the operational level in multiple functions to fully understand the day-to-day processes, challenges, and issues. This functional experience should include a combination of hands-on operations and managerial experience.

Technical Skills

Given the increasing dependence of supply chain on technology, a true SCM professional must have experience in applying information technology effectively. This does not suggest that a supply chain management executive must be experienced in technology development. A senior leader ideally will have dealt with the challenges of technology selection, implementation, and application. A well-developed understanding of the relationship between supply chain processes and execution management solutions is also a critical part of this skill set.

[11] M. B. Myers, D. A. Griffith, P. J. Daugherty, and R. F. Lusch, "Maximizing the Human Capital Equation in Logistics: Education, Experience, and Skills," *Journal of Business Logistics*, 25, no.1 (2004), pp. 211–32.
[12] John Dischinger, David Closs, Eileen McCullogh, Cheri Speier, William Grenoble, and Donna Marshall, "The Emerging Supply Chain Management Profession," *Supply Chain Management Review*, January/February 2006, pp. 62–68.

Leadership Skills

A supply chain management executive must demonstrate a broad range of leadership capabilities. Most supply chain management assignments require a capability to lead projects involving customers, partners, and/or competitors while effectively interacting with both internal and external executives. A supply chain management executive must also demonstrate leadership and experience in complex, matrixed business environments. This experience will ensure that supply chain initiatives and resources are managed and integrated effectively. Other broad leadership skills relate to communication, negotiation, problem solving, team leadership, and project management.

Global Management

In today's boundary-spanning supply chain environment, a supply chain management executive must have global planning and operations experience. This experience provides the insight into the global supply chain environment and its challenges. Ideally, professionals will have had one or two experiences working outside their home country. The next best thing is to have extensive involvement in and responsibility for global planning and operations.

Experience and Credibility

A supply chain management executive must possess sufficient knowledge, breadth, and experience to evaluate the competitive environment, to conceptualize strategy, to assess and organize solutions, and to implement change both in the organization and with supply chain partners. This capability is achieved by developing experience and credibility within the enterprise as well as developing substantial credibility externally. External credibility can be achieved through a variety of activities, such as participation in industry conferences and associations, receipt of awards and patents, and publication in business/professional journals.

Similarly, supply chain management executive development will proceed differently today than in the past. As a result, human resources and supply chain departments will need to collaborate more and change their expectations regarding the source of future talent. The solid lines in Figure 17.5 illustrate what a typical career path looked like in the past. Talent often rose through the ranks in one of the single functional areas of demand/supply planning, procurement, manufacturing, logistics, or fulfillment. While the resulting individuals were thoroughly grounded in their functions, they did not always understand the integrated processes or the functional trade-offs. The dotted lines in Figure 17.5 illustrate the cross-functional career path necessary to develop today's supply chain professional.

As organizational structures become flatter and supply chain leadership requires more holistic business skills, firms need to develop a range of training models. Certifications are particularly useful for a workforce without formal supply chain training and may also broaden the skill sets of mid-level managers who have earned university SCM degrees. Additionally, continuous education is needed to expose emerging leaders to changes in technological advances and to challenge their acceptance of current industry paradigms. Consequently, companies will find it beneficial to develop strategic relationships with educational institutions to ensure long-term value creation.

To develop a strong supply chain organization particularly globally, firms must face the daunting task of identifying new talent and training their emerging leaders to meet needs that are as yet unidentified. Firms also need to perform effective succession planning that allows them to retain and develop their critical talent base. Firms with the most successful and competitive supply chains recognize that technical knowledge and training

FIGURE 17.5 **Cross-Functional Supply Chain Career Paths**

Source: John Dischinger, David Closs, Eileen McCullogh, Cheri Speier, William Grenoble, and Donna Marshall, "The Emerging Supply Chain Management Profession," *Supply Chain Management Review,* January/February 2006, pp. 62–68.

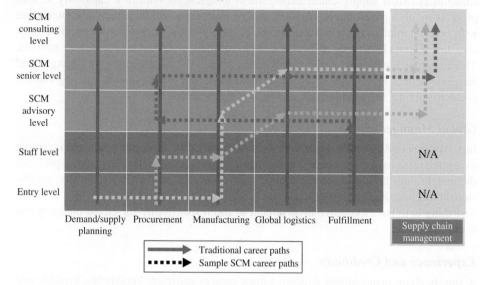

by themselves are insufficient. Supply chain management executives must be able to meet the rapid changes of a global economy that demands greater connectivity across companies and geographies and rapidly evolving technologies. They must also have a greater breadth of knowledge in related operational areas and must possess enhanced leadership and communication skills to enable them to become an adaptable resource and ensure competitive advantage into the future.

Transport Capability

The variability of diesel fuel prices has been a subject of daily concern. After increasing over 300 percent since December 2000, the upward trend abruptly reversed in late 2008 as the economy slid into recession. Figure 17.6 illustrates the month-end fuel prices based on U.S. Department of Energy data. Diesel is the primary fuel source supporting global supply chain operations and represents approximately 30 percent of overall transportation cost. Therefore, a diesel fuel price increase of 100 percent increases overall transportation cost by 30 percent. The result of such dramatic fluctuation in fuel and resulting transportation cost is that supply chains must be regularly reassessed to determine what network structure and strategy are best for a firm.

Fuel price volatility influences supply chain decisions in two ways. First, it may dramatically influence the viability and flow of global trade. At $4.50 per gallon for diesel fuel, firms are reconsidering where they source product from and the transportation modes utilized. Higher fuel prices favor more localized operations as exemplified by IKEA locating a plant in Virginia and increased volume manufactured by steelmakers in the middle of the United States.[13] Increases in transportation cost also reduce the relative advantage of low-cost-labor countries. Higher fuel cost also diverts more international freight to ocean transport from air. The implication is that supply chain decision makers may source from

[13] David Lynch, "Transport Costs Could Alter World Trade," *USA Today,* August 11, 2008,

FIGURE 17.6
**U.S. Diesel Fuel
Prices Since 1994 (in
USD per gallon)**

Source: U.S. Department of
Energy.

U.S. No. 2 Diesel retail sales by all sellers (USD per gallon)

less-distant suppliers with manufacturing postponement or late accommodation being used
to customize products in local markets.

Second, transportation cost increases may also change the domestic logistics network. Building on Chapter 13's discussion regarding the total cost curve, transport cost
increases will shift the total transportation cost curve up and to the right. Figure 17.7
illustrates how transport cost increases of 25, 50, and 100 percent cause the total cost
curve to shift. At the base fuel price, the figure illustrates that the least-total-cost number of distribution centers is seven. As the fuel price increases, the least-total-cost
structure increases to 10 distribution centers. To apply this concept, Procter & Gamble
are considering new distribution centers to respond to the recent increases in transportation cost.[14]

Outsourcing

Another means that firms are using to manage risk is the use of logistics and supply
chain outsourcing to third-party logistics **(3PL)** firms or logistics integrators. Third-
party logistics firms and logistics integrators provide supply-chain-related activities such
as transportation, warehousing, light manufacturing, information technology, customer

[14] Ibid.

FIGURE 17.7
**Optimal Number of
Distribution Centers
by Fuel Price**

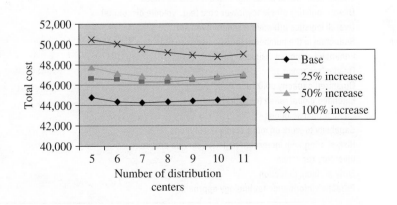

service, and returns processing to other companies on a contractual basis. Third-party logistics providers typically provide integrated transportation and warehousing services. Integrated service providers are more like resource orchestrators that solicit and coordinate the logistics services from 3PLs as well as providing resource management expertise.

While some firms view logistics outsourcing as a means to reduce cost, on a much broader basis it can also assist in managing risk. From the cost perspective, logistics outsourcing can reduce cost because most firms that offer logistics outsourcing arrangements are nonunionized. So, unionized manufacturers can shift material handling, warehousing, and transportation activities to a logistics service provider at a lower wage rate. Logistics outsourcing can also shift supply chain risk by assigning a supply chain activity to a partner that can take advantage of economies of scale, scope, or expertise. Specifically, a supply chain partner that primarily focuses on a supply chain activity such as warehousing, transportation, technical expertise, or process expertise can likely complete the task with less risk and a lower cost. Logistics outsourcing can also reduce risk by pooling capacity across a number of clients, resulting in a lower risk of not being able to meet customer demands due to a surge. Table 17.3 lists the benefits that firms are experiencing from the use of integrated logistics services or outsourcing. These benefits contribute to the outsourcing firm by reducing risks related to uncertainty, capacity, process, and expertise.

Table 17.4 lists the types of services that are outsourced to 3PLs and logistics integrators. The relative percentage of respondents outsourcing illustrates that the majority of outsourcing is for transportation and warehouse-related activities. However, there are a growing number of firms that are outsourcing order management, light manufacturing, and consulting services to 3PLs and integrated service providers. While cost will continue to be a major objective, firms are also seeking to manage overall risk through access to expertise.

In summary, expertise and fuel availability are critical to supply chain sustainability. The relative accessibility and cost will likely continue to challenge logistics and supply chain executives in the design and operation of supply chains. The extreme volatility of fuel cost will continue to place a premium on flexibility. It is also likely that firms will have to become more proactive in designing for and guaranteeing access to expertise and

TABLE 17.3
Benefits Experienced from the Use of Integrated Logistics Services

Source: C. John Langley, *The State of Logistics Outsourcing 2008 Third-Party Logistics* (Atlanta, GA: Georgia Tech, 2008), p. 18.

Benefits	Percentage of Firms Realized
Greater ease of managing outsourced logistics services (i.e., one point of contact)	75
Reduced management time and effort	69
Enabled our firm to focus more on our core business	67
Overall logistics efficiency/lower cost (e.g., volume discounts)	56
Overall logistics effectiveness/improved service	56
Reduction in the number of logistics service providers	51
Enhanced shipment visibility	39
Quicker response	37
Optimized capacity utilization	34
Extended global reach (network)	31
Custom-built solutions	24
Capability to work on more complex solutions	24
Risk-sharing with integrated logistics service providers	23
Inventory reduction	22
Early problem detection	22
Proactive information technology approach	18

TABLE 17.4
Types of Services Outsourced to Logistics Integrators

Source: C. John Langley, *"The State of Logistics Outsourcing 2008 Third-Party Logistics"* (Atlanta, GA: Georgia Tech, 2008), p. 13.

Outsourced Logistics Service	Percent of Respondents Outsourcing
Domestic transportation	85
International transportation	81
Warehousing	72
Customs clearance and brokerage	65
Forwarding	52
Shipment consolidation	46
Reverse logistics (defective, repair, return)	38
Cross-docking	38
Transportation management (shipment planning and execution with one or more carriers)	37
Product labeling, packaging, assembly, and kitting	36
Freight bill auditing and payment	30
Supply chain consulting provided by 3PL	17
Order entry, processing, and fulfillment	15
Fleet management	13
Lead logistics provider/logistics integrator services	13
Customer service	12

resources. Specifically, firms need to develop contracts that guarantee access to critical resources and offer education to create qualified human resource expertise. The trend also indicates that firms will continue to increase the amount of outsourcing to reduce both expenses and risk.

Security

Global operations increasingly require more secure supply chains to protect the firm, its products, and its reputation. Secure supply chains require that the firm not only design such internal processes to reduce security risk but also to collaborate with supply chain partners as well as the government to minimize risks involved in interfirm and cross-border operations. This section discusses the actions firms are taking to develop more secure supply chains and the initiatives governments are taking to reduce risk. It is important that supply chain executives understand the need for collaboration. Failure to collaborate leads to either increased risk or redundancy, each of which exposes consumers to increased risk and higher cost.

Developing a Secure Supply Chain

Supply chain security is the application of policies, procedures, and technology to protect assets, product, facilities, equipment, information, and personnel from theft, damage, or terrorism and to prevent the introduction to the supply chain of unauthorized contraband, people, or weapons of mass destruction. The supply chain security challenges posed by the threat of terrorism have significant implications for firms, suppliers, customers, carriers, terminal operators, governments, and global trading partners. Indeed, the global economy is dependent on supply chain security and resiliency. While supply chain security was defined previously, supply chain **resiliency** refers to a supply chain's ability to withstand and recover from an incident. A resilient supply chain is proactive in anticipating and establishing planned steps to prevent and respond to security incidents. Resilient supply chains quickly rebuild or reestablish alternative means of operations when they experience a security incident.

Rationale for Supply Chain Protection[15]

Increased threats of terrorism require heightened awareness of firm and supply chain security. In the past, firms may have considered only the potential threat to their firm when considering defense protection. However, given the interconnectedness of firms, products, and transportation infrastructure in today's high-speed global supply chains, there is growing concern that disruptions can and typically will impact operations beyond individual firms, leading to the need for a broader supply chain defense framework.

Firms must proactively enhance their supply chain resiliency against terrorism. They need to enhance overall security as well, to protect customers, the public, and brand equity. This starts with understanding the five key potential adverse consequences of supply chain security failures: 1) A terrorist attack against a firm's supply chain might cause widespread disruption to customer delivery capabilities leading to a loss of short-term revenue and creating a service failure; 2) There could be reduced brand equity if customers believe the attack occurred because of a supply chain security failure resulting from neglect; 3) Loss of revenue could lead to investor discontent with the firm's performance, and the subsequent sale of equity investments; 4) This disruption could also increase regulatory scrutiny; and 5) A terrorist attack could result in significant legal liability.

While the above are likely primary consequences for the target firm, secondary consequences extending beyond the target firm including other supply chain partners are also likely. If supply partners perceive the attack was due to the firm's insufficient security efforts, the supply chain relationship would suffer and could potentially be dissolved.

The challenges associated with supply chain defense are significant, particularly in today's environment where numerous entities are involved in cross-organizational and particularly cross-border movement where a product is handled multiple times and many ownership changes. The number of parties involved in these exchanges creates significant challenges when one considers that defense efforts of one firm can be nullified by the inattention or inadequacy of a single supply chain partner.

Brand protection and safety are the primary reasons for enhancing security. Practitioners fear that product contamination may damage customer perceptions of their brand. Related to brand equity are the issues of brand piracy, gray markets, and product counterfeiting. Firms secure supply chain assets in order to reduce theft and provide product origin assurance for customers.

To protect themselves, firms now require greater security from their suppliers. Whether this requirement comes in the form of quality certification programs, audits, or other security initiatives like the Customs-Trade Partnership Against Terrorism, **(C-TPAT)**, firms need to be more vigilant regarding who is involved in the manufacturing and/or distribution of their products and set requirements that can be regularly monitored. Certainly, the recent recalls in the toy industry highlight the need for greater scrutiny in this context.

Government pressure is another significant driver. While many initiatives such as C-TPAT are voluntary, the government has formally enacted regulatory measures. The Bioterrorism Act of 2002, for example, requires that firms engaged in food processing be able to trace raw materials and finished goods one step up, and one step down, the supply chain. Additionally, in an effort to provide consumers with more information regarding product origin, regulatory and voluntary guidelines have been developed for "country of origin labeling" **(COOL)** labels for some agricultural and food products.

[15] This research was supported by the U.S. Department of Homeland Security (Grant number N-00014-04-1-0659) through a grant awarded to the National Center for Food Protection and Defense at the University of Minnesota. Any opinions, findings, conclusions, or recommendations expressed in this publication are those of the authors and do not represent the policy or position of the Department of Homeland Security.

While these initiatives are prompting firms to be proactive in establishing security programs, many managers are still myopic regarding their firm's vulnerability and have been slow to initiate security programs. One possible explanation is that managers feel their firm will not be the target of a terrorist attack. Other managers may believe that their security obligations end when goods are transferred to another supply chain partner.

The Security Framework

This framework identifies core competencies that firms must develop to protect themselves, their supply chains, and their customers. As defined by this framework, supply chains require 10 security competencies to protect their products and themselves.

Security competencies are created through the development of security capabilities such as infrastructure, processes, assets, and resources that achieve and maintain supply chain security. Table 17.5 defines specific security competencies while Table 17.6 provides examples regarding specific initiatives firms are using to apply each competency.

Cross-Border Operations

Given the global nature of supply chains, firms are similarly dependent on the procedures, laws, and regulations that may be unique in different countries. Decisions regarding suppliers are likely to increasingly depend on the trusted partner status of the supplier's firm and country. The specific concern is whether supply chain partners and service providers have demonstrated that they can be trusted to ensure the security of product when it is within their control. Finally, supply chain managers must engage in self-appraisal of supply chain security and contingency planning, and cross-functional teams must develop crisis management plans that include planning, mitigation, detection, response, and recovery components.

TABLE 17.5
Supply Chain Security Competency Definitions

Competency	Definition
Process strategy	The executive commitment to enhancing security and instituting a culture of security within the enterprise
Process management	The degree to which specific security provisions have been integrated into processes managing the flow of materials and products into and out of the firm
Infrastructure management	Security provisions that have been implemented to secure the physical infrastructure and products (e.g., buildings, transportation vehicles)
Communication management	The internal information exchange between employees, managers, and contractors to increase security
Management technology	The effectiveness of existing information systems for identifying and responding to a potential security breach
Process technology	Specific technology (e.g., electronic seals, RFID) implemented to limit access and trace the movement of goods
Metrics	The availability and use of measures to better identify and manage security threats
Relationship management	The information sharing and collaboration between the firm and its supply chain partners (e.g., customers, suppliers)
Service provider collaboration management	The information sharing and collaboration between the firm and its logistics service providers (e.g., transportation firms, warehousing providers, 3PLs, etc.)
Public interface management	The security-related relationships and exchanges of information with the government and the public

TABLE 17.6 Examples of Security Competency Initiatives

Competency	Corporate Example
Process strategy	• Senior management believes that supply chain security is critical for consumer and brand protection • Firm has cross-functional representation on senior-level security crisis management team • Management support for security consciousness is indoctrinated through ongoing training
Process management	• Defined procedures to complete product recalls • Standardized procedures to control receipt and shipment of product • Applies hazard analysis and critical control point (HACCP) system
Infrastructure management	• Application of gates, locks, access controls, and guards to restrict access to sensitive areas • Application of monitoring equipment to detect unauthorized activity • Controls for nonemployees to limit access to facilities and operations
Communication management	• Incorporates modules on preventing contamination/security incidents into employee training • Establishes defined communication protocols in case of a contamination/security incident • Establishes defined reporting protocols in case of a contamination/security incident
Management technology	• Able to quickly share information with employees in case of a contamination/security incident • Secure information systems • Ability to track transactions by origin, destination, date, description, and route
Process technology	• Ability to track and trace commodities and products up and down one stage in the supply chain • Ability to track salvage and returned products • Transportation assets are sealed while not under control of the firm
Metrics	• Measures to track and monitor vulnerable areas (e.g., products, facilities, supply base) • Supply chain security metrics are based on a combination of internal, industry, and government guidelines
Relationship management/service provider collaboration management	• Applies external audits (as opposed to self-audits) to verify security procedures • Maintains a database of emergency contact information for service providers • Requires service providers to use government or industry security guidelines
Public interface management	• Complies with government-required record-keeping regulations regarding threats and incidents • Establishes communication strategy for providing information regarding contamination/security incidents to appropriate government/public agencies

In order to promote economic growth and increase international trade, governments are responsible for facilitating the movement of people and goods across borders and are ultimately responsible for the safety of people, country, and commerce. For government agencies, the traditional focus has been on the control of trade, insuring the collection of taxes and fees, restricting the flow of illegal items, with sampling inspection of imports for security.[16] The contemporary focus, however, is shifting to trade facilitation and secure supply chain operations using trusted partners to increase security through export inspection and information trails. The very notion of trusted partners, however, must be developed on a platform of global cooperation.

[16] The level of control of imports and exports of course varies with the movement of certain tightly controlled technologies.

The United States and many of its trading partners have responded to the threat of terrorism by initiating efforts to build security and facilitate trade. Congress mandated that the Department of Homeland Security **(DHS)** Directorate of Border and Transportation Security ensure the speedy, orderly, and efficient flow of lawful traffic and commerce. United States Customs and Border Protection, now part of DHS, has attempted to facilitate trade and increase security through C-TPAT, Container Security Initiative **(CSI)**, and related programs.[17] C-TPAT seeks to advance-certify selected shippers through self-appraisals of security procedures coupled with customs audits and verifications. CSI calls for prescreening of containers coupled with fast tracking when the cargo reaches the United States. The Advanced Manifest Rule **(AMR)** and more recent Advance Cargo Information **(ACI)** require detailed cargo data before the cargo is brought into or shipped from the United States by ocean, air, rail, or truck.[18] The Free and Secure Trade **(FAST)** program allows low-risk goods transported by trusted carriers for trusted firms to pass rapidly through border crossings while reserving inspection resources for unknown or high-risk shipments. These provisions all require international cooperation. The next evolution in these developments will be to use technology to enhance the detection of tampering, increase tracking efficiency and effectiveness, and extend the scope of "trusted partners" at a greater number of shipping locations.

These global efforts are not confined to initiatives of the U.S. government. The World Trade Organization **(WTO)** also seeks to facilitate trade by moving controls and inspection to the export stage by sharing uniform information among government agencies, firms, suppliers, carriers, and customers. The World Customs Organization **(WCO)**, including the 161 member countries involved in the Global Standards for Supply Chain Security initiative, similarly seeks to facilitate trade by developing and promoting guidelines to help customs administrations work together to achieve rapid clearance of low-risk cross-border shipments.

The U.S. Customs programs as well as the efforts of the WTO and WCO have broadened customs verification processes to include exports, relying on declarations that include essential data for adequate cargo risk assessment. The data include commodity description, price, origin and destination, shipper and consignee, and transportation provider to be used by certifying manufacturers, carriers, and other entities. The International Organization for Standardization **(ISO)** is working with Strategic Council on Security Technology on a Smart and Secure Tradelanes **(SST)** initiative. SST is developing a technology platform to track containers globally and generate chain-of-custody audit trails.

Summary

Logistics and supply chain executives have substantially increased their visibility in the firm over the past 20 years. One advantage of this increased visibility is a greater role in designing and executing corporate strategy. However, this advantage comes with a broader responsibility for collaborating in the management of the firm's global risk. This chapter described and discussed some of the dimensions of firm risk that have major logistics and supply chain implications. The chapter began with a review of the expanding focus in supply chain from primarily cost minimization to overall firm risk management.

[17] For a more detailed and current discussion regarding these initiatives to enhance supply chain security, see the U.S. Department of Homeland Security Web site at www.dhs.gov.

[18] The AMR applies to sea cargo. The Advance Electronic Presentation of Cargo Information encompasses ocean, air, rail, and truck. Similar requirements were imposed by Israel in November 2003 and others have followed.

Today's logistics and supply chain leaders must understand overall corporate risk management and be able to position their recommendations and strategies in this corporate context.

Following the discussion of risk, the dimensions and trends of individual firm risk in a supply chain context were discussed. These include product complexity, regulatory, resource availability, and security. Product complexity refers to the number of product variations offered domestically or globally. While more product variations may be more attractive to a broader range of consumers, increased complexity often drives up supply chain cost. Today's supply chain manager must work with marketing colleagues to develop the appropriate balance.

The regulatory environment is also introducing supply chain challenges as cities, regions, and countries expand and refine environmental and taxation policies. Regulatory changes, which can be quite dynamic, can substantially affect the location and strategies for global supply chain activities. It is important that logistics and supply chain executives understand the impact of the regulatory environment and work with their finance, taxation, and environmental counterparts to make appropriate risk trade-offs.

Logistics and supply chain executives cite two major concerns as they attempt to develop sustainable supply chains. The first is access to supply chain expertise that is cross-functional and globally aware. As firms have globalized, the shortage of expertise has become increasingly apparent. The second is the dramatic volatility in energy cost. Since most supply chains were designed in a time of lower cost energy, today's logistics and supply chain manager must consider the supply chain changes that are necessary in a time of increasingly expensive and more dynamic energy cost. This assessment must also consider short- and longer-range strategies related to the availability and cost of alternative fuels.

The last, but certainly not least, is the need to develop secure and resilient supply chains. Firms must refine internal processes and strategies, collaborative strategies with supply chain partners, and governmental relationships to develop secure and safe global flow of product while trying to minimize the cost impact.

Challenge Questions

1. Discuss the implications for supply chain leadership as their focus shifts from minimizing total supply chain cost to managing overall firm risk.

2. Discuss the marketing and supply chain benefits and costs related to product complexity.

3. Compare and contrast the roles that logistics management, supply chain management, product quality, corporate security, logistics service providers, and the government need to play to enhance supply chain security.

4. Identify and discuss the trade-offs associated with operating a supply chain that handles both forward and reverse movement as compared with separate supply chains for forward and reverse movement.

5. Discuss the role that firms should play in responding to changes in public policy regarding environmental initiatives in the locations where they operate.

6. Discuss how regional and local tax strategy regarding property, value-added, inventory, and income taxes can influence supply chain design.

7. Describe the role that logistics and supply chain management should take in complying with C-TPAT, CSI, AMR, and ACI security initiatives.

8. Describe the role that information technology can play in enhancing supply chain security. Focus the discussion on the following technologies: RFID, shipment tracking and tracing, and supply chain planning systems.

9. Describe the initiatives that firms need to take to develop a sustainable pool of supply chain expertise.

10. Discuss the trade-offs that a firm must consider when determining the focus and comprehensiveness on supply chain security initiatives.

In the final analysis, the logistical management challenge is to rise above a traditional functional perspective to help capture and promulgate the need for managers to reinvent what they are all about. What they should be about is very simple—servicing customers. While it is sometimes hard to comprehend why, the fact is that most business firms are in need of a significant transformation to reposition resources to best accomplish this basic goal. For a host of reasons, complexity dominates the modern enterprise. Reinvention of a business is all about simplification, standardization, and integration. It is all about getting back to basics. Logistics is basic.

The logistics manager of the future will be much more of a change leader and much less of a technician. The challenge of change will be driven by the need to synchronize the speed and flexibility of logistical competency into the process of creating customer value. Technology and technique will not be limiting factors. If no new technology is invented for a decade or more, we still will not have fully exploited technology currently available. The concepts being promoted as new ways to improve productivity are for the most part old. Such concepts as activity-based costing, time-based competition, ABC inventory analysis, process integration, collaboration, quick response, segmentation, and so forth, are not new. What is new is that today's leader is supported by information technology that makes them work.

Of course, the challenge to reinvent the enterprise is not the sole responsibility of logisticians, but it is a responsibility of logistical managers to participate in the process, especially those who lead global operations, have stewardship for extensive capital and human resources, and facilitate the delivery of products and services to customers. The logistical executive of the future will not be able to neglect responsibility for contributing to and participating in the change management required to transform the enterprise to the digital information age.

To this end, authors typically collect quotations and statements that they feel capture the meaning and intensity of their message. To the logistics manager of today and tomorrow who will face the challenges of change, we offer the following quotes as a source of compassion and inspiration:

Concerning Change: Logistics Is Not an Ordinary Occupation

> Experience teaches that men are so much governed by what they are accustomed to see and practice that the simplest and most obvious improvements in the most ordinary occupations are adapted with hesitation, reluctance and by slow graduations.—*Alexander Hamilton,* 1791

Concerning Organization: It Is a Matter of Perspective

> We trained hard . . . but it seemed that every time we were beginning to form up into teams we would be reorganized. I was to learn later in life that we tend to meet any new situation by reorganizing; and a wonderful method it can be for creating the illusion of progress while producing confusion, inefficiency and demoralization.—*Petronius,* 200 B.C.

Concerning New Ideas: Some Are Not So New

> One may even dream of production so organized that no business concern or other economic unit would be obligated to carry stocks of raw materials or of finished goods . . .

picture supplies of every sort flowing into factories just as machines are ready to use them; goods flowing out to freight cars and trucks just pulling up to shipping platforms; merchandise arriving at the dealer's shelves just when space was made available . . . under such conditions the burden of expense and risk borne by society because of the stocks necessary to the production process would be at a minimum.—*Everett S. Lyon,* 1929

Concerning Appreciation: What Have You Done for Me Lately?

The Logistician

Logisticians are a sad and embittered race of men who are very much in demand in war, and who sink resentfully into obscurity in peace. They deal only in facts, but must work for men who merchant in theories. They emerge during war because war is very much a fact. They disappear in peace because peace is mostly theory. The people who merchant in theories, and who employ logisticians in war and ignore them in peace, are generals.

Generals are a happily blessed race who radiate confidence and power. They feed only on ambrosia and drink only nectar. In peace, they stride confidently and can invade a world simply sweeping their hands grandly over a map, pointing their fingers decisively up terrain corridors, and blocking defiles and obstacles with the sides of their hands. In war, they must stride more slowly because each general has a logistician riding on his back and he knows that, at any moment, the logistician may lean forward and whisper: "No, you can't do that." Generals fear logisticians in war and, in peace, generals try to forget logisticians.

Romping along beside generals are strategists and tacticians. Logisticians despise strategists and tacticians. Strategists and tacticians do not know about logisticians until they grow up to be generals—which they usually do.

Sometimes a logistician becomes a general. If he does, he must associate with generals whom he hates; he has a retinue of strategists and tacticians whom he despises; and, on his back, is a logistician whom he fears. This is why logisticians who become generals always have ulcers and cannot eat their ambrosia.—*Author unknown; made available by Major William K. Bawden, RCAF*

Problem Set 1: Information and Forecasting

1. Mike McNeely, logistics manager for the Illumination Light Company, has considered replacing the firm's manual customer order management system with electronic ordering, an EDI application. He estimates the current system, including labor, costs $2.50/order for transmission and processing when annual order volume is under 25,000. Should the order volume equal or exceed 25,000 in any given year, Mr. McNeely will have to hire an additional customer service representative to assist order reception in the manual process. This would raise the variable cost to $3.00/order. He has also estimated the rate of errors in order placement and transfer to be 12/1,000 orders.

   EDI would cost $100,000 upfront to implement and variable costs are determined to be $.50/order regardless of volume. EDI could acquire and maintain order information with an error rate of 3/1,000 orders. An EDI specialist would be required to maintain the system at all times as well. Her salary is $38,000 in the first year and increases 3 percent each year thereafter.

   Order errors cost $5.00 per occurrence on average to correct in the manual system. EDI errors cost $8.00 on average to correct since the specialist inspects the system for flaws on most occasions.

   a. If the firm expects order volume over the next five years to be 20,000, 22,000, 25,000, 30,000, and 36,000 annually, would EDI pay for itself within the first five years?

   b. What effects aside from cost might Mr. McNeely consider when implementing EDI?

2. Mr. McNeely currently batches orders for processing under the manual order management system. The orders are batched for daily processing. If Mr. McNeely opts to implement EDI, might this affect his current means of order processing? If so, how?

3. Quality Marketing Technologies, Inc., has hired you as a sales representative. You have been asked to call on Quikee Stop, a small convenience store chain with five locations in your region. What benefits of UPC and bar coding applications might you illustrate to encourage Quikee Stop to utilize these technologies to track sales at its retail outlets?

4. Comfortwear Hosiery, Inc., produces men's socks at its manufacturing facility in Topeka, Kansas. The socks are stored in a warehouse near the factory prior to distribution to DC locations in Los Angeles, Memphis, and Dayton. The warehouse uses a top-down forecasting approach when determining the expected quantities demanded at each DC.

   The aggregate monthly forecast for June is 12,000 pairs of socks. Historically, the Los Angeles DC has demanded 25 percent of the warehouse's stock. Memphis and

Dayton have demanded 30 percent and 35 percent, respectively. The remaining 10 percent is shipped directly from the warehouse.

a. Based on the aggregate forecast, how many pairs of socks should you expect each DC to demand in June?

b. Suppose the aggregate forecast for July results in a 6 percent increase over June's forecast. How many pairs of socks would each DC anticipate in July?

5. Ms. Kathleen Boyd, director of logistics for the Scenic Calendar Company, wishes to evaluate two methods of time series forecasting. She has collected quarterly calendar sales data from the years 2003 and 2004.

2003		2004	
Qtr.	**Actual Sales**	**Qtr.**	**Actual Sales**
1	1,200	1	1,300
2	800	2	800
3	200	3	250
4	1,000	4	1,200

a. Use the moving averages technique to find forecasted sales for the third quarter of 2004 based on actual sales from the previous three quarters.

b. Use simple exponential smoothing to forecast each quarter's sales in 2004, given that Ms. Boyd qualitatively forecasted 900 calendars for quarter 4, 2003. Ms. Boyd has assigned an alpha factor of .1 for time series sensitivity.

c. Repeat the simple exponential smoothing problem above (part 5b) with Ms. Boyd employing an alpha factor of .2.

d. How well do the moving averages and simple exponential smoothing techniques seem to work in Ms. Boyd's situation? In what ways do the techniques appear to fail?

6. Michael Gregory, logistics manager of Muscle Man Fitness Equipment, has determined that his current forecast system for national sales has historically shown a 20 percent error rate. Due to this level of error, Muscle Man's DC managers maintain inventory at their locations costing the company, on average, $3,000 per month.

By improving his forecast methodology and shortening forecast horizons, Mr. Gregory anticipates cutting the error level down to 12 percent. With improved forecasting, Muscle Man's DC managers have indicated that they feel comfortable with lower inventory levels. Mr. Gregory anticipates monthly inventory carrying cost reductions of 40 percent.

a. If the forecast system improvement will cost $1,000 more per month than the old system, should Mr. Gregory implement the change?

b. Why might Muscle Man's customers encourage the firm to improve its forecasting capabilities?

Problem Set 2: Operations

1. Mr. Stan Busfield, distribution center manager for Hogan Kitchenwares, must determine when to resupply his stock of spatulas. The DC experiences a daily demand

of 400 spatulas. The average length of the performance cycle for spatulas is 14 days. Mr. Busfield requires that 500 spatulas be retained as safety stock to deal with demand uncertainty.

  a. What is the reorder point for spatulas.

2. Mr. Busfield recently completed a course in logistics management and now realizes that there are significant costs associated with ordering and maintaining inventory at his distribution center. Mr. Busfield has learned that the EOQ is the replenishment logic that minimizes these costs. In an effort to find the EOQ for measuring cups, Mr. Busfield has gathered relevant data. Mr. Busfield expects to sell 44,000 measuring cups this year. Hogan acquires the measuring cups for 75 cents each from Shatter Industries. Shatter charges $8 for processing each order. In addition, Mr. Busfield estimates his company's inventory carrying cost to be 12 percent annually.

  a. Find Mr. Busfield's EOQ for measuring cups. Assume that Mr. Busfield accepts ownership of products upon arrival at his DC.

  b. Now assume Mr. Busfield must arrange for inbound transportation of the measuring cups since Hogan accepts ownership of products at the supplier's shipping point. Quantities of fewer than 4,000 measuring cups cost 5 cents per unit to ship. Quantities of 4,000 and above cost 4 cents per unit to ship. Determine the difference in total costs associated with an EOQ of 4,000 units and the EOQ level found in part (a) when transportation costs must be considered.

  c. Given the information above and the low cost EOQ alternative determined in part (b), use period-order-quantity logic to determine the number of orders Hogan would place each year for measuring cups and the time interval between orders.

3. Mr. Dave Jones manages the warehouse inventory for Athleticks, a distributor of sports watches. From his experience, Mr. Jones knows that the PR-5 jogging watch has an average daily demand of 100 units and a performance cycle of 8 days. Mr. Jones requires no buffer stock at this time.

  a. Assume Mr. Jones perpetually reviews inventory levels. Find the reorder point for the PR-5 jogging watch.

  b. Find the average inventory level of the PR-5 watch.

  c. How might the reorder point change if Mr. Jones reviews inventory once each week? Find the reorder point under these conditions.

  d. Find the average inventory level of the PR-5 watch under this periodic review.

4. Mr. John Estes oversees the distribution of Tastee Snacks products from the plant warehouse to its two distribution centers in the United States. The plant warehouse currently has 42,000 units of the company's most popular product, Chocolate Chewies. Mr. Estes retains 7,000 units of the product at the warehouse as a buffer. The Cincinnati DC has an inventory of 12,500 units and daily requirements of 2,500 units. The Phoenix DC has an inventory of 6,000 units and daily requirements of 2,000 units.

  a. Determine the common days' supply of Chocolate Chewies at each DC.

  b. Given the above information and your answer to part (a), use fair-share-allocation logic to determine the number of Chocolate Chewies to be allocated to each DC.

5. Stay Safe International manufactures industrial safety equipment at its plant in Evansville, Indiana. The company has initiated DRP to coordinate finished goods distribution from the plant to DCs in Dallas, Texas, and Lexington, Virginia.

  a. Given the accompanying information regarding hardhats, complete the DRP schedule for the warehouse and each DC.

Dallas Distribution Center

On-hand balance: 220   *Performance cycle:* 1 week
Safety stock: 80   *Order quantity:* 200

	Past due	Week					
		1	2	3	4	5	6
Gross requirements		60	70	80	85	90	80
Scheduled receipts							
Projected on-hand							
Planned orders							

DC1

Lexington Distribution Center

On-hand balance: 420   *Performance cycle:* 2 weeks
Safety stock: 100   *Order quantity:* 400

	Past due	Week					
		1	2	3	4	5	6
Gross requirements		100	115	120	125	140	125
Scheduled receipts							
Projected on-hand							
Planned orders							

DC2

Evansville Warehouse

On-hand balance: 900   *Lead time:* 2 weeks
Safety stock: 250   *Order quantity:* 650

	Past due	Week					
		1	2	3	4	5	6
Gross requirements	0						
Scheduled receipts							
Projected on-hand							
Planned orders							
Master sched.-rept.							
Master sched.-start							

b. Suppose that, without warning, no more than 500 units can be distributed from the warehouse to the DCs in a given week due to a manufacturing breakdown. Hardhats sell for $12 each out of the Dallas DC and $14 from Lexington. Discuss whether the warehouse should delay shipments until both DC requirements can be satisfied or allocate based on need.

6. Scorekeeper, Inc., manufactures stadium scoreboards. Table 1 illustrates the demand for Scorekeeper's scoreboards over the past 25 days. The mean of daily demand is 6 units.

a. Is the demand distribution normal? How do you know?

b. Calculate the standard deviation for daily demand. Assume in this case that the performance cycle is constant.

TABLE 1

Day	Demand	Day	Demand
1	4	14	6
2	3	15	4
3	4	16	2
4	6	17	5
5	7	18	6
6	8	19	7
7	6	20	6
8	5	21	6
9	6	22	5
10	10	23	7
11	8	24	8
12	7	25	9
13	5		

Table 2 summarizes Scorekeeper's performance cycles over the past 40 replenishments. The expected cycle duration is 12 days.

  c. Is the performance cycle distribution normal? How do you know?

  d. Calculate the standard deviation for the performance cycle.

  e. Given your answers to parts (b) and (d), find the safety stock required at 1 combined standard deviation under conditions of demand and performance cycle uncertainties.

  f. If the typical order quantity is 36 units, find the average inventory at 3 standard deviations under demand and performance cycle uncertainty.

  g. Scorekeeper is striving for a 99 percent product availability level. Given the above information as well as your answer to (e), find the function value of the normal loss curve, $f(k)$.

  h. Use Table 7.14 to find the value for k, given your answer to part (g), and calculate the required safety stock for the desired 99 percent availability level.

  i. What would be the required safety stock for 99 percent availability should the order quantity change to 30 units?

7. The XYZ Chemical Company must ship 9,500 gallons of pesticides from its plant in Cincinnati, Ohio, to a customer in Columbia, Missouri. XYZ has a contract in place with Henderson Bulk Trucking Company as well as with the Central States Railroad. Both carriers are available for the move. Henderson will charge $600 per tank truck, and Central States' rate is $1,000 per tankcar. Henderson tanks can hold a maximum quantity of 7,000 gallons. XYZ has a fleet of 23,500-gallon tankcars available in Cincinnati.

  a. Given the above information, evaluate the cost of each alternative.

  b. What other qualitative factors should be considered in this decision?

TABLE 2

Performance Cycle (in days)	Frequency (f)
10	4
11	8
12	16
13	8
14	4

8. Shatter Industries, Inc., manufactures household and commercial glass products that serve a variety of purposes.

   a. Refer to the National Motor Freight Classification 100-S (Table 9.1) to determine the LTL and TL product classifications for the following Shatter items:

      i.   Item 86960, glazed glass, boxed.

      ii. Glass slides for microscopes.

      iii. Bent mirror glass, dimensions 7 feet by 5 feet.

   b. Shatter ships many of its products from a warehouse in Atlanta, Georgia, to a distribution center in Lansing, Michigan. Refer to the rate tariff in Table 9.2 to find applicable charges for the following shipments over the route:

      i.   5,200 lb. of mirrored shock glass (Item 86900, Sub 1—class 85).

      ii. 32,000 lb. of class 65 product.

      iii. 200 lb. of class 60 product.

      iv. 19,000 lb. of class 150 product.

      v.   2,500 lb. of class 200 product with a 5 percent temporary fuel surcharge added to the line-haul charge.

9. Gigoflop Electronics has three shipments of class 100 product to be transported from Atlanta, Georgia, to Lansing, Michigan. The shipments weigh 5,000 lb., 10,000 lb., and 7,000 lb., respectively. Gigoflop can ship each quantity individually or consolidate them as a multiple-stop shipment. Each shipment is to be delivered to a different location in Lansing. The carrier, Eckgold Trucking, charges $50 for each stop-off (not including the final destination). Refer to Table 9.2 and evaluate the costs of shipping individually versus consolidation. Which option should be used by Gigoflop?

10. Stanley Harris, traffic manager of This n' That Manufacturers, is considering the negotiation of a freight-all-kinds (FAK) rate for shipments between Atlanta and Lansing. The company ships 200 (class 65) shipments of 5,000 lb., 40 (class 400) shipments of 1,200 lb., and 30 (class 100) shipments of 10,000 lb., and receives a 45 percent discount on published rates.

    a. Refer to Table 9.2 to determine the current freight bill for the above shipments. *Note:* Take the discount from the published rate and round *up* for the applicable hundredweight rate.

    b. Should Mr. Harris accept an FAK rate of $10 per hundredweight?

    c. What factors aside from price should Mr. Harris consider with an FAK rate?

11. Carole Wilson, Transportation Manager of Applied Technologies, has a shipment of 150 computer monitors originating at the company's plant in Santa Fe Springs, California. The shipment, valued at $29,250, is destined for a DC in St. Louis, Missouri. John Miller, receiving manager at the St. Louis DC, has established a standardized transit time for the shipment to be 2.5 days. Mr. Miller assesses an opportunity cost of $6.00 per monitor for each day beyond the standard. Ms. Wilson has three transportation options available.

    a. Cross Country Haulers, a long-haul trucking company, can ship the monitors at a contracted rate of $1.65/mile. The distance from Santa Fe Springs to St. Louis is 1,940 miles. Cross Country estimates that it can deliver the shipment in 3 days. A truck can carry 192 monitors.

    b. The Sea-to-Shining Sea (STSS) Railway can pick up the shipment at the plant's dock and deliver the monitors directly to the St. Louis DC. STSS can ship the railcar of monitors for a flat charge of $1,500. Ms. Wilson has recently experienced delays with the switching of its railcars and expects delivery to take 5 days.

    c. Ms. Wilson has also negotiated an agreement with Lightning Quick Intermodal, Inc. (LQI), a third-party carrier that utilizes both motor and rail transportation. LQI can pick up the shipment by truck at the plant and deliver it to an intermodal rail-yard in Bakersfield, California, where the trailer is placed onto a flat railcar. The servicing railway, the Rocky Mountain Railway (RMR), then delivers the trailer to another intermodal yard near St. Louis, where the trailer is unloaded and transported by truck to the DC. Lightning Quick offers the origin-to-destination transportation for $2,500. Transit time is anticipated at 2.5 days. From past experience, Mr. Miller has discovered that the additional handling inherent with Lightning Quick's service results in 3 percent product loss and damage. Recovery of these losses is difficult and typically results in only 33.3 percent immediate reimbursement of the losses. Evaluate the cost of each transportation alternative.

12. Moving Hands, Inc., ships alarm clocks from Atlanta to Lansing. The company has begun packaging the clocks in a stronger corrugated box to reduce the likelihood of damage in storage and transit. As a result of the improved packaging, the clocks' product classification has dropped from 100 to 85 without significantly adding weight to the package.

    a. What effect does the new packaging have on the transportation cost of a single 1000 lb. shipment? Refer to Table 9.2.

    b. Suppose Moving Hands ships 300 loads of the 1,000 lb. quantity each year and the new packaging costs $10,000 to develop and produce. Will Moving Hands realize a full payback of the packaging investment in its first year?

13. Bill Berry, transportation sales manager of Speedy Trucking Company, has considered serving a new customer, El Conquistador, Inc., an importer of Venezuelan goods, by hauling 12 truckloads of product each month from the receiving port in Bayonne, New Jersey, to a distributor in Pittsburgh, Pennsylvania, for $850 per truckload. Each serving truck must depart from the Speedy terminal in Secaucus, New Jersey, 12 miles from the seaport. The distance from Bayonne to Pittsburgh is 376 miles. Upon unloading at Pittsburgh, trucks return empty (deadhead) to the Secaucus terminal 380 miles from the distributor.

    a. If it costs Speedy an average of $1.20 per mile to operate a truck, should Mr. Berry accept the business at the negotiated rate? Why or why not?

    b. Mr. Berry has coordinated back-haul moves for the Conquistador shipments above with a new customer in Youngstown, Ohio. The new customer, Super Tread, Inc., ships tires from its plant in Youngstown to the port in Bayonne for exporting. Each Conquistador shipment will be accompanied with a return shipment from Super Tread (12 truckloads/month). Speedy will charge Super Tread $1.30 per mile. Bayonne is 430 miles from Youngstown. The distance from Pittsburgh to Youngstown is 65 miles. Trucks must return to the terminal in Secaucus upon delivering product from the back-haul (before picking up again at Bayonne). The terms of the Conquistador agreement outlined in part (a) remain intact. How much can Mr. Berry expect Speedy to profit (lose) per trip from the new arrangement?

    c. How much can Mr. Berry expect Speedy to profit (lose) per month from the new arrangement should the company accept the business?

    d. Is it worthwhile for Mr. Berry to arrange for the back-haul? Why or why not?

14. Super Performance Parts (SPP) produces braking devices exclusively for the Ace Motor Ccompany, an automotive manufacturer. SPP has been leasing warehouse space at a public facility 20 miles from the company's plant. SPP has been approached by a group of four other Ace suppliers with the idea of building a consolidated warehouse to gain transportation and materials handling economies. An investment of $200,000 would be required by each of the five companies to acquire the warehouse. Payment of the initial investment secures 10 years of participation in the agreement. Annual operating

expenses are anticipated to be $48,000 for each party. SPP is currently charged $6,000 per month for use of the public warehouse facilities. SPP's outbound transportation from the public warehouse often consists of LTL quantities. Its annual outbound transportation bill is currently $300,000. SPP expects consolidated warehousing to more fully utilize truckload quantities with transportation expenses shared among the supplier pool. SPP's annual outbound bill would be reduced by 25 percent in the consolidated plan. Differences in inbound transportation costs are assumed negligible in this case.

a. Compare the storage and shipping costs associated with consolidated warehousing as opposed to SPP's current, direct shipping plan. Are any efficiencies apparent through consolidation?

b. Aside from potentially reducing costs, how else might SPP benefit by participating in the consolidated warehouse?

c. What disadvantages might exist in a consolidated warehouse as opposed to a direct-shipping situation?

15. Essen Beer Company has a brewery in Michigan's Upper Peninsula and is setting up distribution at Jackson, Michigan, in the state's Lower Peninsula. Essen packages its beverages in barrels and in 24-can cases. Barrels must be maintained at temperatures below 60 degrees Fahrenheit until retail delivery. The company's logistics department must determine whether to operate individual private warehouses for barrels and cases or to utilize a single warehouse with barrels placed in a carefully controlled environment separate from cases. Assume that cases are not to be stored or transported in refrigerated environments.

   Essen experiences a weekly demand of 300 barrels and 5,000 cases. The company has arranged truckload transportation with Stipe Trucking Service. Stipe operates refrigerated and nonrefrigerated trailers, as well as multicompartmented trailers that are half refrigerated and half not. A refrigerated truckload can hold 72 barrels, while a nonrefrigerated truckload holds 400 cases. The multicompartmented trailer can hold 36 barrels and 200 cases. The costs for these services and other related expenses are detailed below:

Truckload costs	
Refrigerated	$550
Nonrefrigerated	$400
Multicompartmented	$500
Warehouse expenses	
Individual warehouses	
For case storage only:	
Capital	$1,250/week
Labor	$2,500/week
For barrel storage:	
Capital	$2,500/week
Labor	$1,600/week
Single, consolidated warehouse	
Capital	$3,500/week
Labor	$3,200/week

a. Considering demand and all costs depicted above, does the single, consolidated warehouse or the two individual warehouses represent the least-total-cost alternative?

b. Now assume that Stipe Trucking Service will provide *only* the multi-compartmented trailers to serve the proposed consolidated warehouse. Which plan is the least-cost alternative in this scenario?

16. Comfy Mattresses, Inc., is opening a new plant in Orlando, Florida. Ron Lane, distribution manager, has been asked to find the lowest cost outbound logistics system. Given an annual sales volume of 24,000 mattresses, determine the costs associated with each option below.

    a. Build a private warehouse near the plant for $300,000. The variable cost, including warehouse maintenance and labor, is estimated at $5 per unit. Contract carrier transportation costs $12.50 per unit on average. No external transportation services are necessary for shipment of mattresses from the plant to the warehouse in this scenario. The fixed warehouse investment can be depreciated evenly over 10 years.

    b. Rent space in a public warehouse 10 miles from the plant. The public warehouse requires no fixed investment but has variable costs of $8 per unit. Outbound contract carrier transportation would cost $12.50 per unit on average. The carrier also charges $5 per unit to deliver the mattresses to the warehouse from the plant.

    c. Contract the warehousing and transportation services to the Freeflow Logistics Company, an integrated logistics firm with a warehouse location 25 miles from the plan. Freeflow requires a fixed investment of $150,000 and charges $20 per unit for all services originating at the plant. The fixed investment covers a 10-year agreement with Freeflow.

    d. Name a few advantages aside from cost that the low-cost alternative above may have over the other alternatives.

17. Ms. Sara Ritter is the distribution manager for the Fiesta Soft Drink Company. She is considering full automation of the plant's warehouse. At present, the warehouse utilizes a mechanized system of materials handling. The current system employs 20 laborers at an average wage rate of $13/hour. Laborers work an average of 2,000 hours per year. The mechanization costs $18,000 annually to maintain. The equipment was purchased two years ago with uniform payments of $25,000 made annually. In year 9 the mechanical equipment will be replaced by new machinery with fixed annual costs of $35,000. In addition, it will cost Fiesta $12,000 per year to maintain the new equipment with the same 20 laborers.

    The automated equipment would cost $1.2 million upfront for implementation. Only eight laborers and an automation specialist would be required to maintain operations in the new system. The laborers would earn $16/hour over 2,000 hours each year. The automation specialist would earn a salary of $56,000 per year, increasing 2 percent annually after the first year. Much of the old mechanized equipment could be sold immediately for a total of $125,000. Maintenance of the automated system is estimated at $60,000 each year with this cost growing by 3 percent annually after the first year. The automated system is expected to serve Fiesta for 15 years.

    a. Examine the cash flow under each system. What is the payback period for automation?

    b. What advantages aside from long-term cost savings might an automated warehouse have over more labor-intensive systems?

18. Dandy Collectibles is opening a new warehouse. Bob Lee, the warehouse manager, is trying to determine the labor compensation package that most productively utilizes resources. The typical compensation plan offers an hourly wage rate of $13. Mr. Lee is also considering an incentive plan. The incentive plan rewards solely on performance with order pickers earning $0.40/unit prepared for shipping. A typical week shows the number of ordered units that must be prepared for shipping.

    Errors sometimes happen in Dandy's order picking. Product mishandling occurs in 1 percent of the orders under the incentive plan and in 0.5 percent of the orders under the hourly wage plan. Errored orders are scrapped and result in lost revenue of $60 per occurrence. Hourly workers pick 20 units per hour. Incentive workers pick 28 units per hour. Regardless of the plan designation, employees work 40-hour weeks. Union restrictions prevent Dandy from operating on Saturday and Sunday. The labor union also restricts Dandy from hiring part-time workers. Orders need not be filled daily, but all orders must be shipped by week's end (Friday). Assume that hiring and training costs are negligible.

a. How many workers are needed under each plan for the typical week's demand?

b. Which plan meets the typical week's demand at the lowest cost, including lost sales resulting from errors?

19. Mitchell Beverage Company produces Cactus Juice, a popular alcoholic beverage. Recently the firm has experienced problems of product pilferage at the warehouse. In one month, 3,200 bottles of Cactus Juice, representing 0.4 percent of the month's volume, could not be located for shipping. Should the problem go unresolved, it is anticipated that it will continue at this rate. The forecasted annual sales volume for Cactus Juice is 9.6 million bottles. Each bottle sells for $4.50.

Steve Davis, vice president of distribution, has asked you to look into the following security options to reduce the pilferage problem.

a. Hire four security guards to patrol the warehouse floor all hours of the day, 7 days a week. The firm would offer a wage of $14.50/hour to the guards as well as a benefits package expected to be worth $2,000 per employee per year. The presence of security guards should lower pilferage to 0.2 percent of volume. Only one guard would be on duty at any one time.

b. Implement an electronic detection system based on bar code technology. This would require purchasing bar code equipment for the packaging facility and warehouse. Electronic scanning devices must also be purchased and placed at warehouse entrances. Alarms sound whenever a bar-coded item passes through a warehouse entrance without clearance. The electronic detection package, including bar code printers and readers, will cost $120,000. In addition, employees at the plant and warehouse will be trained to use the new equipment at a one-time cost of $8,000. Monthly maintenance of the system is expected to cost $800. Also, a bar code specialist must be hired. The specialist would earn a salary of $49,000 per year. Product pilferage is expected to be lowered to 0.1 percent of volume with the electronic security system. The system has an estimated life of 8 years. Accrue all costs evenly over the life of the equipment.

c. Install security cameras in key locations throughout the warehouse. It has been determined that six cameras could adequately record warehouse operations. Each camera costs $1,200. The support devices and installation will cost $36,000. Four security guards would be hired for the purpose of viewing the security monitors for suspicious activity. One guard would be on duty at all times. The guards each earns $12/hour, in a 42-hour workweek, and receives a benefits package worth $1,000 per year. Pilferage under this system would be 0.05 percent of volume. The monitoring equipment is expected to have a life of 12 years. Accrue all fixed costs evenly over the life of the equipment.

Should the firm implement any of the options above, or make no investment and allow the pilferage to continue at the rate of 0.4 percent of volume? Compare the costs and benefits of each option on an annual basis.

20. Chronotronics produces two models of clock radios, the X-100 and the X-250 deluxe. Both products are currently packaged in a single-wall corrugation. Through close observation, the firm has discovered that 0.5 percent of both X-100s and X-250s are damaged between packaging and customer delivery. Chronotronics can package either model, or both, in double-wall corrugated fiberboard, which would reduce

product damage by half. The current single-wall packaging costs $0.80 per unit. Double-wall packaging costs 20 percent more. The X-100 and X-250 have market values of $40 and $70, respectively. Damaged units are a total loss. Chronotronics sold 12,000 X-100s and 7,000 X-250s last year. Forecasts indicate consistent sales for the X-100 and a 5 percent increase in X-250 sales over the next year. *Note:* Round up for whole units lost.

    a. From a least-cost perspective, should Chronotronics utilize double-wall corrugation with the X-100 next year?

    b. From a least-cost perspective, should Chronotronics utilize double-wall corrugation with the X-250 next year?

    c. From discussion earlier in the text, how might packaging improvements affect transportation costs?

21. Your firm is planning to introduce a new product line. Your task is to determine the inventory implications of the new product. The typical product will ship an average of 20 units per day from the firm's central DC. Historical sales patterns indicate that the standard deviation of daily sales should be approximately 3. The typical performance cycle for comparable products has been a mean of 7 days and a standard deviation of 2.

    a. Assuming a replenishment quantity from the plant of 200 units, what are the safety stock and resulting average inventory for a 95 percent case fill rate?

    b. What are the inventory implications (safety stock and average inventory) of increasing the case fill rate objective to 99 percent?

    c. What would be the inventory implications for daily replenishment with a 99 percent fill rate objective, assuming that the same level of demand and performance cycle uncertainty is maintained?

22. As the logistics representative on a manufacturer's sales team, you have been asked to quantify the benefits that can be sold to a customer using more consistent service and transportation. The customer wants 99 percent case availability from its distribution centers that are resupplied from the manufacturer. The average daily demand in cases from the customer's DC is 1,000 units with a standard deviation of 250. Historically, the replenishment performance cycle has been 10 days with a standard deviation of 4 days. The customer has traditionally used a 20 percent inventory carrying cost, and the average value of each case is $25. The customer orders weekly an order quantity of 7,000 units.

    a. What is the average inventory and annual carrying cost for the current situation?

    b. What is the average inventory and carrying cost impact of reducing the manufacturer's performance cycle variation by 2 days?

    c. How does reducing the performance cycle variation by 2 days compare with reducing the average performance cycle length by 2 days in terms of average inventory and inventory carrying cost?

23. Spartan Plastics provides components to assembly plants in the automobile industry. Currently, they ship directly from their plant in St. Louis, Missouri, to plants in Lansing, Michigan; Toledo, Ohio; and eight assembly plants surrounding Detroit, Michigan. In total, there are 10 assembly plants that each receives approximately 3,000 pounds per day in shipments. Currently, the company ships LTL from its plant to each assembly plant for a cost of $0.0013 per pound per mile. The company is considering two transportation alternatives to reduce cost. The first alternative is using a milk-run approach where a truckload begins in St. Louis, stops in Lansing, then the Detroit plants, and finally Toledo. The transportation cost for the milk-run approach would be $1.30 per truck mile plus $100/stop, not including the final stop in Toledo. The second alternative is to consolidate a truckload to Ypsilanti, Michigan, and then cross-dock the components

TABLE 3

Materials Handling Alternative	One-Time Acquisition Cost	Annual Fixed Cost	Per Case Variable Cost	Usage Life Span (Years)
Mechanized	$1,000,000	$50,000	$0.30	10
Semiautomated	$3,000,000	$200,000	$0.08	5
Information-directed	$1,500,000	$150,000	$0.15	7

for delivery to the assembly plant by the logistics provider. The truckload cost is still $1.30 per mile, and the cost per delivery to each assembly plant from Ypsilanti is $200.

   a. What are the cost characteristics of each delivery option?

   b. What are the qualitative and service characteristics of each delivery option?

24. Presswick Industries supplies plastics used for medical applications such as pharmaceutical injections and collecting laboratory samples. Presswick produces the containers and tubes and then ships them to customers who incorporate the plastics into kits that are used in hospitals and labs. Currently, Presswick simply loads the containers and tubes into corrugated boxes and ships them to customers who are then responsible for disposing of the corrugated. Presswick is considering the possibility of using returnable packaging with some of its key customers to be more environmentally friendly and perhaps reduce cost as well. The current corrugated cost per unit (container or tube) is $0.05 with an additional $0.02 per unit for disposal. The cost of the recyclable container is $0.25 per unit of capacity that can be used multiple times. The recyclable container does not have to be disposed of, but it must be transported back to Presswick at a cost of $0.02 per unit of capacity. Assume that the recyclable containers can only be used for one year because the plastic in the containers begins to break down.

   a. At what annual volume level does it make sense to use the recyclable containers versus the corrugated containers?

   b. What other qualitative factors should be considered in the decision?

25. Forest Green Products provides private label vegetables for grocery chains throughout the Midwest. They currently have distribution centers in Columbus, Ohio; St. Louis, Missouri; and Minneapolis, Minnesota. The typical annual capacity requirements for Forest Green are 5 million cases with a case split of 35 percent, 40 percent, and 25 percent for Columbus, St. Louis, and Minneapolis, respectively. The company is reassessing its materials handling and storage capability in each facility. The technology alternatives being considered are mechanized, semiautomated, and information-directed systems. Table 3 summarizes the acquisition, annual fixed cost, per case variable cost, and life span of each system alternative. The acquisition and annual fixed cost are quoted in terms of dollars per million units of capacity. In other words, a DC requiring two million units of capacity would double the specified cost. The annual fixed cost does not include depreciation for the acquisition cost. Assume that the total square footage of the three DCs is the same.

   a. What system alternative should be used for each DC based on annual cost? How does this decision change if net present value (NPV) is considered over the life of the system? Assume a 10 percent discount rate.

   b. Assume that, for simplicity's sake, Forest Green wants to use only one system alternative for all three DCs. What is the system with the lowest NPV for the life of the system for the combination of DCs?

   c. What other qualitative factors should be considered?

Case 1

Integrated Logistics for DEP/GARD

Steve Clinton

Tom Lippet, sales representative for DuPont Engineering Polymers (DEP), felt uneasy as he drove to his appointment at Gard Automotive Manufacturing (GARD). In the past, sales deals with GARD had proceeded smoothly. Oftentimes competitors were not even invited to bid on the GARD business. Mike O'Leary, purchasing agent at GARD, claimed that was because no competitor could match DEP's product quality.

But this contract negotiation was different. Several weeks before the contract renewal talks began, O'Leary had announced his plan to retire in 6 months. GARD management quickly promoted Richard Binish as O'Leary's successor. Although Binish had been relatively quiet at the previous two meetings Lippet sensed that it would not be business as usual with Binish. While the contract decision ultimately depended upon O'Leary's recommendation, Lippet felt Binish might pose a problem.

Binish, 35, had worked for a Fortune 500 firm following completion of his undergraduate degree in operations management. While with the Fortune 500 firm Binish had become extensively involved with JIT and quality programs. He had returned to school and earned an MBA with a concentration in purchasing and logistics. Eager to make his mark, Binish had rejected offers to return to large corporations and instead accepted GARD's offer in inventory management.

GARD, an original equipment manufacturer (OEM) for U.S. auto producers and aftermarket retailers, makes a wide variety of plastic products for automobiles and light trucks. Examples of GARD products are dashboards, door and window handles, and assorted control knobs. When Binish began working with GARD's inventory management he applied the 80/20 rule, illustrating to management that 80 percent of GARD's business was related to 20 percent of its product line. Over the next 3 years, as contracts expired with customers and suppliers, Binish trimmed GARD's product line. GARD management was impressed with the positive impact on GARD's profits as unprofitable contracts and products were discarded. A trimmer product line composed primarily of faster-moving products also resulted in higher inventory velocity.

So, when O'Leary announced his retirement plans, management immediately offered Binish the position. After taking a few days to review GARD's purchasing practices Binish felt he could make an impact. He accepted management's offer. As he learned his way around the purchasing department Binish tried to stay in the background, but he soon found himself questioning many of O'Leary's practices. He particularly disdained O'Leary's frequent "business lunches" with long-time associates from GARD suppliers. Despite these feelings Binish made an effort to not be openly critical of O'Leary. Such efforts did not, however, prevent him from asking more and more questions about GARD's purchasing process.

O'Leary, for his part, felt his style had served GARD well. Prices were kept low and quality was generally within established parameters. Although O'Leary typically maintained a wide network of suppliers, critical materials were sourced from a limited number of them. In those cases contract bids were a ritual, with the winner known well in advance.

DEP was one such winner. Its polymers were a critical feedstock material in GARD's manufacturing process. When O'Leary began sourcing from DEP nearly 15 years ago, there was no question that DEP polymers were the best on the market. GARD's production managers rarely complained about production problems caused by substandard polymers. O'Leary reasoned that the fewer complaints from manufacturing, the better.

"Hi, Tom! Come on in! Good to see you. You remember Richard Binish, don't you?" Lippet's spirits were buoyed by O'Leary's cheery greeting.

"Absolutely! How are you, Richard? Coming out from the old horse's shadow a bit now?"

Binish politely smiled and nodded affirmatively. Light banter continued as the three moved down the hallway to a small conference room.

"Well, great news, Tom! DEP has the contract again!" O'Leary paused, then continued, "But there's going to be a slight modification. Instead of the traditional 2-year contract we're only going to offer a 1-year deal. Nothing personal, just that management feels it's only fair to Richard that these last contracts I negotiate be limited to a year. That way he doesn't get locked into any deals that might make him look bad!" O'Leary roared with laughter at his last comment.

"It is certainly no reflection on DEP," Richard interjected. "It simply gives me a chance to evaluate suppliers in the coming year without being locked into a long-term contract. If my evaluation concurs with what Mr. O'Leary has told me about DEP I see no reason that our successful relationship won't continue."

"Entirely understandable," replied Tom as his mind pondered the meaning of Binish's *evaluation.* "I'm confident you'll find DEP's service and product every bit as good as Mike has told you."

Following the meeting O'Leary invited Lippet to join him for a cup of coffee in GARD's lunchroom. Binish excused himself, saying he had other matters to attend to.

As they enjoyed their coffee, O'Leary sighed. "You'll be seeing some changes coming, Tom. The best I could do was get you a year."

"I'm not sure I understand. As far as I know GARD's never had a major problem with DEP's products."

"We haven't," O'Leary replied. "At least not under the guidelines I hammered out with management. But there will be some changes by next year."

"Such as?"

"Well, you remember when I started buying from DEP? You were the leaders, no question about it. Now I knew some other suppliers had moved up since then but I figured, hey, if it ain't broke don't fix it! As long as DEP's price was in line, I knew I wouldn't have any troubles with manufacturing. Less headaches for me. Now it turns out that Binish has some other ideas about purchasing. I can tell you for a fact that he's sampled several lots of DEP feedstock. He's also invited other potential suppliers to submit samples. The long and short of it is that there's not much difference between DEP and the competition in terms of product."

"I still don't clearly understand the problem, Mike."

"In Binish's terms, product merely becomes a 'qualifying criterion.' If everyone's product is comparable, especially in something such as polymer feedstock, how do you distinguish yourself? Binish claims companies will need to demonstrate something called 'order winning criteria' to get our business in the future."

"I still don't see a problem. We have our reviews with GARD every year. Our service performance has always been found to be acceptable."

"True. But acceptable according to my guidelines. Let me throw a number at you. On average GARD schedules delivery 10 days from date of order. I count on-time delivery as plus or minus 2 days from scheduled delivery date. That's a 5-day service window. GARD's minimum service threshold within this 5-day window is 95 percent. DEP had a 96.2 percent record last year using my window. Do you know what Binish is talking?"

"Probably 3?"

"Exactly. And do you know what DEP's performance is if we use a 3-day service window?"

"No, Mike, I really don't."

"Well, Tom. Sorry to tell you it's 89.7 percent. Worse yet, with Binish not only will the window decline but also the threshold level will be bumped up to 96 percent. And, that's only going to be for the first 3 years after I retire. After that Binish is shooting for exact-day delivery only with 96.5 percent service capability. Right now using exact day DEP only has 80 percent flat. You aren't even close to being in the game."

"So we've got a 1-year contract essentially to demonstrate that we can deliver service as well as product?"

"You understand the problem now."

Polymer feedback production requires a mixture of chemical compounds. DEP's manufacturing process relies heavily on six principal compounds (A–F). DEP's current procurement policy is to source each of these compounds from three sources determined through an annual bidding process. Typically the firm with the lowest price is considered the best bid. The top bid receives 60 percent of DEP's business while the other two firms receive 25 percent and 15 percent, respectively. Management feels this policy protects DEP from material shortages and unreasonable price increases. Table 1 indicates the current compound suppliers and their performance statistics (percentage of business, delivery time from order date, fill rate).

DEP currently uses the following performance criteria:

1. Delivery of A: On-time considered 4 days from date of order $\pm$ 2 days.

TABLE 1
Performance Statistics of Compound Suppliers

	Chemical Compounds					
Supplier	**A**	**B**	**C**	**D**	**E**	**F**
Company 1	60%	60%			15%	15%
	3–8 days	2–9 days			5–8 days	6–9 days
	93%	94.5%			92%	94%
Company 2	25%	25%	15%	15%		
	4–6 days	3–4 days	2–4 days	2–4 days		
	95%	96%	98%	98.7%		
Company 3	15%	15%			25%	25%
	2–5 days	2–4 days			5–9 days	4–6 days
	95.5%	98%			97.5%	98.7%
Company 4			60%	60%		
			4–9 days	2–9 days		
			96.5%	97%		
Company 5					60%	60%
					4–7 days	4–6 days
					98.3%	97%
Company 6			25%	25%		
			3–6 days	3–5 days		
			98.4%	96%		

Entries list percentage of business, delivery time from order, and fill rate, respectively.

2. Delivery of B: On-time considered 4 days from date of order ± 2 days.
3. Delivery of C: On-time considered 4 days from date of order ± 2 days.
4. Delivery of D: On-time considered 5 days from date of order ± 2 days.
5. Delivery of E: On-time considered 6 days from date of order ± 2 days.
6. Delivery of F: On-time considered 6 days from date of order ± 2 days.
7. Minimum acceptable fill rate on all compounds is 92 percent.

The manufacture of polymer feedstock is highly standardized. DEP has continually invested in technologically advanced manufacturing equipment. As a result, DEP can quickly change processes to manufacture different polymers.

To avoid material shortages and thereby maximize production, DEP normally maintains a 7-day supply of each compound. An earlier attempt at JIT manufacturing was abandoned after DEP experienced material shortages and production shutdowns. As a result, the manufacturing department is opposed to any reimplementation of JIT-type concepts.

The manufacturing department is electronically linked to the procurement and marketing/sales departments. Marketing/sales receives customer orders by phone or facsimile. The orders are then entered into the information system. This allows manufacturing to monitor incoming materials shipments as well as schedule production runs. Under this system most customer orders are produced within 6 to 8 days of order.

Following production, orders are immediately sent to a warehouse a short distance from DEP. At the warehouse shipping personnel verify manufacturing tickets, match the manufacturing ticket with the purchase order, and prepare shipping documents. Once the shipping documents are completed, the order is prepared for shipment (e.g., palletized, shrink-wrapped, etc.) and labeled. Once a shipment is labeled, delivery is scheduled. Three to 6 days normally elapse from the time an order leaves manufacturing until it is shipped from the warehouse.

Market distribution is divided between the private DEP truck fleet and common carriers. The majority of DEP's customers are within a 200-mile radius. DEP trucks service these customers via twice-a-week delivery routes. Customers beyond this delivery zone are serviced through common carriers; delivery time fluctuates according to location and distance but rarely exceeds 6 days from time of shipment.

Questions

1. Diagram the DEP/GARD supply chain. What stages are adding value? What stages are not?

2. Using the primary DEP suppliers (60 percent of business), what is the minimum performance cycle for the supply chain diagrammed above? What is the maximum?

3. Can the performance cycle be improved through the use of the 25 percent and 15 percent suppliers? What trade-offs must be made to use these suppliers?

4. If you were Tom Lippet, what changes would you make in DEP's operations? Why? What problems do you foresee as you try to implement these changes?

5. Assuming you can make the changes mentioned in question 4, how would you "sell" Richard Binish on DEP's next bid? What will likely be "qualifying criteria" and "order winning criteria"? Will these change over time? What does this suggest about supply chain management?

Case 2

Woodmere Products

Judith M. Whipple

John Smith had just returned from what may prove to be one of his most important sales calls. John, a sales representative for a top furniture manufacturer, had been meeting with a representative from HomeHelp, a major home decorating retailer. It seems the buyer, Nan Peterson, and the product team she heads had just returned from the annual Council of Supply Chain Management Professionals. At the conference, Nan's team had attended several sessions on time-based logistics strategies. Even though Nan and her team had just been exposed to the new strategies, they felt it had the potential for significant competitive advantage in their industry.

At the meeting with John, Nan explained that HomeHelp is an entrepreneurial company that encourages product teams to try new products and channel relations. The few rules a team has to follow are simple: (1) deal only with manufacturers (no independent distributors are contacted) and (2) keep costs low and service high. The second rule highlights HomeHelp's basic business philosophy. HomeHelp is a design and home decorating retail chain that follows the warehouse club format. As such, a premium is placed on maintaining low overhead to support an everyday low price (EDLP) strategy. Service is also a premium since HomeHelp targets two distinct customer segments: do-it-yourself consumers, who need special in-store guidance; and interior decorators, who need speedy checkouts and convenient delivery or pickup.

Nan explained that the team has been considering applying time-based logistics strategies to furniture. Such an arrangement had the potential to improve product availability for in-store customers while reducing overall inventory. HomeHelp's close relationship with professional decorators required continued attention to improve its profitability and to ensure long-term growth. Interior decorators need convenient and exacting service, and HomeHelp feels that time-based logistics applied to furniture could be an important step to improving profitability.

HomeHelp's main concern is that the furniture industry as a whole appears to be trailing other industries in terms of sophisticated logistics operations. For example, the furniture industry has invested little in information technology and maintains high inventories throughout the channel, including at the retail level. The results other firms reported for their innovative logistics applications gave HomeHelp a new insight into how an alliance with a furniture manufacturer might create a best practice distribution system with lower costs and less inventory.

Nan told John that his company, Woodmere, had the potential to achieve an exclusive distribution arrangement with HomeHelp if the two companies could create time-based logistical capability. Woodmere was chosen since the business press had recently featured articles on its new organization plan that focused on channels of distribution and leading-edge logistics strategies. In addition, Woodmere was beginning to invest in information technology. Nan felt both companies should be able to reduce overall channel costs and offer customers superior product availability. Her specific request was for John to formulate a tentative proposal within 3 weeks to strike while the iron was hot. Nan knew the timing and unexpected opportunity created a great challenge for Woodmere, but she explained that HomeHelp strives to remain leading edge. Furthermore, HomeHelp wants to increase annual growth to 20 percent and feels that furniture offers the best opportunities. As such, top management attention is on this potential business arrangement.

As John walked to his regional sales manager's office, it was hard to conceal his excitement. The potential agreement HomeHelp offered was enormous. However, the effort required to get all groups at Woodmere involved would be great. The first step was to convince top management of the unique opportunity so that a team could be formed to create the proposal HomeHelp was expecting.

John's boss, Frank Harrison, was on the phone as John walked in. John carefully planned his words while Frank finished his conversation. As Frank hung up the phone, John blurted out, "We've got the potential for an exclusive with HomeHelp, but they want a customized delivery system. The proposal's due in 3 weeks. I think we need the top brass in on this one. It's big."

Frank's reply was typical. "It's not April 1 again already, is it John? What's the problem with our current system? Three weeks! It will never happen." After John explained the meeting with Nan, Frank got on the phone to arrange a senior management review. Surprisingly, a business planning meeting was scheduled for the coming Friday. Frank and John could get on the agenda under new business. What a break! It was Wednesday and John began to reorganize his calendar to concentrate on the Friday meeting.

The first item John focused on was researching HomeHelp. He discovered that Home-Help operated over 200 warehouse-style stores in 18 states with the average store being over 100,000 square feet and offering 25,000 different products. Typical sales breakdown is 50 percent wallpaper and draperies, 25 percent accessory pieces, 20 percent lighting and electrical fixtures, and 5 percent furniture. The potential for growth in furniture was clear. Furniture included fabric-covered items such as sofas, loveseats, and reclining chairs as well as wooden products such as tables, dinettes, and end pieces. HomeHelp was the industry leader with 10 percent of the $120 billion home decorating retail market. Forecasts indicate that the market will reach $150 billion within three years. Industry observers predict that HomeHelp is positioned to enjoy up to 20 percent of total industry sales.

HomeHelp is dedicated to service. In-store classes illustrate design techniques, repair and installation procedures on wallpaper, drapes, and lighting and electrical fixtures. The classes are taught by HomeHelp's employees, most of whom are retired or part-time professional decorators and contractors. HomeHelp provides installation service in a majority of its stores as well as professional decorating services. Both services are offered on a fee basis.

Forty percent of HomeHelp's sales involve professional decorators. The remaining 60 percent come from do-it-yourself consumers. The professional segment is quite large, and HomeHelp works closely with this group to meet service requirements. Affiliated professionals, called Propartners, have separate checkout lanes, a commercial credit program, and delivery services. Currently, Propartners customers purchase only 10 percent of Home-Help's home furniture. Nan feels that this low sales level results from two factors. First, the delivery service offered by HomeHelp is contracted out to local moving companies, with the cost to HomeHelp passed on to the customer. Delivery for a piece of furniture typically adds 8 percent to the price HomeHelp charges for the product. This increase makes the overall price of purchase within $10 to $30 of the price charged by the competition, which offers free delivery. The close price range, accompanied by the psychological effect of free delivery, prompts many Propartners customers to purchase furniture elsewhere. While not a major concern, the use of moving companies sometimes also creates delays so delivery promises are not always met.

Second, each HomeHelp store's inventory is restricted to display items plus a limited stock of fast-moving products. Typically, only 7 percent of all customer orders can be filled from store inventory. As such, if a store does not have a specific piece of furniture, an order for the item is forwarded to a regional warehouse where the item is taken from inventory and sent to the store the following day. Furniture is available for delivery or customers can pick it up 2 days after the original order, assuming the regional warehouse has stock. If the regional warehouse is out of stock, the piece is typically not available for shipment or pickup for 5 to 7 days because an interfacility transfer or manufacturer shipment is required.

Since many Propartners are working on remodeling/redecorating projects, unexpected problems and delays can easily cause schedule changes. On a day-in and day-out basis, the exact time of furniture delivery and installation is difficult to accurately gauge. Propartners would like to be able to place an order 48 hours (or less) before the expected completion to reduce cost of rescheduling. Working on shorter timetables would improve their efficiency and cash flow and is perceived by Propartners as a major benefit. Currently, Propartners buy mostly from independent distributors who have more flexible delivery programs.

Friday's meeting was long. Frank and John weren't scheduled to present until near the end and they hoped it wouldn't run overtime, forcing them to be rescheduled. Finally, it was their turn. Frank started the presentation and discussed how long and hard a struggle it had been to develop a relationship with HomeHelp. Then John spoke of the benefits. He built on the need to develop new business relationships because Woodmere was involved in an alliance with a retailer in financial trouble. This retailer, Happy Home & Living, had historically accounted for 25 percent of Woodmere's sales, but this figure was dropping dramatically. Happy Home & Living's erratic purchases were creating undercapacity in Woodmere's manufacturing facilities.

Furthermore, HomeHelp had a relationship with decorators, a customer group that Woodmere had been targeting under its reorganization plan. Woodmere's image was as a value leader—good quality furniture at a low price. Attracting professional decorators to its products would definitely enhance Woodmere's image. Furthermore, Woodmere hoped to have some direct contact with professional decorators to get firsthand information on upcoming fashion trends.

Finally, an exclusive arrangement with HomeHelp appeared critical for the future. Home furniture manufacturing is heavily consolidated among a few key players, meaning stiff competition. While the home decorating industry remains heavily fragmented, HomeHelp is a leader and appears positioned to grow faster than competitors. Even though HomeHelp currently only has 10 percent of the market share, they have unlimited growth potential and are often referred to as the WalMart* of the home decorating industry.

Reaction from senior management was mixed. While many were excited about the potential, they were also cautious. The long-term relationship with Happy Home & Living that had prospered for 50 years was clearly becoming a potential problem for Woodmere. Relying on Happy Home & Living had created a false sense of security, and when Happy Home & Living suffered financially during the recessions of the eighties, Woodmere also suffered. Furthermore, Happy Home & Living's reputation as a quality retailer was beginning to decline. In fact, it was getting the reputation for providing low-quality, outdated products. Top management was afraid to launch another close relationship that tied Woodmere's success to another company. Frank responded that HomeHelp had achieved at least 10 percent growth each year for the last 15 years, even through the recessions. The main reason for this growth was its advertising strategy, which convinced consumers who couldn't afford a new home that they could afford to remodel/redesign their current one.

Another concern was the shift in traditional operations necessary to support a customized delivery system. While no concrete evidence was available on the exact requirements of customized delivery, it was still apparent that the service being requested was unique and nontraditional and might require major reorganization and financial investment. Also, several board members wondered how traditional customers, not interested in time-based logistics, would benefit. Their specific concern was that the commitment to HomeHelp would increase the overall cost of doing business with all customers. In short, some customers would be overserviced at a cost penalty. John agreed these were serious concerns, but reminded the group of the potential benefits that could result from a successful shift to time-based logistics. Not only was the exclusive agreement with HomeHelp important, but this "test case" with a major retailer could forge a leading-edge path for Woodmere, resulting in difficult-to-duplicate competitive advantage. Furthermore, John was convinced that HomeHelp would make a move to time-based logistics in the furniture segment with or without Woodmere. After extended discussion, the group decided to assign a task team, with John as the leader, to take the steps necessary to determine if an arrangement with HomeHelp was in Woodmere's best interest and, if so, to develop the requested business proposal. The proposal would need approval before the presentation to HomeHelp. A special review meeting was scheduled in 2 weeks.

First, John felt the team had to detail Woodmere's current operations. Then, an appropriate time-based system would need to be defined and compared to current operations to isolate changes necessary to offer excellent service support. A modified system would also need to be outlined and the cost and benefits determined. The issue of coexistence of current and time-based response capabilities was also a concern.

Current Operations

Woodmere currently has two manufacturing facilities and six regional distribution centers. One manufacturing facility is located in Grand Rapids, Michigan, while the other is in Holland, Michigan. The Grand Rapids facility produces fabric-covered items, such as sofas, cushioned chairs, and recliners. The plant in Holland produces wooden items, such as tables and end pieces. The six distribution centers are located throughout the United States with one adjacent to the manufacturing facilities. Orders are received from customers electronically as well as by phone through sales representatives. Only 40 percent of Woodmere's customers are electronically linked to the ordering system.

Woodmere's manufacturing facilities forecast sales to create the production schedule. Forecasts are locked in 6 weeks prior to assembly. Three of the distribution centers carry a full line of product inventory and seek to maintain a minimum on-hand quantity for each product. When inventory hits the predetermined minimum, a restock order is sent to the appropriate manufacturing facility. The other distribution centers stock only the fast-moving products. When a customer order is received it is assigned to the distribution center closest to the customer. If the product ordered is not available, the required item is transferred from the closest distribution center that has the required stock. If multiple products are ordered, the original order is held until the out-of-stock item is available to ship so customers receive all requirements in one delivery. No shipments are sent directly from the manufacturing plant to the customer; all orders are processed through a distribution center.

Woodmere's customers are dealers at the retail level who maintain their own inventory of Woodmere's products. When customers' inventory is low, they place replenishment orders. These orders are transmitted to Woodmere's designated distribution center. Distribution centers review their orders nightly in an effort to consolidate truckloads and schedule efficient delivery routes. When a full load is available, orders are assembled and loaded to facilitate sequenced delivery. Typical order cycle time is 3 to 6 days when inventory is available at the initially assigned distribution center. Interfacility inventory transfers typically add 2 to 3 days to the order cycle. When an item is backordered to a manufacturing plant, 8 to 12 more days are added to the order cycle. When factory backorders are required, a partial order may be sent to the dealer or retailer; however, no firm policy exists concerning when to ship and when to hold partial orders. Currently Woodmere uses a national for-hire carrier to handle all its outbound deliveries to customers and interfacility movements between distribution centers. This carrier is already working with food and clothing customers that operate on a time-based logistics system.

Time-Based Logistics

John felt it was important for the task team to talk with a representative from another company concerning its experience with time-based logistics. John contacted an old college roommate working at JeanJean, a clothing manufacturer, to see if he could help. John's old roommate, Phil Williams, arranged for John's team to visit JeanJean to discuss QuickJeans, its proprietary time-based system.

In JeanJean's system, retailers play a major role. When a product sells in a retail store, the bar code on that product is scanned, and the POS information is transmitted electronically to JeanJean. POS data detail the size, color, and style of product sold and are transmitted directly to JeanJean's manufacturing facilities where they are used to derive production schedules in response to consumer sales. Rapid movement of information replaces the need to forecast. To the Woodmere team, it looked as though information was being traded for inventory. Product replenishment was exact and done within days of the sale depending on each retail store's volume. For example, high-volume stores receive daily replenishment shipments whereas lower volume retail outlets are served less frequently. The time-based system was flexible and able to accommodate a variety of different replenishment styles based upon individual retail customer requirements.

This type of system reduces response order cycle time and inventory. Since delivery is tied to actual sales, consumer trends are responded to quickly, reducing obsolescence. Furthermore, daily or weekly replenishment cycles allow the retail outlet to carry significantly less inventory while improving stockout performance. JeanJean was also able to reduce inventory by 20 percent by timing production to POS data. This reduction was even more impressive when JeanJean explained that its sales increased by 25 percent. Even though transportation cost doubled, it was more than justified by the savings in inventory and the benefits of knowing for sure that product was needed to service customers.

The QuickJeans solution was technology-driven. EDI used to transmit POS data and bar codes were essential to making the system work. EDI was also utilized for invoicing and payments, advanced shipment notification, and delivery verification. This reduction in paperwork and clerical tasks benefited both JeanJean and its customers.

To implement QuickJeans, JeanJean had to change its fundamental business processes not just with its customers but also within its manufacturing plants. Flexible manufacturing required quick product changeovers to be fully responsive to the POS data. Furthermore, the ability to produce small runs of necessary product was a key requirement.

The management at JeanJean pointed out that one of the most difficult parts of implementing time-based logistics was the sales decline that resulted from "deloading the channel." This "sales hit" was created by the false sense of expected sales and anticipatory inventory that resulted from manufacturing according to forecast, not to actual need. JeanJean had to wait until inventory at the retail stores, retail warehouses, JeanJean warehouses, and manufacturing facilities moved through the channel system before QuickJeans began to work and show the expected benefits. This created tension among JeanJean's top management because it was a cost not originally expected when they bought into the QuickJeans program.

The main cost to implement QuickJeans was the investment in technology. For example, JeanJean invested over $1 million in scanners, lasers needed to make distribution operations fast and efficient, and ticket printers to label products with retailers' unique bar codes. Key retailers spent close to the same amount to purchase new equipment to scan the bar codes. This investment was not a one-time deal, either. The need to reinvest to upgrade technology has remained constant from the start. Some retailers, especially locally owned stores, didn't want to participate in QuickJeans because of the initial investment. However, the retailers that participated were so pleased that most have placed JeanJean on their preferred supplier list.

JeanJean provided John's team with a flowchart of its QuickJeans operation as shown in Figure 1. The chart shows that daily transmission of POS data, as well as any promotional specials, is provided by the retailer. This information is used to calculate an initial production schedule. Inventory already on-hand in JeanJean's warehouse as well as in its retail customers' storage areas is subtracted from the schedule, creating production requirements for all JeanJean's products. These requirements are reviewed by an order specialist, who creates a final production schedule that is transmitted to the appropriate manufacturing plant. This order specialist also manages orders from retailers that are not involved in QuickJeans. All products are bar coded after manufacturing as required. Delivery is initiated by an electronic Advanced Shipping Notification (ASN) to tell the retailer what products are on the way. Delivery is direct to the retail store unless an alternative delivery site is specified. When the order is received at the designated location, the bar code is scanned and compared to the ASN and invoice. If the information matches, the retailer pays the invoice electronically.

The Proposal

John's team was finally ready to present its time-based delivery system to top management and they hoped the proposal would be accepted. The presentation to HomeHelp was scheduled in 3 days. The Woodmere task team had worked hard and was confident their proposal had strong selling features for both Woodmere and HomeHelp. The special meeting with top management was called to order.

The task team called the project "Customized Distribution: Creating Time-Based Customer Response" and began discussing how the proposal was developed, including the meeting with JeanJean. The team felt that Woodmere could benefit greatly from accepting the HomeHelp challenge.

FIGURE 1
QuickJeans: A Time-Based Logistics System

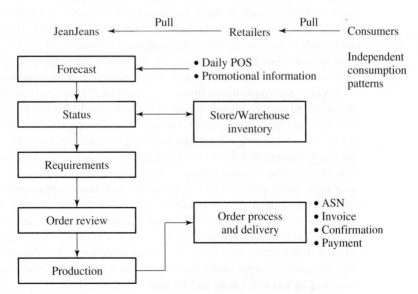

Each HomeHelp store will transmit POS data on furniture sales at the close of each day. HomeHelp will not carry any Woodmere inventory in its regional warehouses and will carry only a limited amount of furniture and display items in each store. The POS transmission will include furniture items actually sold from inventory at the store and the furniture ordered, but not in stock. The POS transmission will be sent to a central information service. The information service will sort the POS data and compare them to inventory on hand at each Woodmere distribution center. Furniture in stock will be consolidated, while those items that are not in stock will be added to the production schedule and manufactured the next day. After manufacturing, the products will be delivered to the distribution center where initial consolidation of in-stock items will occur, and the entire order will be shipped out to the customer. After shipment, the on-hand quantities at the distribution centers will be examined to determine if a replenishment needs to occur. If the on-hand quantity is too low, a replenishment order will be sent to the appropriate manufacturing plant.

Questions

1. What are the major business propositions for Woodmere and HomeHelp to consider in evaluating this proposal? Is time-based logistics the right strategy for each company?
2. What are the benefits and barriers (short- and long-term) to this proposal for both Woodmere and HomeHelp? What other factors need to be considered?
3. If you were Woodmere's top management, what suggestions would you make to improve the current proposal for long-run viability?
4. If you were HomeHelp would you accept or reject the proposal? Why?

Case 3

Alternative Distribution for SSI

Judith M. Whipple

Sugar Sweets, Inc. (SSI), was considering ways to increase market coverage and sales volume on its candy and snack products. Historically, the majority of SSI products were sold to consumers through various grocery and convenience stores. Vending machines and institutional sales, such as airports, represent the remaining consumer market segments. The selling environment for candy and snack foods was becoming increasingly competitive and traditional channels of distribution were being distorted, especially in the grocery and convenience trade.

Grocery and convenience stores were traditionally serviced through distributors known as candy and tobacco jobbers. These distributors purchased SSI products in large quantities and then sold them to retail stores for sale to consumers. The number of candy and tobacco jobbers was decreasing, which was distorting the traditional distribution channel. Two factors were causing this distortion. First, the wholesaler and distributor industry in general was going through consolidation as large distributors continued to get larger and more profitable, while smaller and less profitable distributors either were bought up or closed. Second, the popularity of warehouse club stores threatened candy and tobacco jobbers. Small mom-and-pop grocery or convenience stores were able to purchase many products they needed at these warehouse clubs at the same price or less than what the distributors offered. Furthermore, the warehouse clubs provided a one-stop shopping experience so that the grocery stores could purchase a wider range of products at the club store than was sold by any one candy and tobacco distributor. For example, a club store may offer a narrow selection of the most popular SSI products as well as its competitor's products, while an individual distributor may handle SSI products exclusively. While SSI encouraged grocery and convenience stores to carry its products, regardless of whether these stores purchase products from distributors or club stores, there was a concern about how the products were serviced. Distributors provide a significant benefit in that they carry a broader line of SSI products than most club stores. Also, some candy and tobacco jobbers visit their retail customers regularly to ensure the stores remain stocked with a large variety of fresh product. In this sense, candy and tobacco jobbers provided a marketing service for SSI that is not achieved with club stores.

As such, SSI began looking for an alternative channel system that would not only increase market coverage in light of the new competitive environment but also provide the important marketing service to ensure a large variety of fresh product available for consumers. To accomplish this, SSI questioned the reliance on its traditional marketing channel, as well as the typical outlets through which its products were sold. Andy Joslin, the vice president of integrated logistics, had an idea. Andy began to focus on new retail outlets where SSI products could be sold and how these sales could be uniquely managed via a new channel arrangement. It was determined that direct store delivery of SSI products could be handled by using telemarketing for order processing and small package delivery. The notion was that any retail outlet that had sufficient counter space and high customer traffic was likely to sell high-impulse snack items such as SSI products. Examples of potential retail outlets that traditionally did not carry snack items included dry cleaners, barbers and beauty shops, hardware stores, and drinking establishments. The concept is summarized in Table 1.

The alternative distribution plan offers various benefits. First, it is a unique selling concept in that it provides retailers a way to increase their business through incremental sales of snack products with little risk of cannibalization by other retail outlets due to the impulse nature of the product. Furthermore, retailers are not required to make a significant capital investment to try the concept and there is little risk to the retailer if the plan fails. SSI will provide countertop units or shelving to display the products for sale and will suggest pricing for maximum sales volume and profit. The alternative distribution concept benefits SSI as well by providing market growth and exposing its products to a wider range of customers. Also, SSI will have direct contact with retailers, providing a great opportunity for testing and tracking new products while ensuring timely delivery.

One potential drawback is that the retailers may feel the incremental revenue received is insufficient, which will dissuade product reordering. Also, retailers may have pilferage problems that would discourage their participation. Finally, the arrangements could threaten candy and tobacco jobbers that rely on similar retail accounts. Resentment from candy and tobacco jobbers could potentially result in decreased service to grocery and convenience stores.

From initial interviews with target retailers, SSI became convinced the alternative distribution concept had merit. The next step was to evaluate whether the idea was a viable business decision in terms of retail interest versus actual participation. An internal operating plan for managing the alternative distribution program would also need to be devised to identify and determine the internal costs and potential profit.

Retail Interest

The research summarized in Table 2 illustrates important considerations for retail sales. Fifteen types of retail stores were targeted for participation, and 30 product lines were considered for distribution. Estimates concerning expected retail participation and sales were a critical part of business viability. To start, SSI estimated it could contact only 20 percent of all target retailers. The remaining retailers would be approached after a 1-year test period if the alternative distribution program was successful.

TABLE 1
Alternative
Distribution Concept

What is it?

A unique new concept for distributing and selling SSI snack foods through new retail outlets to broaden market coverage.

How does it work?

Display units of popular snack foods are provided to retail outlets for direct purchase by consumers. Fast-selling items are easily restocked by telephone order with an 800 number and rapid small package delivery service.

What are the special features?

Minimal effort is required on the retailers' part since the popularity of well-known SSI brands makes selling easy. Freshness is guaranteed by direct shipment from SSI's warehouses through rapid delivery service. Incremental money is made by selling high profit "impulse" snack foods to customers at no risk since SSI will remove slow-moving products at no cost to the retail outlet.

Two types of display units were designed as well as two reorder packages. An initial order would include two boxes shrink-wrapped together. One box would hold the product and the other would hold the display unit. Table 3 provides display and product package characteristics. Reorder packs would contain the same product weight and units as shown for the initial order.

Operating Procedures

Two logistics networks are under consideration for the new channel. Both networks facilitate direct retail customer contact: no distributors are included in the channel. One network uses three distribution centers while the other uses four. Service for the first network is estimated at 2 to 4 days, with some outlying areas serviced in 5 days. Service through the second network is estimated at 1 to 3 days and to outlying areas in 4 days. The number of outlying areas is reduced under the second network. Table 4 compares the costs of both networks.

The information flow would start with order entry at the telemarketing department. Retail orders would be transmitted to the appropriate distribution center and compiled each night. Orders would be picked and packed, then delivery would be arranged based on the aforementioned service levels.

Summary

Before SSI can determine whether the alternative distribution concept should be initiated, it must analyze the information gathered and project the potential sales and profits. Profits must be determined for SSI as well as for the retail customers. If retailers do not make sufficient incremental profit, it is unlikely they will continue participating in the plan. A team has been assigned to perform the data analysis. Andy Joslin has identified five questions he feels are critical for the team to analyze. These questions are provided below.

Questions

1. Determine the total number of retailers in the program initially as well as after the trial period.

2. Determine what the average retailer will sell on a daily basis as well as annually. Provide sales in terms of unit and dollar amounts. (Assume 260 business days per year, with 5 business days each week.)

3. Translate the annual sales for an average retailer into the number of large packs that retailers will order per year. Repeat for the small pack order. (Round if necessary.) Include the initial order in the calculation.

TABLE 2
Retail Characteristics

Sales Regions	Total Number of Target Retailers
Eastern	320,000
Midwestern	290,000
Western	210,000

Percent of retailers for initial contact: 20%.
Projected retailers who will participate after initial contact: 30%.
Retailers who will continue after 6-month trial period: 55%.
Expected average retail sales transactions: $1.40 per customer purchase.
Expected average unit sale: 1.12 units per customer purchase.
Expected average customer traffic/retail store: 100/day.
Expected average number of customers who will purchase product: 10%.

TABLE 3
Initial Display and Product Package Characteristics

	Large	Small
Weight	25 lbs.	14 lbs.
Cubic Feet	2.75	2.00
Product Included	24 lbs.	12 lbs.
Cost of Display Unit	$35	$18
Units of Product	180	92
Production Costs	$190	$98

TABLE 4
Operating Costs per Order

Costs	Three Distribution Centers	Four Distribution Centers
Handling	$3.00	$3.00
Storage	.11	.21
Transportation of average package	6.25	5.90
Ordering costs/order	.75	.75
Total logistics costs/order	$10.11	$9.86

4. SSI would like to determine its potential sales for the first year on the basis of the information in question 3. However, there is some concern that the estimate of average retail sales is too high. SSI assumes only 40 percent of the participating retailers will actually achieve the average sales and reorders (this group is designated as high performers). Twenty percent of the retailers are expected to have medium performance success and will only sell/reorder 75 percent of the average suggested order. Low-performing retailers represent the remaining 40 percent and will achieve half the sales/reorder expected on average. Calculate the orders (separate initial and reorder quantities) for the 6-month trial period if 45 percent of retailers exclusively order/reorder large packs and the remaining retailers exclusively order/reorder small packs. Calculate the second 6 months accounting for the dropout. (Round if necessary.) Assume the "performer" ratios remain the same after the trial period (i.e., 40 percent are average performers, 20 percent sell 75 percent of the average, and 40 percent sell 50 percent of the average.)

5. Assume retailers pay $205 for a large pack (initial or reorder) and $115 for a small pack. On the basis of the first year's sales calculated in question 4, determine the profit to SSI if three distribution centers are used. Repeat for the four-distribution center network. Which network, if either, should be used? What factor(s) aside from cost/profit might influence the network decision?

![Case 4]

Westminster Company

Company Profile

Westminster Company is one of the world's largest manufacturers of consumer health products. Their distinctive name and company logo are recognized throughout the world. Originally founded as a family-owned pharmaceutical supply business in 1923, the company has expanded, by virtue of aggressive new product development, into a global provider of health care consumer products. Westminster maintains regional offices in Europe, Latin America and the Pacific Rim to support overseas manufacturing and distribution.

Westminster's domestic operations consist of three separate but wholly owned companies that each manufactures and distributes unique product lines. Decentralized management has been a proud historical tradition at Westminster. According to President Jonathan Beamer, the policy of maintaining unique and independent companies encourages responsibility, self-ownership of the product development and marketing process and provides the incentive for entrepreneurial management. Westminster's products are marketed through a network of diverse retailers and wholesalers. Trade class as a percent of sales is 37 percent grocery, 20 percent drug, 35 percent mass merchandise and 8 percent miscellaneous. All three companies sell and distribute products to several of the same customers.

Westminster Today

Pressure from domestic and global competitors, as well as large domestic Westminster customers has recently forced the company to reevaluate their traditional supply chain practices. In particular, attention has focused on the changes that customers are demanding as well as other operational modifications in current practice that management feels are required to effectively compete in the 21st century marketplace.

Westminster just completed several months of extensive study focusing on their customers' current and future supply chain requirements. The findings addressed a variety of issues, but two key topics were identified: (1) customer composition; and (2) customer service requirements.

The most significant trend with regard to customer composition over the past decade has been the growth of key customers into very large accounts. Mass merchants now account for 35 percent of total corporate sales volume and have become the fastest growing category of trade. All three companies sell to this category of trade. This trend is expected to continue into the foreseeable future. The major shift in the mix of accounts is not expected, however, to dramatically alter the historical composition of product sales. Approximately 70 percent of domestic consumer sales volume is concentrated with 10 percent of Westminster's customers. What may affect the composition of product sales to large retail accounts, however, is the rapid growth of private-label nonprescription drugs and consumer health competitors. Cost-efficient private-label manufacturers offer large retail accounts higher profit margins, and willingness to provide private labeled products. The private-label health and beauty aids business sales exceeded $5 billion in 2008.

The second research conclusion confirmed senior management's belief that these large accounts have an increasing commitment to improved supply chain efficiency. To maintain and increase the percentage of sales volume Westminster generates from these important customer accounts, management has identified several key customer service improvements. These improvements specifically address the second issue of customer service requirements. Company research has also concluded that the formulation of supply chain collaborations between Westminster and its large customers has now become a competitive necessity. In many instances, powerful retailers demand such collaboration and oftentimes have the leverage to dictate relational arrangement. Westminster will have to maintain considerable flexibility in order to develop unique supply chain solutions for a variety of large, powerful customers. Ideally, Westminster would like to establish a position of leadership within these collaboration arrangements.

Westminster's management is well aware that successful retailers and wholesalers are focusing strategic effort on more timely, efficient and accurate inventory delivery. Many large firms have identified their supply chain management capabilities as a primary strategy to achieve successful inventory management and improving overall financial performance. "I visualize three important changes for our operations with regard to large accounts," says Alex Coldfield, Westminster Vice-President of SCM:

- "First, traditional inventory replenishment procedures must be replaced by POS driven information systems. Customers have the ability to transmit daily or biweekly actual product sales at the SKU level in order to ensure timely inventory replenishment and allow production to be scheduled according to response based sales information rather than forecasts. We will also establish and utilize customer support 'work-teams' that operate on-site with key customer accounts to better manage ordering and distribution.

- Second, order cycle times can be reduced from current levels. Large accounts will increasingly demand three rather than one delivery per week. In addition, many large accounts want to simplify their procurement practices and are questioning why we cannot provide integrated deliveries of merchandise from our three consumer product companies when cost reductions are achievable. The demand for direct store delivery (DSD) may also significantly increase. A long term goal is to arrange a mix of products from all Westminster companies delivered on a single trailer to key customers, perhaps direct to retail. The long term has become now.

- "Third, products will increasingly have to meet specific customer requirements, such as assembly of individual store customized pallets, and customer specific inner packs and display units. Bar codes will have to utilize industry standards such as UCC 128 and there will be increased demand for RFID capability on unit loads and master cartons. Invoicing and payment, particularly with regard to promotional allowances and discounts, must increasingly move toward paperless transactions. Our pricing will evolve to reflect value added services as provided, rather than purely traditional logistical order fulfillment, transportation and handling."

For the balance of Westminster's customers, the smaller retailers, service will be provided much as it is today. Although other customers may not be willing or able to initiate close working relationships, they are entitled to a high standard of basic service that provides timely and consistent performance. For these accounts, purchase price will remain the priority, although there will be some increased pressure for improved order fill rates and decreased cycle times. Traditional purchase order invoicing and payment will also remain the rule.

In response to the issues raised by company research, CEO Wilson McKee directed the company's executive management committee to organize a supply chain taskforce. The taskforce, to include top-level managers from each company, has been directed to identify changes necessary within the three domestic sales' supply chain practices and operational network that will achieve improved distribution performance and responsiveness.

As a framework to guide the integrative redesign McKee decided to seek recommendations around the eight key processes that link a firm into a supply chain structure with customers and suppliers. McKee remembered a framework he was introduced to at a leadership seminar he attended the previous year. A speaker on supply chain strategy

TABLE 1
Eight Supply Chain Processes

Description	
Demand planning responsiveness	The assessment of demand and strategic design to achieve maximum responsiveness to customer requirements.
Customer relationship collaboration	The development and administration of relationships with customers to facilitate strategic information planning, joint planning, and integrated operations.
Order fulfillment/service delivery	The ability to execute superior and sustainable order to delivery performance and related essential services.
Product/service development launch	The participation in product service development and lean launch.
Manufacturing customization	The support of manufacturing strategy and facilitation of postponement throughout the supply chain.
Supplier relationship collaboration	The development and administration of relationships with suppliers to facilitate strategic information sharing, joint planning and integrated operations.
Life cycle support	The repair and support of products during their life cycle. Includes warranty, maintenance and repair.
Reverse logistics	The return and disposition of inventories in a cost-effective and secure manner.

highlighted a set of "Eight Supply Chain Processes" (see Table 1) as a requisite for supply chain excellence. McKee then thought about the performance gaps that existed between present-day and the idealized processes, as well as the measures he proposed to achieve operational integration.

Clearly McKee's initiatives, if implemented correctly, would enhance demand planning and strengthen relationships with customers and channel partners. Moreover, the initiatives also would improve the timeliness and attentiveness of how Westminster fills and delivers its orders. However, implementing the new processes would be no mean feat, and would represent a paradigm shift from an anticipatory mode, based on forecasts to a more customer-responsive based operation.

The program would require buy-in from the top down to the delivery truck drivers. Furthermore, thinking in terms of key organizational processes, spanning across all divisions and departments, was a significant departure from the autonomous way Westminster companies had operated in the past. Nevertheless, McKee was steadfast in his belief in the new processes, and was eager to deal with the challenges associated with implementing his new program.

Westminster's Distribution Network

Table 2 outlines Westminster's existing distribution network for the three domestic consumer sales companies. Each company consists of a number of company-owned and operated manufacturing plants and distribution facilities. Table 3 presents a number of key demand and inventory statistics for the facilities.

Each manufacturing plant produces stock-keeping units (SKUs) unique to that particular facility. All SKUs are distributed on a national basis. Due to significant capital outlays and fixed costs associated with each manufacturing plant, the supply chain taskforce has already eliminated the possibility of relocating any manufacturing facilities from their present locations.

Manufacturing plants route products through a distribution center before final delivery to a retail or wholesale customer. Any distribution center may be utilized within its own

TABLE 2
Westminster
Company Facility
Locations

Company A			
Manufacturing Plant	**% of Total Pounds Produced**	**Distribution Center**	**% of Total Pounds Shipped**
Los Angeles, CA	53%	Newark, NJ	28%
Atlanta, GA	24%	Atlanta, GA	31%
Jacksonville, FL	23%	Dallas, TX	41%

Company B			
Manufacturing Plant	**% of Total Pounds Produced**	**Distribution Center**	**% of Total Pounds Shipped**
Philadelphia, PA	39%	Philadelphia, PA	78%
Newark, NJ	37%	Los Angeles, CA	22%
Atlanta, GA	24%		

Company C			
Manufacturing Plant	**% of Total Pounds Produced**	**Distribution Center**	**% of Total Pounds Shipped**
Chicago, IL	75%	Newark, NJ	38%
Houston, TX	10%	Chicago, IL	54%
Trenton, NJ	15%	Los Angeles, CA	8%

TABLE 3
Westminster
Customer Demand
(2003)

Characteristics	Company A	Company B	Company C
Total demand (000,000 lbs)	150	72	60
Sales ($000,000)	475	920	271
Cases (000,000)	13.2	8.5	9.8
Shipments (000)	80	88	73
Lines ordered (000)	1060	683	340
Inventory turns p/yr	6.5	10.8	7.2
Total SKUs	1260	430	220

company. Distribution centers may ship product to any region of the country; however, customers are typically serviced by the closest distribution center based on Westminster's regional boundaries. Transfer shipments between distribution centers are frequently made to achieve an assortment of products for customer shipment.

Most shipments from manufacturing plants to distribution centers are delivered via motor carrier on a truckload basis. Air freight is sometimes utilized for emergency shipments from plants and between distribution centers before delivery to customers. Most shipments between distribution centers and customers are delivered by motor carrier on a less-than-truckload basis and vary in size from a few pounds to nearly truckload quantities. Table 4 shows the three domestic sales companies' shipments by typical weight brackets and the number of bills of lading issued within each bracket. The first weight bracket (0–70 pounds) represents shipments typically delivered by small parcel carriers; the majority of these shipments represent order fulfillment of back ordered SKUs. Approximately 47 to 50 percent of all shipments are 500 pounds or less.

Distribution center locations are based both on market and production factors. The majority of distribution centers are strategically located throughout the country to service geographic territories that contain the strongest demand for Westminster products. Demand patterns for consumer products follow major population centers and are generally consistent across the country for all three companies. Most distribution centers were originally

TABLE 4
Shipment Profiles

Shipment Size	% of Weight	% of Shipments
Package Delivery	6	25
< 500 lbs.	8	22
500 – 2,000 lbs.	13	20
2,000 – 5,000 lbs.	18	15
5,000 – 10,000 lbs.	22	10
> 10,000 lbs.	32	8

TABLE 5
Westminster 2003 Distribution Costs ($000,000)

Transportation	Company A	Company B	Company C
Transfer freight	4.2	3.2	2.8
Customer freight	9.9	8.3	8.5
Total transportation costs	14.1	11.5	11.3
Warehousing			
Storage & handling	6.2	4.4	3.2
Fixed	2.3	1.6	4.2
Total warehousing costs	8.5	6	7.4
Total logistics costs	22.6	17.5	18.7
Average number of days' transit time (DC to customer)	2.8	2.9	2.3

located near manufacturing plants to reduce transfer transportation costs. Demand patterns for consumer products follow major population centers and are generally consistent across the country for all three companies.

Table 5 lists the current system's transportation and warehousing costs for each of the three companies. Freight rate classification for product shipments is different for each of the three companies. Company A freight has a rating of class 60; Company B freight has a rating of class 70; and Company C freight has a rating of 150. In general, these ratings reflect the relative expense of moving products based on density and value. Transfer freight costs are based on truckload rates from the manufacturing plants to the distribution centers. Customer freight costs are based on less-than-truckload shipments from distribution centers to retail and wholesale customers. Average number of days' transit time from the distribution centers to the customer is the shipment time from the point an order leaves the distribution center's loading dock until it reaches a customer. Any potential systems redesign must consider the effect of labor costs.

Questions

1. What impact would the three new alternatives have on transfer and customer freight costs? Why?
2. What impact would warehouse consolidation have on inventory carrying costs, customer service levels, and order fill rate?
3. How are warehousing costs affected by the decision to use third party or private warehouse facilities? What effect would this have on handling, storage, and fixed facility costs?
4. What effect would shipping mixed shipments from consolidated distribution centers have on individual company cost and performance?
5. Evaluate the eight supply chain processes in terms of customer classification and degree of centralization/decentralization of required functionality (use the matrix on page 459).
6. Given all available information briefly describe the logistical system design you would recommend for Westminster's integrated consumer products.

	Eight Supply Chain Processes—Classify as "Centralized or Decentralized"							
Retail Segment	**DPR**	**CRC**	**OF/SD**	**P/SDL**	**MC**	**SRC**	**LCS**	**RL**
Grocery								
Drug								
Mass Merchant								

Case 5

Michigan Liquor Control Commission

On a Friday afternoon in October 2000, Joseph Duncan, a third-year distribution systems analyst for the Michigan Department of Commerce, was sitting at his office desk reading through some background material on distilled liquor distribution in Michigan. Prior to his current position, Joseph had worked as a distribution analyst in private industry for several years after graduating from a large midwestern university with a degree in materials and logistics management. His direct supervisor, Donna Mills, had given Joseph his next assignment earlier that day. "Be prepared to head up a project team and prepare a proposal on distilled liquor distribution," Donna said, "We'll meet Wednesday afternoon at 2:00 P.M. to lay out an initial plan." This was Joseph's first "lead" project assignment, and although he was unfamiliar with the topic, he was excited about the opportunity to demonstrate his ability. He placed the background material in his briefcase and decided to reexamine it at home over the upcoming weekend.

History of Michigan Liquor Distribution System

In the early 1900s, brewers in Detroit were the dominant force in the state due to efficiencies of size, new bottling technology, and local "option laws," which restricted or outlawed in-county production. This created a sharp division between outstate and Detroit brewers and prevented the formation of a strong state liquor association. Prohibition forces also benefited from this divisiveness; by the year 1917, Michigan had 45 dry counties. Michigan enacted a statewide prohibition on liquor in May 1918, approximately 18 months prior to passage of federal Prohibition (the 18th Amendment). By the late 1920s and early 1930s, significant pressure existed throughout the country to repeal Prohibition. In early 1933, Congress passed a bill authorizing 3.2 percent beer. In the same year, a similar bill was considered in Michigan and along with it, the introduction of a state board which came to be known as the Michigan Liquor Control Commission (MLCC). In April 1933, Michigan became the first state to ratify the repeal of federal prohibition and the present-day liquor distribution system was designed and put into place.

A bill for beer and wine (defined legally as under 21 percent alcohol by volume) was passed that allowed distribution from brewers and wineries to private wholesalers who then resell to retailers. However, all distilled "spirits" (defined legally as over 21 percent alcohol by volume) were to be purchased by the State of Michigan. Michigan "come-to-rest" laws required that any distilled liquor moving through or stored in state bailment warehouses must be handled by state employees. Package liquor sales were allowed through any hotel or established merchant. Many of the merchants were druggists who also had the right to dispense "medicinal" liquors as well as valid medical prescriptions. A local option was also set up to provide for on-premise consumption.

The State of Michigan's decision in 1933 to exercise public, rather than private control over distilled liquor distribution was due to a variety of reasons. First, Michigan's geographical proximity to Canada made politicians familiar with Ontario's system of monopoly control. Second, there was a strong influence of "dry" sentiment and a fear of bootlegging, which was common during Prohibition years. Third, druggists exerted considerable political influence at the time and were positioned to benefit from state control. Finally, the state believed government control would protect the public from middleman profiteering and excessively high private enterprise pricing.

Currently, Michigan is one of 18 states in the United States that completely controls the wholesale distribution of distilled liquor between distillers and retail licensees. The remaining 32 states utilize an "open" private license system in which the state government is not involved in wholesale distribution at all.

In 1993, Michigan and many other states throughout the country faced the problem of rapidly increasing costs of government services and strong citizen resistance to any tax increases to provide those services. Unlike nearly all other Michigan government functions, the control and distribution of liquor generates a considerable general revenue contribution for the state. Distilled liquor tax contributions go directly to the General Fund in the Executive Budget for running the State of Michigan. At present, taxes of 11.85 percent are assessed on the full price of liquor as follows: 4 percent for excise taxes, 6 percent for a Michigan school-aid fund, and 1.85 percent on packaged liquor.

Public sensitivity toward liquor as a social issue and its ability to provide the state with significant revenue make liquor control a high-profile government activity. Under a recent directive from the governor, all state functions must be examined to determine how state government efficiency could be improved. Despite the contribution of current operations, considerable room for improvement appears to exist. For example, even in light of technological improvements and the addition of more modern facilities, the cost of liquor distribution has continued to increase. Specifically, administrative cost as a percentage of sales has risen 121 percent over the past 11 years, while the number of inventory turns has decreased from 6.7 to 5.5.

The Liquor Distribution Process

Distilled liquor distribution in the State of Michigan during the fiscal year 2000–2001 involved the shipment of 6.97 million cases of liquor to retail markets, and generated $515.0 million in revenue for the state. After purchase costs and operating expenses, the net contribution to the state came to $61.5 million. The state also realizes roughly $50 million per year from taxes on distilled liquor.

Contributions from the sale of distilled liquor are generated in the following manner: the state buys liquor directly from a distiller at a delivered price of, for example, $10.00 per bottle. Then, the state factors in transportation and other costs and marks up the $10.00 bottle a state mandated 51 percent to $15.10. Retailers buy liquor from the state at a 17 percent discount off the "markup" price, and in this example would pay a wholesale price of $12.53. Thus, the state markup (51 percent) and retail gross profit margin (17 percent) are fixed by Michigan law. The net result is that consumers pay the same retail price for distilled liquor everywhere throughout the state. The state-imposed taxes of 11.85 percent are assessed on the $15.10 price and collected by the retailer upon sale to consumers.

Any alteration of Michigan liquor distribution must consider potential effects on liquor prices at the retail level. In terms of consumer purchase behavior, liquor quantity is generally price inelastic. The price elasticity of liquor sales with respect to total expenditures is, however, fairly elastic. These conditions imply that as prices are raised, consumers will generally purchase the same quantity of liquor but will shift their consumption to cheaper brands. This shift reduces projected consumer expenditures and tax revenues. If system changes require that prices be raised, the effect on tax revenues could be detrimental.

Currently, distilled liquor is distributed through a two-tier network consisting of three state-owned-and-operated warehouses, 75 smaller second-tier state warehouses (known as "state stores"), which function as wholesale outlets, and 12,000 retail licensees serving the consuming public throughout the state (see Figure 1 at www.mhhe.com/bowersox3e <http://www.mhhe.com/bowersox3e>). Licensees are divided into two categories of approximately 6,000 members each: (1) on-premise bars, restaurants, and hotels that serve liquor by the glass and (2) off-premise package liquor dealers/stores. The package liquor dealers represent a wide variety of businesses, ranging from traditional liquor or party stores to large retail grocery superstores like Meijer, Inc. The first 600 retail licensee outlets were authorized in 1934 and have steadily increased to their current level. The number of state stores has remained fairly constant over the years and most of the original 75 stores are still in their original cities.

The cost to operate the current distribution network is approximately $20 million per year. Average distilled liquor inventory within the 75 second-tier warehouses is $25 million. Inventory carrying cost is assumed to be 15 percent and is considered a conservative estimate compared to figures used in private industry liquor analysis.

Distillers ship their products to the three state-owned-and-operated warehouses based on state-suggested shipping quantities. The distillers are charged a handling fee for storage of their product because the State of Michigan does not take title to the liquor until it has been shipped from the three warehouses to one of the state stores. The process of title transfer in the system is essentially a consignment arrangement. Under consignment, a product is sent to a sales agent (in this case, the State of Michigan) for sale or safekeeping. From the State of Michigan's perspective, the consignment arrangement reduces inventory ownership risk and inventory carrying costs because the state does not take title until retail licensee demand is established. This operational arrangement was implemented several years ago; however, distillers circumvented the state's fiscal efforts by sufficiently raising prices to cover their increased storage costs. No direct shipments are made from the three state-owned-and-operated warehouses to retail licensees. Transhipment among the three state-owned-and-operated warehouses and the state stores is minimal. Licensees place their orders weekly through a centralized order processing system and may either pick up an order in person or have it delivered by common carrier. The only exception to this delivery system occurs in the Detroit metropolitan area, where state delivery service is mandated from the largest state store to all its retail licensees.

Geographically, Michigan's liquor distribution network is broken down into three operating districts. Figure 2 (Figure 2 can be found at www.mhhe.com/bowersox3e <http://www.mhhe.com/bowersox3e>) illustrates the districts which each contains one of the major state-owned-and-operated warehouses. The Lincoln Park warehouse serves the Detroit area (District 1); the Lansing warehouse serves the western and central portion of the state (District 2); and the Escanaba warehouse serves the northern portion, or Upper Peninsula, of the state (District 3). District population, case liquor sales, and facility costs are shown in Table 1.

While the state does not directly pay the cost of inbound freight from distillers, research indicates that the cost is approximately $1.00 per case. Transfer freight is defined as freight movements from and between the three state-owned-and-operated warehouses to the 75 state stores. Customer freight is defined as freight movements between state stores and a retail licensee. Transfer and custom freight charges are listed in Table 2.

TABLE 1
MLCC District Operating Characteristics

	District 1	District 2	District 3
Population	4,363,850	4,267,531	334,518
(% of state)	(48.7%)	(47.6%)	(3.7%)
Cases sold of distilled liquor	3,945,441	2,749,611	286,013
(% of state)	(56.6%)	(39.9%)	(4.1%)
Fixed cost of district warehouse	$924,542	$576,294	$93,825
Variable cost per case at warehouse	$0.41	$0.35	$1.48
Warehousing cost per case	$2.20	$3.91	$13.13
Average fixed cost per state store	$163,810	$65,274	$54,341
Variable cost per case per state store	$1.37	$1.43	$3.64
Number of state stores	12	46	17

TABLE 2
MLCC Transfer and Custom Freight Charges

	District 1	District 2	District 3
Transfer freight (per case)	$0.35	$0.28	$0.60
Customer freight (per case)	$1.00 (south) $1.10–1.30 (north)	$0.40–0.70	No service available; "pickup" only

Current Issues

Redesigning the liquor control system in Michigan is not a new idea. Lawrence Desmond, business manager for the MLCC, says, "When you talk about the liquor commission you're really talking about two distinct aspects. One is a regulatory agency that enforces the state's liquor laws. The other is the fact that we're the state's sole wholesaler of spirits, and along with our licensing process, we directly contribute to the state's general fund." The subject of system redesign has been raised numerous times for a variety of reasons, and many powerful economic and political special interest groups have strong opinions on the two issues of liquor enforcement and sales and licensing.

Liquor enforcement is a highly sensitive social issue. From 1992–2000, nationwide per capita consumption of distilled liquor declined about 3 percent per year. Michigan sales figures mirror the national trend (see Figure 3 at www.mhhe.com/bowersox3e <http://www.mhhe.com/bowersox3e>). Increased public awareness of alcohol abuse has been heightened through the efforts of the distillers and brewers, government agencies, and groups such as Mothers Against Drunk Driving (MADD). Anti-alcohol groups such as MADD argue that the state's highly controlled system contributes to strong enforcements of liquor violations, and thereby acts as a deterrent to alcohol abuse. "Alcohol is a problem-causing narcotic drug, and we need to retain as much control as possible," says Reverend Allen West of the Michigan Council on Alcohol Abuse and Problems.

The chairperson and the five commissioners of the MLCC are appointed by the governor of Michigan. Given the nature of the political process, the MLCC and its licensing procedures have historically been subject to frequent charges of political patronage, graft, and corruption by whichever political party is out of power in the state legislature. The MLCC employs approximately 620 people and a considerable number of the positions are well-paying, low-skill jobs. Although the population of Michigan is concentrated in the lower third of the state, many of the MLCC positions are located in geographically remote areas where it is unlikely that employees would be able to secure similar, private sector jobs if system redesign eliminated their positions. Also, approximately 500 MLCC employees are represented by United Auto Workers local unions. Teamsters Union delivery firms with long-term contracts for hauling liquor also exist, especially in the Detroit metropolitan area.

A number of state budget analysts and legislators, as well as academic and professional consultants, believe that the state liquor distribution system is considerably less efficient than private industry. They argue that, for example, mandated state delivery contracts and state employees with little job performance incentive hinder productivity improvement.

Lower volume retail licensees fear that redesigning the current system may hinder their ability to purchase small quantities of liquor, particularly if minimum order sizes or delivery freight breaks are instituted. They believe that changing the current setup will severely disadvantage them relative to larger, high-volume chains and retailers. Jerry Faust, spokesperson for a state organization representing retailers says, "If the system ain't broke, don't fix it." Many consumer advocates argue that the current distribution system of state-set, single pricing at all retail outlets provides consumers with an economically equitable system.

Challenges of System Redesign

Before leaving the office, Joseph outlined two general objectives of distribution network redesign: (1) increase the state's return from liquor distribution by reducing distribution costs and inefficiencies and (2) improve inventory management by utilizing Management Information Systems (MIS) to further increase efficiency. He also identified four specific objectives: (1) maintain the current service level; (2) increase inventory turns; (3) decrease administrative costs; and (4) maintain the current level of control over a highly sensitive socioeconomic policy area.

Joseph realized he would need to contact a variety of people upon his return to work on Monday in preparation for Wednesday's meeting. He sketched out plans to meet with representative MLCC staff and operations personnel, MIS staff, external industry experts in liquor and custom delivery operations, and academics in marketing and logistics at the nearby state university.

Joseph decided that any changes in distilled liquor distribution would have to reflect key operational issues of pricing, service level, projected retail sales and tax impact, direct delivery from distillers to major chain warehouses, and delivery cost considerations—not to mention a host of economic and political special interest group concerns. He began to realize that the topic of liquor distribution in Michigan was a much more complex issue than it had seemed a few hours earlier.

Questions

1. What alternative designs for distilled liquor distribution in Michigan might be considered? Explain the rationale for your suggestions.
2. Discuss the benefits and risks of alternative designs for distilled liquor distribution.
3. Are the historical conditions which the current liquor distribution system is based upon still important today? What, if any, other factors exist that require consideration?
4. Does an inherent social conflict exist when state governments rely upon tax contributions from liquor sales to fund educational programs?
5. How would you organize the final report on distilled liquor distribution in Michigan if you were Joseph Duncan?

Case 6

W-G-P Chemical Company

John White, vice president of distribution for W-G-P Chemical Company, was preparing for the annual strategy review session conducted by the firm's executive committee. He was charged with the task of evaluating his firm's logistics costs and customer service capability for his firm's packaged dry and liquid agricultural chemicals.

W-G-P Distribution Systems

Figure 1 (Figure 1 can be found at www.mhhe.com/bowersox3e <http://www.mhhe.com/bowersox3e>) outlines the existing logistics system for W-G-P Chemical Company. Four types of facilities: (1) two continuous, company-owned manufacturing plants; (2) nine seasonal contracted manufacturing plants; (3) numerous in-transit distribution centers; and (4) 28 full-time distribution centers. Growing environmental activism has influenced management to reject any relocation of the manufacturing plants. W-G-P distributes 129 different products or SKUs on a national basis. For distribution considerations, the products may be grouped into two different categories. Category A consists of 13 SKUs of a product called *Prevention*. The sales of *Prevention* are highly seasonal and account for 85 percent of W-G-P's total revenue. The 116 Category B products (called *Support*) sell throughout the year but also have a seasonal pattern similar to that of *Prevention*'s sales. Although the sales volume of Category B is only 15 percent of W-G-P's total revenue, this group of products contributes approximately 30 percent of total before-tax profits. The typical end user of W-G-P's products purchases a variety of both A and B products. In many cases, the products are used jointly in agricultural applications. W-G-P's total product line is marketed through a network of agricultural dealers. The company sells to the dealers, who then resell the products to farmers. The typical dealer provides farmers with a broad line of products, including those that are directly competitive with W-G-P products. Historically, farmers tend to purchase both A and B products 1 to 2 weeks before field application. Application occurs at different times in different parts of the country and is directly related to the intensity of rainfall. Thus, W-G-P's products must be available precisely when the farmers need them. Likewise, the quantity needed per acre varies depending on the rainfall received in an area. Therefore, although W-G-P produces *Prevention* and *Support* all year, sales to farmers take place during a very short time period. Farmers' requirements vary in time and duration of use throughout the country.

To even out distribution to dealers across the year, W-G-P offers discount incentives and warehouse allowances to dealers who purchase at least 90 days in advance of estimated application dates. This early-order program accounts for 30 to 40 percent of the total annual sales of *Prevention* and *Support*. For the dealer, placing an early order means taking an inventory position on *Prevention* in advance of farmer purchases. However, since both *Prevention* and *Support* products are available, in effect, the early-order warehouse allowance means a special discount of the *Support* products which sell all year. To avoid abuse of the program, W-G-P requires that a proportional amount of *Prevention* products accompany each order. W-G-P also agrees to accept returns up to 15 percent of the total quantity of early-ordered *Prevention* products. The return policy requires a refund of the full purchase price providing dealers repay the return freight to W-G-P's warehouse.

The advantages afforded W-G-P through the early-order program are two-fold.

1. W-G-P can schedule shipments at its convenience to achieve the lowest possible transportation cost.
2. Dealers are given an additional discount if their own transportation equipment is used to pick up early orders, provided the cost is less than transportation paid for by W-G-P.

Seasonal sales, those sales which dealers buy within 90 days of estimated application dates, account for 60 to 70 percent of sales. Thus, to a significant degree, seasonal sales volume depends on W-G-P's ability to deliver products rapidly. During the seasonal period, dealers expect *Prevention* and *Support* to be available for pickup at distribution centers within a few hours of order placement. During this period, approximately 50 percent of the dealers pick up products. When transportation is arranged by W-G-P, dealers expect overnight delivery. Although the service level required during the seasonal period is high, these sales are very profitable for dealers because the farmers who purchase the products are willing to pay the full retail price. The capability to provide products during the application period is one of the most important criteria dealers use when selecting a chemical firm. Historically, sales have been concentrated in eight midwestern states which account for 80 percent of annual revenue. Table 1 presents a summary of the most recent data.

The distribution pattern for W-G-P products is relatively simple. Two company-owned manufacturing plants are located in Alabama and Louisiana. The Alabama plant produces *Support*, while the Louisiana plant produces both *Prevention* and *Support.* Both facilities are continuous-process plants, and their location at deepwater ports facilitates economical inbound raw material movement. The nine contracted seasonal manufacturing plants have passed the environmental audits and are strategically located at key transportation gateways.

The three in-transit warehouses are utilized because the manufacturing plants have only enough storage space for 2 or 3 days' production. Table 2 lists the in-transit facility locations.

In terms of total system, the in-transit warehouses have three functions: (1) to provide storage until forward shipments are required; (2) to postpone the risk of advance shipments; and (3) to provide a combination of transportation rates that are lower to field distribution centers than the sum of published rates into and out of the in-transit warehouse. In a sense, the in-transit warehouses are economically supported by special transportation rates. All warehouses and distribution centers in the W-G-P system are public facilities. Therefore, W-G-P's costs are based on volume throughput and duration of storage. The 28 full-line distribution centers are primary facilities from which dealers are served. Although some early orders are shipped directly from plants and in-transit warehouses to dealers, they represent less than 10 percent of the annual tonnage shipped to dealers. Ninety percent of all

TABLE 1
Annual Sales

Dollars	525,146,747
Weight (lb.)	242,717,768
Cubic Feet	26,887,513
Cases	2,912,753
Product Lines per Order	25,392
Orders	19,139

TABLE 2
In-Transit Warehouses

Birmingham, AL
Memphis, TN
Alexandria, LA

TABLE 3
Warehouse Locations

Indianapolis, IN	Brooklyn Center, MN
Memphis, TN	Rockford, IL
Ennis, TX	Memphis, TN
Alexandria, LA	Phoenix, AZ
Fresno, CA	Orlando, FL
Baton Rouge, LA	Milwaukee, WI
West Helena, AR	Goldsboro, NC
West Sacramento, CA	Des Moines, IA
Greenville, MS	Decatur, IL
Weslaco, TX	Columbia, SC
Omaha, NE	Pennsauken, NJ
Evansville, IN	Houston, TX
Albany, GA	Lubbock, TX
Montgomery, AL	Charlotte, MI
Birmingham, AL	Lima, OH
Kansas City, MO	

tonnage is either shipped from or picked up by dealers at the full-line distribution centers. Table 3 provides a list of distribution center locations. Replenishment of distribution center inventories is primarily on an allocation basis controlled by central inventory planning. All orders are processed in an online basis at the central office after they are received over a telecommunications network. The elapsed time from order entry to shipment release from the distribution center is less than 24 hours. The primary method of shipment from plants to in-transit warehouses and distribution centers is motor carrier.

The System Review

A primary objective of the physical distribution system review is to evaluate the cost and service levels of the existing program in comparison with alternative methods of operation. Despite relatively smooth operations, the fact remains that at the end of each application season, many dealers' requirements have not been satisfied, while other dealers have returned inventory. Thus, sales are lost that could have been enjoyed if products had been available to the dealers in need. A critical element of customer service is forward inventory availability to accommodate customer pickup. In preparing the study, John White asked the Accounting Department to provide standard costs. The following standards were developed:

1. Order processing at a standard fixed cost per month with a variable cost per order.
2. Inventory at before-tax cost of 18 percent per annum of average inventory per field warehouse location.
3. Handling and storage at actual local cost for each existing and potential facility. Appropriate storage rate applicable at in-transit warehouses.
4. Inbound transportation from plants and in-transit warehouses to field warehouses based on point-to-point rates.

Table 4 contains the costs for the reference year.

Questions

1. What is the total distribution cost for W-G-P Chemical Company? What is the cost per pound, cubic foot, case, line, and order? How can these measures contribute to the distribution review process?

TABLE 4
Distribution Cost

Storage	$ 3.1 Million
Handling	$ 1.3 Million
Ordering	$ 3.5 Million
Average Inventory Level	$ 90.0 Million
Transportation to Warehouse	$ 2.3 Million
Transportation Transfer between Distribution Centers	$ 1.2 Million
Transportation to Customers	$ 5.6 Million

2. On a map, plot the distribution facilities and network for W-G-P Chemical Company. What product and market characteristics can help explain this distribution structure?

3. What alternative methods of distribution should W-G-P consider for *Prevention* and *Support*?

4. Discuss the rationale for:

   A. The early order program,
   B. Customer pickup policies,
   C. Use of public versus private warehouse facilities.

Case 7

Western Pharmaceuticals (A)

George Castro had a lot to be proud of. His company, Western Pharmaceuticals, had just merged with the largest producer of over-the-counter (OTC) cold remedies on the East Coast. The merger with Atlantic Medical should guarantee coast-to-coast market penetration for both Western's upset stomach products and Atlantic's cough syrups. George had been selected to serve as CEO of the newly formed United Pharmaceuticals, and was rapidly becoming recognized as being one of the top Mexican-American business leaders in the country.

History

Western Pharmaceuticals had been founded by George's grandfather in post-war Los Angeles. Tony Romero's reputation for hard work combined with his strong pharmaceutical background made the introduction of his first antacid tablet an unqualified success in the booming downtown area. The company grew quickly, and soon became the largest producer of antacid tablets in Central and Southern California.

George's father, Rudy, married in to the Romero family in 1961. Although not a pharmacist, Rudy received a degree in urban planning from Pepperdine University. After many heated discussions with his new son-in-law, Tony acted on Rudy's advice to expand the company outside of the now congested Los Angeles city limits. Tablet production would now take place in tiny Ontario, some distance to the east of L.A. The urban site, conveniently located in proximity to several major freeways and a railhead, would now serve only as a distribution center.

Rudy's suggestion to separate production and distribution worked. Ontario offered markedly lower rent and labor costs than Los Angeles, but was close enough to the city to prevent any significant inconveniences. Additionally, allowing the Los Angeles site to focus only on distribution led to significant economies. Western Pharmaceutical flourished.

Upon his father-in-law's recommendation, Rudy enrolled in business school and received his MBA from Cal-State Los Angeles in 1968. Rudy was subsequently appointed executive vice-president of Western and quickly focused on expanding and diversifying the company. Aside from seeking new products, Rudy recognized the importance of a viable distribution system to market penetration. A second distribution center was constructed in Indianapolis, and Western Pharmaceuticals became the market leader of Nevada and Arizona by mid-1971. By 1972, Western had a dominant position in the Northwest, Utah, Idaho, and New Mexico, and was making significant inroads in Colorado. Upon Rudy's recommendation, Tony pursued the acquisition of Central Solutions, a small Midwestern outfit that manufactured liquid antacids. Although Central was a struggling company, its acquisition allowed Western Pharmaceutical to diversify into the liquid market. More importantly, Western obtained distribution centers in Nebraska and Sparks. Midwestern market share and profits followed.

George started working part-time as a warehouseman in the Los Angeles distribution center in 1978. After graduating from UCLA in 1982, George worked as a production manager at the Ontario site. By the time George earned his MBA in 1986, Western Pharmaceuticals had conquered the majority of the West and Midwest and was now eyeing the South. In 1988, Western opened its newest distribution center near Atlanta's inner beltway. Construction of the Atlanta site made access to the South and Southeast significantly more efficient, and market share increased accordingly.

By 1996, Western Pharmaceuticals was recognized as a "cash-cow" in the stomach upset industry. No longer an innovator, Western had well-recognized products that retained their market share through creative and aggressive advertising campaigns. Rudy, now president of the company, was content to leave the company in its current state. This led to some amount of disagreement between him and his son. George, always the "go-getter," had developed an aggressive reputation within the company and frequently encouraged his father to tackle the East Coast.

George became the president of Western Pharmaceuticals after his father's retirement in mid-1997, and immediately began his pursuit of the East Coast. Atlantic Medical offered everything that he felt Western needed in order to guarantee its continued success. First, the company offered cold remedies, something that Western had considered but never pursued. Second, the company had key East Coast distribution centers in Mechanicsburg, PA., and Atlanta, GA. George was convinced that the successful merger of the companies would guarantee nationwide success in the OTC market for antacids and cough syrups.

Present

The newly formed United Pharmaceuticals was comprised of six factories and seven distribution centers. The newly formed company produced six products (A–F) with nationwide market penetration. Now that the company had achieved a coast-to-coast presence, George looked internally for further efficiencies. Namely, based on production and handling costs, inbound, outbound and service costs, were all of the distribution centers necessary?

Table 1 lists the pre-merger, Western Pharmaceuticals plants and distribution centers. Table 2 lists the pre-merger plants and distribution centers for Atlantic Medical.

Table 3 lists the production capability and percent of volume for each plant.

Even though both firms utilized contract warehouse facilities, there are fixed costs incurred for each facility due to management and technology. Each Distribution Center operates with fixed costs of $300,000. The handling cost at each distribution center is estimated at $1.00/cwt. The handling cost covers the labor and equipment required to receive shipments from plants, put-away, order picking, and truck loading.

TABLE 1
Western
Pharmaceuticals
Current Plants and
Distribution Centers

Plants	Distribution Centers
Columbus, OH	Atlanta, GA
Omaha, NE	Indianapolis, IN
Ontario, CA	Los Angeles, CA
South Bend, IN	Omaha, NE
	New Brunswick, NJ

TABLE 2
Atlantic Medical
Plants and
Distribution Centers

Plants	Distribution Centers
Buffalo, NY/Toronto, ONT	Atlanta, GA
Newark, NJ	Mechanicsburg, PA
	Sparks, NV

TABLE 3
Plant Production
Profile

Plant	Products Produced	Source Division	Percent of Weight
Ontario, CA	A	WP	48
Columbus, OH	B	WP	6
South Bend, IN	C	WP	4
Omaha, NE	D	WP	7
Newark, NJ	E	AM	11
Buffalo/Toronto, ONT	E	AM	10
Buffalo/Toronto, ONT	F	AM	14

For accounting and inventory carrying cost purposes, each pound of inventory is valued at $5/lb. Finished goods inventory turns in the distribution centers have historically been 3.5 turns annually for Western Pharmaceuticals and 3.0 turns annually for Atlantic Medical. Each product at the distribution centers is typically replenished on a bi-weekly basis.

Table 4 lists the current service areas for each division and state. While there are numerous exception shipments, each state is generally served by its assigned distribution center.

At this time, the production capacity of the combined firm is 100 percent utilized. As a result, it is not possible to shut down any production capacity. It is possible, however, to shift capacity around to different plants for a one-time charge of $500,000. This covers the cost to prepare the new site, tear down the equipment, transfer it, set up, and recalibrate it at the alternative plant location.

Customer satisfaction requires that all products for a single customer must be shipped from a common distribution center. This implies that shipments cannot be made directly from any plants. The integrated firm has operationalized this policy by requiring that each state should be assigned to only one distribution center source. The firm also requires that 95 percent of the volume be within two days transit of the servicing distribution center. This effectively means that 95 percent of the volume must be within 750 miles of the servicing distribution center.

The accompanying Excel spreadsheet (Spreadsheet can be found at www.mhhe.com/bowersox3e <http://www.mhhe.com/bowersox3e>) contains three worksheets. The first, "Weight by State," lists the number and total weight of the current shipments going to each state. The volume is broken down into LTL (Less-than-truckload) and TL (truckload) shipments and includes a standard mixture of all products. For products that have multiple production sites, each distribution center is sourced from the nearest plant. The second worksheet, "Customer Rates," contains the LTL and TL rate (per cwt.) from each distribution center to the major city representing each state. These rates are based on the discounted ZIP to ZIP rates provided by Western's major carrier. The third worksheet, "Inbound," provides the inbound TL rates from each plant to each distribution center. These rates are also in $/cwt.

TABLE 4
Historical Service Areas

State	AM Service Location	WP Service Location
AK	Sparks	Los Angeles
AL	Atlanta	Atlanta
AR	Atlanta	Atlanta
AZ	Sparks	Los Angeles
CA	Sparks	Los Angeles
CO	Sparks	Omaha
CT	Mechanicsburg	New Brunswick
DC	Mechanicsburg	New Brunswick
DE	Mechanicsburg	New Brunswick
FL	Atlanta	Atlanta
GA	Atlanta	Atlanta
HI	Sparks	Los Angeles
IA	Mechanicsburg	Omaha
ID	Sparks	Omaha
IL	Mechanicsburg	Indianapolis
IN	Mechanicsburg	Indianapolis
KS	Mechanicsburg	Omaha
KY	Mechanicsburg	Indianapolis
LA	Atlanta	Atlanta
MA	Mechanicsburg	New Brunswick
MD	Mechanicsburg	New Brunswick
MI	Mechanicsburg	Indianapolis
MN	Mechanicsburg	Omaha
MO	Mechanicsburg	Omaha
MS	Atlanta	Atlanta
MT	Sparks	Omaha
NC	Atlanta	Atlanta
ND	Mechanicsburg	Omaha
NE	Mechanicsburg	Omaha
NH	Mechanicsburg	New Brunswick
NJ	Mechanicsburg	New Brunswick
NM	Sparks	Los Angeles
NV	Sparks	Los Angeles
NY	Mechanicsburg	New Brunswick
OH	Mechanicsburg	Indianapolis
OK	Atlanta	Omaha
OR	Sparks	Los Angeles
PA	Mechanicsburg	New Brunswick
PRO	Atlanta	Atlanta
RI	Mechanicsburg	New Brunswick
SC	Atlanta	Atlanta
SD	Mechanicsburg	Omaha
TN	Atlanta	Atlanta
TX	Sparks	Los Angeles
UT	Sparks	Omaha
VA	Mechanicsburg	New Brunswick
VT	Mechanicsburg	New Brunswick
WA	Sparks	Los Angeles
WI	Mechanicsburg	Indianapolis
WV	Mechanicsburg	New Brunswick
WY	Sparks	Omaha

Case 8

Western Pharmaceuticals (B)

Once George initiated the supply chain design project (see Western Pharmaceuticals A), his next task was to investigate the firm's inventory management capability relative to the refined supply chain. The integration of the Western and Atlantic Medical distribution systems required a refinement of the firm's inventory management system. (Spreadsheet can be found at www.mhhe.com/bowersox3e <http://www.mhhe.com/bowersox3e>).

Although the firm wanted to have a comprehensive inventory analysis, the information available was limited due to the merger and a simultaneous move to an Enterprise Resource Planning system. In fact, in terms of quickly available data, there was only a limited sample from the Atlantic Medical sales and inventory records. For a sample of 100 stock keeping units (SKUs), the data base includes the average and standard deviation of weekly sales, average order cycle time (OCT), replenishment order quantity (OQ), and the average inventory. Based on history, the current standard deviation in the replenishment cycle time is 1 week. The sales, order quantities, and inventory are recorded in cases. The historical information is provided for each of the three existing distribution centers.

Atlantic believes that the historical case fill rate is 95 percent but they are not really sure.

Questions

1. What should the case fill rate be for each product given the current uncertainty levels and order quantities and how does the calculated aggregate case fill rate differ from the historically observed level?

2. What are the safety stock and average inventory levels for each product and in aggregate necessary to achieve 95 percent case fill rate for each product? To what extent do the actual inventory levels deviate from the theoretical inventory levels? What conclusions can you draw from the differences?

3. What is the inventory carrying cost impact for increasing the case fill rate from the current level of 95 percent to 99 percent? Assume an annual inventory carrying cost of 20 percent. Assuming that 5 percent is potentially lost due to stockouts (100 – 95 percent) and that there is a 25 percent margin on the average item (COGS = 75 percent), would you recommend that the service level be increased? Justify your answer.

4. What would be the impact on inventory and service of consolidating all of Atlantic Medical stock into a single facility? Apply both the "square root of N" and item level approaches. The square root of N should be applied to aggregate inventory values for a total of all products. The item level approach uses the individual standard deviations. Discuss the differences between the two approaches. Why?

Case 9

Customer Service at Woodson Chemical Company

From the perspective of Melinda Sanders, the problems of Woodson Chemical Company (WCC) were straightforward and easily identifiable. Solutions, however, appeared to be far more difficult and complex. Sanders had just turned 29 years old and was in her sixth year of employment with WCC. After graduating from a top university in the western United States with an MBA in marketing, she had steadily progressed through a series of positions in marketing, sales, and distribution operations. Her current position is lead distribution planner in the Chemicals and Performance Products Division of WCC North America.

The most recent WCC North America customer service report revealed that "customers continually give the company average-to-poor marks in customer service performance. In particular, customers express extreme dissatisfaction with the order-information process." Sanders was of the opinion that the more WCC sales and distribution systems were expanded, the more management and communication bottlenecks seemed to be created. She was also well aware that the issue of order information status was problematic throughout all of WCC's North American operations. Each division had been hard at work over the past 18 months developing and instituting a variety of software packages aimed at improving its service performance. During a recent meeting with Barry McDonald, WCC North America Chemical and Performance Products Director of Customer Service, Sanders had been given a copy of a report regarding projected directions and importance ratings of customer service requirements in the chemical industry. The report stated

> Customers specifically desire instantaneous access to real-time order information status. This information accessibility is necessary throughout the supply chain—from the customer's initial inquiry to production status, shipment loading, and arrival at the final destination. A critical goal is to be able to both commit and monitor inventory from the point in time an order is placed. While the goal of integrated logistics is a major goal for many chemical companies, efforts are frequently being hindered by inadequate information systems and organization structural design.

Woodson Chemical Company

WCC was founded in 1899 by Alexander Woodson. The company originally was located in southeast Texas; in the early 1960s the corporate headquarters were moved to St. Louis to capitalize on the city's central geographic location. Approximately one-third of WCC's business is conducted overseas. Most arrangements are wholly owned subsidiaries; there are few industrialized countries in the world where WCC does not have some manufacturing or sales presence. WCC North America, a wholly owned subsidiary of Woodson Chemical Company, is the sixth largest chemical company in North America, and produces a diversified range of chemicals used as raw materials for manufacturing in the food, personal care products, pharmaceuticals, pulp and paper, and utility industries.

The company operates four product groups which are broken down into three divisions (see Table 1). Division 1 comprises chemicals and performance products, which are mainly used as raw materials in the manufacture and/or processing of consumer products. Division 2 is composed of two product groups: plastic products, and hydrocarbons and energy. Plastic products are utilized in numerous markets such as packaging, automotive, electrical appliances, building and construction, housewares, recreation, furniture, flooring, and health care. The hydrocarbons and energy group is concerned with the purchase of fuels and petroleum-based materials as well as the production of power and steam used to manufacture WCC's plastics, chemicals, and metals. Division 3 comprises consumer specialties, which serve the food care, home care, and personal products markets.

In terms of functional support, each division maintains its own marketing, manufacturing, logistics, and administrative departments. Currently, divisional information processing responsibilities for customer service, transportation, and warehousing are provided by the logistics group. Information processing responsibility for finance and accounting are provided by the administration group. Figure 1 (Figure 1 can be found at www.mhhe.com/bowersox3e <http://www.mhhe.com/bowersox3e>) presents the organization structure for WCC North America's operations.

TABLE 1
WCC Sales 2001–2005 ($000,000)

Division	2001	2002	2003	2004	2005
1: Chemicals and Performance Products	$3,630	$3,785	$3,562	$3,165	$3,130
2: Plastic Products,	4,857	4,896	5,174	4,775	4,701
Hydrocarbons and Energy	1,051	1,243	1,547	1,353	1,214
3: Consumer Specialties					
Medical Health					
Agriculture					
Consumer Products	2,120	2,387	3,537	3,838	4,184
Total	$11,658	$12,311	$13,820	$13,131	$13,229

TABLE 2
Selected WCC Operating Costs and Expenses—2001–2005 ($000,000)

	2001	2002	2003	2004	2005
Costs of Goods Sold	$6,864	$7,335	$9,125	$8,863	$8,893
Research and Development	540	611	795	811	902
Promotion and Advertising	291	346	447	505	557
Selling and Administrative	1,138	1,231	1,459	1,527	1,630
Total	$8,833	$9,523	$11,826	$11,706	$11,982

Across the four product groups, performance has varied considerably over recent years. Although chemical and performance product sales have been declining or flat, increased volume and profit improvement is projected due to growth opportunities. In Division 2, plastic products has exhibited reduced sales; although moderate growth is attainable, prices are projected to remain under pressure due to a weak global economy and considerable industry oversupply. Hydrocarbons and energy sales have declined significantly in the past three years; although feedstock and energy purchase costs have been reduced, lower sales have more than offset procurement savings. Industry overcapacity remains a severe problem; additional capacity coming online in developing industries in Korea and China will only exacerbate the situation. Consumer specialties continues to exhibit very strong sales gains, particularly in medical and health and consumer product categories. Agricultural sales are relatively unchanged. Steady growth for consumer specialties is projected to continue, although perhaps not at the rapid rate of the past five years.

A significant concern of WCC management is the major cost and expense areas of distribution and marketing (see Table 2). The company has made considerable progress in reducing the cost of purchased raw material inputs, but other category expenses are increasing at a rate in excess of sales.

Industry Background

Chemical manufacturing has historically been a very cyclical industry; recessions and periods of slow economic growth typically depress chemical industry sales for several years at a time. As economies begin to rebound, manufacturing picks up and chemical production often leads the U.S. economy into a recovery period.

The chemical industry's attempts to alter its strategic planning with regard to markets and strategy are changing. The expansion of a global economy and leading-edge chemical technology have dramatically altered the manner in which the chemical industry operates today. In the past, a large, fully integrated chemical company with control of raw materials, economies of scale, and modern plants possessed significant cost advantages that could eliminate marginally efficient chemical producers throughout the world. Today, such a strategy is easily negated. The availability of cutting edge chemical technology that goes into building premier chemical plants can make a low-cost producer out of most any company that can structure an arrangement for a constant supply of chemical feedstock from an oil-producing country. Contemporary competitive advantage is typically derived from a focused market position, good raw materials supply without the heavy investment required in a completely vertically integrated structure, and a lean efficient organization structure. Industry leaders must maintain efficient resource and organization structure while they leverage their technological expertise across as many chemical applications as possible. In addition, many chemical manufacturers are diversifying into specialty chemicals in an attempt to balance the cyclical nature of their earnings.

Faced with mounting pressure to become increasingly globalized, especially during difficult economic conditions, chemical industry information systems leaders are scrambling to implement more cost-efficient and effective strategies to track and share business information. Angela Lowrey, director of WCC North America's Information Resources Planning, says, "better logistics information across business divisions is integral to instituting a strategic business plan. With current spending on computer information systems accounting for approximately 2 percent of corporate revenues, [business] information is a premium commodity and a potential strategic asset that many firms in our industry are just beginning to recognize."

The determination of where to focus chemical operations is also becoming increasingly complex as the geographic nature of the industry changes economically. Uncertainty in Eastern Europe, rapid growth in the Pacific Rim, and potential markets in Latin and South America and the Caribbean have upset the traditional patterns of global chemical manufacturing. Very high research and development costs are necessary to maintain a steady stream of high-margin, new products. Environmental problems and liability issues are a significant concern for the chemical manufacturing industry. Although compliance with increasingly stringent emission controls has improved the relationships among chemical manufacturers, government, and public interest groups, the transportation and handling of hazardous materials remains a high-profile issue, particularly in North America and Western Europe.

WCC North American's Distribution Network

WCC North America produces and sells more than 1,500 products in many different formulations, packaging containers, and labeling arrangements. The products are manufactured at one or more of the 22 manufacturing locations in the USA, and are distributed through 5 WCC distribution centers to field warehouses and then to 325 stocking points (cooperatives and dealers). Table 3 lists the WCC manufacturing plants and distribution centers located in North America.

Chemical manufacturing does not maintain significant levels of WIP (work-in-process) inventories and managing them is typically not difficult. However, managing finished goods inventories is a considerable problem. Short customer lead times, high customer service levels, large manufacturing and distribution replenishment quantities, and long manufacturing and distribution lead times require that many products be in inventory when customer orders are received. The size and complexity of the WCC distribution network makes distribution management complex and difficult.

According to Melinda Sanders, WCC's management structure does not match up well to the company's needs of supply chain management. Recently, however, the company has begun to implement an integrated logistics system to coordinate planning, purchasing, manufacturing, marketing, and distribution functions. Increased attention has been directed to the problems of providing manufacturing with the necessary information to

TABLE 3
WCC North
America's
Distribution Network

Manufacturing Plants	Distribution Centers	
Schaumburg, IL	Gary, IN	Reno, NV
Los Angeles, CA	Omaha, NE	Louisville, KY
Harrisburg, PA	Spokane, WA	Shreveport, LA
Memphis, TN	Denver, CO	Charlotte, NC
New Orleans, LA	Little Rock, AR	Omaha, NE
Shreveport, LA	Raleigh-Durham, NC	
St. Louis, MO	Morristown, NJ	
Houston, TX	Toledo, OH	
Lubbock, TX	Wilmington, DE	
Tulsa, OK	Jacksonville, FL	
Montgomery, AL	Billings, MT	
Field Warehouses (as necessary) Primary public facilities		
Dealers and Cooperatives Contractual throughout North America		

determine the level of individual SKU production (via MRP) as well as how much and where to deploy products (via DRP). Improved communication among marketing, manufacturing, and distribution has led to better forecasts of IT customer demand.

However, although each division of WCC is beginning to operate in a more integrated manner, each division continues to maintain separate responsibility for customer orders and information status. Each division also designs, plans, and executes its manufacturing, warehousing, picking, and loading activities. The majority of warehouses utilized are public facilities. Transportation is provided by common and contract carriage and railroad. A significant portion of WCC's product moves by rail; in fact, WCC owns and operates a sizeable private railcar fleet due to the specialized nature of its products. The link between transportation and customer service is a vital component at WCC. "Logistics at WCC North America's Chemicals and Performance Products Division is a competitive tool," says Logistics Manager Michael Davidson. "I make sure that we always have more than enough carriers on our inbound and outbound traffic lanes to keep product moving throughout our system."

Traditionally, a general level of attention to customer service was acceptable but as WCC restructured its divisional operations by product grouping and, in particular, diversified into specialty chemicals, the requirements across divisions have become very differentiated. The complexity of customer service is additionally complicated because each division serves a considerable number of common customers, many of whom are high-volume, key accounts. WCC North America's decentralized divisional structure has historically allowed each division to provide tailored, high-quality customer service to meet the differentiated and demanding requirements of WCC customers. The ability to tailor such services is considered a competitive strength at WCC. Sales, marketing, and cost control efforts are becoming increasingly customer responsive—the level of focus is now not only division-specific but also individual customer account-specific. In particular, the Consumer Specialties Division serves a highly time-sensitive market that includes many powerful, large retailers and mass merchandisers.

Melinda Sanders and her staff have a meeting scheduled tomorrow morning with Douglas Liddell, vice president of WCC's Corporate Information Systems Group, to discuss the direction of WCC North America's Chemicals and Performance Products Division. Sanders strongly believes that any investment in information systems should directly support a specific business strategy. The question is, which investments should be made and what exactly should WCC's strategy be?

Questions

1. What is the critical issue(s) confronting WCC North America?
2. What changes, if any, should be initiated to address the critical issue(s)?
3. Identify the risks and benefits of your proposed changes from the perspective of (a) WCC North America corporate management; (b) WCC North America line distribution management; (c) WCC North America customers.
4. What would be the impact on WCC North America operations if the proposed changes were successfully implemented?
5. What changes, if any, would you recommend in WCC North America's information processing arrangements?
6. Is Melinda Sanders in a position to properly understand WCC North America's problems? Why or why not?
7. Do you think WCC North America's current situation is applicable across its global operations? How, if at all, does it change the nature of the problem?

Case 10

Performance Control at Happy Chips, Inc.

Wendell Worthmann, manager of logistics cost analysis for Happy Chips, Inc., was faced with a difficult task. Harold L. Carter, the new director of logistics, had circulated a letter from Happy Chips' only mass merchandise customer, Buy 4 Less, complaining of poor operating performance. Among the problems cited by Buy 4 Less were: (1) frequent stockouts, (2) poor customer service responsiveness, and (3) high prices for Happy Chips' products. The letter suggested that if Happy Chips were to remain a supplier to Buy 4 Less, it would need to eliminate stockouts by: (1) providing direct store delivery four times per week (instead of three), (2) installing an automated order inquiry system to increase customer service responsiveness ($10,000.00), and (3) decreasing product prices by 5 percent. While the previous director of logistics would most certainly have begun implementing the suggested changes, Harold Carter was different. He requested that Wendell prepare a detailed analysis of Happy Chips' profitability by segment. He also asked that it be prepared on a spreadsheet to permit some basic analysis. This was something that Wendell had never previously attempted, and it was needed first thing in the morning.

Company Background

Happy Chips, Inc., is the fifth largest potato chip manufacturer in the metropolitan Detroit market. The company was founded in 1922 and following an unsuccessful attempt at national expansion has remained primarily a local operation. The company currently manufactures and distributes one variety of potato chips to three different types of retail accounts: grocery, drug, and mass merchandise. The largest percentage of business is concentrated in the grocery segment, with 36 retail customer locations accounting for 40,000 annual unit sales and more than 50 percent of annual revenue. The drug segment comprises 39 customer locations which account for 18,000 annual unit sales and more than 27 percent of annual revenue. In the mass merchandise segment, Happy Chips has one customer with three locations that account for 22,000 annual unit sales and almost 22 percent of

TABLE 1
Income Statement

Income	
Net Sales	$ 150,400.00
Interest and Other Income	3,215.00
	153,615.00
Cost and Expenses	
Cost of Goods Sold	84,000.00
Other Manufacturing Expense	5,660.00
Marketing, Sales, and Other Expenses	52,151.20
Interest Expense	2,473.00
	144,284.20
Earnings before Income Taxes	9,330.80
Income Taxes	4,198.86
Net Earnings	5,131.94

TABLE 2
Annual Logistics Costs by Segment

Cost Category/Segment	Mass Grocery	Drug	Merchandise
Stocking Cost ($/Delivery)	$ 1.80	$ 1.20	$ 2.80
Information Cost (Annual)	1,000.00	8,000.00	1,000.00
Delivery Cost ($/Delivery)	5.00	5.00	6.00

annual revenue. All distribution is store-direct, with delivery drivers handling returns of outdated material and all shelf placement and merchandising.

Recently, Happy Chips has actively sought growth in the mass merchandise segment because of the perceived profit potential. However, while the company is acutely aware of overall business profitability, there has never been an analysis on a customer segment basis.

Performance Statistics

Wendell recently attended a seminar at a major midwestern university concerning activity-based costing. He was anxious to apply the techniques he had learned at the seminar to the current situation, but was unsure exactly how to proceed. He did not understand the relationship between activity-based costing and segment profitability analysis, but he knew the first step in either is to identify relevant costs. Wendell obtained a copy of Happy Chips' most recent income statement (Table 1).

He also knew specific information concerning logistic costs by segment (Table 2).

All deliveries were store-direct with two deliveries per week to grocery stores, one delivery per week to drug stores, and three deliveries per week to mass merchandisers. To obtain feedback concerning store sales, Happy Chips purchased scanner data from grocery and mass merchandise stores at an aggregate annual cost of $1,000.00 per segment. The drug store segment required use of handheld scanners by delivery personnel to track sales. The cost of delivery to each store was dependent on the type of vehicle used. Standard route trucks were used for drug stores and grocery stores, while extended vehicles were used to accommodate the volume at mass merchandisers.

Trade prices for each unit were different for grocery ($1.90), drug ($2.30), and mass merchandise ($1.50) customers. Wendell was also aware that Buy 4 Less required Happy Chips to cover the suggested retail price with a sticker bearing its reduced price. The machinery required to apply these labels had an annual rental cost of $5,000.00. Labor and materials cost an additional $.03 per unit.

Conclusion

As Wendell sat in his office compiling information to complete the segment profitability analysis, he received several unsolicited offers for assistance. Bill Smith, manager of marketing, urged him not to bother with the analysis:

Buy 4 Less is clearly our most important customer. We should immediately implement the suggested changes.

Steve Brown, director of manufacturing, disagreed. He felt the additional manufacturing cost required to meet Buy 4 Less's requirements was too high:

We should let Buy 4 Less know what we really think about their special requirements. Stickers, of all things! What business do they think we are in?

The sales force had a different opinion. Jake Williams felt the grocery segment was most important:

Just look at that volume! How could they be anything but our best customers?

The broad interest being generated by this assignment worried Wendell. Would he have to justify his recommendations to everyone in the company? Wendell quietly closed his office door.

Based on the available information and his own knowledge of ABC systems, Wendell Worthmann needed to complete a segment profitability analysis and associated spreadsheet before his meeting with Harold in the morning. With all these interruptions, it was going to be a long night.

Questions

1. What is the difference between activity-based costing and segment profitability analysis? How would you counter the arguments by other managers concerning the most attractive segments? Using relevant costs provided above, determine the profitability for each of Happy Chips' business segments.
2. Based on your analysis, should Happy Chips consider the changes desired by Buy 4 Less? Why or why not?
3. Should Happy Chips eliminate any business segments? Why or why not?
4. If the price to mass merchandise stores were to increase by 20 percent, would that change your answer to the previous question?
5. Are there factors other than segment profitability that should be considered? If so, what are they?

Case 11

The Cooper Processing Company

The Cooper Processing Company (CPC) is a manufacturer/processor of food products. Located in the city of Lansing, Michigan, the company services a national market with processed and packaged meat items such as hot dogs, bologna, sausage, etc. Because the company has been experiencing increased costs in marketing and logistical activities it has hired you as an expert to analyze costs and investments and make recommendations to management. In its most recent fiscal year, the company achieved sales of $100,000,000.

The company sells its products through two separate channels of distribution and each is treated as a profit center with full financial responsibility for income statement and balance sheet. The first channel is to retail grocery stores and supermarkets. The second channel is to foodservice wholesalers who, in turn, sell to restaurants and other foodservice establishments. According to the company accounting records, the retail segment accounts for 60 percent of sales, foodservice for 40 percent. The cost accountant believes that both channels are profitable. He says that the company achieves an overall average gross margin of 60 percent on its sales.

The cost accountant also provides you with the following total costs for various marketing and logistics functions at CPC:

Personal Selling	$5,000,000
Sales Promotions	$8,000,000
Order processing	$10,000,000
Packaging	$5,000,000
Labeling	$2,000,000
Delivery	$10,000,000
Total Marketing & Logistics Costs	$40,000,000

The total of all other expenses at CPC is $15,000,000.

The company's cost accountant has always allocated all expenses and investments to the channels based on the percentage of sales volume and has used the overall company average of 60 percent gross margin to determine the profitability of each channel of distribution.

You, being much wiser than the company cost accountant, decide to do a little further analysis. The first thing you discover is that, due to differences in product mix sold in each channel, gross margins actually are different in each. You find that the gross margin in the retail channel is 70 percent, in the foodservice channel it is 45 percent.

Next, you find that all of the salespeople are paid a straight salary and all receive exactly the same amount of salary. However, you find that of the 50 sales people employed by CPC, 40 of them are devoted to the retail channel, 10 of them are devoted to the foodservice channel. Since there are no sales managers and each salesperson pays for selling expense out of their salary, this accounts for all of the personal selling expense.

You learn that all sales promotions were conducted in the retail channel.

Next, you discover that there is a great difference in the number of orders placed by customers in each channel and the deliveries to each channel. You find that the retail channel accounts for 70 percent of the orders placed and 80 percent of the delivery expense. The foodservice channel accounts for 30 percent of the orders placed and 20 percent of the delivery expense. Your activity-based approach suggests that this is a reasonable way to trace the costs directly to each segment.

Next you learn that packaging differs for each channel. You discover that retail accounts for 80 percent of the packaging cost, foodservice for 20 percent. (Don't worry about how you discovered this.)

Next, you discover that only the retail channel requires "labeling." The company has a machine which applies these labels. The labeling expense of $2,000,000 includes materials, labor, and depreciation of the machine. The machine has an asset value of $10,000,000.

Next, you find that the company has inventory of $10,000,000 (this has also been the average amount of inventory held by the company during the year). You learn that the inventory is specialized by channel. For the retail channel, the inventory is $4,000,000.

For the foodservice channel the inventory is $6,000,000. Inventory carrying costs for the firm are 20 percent.

Finally, you learn that the different channels have different terms of sale. Accounts receivable for the retail channel are (and have averaged) $3,000,000. Foodservice accounts receivable are (and have averaged) $1,000,000. You found that the cost of financing accounts receivable is 10 percent.

As hard as you have tried, you cannot find a reasonable basis to trace any other costs or assets directly to the channel segments.

Questions

1. How "profitable" is each channel?
2. What is the ROA of each channel?
3. Any recommendations?

Case 12

Supply Chain Management at Dream Beauty Company

Dream Beauty (DB) Company is a manufacturer of consumer beauty supplies and cosmetics. Based out of Money City, Nevada, the company services its customers across the U.S. Recently, a supply chain expert was elected to the board of directors. With his insight into supply chain operations, heightened attention was turned toward that area. The costs in this area have been increasing, and management became very concerned about the issue. The company annual sales reached $130,000,000 for the first time since inception. Management believed that some of the increase in supply chain costs may be attributed to additional sales, but they were confident that other factors existed that needed to be addressed. The situation had management's full attention, especially since supply chain costs (and savings for that matter) flow directly to the bottom line.

DB supplies its products through three distinct channels: retail stores (direct), convenience stores, and mass merchants. Each channel is considered an independent profit center with full financial responsibilities for income statement and balance sheet. From DB sales, retail accounted for 50 percent, convenience stores for 30 percent, while mass merchants picked up the remaining sales. Cost of goods sold accounted for 40 percent of sales. All three channels seem to be profitable, and contribute equally to DB, according to the company's cost accountant.

The order fulfillment cycle at DB consists of four areas:

Cost Category	Total Cost
Order Processing	$10,000,000
Packaging	8,000,000
Labeling	2,000,000
Delivery	30,000,000
Total Supply Chain–Related Costs	$50,000,000

The total order fulfillment averages three days. All orders are processed through a central location, and delivered from distribution centers located across the U.S. Usually retail and convenience store orders are shipped unlabeled on standard nonmixed pallets. Mass merchants, on the other hand, have placed a lot of pressure on DB and want the company to take an active role in helping them manage their inventory. To accommodate this channel, DB has assumed some of the jobbers' functions in the store and started labeling the orders for mass merchants. To accomplish that, the company recently purchased a labeling machine that can process labels at a speed of 30 labels/second. The machine's historical value was determined to be $10,000,000. The company usually depreciates similar equipment on a straight-line basis over a period of five years.

The company has a discount policy for all three channels that it services. The net is due in 30 days. While this policy is explicitly stated on all DB's invoices, retail stores are the only ones that pay according to invoice terms. Mass merchants usually pay within 15 days, while convenience stores usually pay within 45 days. The company's cost accountant reported that all sales were sold on credit. Cash sales and C.O.D. sales were rare; therefore, they can be ignored for the purpose of this analysis. DB does not engage in any barter transactions.

The company received a total of 3,600 orders. Retail orders amounted to 1,000; convenience stores to 2,500; and mass merchants had 100 orders. Each order has a corresponding delivery that is usually completed within the three-day fulfillment cycle. The company's practice has been to allocate logistics-related costs to its three channels based on their relative percentage of sales volume. The orders were shipped in 2,000 packages, with retail accounting for 800 packages, convenience stores for 1,100 packages, and mass merchants for 100 packages. Packaging cost is estimated to be the same regardless of size. To service these orders, the company has maintained an inventory safety stock so that it can meet the level of service that it promises its customers (the three-day fulfillment cycle). It is estimated that the company holds an average of 90 days' inventory for retail, 60 days' inventory for convenience stores, and 40 days' inventory for mass merchants. The company's cost accountant estimated the total carrying costs of inventory to be approximately 15 percent of total average annual inventory. These costs also include the cost of capital.

The company's customer base in convenience stores includes 13 different stores located in major U.S. cities. Table 1 provides a breakdown of sales per store, as well as the number of orders, and packages for each store.

Historically, DB has offered its customers a level of service that is of the highest standards. One of the fulfillment managers has been quoted, "We do not discriminate between customers; our three-day fulfillment cycle in my opinion is becoming an industry benchmark, and I like it that way. I do not think that our strategy should change in that regard."

TABLE 1
Activity Summary by Account

Store Name	Sales	Orders	Packages
Love Your Style	$5,000,000	300	50
Looking Good	$1,500,000	75	10
Wild by Nature	$3,000,000	200	100
Beautyss Bliss	$10,000,000	450	150
Cosmo Naturelle	$3,500,000	60	30
Beautee Fatale	$1,000,000	100	100
La Belle Femme	$5,000,000	200	20
Le Beau Monsieur	$2,500,000	320	200
Fruity Beauty	$1,500,000	120	120
Tuti Fruity	$2,000,000	250	200
L'Air Du Jour	$1,000,000	150	75
Make-up Galore	$2,000,000	175	10
Nuttin' Homely	$1,000,000	100	35

The board has some second thoughts about this strategy, and what type of value-added it is generating to the company.

On your first day, you get accustomed to your surroundings, and you become familiar with the computer system. On your second day, the vice president for supply chain (and your hiring manager) comes up to you. He proceeds to brief you on a high-level meeting that he just concluded with the top brass at the company. He states that management wants to know why supply chain costs seem skewed, as well as a full analysis of the three logistical channels that the company employs. Management would like you to answer the following questions.

Questions

1. Analyze the way that current costs are being allocated; what potential changes can you recommend to make the system more efficient and more accurate?
2. What is the profitability level and return on investment by distribution channel, under both the current and the recommended allocations?
3. What are your recommendations regarding the company policy of offering all its customers the same service level (three-day fulfillment cycle)?

Note: The company's cost of capital for both borrowing and lending can be estimated at 9 percent. Ignore tax effects on all transactions.

Case 13

DOW Greenhouse Gas Emission Scenario Study[1]

Don Weintritt Jr., Amarendra Kumar Martin Fernandes, and Pooja Anand

An increasing number of studies in the area of environmental research indicate that the earth's environment is at risk due to human activities. The research specifically points towards the increase in greenhouse gas emissions in the post–industrial revolution era and calls for a pressing need for the human society to establish a symbiotic relationship with the environment. With growing concern in the global community, it is anticipated that stringent environmental standards will be incorporated into the Federal Regulations in the next five to ten years.

DOW believes that it is a major stakeholder in any changes that come about from the efforts to redress the global climate issues; therefore it aims to contribute to slowing, stopping and reversing the growth of its Green House Gas (GHG) footprint as part of its commitment to the planet. In alignment with its 2015 sustainability goals, DOW wants to study its supply chain from an environmental perspective.

The company wants to reevaluate its current supply chain for certain products, one of which is Gas Treated (GT) Amine. Sixteen raw materials are required for this product, two of which are supplied by DOW's raw material suppliers, and the rest are acquired internally from other DOW plants. These supplier plant locations cannot be changed based on other constraints. There is one manufacturing plant in Plaquemine, Louisiana, that manufactures a particular grade of this product. This grade can be blended with raw materials supplied

[1] The authors would like to thank The Dow Chemical Company for preparing the case and granting permission to include this case in the textbook.

by external suppliers, in different proportions, to produce a total of 28 finished products. Different customers require various grades of this product. There are two blending plants, one of which is in Pearland, TX. This site also has a drumming facility attached to it where the blended product is packed in drums to ship out to customers. The product can also be shipped via bulk from this facility. Another blending site is in Calgary, AB, that supplies a group of customers in that vicinity in a bulk mode of transportation.

There are three terminal locations:

Terminal1	Houston	TX
Terminal2	Texas City	TX
Packaging Site	Deer Park	TX

Houston and Texas are bulk terminals but the one in Deer Park is a packaging facility. Bulk mode of transportation includes tank truck, bulk vessel, Intermodal (IM) ISO, and rail tank car, while packed mode includes drums put in containers loaded on to a rail, ship, truck or as air freight.

Raw material suppliers can supply to blending facilities only in tank trucks. Production, blending, and drumming facilities are connected through the rail. Bulk terminals can receive the products by rail and tank truck and ship out to the customers in tank truck within North America (USA, Canada, and Mexico). Overseas customers are served in both bulk (mode of transportation used—IM ISO and vessel) and packed/drummed mode (mode of

Global Customer Base

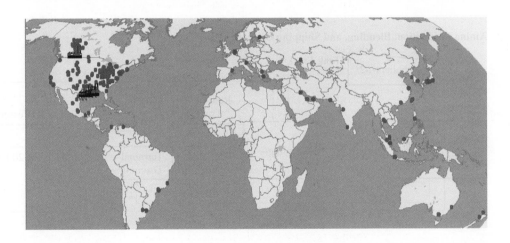

A Close Look at the Facilities

**North America
Supply Chain
Network**

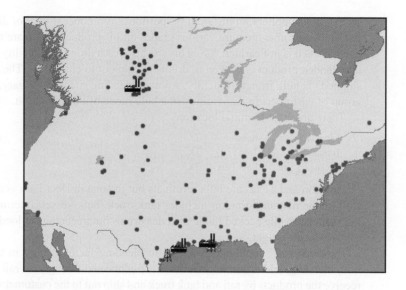

transportation—IM 20 FT). Customers within North America which need product in drums are served by FTL (Full Truck Load). Here is a schematic to show the complete operation:

Amine Production, Blending, and Shipping Operation

The relative cost of transportation is currently:

MOT	Unit Cost
FTL/Tank Truck	$ 0.29/lb
Rail	$ 0.12/lb
Vessel	$ 0.09/lb
IM ISO/ IM 20 ft	$ 0.24/lb

Optimizing DOW's supply chain network both at strategic and tactical levels is key to achieving 30 percent lower cost to serve goals by 2010. The challenge, however, is balancing multiple objectives, i.e., minimizing cost and minimizing GHG emissions, while maintaining or improving customer service levels for DOW's global supply chains.

We will meet agreed-upon service standards and translate strategic product plans into improved tactical and operational planning and execution to meet demand. Finally, we will design/redesign low cost-to-serve, effective, and flexible supply chains for emerging geographies. As a responsible corporate citizen, Dow continues to work towards reducing green house gas (GHG) emissions by aligning its strategies and incorporating measures from product conceptualization to final consumption.

CO_2 emission estimates associated with various modes of transportation are given below:

MOT	CO_2 Emission Estimates (in grams/tonkm)		
	Low	Med	High
Air	1,000	1,400	1,800
Bulk vessel/barge	10	40	60
Container vessel	40	70	100
Rail	30	530	70
Truck/IM	70	90	110

Source: Dutch.

Based on the table above, we have determined the current CO_2 emitted in transportation for each mode of transportation (MOT) used by DOW's global transportation network:

Mode of Transportation	% of Weight Shipped	% of CO_2 Emissions
Truck/IM	39.05%	20.21%
Bulk Vessel/Barge	28.55%	25.96%
Container Vessel	6.49%	33.83%
Rail	25.89%	17.77%
Air	0.03%	2.23%

DOW would like you to evaluate its supply chain to answer the following questions.

Questions

1. What sort of framework should a company like DOW follow to start on a green initiative and what are the associated challenges?
2. What technologies and solutions can DOW use to minimize fuel consumption and GHG emissions in its supply chain? What challenges could DOW face while applying these technologies and solutions?
3. What types of relationships will DOW need to build with its customers and suppliers, in order to achieve a greener supply chain?
4. How can a company like DOW benefit from an initiative like emissions trading?
5. What changes in mindsets are required to institutionalize greening of the supply chain?

Name Index

486

Subject Index

Page numbers followed by n refer to notes.

PAIN MEDICINE
AND MANAGEMENT
Just the Facts